Tying Flies Like a Pro

Marty Bartholomew

Dedication

My wife Ann, children Vanessa, and Cole are to be thanked for letting me pursue my fly fishing and fly tying projects. It is me who misses their companionship.

And to the great tyers that I have learned from over the years and all the contributors of this book, who made a loosely knit plan come to fruition.

Frank Amato Publications, Inc, P.O. Box 82112, Portland, Oregon 97282

503.653.8108 • www.amatobooks.com

Photographs by the author unless otherwise noted.

Book & Cover Design: Kathy Johnson

Printed in Hong Kong

Softbound ISBN: 1-57188-370-3 UPC: 0-81127-00204-7

Limited Edition ISBN: 1-57188-372-X UPC: 0-81127-00206-1

1 3 5 7 9 10 8 6 4 2

Tying Flies Like a Pro

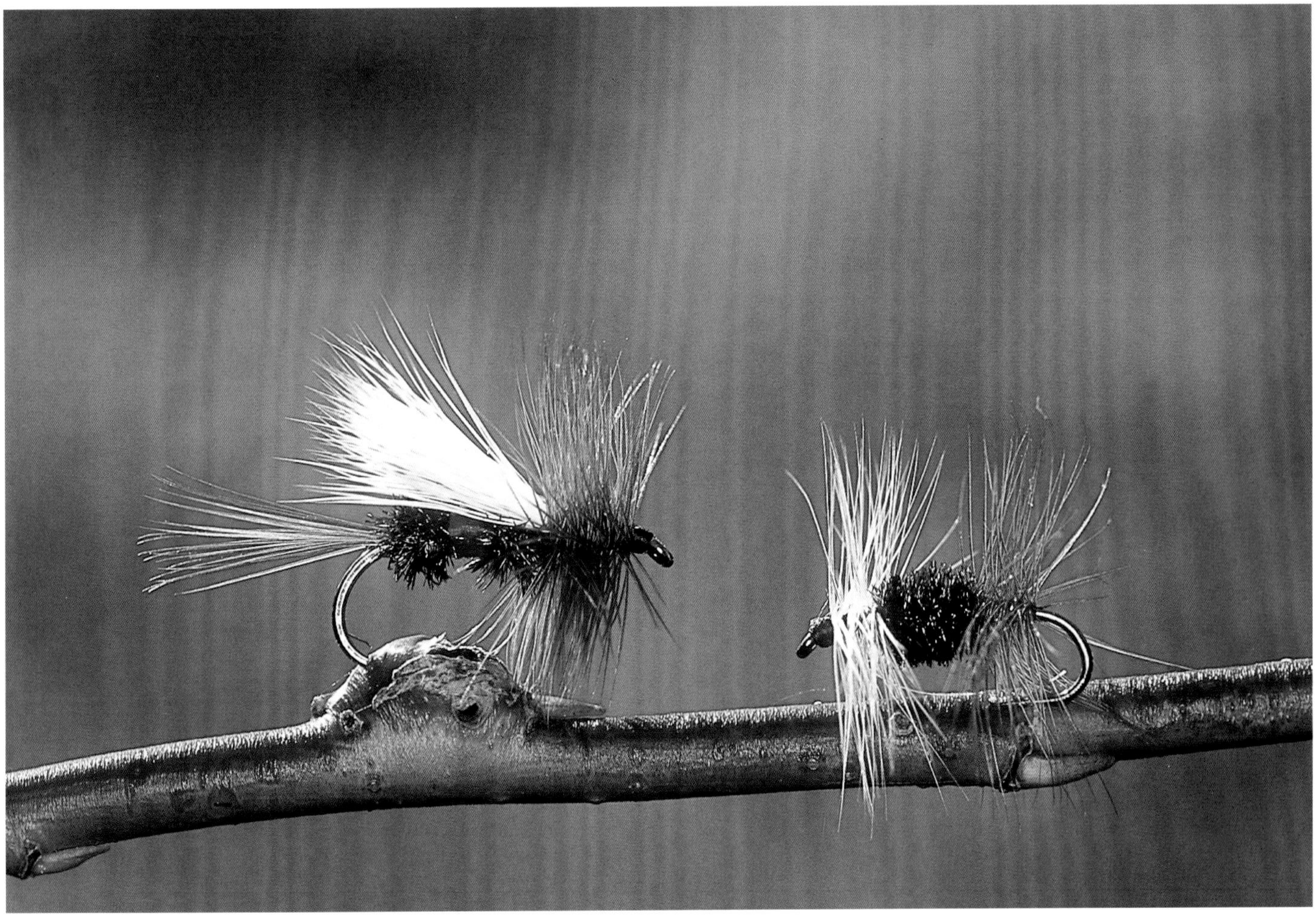

Marty Bartholomew

Frank Amato
PORTLAND

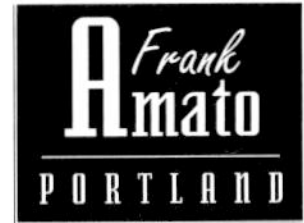

CONTENTS

Contents

In Memory

I JUST FOUND OUT THAT Gary LaFontaine passed away yesterday.

I instantly recalled one of our last times together. It was in Missoula at the assisted care home he was staying at the time. I had traveled to see him so we could go over some of the flies and information he wanted to contribute to this book.

You see, I had mentioned this project to him and he immediately wanted to help in any way he could. I asked how much it was going to cost me and he said, "All I want is the exposure." Like he needed exposure? He was just that kind of a guy.

Gary learned a lot over the years for us fly-fishers and fly-tiers and was not very good at keeping secrets. Plain and simple, he loved sharing what he had learned. The conviction in his voice was tempered by the hours on the water he spent with his team in search of answers to many of our questions. His findings were always backed up by facts, not blow-hard stories. With tape recorder in hand, I sat in awe listening to the research and processes it took to engage trout up close and personal and begin to understand their behavior. I have eight hours of recordings and we just covered the intricacies of four fly patterns. I will forever treasure those tapes.

After our last session, he suggested we grab some dinner. He looked whipped after two days of my pestering questions, but I agreed. I went to the motel, took a shower and headed back to pick him up. Gary was waiting at the front door. Dinner was nothing fancy, in fact I think it was Denny's. We had a couple of steaks, darn good ones if I may so, and Gary continued to share. His voice was more peaceful as he talked about family and friends. He truly loved the people surrounding him and cared deeply for his fly-fishing friends.

DON ROBERTS

After dinner I expected we'd call it a night, after all I had to get up to catch a flight in the morning, but Gary wanted to go to a movie. One thing you can say about Gary: quit was not in his vocabulary.

The movie had a surprise ending and as we headed back to the car, Gary said, "I love surprises. I guess that is why I like fly-fishing for trout so much. I love when a trout crashes on a fly and gives me a jolt of energy."

After I said good-bye, he said, "Come by before heading to airport and we'll drive out to Rock Creek and I'll show you some of my favorite fishing holes." What a great morning listening to him weave his beautiful stories of trout caught and some that weren't.

There has been a good deal of talk about heroes in recent times. Gary fought his disease tooth and nail; he never talked ill of anyone nor pushed any blame. He always had time for the regular guy and always seemed to know everyone by his or her first name. I will remember him as he stood tall in front of crowds of people sharing his newly found discoveries. If ever there was an inspiration and hero for fly-fishermen, it has to be Gary LaFontaine. I am proud to have been able to call him my friend. I will miss him.

I dream the water flowing through his legs,
testing his newfound stability, is cool.
I wish him one more caddisfly hatch and one
more trout to fool.

—Marty Bartholomew
January 5, 2002

Foreword

I FIRST LEARNED TO TIE FLIES AS A young teenager. Until then I sponged them from my dad or grandfather or I bought them at the local mercantile or the hardware store. I learned fly tying basics from a local taxidermist who was the only guy I knew who tied his own flies. He helped me search through my Herter's Catalog and identified the basic tools and materials I needed.

I carefully dissected my favorite patterns by carefully taking them apart to learn how they were constructed and I ordered more materials from there. I didn't need much because most of my patterns were wet flies that required a minimum of materials and fly tying skill. Many of them were tied out of horsehair. It wasn't uncommon for me to stop at a pasture to lure a distinctive colored mare over to the fence so that I could cut a cluster of hair from her mane.

In those days I tied flies for the same reason I reloaded my shotgun shells. It was more convenient and cheaper than buying them. I simply duplicated my favorite patterns. I never considered creating new patterns by incorporating my own ideas.

I learned how to mount dry fly wings, how to tie various types of tails, dubbing techniques and other basics from my first fly tying book, *Jack Dennis' Fly Tying Manual*. How I wished I had discovered his book a few years sooner! Since then I've owned, read and traded dozens of additional fly tying books. Some of them were great while others were complicated and hard to understand. I still have some of the great ones. The best books help stimulate your own creative juices to develop new and better patterns. Now and again another great one comes along. *Tying Flies like a Pro* by Marty Bartholomew is such a book.

Like several of my other favorite fly tying books including Dave Whitlock's *Fly-Tyer's Almanac*, *Masters on the Dry Fly* by J. Michael Migel, and Jack Dennis' *Tying Flies with Jack Dennis and Friends*, *Tying Flies Like a Pro* offers great insights from the author and other experts to help you tie better flies whether you're a newbie or an experienced pro. His contributors share their ideas with many new patterns as well as better ways to tie some great proven classics from some of the best fly tiers in the business.

I first met Marty at a large sports show in Denver. Like me he was on the schedule as a featured fly tier. He was scheduled to tie at the end of my presentation so after I finished I decided to stay and watch. I originally intended to watch him for a few minutes but I stayed until Marty was finished with his presentation. I was amazed that such a soft-spoken guy could execute such a powerful presentation. He exhibited a lofty level of confidence with quiet humility that is rarely seen. We exchanged handshakes and became friends. I always look forward to seeing him on the show circuit.

I was excited to hear about his book when he called me and asked me to write his Foreward. I am honored at his request and I am proud to be a part of this excellent project. With fly tying a good book needs to come out every year or so to keep the energy flowing and to provide guidance for new participants. I've tied flies as a pro since the first order I tied for Pat Barnes in West Yellowstone in 1973. A guy like me who has tied flies professionally for so many years shouldn't need a new fly tying book. Hasn't it all be written many times over? I can answer that with an emphatic NO! There is always something new to learn for all of us whether you're a crusty old pro or a fresh greenhorn. *Tying Flies Like a Pro* has something for everybody.

—Mike Lawson
St. Anthony, Idaho

INTRODUCTION

I HEARD A STORY MANY YEARS AGO about a young lumberjack. He was hired by a well-known lumber company and showed up at the assigned camp right on time carrying a brand-new ax.

He was in great shape and proved it after his first day. He chopped down fifteen trees while all the experienced lumberjacks averaged ten apiece. He came into camp with the cockiness of youth, flexing his muscles and bragging about his accomplishment. The guys rolled with the punches and didn't make much of the kid, as they had seen many come and go.

The second day was much the same. The youngster felled twelve trees, while the older fellows again averaged ten each. As the sun was setting, he strutted into the mess tent with his ax slung over his shoulder telling the old guys they had better start earning their pay. As he sat down to eat he rolled up his sleeves, displaying his massive forearms and biceps.

The third day was a bit sobering. Adonis had slipped to ten trees, while the rest of the camp averaged their usual ten. The kid was met by a few jabs of his own as he leaned his ax against the wall. "What's wrong boy, your arms stiffen up on ya today?" "Hey kid, I didn't know there were oak trees up here!" "Better quit sleeping on the job or we'll be sharing ***your*** pay."

On the fourth day, the young lumberjack came in looking like he had been run over by one of the logging trucks. His ax was dragging behind him, sweat running down his dirtied face, shirt open and untucked. He had only dropped seven trees, while the rest of the camp averaged their usual ten. "Hey kid, the elevation getting to you?" they jeered.

Friday was another long day with only five trees to his credit. Yes, the camp averaged ten.

He was sitting on his bunk packing the last of his belongings. He had decided he was not cut out for this kind of work. He grabbed his bag and headed for the door. A seasoned lumberjack, a man half his stature and twice his age, stopped him and asked, "Where are you going?"

"I'm going back to the city to find a job."

The old lumberjack said, "Son, you have a lot of potential as a lumberjack and I would like to ask you a question."

"What's that, old man?"

"Son, when was the last time you sharpened your ax?"

If I had to tell you in just a few words what I would like to accomplish with the lessons in this book, it would be to help you "Sharpen your ax!" Or "your scissors," may be a better phrase.

I have heard a few statements over the years that reminded me of the story about the lumberjack. One of them is, "I only tie nymphs." When I look at the nymphs the person has tied, I can see their potential. They are proportioned beautifully, tails are of perfect length and the heads are finished very nicely. There is absolutely no reason they couldn't pick up some hackle and turn out a dry fly. All they would have to do is learn a new skill.

"Others say, I only fish about ten patterns so I don't need to know anything else." When I ask if they like to tie flies, they always say yes. I ask, "Wouldn't it be fun to tie a multitude of patterns, if for no other reason than to just tie?"

I have people who show up in my fly-tying classes that tell me, "I got a fly-tying kit for Father's Day and I just can't figure this stuff out." To be honest, there are a few out there that will never figure it out. Flies are still tied by hand, not machines, and some people just don't have the hands for it. However, I think most anyone can learn the techniques it takes to put a fly together. If you approach fly tying in steps, sharpening your skills gradually instead of trying to tie as many patterns as you can, you will go a long way towards becoming an accomplished tier. That has always been my approach to teaching; show new people one technique at a time, in essence, taking small steps towards the completion of the masterpiece.

There are many new patterns in this book for you "pattern addicts", but look for the techniques used to put the fly together. With creativity and a few good techniques, you can come up with your own patterns. Fool a couple fish with them and all of a sudden you're an old pro at this!

One of my favorite books, when it comes to learning how to catch trout, is *The Masters of the Nymph*. I have highlighted passages on every page in that book. As many of you know, if you fly-fish in Colorado, you must be proficient with a nymphing rod. The book includes several essays by some of the great names in fly-fishing. If you're looking for a hero in this sport, there is surely one to be found here: Ernest Schwiebert, Lefty Kreh, Dave Whitlock, Chuck Fothergill, Charles Brooks, Carl Richards, Frank Sawyer, Ed Zern, and Al Troth, to name a few. It was very insightful to get ideas from so many experienced anglers and then try them on the stream.

It was followed by another multi-authored book called the *The Masters on the Dry Fly*. Also jam-packed with great ideas from the best minds in the sport. Several years later Jack Dennis put together a great work for the fly tier called *Tying with Friends*. Again the basis of the book was to show patterns and techniques by several very good tiers. Some were very well-known tiers, and a few were up-and-comers.

So the idea for this book: Put together a team of the best pro tiers I know and give you the techniques, secrets, and patterns of some of the best in the business. These tiers have, at one time or another, paid for the groceries tying flies, so they have to be good.

I had several accomplished tiers in mind for this book; a couple that inspired me when I first started tying, a few that were still in the commercial tying business, and a couple of good friends. A few surprises jumped in also. Dale Darling had a huge influence on my early tying so I knew I wanted to work with him. I asked and he agreed. I remember watching Brad Befus when I first started also. Here was a young guy (I don't think he was shaving yet) tying beautiful flies who followed his passion to great heights in the fly-fishing business. He has co-authored a couple books and was part owner of a fly shop. He said he would love to help out. A pleasant surprise occurred when Gary LaFontaine volunteered his time and information "for the exposure". Before Gary's passing, he introduced me to Paul and Char Stimpson. I met Ken Mead while on the road doing sportsmen's shows and Mark Hatter on a guide trip. Dennis Potter and Fred Vargas were referred to me through people in the business when we decided to round out the book with some Midwestern flies. Randy Smith, Pat Dorsey, and John Hagen were all tying commercially in the Denver area at the same time I was in the tying business. We got to know each other at tying clinics, ran into each other delivering flies to local shops, and sharing the presenter's chair at sportsmen's shows in Denver. Rich Pilatske was churning out hundreds of dozens of foam terrestrials for Pat Dorsey so I couldn't resist the addition of those patterns to this project.

There were many others I would have liked to work with, but time restraints had to be considered and the size of the book would have gotten way out of hand.

My plan of action for *Tying Flies Like a Pro* was to go to the contributing tier's tying desk with camera and tape recorder in hand and basically do an interview. Randy Smith was my first guinea fowl; things went just as planned. Tape recorder worked, the photos were great, and we got to know each other just a little bit better. I took the tape home and sat in front of the computer and translated the information. I sent the information back to each tier, and they would approve, edit, or add to the details of the fly pattern. Aside from the roll of film I didn't put in the camera at Rich Pilatzke's house, and the tape recorder set in the wrong recording position while interviewing Dale Darling, the process worked out very well.

You hear something over and over again in this business: "So and so showed me this, so and so told me that." We have all picked up tying techniques from other tiers and have incorporated some of them into our own tying. We have also modified some of these techniques to fit our own style of tying. Therefore, one of the goals of this book is to open doors to your creativity. Use or modify any of the techniques in this book to suit your style.

It always amazes me how well fly tiers are respected in this sport. Fly tiers always draw a crowd at tying clinics, conclaves, and sportsmen's shows across the country. People are taking notes, wanting to see certain techniques, or how to tie such and such a pattern. They are looking for the secret someone else has been holding out on him or her. I don't think there are any secrets, you just haven't run into the tier that has the elusive answer to your problem.

The group of tiers who contributed to this book have "been there, done that." We have seen just about all the problems, a tier can face, fixed many of them and are working on the ones that remain a challenge. You will find a lot of new ideas that contradict old thoughts on fly tying. Some things are just taken for granted in fly tying, but this group will lead you in new directions with new ideas. We will show you how to increase your speed, improve your consistency of proportion, and your tying rhythm. Most important, we have a vision of where fly tying and fly-fishing is headed in the future. With the incorporation of synthetics, colored wires, more colors and sizes of beads than can be counted, there are new techniques and ideas coming to the forefront daily. You can be a traditionalist if you must; however, you are missing out on a whole new world of fly tying. Some of the creative patterns that have surfaced in the last few years using these new materials are nothing short of genius.

I would like to thank each and every one of these brilliant tiers for their contributions to this work. It has been a pleasure getting to know each one of them better and I've enjoyed the opportunity to work so closely with each of them. There was some tedious work involved, but it was a great learning experience overall. My hope is that you learn as much while reading this book and practicing the techniques inside, as I did while working with these folks.

Marty Bartholomew

MARK LANCE

My older sister, Carol and my brother in-law, Dwight introduced me to the sport of fishing at a pretty young age. I'm not sure how old I was when they would

Introduction

take my brother and me to their home in Pueblo, Colorado for a two-week stay during the summer, but we always went camping and fishing on the weekends. The one thing I do remember was NOT catching fish. My sister hooked herself in the backside with a Mepp's Spinner one time which was pretty entertaining.

While still in high school, I carried a 7 1/2-foot Eagle Claw fiberglass fly rod backpacking, and again, never had so much as a little brook trout take a look at my fly. I had no idea what I was doing; at the time I just thought it was the next step a fisherman should take in the pursuit of trout. I wasn't really taking it seriously enough. The only times I would try fly-fishing was on those four or five backpacking trips every year.

Eleven years after I finished high school, my neighbor Jim Wilborn had me over for a beer and showed me a few flies he had tied. He actually tied a few to show me how it was done. Wilborn had been fly-fishing for a while and it sounded like he knew what he was talking about. He was gracious enough to invite me to go out with him so he could show me a thing or two. We planned a quick bike ride up Waterton Canyon on the South Platte River. We strapped our gear to the bikes, hopped on, and rode the six miles to Strontia Springs Dam.

Putting on waders, stringing up a "pole", tying on a fly, what a challenge. Wilborn's simple suggestion, "Look around to see what is flying around and use a fly that looks like it."

Simple, right? Wrong! There was a yellow thing flying around, but with a meager selection of flies to choose from, it wasn't simple. I had this extended-body thing that was yellow, so what the hell! After thrashing around a while, I was getting the fly on the water and could see it. Progress!

Then, all of the sudden, there it was, my first trout on a fly! A twelve-inch brown trout. I wish that moment had been video-taped. Not that is was the sacred event in my life as a fly-fisher, but because the netting, landing, and releasing of that fish would have, without a doubt, made the "World's Funniest Videos"! Needless to say, my future as a fly-fisherman was very suspect at that moment.

In September of 1986, I got my second chance at fly-fishing, this time in Yellowstone National Park. I had bought a cheap graphite rod, a couple dozen flies, and a few necessities. I loaded up my future wife, (we were married October 3rd) grabbed the old hip boots, and headed for Wyoming.

While sight-seeing around the park, I would hop out and fish a little here and there. I felt as if I knew a little bit more about what I was doing and I did catch a few trout. However, most of the store-bought flies went by the wayside, and quickly. I popped some of them off with the snap of my backcast or hung others high in the pine trees behind me. After a few acquisitions, my fly box looked to be in pretty good shape again, however a gust of wind on the Madison River lifted more than two-dozen flies out of my meager fly box and sent them downstream out of reach. This trip was getting expensive! I decided at that point, if I were going to continue with this sport, I would definitely need to start tying my own flies.

On the way home we stopped at Jack Dennis's shop in Jackson Hole, Wyoming. Although I had been in the sport only a few weeks, I had heard of Jack Dennis and wanted to meet him. He was there, but was very busy.

I waited until I got a chance to meet Jack. I discussed my tribulations with him and he told me to go back to Denver, find the fly shop closest to my house and buy some tying equipment. He said, "Strike up a relationship with them; they are the ones that will be able to help you in the long run. However, I will sell you one of my fly-tying videos."

Four months later, I showed some of my creations to Len Sanders at the Trout Fisher, my local fly shop at the time. He saw enough potential to put me to work. We struck up a deal where I tied flies for equipment. I needed a new reel, so I agreed. It would take eighteen dozen Gold Ribbed Hare's Ears to get a new Ross G-2.

I sweated over that old Thompson vise night after night. I thought I would never get them done. Fortunately, the West Denver Chapter of Trout Unlimited had their annual fly-tying clinic in February. There I met Dale Darling, and he was tying a Hare's Ear. Thank the "Tying Gods" for Dale Darling. He gave me my first lesson in commercial tying and showed me how to put this fly together in two minutes. It took me a while to get down to two minutes per fly, but I was tying them much better and doing more than a half dozen a night! I also learned that day how to keep my scissors in my hand.

When I showed up the next year, Dale actually remembered who I was and knew my name. I will always respect Dale for that and consider him one of my heroes in the sport. Within a couple of years I was tying at the West Denver Tying Clinic, and to this day I try to support the event as often as I can. I know there will be someone there, someday, in the same predicament that I was in, that I will be able to help.

Soon, I was teaching the fly-tying classes for the Trout Fisher and continue that to this day. I spend a couple of nights a week during the winter at the Trout Fisher and Trout's Flyfishing teaching people how to tie. It's fun watching folks go through the frustration of the whip finisher as they put their first fly together. Then, to see them after four weeks really enjoying the process is very gratifying.

Somewhere in there, I actually learned how to fly-fish. I worked with Mark (Gus) Ridlen for years and knew he was a fly-fisherman. I talked him into going fishing and he took me into Cheesman Canyon on the South Platte River. I know he landed twenty-plus trout that day, while I broke two off. I knew from that day that I would fish as much as I could until I got that good. Gus is not much of an instructor, but he has taught me a lot over the years. I tagged along watching him until I got the hang of it. I watched him cast, noticed the water types he fished, got a Winston Rod like his, but he must not have shown me everything. He always seems to have a bent rod while I'm still tying on a fly!

A float trip down the San Juan River below Navaho Reservoir with Paul Faust was a great lesson in nymph fishing and how to fight big fish. Paul was a guide on the river whom I met at one of the sportsmen's shows in Denver. He invited me down for a couple of days as a professional courtesy.

This trip was in the spring of 1987, about seven months from the time I had started fly-fishing, and I felt like I had a great start in the sport. I caught trout on a regular basis and pretty much kept up with whomever I was fishing with, except Gus. I think that fly tying was an intricate part of my maturity as a fly-fisherman. It forced me to learn and understand the entomology and scientific side of the sport.

I had just started doing fly-fishing classes when what many of us refer to as "The Movie" came out. "A River Runs Through It" brought people out of the woodwork to try out this "beautiful sport". I am very fortunate to have been in the position I was in and to gain the exposure I received in the educational part of fly-fishing.

I continued to tie flies professionally, expanding to several shops in the Denver area, to Cold Spring Anglers in Pennsylvania, and Hunter's in New Hampshire. Peak years of tying 1500 dozen flies while working a 40-hour-a-week job, raising two children, and trying to maintain a family life was a tremendous burden, but it kept my wife at home with the kids. The kids were healthier and better cared for, so I feel it was a great trade off.

I started doing tying presentations and slide shows at the sportsmen's shows in Denver. Eventually, I participated in fly-fishing shows across the country.

In February of 1996, I received a call from Chuck Johnson, the publisher for Wilderness Adventure Press. He said he had heard I fly-fished Colorado quite a bit and asked if I would write a fly-fisher's guide for Colorado. After I picked myself up off the floor, I told Chuck that I "Ain't never wrote nothin" before. After a long pause (I'm sure he was wondering if he had made the correct choice in authors) he said, "That is OK. I would rather work with someone who has something to say and not know how to write, than to work with someone who knows how to write and has nothing to say."

We worked out the details and signed a contract for what is now the *Fly Fisher's Guide to Colorado*. The book came out in January of 1998 with broad acceptance. What a life-altering event! Someone told me that as soon as the book came out I would instantly become an expert. Hey, I just like to fish!

I have written stories for *Trout, Fly Fish America and Southwest Fly Fishing*. I am currently on the pro staff with Ross Reels and Scott Rods.

My latest project was the production and filming of a Dud set called "Fly Fishing Colorado's Major 6."

I live in Aurora, Colorado with my wife Ann and children Vanessa and Cole.

Gary LaFontaine

DON ROBERTS

Gary LaFontaine is internationally renowned for his innovative research into aquatic entomology, fisheries behavior and fly-fishing techniques. He is published widely in various periodicals in both the United States and abroad. Gary's books include:

Challenge of the Trout (1976)
Field & Stream Book Club main selection

Caddisflies (1981)
1981 Book of the Year Award from the United Fly Tiers selected by Robert Berls

Trout Magazine as one of the best 15 books of the last 30 years (1959-1989)

The Dry Fly: New Angles (1990)
1990 Book of the Year Award from the United Fly Tiers selected by Robert Berls as one of the best books from 1989 to 1996.

Trout Flies: Proven Patterns (1993)
Main selection of the *Outdoor Life* Book Club
Translated into Norwegian, main selection of Vilmark Livs book club
1993 Book of the Year Award from the United Fly Tiers

Fly Fishing the Mountain Lakes (1999)
The first book in his "Summer of Discovery" series.

Gary is co-creator with Ron Cordes, of the Cordes/LaFontaine "Pocket Guide" series, which includes the following fly-fishing titles:

Fly Fishing
Dry Fly Fishing
Basic Fly Tying
Fly Fishing the Lakes
Fly Casting
Nymph Fishing
Steelhead Fly Fishing
Fly Fishing Knots
Saltwater Fly Fishing

When I first told Gary what I had in mind for a new book, he immediately said he wanted to be a part of it. If there was anything he could contribute to help me, he was more than willing to do so. And that is how Gary was. His strong presence in the angling world was matched by his enjoyment of personal contact with his readers. It seems that Gary had never forgotten a face or conversation. I'd see him in Denver every year at one show or another and everyone who came to the booth had a first name and a story. Gary would ask how their spouse was, by name mind you, then how the new technique worked on such and such river. He never ceased to amaze me.

Gary started fly-fishing when he was 9 years old in his home state of Connecticut. At various times in his career he worked as a professional fishing guide, starting at the age of 9 when he guided in the swamps of Georgia for largemouth bass. He logged several years as a guide on both the Madison and Big Hole rivers.

Gary published his first article when he was 15 years old. Since then he has published over 100 articles on fly-fishing in virtually every major outdoor publication in the U.S. His literary efforts go beyond fly-fishing to include poetry and fiction. He was even a partner in his own publishing company, Greycliff Publishing Co.

In 1963 Gary moved to Montana to attend college at the University of Montana in Missoula, majoring in English and Psychology. He did his Masters Thesis in Psychology on the "Selective Feeding of Trout". He also did a little fishing while at University of Montana.

In addition, he has received a number of awards for his writing, including:

- The Arnold Gingrich Memorial Award for Lifetime Writing
- Achievement from the Federation of Fly Fishers
- The 1996 Angler of the Year award from *Fly Rod & Reel Magazine*

For Gary the best part of his career was traveling the four corners of the world, sharing his techniques and knowledge with fellow anglers. One of his many contributions to fly tying was the use of Antron yarn. The effect it gives to a fly is truly amazing. Gary spent several years traveling the world with Jack Dennis and Mike Lawson, speaking and giving demonstrations at sportsmen's shows. Gary has also appeared in a number of videos with Jack and Mike. He truly enjoyed talking with anyone who talked fly-fishing, and no matter where he went, someone would desperately try to elicit his advice. In between talks and seminars, he was sure to spend time "brushing up" his own skills on whatever water he was closest to.

Gary made Deer Lodge, Montana his home because of its close proximity to some of his favorite fishing waters, and the fact that the town was so small. Everyone there knew him by name. Then Gary moved to Missoula, Montana where his daughter Heather resides. One of Gary's true loves, besides his daughter, is the Bookmailer. He spent his time creating this outrageous newsletter where he stayed in contact with his readers who sent suggestions, stories, and cheer. His companions were the world's smartest fishing dogs, Zeb and Chester.

Brad Befus

Talk about starting early, Brad Befus got a fly rod and fly-tying kit for his eighth birthday. He started fly-fishing right away, but was actually more interested in making blow darts with the feathers and hooks in his tying kit than actually tying flies. His dad fly-fished a little, but was more into spinner fishing, so much of his early experiences with fly-fishing were self-taught. Brad claims, "It was a lot of trial and error!"

Brad started working at a fly shop in Boulder, CO when he was fourteen years old. He stocked shelves, cleaned up, and helped set up for Saturday morning clinics. Much of his time at the shop was basically a trade-out for fly-tying and fly-fishing equipment. One of his first trades was for a Fisher graphite blank that he put together in a rod-building class at the shop. With a few more days of work, he added a Scientific Anglers System One fly reel to his repertoire. "This was my first high-tech set-up," Brad exclaims.

At fourteen he started tying flies commercially. His first order was 240 dozen Deer Hair Mice for a lodge in Alaska. Soon, local shops started ordering some "easy stuff" like LaFontaine's Deep Sparkle Pupa and Pheasant Tail Nymphs. By the time he got into high school he was tying for A.K. Best. He tied dry flies like Green Drakes, variants, and Light Cahills. Brad, being the typical high school student, waited until two days before an order was due and tied for 18 hours straight two days in a row to get them done in time for delivery.

By the time Brad was a junior in high school, he had his own tying operation with seven of his school buddies tying for him. He was filling orders for five or six fly shops in the Denver area. With the money he made as a young pro tier, he started fishing in the Florida Keys for tarpon and snook. He expanded his fly-tying business into the saltwater arena, tying for some guides in Florida.

Brad says this all may sound like fun, but it was not achieved without paying a price. "When all the kids at school were going out on Friday nights, I would have to tell them I had to get home and tie flies. They all thought I was a geek! What they didn't realize was, they were working at McDonald's for peanuts and I was home doing something I loved to do. On top of that, I was fly-fishing in Florida!"

In 1989 he cut back his production tying to custom orders and filling a few odd boxes in the store when he became manager of Front Range Anglers fly shop in Boulder.

In 1990, Umpqua Feather Merchants picked up one of Brad's patterns, the Epoxy Scud, and put it in their catalog. This was the first of many flies that Brad has designed to be sold through the catalog. The exposure with Umpqua opened up opportunities to do articles in the fly-fishing magazines and to participate in many tying clinics.

Brad then co-authored a book with Barry Reynolds and John Berryman called *Carp on a Fly*. Soon he was doing local television spots promoting warmwater fly-fishing and speaking at major fly-fishing shows in Denver, Chicago, San Mateo, Portland, Summerset, and in Texas. The addition of a second book "*Basic Techniques for Successful Fly Tying a Lesson by Lesson Approach*" has put Brad in even greater demand. He was busy in the fall of 2002 with the release of three tying videos, "*Basic Techniques for Successful Fly Tying*",

"*Tying Flies For Carp*" and "*Micro Patterns - Creative Techniques*". Brad has published articles in *Warmwater Fly Fishing*, *Western Fly Fishing*, *Southwest Fly Fishing*, *Fly Fisher* magazine (The FFF publication), *Fly Fisherman*, and the *Japanese Fly Fisherman* magazines.

Brad is currently working with Ross Reels and lives in Montrose, Co with his wife, Lisa and two children.

Dale Darling

Dale Darling was born and raised in Ohio and told me, "I can't remember when I didn't fish." What a dilemma to be in! He started with spinning gear at about the age of five when he got to go out with his father. Dale continued chasing the warmwater fish near his home through his years in school.

Dale attended Glen Oaks College in Michigan pursuing an education in science. After deciding science was not what he wanted to do, he moved to the University of Akron to major in music. There, he received a Bachelors and a Masters Degree in music.

Dale became interested in fly tying even before he started fly-fishing. He did start fly-fishing for bass and bluegills, but did not take it seriously. He thought he may be able to make a little money tying flies.

After graduating he had two dreams: he wanted to get a Doctorate in music and learn how to fly-fish for trout. He and his wife, Shan, made the decision to move to Colorado in 1979. Dale attended University of Colorado and worked in the School of Music. He did start to fly-fish for trout and continued his development behind the vise, while selling trout flies to some local fly shops. "We were broke," Dale admits. "I had to work and tie flies while Shan held a full-time job just to make ends meet."

Dale did receive his Doctorate and to this day, still loves performing, composing, and teaching music. The work at the college was not what he had envisioned, so he started looking into fly-shop ownership. After some wheeling and dealing, St. Vrain Anglers came to be in May of 1991. Dale now owns three fly shops in Colorado: the original store in Longmont, one in Westminster, another at the gates to Rocky Mountain National Park in Estes Park. A very important part of his businesses is helping people learn all phases of the sport. Instruction in fly tying and fly-fishing are seasonally available at his stores. They specialize in guide trips along the front range of the Rocky Mountains, with Rocky Mountain National Park their specialty. "I want to enhance people's lives." says Dale. "I like helping people enjoy this sport to its fullest."

Aside from his love of music, one of Dale's favorite things to do is teach fly tying. This is how I met him. He was tying at the West Denver Tying Clinic, a fund-raiser for the West Denver Chapter of Trout Unlimited. I had just started tying flies myself, it must have been early 1986 or 87. I was in the process of doing eighteen dozen Hare's Ears for a shop, when I noticed Dale was tying one. He was tying it very differently from me, and it was only taking him a fraction of the time it took me to get one done. I sat down and asked questions, donated my dollar so I could take one of his flies home with me. I thought his shaggy old Hare's Ear was a true work of art. As it turned out, the few minutes I spent with Dale that day was a turning point in my career as a fly tier. Thanks Dale!

All in all life is good for Dale. He is very active in the day-in, day-out buzz of his businesses, but does get out to go fishing on occasion. He enjoys small-stream fishing for trout, still pops a bug on local bass ponds, and genuinely loves saltwater fly-fishing. Although, he says that his most memorable trip was casting to Atlantic salmon in Scotland.

Dale and his wife, Shan, reside in Longmont, Colorado. They have three daughters, Rachel, Brittany and Jessica.

Pat Dorsey

For Orvis-Endorsed Guide Pat Dorsey, fly-fishing is a way of life. Pat's enthusiasm for fly-fishing is unmatched, and his ability to share knowledge makes him unique. From the complexities of fooling large trout on tiny nymphs to dry-fly fishing under the most challenging of conditions, Pat loves to instruct and introduce anglers to the heart of fly-fishing. "Fly-Fishing is a problem-solving exercise. The more you know about the fish, their environment, and the specific techniques required to catch them, the better an angler you will become. There is absolutely no luck involved in fly-fishing, it's a set of learned skills and your ability to execute them that makes you a great angler." Pat won the prestigious "Orvis Guide of the Year" award in 2001. This national award separates the best guide for the Orvis Company based on customer satisfaction and feedback.

Pat hooked and landed his first brown trout with his father, Jim Dorsey, on the East River near Gunnison over thirty years ago. Pat's family made annual pilgrimages to the "Gunnison Country" to fish the Taylor, East and Gunnison rivers. Family vacations always revolved around trout fishing. The driving passion behind the Dorsey family's love of fly-fishing started back with Pat's Grandfather, John T. Dorsey who is currently 92 years old.

Pat is not only a consummate angler, he is a master fly-tier as well. Pat's uncle, Jim Cantrall, started tying flies with him when he was ten years old. His fly-tying addiction was like a fire out of control. Even as a youngster, Pat tied flies every day. Pat has been tying flies professionally for over fifteen years, producing up to 28,000 flies a year. That's well over 2000 dozen. Pat's Fly of the Month Club‰ has attracted anglers world-wide, supplying helpful insight to effective fly tying, and even more important, how to fish them.

Another talent of Pat's is photography. He gives several slide presentations and lectures to fishing clubs throughout the central Rocky Mountain region. Pat is among the elite, a Celebrity Speaker for the International Sportsman's Exposition, which makes seven stops in major western cities like Denver, Seattle, Portland, Phoenix and Salt Lake City.

Pat recently did a special for ESPN and Trout Unlimited Television on the South Platte's infamous Cheesman Canyon. Also, Pat recently did a national advertising campaign for Fetzer Vineyards (Napa Valley) on the Snake River in Jackson Hole, Wyoming. The ads were nationally viewed in both magazines and on television. Pat has also appeared in Fly Fisherman Magazine and other national magazines promoting the new Orvis Wonderline Advantage. Look for his new book which exemplifies his talents on the South Platte River called A *Fly Fisher's Guide to the South Platte River - A complete Angler's Guide* published by Jim Pruett.

Pat is very active in Trout Unlimited and the conservation of cold-water fisheries. He has won the annual Master Fly Tournament five out of eight years. This event, sponsored by Trout Unlimited, is held in the beautiful Cheesman Canyon on the South Platte River. This two-fly competition involves twenty-four of Colorado's best anglers with the primary purpose of raising money to enhance the South Platte River drainage. Anyone who fishes the South Platte knows what an accomplishment this is. Bravo Pat!

Pat is also the Guide Director and a partner in the Blue Quill Angler, Inc. in Evergreen, Colorado. He oversees more than thirty guides and sets the standard for integrity and professionalism for the Blue Quill guiding operation. Pat also produces an on-line weekly fishing report keeping anglers up-to-date on fishing conditions.

Pat is a native of Colorado and has been guiding for more than ten years. He spends at least two hundred days a year on the stream, both personally and professionally, enjoying a unique quality of life. "I'm blessed to make my living as a fly-fishing guide. I'll never lose sight of how fortunate I am to really love my job."

Pat is a proud father of three beautiful boys, Forrest, thirteen, Zach, nine, and Hunter, seven. They too, carry on the family tradition and also love fly-fishing. Pat, his wife Kim and their five children reside in Parker, Colorado.

Dennis Potter

Dennis Potter, alias the Rivergod, has been has been fly-fishing nearly thirty years. He became a fly-tying fanatic when he spun his first "bug" over twenty-five years ago. Every one of the hundreds of dozens of flies he ties through Riverhouse Fly Company reflects his commitment to maintaining quality, simplicity, proportion and, above all, durability. He stresses technique and durability over speed and numbers. In fact, his catch phrase for his fly company is "Durable flies for the discriminating angler". These days, much of his bench time is taken up in fly design for Umpqua Feather Merchants.

He has taught and shared his skills as a fly-tying instructor for over twenty years. He passes along to his followers that durability is of the utmost importance. He urges tiers to do anything they can—using a more durable material, slowing down, or use some special technique—that will keep flies together longer. An accomplished video photographer, Dennis now specializes in giving group classes and seminars using studio-quality, macro video equipment. A very proud moment in his life came in 1999 when the Great Lakes Council of the Fly Fishing Federation awarded him as the Educator of the Year.

Dennis has produced a video, "Durable Flies", introducing a number of his favorite Rivergod creations. This very well-done work shows off his personal techniques for durable pattern design and includes helpful tips for fly tiers of any skill level. Several of the Rivergod patterns can be found in *Flies of the East* by Jim Schollmeyer and Ted Leeson and in the *Versatile Fly Tier* by Dick Talluer. He shoots the still photography for the Fly Box, a column that comes out once a month in *Michigan Outdoors Magazine*.

Dennis's robust personality has kept him very active in the Fly Fishing Federation where he is a life member, Trout Unlimited as a life member, and a past president of the West Michigan TU Chapter. He is a founding member of the Anglers of the Au Sable, founder of the Pathological Tiers, and member of the Fly Girls.

Dennis has been a fly-fishing instructor and guide on his home waters of the Au Sable River for a number of years. He has fished extensively throughout the Midwest, West and Alaska, where he had the distinction of catching and releasing all five species of Pacific salmon on flies. These days he spends time on his beloved Au Sable in northern Michigan, seeking out the challenge of fishing the little fly hatches. The Tiny Black and the Tiny Green Curse, as they are better known, drive some anglers to take up the equally frustrating game of golf. Midges, Tricos and tiny olives push Dennis to the edge of "angling ecstasy".

Dennis is married to his high school sweetheart, Karen. He says, "I would be long dead in a ditch somewhere if it wasn't for her." She has supported his fishing and allows him to go about doing his thing whenever he needs the time away. They have raised two kids. A son twenty-three, and daughter nineteen, both students at Northern Michigan University. Both are very good fly-fishers; however, their son has developed the need to mountain bike, rock climb, and winter camp. Their daughter loves fly-fishing and would fish with River Dad every time Dennis stepped out the door with a fly rod if time permitted her to.

Fred Vargas

Fred's is a very unusual story. He had moved to Michigan in 1988 with his wife. She wanted him to get involved in some recreation or sport. Sue, a Michigan native, was worried he would pack his stuff and leave if she couldn't find something to keep him busy. He had no desire to hunt so he decided fishing would be the best thing he could do since there is so much water in Michigan. To get him started, his wife actually had to show him how to knot the hook on and load up a worm. Now that is what you call a "Pilgrim". Fred fished with spin gear for a while and hooked his first steelhead. The sport of steelhead fishing intrigued him to the point of searching out other methods of hooking the mighty silver beast. After watching the video by Lanny Waller on steelheading, he knew he had to get a fly rod in his hand. This started an amazing chain of events that brought Fred into the limelight of fly-fishing.

"I started tying flies in 1991, the same year I started fly-fishing. That same year on November 2nd, I was hit by a semi truck during a snowstorm on my way to work. I had three hairline fractures on my hip and a broken leg. One fracture was along the sciatic nerve so for two months I had to lie in bed watching TV. The pain was such that I couldn't sleep, a catnap now and then, but basically watching TV twenty-four hours a day. Once I was finally able to sit up, I had no desire to watch TV."

To fend off boredom, Fred tied flies every day, 10-14 hours a day, for the next six months. Fly tying got him through the recovery time. In a strange way, it was therapy. "If it hadn't been for the accident, there is no way I would be at the level I am today," Fred admits.

Naturally, he got good at it. "I learned on my own through books and videos, when I could find them. I sold my first commercial flies to a local bait store in town, some ten years ago. Shortly thereafter, once I had a little more confidence in my tying, I visited a new fly shop in Rockford, Michigan. I asked if they could use another fly tier."

Basically, Fred has been tying with The Great Lakes Fly Fishing Company since the store opened. At one time, Fred was tying full-time, turning out 2000 dozen a year. In the meantime, he learned how to fly-fish. Again, pretty much on his own, even learning to cast a fly rod. Fred now guides on the Muskegon River for the store, works in the fly shop on weekends, and still ties about 500 dozen per year. He has taken an official lesson on spinning deer hair with Chris Helm, a very well-known tier from Ohio. Mike Martinek helped Fred on tying classic streamers and the late great Eugene Sunday showed him techniques on classic salmon flies. Fred now teaches fly-tying classes for the shop and does several demos every year around the state.

Fred is a member of the Fly Fishing Federation and is a certified casting instructor with the organization. Fred says the accomplishments he is most proud of are: Being a part of the Great Lakes Fly Fishing Company from day one and having a fly that he tied on the cover of a book, *Great Lakes Steelhead* by Bob Linsenman & Steve Nevala. Fred helped test new patterns for a book *Caddis Super Hatches* by Carl Richards and Bob Braendle and is mentioned and has a fly in Spey Flies & Dee Flies by John Shewey.

"I enjoy fly tying almost as much as I do fishing, but not quite!" Fred adds, "I consider fly tying as an art form and each fly a sculpture."

Fred and Sue reside in Montague, Michigan.

Ken Mead

PHILIP J. CAMPBELL

I met Ken Mead while we were gallivanting around the country on the pro staff with the A.K. Tool Company. We got to know each other pretty well and I found a good friend and an absolutely wonderful tier. He has a very sincere way about him and explains his fly-tying techniques to others very well. People would slowly gather around his tying desk at the big sportsmen's shows around the country and hang out for hours. They love watching him tie.

Come to find out, Ken has been tying flies for about twenty-three years and waving the long rod nearly twenty-six. He is very efficient behind the vise, and shares some of his preparation and material handling techniques.

Ken tied flies for Barry and Cathy Beck's old fly shop from the early 1980's to the early 90's. He also helped Barry teach tying classes on several occasions during that time period. "Barry has been the major influence on my tying style. I learned from him how to choose and grade materials, as well as how to tie quickly and efficiently. During the time I worked for the Beck's, they arguably had the finest tying staff in the East and much information was shared back and forth among the tiers. While each of us had our specialties (mine were Wulffs, fixed-wing streamers like Matukas and Zonkers, Atlantic salmon flies and Schwiebert-style thorax duns), we could all flip-flop back and forth among the various genres of fly styles. This, of course, made us all pretty versatile fly tiers."

Other major influences on my tying style were books by Ernest Schwiebert and Dave Whitlock. "This may sound a little strange in some respects because Whitlock is more of an impressionist tier and Schwiebert, in many cases, is more into realism," says Ken. "I try to use both aspects with my creative endeavors. To this day, their books, along with *Hatches*, are my main references." During the 90's, Ken worked out of several Eastern Pennsylvania Shops and was a frequent participant in the major eastern fly-fishing shows.

Ken has been published in the *Mid-Atlantic Fly Fishing Guide and* some of his original patterns are in the book *Flies of the East* by Ted Leeson.

Ken lives in the vicinity of Jim Thorpe, PA, in the Pocono Mountains of Pennsylvania. It affords him the opportunity to fish some of the great waters of the East. The Upper Delaware River system (including the East and West Branch), which is probably the finest fly-fishing in the East, are close by. A quick trip to the Southeast puts him the area of the Little Lehigh Creek and other Lehigh Valley Limestone creeks. Fabled Pocono streams such as the Brodheads and the Lackawaxen are a short distance away. The Letort Spring Creek and Yellow Breeches are not far down the road from there. Sounds like heaven to me, however, most of these waters require very technical fishing, perfect flies and perfect drifts. His skills as an angler are top notch.

I have had the pleasure of fishing with him on some of Colorado's finest waters and he spanked them there also.

John Hagen

John is a native of South Dakota who started fishing at the age of four. A natural born outdoorsman, he has hunted waterfowl, deer, elk, and upland game birds for as long as he can remember. He moved to Colorado in 1984 and started fly-fishing right away.

While working at Lens Crafters, John met Chas Clover. They started fishing together and John eventually learned how to tie flies from Clover. He started working as a guide at St. Vrain Anglers fly shop in Longmont, Colorado for Dale Darling. While working for Darling, a professional fly tier himself, John picked up several tying tricks to improve the speed of his tying, and started trading flies for fly rods. He ended up teaching many fly tying and fly-fishing classes for the store.

Soon thereafter, John was tying professionally and selling flies to five or six shops around Denver. He has made a quiet living as a lifetime outdoorsman. John says, "It may take me a while to get going, but after I get started tying, I can put a serious hurtin' on a pound of peacock herl and a case of hooks."

The quality of his dry flies in this book shows that is where his passion for fly-fishing lies. "I can hook a 14-inch brown trout on a dry fly and I feel like I have died and gone to heaven."

Some of his expert knowledge of dry-fly hackle came from grading hackle for Whiting Farms in Delta, Colorado. He has shown his skills during Saturday morning tying clinics at local fly shops and has been a featured presenter at major sportsmen's shows in Denver.

I have fished and worked with Too Tall, as John is known amongst friends, many times over the years and have experienced his passion. He is a natural as a guide and instructor. I watch the people he works with become better anglers right in front of my eyes. His quiet enthusiasm is remarkable. I asked him about his interest in jotting down his immense knowledge of fly tying and fishing and possible pursuit towards being an outdoor writer. He said, " I have contemplated writing a book but I soon realized it would be a great deal of work and end up going goose hunting instead."

John now guides at Boxwood Gulch Ranch and lives in Shawnee, Colorado with his wife Cindy and his two hunting dogs.

Paul and Char Stimpson

"I had every opportunity to start tying as a youngster," says Paul Stimpson. "My father fly-fished and tied his own flies. I used to sit and watch him for hours. I know he would have taught me, but I didn't think I wanted to learn. In his later years he gave me his tying kit in hopes that I would learn to tie, but I never seemed to have the time. I waited too long and he passed away without having the chance to teach me. I felt so bad that when the local fly shop offered fly tying classes, my wife Char and I both signed up.

Paul and Char learned fly tying from Mims and Bruce Barker at the Flyline Fly Shop in Ogden, Utah. Char learned quickly and was soon tying neat, well-proportioned flies. Paul, on the other hand, struggled and was easily the worst tier in the class. (As a fly-tying instructor, I love when I get a husband and wife team tying together. The nimble-fingered women always tie better.) However, he was determined to get better and practiced daily. "Even in my very early days of tying, I was fascinated with hair and the skills required for tying with it. I spent so much time tying hair flies, it soon became my personal expertise," explains Paul.

Char Stimpson

Paul and Char enjoyed fly tying so much that they were tying more flies than they could ever use. Flyline ended up taking some of their flies to pay for all the hooks and materials they were going through.

Before long, Paul was a fly-tying instructor. "I worked as an instructor for the U.S. Air Force so it was only natural that I started teaching fly tying. I worked with Eagle Outfitter in Layton, Utah and Wild Country Outfitter in Ogden, Utah,

Paul Stimpson

but was most proud when I returned to Flyline where I learned to tie and taught classes for Bruce and Mims Barker."

After attending several shows with the "Traveling Flyfisherman" featuring Gary LaFontaine, Jack Dennis, and Mike Lawson, Paul and Char became even more interested in the sport. It was during these shows that they became acquainted with Gary and formed a close relationship. "When Gary was stricken with ALS, he still wanted to do his tying programs, and asked me to do the tying for him while he explained the patterns. I gratefully accepted," says Paul.

Paul and Char's exposure to the public elevated when they tied with Gary at the Federation of Fly Fishers International Conclave in Livingston, Montana. Paul also assisted him in shows in Ogden, Utah and Denver, Colorado.

It was during a FFF Conclave in Idaho Falls, Idaho that they struck up a friendship with Al and Gretchen Beatty. During their discussions about fly tying, someone made the comment that Gary had a number of flies that had never been shown on video. So with Gary's help, they started the project of filming all of Gary's fly patterns. "We have completed all seven videos in the series and are very excited to present all of Gary's flies to the fly-fishing public," Paul adds.

The videos can be ordered through Al and Gretchen Beatty at BT's Flies.

Also during this same show, Al Beatty sat down with Char and showed her his techniques for spinning hair. This quickly became her favorite pastime and she is now very proficient at spun and clipped hair flies. Incidentally, this conclave was her first tying demonstration in front of people. She now ties Mohawks and Deer Hair Woollys.

Paul ties a 1000 dozen flies a year or more, with one grueling year of 2000 dozen. This included fly deliveries to Edgewater Fishing Products in Clearfield, Utah, Arricks Fly Shop and Eagle Store in West Yellowstone, Montana and Gary LaFontaine's Bookmailer in Helena, Montana.

Paul and Char live in Ogden, Utah. They enjoy traveling and fishing around the West, attending Fly Fishing Federation conclaves helping people improve their tying and spending as much time as possible on their local waters such as the Logan River and Willow Valley.

Randy Smith

Randy Smith started fly-fishing in the early 1980s. Not as early as some, but it came very naturally to him. Randy says, "From the very first time I had a fly rod in my hand, I started catching trout right away." He spends much of his time fishing these days with a backpack on his back. He loves hiking into high-mountain lakes and streams with his wife, Gale.

On top of being a well-respected tier, Randy has been a member of the pro staff for Whiting Farms and the Spirit River Company. He has been a featured presenter and fly tier at the International Sportsman Exposition in Denver and Seattle. Randy's accomplishments with a camera have been published in *Colorado Outdoors, Rocky Mountain Fish and Game*.

Tying came very naturally to Randy also. After getting his first vise and tools, he tied mostly for himself but had a friend heading for New Zealand. He asked if Randy would tie him some flies. "Well, of course!" agreed Randy. "So, my first order was five dozen Adams dry flies. It seemed insurmountable. I remember tying three dozen one day and saying, 'Wow, that's a record.' There was no method, no set up. I just pieced them together. Those three dozen took about eight hours. I was so proud of those first five dozen flies, and they actually caught fish on them."

He started tying professionally. The thought it might be a way to make a living and not work for the 'Man' intrigued Randy. He got his name out and a few orders started coming in, a few dozen Woolly Buggers here and a couple of dozen scuds there. Some shop owners were willing to give a guy a shot, not to mention that most owners were looking for flies. The influx of foreign flies had not been perfected at that point in time, as it is these days.

Randy adds, "I think it's a gradual progression. With many pro tiers, the business of fly tying is something you mix in with other ventures as a second income. Then the thought came to me that I might be able tie enough to make a living. It didn't take too long to figure out that tying perfect flies, a large number of flies, and tying them as fast as you can is an attitude. Of course, there is skill involved, but it revolves around self-discipline and making yourself reliable. The better you get and the more focused you are, the less you have to force yourself to sit down and do it."

"My schedule these days, especially during the winter, is to start tying about 6:00AM and go until about 10:00AM. Since I live in the mountains and I'm also a ski instructor, I strap on the skis for a few hours and get a little exercise. However, on my last run down the mountain my mind is already geared back to the vise figuring out how many dozen I need to get done that day. Before it is all said and done, I will get 8-10 hours of tying in each day."

After tying flies professionally for over a dozen years, Randy has found that he can make a decent living at it. He reminds me that he's not getting rich, however, this is what he had envisioned: To work for himself, using his time as he likes instead of having someone make his schedule for him.

Randy specializes in tailwater flies and micro patterns. You can get his flies at several locations in Colorado, including the entire group of fly shops in Breckenridge and Silverthorne. Other well-known shops around the state, such as Trout's Flyfishing, Complete Angler, Blue Quill Anglers, The Hatch Fly Shop, Taylor Creek Fly Shop, Angler's Covey, Flies and Lies, and Roaring Fork Anglers, also carry Randy's flies.

Here is a pro tying tip that Randy would like to share: "Keep a personal pattern book of the flies you specialize in. Note the hook, dubbing mix, dye color of a feather, or certain brand of a material! It makes for more consistent looking flies from year to year."

Randy and his wife Gale live in Fairplay, Colorado.

Mark Hatter

Here is a guy who eats, sleeps, and breathes tarpon fishing. Mark Hatter's passion is taking big tarpon on the fly each spring and summer in his home waters of the Gulf of Mexico. He has been an avid fisherman for over thirty years and has fly-fishing experience in both salt and fresh water. From blue marlin to trout, there are few species of fish he hasn't attempted to catch on a fly.

His last twelve years have been devoted exclusively to saltwater fly-fishing in his home state of Florida. He does trek to the Bahamas, Colorado, and Alaska to fish on occasion, but it's pretty tough getting him to put down that 12 weight.

Currently, Mark is a masthead contributing writer to *Fly Fishing in Salt Waters* magazine with published features and stories in five different fishing magazines over the last eight years.

He began tying his own flies after an expensive trip to Charlotte Harbor on Florida's southwest coast one fall, shortly after he went exclusively to the long wand. Bad weather had murked up the flats, making sight fishing nearly impossible. Consequently, Mark and his son plied the seemingly productive, albeit dirty, flats by blind casting to barely visible potholes in hopes of finding laid-up redfish. What they found instead of redfish were legions of blowfish eager to take any fly presented.

Unfortunately, blowfish sport dentures like a parrot and in less than two hours, Mark's $75 arsenal of purchased Clouser Deep Minnows and Lefty's

Mark Hatter

Deceivers were reduced to bare hooks and wisps of tying thread. The next trip Mark made was to the local fly shop for a vise, bucktail and an assortment of chicken necks!

A saltwater specialist, Mark now ties everything from #6 bonefish flies to 6/0 tandem hooked marlin flies. But he spends the majority of his time either at the vise tying his beloved tarpon patterns or tying Bimini twist class tippets Huffnagled to fluorocarbon bite tippets for his tarpon leaders.

Mark and his wife Vicky, live in Oviedo, Florida.

Richard Pilatzke

Richard was born in Montreal, Canada and grew up in upstate New York. Pete Peterson, Richard's father-in-law, introduced him to fly-fishing some twenty-three years ago. Richard has been fly-fishing and fly tying ever since. He has lived in Colorado now for over twenty years and for the last several years has specialized in tying flies for high-mountain lakes in Colorado. Richard is most comfortable sitting in a kick boat with one of his favorite boxes of foam flies beside him.

Rich found a niche in the fly-tying business when he saw his first sheet of tying foam. "I have been fascinated with foam as a fly-tying material for over fifteen years. It was sheets of craft foam in yellow, green, and orange. My mind was racing furiously thinking about flies I could tie with this new material. Eventually, I would tie Madam X's and Elk Hair Hoppers from this foam. They turned out to be highly successful fished as terrestrial imitations."

As you will see from his flies, Richard has found foam a highly versatile and durable material. He likes to search out little-known materials and create new patterns. His flies are available at the Hatch Fly Shop in Pine Junction and Evergreen, Colorado. You can also find his unique foam patterns at the Blue Quill Angler in Evergreen, Colorado.

Richard is very active in local Trout Unlimited organizations and donates dozens of flies for fundraisers in Colorado. Overall, he likes the creative aspect of fly tying, so his biggest influences have been Gary LaFontaine, John Betts, Craig Matthews, and Al Makkai.

He lives in Littleton, Colorado with his wife Cheryl and his black lab, Ebony.

Chapter 1

20 Tricks of the Trade

1. Proportions

Professional fly tiers take fly proportions very seriously. Not only do proportions make a fly anatomically correct, oftentimes it is the difference between the fly riding on the water correctly or on its side. Dealing with proportions on a fly has a direct relationship with the hook and its proportions. As you follow the instructions for each fly pattern, I will relate to hook positions and the direction you need to move the thread to get there. It is mostly fly-tying jargon, but it has a purpose and it is an important "trick of the trade".

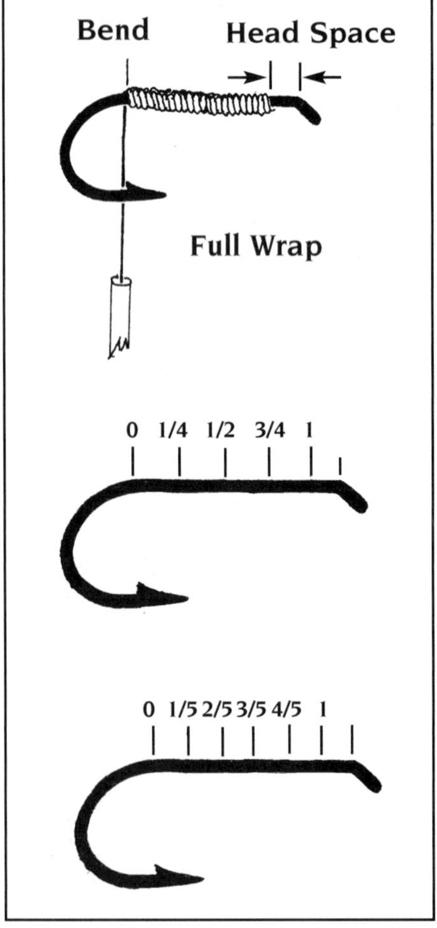

DAVE HILTON

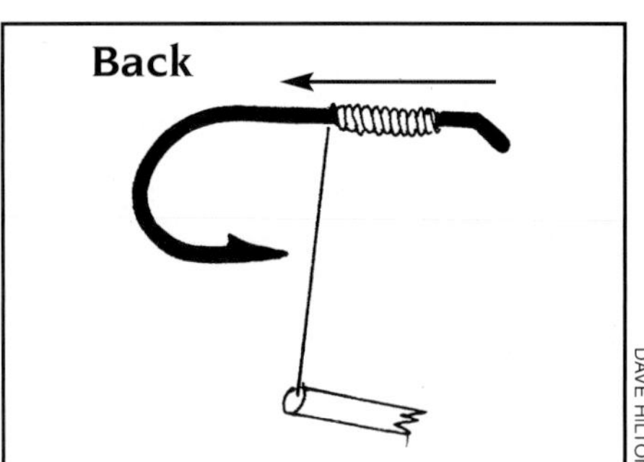

DAVE HILTON

Hook position, starting at the back of the hook, is primarily referred to as the 0 point, the back of the hook, or the barb. Moving forward to the hook eye, the 1/4 point is next, followed by the1/2 point, and then the 3/4 point. The front of the fly or behind the eye is most often referred to as the 1 point. Notice the front of the fly is not directly behind the eye, it is back slightly to accommodate the head of the fly. Contributors to this book will often be more precise, referring to the 3/5 point or dividing the hook into fifths instead of quarters. They do this for a reason, so try to use the proportions correctly.

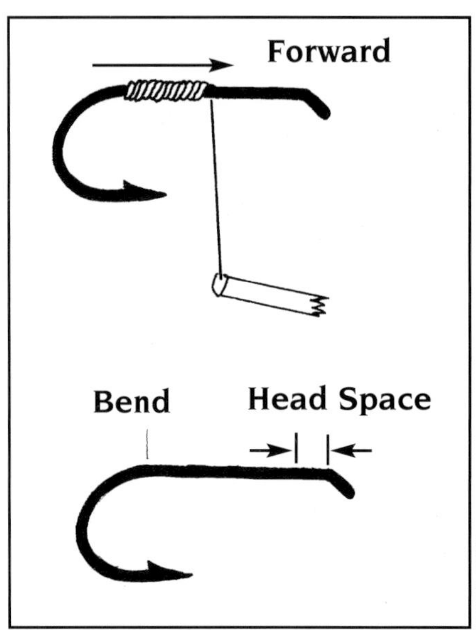

DAVE HILTON

When there is reference to moving the thread forward, wrap the thread towards the eye of the hook, while moving back is towards the bend of the hook.

2. Get Comfortable

Find the correct height for the vise. In order to tie comfortably, the angle of your eyes and the distance your hands need to move should be taken into consideration.

Make sure your shoulders do not knot up. Armrests on your chair help considerably.

Make sure your neck doesn't get stiff.

Make sure your lower back is in a good posture. A chair with lumbar support takes your comfort to a whole new level.

3. Choosing a Vise

A vise should be a one-time purchase. I started with an inexpensive vise and had to move up as soon as I started tying commercially. It was too frustrating to have the hook sliding around in the vise under the lightest of thread tension. So I spent a hundred bucks on another vise.

It was better than the first one, but still had significant downfalls. It held a hook very well, but had such strong holding power it would crack the jaws when tying small hooks. And that is what I tied with most, hooks from size 16 down. Within a very short time I had to step up again. Three hundred dollars and thousands of dozens of flies later, I still have a usable vise that works for every size hook. That was 15 years ago.

I know buying a vise is a tough decision, but these days vises are so advanced, you can purchase a vise at a very reasonable cost that will last a lifetime. Yes, you can easily spend those three hundred dollars on a vise, but that is the last vise purchase you will need to make. Pick the one that fits your style of tying and get it.

Avoid the situation in which I found—myself. I spent nearly five hundred dollars on three vises before I found the one that was most suited to my needs.

3. Star Light, Star Bright

Use the brightest light you can stand. Halogen lights are better than incandescent light. Small fluorescent lights are not too bad. The Ott Light is color corrected to natural light. It deals with Kelvin light temperatures. A photographer would know about light temperatures, but a fly tier only needs to know that it is very good lighting for tying flies.

One more thing to take into consideration is the color of your desktop used for tying. A desktop of white, light yellow, or light blue is best to tie against. Wood-grain tops and dark colors cause eyestrain and materials are hard to see against them.

4. Shooting Pool

Tying flies is very much like shooting pool; you need to plan your next shot before you chalk your cue.

Laying out the hooks, materials, and tools needed for the fly pattern is of utmost importance. The location of these materials on the tying desk is totally up to the tier. You must develop your own system. When the material or tool stays in a certain location, you subconsciously reach for it and it's always there. (Check the layout technique by Randy Smith in the Flashback Pheasant Tail Nymph.

This trick is the key to rhythm. When you watch a pro tier at work, everything looks so smooth. Seldom does it look like they are tying fast, however, they are very efficient with their movements. Their hands are reaching for the correct material and the bobbin is always in the right position to tie in the next material. You can always tell if the tier is accomplished because they are instructing, talking, shaking hands and they still get the fly tied in two and a half minutes.

Brad Befus adds, "Not only do you have to plan your next shot, you need to plan out the strategy for the whole game. Know what you are going to tie before picking and buying the material. Choosing the correct material for the fly pattern is very important. Some materials are interchangeable, while others are not. Deer hair, winging materials, hackle, and tailing should be chosen with a particular fly in mind."
The best materials make the best flies!

5. Write Your Own Book

Randy Smith suggests preparing your own pattern book. Keep track of your own material lists. As a pro tier, delivering consistent flies to the shop owner will make your life much easier. Specialty flies are not uncommon amongst fly shops. They all have their special patterns, colors, or hook styles. Keeping track of these patterns in your head will lead to many challenges.

If you develop a pattern that works very well with a certain color or material that makes it unique to you, make notes so you will not forget how to put the pattern together.

Add notes concerning any brainstorms about tying the fly, preparing the materials, thread choice, and durability.

6. Do Two Things at Once

Combine steps whenever possible. Dub the thread, leaving a half-inch of bare thread between the dubbing and the hook shank before you tie in ribbing. Tie in the ribbing and dub the fly all in one move. Now, do not let go of the ribbing. As soon as the abdomen on the fly is done, immediately wrap the ribbing. In essence you are reducing the number of trips to the vise. This can be done with dubbing and a tail. It also can be used by dubbing the thread for a thorax and then tying in the wingcase with the bare thread. See RS-2, Hare's Ear Nymph.

7. Measuring Wings for Streamers

Brad Befus suggested clamping a ruler to your tying desk to measure feather wings for streamers, such as Lefty's Deceivers or tarpon flies. Pre cut all feathers to length before you start tying.

8. Fingernails are Tools

Use fingernails as measuring tools for tails and wings. With your thumbnail at

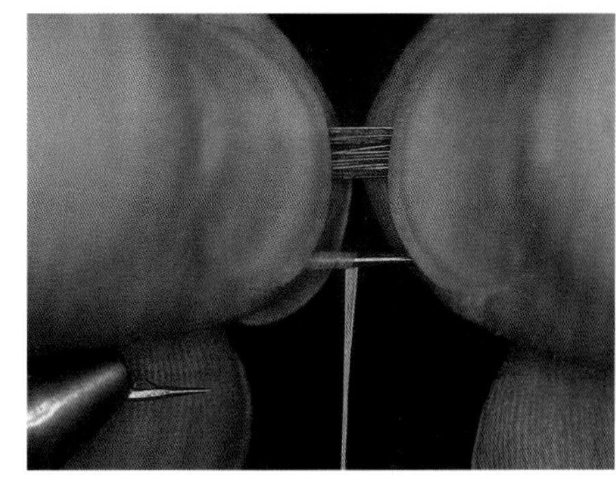

the eye of the hook, make measurements in proportion such as thread placement or hook position to measure materials against. For instance, have the tips of the tailing material at the 1/2 point of the hook for tails that you would like to be 1/2 hook shank length. Transfer to the other hand by putting thumbnail to thumbnail. Move thumbnail of the left hand to the back of the hook, which should be right above the barb. Secure tails to the hook, they should be the precise length you measured. This is a key point for consistent proportions.

9. Don't Put Your Scissors Down

Learn to keep your scissors in your hand at all times. There are several styles of scissors out there to accommodate every hand.

Notice how the pair of scissors with the black handles is held between the first and second knuckles of the third finger. You will find most fly tiers hold their scissors this way. Do not let the loop of the scissors go all the way into the palm of your hand. It is too restrictive when

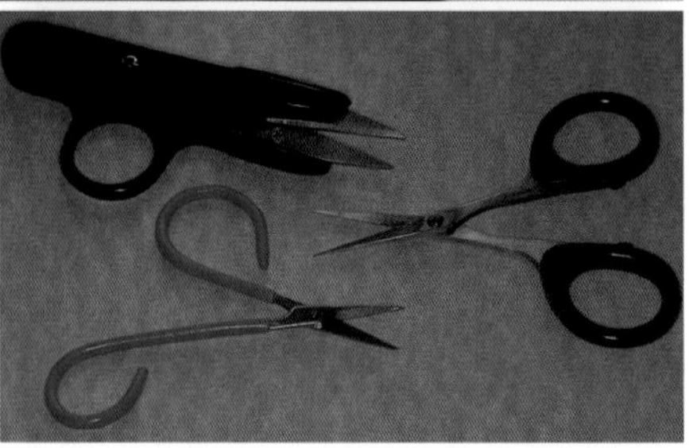

trying to get the thumb into the other loop and positioning the scissors for cutting. Wiss scissors, or nipper-type scissors, are very popular and are easily held in the hand at all times. Looping the index finger was the first method I learned to hold my scissors while tying. It is a little restrictive but a very adequate method. Randy Smith still uses this technique.

Have you ever had a pair of scissors flop around in your hand while you're tying? One possibility is that the springing action of the blades has worn out. Another may be that you purchased a cheap pair of scissors. Randy Smith suggests storing your scissors in the open position to maintain the tight cutting action. Scissors are a very important tool for the fly tier, so shake out the piggy bank and buy a good pair. You don't have to buy a $200.00 pair of German hair scissors, but there are some very good ones from $20.00 to $50.00.

10. Hang On To Your Bobbin

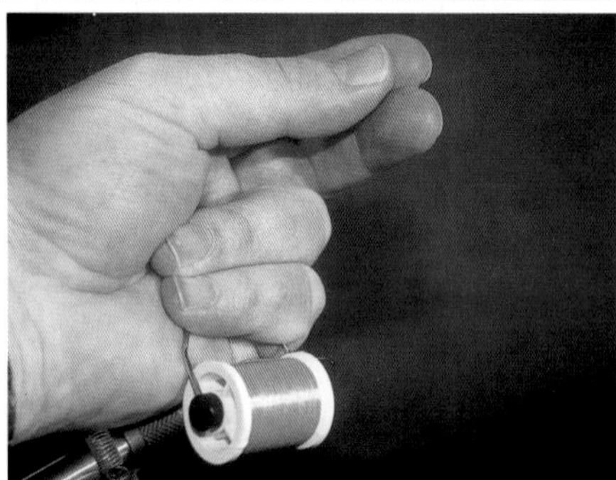

Most pro tiers keep their bobbin in their hand at all times.

Ken Mead suggests bending your bobbins to fit your hand comfortably. He has bent all of his bobbins to fit his hand. Try a couple to see if they feel better and are easier to hang on to while tying.

11. Tying One On

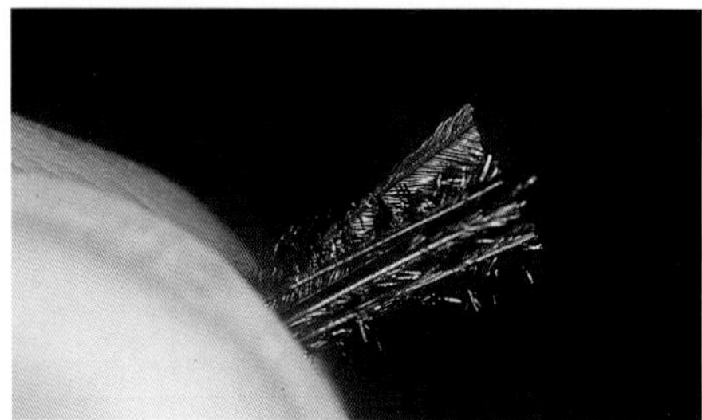

Hold a material with just a small amount, maybe 1/16 to 1/8 of an inch, out of your thumb and index finger before you tie it on the hook. By tying in material by the tip, you don't have to go to the vise and cut excess material off.

12. Hold It At An Angle

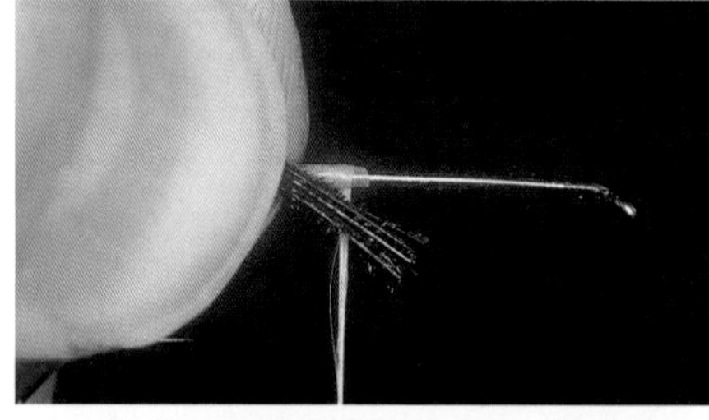

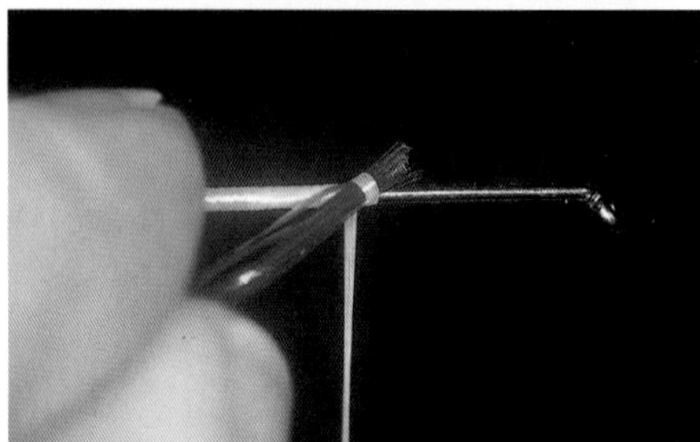

Hold material at a 45 degree angle to the hook to ensure a good tie-in. The material is held on the foreside of the hook at a downward angle even with the tie-in point. Taking the thread over the top of the material with a soft wrap will fasten said material to the side of the hook and roll it to the top of the hook. Try holding the material on top of the hook at the same angle and take the thread over the top of it. This position works especially well with wire and other types of ribbing that need to be maneuvered to the backside of the hook.

13. Epoxy Bubbles

Brad Befus suggested this trick for getting air bubbles out of epoxy before it sets up. Blow through a straw using the warm, moist air from your lungs directed at the epoxy. The air bubbles will come to the top and burst leaving a smooth, clear epoxy finish.

14. Just Because It Looks Clean?

Remember that no matter how clean a raw material looks, store it in a plastic shoebox or sweater box with moth balls. Bird skins, strung feathers, loose feathers in a bag, feathers and skins acquired from a hunter should all be protected in this fashion. I purchase raw materials in bulk, not only for cost savings but to acquire a variety of that material. By buying the side of a whitetail deer hide, I can get caddis winging hair, Comparadun hair, and hair that can be used for spinning. Bulk feathers also give you a variety of sizes and colors. Skins that have been tanned do not need to be moth-balled.

15. Prepping and Storing Materials

There is one thing all good tiers do: Store materials away in an orderly, well-marked fashion. Plastic shoeboxes store materials like pheasant tails, calf and squirrel tails, flash, biots and quills,

dubbing, and thread. They are stackable and easily marked with labels. Plastic sweater boxes are great for hackle, bulk hair, rabbit and squirrel skins, and bucktails.

Take time out to prep materials. Sit down and do the chores that make setting up to tie flies easier. They are usually annoying, tedious things like measuring hackle, preparing turkey tail feathers

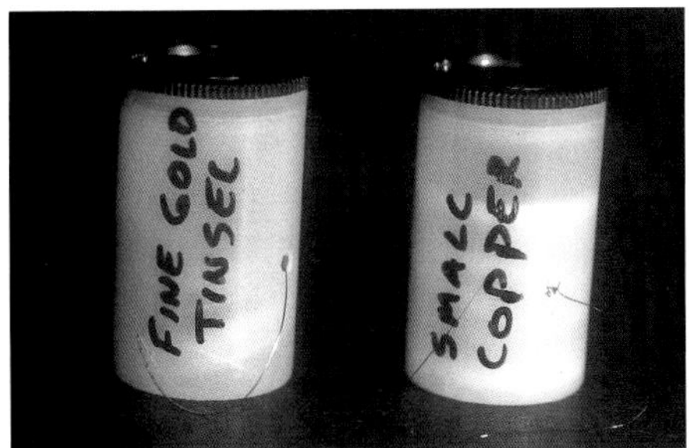

for wingcases, dying materials, and high selecting feathers like pheasant tails, turkey flats, mallard flanks.

16. Break Your Thread

Now what kind of a trick is this? This is a way of learning thread torque. I always suggest to beginners that they break their thread (they usually do anyhow) so they can find out just how tight they can wrap-in a material. All materials should be secured to the hook with as much thread torque as possible: Flies are more durable and fewer wraps of thread are needed to tie it.

17. Rotating the Vise

For those of you using a rotating vise, John Hagen suggests making a couple extra wraps of thread before rotating a material into place to avoid using a bobbin cradle.

18. Break It Instead of Cutting It

Break the thread after starting it instead cutting the tag end. Hold rearward pressure with the thread and bobbin while pulling the tag end of thread towards the eye of the hook, in essence cutting the thread with thread. Some materials can be broken instead of cut; peacock herl, ostrich herl, and the tip of a hackle after it has been wrapped.

19. The Secret to Dubbing

Spread a smaller amount of dubbing over a longer length of thread. It is much easier to add dubbing if you run short than it is to take it off if you have too much.

20. The Secret to Hair

Always start with more hair than you will need because it easier to take hair away if you have too much than it's to add more if you come up short.

Chapter 2

MATERIAL PREPARATION

ONE OF THE OUTSTANDING TRAITS of all professional tiers is their ability to handle and prepare materials prior to and during the act of tying flies. Pros make it look so easy, but the truth be known, we were at the beginning of this process at one time ourselves and went through the *University of Hard Knocks.* Although the repetitive nature of tying flies develops the skills needed to hold, secure, and understand what a material should look like on the hook, a little instruction along the way doesn't hurt. All pro tiers have learned tricks along the way from books or watching another tier. I'm sure that is why you are reading this, so I aim to please.

One of the most important issues to consider is the material itself. It is imperative that you acquire the finest-quality materials available. This is the only way you can tie the best flies you possibly can.

I've had several people over the years come up to me with a box full of flies and ask me what I think of them. My first question is always, "What do YOU think of them?" And my second is, "It's not really what I think of them, have you caught fish on them?" Answers vary, but they usually catch fish. Their concern was not so much how many fish they can catch on them, but how neat they look. Most people who start tying their own flies want them to look as good as possible; it's just the nature of tying. However, there is always some aspect of the fly that they had trouble with. "I couldn't get the dubbing tight," or "This dry fly always rides on its side or doesn't float very long," or "This hackle just doesn't look like the one in the book." All great observations by the inquisitive tier.

More often than not, the answer can usually be found in the materials used to tie the fly. A friend or family member finds out you are interested in fly-fishing and fly-tying, so the natural gift for Father's Day or a birthday is a fly-tying kit. I hate to say it, but fly-tying kits are usually the reason a fly doesn't look too great. Sad but true, a well thought out gift turns out to be a headache, but taken in perspective, it is a great learning experience. Beginner fly tying kits are just that, materials and tools used to gain a certain amount of knowledge about fly-tying in the beginning. It is more of a marketing thing than practical, smart shopping. However, to progress into a good tier, knowledge of fly tying materials is a necessity. Do remember this though, most of the flies tied in the beginning don't look like much (you should have seen mine) partly because of the two left hands you start with, but also because these flies are tied with inferior materials. If you already have a fly-tying kit, use what you can. However, if you don't have a kit, please hang in there with me for a while and I will pass along the do's and don'ts of picking materials.

After talking with the rest of the contributors for this book, I found they have heard the same questions and experiences. These common occurrences led me to write this chapter. A number of books on the market have researched materials to the ends of the earth and I really didn't want to hash that over again. I will examine a number of the most common materials used to tie flies, help you understand what good materials are and what to look for so you can acquire top-quality goods. I will also pass along ideas on handling and storing materials, all in hopes you will become a better, more proficient fly tier.

Biots

I always get requests and questions about goose biots during tying demos and classes, so I thought I would quickly try to clear up the use and tying procedures for them.

First of all, goose biots, also called stripped goose, are from the leading edge of the first two flight feathers on a goose wing. They are literally stripped from the stem of the feather. Biots are primarily used for tailing on stoneflies and Prince Nymphs, which will be covered in the Material Preparation chapter on tailing. The fancy pointed wings on a Prince Nymph are also biots. However, a nicely segmented body can be made on a dry fly or nymph. This strip has a range of different sized biots as shown in photo 1, which can be used for a body on hook sizes ranging from #16-#24.

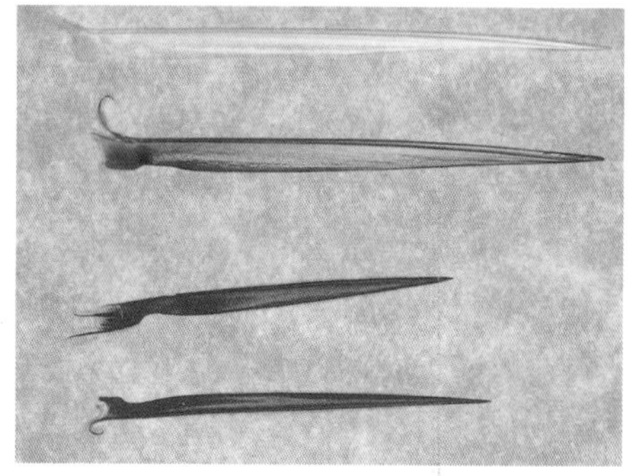

Turkey biots are much longer and wider than goose biots as shown in photo 2. Turkey biots can be wrapped for larger fly bodies, basically up to a #12.

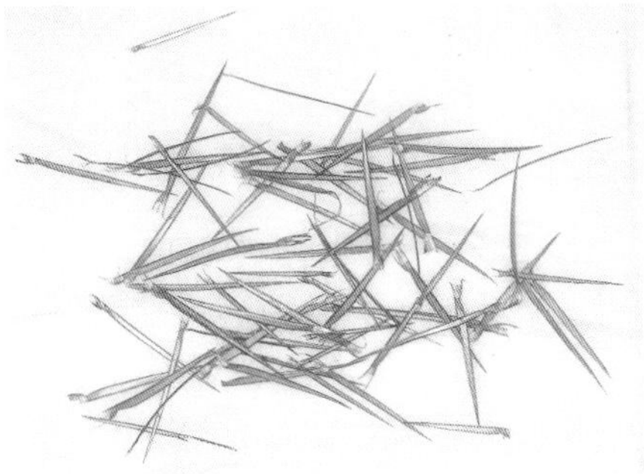

This step in preparation is not entirely necessary, but I find the biots much easier to use and wrap around the hook more consistently. When I am going to wrap biots for fly bodies, I like to strip the correct sized biots for the hook I am using off the main stem and lay them on a damp cloth or paper towel. This softens the biots just enough to make them pliable and wrap easier. It also prevents the biots from splitting and the softness helps the thread bind the biot to the hook more securely. I have watched many good tiers using biots that do not moisten them and get along just fine. I would suggest trying it both ways and find which method works best for you.

Biots can basically be wrapped in two ways. One method has a raised edge to the segmentation. The other is fairly smooth but still has the appearance of segmentation. The method you use, is totally dependent on which look appears best to you personally. I tie all my nymph patterns and 75% of my dries using the raised rib. There are a few dry flies that look great using the smooth segmented look.

A biot has a straight edge on one side and curved edge on the other. The curved edge also has a notch very near the point where it came off the stem. In order to determine which method to use for the body, it is very important to pay attention to the edges of the biot.

To make a body with a raised rib, position the biot parallel to the hook shank with the straight edge on top, notch on the bottom, and the point of

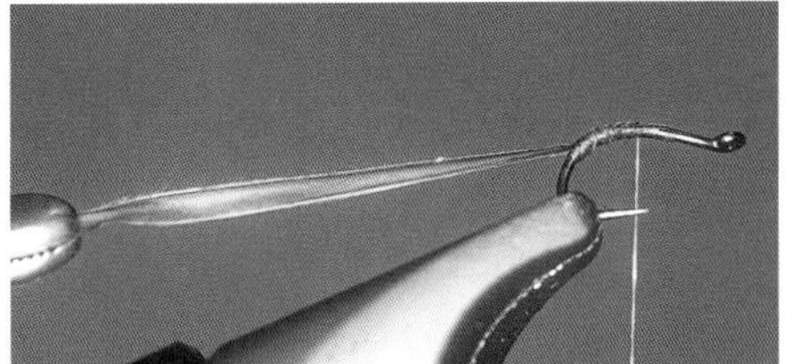

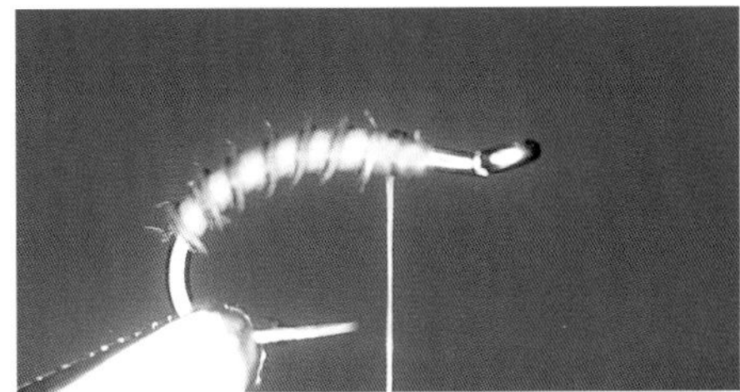

the biot toward the eye. Tie in the tip of the biot at the 1/2 point of the hook and wrap back. Move thread forward to a point on the hook you want to end the body. This will vary from one fly to the next. On this simple midge pattern, the thread stopped at about the 5/8 point. Attach hackle pliers to the butt end of the biot. Reposition the biot perpendicular to the hook shank and rotate the pliers counter-clockwise about 90° so the straight edge of the biot is now to the rear of the fly. Wrap the biot forward around the hook, spacing the segmentation to the desired width. Secure biot.

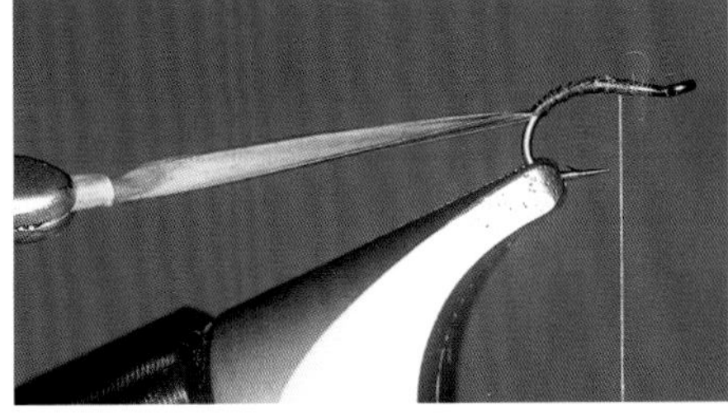

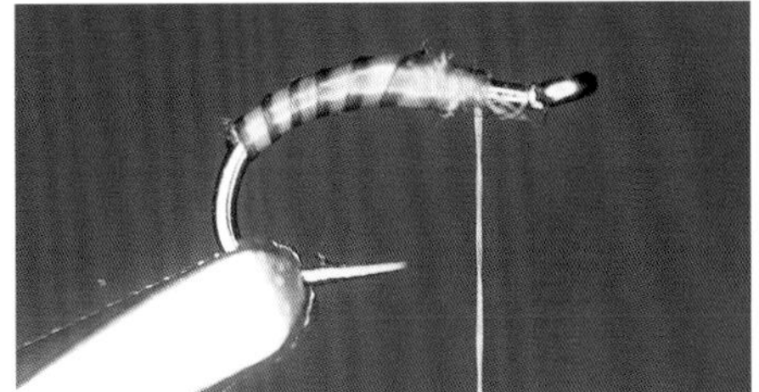

To make a body with a smooth segmentation, position the biot parallel to the hook shank with the straight edge on the bottom, the notch on top, and the point of the biot toward the eye. Tie in the tip of the biot at the 1/2 point of the hook and wrap back. Move thread forward to a point on the hook you want to end the body. Attach hackle pliers to the butt end of the biot. Reposition the biot perpendicular to the hook shank and rotate the pliers counter-clockwise about 90° so the straight edge of the biot is now pointing to the front of the fly. Wrap the biot forward around the hook, spacing the segmentation to the desired width. Secure biot.

Wrapping biots takes practice. The tension used on the first wrap is the key to success. If pulled too hard the biot will snap off. A soft first wrap with gradual tension applied to tighten the biot on the second and third wraps is the secret. See the Biot Midge in the chapter on Midges for more tying ideas.

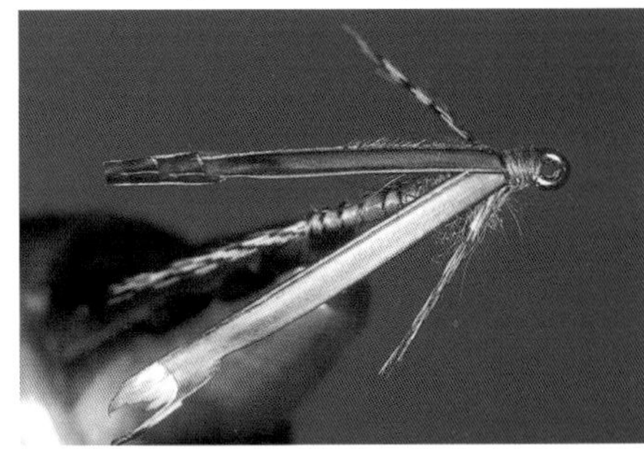

Try making a mayfly wingcase out of biots. Attach the wingcase just like the wings on a Prince Nymph except they are tied in by the tips. Trim them at slight angles to get the shape of a wingcase.

Speaking about Prince Nymphs, try a Golden Prince. This has been a good producer for me going on 10 years now.

See the chapter on Tailing for a look at biots used as tails.

Dubbing

Have you ever bought a bag of dubbing and had the bottom of the bag end filled with dust, little bits of unusalbe hair and fur that you end up throwing away? On top of that, half the fibers in the supposed dubbing are less than a quarter-inch long, again pretty much unusable. I know I have!

The process that left you with that mess is simple and productive as far as time goes. They take a skin, let's say a rabbit pelt, get a pair of electric shears and start cutting the fur off the skin. If the first pass doesn't get it all, they go over it again (this second pass is what causes the short unusable fibers). Throw it in a blender of some kind, mix it up, and bag it for the unknowing fly tier. Hey, you can't blame dubbing makers. They need to make a profit and the person standing over a pile of smelly rabbit skins with the shears is doing the best he can. The shears can only stay sharp for so long! But that doesn't mean we fly tiers are stuck with that as our only option.

I started tying before the synthetic age so dubbing was the number-one product for building flies. As far as I know, dubbing may very well still be the most important fly-tying material out there. A lot of it is still sold and fly tiers are still demanding a large variety, myself included! I've bought several different types of dubbing just to see what they were like. Some didn't cut the mustard! I still have many "test" bags of dubbing stored away in shoeboxes somewhere, never to be used. In fact, dubbing makers were just starting to mix synthetics into the natural furs, further confusing the issue. Some of these blends are very good, especially the furs blended with Antron.

Out of all the different types of dubbing, natural rabbit and Aussie possum work best for me. Muskrat, beaver, red fox and gray squirrel all have their place. There are many very good synthetic dubbings. Primarily I like the very fine denier dubbings for dry-fly bodies. Fine & Dry by Spirit River is one of the best.

I must reiterate here: In order to tie durable, quickly tied, consistently proportioned flies you must use top-quality materials. Dubbing is not an exception. Find the ones you can dub well with and that have an overall look you like and stick with them.

What makes good dubbing?

Quality natural dubbing has two characteristics: It should have long fibers and be clean so that the fur blends well without forming big clumps. I prefer to work with tanned skins mainly for their cleanliness. However, I would rather use raw muskrat for the natural oils that help it repel water.

This brings up another point. For dry flies, I try to use the fur from an animal that lives in or around water—like muskrat, beaver, mink, and otter—because of their natural water-repelling qualities. Nymph dubbing usually comes from land-borne animals—rabbit, squirrel, and badger because water absorbs into their fur better, helping the flies sink. This information is not etched in stone, but it does give you an idea of what type of dubbing you can use for a certain fly. Hey, I have lots of dry flies with rabbit dubbing for the body!

There is a way to produce natural dubbing that has long, usable, easy-to-dub fibers. It is a bit time-consuming, but every minute it takes is time well spent.

First you will need a coffee can, A one-pounder will do nicely. I'm not staking claim on this idea, but I definitely made it popular in the Denver area over the years. I was called the "Can Man" for quite some time. I found the idea years ago in the "Tying Tips" section of an old *American Angler & Fly Tier*" magazine. While doing the research on this book I was unable to locate the issue with this tip in it, so if the real "Can Man" would please step forward and call my publisher, I will do my best to give credit where credit is due.

Cut a one-inch-square hole in the side of the can below the centerline of the can. With a knife I make three cuts in the shape of an H and fold the halves of the H over to make a square hole. The overall shape is not important so if you wanted to use a jig saw and cut a heart-shaped hole, it would work! Use masking tape to cover the sharp edges, then take a piece of cheesecloth, fold it so you have four plies and tape it over the hole, inside and out. (See photo) Now, take the clear plastic lid and cut a hole the size of a pencil near the edge. (See photo) The can is ready.

A few more items you'll need for preparing dubbing are a pair of long-bladed scissors to cut the fur off the skin and a sharpening tool of some kind to repair the edge on your scissors. They will get dull, guaranteed! A dryer sheet to reduce the static cling on the inside of the can while mixing the dubbing is also useful, but not absolutely necessary.

You will need some kind of skin with fur on it. As I mentioned before, some of the most popular dubbings are made of rabbit, squirrel, (shown in photo) muskrat, beaver, otter, and, my favorite, Australian possum. Trim the fur as close

to the skin as possible and put the loose fur in the coffee can. The one pound coffee can will mix up more dubbing than you think, but I suggest you start with small amounts at first.

Put the lid on the can, take a deep breath (turn your head away from the can or you might cough up fur balls like the cat) and blow into the small hole in the lid. The fur is spinning around in the can, blending evenly, while the exhaust is exiting through the hole in the side covered with cheesecloth. One or two puffs will usually do it. Take the lid off and roll the dubbing out with your fingers. You will be amazed at what comes out. Perfect dubbing!

I normally buy white rabbit and light Australian possum and dye it eleven different colors. Beaver will also dye up into black, dark olive, light olive, gray, yellow, pink, dark brown, fiery brown, ginger, tan, and orange. I mix up a little white to make twelve different colors and put them into a twelve-compartment plastic dubbing container.

One last tip to increase your tying speed: As you dub the thread, keep in mind how much dubbing it will take to complete the task. After dubbing a couple of flies you should learn just how long the dubbing noodle should be to complete the fly without having too much left over or too little so that you have to reapply dubbing to finish the task. Dubbing a dry fly and a nymph body up to a size 16 should be done with one noodle of a precise amount.

As your flies get bigger, don't make the noodle so long that you hit yourself in the chin as you are turning the dubbing into place. When you know more than two inches of a dubbing noodle will be needed to complete the task, apply the dubbing two or three times if needed.

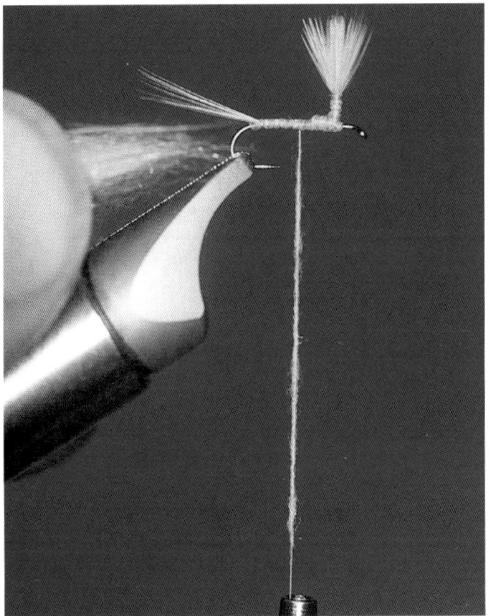

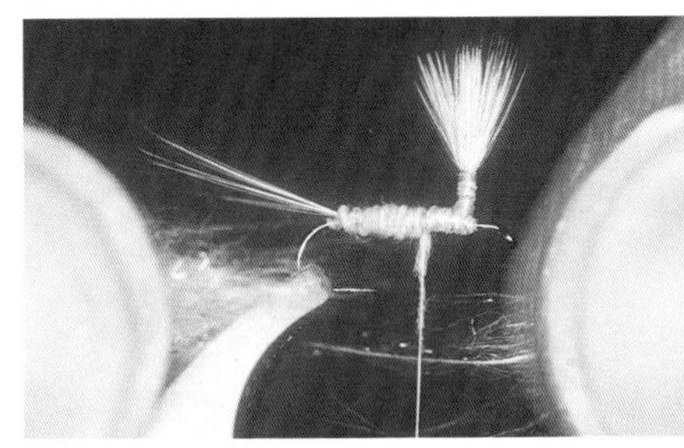

I use a size 16 Paradun as an example. Dub a two-inch noodle and leave the dubbing ball in your left hand if you dub with your right hand and vice versa if you dub with your left. DON'T PUT IT DOWN! (It always seems hard to find anything on my tying table when I set it down.) Wrap the dubbing into place until you have just about finished the noodle. Stop and re-dub the thread. Leave the extra in your hand again just in case you need more. On this particular fly, I have found that I need about one and a half inches more dubbing to finish the fly. Again, it should take a couple of flies to figure out just how much you will need on the second application so a third is not needed.

An exception to this thought would be the tier that uses a rotating vise. In this case, make the dubbing noodle as long as you need and rotate it in place. However, after doing it both ways, I think I can wrap faster than I can rotate.

My Method

My method of dubbing the thread goes something like this: pull apart a small ball of dubbing and lay it back together.

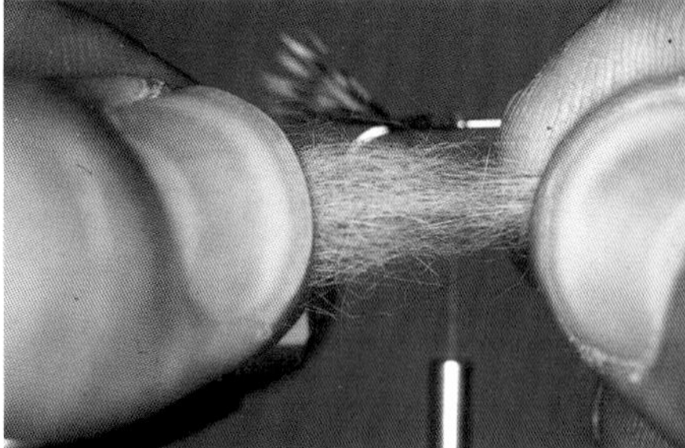

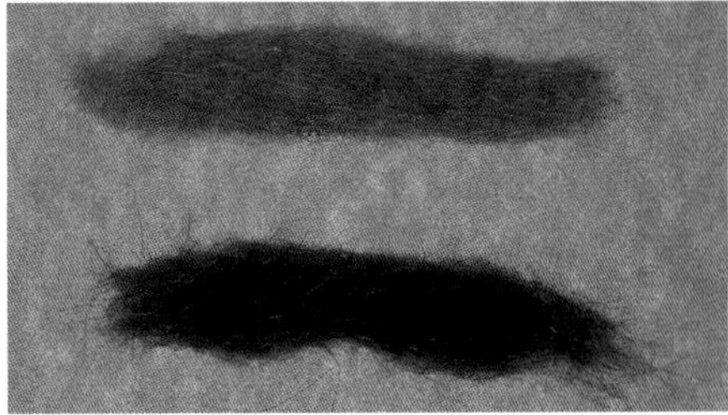

Repeat this four or five times until the biggest percentage of the fibers are going the same direction. Roll the dubbing into a long noodle (see second photo). This action does two things that will improve your dubbing. First, the longer, narrow noodle allows smaller amounts of dubbing to be pulled out, reducing the chances of a bulky looking fly. Second, with the fibers in one direction it can be applied perpendicular to the thread, making the dubbing much tighter and in turn more durable. This is a very important point in consistent dubbing. Your fingers should be tacky for the next action, so apply a small amount of dubbing wax to your thumb and index finger. It is a waste of time to wax the thread.

Notice in the next photo what a small amount of dubbing I'm using and the direction the fibers are going. With your index finger holding the dubbing fibers on the far side of the thread, use your thumb to fold the fibers over the thread. Pinch the fibers tightly and pull your index finger to the right, basically

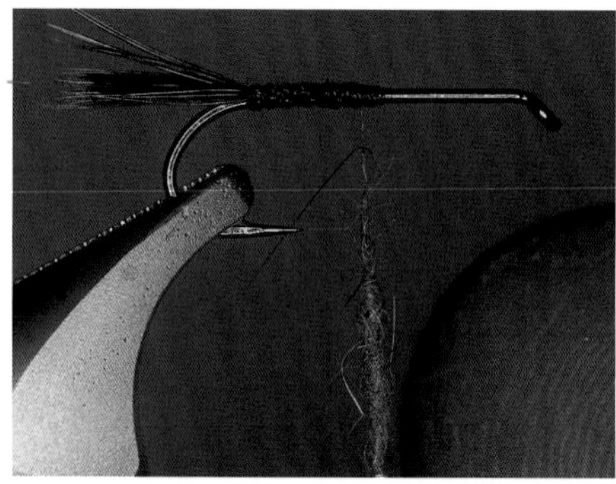

twisting the fibers clockwise. I have used this technique of dubbing for so long it's become second nature, and absolutely no thought goes into it. The next photo shows what the dubbing on the thread should look like after one twist.

Seriously! This is not trick photography. I have shown this technique to people all over the country and it works every time.

See the tying instructions for the Hare's Ear, Randy's Baetis nymph, and the RS-2 for more nifty speed techniques on dubbing. For those who need a visual aid, I also demonstrate my dubbing technique in one of the tying segments in my DVD "Fly Fishing Colorado's Major 6".

Hackle

One of the most fascinating things I have found out in recent years about hackle or feathers in general, is where they actually came from. You have heard the age old question, "What came first the chicken or the egg?" The answer will most certainly surprise you.

"First of all, what are feathers? I'm sure everyone thinks they know. But are you aware that feathers are actually just elongated, high specialized scales? Birds evolved from retiles some 160 million years ago, and in that time the humble scales of the lizard-like ancestor of the bird (archaeopteryx) have been transformed into the staggering diversity and beauty that we now know as the plumage of the modern bird."

By Dr. Tom Whiting *from the Cleveland Project or Fascinating Facts about Fly Tying Feathers"*

Today, birds use this plumage for an array of functions. Birds take flight because of feathers. They also regulate body temperature, protect their skin from the environment and harmful UV rays from the sun, camouflage themselves from danger, and sexual selection (the colorful male of the species) for reproduction.

Man, on the other hand domesticated birds, namely especially the chicken for provisions such as meat and eggs. Then along came the fly tier. Needing a material to float his flies, make his flies look alive, and correctly color his patterns, the fly tier developed a multitude of breeds and varieties within the birds he's had kept on the farm.

More Than You Ever Need To Know About Hackle

A History

I do not proclaim to know the exact history of all dry fly hackle, but I do have some knowledge of the Hoffman line which eventually was bought out by Tom Whiting. From the mid 1960's to 1989, Henry Hoffman devoted his life to producing the best dry fly hackle in the world.

Henry started a commercial fly tying business after a tour in the military. He moved to Oregon and made a living tying predominantly dry flies. Good quality feathers for dry flies were nearly impossible to acquire at that time. Most tiers had to rely on capes from India and China, which were basically just village chickens. Major fly patterns which required the coveted "grizzly hackle" did not exist in village chickens, thus the barred hackle garnered a premium price.

When Henry was growing up, his parents had a small meat chicken breeding operation in California, so he grew up learning the basics of breeder selection and poultry husbandry. With this knowledge, Henry set out to find himself a few Barred Plymouth Rock bantams to raise for his own tying purposes and potentially develop a marketable genetic hackle chicken. While searching county fairs and poultry fanciers, he found a trio of birds in the Pacific Northwest that had excellent dry fly hackle. By Henry's own estimation, these initial birds saved him 10 years of development time.

The breeding started and the fly tying was intense. He plucked feathers to tie with and the best feathers determined which birds would be sires to the next generation. To make a long story short, by the 1980's the Hoffman Grizzly was world famous, almost legendary, with only 2,200 roosters harvested a year.

Henry wanted to get out from under the all-consuming work load and enjoy a retirement of fishing, so he put the business up for sale. After five years of tying to find someone with the necessary skills and a serious willingness and commitment to devote their life to this long term endeavor, Henry created a workable deal with Tom Whiting of Colorado.

Dr. Tom Whiting had considerable industrial poultry experience, managing a commercial egg complex here in Colorado that produced 3 million eggs a week. Whiting was finishing his Ph.D. in poultry genetics and husbandry from the University of Arkansas. His education also included an M.S. from the University of Georgia and a B.S. from Colorado State University, also in poultry genetics.

Whiting Farms started in April 1989, when Tom hatched out his first Hoffman chicks in western Colorado from eggs sent to him by Henry from Oregon. From about 5,000 birds that first year, Whiting Farms Hoffman Hackle has risen to be the best and most dominant hackle producer in the world.

Although my intent in this article is to inform you about hackle, it may seem like a commercial at times. I have used several brand names of hackle since the mid-eighties but the dry fly hackle available today from Whiting Farms is of the finest quality. Dr. Tom Whiting has put together a class and diversity of feathers unmatched in the industry today. With the acquisition of the #2 quality genetic hackle stock, known as Hebert Hackle, to compliment its gene pool and product line, Whiting Farms is renowned for incredible dry fly capes and the widest and most unique array of natural colors of any stock in the world. Dr. Whiting has developed a line called "American Hackle" for use in the salt water tying industry. Several other feather products are available at Whiting Farms. Coq de Leon and soft hackle that is a near replacement for Hungarian partridge are just a couple. The arduous work he has put forth in developing superior fly tying feathers for us is admirable. The mutation of the domestic chicken continues and the development of better hackle is just round the corner. With better stock to work with today means better feathers tomorrow.

Tom has given me research documents and hours of his time to help with the technical information about hackle, such as cost analysis and feather quality. To give credit where credit is due, much of the information in this chapter is directly from research done by Dr. Whiting. He has generously given me permission to reprint any of the information in the documentation; however, I have shortened it considerably. For those of you who may have read this study should know that it is Tom's work and I am, in effect, just the messenger. My job will be to pass along the sound use of and preparation of hackle as it pertains to a fly tier. Without apology, if what you read here and throughout the book as it pertains to hackle sounds slightly biased, you are in all probability probably correct.

Premium dry fly hackle is one of the single most important materials, and often the most expensive, which a fly tier needs to deal with. Hackle is innately more complex than other materials and what represents good quality and bad quality is very confusing. Grading standards over the years has lead to much of the bewilderment. The result to the consumer is that capes graded #1 from four different producers with very small differences in price, can have large differences in the number of useable hackle per cape, colors can be quite different in shade, and overall tying quality is very noticeable.

As an example, in storage I have a #1 cream cape I bought in the mid 1980's, which looked great, it felt great, didn't particularly smell good (and still doesn't), and the hackle ended up almost totally worthless. The hackle twisted terribly and would inevitably break or split about half way through wrapping the collar on a dry fly. (I pulled a hackle off of this cape as of this writing and it still twisted and broke. I should throw it away, but fly tiers have such a hard time throwing things away. There must be some use for it; I just haven't found it yet.) This event made me very leery about the next cape I purchased. I should have been confident that since it was graded #1, it would have been near perfect hackle. However, that was not the case. It took several years for someone to come up with a viable method of grading hackle. As you will see in the information presented next, a hackle study in 1998 discusses, and in my perspective, sets the standards for hackle grading.

The Hackle Study Done By Dr. Tom Whiting

A fair and balanced way of acquiring several producers' hackle had to be established. It was decided to buy hackle through mail order companies when ever possible. The thought was when someone was pulling stock from the shelf it would be totally random rather than entering a retail fly shop down the street and have an employee "pick" the hackle.

The basic colors for the study would be Grizzly, White, and Brown. These colors were chosen due to the fact that because they are most often used by fly tiers and it would represent the producer's oldest genetic stock and, hopefully, the best available from the producer.

Hackle from Whiting Farms was pulled from stock by extracting only the 25th pelt in any color and particular grade.

Hackle was evaluated with several criteria. To start, the hackle was given points for workmanship in skinning, put up, and final trim. Points were also given for overall cleanliness. I must add here that up to this point in time (1998) there was only one producer that washed and sanitized their pelts. That producer was Whiting Farms. I have personally witnessed this process and it did seem a little overboard until Dr. Whiting explained his thoughts on this measure. "Such cleanliness, or lack of, is an important aspect of hackle quality because the tier works intimately with this material, often even orally wetting his/her fingers in the tying process after handling the hackle." It made sense to me because I do wet my fingers on occasion for finer control of any given material, so I do appreciate this added step in the processing. While doing this study, one producer's feathers were so dirty that a respirator was worn. Another was so greasy that the feathers literally soaked the face of the hackle gauge to the point that it peeled away and had to be replaced. YUCK!! That is definitely more than I needed to know about hackle!

Once the cosmetics were assessed, each pelt was split vertically down the center into two equal half capes. If there were any discrepancies whether one half was better than the other, the best looking or fullest half was used for the study. The other half was repackaged, marked, and stored for future reference if needed.

The hackle analysis began with each half cape being stripped of all feathers from the crest to the size 6 line of hackle. This assured that all of the feathers from size 8 to size 28, the most widely used by fly tiers, were accounted for. The feathers were sorted by size using a Troth Hacklemaster hackle gauge and a total count for each size was recorded.

Much care was taken in measuring the usable length of each feather and then examined for characteristics that would be important to the fly tier. The shape, width, and character of the rachis (also known as the quill or stem) were rated. The length, shape, character of the barb, and barb symmetry were rated. And finally, barb count per cm was recorded on size 16 hackle only.

The next test for the hackle was wrapping ability. A needle, the same diameter of a size 12 hook was used for a standard. A hackle collar was wrapped and judged for its appearance. The best were given 6 points for an ideal, perfect collar and the worst or unusable were given 1 point for unfunctional and unattractive. Five to 2 points were given for anything in between.

The number of wraps presumed necessary to wrap each fly size for an "eastern dry fly" is as follows:

#8	14 wraps
#10-#18	12 wraps
#20	10 wraps
#22	8 wraps
#24	6 wraps
#26	4 wraps

By counting the number of wraps from all of the feathers on the half cape gives us the total number of flies it is capable of tying and then that total is multiplied by two to find the total number of flies for the entire pelt. This is the most important part of the study as it pertains to the fly tier. This number is divided into the retail price of the pelt to calculate the overall cost per fly.

I will not go into a full blown analysis of the cape but I mention a few interesting aspects of what the research revealed. A pelt graded Gold from Whiting Farms could tie 1590 flies, the feathers had 87% usable length, and had a barb count of 72, with an average cost of 5 cents a fly. Another producer's grade #1 could tie 500 flies, with only 71% of usable length per feather, and a barb count of 40, with an average cost per fly at 13 cents. Here is one more point about the discrepancies in the standard grading system. One producer's grade #1 Grizzly could tie 501 flies while the same producer's grade #1 Brown would only tie 323 flies. That is a big difference in quantity for the same cost.

The latest numbers we could come up with in the development of Whiting Farms hackle is that a 30% increase in usable hackle per year had existed over the last few years. This means that Gold graded capes are easily tying about 2200-2500 flies and they did not raise their prices for the 2004 season, so the cost per fly should be under 5 cents. It also means that the grading system is escalating dramatically. What used to be Gold is now a Bronze. There are a few capes that are graded Ultra Platinum. They have a full pelt of long usable hackle, which could be getting close to producing 4000 flies. They are more of a collector's item at this time, constituting only 1% of the total production, but are a vision of what is to come.

What You Do Need To Know About Hackle

Dry-Fly Hackle

It was not planned this way, but every professional tier that contributed a pattern to this book used Whiting Farms dry-fly hackle. I saw the stores of hackle each one of the pros had in stock: pelt after pelt of Whiting Farms hackle. We are not the only ones. As I walk through tying clinics and watch demonstrations around the show circuit, I see a very large parentage of tiers using Whiting hackle. If you have been locked in your tying room so long that you have not had a chance to use this premium hackle, it is time to get out and mingle with the "in crowd".

Dry-fly hackle basically comes in two different styles, neck hackle and saddle hackle. Typical neck hackle comes in a wide range of sizes, while saddle hackle is normally restricted to 3 or 4 sizes, but you get a horde of each size. Depending on the neck, size 16 and 14 account for 25%-35% of the useable feathers, size 20 and 22 account for another 25%, size 12 and 18 can make up another 25%, while size 8 and hackle smaller than size 22 finish out the totals.

Saddles can be ordered from Whiting farms that have a particular size range. If you would like more size 18-16 hackle you can ask for it. There will be few size 20 and several size 14 on the saddle and great numbers of 18-16. If you would like to have additional size 12 hackle for a particular project, you can order that also. A very good option for dry-fly saddle hackle is the 100 Packs. These are pre-sized feathers packed in bunches that will tie 100 flies. You can even get a pack of size 22 or 24. What a concept! It would be worth a tier's time and money to try both neck and saddle hackle on their flies to find out which one they like better. They both work perfectly fine, but they do have slightly different characteristics. I know John Hagen, who contributed several dry flies to this work, prefers neck hackle. It is what he likes. I like saddle hackle for parachute flies because I do not need hackle pliers for the first five of six flies on a single feather. Also, the quill on a saddle hackle is slightly thinner and wraps very easily and does not build up much bulk. You be your own judge.

I find it most efficient to strip a pelt, either a neck or saddle, of its hackle and measure it prior to storage. I do this for the whole cape. After it is sorted by size, I will put the loose hackle in a square plastic bag and mark the size on the bag. It is not necessary to get this nit-picky, but I will even take the hackle from the sides of a neck, which are shorter and about a size bigger than they should be according to their length, and use them for parachute hackle. For argument's sake, let's say there is a size 14 hackle that is only long enough to make 10 wraps instead of the needed 14 wraps to complete the collar

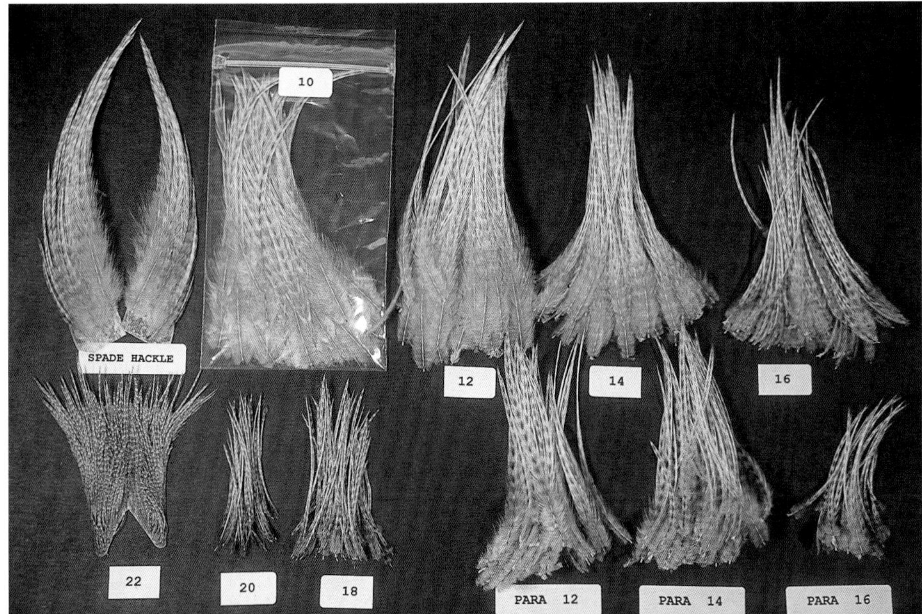

on a dry fly. This hackle will easily make the 8 wraps needed to complete a parachute hackle, so wouldn't it be smart to separate it and designate it a parachute hackle? I thought so, that is why I do it. I will leave the very small hackle on skin and save it for the small dry flies. I very seldom use size 8 hackle or large so I save these feathers on skin also to make quill bodies or dye them black for Woolly Bugger hackle. See the chapter on the PMD Quill tied by John Hagen to find out to prepare this oversized hackle for quill bodies. It is amazing.

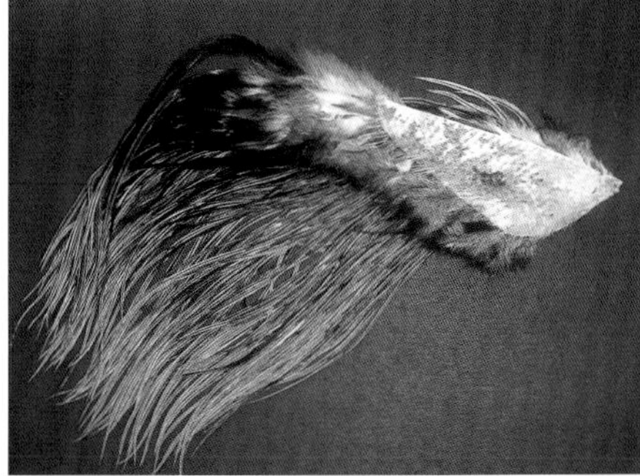

I normally strip half of a saddle at a time and store the other half in its original packaging. I size the hackle, sort it and bundle them together at the butt ends with a small rubber band or twist them together with wire. If I have a need for dyed hackle, such as the case for the Western Green Drake, I will take a bundle of size 12 grizzly and dye it a shade of olive. After they are bundled I transfer them into a narrow, long plastic bag

and mark the size of the hackle on the bag. I then keep all the sized hackle together in one big bag for personal and traveling purposes. I should warn all readers that this is one tedious job and should be done whenever there is absolutely nothing else to do. Try to get as much done at one time as you can so you won't feel too bad when procrastination sets in the next time it needs to be done. As mentioned in many parts of this book, material preparation is a key component to speed and rhythm in fly tying. Time needs to be set aside to accomplish some of these mind-numbing chores.

The best way I have found to prepare a hackle before use is to open the butt end of hackle feather to a point where the size is consistent and with minimal web. Snip the quill at this point. Open the fibers up again at the newly cut butt and trim the barbs short from the quill instead of pulling them off. This has a duel purpose. Trimming the barbs leaves tiny micro barbs attached to the quill so when they are fastened to the hook, the thread has something to hang onto preventing the hackle from pulling out easily. Second, the integrity of the quill stays intact, making the hackle more durable. It takes just a little extra time, but it is time well spent.

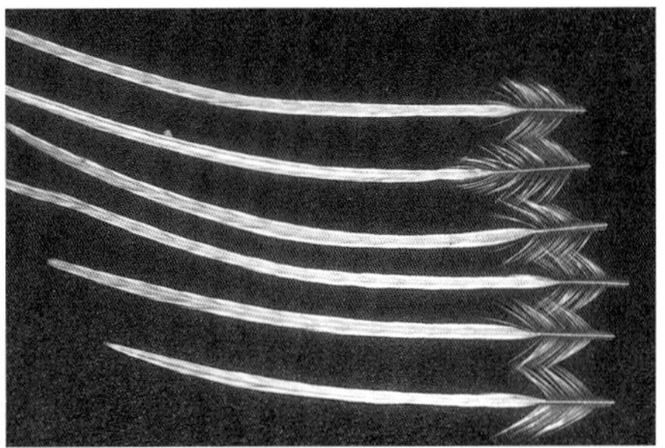

Before tying a batch of hackled dry flies, it is a great idea to prepare enough hackle in the previous manner to complete the job. In this photo I have prepared hackle for a dozen flies. I should be able to get two flies per feather. The bottom hackle has already tied one fly and I would like you to notice that as soon as I finished wrapping the hackle for that fly, I readied it for the next fly one by trimming it before I set it down. Always be aware of situations, whenever possible, where two steps can be done at one time. As you read through this book, you will find great ideas for speeding up the preparation and tying process.

Standard Hackle Collar

Tying in and wrapping a standard hackle collar has always been a very controversial subject. In fact, when I first started tying it was so confusing I had to go back to my notes to find out if I should tie the hackle in with the shiny side up, dull side up, on top of the hook, on the side of the hook, in front of the wing, or behind the wing. There are differing ideas from the professional tiers inside this book on wrapping hackle, so my intention is not to come across as a hackle wrapping guru. Which brings me to the whole idea I am about to present.

I have not seen a book yet called "The Rules of Fly Tying", so there must not be any rules. I do not intend to write one anytime in the near future nor do I suggest that what you read here depicts any rules. There is any number of ways to wrap hackle correctly, so my suggestion is not to get caught up in nonsense. I know there are a few old timers that would argue about hackle all day long with me, (the same ones that think hackle is too good these days) but I just think it can be simpler than it has been presented in the past. There are techniques that work well for certain patterns, but I could wrap a hackle on the same pattern with my simple-minded approach and a judge would be hard pressed to tell the difference. Who's to judge your flies anyhow? If they look good to you and they catch fish, it does not matter what anyone thinks.

What does all this mean? The real answer is as individual as a person's DNA. I have mentioned this before, but it is worth another look. We have all learned to tie flies from other people; even the so called "self taught" tiers have grabbed a couple of ideas from others along the way somewhere. So, find a method you are comfortable with and use it as often as you can. Pretty soon you are subconsciously wrapping a hackle instead of thinking about it.

The main thoughts I use over and over when tying in and wrapping hackle is to attach the hackle on top of the hook shank shiny side up (concave side down), wrap the hackle, and secure it on top of the hook shank after it is wrapped. This is not only a no brainer getting it on the hook, but also makes it

easy to clip the hackle off the fly when done. It is up and out of the way of the thread, reducing the chance of a scissor blade nicking it. I think it reduces the number of renegade barbs that get trapped in the eye of the hook also. If there are barbs that interfere with the hook eye, they are usually right on top of the hook and easily trimmed. Keep it as simple as you can.

Whether the hackle should be tied in front of the wing or behind the wing is up to the individual. When tied in behind the wing and up against the body, the hackle is wrapped forward, one wrap in front of the last, which tend to produces a square looking hackle collar. This is the method used by a number of tiers and is presented in a number of fly tying books.

The hackle tied in front of the wing produces a hackle collar that is flared, especially behind the wing because the hackle is wrapped back to the body and

then forward in between the previous wraps, in essence, over the top of itself. It is not a matter of right or wrong. Notice the position of the hackle on the first half wrap. It starts just in front of the wing, passes directly under the wing and completes the wrap behind the wing. It depends on the look the individual wants and the difference in the way it will perform on the water.

Parachute Hackle

There are basically just two thoughts for tying in and wrapping a parachute hackle. The only options are to make the wraps in a clockwise direction or counter-clockwise direction around the wing post. Again, there is no right or wrong; both ideas work just fine depending on individual preference. In fact, the predominant hand used to tie with must be taken into consideration.

I have personally tried both ways and as a right handed tier decided to follow the counter-clockwise method shortly after I started tying flies (a left handed tier would wrap the hackle clockwise). There is one technical aspect of this method that I feel justified my decision. When the hackle is wrapped counter-clockwise, the last wrap of hackle is going away from the tier, basically in the same direction as the thread wraps. So, as the thread is brought over the hackle to secure it in place, it also has a tightening effect.

When the hackle is wrapped clockwise, the hackle is coming around the hook towards the tier and as the thread is brought over the hackle to secure it in place, it actually has a loosening effect. A tug here and pull there will secure the hackle sufficiently, but extra care must be taken to insure that the hackle is tight.

Prepare the hackle by trimming away about 1/8 inch of the barbs at the butt end of the feather. Tie the hackle in front of the wing on the far side of the hook and make the wraps counter-clockwise.

The same procedure is used except the hackle is tied on the fore side of the hook and wrapped clockwise.

It is common practice to make the first half wrap of hackle to the top of the thread landing area on the wing post and then wrap the hackle down the post with one wrap directly below the last

until the post is completed. I have clipped the barbs on this hackle so this idea could be seen clearer.

Another? common practice for parachute hackle is to use a hackle sized at least a half size to a full size larger than the actual hook size. For instance, wrap a size 14 hackle on a #16 parachute pattern. This method is used by a number of fly tiers I know.

Soft Hackle

There are several flies included in this work that use a soft hackle, and books written about soft hackle, so I do not want need to get into a long dissertation on it. Most soft hackle used comes from Hungarian Partridge or from the saddle of hen chickens.

From top right moving clockwise we have a brown feather from the back of a partridge, a gray feather from the neck and shoulders of a partridge, a hen chicken dyed olive, a natural hen, and a dark mottled brown hen saddle.

However, any fly tier who has tried to tie a soft hackle under a size 16, often times even the size 16 itself, will have a hard time finding a feather that will wrap with the correct proportion. The barbules are almost always too long. Here is a very simple idea for those of you that like small soft hackle flies.

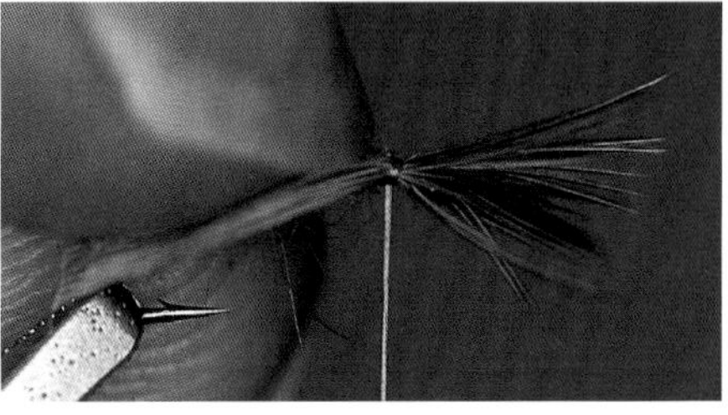

Pull several fibers off of a regular soft hackle feather, keeping the tips even. Using two soft wraps of thread, tie the tips over the front of a fly intended for a soft hackle. The ideal length is a full hook shank extended over the front of the hook. Take a thumbnail and spread the fibers around the hook shank and tighten the thread.

Trim butt ends of the soft fibers. Sweep the fibers back, evenly encompassing the hook shank, and make two wraps of thread to lock the fibers in place. Whip finish and you have a small soft hackle.

NOTE: In a perfect situation, the soft hackle fibers should be tied in first and then the fly body and thorax are wrapped in place. The last step would be to sweep the fibers back and locked into place.

Hair For Wings, Spinning, And Tails

Winging Hair

Deer and elk hair are very good types of hair for winging dry flies. Upright wings on Comparaduns and Wulff patterns can be tied with white-tail deer hair, while most down wings on caddis and stoneflies are tied with the more durable and stiffer elk body hair. Large parachute drake patterns and Humpys are also candidates for elk hair.

Not all hair is what you think it is. Let's say a fellow fly tier recommends you use white-tail deer hair for a certain creation. You run down to the local fly shop and grab a bag of white-tail deer hair. You take it home and it doesn't work worth a darn. You cuss your so-called friend for telling you to use the wrong material. It's not your friend's fault.

Just because the package hanging on the wall at the local fly shop says white-tail deer doesn't mean it is the type of hair you are after. Over the years, I've picked up all kinds of hair. The packages on the wall, hair from taxidermists, hair right out of the back of a hunter's pick-up, and a chunk of road kill (just once). What I have found is that no two chunks of hair are alike.

Here is a prime example of the incorrect and correct use of elk hair for the wing on a caddis. Both clumps of hair are from an elk body. Different animals, mind you. The first photo shows the hair flaring a bit too much, while the second shows the proper amount of flaring. This is the problem to which I was alluding.

The character of the hair, even though both are elk body hair, is so different that you must pay close attention to the tips of the hair to choose the right hair for a certain application.

Most fly shop personnel have a good working knowledge of the different types of hair and their uses, so if in doubt, ask questions. Tell them what you are trying to tie, and they should be able to lead you in the right direction. When ordering from mail-order catalogs, make sure you tell them exactly what you are looking for and request a certain type of hair.

How to Pick Hair for Wings

First, I would let you know that I prefer raw deer and elk hair, which has not been tanned for winging. Tanned hair works fine, but I have seen the tips of the hair damaged from improper tanning and the tips of the hair if what makes or breaks a good hair wing. However, take precautions when storing raw hair. See Chapter 1, (page 22) "Just Because it Looks Clean" for ideas on storing raw materials.

I classify deer, elk, and moose hair into three different categories: fine, medium, and coarse. The examples we are about to cover deal only with the tips of the hair since that is what we are going to use for the wings. With most hair, be it white-tail deer hair, mule deer, or even elk hair, about 1/2 inch from the tip to the base of the hair is considered coarse because that part of the hair will flare more than 45 degree. It is best used for spinning.

Body hair from bull elk is a good hair for down-wing flies because it seldom flares more than 45 degree so I consider it medium hair. Hair from the back of a white tail and, believe it or not, moose body hair is fine hair because it flares less than 30 degree.

I have found mule deer hair unfavorable for winging dry flies in most cases. It is coarse hair and is best used for spinning because it flares so easily.

Fine hair does not flare more than about 15 degree to 30 degree from the hook shank when thread is wrapped over the top of it tightly. Examples of this type of hair are elk mane and the hair from the very top of the back of a white tail (shown). Where the deer was taken, geographically, also makes a difference in the type of hair you will get. A white tail from Texas will have a predominately fine texture to it and be fairly short, while a northern woodland white tail will be coarser hair overall and have much longer hair. However, a northern deer harvested during the earlier season, late September to mid-October, can have some of the best winging hair for Comparaduns and Wulff patterns that you can find.

Hair that does not flare more than 15 degree to 30 degree is very good for down-wing flies, such as Elk Hair Caddis (which can be tied with fine white tail hair and still be called an Elk Hair Caddis). I have a few pieces of elk body hair from a cow that was taken in the early season and it flares very little. It is some of the best winging hair for small caddis and stoneflies that I have ever found. Elk mane hair is ideally suited for adult stonefly patterns since its hair is long and is fine much of its length so it does not flare much at all.

Medium hair flares about 30 degree to 45 degree from the hook shank when thread is wrapped tightly over it. Generally the body hair from the sides of a white tail can be used as a medium hair (early season harvest). I tie Comparaduns professionally and have searched for the perfect hair to tie them with for years. I found the hair from the side a white tail closer to the back of the deer works well for size 14 and bigger. This is because the tips of the hair stay a bit finer and will flare only 30 degree to 45 degree for the longer wings needed on these sizes. I thought I had found the perfect hair until I tried tying smaller patterns with it. The length of the wing is shorter so I ended up using less of the tip and found this hair didn't flare enough for these shorter wings. Actually, the hair was too fine. See how complicated this whole hair thing is? Grab some more hair and experiment!

As you get to the hair about mid-way between the back and the belly, on the same deer, the finer tips are shorter and work for size 16 and 18 flies.

I have not had the joy of tying Humpys commercially, but I do tie quite a few for personal use on the stream. The medium body hair just described works very well for these types of patterns in smaller sizes. Using the right hair does make the job easier.

The hair becomes too coarse as you get to the belly of the deer and is unsuitable for wings because it flares too much. Again, this hair is very good for spinning. The hair near the belly becomes light in color and the belly hair itself is white, great hair to dye up in greens and yellows for bass bugs.

OK, now we get to the real stuff that separates the professionals from the amateurs.

I like to use patches of hair that have been cut into narrow strips about 1 1/2 inches wide and 4 to 6 inches long instead of the typical squares you find in the stores. Ideally, I would rather cut it into 1/4-inch strips like the patch marked in the photo. Such strips would ensure consistency of proportion. If the hair were in strips, I could slip my scissors into the hair every 1/4-inch and have a clump of hair 1/4 by 1/4. A great idea, but cutting the hair into the thin 1/4 inch strips is not very practical or time efficient.

Are you getting the idea? Remember that last batch of Comparaduns you tied? How you had a hard time getting the weight (size) of your wings the same from fly to fly? I know I have!

I was talking with John Gierach one day years ago and he said, "Fly tying is a process of problem solving. When you have a problem, FIX IT before you go on." Great advice when you have the time, but often the answer comes in pieces. Sometimes the light comes on in a few minutes. More often than not, you just have to keep tying and bits of the puzzle present themselves over time. You haven't really learned how to tie a fly until you've tied a few hundred dozen of them. Now that takes a lot of time!

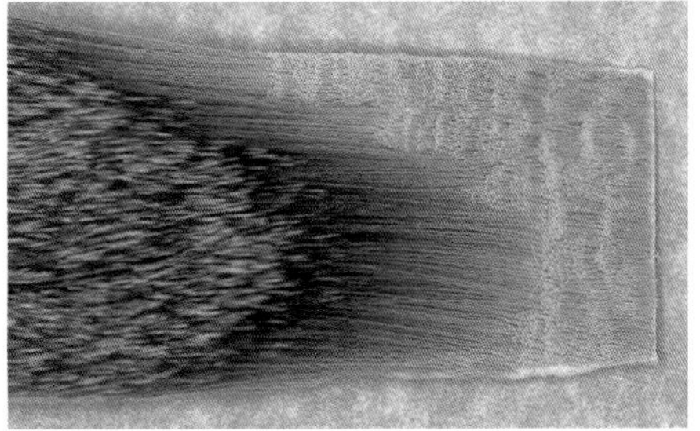

This is the answer that came to me over time: Simply "imagine" this narrow patch of hair is in 1/4-inch strips and trim out 1/4-inch by 1/4-inch clumps. I usually start on one side of the hair patch and take 4 to 6 clumps right down the edge of the patch. Then I start another 1/4-inch row and take a few clumps. You should be able to see the pattern of rows that I have trimmed out in the photo. If you find the clump is too little or too big, adjust the amount by taking more or less out of the row, but maintain the 1/4-inch rows.

Just before you start to tie a fly using hair for wings, remove the static from the hair. Static makes the hair hard to handle and stack; a dryer sheet from the laundry room works great. Lay the patch of hair out and rub the dryer sheet over the hair a few times. Static is gone! I usually keep a sheet in my box of hair so it's always handy.

Trim the hair as close to the skin as possible, comb out the under fur and stack the hair. Make sure to take the hair out of the stacker in the right direction. If you are tying a caddis fly, make sure the hair is pointing over the back of the fly (to the left if you are a right-handed tier) before you take it out of the stacker. Then you won't need to change the direction of the hair between hands before you tie it in.

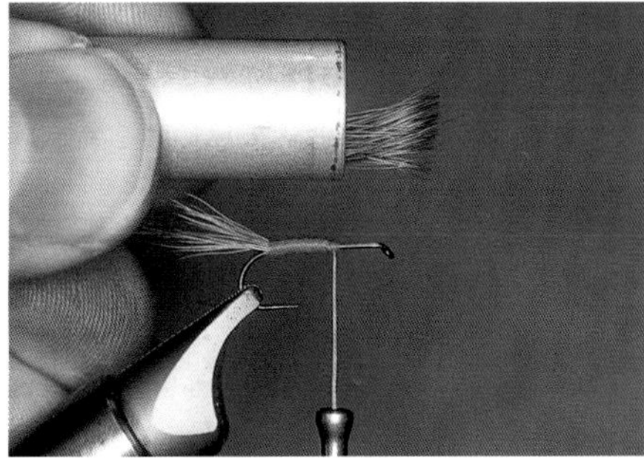

If you are tying a Humpy, Comparadun, or Wulff wing, the hair needs to point over the eye of the hook (to the right for a right-handed tier).

If you tie a lot of hair-winged flies, hopefully this little bit of information will save you the cost of a couple of bottles of Advil next year.

Hair Used for Spinning

I'm sure you have tried spinning hair or at least seen someone do it. There are more "Ooh's and Ahhs" from people watching someone spin hair than any other fly-tying technique. I think this is part of the mystique of spinning hair. It looks cool! Everybody wants to be able to do it. It is not real difficult, but the hair you use for spinning is the key to success.

Spinning hair should feel spongy when pressed between your fingers. When wrapped tightly with thread this type of hair, will flare to 90 degree or perpendicular to the hook shank. Mule deer hair comes to mind right away. It is long and very spongy (coarse), especially when harvested in late October or early November. Lower body and belly hair from a northern white tail is good spinning hair. Rump hair from muley and white tail is also good. Cow elk body hair is often used for spinning up big bass poppers. Caribou hair is great for spinning. One of the coarsest hairs out there is from the pronghorn antelope, however, it can be very brittle. I have used antelope hair that literally exploded when I tightened the thread over it. The thread cut it instead of flaring it. I was left with just a few fibers connected to the hook while the rest was floating around my tying table. So if you decide to try antelope, good luck!

Which brings me to my next point: The thread used for spinning hair is very important. For demo purposes only, I have spun hair with 8/0 thread, but I do not recommend it. It can be done, but Danville Size A, single-strand floss, Gudebrod G, and Monocord are some of the best threads for spinning. Find one you like and stick with it. You will become accustomed to its strength and should never break the thread.

One last note: There is a great video out by Chris Helm called "Spinning Deer Hair" that explains in detail about different types of deer hair. The explanation is maybe ten minutes into the tape, and well worth the price of admission. Then you can watch as he ties a few flies. He is a true master with hair. The tape is one in the series "Hooked on Fly Tying" by Jim & Kelly Watt.

Tailing

I would like to share some information on tailing materials for both nymphs and dry flies in this section. If there is one mistake I see inexperienced tiers make, it is their choice of tailing materials. The correct material is essential, especially for dry flies. With so many options in both categories, I feel compelled to go over a few of the more important ones.

Nymph Tailing

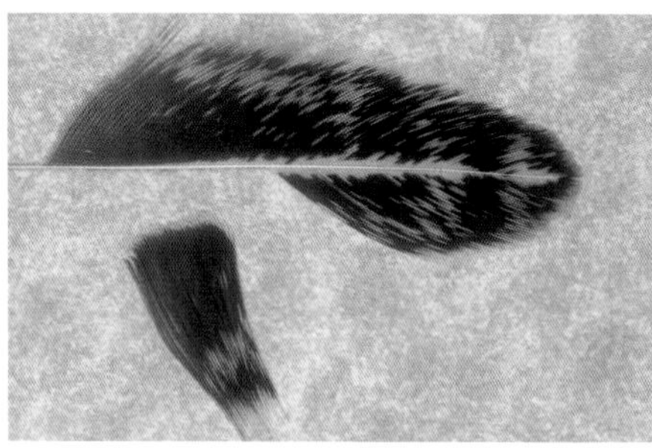

Nymph tailing consists of any material that is soft or webby in nature; something with an easy flowing motion in the water. Hen saddles, pheasant tails, clumps of fur, and marabou come to mind. Sparkle yarn, Antron, and Darlon are a few synthetic materials that can be used. However, these synthetics are most often used for emerging patterns to add the shimmer and brightness of an insect losing its nymphal shuck.

Hen saddles are easily acquired, come in an array of mottled colors ranging from light tan to dark brown, standard colors like grizzly and dun, and they are easy to use, something all pro tiers look for.

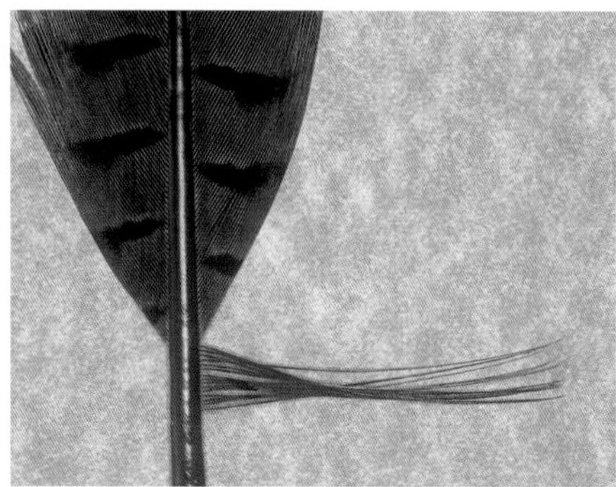

Pheasant tails are also easy to find and can be bleached and dyed to any number of colors. They are most often used on the Pheasant Tail Nymph, but can be a useful replacement material on many nymphs. Whenever using this type of feather, simply separate the number of fibers you want to use, reposition them so they are perpendicular to the stem, and pull them off. This ensures the tips are even and ready to tie on the hook.

Nymph tails made with clumps of fur do look good and act nicely in the water, however, they are time-consuming and can create quite a mess. The original Hare's Ear Nymph used the fur from in between the eyes on the hare's mask, which made a great-looking nymph but most pro tiers do not like tying them because of the added time and expense of hare's masks just for tailing. This is why the tails on most Hare's Ear Nymphs today are tied with mottled hen back feathers. When using fur clumps like muskrat and squirrel for tails, I like to cut the skin into 1/4-inch strips and nip off the individual fur clumps. It is much easier to get consistently sized clumps that way.

Chickabou, a specialty product from Whiting Farms, is basically a miniature marabou feather. The pelt not only has a nice cluster of these mini marabou

Material Preparation

feathers, it also has broad soft feathers that can be used for Matuka wings. Chickabou is a very good tailing material for swimming nymphs like damselflies. I have actually used parts of the Chickabou feather for the legs on the nymph pattern shown in the photo. Try one on a Hare's Ear Nymph sometime, it adds a great new look to an old fly.

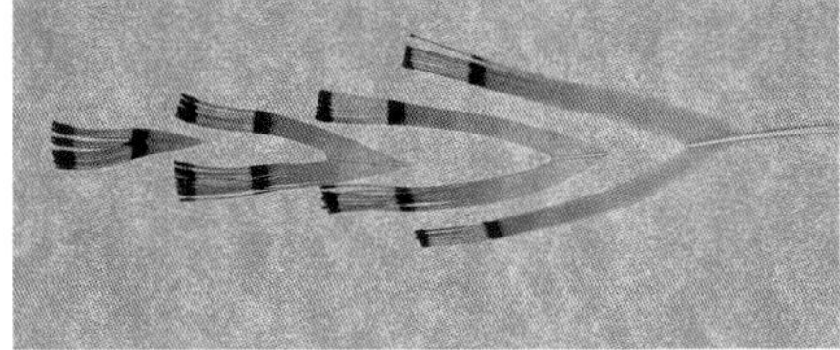

Golden pheasant tippets are used on both dry flies and nymphs, most notably, the Coachman series of flies. They are especially popular on wet flies, old steelhead patterns, and Atlantic salmon flies. I believe this orange feather has a great attracting color, even to the point of saying it has strike-triggering capabilities. (This is my opinion after years of using it on a number of the attractor patterns I tie.

Here is a great trick for tying in golden pheasant tippets as tailing. After stripping the unusable fluff and unmarked barbules off the base of the feather, cut the center stem making individual V's, which leaves the natural orange and black barring intact. This idea works much better than cutting the barbules directly off the stem. They are easily secured to the hook and there is no waste since the very tip of the feather can be used as a tail also.

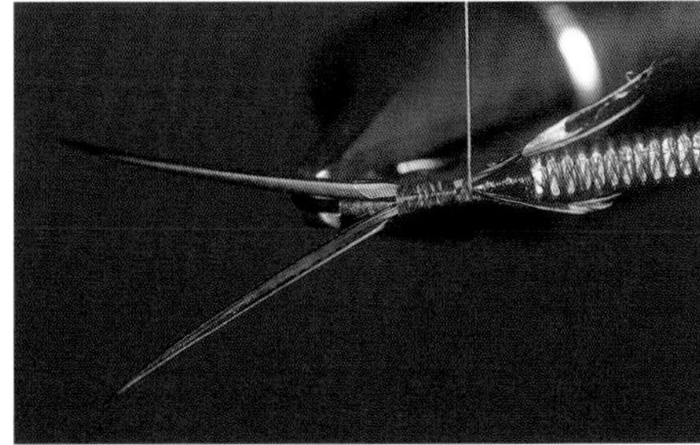

One of the more common uses for biots is for tails on a stonefly. I like to build up a slight thread dam at the back of the hook and wrap the biots against it to make them flare in the desired fork shape. Another point of interest is the transition between the tail and the case

over the body (which I usually refer to as camouflage) on a stonefly. Make sure the case is secured tightly right in front of the tails. I see a lot of beginners that have a hard time with these types of transitions.

Dry-Fly Tailing

Good dry-fly tailing needs to be a stiff, straight material. A synthetic tailing material called MicroFibbetts is very popular. They are made under several names and distributors and I haven't found a nickel's worth of difference in any of them. They are easy to use, come in several colors, and work extremely well in several applications. The bundle of tailing looks like a miniature paintbrush without the handle. The tips are even with a natural looking taper to them, they are easy to separate, and can be trimmed off the bundle quickly in precise numbers.

Natural tailing material for dry flies is usually referred to as spade hackle. They are the short hackles with long, stiff barbules on the side of a rooster cape and at the base of some rooster saddle patch. The barbules on these feathers are excellent tailing material for dry flies. Some say that because of the advanced genetic progress in dry-fly hackle, these spade hackles are in short supply.

In reverse of popular belief, these feathers are still there and work just fine. The only real problem is the barbule length is shorter. Very few spade hackles produce tailing long enough for a size-14 dry fly. After doing a Saturday morning tying clinic at a local fly shop, I was given a few rooster capes from the American Hackle line, also from Whiting Farms. This was right after they acquired the line, which was primarily being raised to produce wide feathers for large streamers and saltwater flies. I wasn't tying many saltwater flies at the time, so the capes got pushed into storage for quite sometime. I had them out for some reason months later and looked at the feathers. Upon closer inspection, I found a high percentage of the feathers to have stiff, long barbules, which would tie size-12 dry flies very easily.

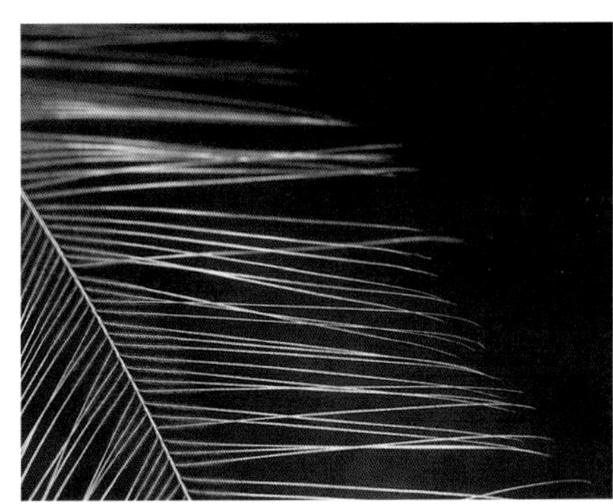

The main thing you need to look for in a good dry-fly tailing feather is the uniformity and straightness of the tips. Notice the comparison of these two feathers: one has very straight, sharp tips, while the other feather has tips that are curling, uneven, and not nearly as rigid. These feathers came from the same pelt, however, the better one is from the side of the skin and the other is from the middle. The difference between the two seems minimal visually, but when tied on a hook and put on the water, the disparity becomes apparent.

The tail made with the inferior feather will not support the fly for the long haul.

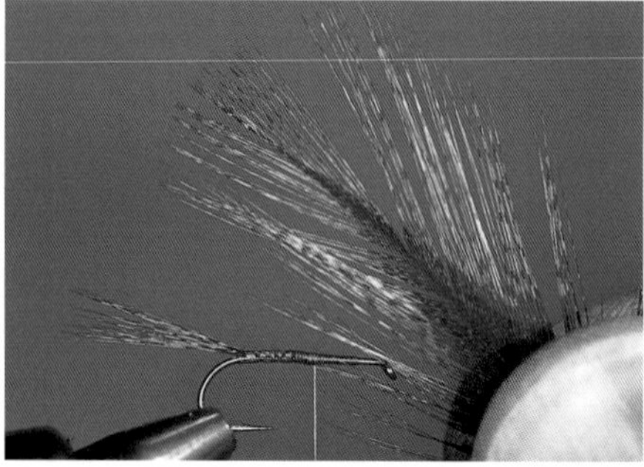

Whiting Farms is saving spade hackle from their birds, packaging them, and selling them as tailing. It has long barbule length and is of good quality. Coq de leon also has beautiful tailing and they are becoming available in numbers at this time. The barbules are lightly mottled and have a beautiful shine, an almost transparent look to them. They are quickly becoming my favorite natural tailing for dries.

Hair for Tailing

Moose body hair is by far the best, most readily available hair for tailing large dry flies. It is stiff, has good floating qualities, and it's durable. Above all else, it does not flare much. Most often it is used for larger hair-winged flies, such as Wulff patterns and Humpys, to help counter-balance the weight of the wings. When in doubt as to what to use for tails, try moose body hair.

It can be used as is or it can be bleached to a wonderful blond color. See photo.

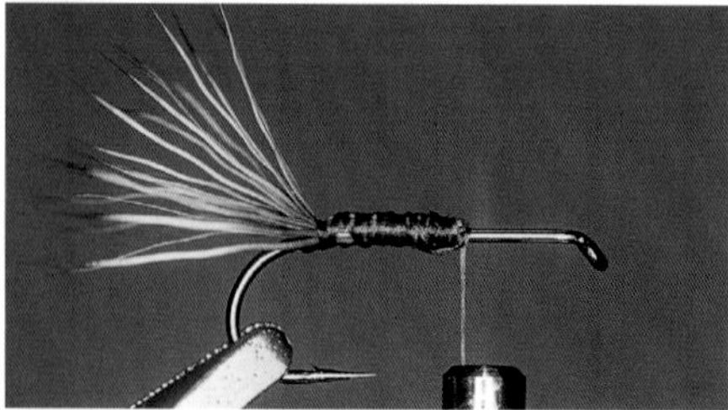

Some elk hair can be used for tailing, mainly the hair near the back. It is fine and does not flare. Be careful though, the wrong elk hair used for tailing will end up looking somewhat bushy like the one shown.

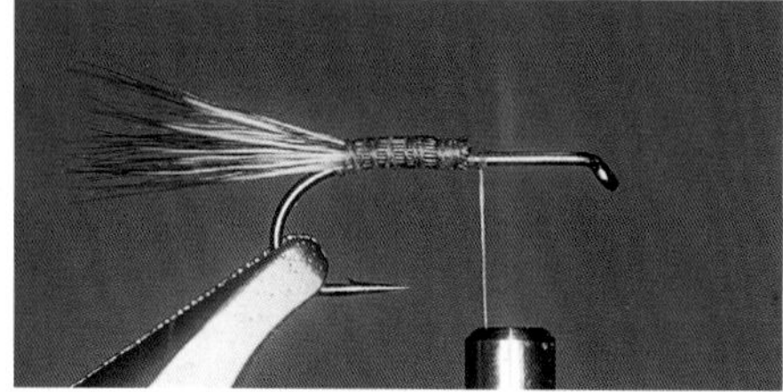

Here is an example of the very fine hair from the back of a white-tail deer. It is ideal tailing hair, very stiff and symmetrical in color. Elk hock is another very good tailing hair. It is a short, fine hair that is very nice for tailing smaller flies. I like to use it for RS-2 tails and small Humpys.

There are several examples of using hair in this book so take advantage of the wealth of information.

Turkey Flats, (Turkey Body Feathers)

Over the years, one of the most common questions I have thrown at me concerns parachute wings. How do you tie a parachute wing with a calf body hair that doesn't build up too much bulk? I don't know! How do you keep calf body hair from spinning around the hook? Don't use calf body hair! Calf body hair is so short, how do you stack it? I don't! I use only turkey flats for parachute flies.

A turkey flat is the ideal material for parachute dry flies, thorax duns, and split wings for the Royal series of flies, e.g. Royal Wulff, Royal Humpy, and Royal Adams. Turkey flats are very fast and easy to use. They are lightweight, they do not create the bulk that many hairs do, and there is no stacking involved.

Whether you are buying strung flats in small bags or bulk feathers, it is a great idea to spend some time selecting these feathers before tying. Separate high-quality flats, medium quality, low grade, and trash. (There will always be unusable feathers.)

What you are looking for is the overall density of the top of the feather. A

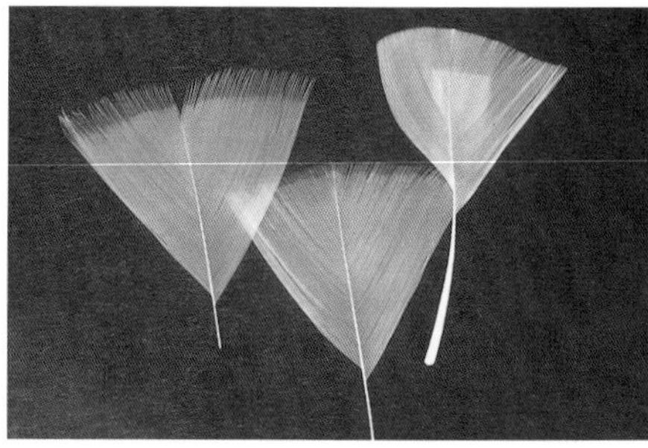

high-quality flat is very dense all the way up to the top. The high-select flats should be used for flies between size 16 and 24. (The feather on the right in the photo.)

A medium-quality feather has a visible line of thin tips at the top. These thin tips should be no longer than 1/16" to 1/8". Still a very usable feather, the medium grades can be used for size 12 down to size 16. (The feather in the middle).

A very low-grade feather has a 3/16" to 1/4"-wide area of thin tips. I save such feathers and use them if I have the luxury of needing a large clump, let's say a size-8 Para-Hopper, and can trim the tops of that wing. These are usually personal flies that I use while guiding clients that need a little help seeing the fly. (The feather on the left)

Ragged feathers, feathers with broken tips, and round tops instead of flat-top feathers are trash. Don't waste any time trying to save them.

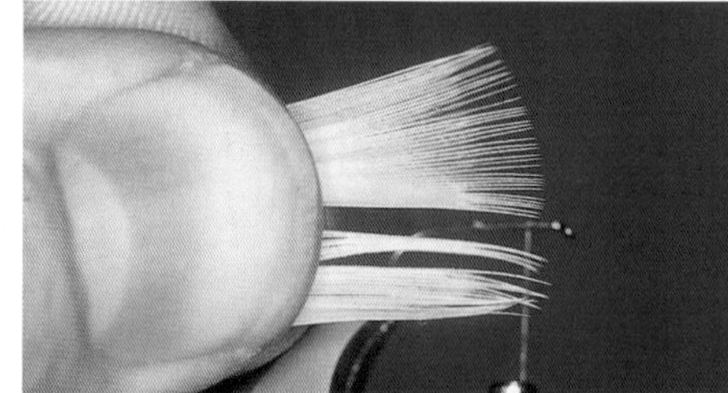

Notice the improper use of a flat (low-grade) feather in photo one. The tips are too thin on this feather, causing all sorts of problems. The wing will be

very hard to wrap thread around to form the post because of its thinness, to say nothing of trying to wrap a hackle around it four or five times. Mistakes like these wreak havoc on your nerves and are very time-consuming.

Now look at this photo. This is a very dense wing (high-grade) feather that will hold its shape and is much easier to work with. Making the post and wrapping the hackle are no problem.

If parachute wings have been a problem up to this point, whether you have been using calf body hair or the wrong feather, these ideas should speed up your tying and enable you to create a much better-looking fly.

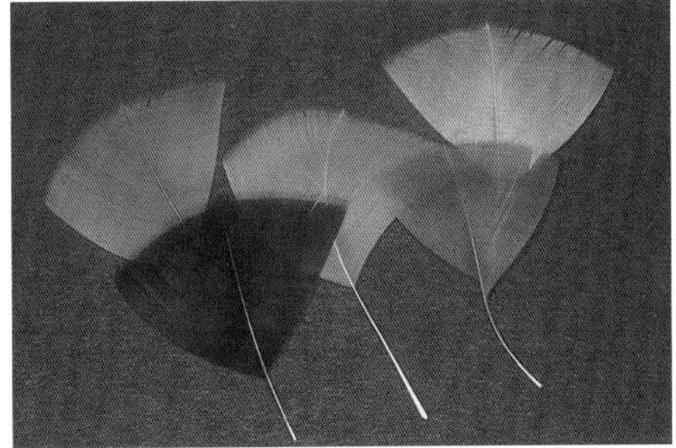

While you are grading turkey flats, pull the fluff from the bottom of the stem to the point where the actual flat part of the feather starts. Bag them and mark the bags high select, medium grade, and low grade: Now they are ready when you need them.

I always set aside a batch to dye. The colors I need for most wings are gray for blue-winged olives, sulphur dun for pale morning duns and light Cahills, and dark gray for large green drake patterns. I always use high-grade feathers for the gray wings on the smaller blue-winged olives. Feathers for the Sulphurs and PMD's are a mixture of high and medium-grade since I tie them up to size 14. I can always get by with medium grade feathers for the larger drake patterns. The colors that you could use are literally endless, but you should match the color of the mayfly wings in your area.

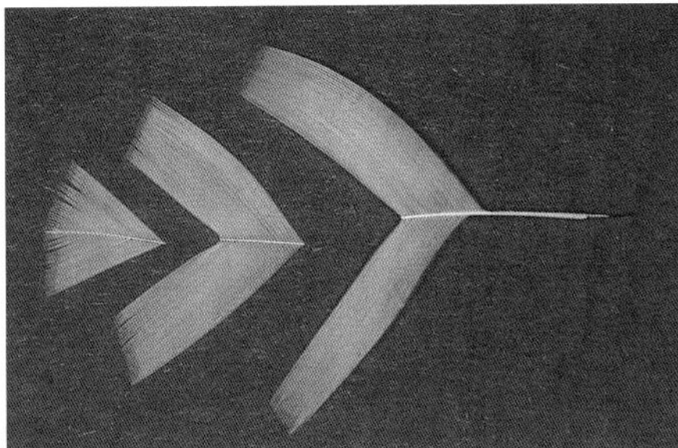

The best way to use this feather is to nip the center stem leaving equal amount of fibers on each side of it, forming a V shape. Repeat this process until the very tip of the feather is left. (See Photo) I normally get two to three sections depending on the size of fly I'm tying. For a size-16 fly, the sections should be cut so the stem in the middle is approximately 1/4 to 3/8 of an inch wide. The actual amount you need for a certain sized hook will come with experience, but any error will be easier to handle than a bulky clump of calf hair. Don't throw the tip away, as the stem is slight enough that it can be used for a parachute wing

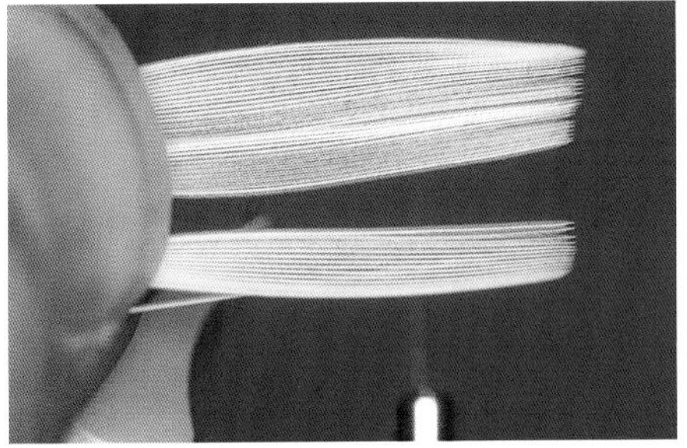

To ready a wing for a parachute post or split wing, sweep the two sides together making one clump out of feather. The tips of the "flats" should line up, eliminating the need for stacking.

Here is a parachute olive quill. Notice how the body remains nicely tapered without the common build up, or ramping, in the thorax area made by calf tail. This is what all parachute-winged flies should look like.

The area of fly tying where the turkey flat truly excels is when you are tying split white wings for a Royal pattern. Use a wider section of the feather than you would for a parachute wing so you have enough fibers for two wings instead of one. If you double the amount, though, it's usually too much. Experimentation will let you know how much you need. This technique will cut your tying time in half.

Turkey Tails

Turkey tails are one of the main sources for wingcases so I like to have them ready when needed. They are fairly simple to prepare so I do several at a time:

1. You will need either Dave's Flexament or a can of spray clear coat. Dave's Flexament is the best glue out there for this procedure. It makes for a very durable wingcase that will seldom split when tying it in. I have tried several,

including a number of water-based flexible cements, and they do not work as well. There are several brands of clear coat on the market, they can be found at a local hardware store in the paint section. I prefer a lacquer-based spray over an acrylic. The spray is much quicker, but not as durable as Fleximent.

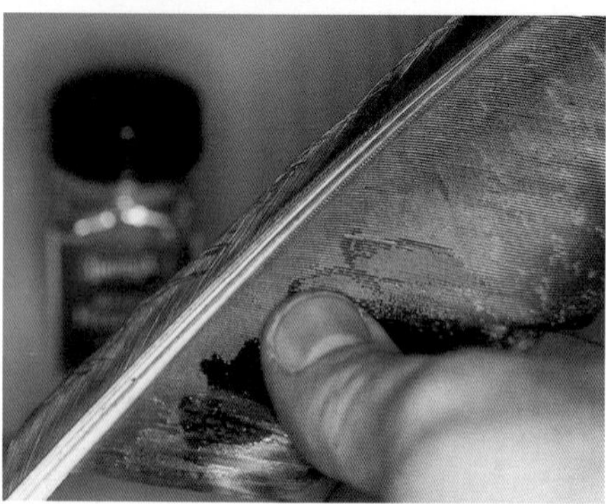

2. Apply the Dave's Flexament on the back of the feather with a bodkin or toothpick. This is the side where you will see the white half of the stem. The colorization of this side of the feather usually has a shiny appearance to it. The color of the front side of the feather is darker, the markings are more pronounced and the stem is dark. Dab on the glue near the stem and spread it towards the tips with the bodkin. Do about two or three inches of the feather at a time. Now, squeeze the glued feather with your fingers and sweep the glue towards the tip to even the application through the feather. Repeat until both halves of the feather are done. If you prefer to use the clear coat, spray the feather with an even coat, also on the back side of the feather.

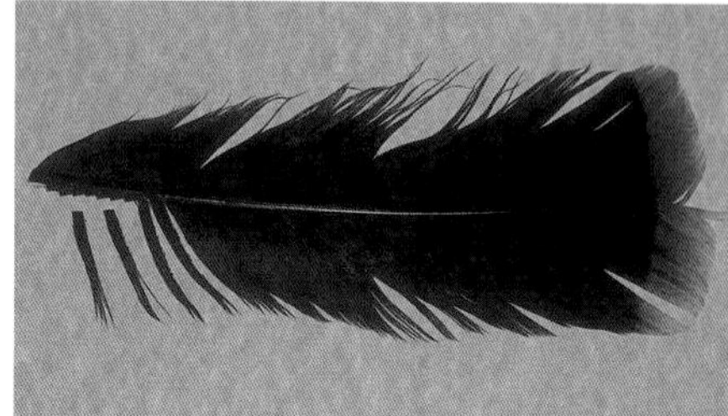

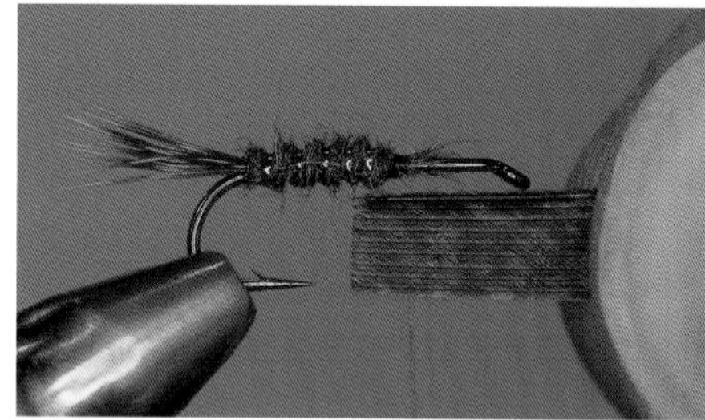

3. Once the glue is dry, wingcases can be separated with a bodkin and cut off the stem. A simple rule of thumb is to make the wingcase as wide as the gape of the hook.

Turkey tails can be bleached to a beautiful ginger color for light-colored flies or bleached and dyed olive to match that spectrum.

Tying With Foam

The first type of pattern I think of when tying with foam is the terrestrial, simply because that is what I have most often seen tied out of foam. However, if you let your imagination run wild there are several very good patterns you could come up with. Besides the terrestrials in this chapter, I have included an adult stonefly pattern and a Balloon Caddis to give you ideas on some of the potential uses for foam. Gary LaFontaine uses packing foam for several of his patterns, including the Cone, Halo Mayfly Emerger and Airhead.

Foam has come a long way in twenty years. There are many different types of foam and the colors of foam seem endless. One of the first sources of quality evasote sheet foam was Blue Ribbon Flies in West Yellowstone, Montana. They carried Traun River Polycelon foam in several different colors. They still market foam, and many of their guides have tied very innovative foam patterns for the West Yellowstone area.

Today, most of the foam used for fly tying is soft polyethylene foam. It is closed-cell foam with very good floating qualities. The two most commonly used types are evasote and cross-link foam. These foams come in all shapes and sizes: sheets of varying thickness, cylinders, disks, and pre-shaped bug bodies. Black evasote sheet foam is used for most terrestrials such as beetles, ants, Chernobyl Ants, cicadas, and crickets. Cross-link foam is good for Madam X, and hopper patterns.

Most good tying foam is available at any local fly shop these days. Foam distributed by Rainy Riding, a material supplier, fly shop owner, and foam pattern innovator from Ogden, Utah is very good. Rainy's sheet foams are available in a number of thicknesses and in both evasote and cross-link foams. Rainy's also markets striped Bumble Bee foam (cylindrical), cylindrical solid color foams and preformed terrestrial bodies with an orange or red end. Rainy Riding has several videos on tying with foam that are useful for seeing how to tie with the stuff. Phil Camera markets Larva Lace foam, soft evasote foam that comes precut and makes a super Black Ant when combined with his yellow foam for an indicator. Craft foam can be found at department store outlets and hobby stores. There are also foam disks from Kreinik that can be used for either strike indicators or foam bodies. There are unusual sources of foam, such as dry cleaners hanger covers, sandals, earplugs, and packing material. Sounds like foam roadkill!

The best way to prepare foam from large sheets is with a rotary cutter and

self-healing cutting mat. These tools, combined with a straight-edge, produce evenly cut strips to any width you may need in a very short period of time. All of these items can be found at fabric stores. If you are just tying a few flies, a pair of scissors will work, but scissors do leave uneven edges and it is difficult to make long strips of the same width.

There are currently several foam cutters on the market that will cut various shapes from sheet foam. There are Gordon Griffith's booby nymph tools, which are a set of sharpened metal tubes that will cut either cylinders (for booby nymph eyes) or disks. Cutters are made that will punch out hopper or Chernobyl Ant bodies.

Another great place to look for ideas is in fly catalogues and fly shops. So if you're a little bored with elk, deer, CDC, and hackle for dry-fly materials, try some simple foam patterns and add them to your dry-fly arsenal. You will find them effective, durable, inexpensive and easy to tie—a combination that can't be beat.

For several examples of fly patterns tied with foam, please see the chapter on "Terrestrials" starting on page 146.

Weighting Hooks

Over the years I have found that weighting nymphs has been very controversial. So here is my take on it. Fly shop owners normally like to have their nymphs weighted, fly-fishermen who buy the flies probably can't tell the difference and fly tiers always want to know how much weight they should put on a hook.

I do weight bigger flies, such as stonefly nymphs, an occasional Woolly Bugger, large caddis larvae. The popularity of Bead Head Nymphs has put weighting hooks out of fashion. However, there are still a few smart fish out there that like a good natural imitation and refuse bead-head flies! For my own flies. I never weight nymphs under size 12. Personally, I rely on split shot to get the fly down where it needs to be.

Preparing hooks with weight is fairly simple. I think the size of the wire should be a minimum of .020 (remember, I don't weight hooks under a size 12) with a maximum .030 wire for nothing but the biggest of flies. Some tiers like to have a thread base under the wire to hold it in place more securely, reducing the possibility of it spinning on the hook. A good idea, but pro tiers don't have the luxury of taking the extra time to accomplish this task. We like to put the weight on the hook first then lock it in place with thread over the top of it.

Here is a great method for doing that: First, to answer the question of how much weight to put on. Pro tiers are very finicky about proportions, so why not use enough wraps of wire to make a set proportion for the fly. Let's use a size 8 3X long nymph hook as an example. I will be tying a golden stone nymph. Basically the fly will be divided into three main parts: the tail, abdomen, and thorax. The abdomen will cover the back half of the hook and the thorax will cover the front half. Wrap enough wire on the hook to cover the area that will eventually become the thorax (half the hook).

1. I like to use an old pair of hackle pliers to grab hold of the very tip of a 4- to

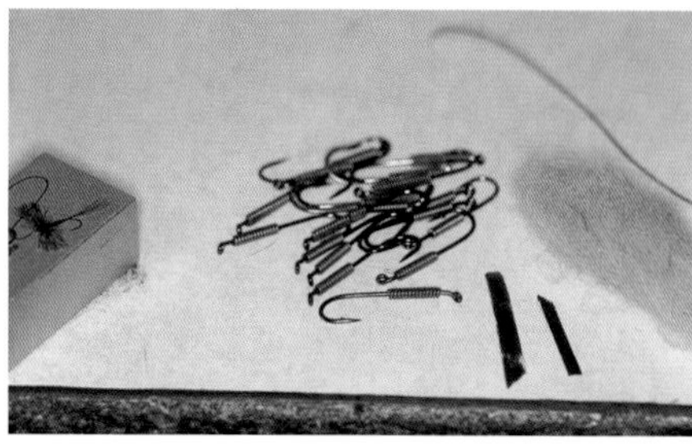

6-inch strand of .020 wire. Hold the hackle pliers up to the mid-point of the hook and start wrapping the wire forward into place. Use enough turns of wire to cover the front half of the fly, leaving enough room at the front, behind the eye, to finish the fly without crowding the head. (See photo in next step.) Keep track of the number of turns (it so happens that 13 turns is just right). Push the hackle pliers down and under the hook away from you. This should break the wire, leaving just a nub in the pliers. No trimming of the wire is necessary. Use your fingernail or scissors to cut away the excess wire at the front. Pro tiers very seldom tie just one fly at a time so we grab another hook and repeat the process. Do a pile of them before you quit.

2. To secure the wire to the hook, start the thread at the mid-point of the hook

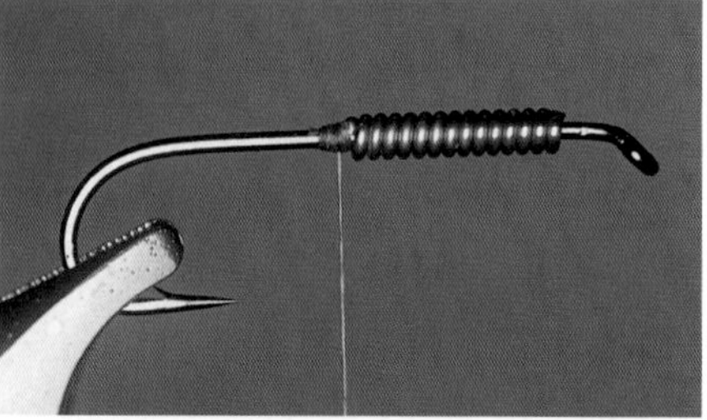

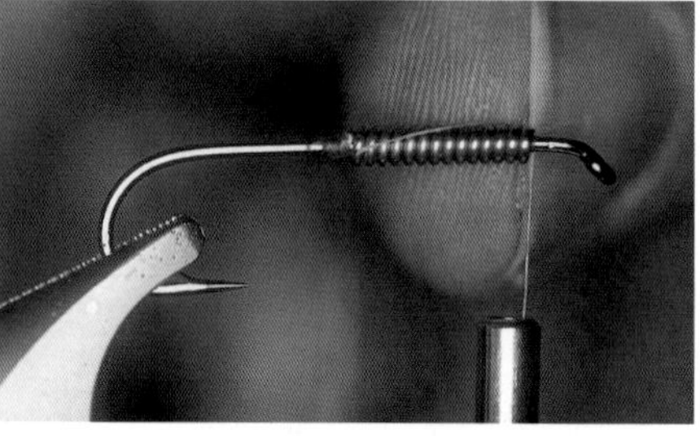

behind the weight, building a dam of thread. Reach behind the hook with the left middle fingernail (for a right-handed tier) and hold the wire back against the dam.

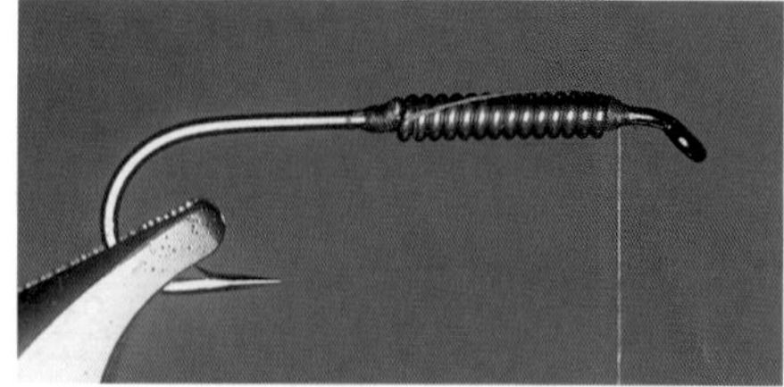

3. Jump the thread over the top of the wire with one move (avoid making wraps through the wire) and build a dam in front of the weight (again, do not crowd the head.)

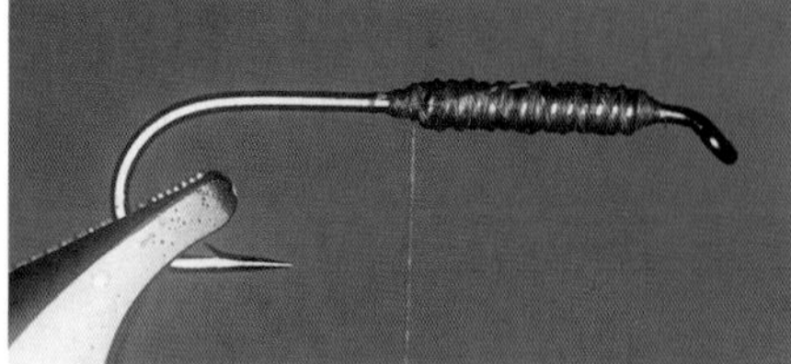

4. The dam in front of the wire will lock the wire in a certain place on the hook and allow you to tightly wrap the thread back and forth through the weight without spreading the lead wire out, which in turn may ruin your proportion.

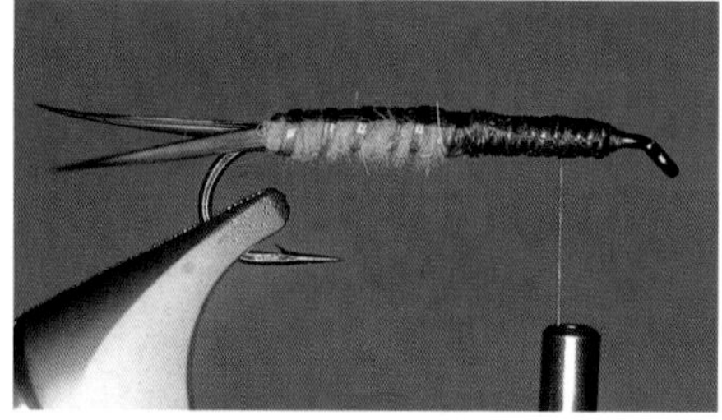

5. Tie the fly, ending the abdomen at the beginning of the wire. Notice how I use the back of the lead wire as a proportion for the end of the body. You can use this procedure to develop a consistency of proportion for all your weighted flies.

With current information on the toxicity of lead, many manufacturers have developed "non toxic" weight, including split shot for on the stream and wire you can wrap on a hook while at the vise. I recommend you use both. Lead weight is banned in certain areas of the country, like Yellowstone National Park. Other state and federal wildlife officials are sure to follow.

Chapter 3

Caddisflies

Bead Thorax Cased-Caddis

Contributed by Paul Stimpson

The Bead Thorax Cased-Caddis is a uniquely designed beaded caddis pattern in that the bead is set back on the hook instead of right behind the eye. This fly was patterned after René Harrop's Cased Caddis by replacing the dubbing with a green bead for added weight. Most of us know that when a caddis is free drifting in its case, the larvae is protruding from the case with head and legs free. There is also a very good possibility the body of the insect might be exposed, so the green section of the fly is introduced to imitate it.

Beaded flies are the "in" thing these days and with the number of colored beads on the market, the creative fly tier has nearly unlimited possibilities for fly patterns. Most people that know me would say that I have a pretty positive attitude, but when I first saw chartreuse-colored beads I thought I would never find a use for them. I may be positive but I can definitely be wrong! Paul's placement of this chartreuse bead for the "peeking caddis" is a great idea.

Actually the placement of the bead is very much like weighting a hook. The position of the heavy bead is forward on the fly enough to keep it balanced and floating correctly in the water.

Cased caddisflies are not free drifting in a stream unless they are knocked loose for some reason or are ready to hatch. According to Gary LaFontaine's research, caddisflies drift primarily during the day when they get ready to ascend. Cased caddis perform a behavioral drift with their heads and bodies extending from the case.

Wading anglers may kick up a few here and there, but another reason for cased caddis to be free drifting is high water conditions. A strategy for this pattern is working the fly in pockets near the bank where trout are most likely holding. Try the Bead Thorax Cased-Caddis post high water when the water clarity is just coming back and the caddis are trying to reposition themselves. The extra weight the bead provides on this pattern also makes it an ideal choice and the bright green bead may make it easier for the trout to pick up as it moves through the water. Hatching activity often occurs after run-off, another good reason for post high-water strategies.

Bead-Thorax Cased Caddis

Hook: Nymph 2X long 14-8
Thread: 8/0 black
Bead: Chartreuse green
Ribbing: Copper wire
Underbody: Brown dubbing
Body: Mottled turkey tail fibers
Legs: CDC feather, black
Head: Black dubbing

1. Slip a bead over the band of the hook and place hook in the vise. Start your thread at the 5/8 point of the hook and wrap back to the 1/4 point. Tie in a length of copper wire and wrap to the back of the hook. Tie in a clump of brown mottled wild turkey tail fibers. Dub a level body forward to the 5/8 point. The dubbing is used to build up a thicker abdomen, reducing the amount of turkey tail fibers needed for the body.

2. Wrap the turkey fibers over the dubbing to the 5/8 point. Rib with the copper wire for durability. Secure wire, trim excess and whip finish. Remove thread. Push bead up against the body. Restart thread in front of the bead. Build up a small dam of thread to lock the bead in place.
3. Prepare two CDC feathers and tie them in front of the bead, tips forward over the eye of the hook. Pull one of the feathers back and secure it on the far side of the hook. Take the other CDC feather, pull it

back and secure it on the fore side of the hook. Trim legs to desired length.

6. Dub the head area and whip finish.

Blue Quail Caddis

A friend of mine at work brought me a bag of feathers from a bird-hunting trip he made in Kansas. Not an unusual thing to happen in November, since I hound everybody that hunts to bring me pheasant, mallard, and turkey feathers. He said the feathers were from a blue quail (Gambel's quail). Now this was unusual, I had never heard of them before. As soon as I saw the feathers I said, "These will make perfect caddis wings."

About a week later I realized the bag was still on the floor in the back seat and decided to mess around with the feathers and see what new and different creation I could put on a hook. I opened the bag and dumped about half of them on my tying desk. "Wow" The P-U meter was about to peg out! There was just enough rotting skin left in there to about knock me out. I wasn't about to throw these gorgeous feathers away so off to the garage I went to pluck the feathers. After a couple of washings in dish soap and laundry detergent the rankness was gone. Needless to say, I didn't get to tie that day. After another couple of weeks airing out in a paper bag, they were ready to become fish bait.

After they were cleaned and I got a good look at them I realized they were gorgeous feathers. I experimented with the feathers, gluing them, not gluing them, folding them, not folding them, trying to come up with the "perfect caddis wing" that I had envisioned when I first saw them. They were OK, but not quite what I thought they would be. Time passed, the feathers were still being pushed around my desk.

The Mother's Day caddis hatch was getting close and I needed to get some caddis in the fly boxes. The feathers were still on my desk (from the previous November) so I dumped out a few. I opened the Dave's Flexament and finally found the secret to forming the wing. When you sweep the Flexament through the feather in the normal fashion you get a more oblong shaped feather when it sets up. However, if you pull the glue out through both sides of the tip of the feather with your fingers you can keep the natural wide look. Then, just as the Flexament is about to set up, a couple of short pulls at the base of the feather produces a nice narrow tie-in point, more of a triangular shape. In my opinion, the "perfect caddis wing".

Blue Quail Caddis

Hook: Dry fly size 14- 18
Thread: 8/0 iron dun
Body: Fine 'n Dry dubbing, olive or dark gray
Wing: Blue quail body feather
Hackle: Dry fly, dark dun (Whiting Farms)

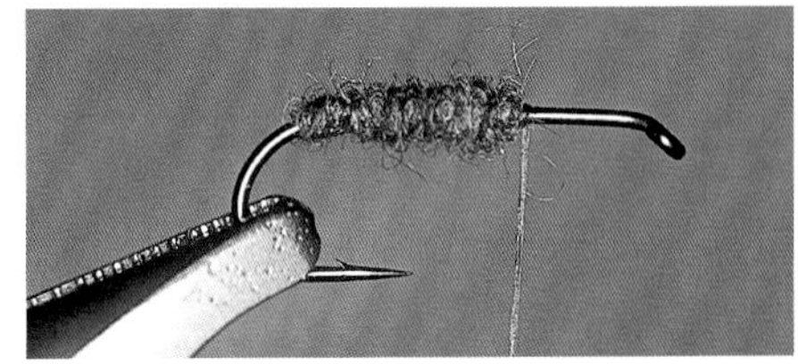

1. Start thread at the 1/2 point of the hook and wrap back a short distance. Dub a slightly tapered body to just past the 1/2 point of the hook.

2. Take a prepared blue quail feather and fold it in half, forming the desired tent shape of the wing. With the wing extending over the back of the hook about 1/3 of the hook shank, tie in the wing just in front of the body. Trim excess stem.

3. Tie in dry-fly hackle on top of the hook, concave side down or shiny side

up, whichever description you prefer. Wrap forward, forming a thick hackle collar. Whip finish.

Variations include a tan caddis using the body feathers with the lighter shades of the blue quail feathers. Another favorite of mine is the Egg Laying Yellow Sally. I use a spot of red dubbing or a red bead at the back of the fly with a yellow, stripped hackle quill for the body. For this fly I do not fold the wing because I would rather have it lie flat over the body like a natural stonefly wing. Notice the nice silhouette the wing makes from the bottom of the fly.

Breadcrust Nymph

Contributed by Pat Dorsey

The incredible Breadcrust Nymph was developed in northeastern Pennsylvania in the Pocono Mountains by Rudy Sentiwany, who is credited with inventing the original pattern in the early 1940s. The nymph basically imitates both a cased and a free-living caddis. "It was THE fly back East," says Ed Rolka, a fly tier in the area. Rolka tied his first Breadcrust at the age of thirteen and popularized the pattern by tying it commercially, making it available to shops all over the country.

In 1970, Rolka moved his family to Denver after being transferred with the Johns Manville Company. Shortly after his move to the Rocky Mountains, Bill Logan, outdoor editor of the *Rocky Mountain News* wrote a column on the Breadcrust Nymph. The piece focused on two very popular streams in the Glenwood Springs Valley, the Roaring Fork and the Frying Pan rivers. Both of these streams have large populations of caddisflies so it was only fitting that the fly would produce there. The Breadcrust consistently fooled the selective, hard-fished trout residing in these two rivers. "After the article, I sold twenty dozen of the flies to Ken Walters at the Flyfisher LTD. He reordered the day after I delivered them because they were all gone," replied Rolka. The word spread quickly and soon Rolka was delivering flies to shops all over the central Rockies as they filled their bins with this productive fly.

The secret of tying this creative pattern is in the preparation of the quills used for the body of the fly. The quill of a red-phased ruffed grouse tail feather is used. These birds are found in the Eastern and Midwestern United States, so if you hunt these birds, save the tail clump. If you don't hunt, then find someone who does. Pat says that he has about forty hunters he contacts every year for his supply of tails. These feathers may be available at your local fly shop and should be sold as a whole tail clump. Pluck the feathers from the clump. Clip off the top inch of the feather and then clip the butt end as well. Take a sharp pair of scissors and trim the barbules off each side of the feather. Make sure to leave 1/16 inch of the barbs attached to the quill.

The following steps in preparing the quills are the reason most fly anglers acquire the Breadcrust at a fly shop. I used to buy them until I learned this process, and I never buy flies. Most fly tiers have a difficult time with these quills, but there is an easy way to get them ready to use. You will wreck a few of the first quills you try, but it does get

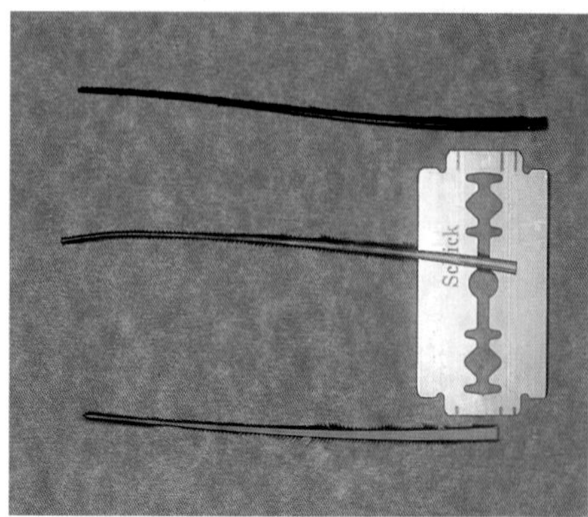

easier. First, soak the trimmed quills in water for quite a while. Take a double-edged razor blade and cut the quill in half. By "in half" I mean split the top of the quill from the bottom not one side from the other. In other words, cut the whitish side of the quill off while leaving the reddish-brown side of the feather with the nubs intact. (See photo) Throw the white half of the feather away. Now, soak the split quill. The longer you soak them the better. Remove the pith from the quill. The pith is the white core remaining inside the brown half of the quill. Pat uses a paint scraper for this step. Lay the quill on a table, pith side up. With the paint scraper and scrape the white spongy substance off the quill. If the pith does not come off fairly easy and wants to tear the quills, soak them longer. When the pith is removed, you end up with what I would describe as a half round, hollowed-out quill. Drop them back in the water so they stay soft while you tie the flies. Once you start tying with these quills, you will be amazed at how easy they are to tie with and the remarkable durability they provide the finished fly.

The keys to prepping these tails and reducing the overall time it takes to tie the fly:

Do as many tails as you can at one time.

Basically keep the quills in water at all times.

Plan around the soaking time. There are lots of things to do while these things are softening.

Scrape all the quills at once.

Tie smaller flies first, using the thin tip of the quill. Often you can tie another, larger fly with the remaining section of the quill.

Ed Rolka will always be known as "the guy" who tied the Breadcrust Nymph, however, since his retirement from commercial tying, Pat Dorsey has been very fortunate to take over tying the Breadcrust. "I hope I live up to Ed's expectations. Thank you Ed for the opportunity to carry the Breadcrust tradition into the twenty-first century," says Pat.

The Bead-Head Breadcrust is a very popular version of this nymph. Many considered bead-headed flies the most productive flies of the 1990s. One school of thought suggests their effectiveness stems from the sparkle of the solid brass bead. Others feel that the fly gets down to the fish more quickly than flies without beads. Pat says, "I think bead-heads work best in tumbling riffles where the flash can be accentuated. They can be especially effective in off-colored water, especially during spring run-off, again because of the better visibility of the fly because of the added flash the bead provides."

The first bead-head patterns were fished in the picturesque Alps of northern Italy. Roman Moser, one of Austria's most innovative fly tiers, is credited with many of the initial bead-head patterns commonly found in fly-fishers' vests today. Tom Rosenbauer introduced this new nymphing concept in the July 1993 issue of *Fly Fisherman* magazine with a story titled "Bead Heads". Bead-heads have been 'Stream Rolling' ever since.

Breadcrust Nymph

Hook: Nymph 2X long, size10-18, Dai Riki 730 or Tiemco 5262
Thread: 6/0 UNI-Thread, black
Underbody: Black yarn
Body: Ruffed grouse
Tail: Feather in the red phase, trimmed and pith removed
Hackle: Grizzly hen neck feather (Whiting Farms)

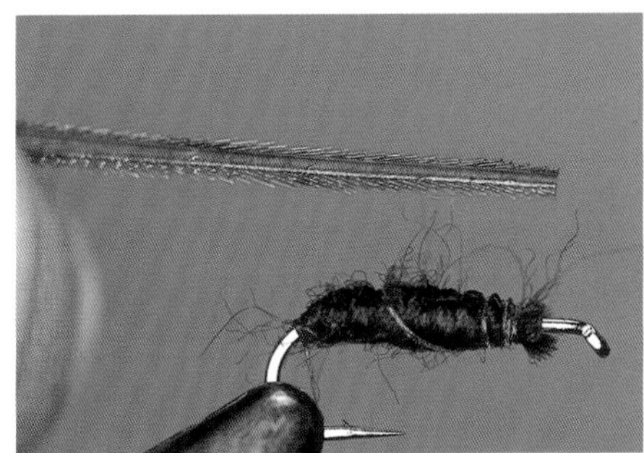

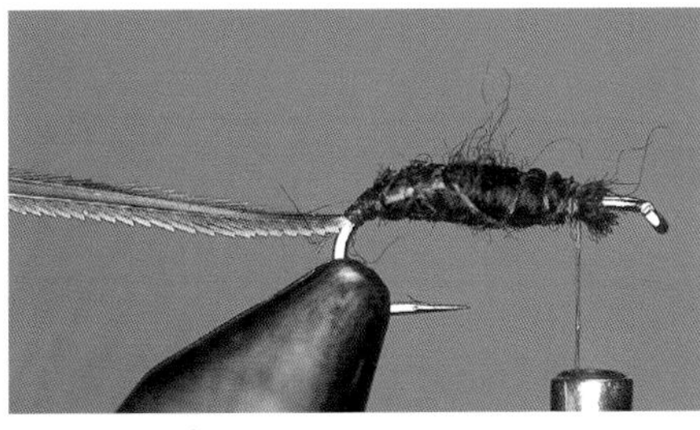

1. Start thread at the 1/4 point of the hook and tie in a length of yarn. Wrap the yarn back to the bend of the hook and then wrap forward to the 3/4 point again. Secure with thread and trim excess yarn. Wrap back through the yarn with thread, locking it in place. Tie in the tip of the grouse quill near the 1/4 point of the hook and wrap back around the bend slightly. Move thread to the 3/4 point of the hook.

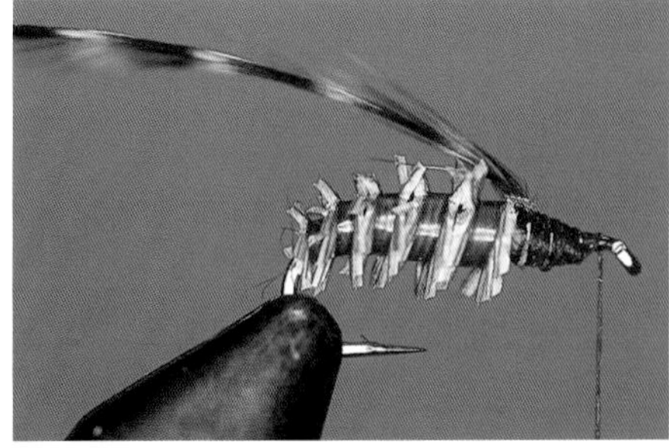

2. Wrap quill forward, making sure one wrap is right next to the last one, thus forming the segmentation. Notice how the 1/16-inch nubs of the barbules stand up. I think this is one awesome looking body!

3. Prepare a grizzly hackle from a Whiting hen neck. A hen neck feather should be used so the hackle size can be gauged more easily. As with a rooster neck, the size of the hackle varies from the bottom of the neck, where the smaller hackles are, to the top of the neck, where the larger hackles are. You are looking for a soft hackle that the hen provides but also the ability to change the size of the hackle with the size of the hook. The hackle should be about twice the size of times the hook gape. Trim off the butt end of the feather, pull a few barbs off to expose the stem, and tie in the hackle on top of the hook in

front of the body. Wrap hackle forward, using as much of it as possible, and secure behind the eye. Sweep the hackle back with your right hand, lock into place with a few wraps of thread and whip finish.

CDC Caddis

Contributed by Ken Mead

Ken Mead wanted to add this version of the CDC Caddis because of its simplicity, there is nothing more than a simple, quick-to-tie fly.

Ken has never cared for the typical tie-in procedure for CDC used on a caddis wing. Tying in a couple of CDC feathers with the tips of the feathers as the wing, which uses the whole feather, stem and all, is very simple. However, the difficulty is in keeping the wings from twisting, which in turn produces a fly that doesn't look or float quite right. So when Ken was shown this new CDC caddis wing, he was elated. Since that time years ago, Ken has shared this pattern with several anglers and tied hundreds of caddisflies in this style for local fly shops.

This technique illustrates a different use for CDC as a caddis wing, was shown to Ken by Tony Gehman. Gehman is one of the owners of Tulpehocken Creek Outfitters, a fly shop in the Reading, Pennsylvania area. He is also well-known for a series of flies that he calls the "Pop-Emergers". Gehman strips the barbules off the stem before tying them on the hook as a caddis wing. This produces a much fuller, better-shaped wing, that floats very well.

I have been using a very similar technique with CDC on the RS-2 emerger (See RS-2 Emerger on page 104) for about 10 years, but I did not take it further to incorporate it into other patterns. One of the best things about putting this book together is getting a chance to work with all the great tiers from around the United States and incorporating all of their innovative techniques into my own tying. I have a bunch of these CDC Caddis tied, ready for our early season Mother's Day caddisfly hatches here in Colorado. I'm sure this pattern will work as well across the country as it has for Ken on the famous streams of Pennsylvania.

CDC Caddis

Hook: Dry fly, size 12-20
Thread: Danville 6/0, olive
Body: Aussie Possum, color to match
Wing: CDC, brown-gray (Spirit River)
Head: CDC fibers dubbed

1. Start your thread at the 7/8 point of the hook and wrap to the back of the hook. Dub a caddis body with Aussie Possum. Aussie Possum makes a fuzzy-looking body that Ken likes. It may add realism to the fly by trapping air bubbles on the underside of the fly as does the CDC.

2. Select the biggest, fullest CDC feathers you can find. Economize your time

by laying three CDC feathers together, tip to tip, stripping the barbules off one side of the feathers, and laying them on your bench. Strip the other side of the feathers and pile that bunch with the other to make one clump of CDC.

3. Tie the CDC barbules on top of the hook with the tips of the barbules going back over the fly and the butt ends of the barbules hanging over the front of the fly. Use 5 or 6 wraps of thread. The fly should look like quite a mess at this point, but if you simply stroke the fibers that are hanging over the front of the fly up and back and wrap them down on top of the hook with a few turns of thread, the fly starts to look much better. By incorporating the butt ends of the CDC fibers into the wing, the CDC is clumped tighter together and produces a very nicely shaped wing that floats very well.

4. Trim the wing to length and shape. Use the excess CDC that was trimmed off as dubbing and form a head for the fly. Whip finish, then take a bodkin and pick out a few fibers on each side of the head to make legs for the fly.

Emergent Sparkle Pupa (ESP)
As described by Gary LaFontaine

At nine years of age Gary LaFontaine knew he was born to be a fly-fisherman. He had the beautiful Farmington River in his central Connecticut backyard, a wonderful coldwater fishery in the upper stretches and warm water in the lower. However, it all really started with his fascination with caddisflies. I asked, "Why caddisflies?"

"As a youngster I watched some of the world's best fly-fishermen cast dry flies on the Beaverkill. They caught trout with ease, on a regular basis, until the evening light started to hit the water," Gary detailed. "This is when the caddisflies would start to emerge and trout became very selective to the hatch. These gentlemen, with their beautiful presentations and the best caddis patterns available, succumbed to the pressures of humility. Frustrated by this evening hatch, they tucked their rods under their arms and headed to the Antrim Lodge for a shot of whiskey. I was amazed at the number of times I witnessed this scene."

Gary stayed on the river observing and trying his best to fool these trout, to no avail. After all, he was not old enough to drink.

So began his obsession with solving the problem of uncatchable trout feeding on caddisflies. He quickly found that collecting samples of the insect and going to the vise with a creative hand trying to stumble upon the "super fly" was not the answer.

The answer took years to find. In 1963, Gary moved west to attend the University of Montana in Missoula. He found the same uncatchable caddis feeders on the Montana trout streams. Everything changed when he went scuba diving for the first time. His first dive was below Holter Dam on the Missouri River. He observed huge trout, some in the twenty-pound class, feeding on various foods. Quite an enlightening experience. He put together a team of enthusiastic fly-fishermen and headed for a big pool on the Bighole River, just below the confluence with the Wise River.

Gary knew scuba diving was going to help reveal the answer he so arduously pursued. "Going under water was like turning on the light switch. You could immediately see what had never been seen before. As the caddisflies were emerging you could seen the brightness surrounding the pupa on its ascent to the surface. It had a glow, an aura around it."

This experience changed the way Gary approached fly tying. He developed ideas for a fly that focused on the point of contact with the fish instead of blindly tying materials on a hook.

The solution in this case had to come from a special material to imitate the glow the natural exhibited. Several materials were tried without a glimmer.

As a result, Gary started working with Dupont in an effort to come up with a material that would work. Dupont was producing a nylon material they were using to make carpets. Antron, the given name, turned out to be the answer.

"We played with Antron several different ways. Finally, I pulled the yarn over the hook and loosened it to form a sheath over the body. When I put into water, it was what I had seen while I was diving," Gary said.

The development of the Emergent Sparkle Pupa, Deep Sparkle Caddis, and the Diving Caddis all included Antron. Because Antron had never been used in fly tying, these were all original patterns. Again, the fact that they were original didn't mean anything to Gary until they were tested beyond a reasonable doubt. A double blind test resulted in a 6:1 ratio in favor of the bright Antron flies over the typical dubbed fly patterns available at the time during these difficult hatch periods.

"What made the ratio so lopsided?" I asked.

"There was something working in these new flies other than just the brightness. So back under water we went for a closer look," Gary continues. "We found the Antron also held onto air bubbles inside the sheath, just like the natural. This produced a super triggering effect. We observed trout feeding regularly on naturals, moving a foot to the left of their feeding lane, then a foot to the right. When an Emergent Sparkle drifted by, the trout would move three feet to get the fly. This is unheard of."

This is not just a theory of imitation, it is something much more powerful. This is pure attraction, which puts it into the category of a Super Fly. Gary insists that you not believe the creator of a fly but instead listen to what other fishermen, such as Craig Mathews and Randall Kaufmann, have to say about it.

One of the most common phrases going in the business is that "the presentation of the fly relates to 90% of the success of a fly-fisherman." (I'm as guilty as anyone is.) This boils Gary's blood. "Hey, the guys I used to watch on the famed Catskill streams were the best presenters of a fly I have ever seen. They made great presentation after great presentation and still ended up going to the bar frustrated. This is a case, pure and simple, in which the pattern does make a difference."

Here's proof from a delighted angler in California. William McCraig says, "When the hatch started, I put on an Emergent as a top fly and fished a Deep Sparkle on a 2-foot dropper. What happened was incredible—there were four "doubles" that evening! In all my years of fishing the North Fork of the Yuba with two-fly rigs, I haven't had four doubles."

Not only is the ESP a great pattern for hatch conditions, but it also works as a searching pattern at any time of the day because of its attracting qualities. Fish it dead drift, twitch it, or lift it. You really can't fish it wrong.

Gary seldom fishes the ESP as a single fly. "I like to fish it in tandem with a high-riding dry fly. Since the Emergent is difficult to see, I tie on an EZ2C Caddis or an Al Troth Elk Hair Caddis with a twelve-inch tippet tied to the eye of the hook, then tie on the Emergent as the dropper. Keeping the flies relatively close together helps in detecting a strike."

Emergent Sparkle Pupa (ESP)

Hook: Dry fly, size 10-20
Thread: 8/0 or 6/0, color to match body
Body: Touch dubbing
Overbody: Antron Sparkle Yarn
Trailing Shuck: Antron Sparkle Yarn
Wing: Deer hair
Head: Natural fur dubbing

1. The Sparkle Yarn you will normally find has four strands of yarn twisted together to make one. Start by cutting the yarn into 2-3-inch pieces then separating the main strand into four individual parts.

2. Start the thread at the 7/8 point of the hook and wrap to the back. The 7/8 starting point is a pre-set proportion so

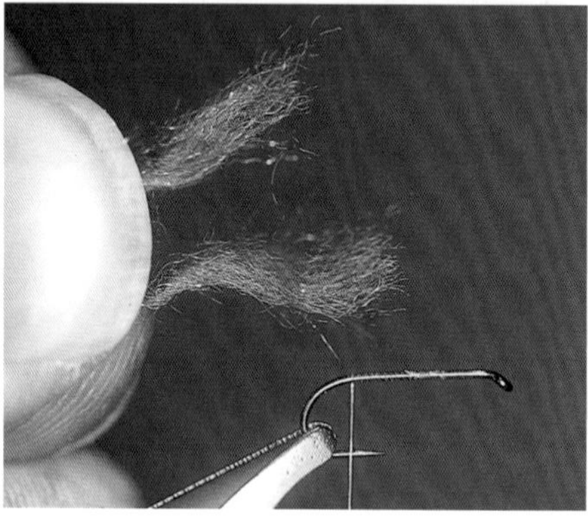

you know where the yarn overbody will be tied down later. Using the dubbing comb, comb out the ends of two individual strands of yarn. Hold both strands in your hand, ready to tie in. They should be offset slightly so you can tie in one strand at a time. Attach one strand of yarn at the back of the hook and with thread torque allow the yarn to roll to the bottom side of the hook. Attach the second strand so that it is right on top of the hook. These strands of yarn will be used for the over body of the pupa.

3. Cut the Sparkle Yarn to a length of 1/2 - 3/4 of an inch. If you find that you have trouble controlling the shorter lengths of yarn, cut them to an inch or better.

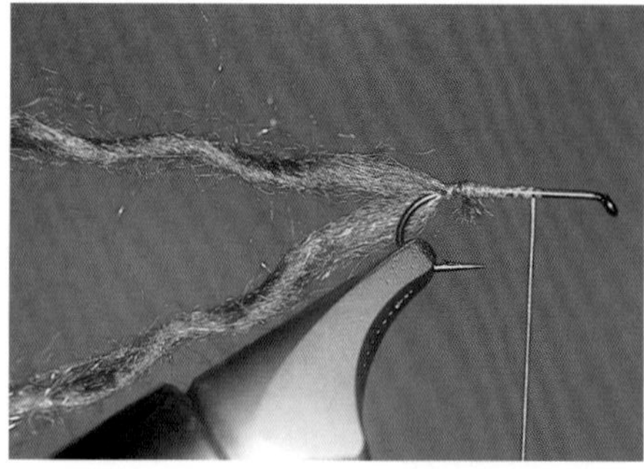

The shorter pieces will conserve on material and make the next step much easier.

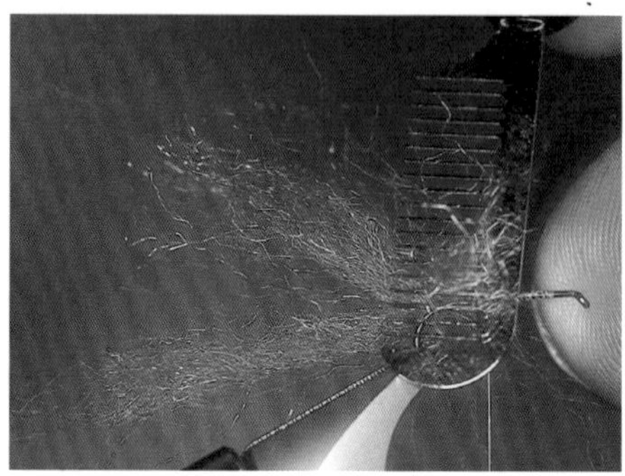

4. Comb out the two strands of yarn completely now so the fibers are loose and well separated. Don't worry about the amount of material you pull out. The sparser, the better.

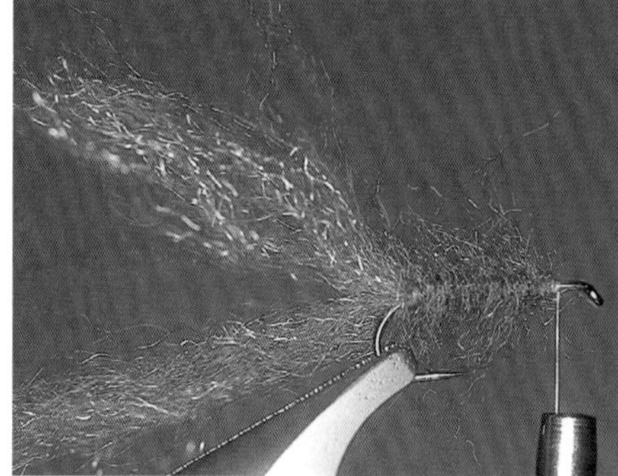

5. Wax a length of thread with BT's Wax. This is the best wax on the market for the touch dubbing technique. Touch

dub the thread with the same-colored dubbing as the Sparkle Yarn over body. Dub forward to the 7/8 point of the hook shank.

6. Make sure the yarn is well separated; you may even pull it apart a bit by hand. Now pull the piece of yarn forward under the hook and secure it loosely at the 7/8 point with a full turn of thread. Take a bodkin and pull down on the fibers to loosen a "sheath" around the body. Repeat with the strand on top of the hook. Make sure the overbody is distributed around the body of the fly evenly. Trim excess as close to the hook as possible. Make several tight wraps of thread to secure the over body into place.

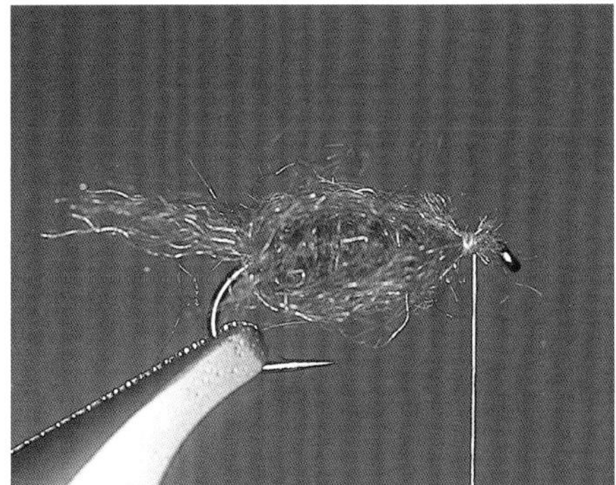

7. Snip a few fibers from the top of the overbody and pull them back to form a trailing shuck.

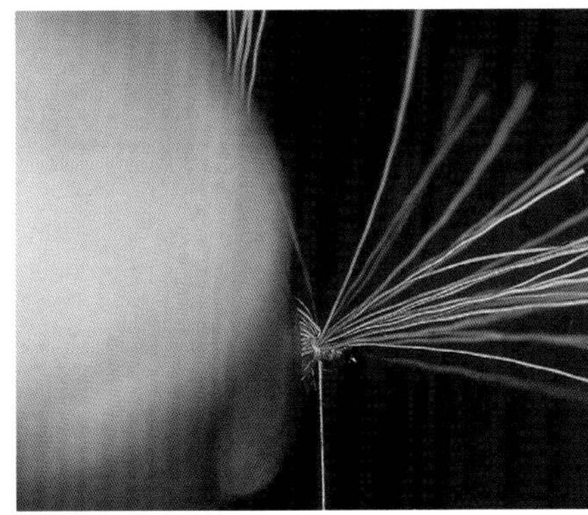

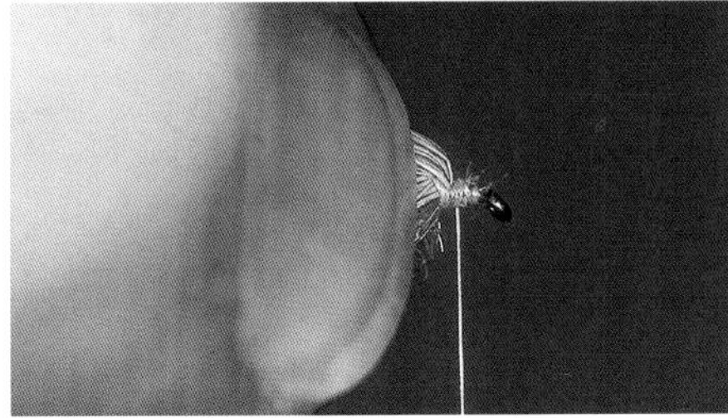

8. Ready a clump of deer hair for the wing. Don't stack the hair. The end of a caddisfly wing does not have a sharp look to it, so it should not be stacked. It should look uneven. A stacked wing in this case is a selling point for the fisherman, not the trout. I have found whitetail deer body hair to work best for the wing on this fly. Bleached elk body hair works well for the cream or ginger versions. Secure hair in front of the body at the 7/8 point of the hook with 4-6 tight wraps of thread. The wing should not extend past the bend of the hook. Pull back about 1/4 of the butt ends of the hair and make a couple more wraps inside the butt ends. Pull back another 1/4 of the butt ends and wrap through them again. Repeat one more time, then pull the entire clump of butt ends back and make a couple of wraps of thread right onto the hook shank. This is one of the finest methods I know to keep the hair on top of the hook and prevent it from rolling. The durability factor goes way up also. The hair is guaranteed not to pull out.

9. Trim the butt ends as close to the hook shank as possible.

10. Dub a small head over the trimmed butts of the wing. Use your favorite dubbing in a shade slightly darker than the body. In this case I used a gray fur with a small amount of black mixed with it to darken it. Whip finish.

Exploding Caddis

Contributed by John Hagen

For many tiers the goal is to create the perfect imitation. Every little detail must be impeccable. These details include calculating the exact length and thickness of the overall fly, the length of the tails, securing antenna and legs meticulously to the hook, and blending the exact color of the body and thorax (checked while wet, of course, to make sure the color is just right). This is more often an attempt to show a tier's ability to fool the fisherman, not the imitation's ability to catch fish.

For commercial tiers, the flies we tie go through the fly angler's hands before a trout ever sees them. However, when tying flies for our own fly boxes, whether for personal use or when guiding, we have a propensity to tie something fast and that works. John says, "The reason I tie this fly the way I do is so that it works for fishing, not so much for how it looks in a box or if I can sell it or not. I'm constantly teaching people how to fish or improving the techniques of people who come to fish with me. I fish a lot of soft-hackle flies and there are reasons for it. For one, they work! Soft-hackle flies seem to give the inexperienced angler a reprieve from the so-called perfect drift. A soft hackle can work with some drag, especially at the end of a drift as the fly is swinging towards the surface. A soft hackle looks as good as anything under this condition." John adds, "People come to me as a fly-fishing guide to learn how to fly-fish, but it works both ways. I have learned through experience that people have caught a lot of fish by accident just as they are getting ready to cast again with the fly dangling below them. So I let them do it on purpose now, and this is one of the best flies to use in this situation." John adds, "To me, a soft-hackle fly more accurately represents the insects in the water than some of the more complicated fly patterns. They simply look more realistic and alive."

We always try to see flies from a fish's point of view. What moves and wiggles, what doesn't? What color gives the fly the best impression with the light the fly may be fished in: Early morning light, bright sun at high noon, or the dusky light as the sun goes over the mountains? Will it be fished in fast pocket water or the deep pools of our favorite river? When developing flies for ourselves to test and eventually sell, these are some of the questions we ask.

The Exploding Caddis is a prime example of a tier trying to make life easier. (Something all pro tiers try to do.) This is an impressionistic fly of an emerging caddisfly, not a perfect imitation. Knowing where the fly will be fished helps the tier make decisions about the design. Details such as legs, antennae, and the trailing shuck are left to the imagination of the trout. This ragged-looking fly may never outsell the Emergent Sparkle Pupa; in fact, I don't think John has put it on the market for sale. "What I'm trying to do with this fly is create the illusion of an emerging caddis with all the facets, but without killing myself trying to imitate all the complexities. The fibers of dubbing hanging out the back imitate the trailing shuck. The tightly dubbed portion of the fly imitates the body, the loose fibers wrapped around the body can imitate the gas bubble that is building up during emergence, and the soft-hackle can imitate the legs and antenna. I've created all this with two steps, dubbing and soft hackle. So far it has worked, hey, when something is working, there's no need to fix it! Soft-hackle flies just seem to be 'easy on the lips'."

This is a very fast and easy fly to tie, using a dubbing technique that I have never seen before and an intensely clean, no no-nonsense soft hackle. The color of the fly can easily be changed with a different dubbing for the caddisflies you may be imitating. The Exploding Caddis will be a quick addition to any fly box.

Exploding Caddis

Hook: Nymph 1x long, size 10-18
Thread: Olive, Danville 6/0 #60
Body: Olive Hairline Krystal Dub
Hackle: Brown, hen saddle (Whiting Farms)

1. Start thread at the eye of the hook and wrap to the back of the hook. There really are no proportions we are trying set here, but a thread base under this dubbing is a good idea. Wax and touch-dub a length of thread. This dubbing is natural rabbit with long fibers and a synthetic with lots of sparkle mixed together, so the wax needs to be very tacky. The tackiest you can find, maybe B.T.'s Wax

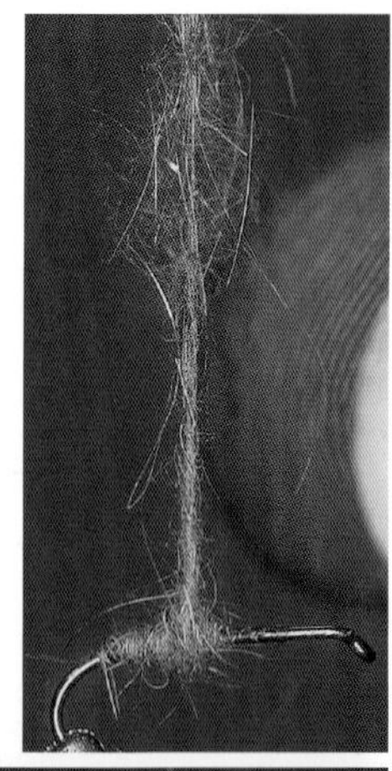

or Loon High Tack Swax. You need more dubbing than you would think. After it is touch-dubbed, tighten up about 3/4 of its length by twisting it as you would for normal dubbing. Wrap this section of "normal" dubbing forward to about the 2/3 point of the hook. Hopefully the shaggy, touch-dubbed section shows up here. Dub forward to the front of the fly, sweeping back the loose dubbing as you go. What an unbelievable look of an exploded caddisfly!

2. Prepare a brown hen back feather as shown. With the shiny side of the feather towards you and tip of the feather over the eye of the hook, strip the barbs off the top half of the feather.
3. Trim the tip of the feather to tie in. With the shiny side of the feather up and the bare side of the feather away from you, tie in its tip at the front of the hook. Wrap soft hackle three or

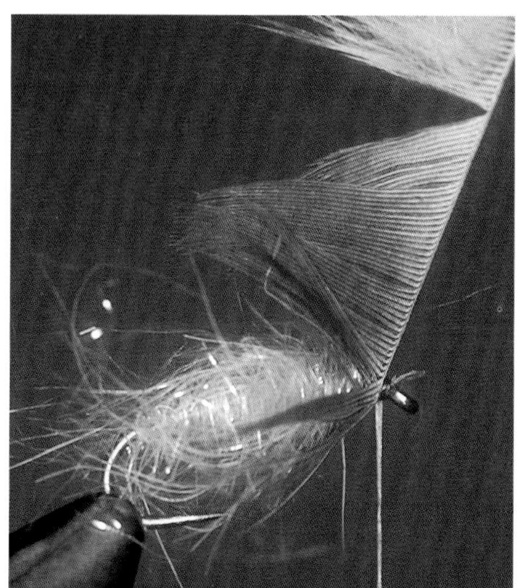

four times and secure right behind the eye of the hook and trim excess. As you wrap this feather you will notice that it lies in place by itself, swept back like a perfect soft hackle, without manipulation. What a great technique. Whip finish and that's it. If you were to blink while tying this one, you might miss it.

Ez2c Caddis (Easy To See Caddis)

As described by Gary LaFontaine

This pattern was initially designed as an indicator dry fly to fish with the Emergent Sparkle Pupa. The ESP rides very low in the water and in most conditions is pretty difficult to follow. This can cause a missed strike. I don't know about you, but I hate to tell the story about the big one that got away! Whenever there is a problem, Gary takes on the challenge of finding the solution.

Gary had used several patterns as an indicator dry fly with success, including the timeless Al Troth Elk Hair Caddis. However, most caddisflies emerge in the waning hours of the day, with low-angled light, which makes anything difficult to see on the water. All the great dry flies would get a fair share of strikes, but they had one inherent problem: They were hard to see in the difficult low-light conditions.

Gary said, "We didn't need to reinvent the wheel, just change the visibility factor."

So what makes things more visible? Color. Why do they make firetrucks bright yellow (in Montana) with all the flashing blue and red lights? So you can see them. Yellow ended up being the most visible color during low-light conditions.

The first wing on the EZ2C Caddis imitates the actual wing on a caddisfly while the second bright-yellow wing is for the fly-fisherman. Calf tail was incorporated as the second wing because of its kinky texture. The kinky hair throws water easier than deer or elk hair, making it faster to dry off while false casting. During tests with single-winged flies, the EZ2C showed increased strikes. Why? Gary always asks why. Could it be that the trout envision two caddisflies? The fly does have a thicker profile and two wings. It could be a mating pair hung in the surface film. With this possibility in mind Gary almost called the fly, The Wedded Bliss.

"Do you think the possibility of the two caddisflies struggling on the water, unable to fly away would have any merit to it?" I asked.

"ABSOLUTELY, that's an excellent point. Vulnerability! Trout recognize vulnerability," Gary said.

"As our caddisfly authority, when do you choose a dry fly caddis over a nymph, or an emerger pattern?" I questioned.

"What you are asking is, why are caddisflies so incredibly important as adults?" Gary replied.

"We do choose an Elk Hair Caddis as a dry-fly pretty often. Not that it was some brilliant brainstorm, but out of habit or because that is what everyone tells you to tie on," I added.

"Al Troth created an absolutely great fly with the Elk Hair Caddis. It has caught as many trout as any fly pattern out there. To answer the question though, an adult pattern is not a good fly during a caddis hatch." Gary continues, "When some egg-layers are coming back to the water is a great time for a dry fly. Some egg-layers, like the Grannom, lay their eggs on the surface. You know that from fishing the Arkansas River in Colorado. At noon during the Mother's Day hatch when the caddisflies come back to lay their eggs, what do you use?"

"A dark Elk Hair Caddis."

Gary adds, "Also, another reason adult caddisflies are so important is because they can live for weeks, even months. Unlike mayflies, which live twenty-four hours and die, caddisflies have mouth parts that enable them to eat and drink, thus sustaining life. They drink water, even take in nectar from flowers. Caddisflies need to stay near dark damp places. What better place than near a trout stream. Undercuts and low-hanging willows are favorite hangouts for adult caddisflies. This makes them available just about any time during the day. This is why the Elk Hair Caddis is such a reliable pattern, day in and day out. The Elk Hair Caddis is a great high-riding, ultimate searching pattern."

The EZ2C Caddis is not a replacement for the Elk Hair, but it is a great addition to your selection of adult caddis patterns. It can be used at any time, but it excels in the late-evening hours.

EZ2C Caddis

Hook: Dry fly, size 12-20
Thread: 8/0 or 6/0, color to match body
Body: Your favorite dubbing, color to match hatch
Wing: Whitetail deer hair or elk hair
Overwing: Calf tail, yellow
Hackle: Dry fly, brown (Whiting Farms)

1. Start the thread at the 1/2 point and wrap to the back of the hook. Dub a nicely tapered body from the back of the hook forward to the 1/2 point.

2. Prepare the wing by stacking a clump of hair. Tie in hair at the 1/2 point of the hook with 4-6 tight wraps of thread. Pull back about 1/4 of the butt ends of the hair and make a couple more wraps. Pull back another 1/4 of the butt ends and wrap through them again. Repeat one more time, and then pull the entire clump of butt ends back and make a couple wraps of thread right onto the hook shank. (See Emergent Sparkle Pupa for sequential photos.) Trim butt ends as close to the hook shank as possible. This is one of the finest methods for keeping the hair on top of the hook, preventing it from rolling. The durability factor goes way up also. The hair is guaranteed not to pull out.

3. Wrap down the butt ends of the hair wing with several turns of thread. Dub over the butt ends, forming a ledge to tie the second wing against.

4. Tie in a clump of yellow calf tail in front of the dubbing. A technique suggested by Gary LaFontaine for securing a calf tail wing is as follows: Tie in the hair wing along the top of the hook shank. Hold bobbin in left hand (for right-handed tiers). Raise the bobbin up and to the back of the shank. Lift hair wing to the vertical position with your right hand. Bring bobbin and

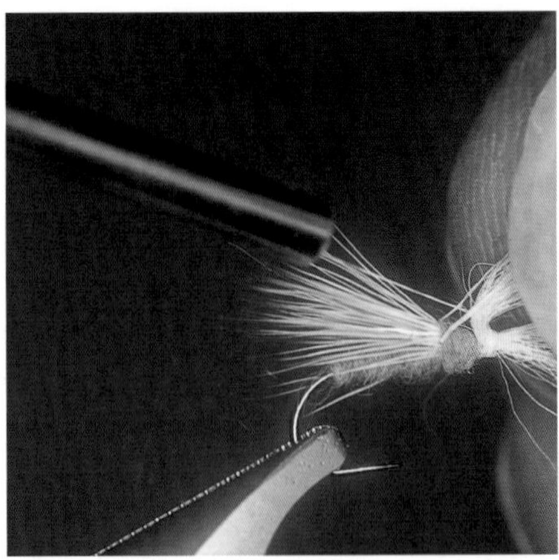

thread over the top of the hook shank but under the wing. Wrap over the top of the wing then repeat, going under the wing again. Make sure you wrap right up against the ledge of dubbing as tightly as possible without breaking your thread so the wing will cant upwards. It shouldn't look like a parachute wing but closer to a 45 degree angle. This upright canted position makes the fly "easy to see" as it is drifting on the water.

5. Measure a hackle to size and attach it in front of the second wing. This should be very close to the 3/4 point of the hook. Wrap hackle forward to the eye and secure. Trim excess and whip finish.

Green Butt Caddis

The caddis were everywhere that weekend! We were fishing the Colorado River near New Castle and the Roaring Fork River in Glenwood Springs.

As I recall, it was April 23, one of those days during the Mother's Day caddis hatch that a fly angler dreams of.

There were millions of caddis, all day long, and the fishing was great, but the catching was off a little bit. I have had the pleasure of fishing the caddis hatch on the Arkansas River several times and it didn't seem this tough.

The trout were stuffed, but they continued to feed. I can't remember a time during the day that I didn't have a rising trout within reach, especially towards the end of the day. The shadows were lengthening and, as we all know, this is the time of day when caddis activity is at its peak.

It was then that I noticed mating caddis for the first time. Hovering about eye level were pairs clinging to their last hours of life. I collected about twenty bugs and put them in a sample bottle for further inspection. They were all about a size 14. The main thing I noticed was the iridescent color of the body.

The next morning I set up the macro lens to photograph a few of the caddis for a slide show I was putting together. Much to my disappointment all the caddis were dead and about half of them had bright green bags hanging from their backends. I thought I had squeezed them too hard while handling them. Not the case. After further inspection I realized the "bag" was actually an egg sack. What amazed me most was the number of eggs in this sack! A thousand I would bet.

This is when I had the idea for an egg-laying caddis using a bead for the egg sack. I had the perfect picture of the fly in my head and it was as simple as getting out the materials. This pattern has been a consistent producer for evening caddis falls for about six years now.

Green Butt Caddis

Hook: Dry fly size 10-18
Thread: 8/0 olive
Bead: Olive, silver-lined glass bead by Spirit River
Tag: Fine & Dry dubbing, olive
Body: Peacock herl
Wing: Elk hair or fine whitetail deer hair
Hackle: Dry Fly, Dark Dun (Whiting Farms)

As all pro tiers know, planning and preparation are the keys to speedy and consistent tying. Count out the number of hooks you plan on dressing. Do at least a dozen! Slide a bead on each hook before you start tying. Get this tedious work out of the way! Prepare and size your hackle for the hook you are using. Get peacock herl and dubbing out in front of you. Pick a hair that doesn't flare too much. (Refer to the section on "Hair".) Doing this prep work beforehand will always save you time when the real tying starts.

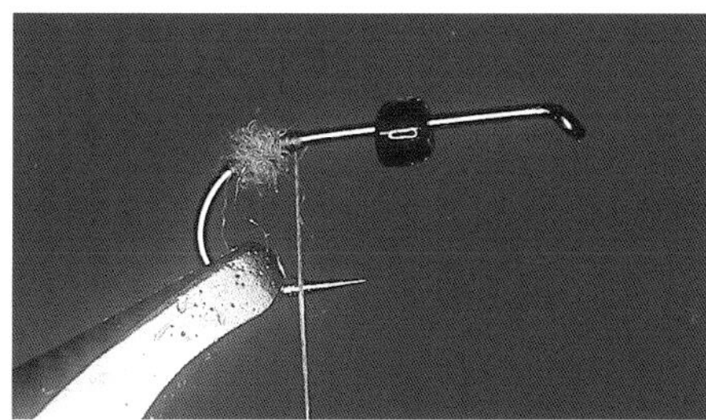

1. Push the bead to the front of the fly and start the thread at the back quarter of the fly. Remember, you don't have to cover the whole hook shank before you tie a fly. Dub a small amount of Fine & Dry to the thread to form a ball at the back of the hook. Make sure the dubbing ball is positioned so that when it is done the thread hangs directly over the barb of the hook. The dubbing ball must be large enough so the bead will not slide down the bend of the hook, but not so big it becomes obvious. When done, whip finish or half hitch a couple of times. A spot of head cement on the knot is not a bad idea.

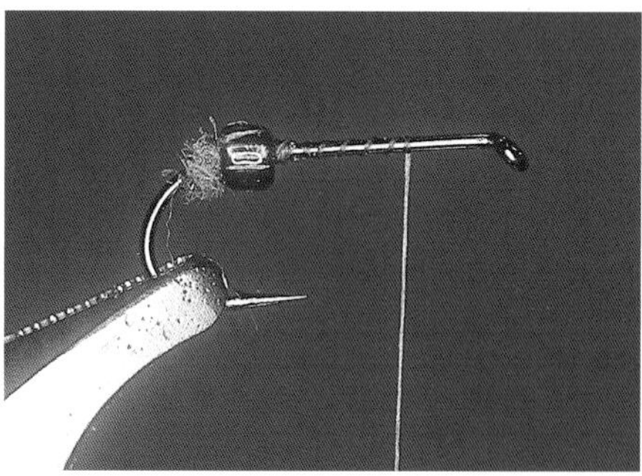

2. Slide the bead back against the dubbing ball nice and tight. Take thread over the top of the bead and start the thread as you would if you were starting a new fly. Build a small dam of thread so the bead will not slide forward. Most tiers that use this method with beads would recommend you cut the thread and restart the thread. There really is no need, the thread over the top of the bead is not going to be visible to the trout and if it happens to break, the whip finish and the restarting method will prevent the fly from coming apart.

3. After examining the live caddis, the choice for the body material was obvious. They were dark and iridescent, a perfect wet peacock lookalike. Tie in 3-4 strands of peacock herl and wrap forward to the 3/4 point of the hook. Since this is a dry fly and you are not reinforcing the herl with wire, you could spin a loop of herl or wrap the herl with the thread to help strengthen the body. (See Soft Hackle Peacock by Randy Smith)

4. Stack a clump of elk hair and tie it on top of the hook in front of body. Make a smooth landing area for wrapping the hackle.

5. Wrap in hackle. This particular version of the fly has a brown and grizzly hackle combination with a wilder looking wing. Late in the evening, when this fly should be fished, this combination is slightly easier to see and does not take away from the effectiveness of the original dun hackle. One last step would be to clip the hackle into a V shape on the bottom so the fly will ride lower in the water as would the natural when laying eggs.

Hare's Ear Nymph

Before you turn to the next fly in this book, I am going to say that I'm not trying to beat a dead horse, but I think there is a lot more to say about the Hare's Ear, especially as a teaching tool. Just about every fly-tying class taught includes the Hare's Ear. Why? The fly has just about everything you need to know to become a very skillful tier. The anatomy of a fly comes to mind first: the tail, body or abdomen, wingcase, thorax, and legs. The overall fly construction, consistency of its proportions, dubbing, and material handling to name a few more. It is truly amazing when you think about it, a fly older than any of us really care to know has all this valuable information beneath all that fuzz.

The Hare's Ear was the first fly I tied commercially. I had an order for eighteen dozen, three dozen of six different sizes. I thought I would never get them done! I wanted them to look good, but the time factor was overwhelming. About half way through the order (It took a month and a half to get about 10 dozen done), I attended a fly-tying clinic put on by one of the local Trout Unlimited chapters. There I found out how to hold my scissors in my hand while I tied and how to tie a Hare's Ear in about two minutes. Dale Darling showed me a few techniques he took for granted (which I will share with you in the tying instructions) that I found to be a major breakthrough in my thought process. My tying career literally took off from there. I got the other eight-dozen done in three evenings after dinner.

Before we start tying there are a few things I should pass along about preparation. You will get sick of hearing about this topic before you get through this book, but it is a major key to improving your tying.

This is the fly where I became very opinionated about the quality of dubbing. The most important material in the Hare's Ear is the dubbing. (Please refer to the chapter in "Material Preparation" called "Dubbing" for more information.) I still use a true hare's mask for the dubbing, even though it's a real pain in the butt. Over the years I've made improvements that may make your Hare's Ears tie up a little more easily and look better.

Trim the fur off the mask as close to the skin as possible. Try to avoid double cutting the fur. This chops it into short fibers and makes it difficult to use.

Make sure you divide the fur into two different sections. Trim the lighter-colored longer fur from the cheeks and put it in the blending can. Mix it up and bag it. This will be used for the body dubbing. You will be surprised at how much dubbing you will end up with! Take the darker mottled fur from in between the eyes and up into the forehead below the ears and put it in the can for blending. Before you blend it though, take about a quarter of a red fox squirrel skin, trim it off and mix it with the hare's mask. This mixture is used for the thorax dubbing.

Again, there is a rhyme to the reason. I found out early on that I would run out of thorax dubbing before the body dubbing and would get out of sync with my supply of masks. I have always liked red fox squirrel for its spiky guard hairs, so it was a perfect complement to the original mixture. It picks out of the thorax area very easily to give that leggy look.

The original Hare's Ear tail was tied with the guard hair from in between the eyes. What a waste of good dubbing, and an incredible waste of time. The best nymph tailing material out there is a hen back feather. It is soft and webby, making it move in the water very naturally. It comes in just about every shade of mottled brown, tan, and gray. Tan or white feathers can be dyed to olive shades. If you are not using them yet, give them a try.

Hare's Ear Nymph

Hook: Regular nymph or 1X-2X long, size 10-20
Thread: 8/0 brown

Caddisflies

Tail: Mottled hen back feather
Ribbing: Holographic Mylar Motion, pick your color
Body: Hare's ear dubbing
Wingcase: White tip turkey tail
Thorax: Dark hare's ear dubbing

1. Start your thread at the 1/2 point of the hook and wrap back to the 1/4 point. The tie-in at the 1/2 point sets up a proportion. This is where the body ends and the thorax begins. Tie in a clump of hen back feather and wrap to the back of the hook. The tail length should be no more than 3/4 of the hook shank, preferably 1/2 the hook shank length. Hold on to the tail clump as you wrap back to ensure it stays on top of the hook. If you let go, the tail will roll to the backside of the hook, which is an absolute a no-no for a pro tier.

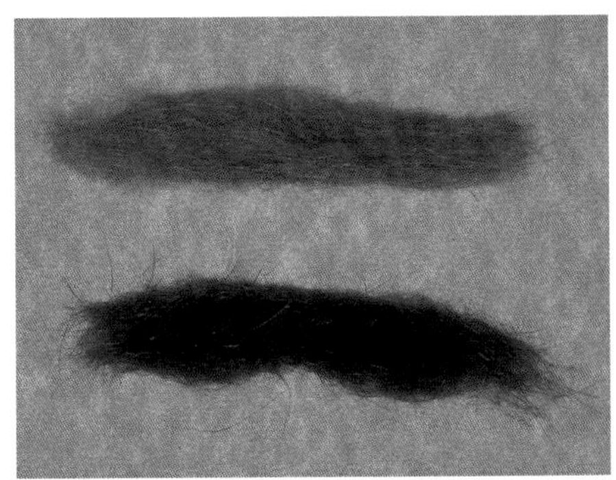

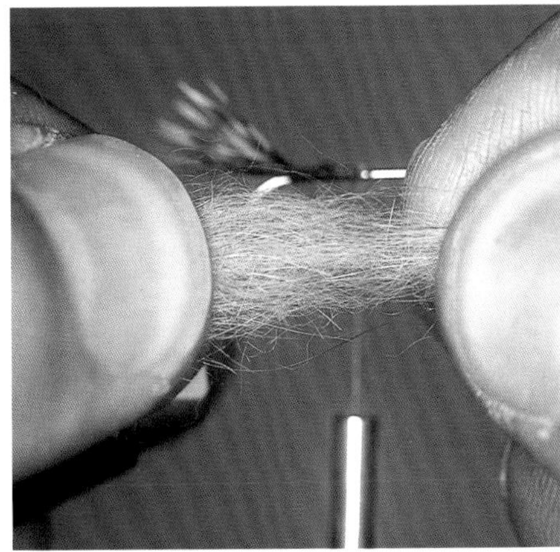

2. Refer to "My Method of Dubbing" under "Dubbing" in the "Material Preparation" chapter before you go to Step 3. Dub the thread which will eventually form the body. The length of dubbing on the thread varies with the size of the fly, so it is important to experiment until you have just the right amount to finish the body without

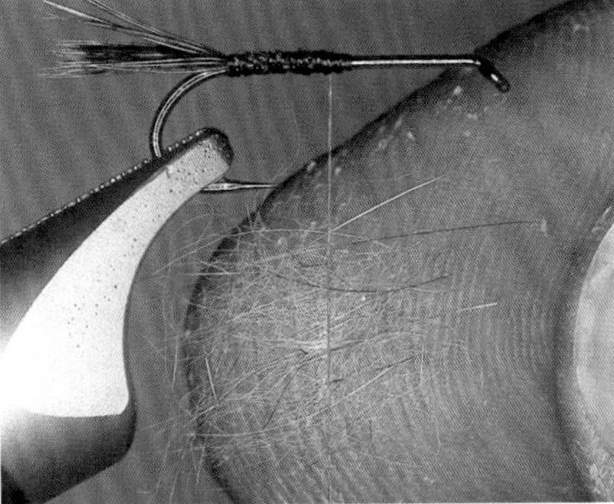

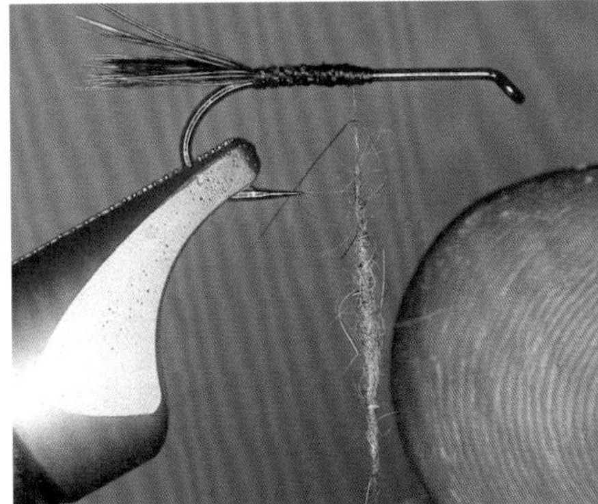

adding or taking away dubbing. In a couple flies you should be able to determine the right amount. Hint: A size 16 1X long nymph should take about a 1 1/4-inch dubbing noodle to complete the body.

3. This is one of the speed-tying techniques that Dale Darling showed me. Come to find out, all professional tiers were doing this. Notice there is bare thread between the hook shank and the dubbing. Use this bare thread to tie in the ribbing as you wrap to the back of the hook. When you get to the back of the hook the dubbing should show up. Do not let go of the ribbing in your left hand. Change directions and start wrapping the dubbing forward, forming the body. Rib the body with 3-4 evenly spaced turns. Secure ribbing. This simple organized set of movements will reduce your tying time immensely.

4. The same tie-in procedure applies to the thorax dubbing and the wing case as did the body and ribbing. Dub your thread with the darker thorax dubbing leaving about a 1/2 inch of bare thread between the hook and the dubbing. Hold the slip of turkey tail on the side of the hook with your thumb. Wrap the thread over the turkey slip, which will lay the wingcase in perfect position. The dubbing should show up by the time you have wrapped the thread back to the body. Change directions and dub the thorax. Again, figure out how much dubbing it takes to fill the thorax area and apply that much to each fly as you go. Hint: A size 16 1X long nymph should take about a 1 3/4-inch dubbing noodle to complete the thorax.

5. There is only one problem I have ever encountered using this technique. If the dubbing gets to the body before the thread, a gap shows up between the body and thorax when you pull the wingcase over. (see first photo) Make sure the thread wraps tightly up against the front of the body to eliminate this

problem. (See second photo) Pull wingcase over the thorax and tie off. Whip finish.

6. Many pro tiers don't take the time to pick out the dubbing in thorax area to imitate legs. I do! I like the extra animation it adds to the fly. Simply take the point of a bodkin into the dubbing just under the wingcase and pick it out. Repeat on the other side. If the fibers are too long, sweep both sides down with your thumb and index finger until you are even with the point of the hook. Tighten your grip and pull. This should make the legs symmetrical in length. This takes less than ten seconds, and I think it makes a much better looking Hare's Ear.

Another world-renowned fly is the Soft Hackle Hare's Ear. As if we haven't beaten this horse enough, I'm going to cover the soft-hackle technique for an added bonus.

1. Tie the Hare's Ear with a ribbed body and thorax, without a wingcase. Prepare a soft-hackle feather. Sweep the fibers of the feather back away from the tip. A good soft-hackle feather should hold this shape without much effort. Hungarian partridge is shown, but a mottled hen back feather or grouse feather would work just fine. Trim the tip to about 1/8 of an inch.

2. Tie in tip of feather right behind the hook eye. Make sure the convex side of the feather is up. Picking the size of a

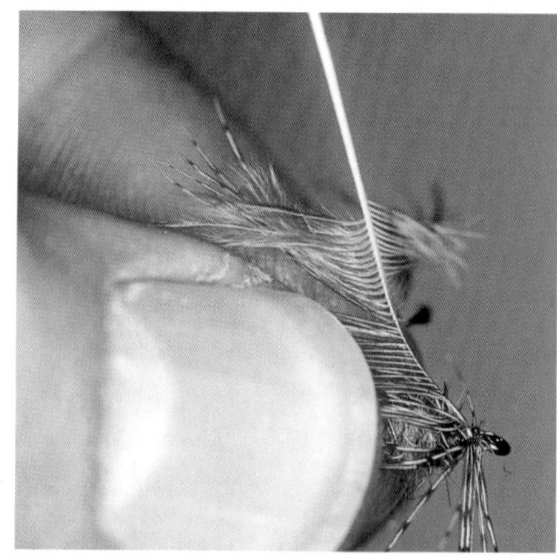

soft hackle can be frustrating. Try to use a feather where the fibers do not extend beyond the bend of the hook.

3. Hold the feather up and sweep the fibers back. Make two wraps of soft hackle, sweeping the fibers back as the feather passes the top of the hook. Secure the feather and trim. Using your thumb and first two fingers, sweep the fibers back and make a nice clean head. Whip finish.

Variations of the Hare's Ear are endless.

Roman Moser Balloon Caddis
Contributed by Rich Pilatzke

This is a fly pattern first tied by Roman Moser, a very talented Austrian fly tier. He is from the Traun River region and is well known for tying flies with synthetic materials. This pattern is tied to imitate an emerging or "ballooning" caddis.

Being a proponent of foam flies, Rich Pilatzke, saw a picture of this simple caddisfly pattern and just had to add it to his tying repertoire. The article listed the recipe of materials to use but did not include instructions on how to tie the balloon in place. He found it challenging to tie. The body and wing were no problem, but that balloon head just didn't want to cooperate. After several attempts, he found the easiest way to secure the foam in place. Recalling other techniques and flies that he had tied, he found the simple bullet-head technique the best for this fly. Tie in a length of foam so that it hangs over the eye and pull it back over the head just like you would a clump of hair on the Thundercreek Streamer series or the Henry's Fork Hopper that Mike Lawson ties. I bring this up at this point to simply reiterate my whole concept on fly tying: If you acquire as many tying techniques as you possibly can, the complexity of the fly pattern doesn't matter. You should be able to look at the fly, just as Rich did in this case, and tie it. Yes, you will have to experiment and may sometimes end up with a real monstrosity, but when you do get it right it can be a real gem of a fly.

The orange-colored dubbing for this pattern is Aunt Lidy's rug yarn cut into 1/4 inch pieces and mixed in a blender. The shortness of the fibers is what gives the fly its shaggy appearance. The orange body also makes it a great searching pattern in the evenings. It works especially well on brookies and cutthroat trout in high-mountain lakes. They seem to love the orange body color.

Roman Moser Balloon Caddis
Hook: Dry Fly, 1x short, size 10-16, Daiichi 1310
Thread: Tan 6/0 UNI-Thread

Body: Orange or yellow Antron dubbing
Wing: Whitetail deer hair
Head: A strip of closed-cell foam, in orange or yellow

1. Here is a quick note on the significance of this particular hook. The Daiichi 1310 is a 1X short dry-fly hook, which is great for tying a fly, let's say the length of a size 16, with a size 14 gape. This gives you the opportunity to tie a smaller fly with better hooking ability. In essence, you are actually cheating, but no one is sending you to the penalty box. Start thread at the 3/4 point and wrap to the back of the hook laying down a thread base. Dub a cigar-shaped, fairly shaggy body forward to the 3/4 point.

2. Stack and measure a clump of elk hair for the wing. The wing should be a full hook shank in length. Secure the hair into place. Pull back about 1/4 of the butt ends of the hair and make a couple more wraps inside the butt ends. Pull back another 1/4 of the butt ends and wrap through them again. Repeat one more time then pull the entire clump of butt ends back and make a couple wraps of thread right onto the hook shank. This is one of the finest methods I know of to keep the hair on top of the hook and prevent it from rolling. The durability factor goes way up also. The hair is guaranteed not to pull out. Now trim the butt ends of the hair.

3. Secure a strip of yellow or orange foam with the length of the foam hanging over the eye. Wrap back through the foam to the base of the wing. Pull the foam back like a reversed wingcase or a half bullet head and lock into place with a few turns of thread. Whip finish and trim the foam to make a balloon head.

Stripped Gear
Here is a typical story about how a fly is developed. It always starts with a vision of a pattern, a special pattern that can't fail. You can see what you want, you know exactly where and when to use it. However hard you try though, this fly requires more skill than you possess to put it together.

Skill in fly tying is not just tying in a material and wrapping it around a hook. (Believe it or not, about 80% of all flies tied are a result of exactly that, tying in a material and wrapping it around a hook, including the Stripped Gear.)

Skill knows what material to tie on a hook to achieve the essential look and performance for that perfect pattern. Another quality of a skillful tier is knowing how to substitute for a material that can't be found, that is no longer available, or the one you ran out of and it's midnight the night before you leave for your favorite fishing hole. As Clint Eastwood once said in "Heartbreak Ridge", "You need to improvise, adapt, and overcome."

The proper material often makes the fly what it is. As hard as it is to bring yourself to do it, that certain material in a fly recipe can be substituted. I do it all the time, if for no other reason than to see if the fly will still look good and work as well on the water. I have often found that the developer of a fly has done the homework required, and usually the best material has been chosen. It's a good thing I do not tie full-dress Atlantic salmon flies. Substituting a material on one of those may end you up in jail.

The Stripped Gear came to me as a drawing, a nice little free-hand job with a couple of notes on it describing color and design. It was from Dave Hilton of Salt Lake City. Dave is a jeweler of many years with a very artistic way about him. However, Dave's challenge in tying this fly was his fingers. He loves to tinker at the vise and came up with a couple of Stripped Gears of his own, but his hands are rough and chapped from years of polishing gold and setting precious stones, so he could not tie a lot of them. Since he also was uninformed about fly-tying materials, he started looking for help.

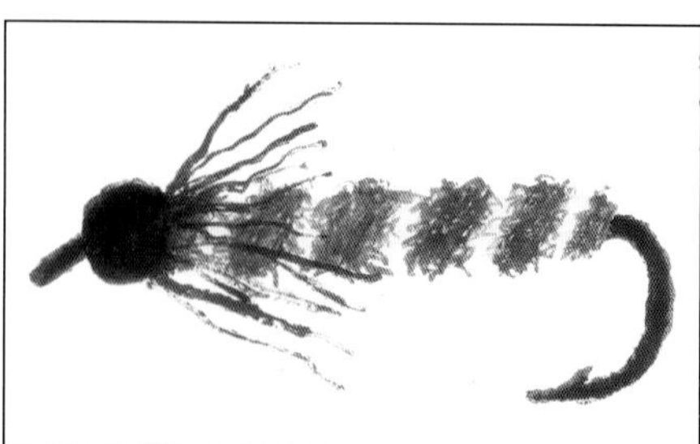

So Hilton searched for someone to put the fly together for him. After inquiring around the ranks of fly-fishermen and fly tiers, Hilton called me. He told me someone recommended me. Dave, a very soft-spoken gentleman explained what he had in mind for his perfect fly. He was looking for a caddis emerger to fish on the local waters around Salt Lake City. (What amazes me is how people see the same thing, *differently*.) He wanted someone from out of town to tie it for him so he could test it properly without other anglers showing it to too many trout. I figured I had some time on my hands and I always love a challenge so arrangements were made. He sent me the drawing. With his thoughts running through my mind, I turned my attention to a bare hook.

It seemed pretty simple to me after seeing the look he wanted. I knew I would use thread for the underbody color to eliminate bulk. Clear Tiers Lace was my first choice for the transparent look he described on the phone. The overbody that formed the segmentation did take some thought, but I remembered tying some Palomino Midges out of a material called New Dub. (The Palomino Midge is another great example of a vision coming to light.) I had a couple of short pieces left and it worked great. It had just enough of the fuzzy appearance that the drawing depicted without being oppressive. New Dub is expensive and is getting hard to find. I have bought most of it here in Denver, but there is a material called Magic Dub that may work if New Dub can't be found. It works well, but does not have the same fuzzy appearance as New Dub. Hungarian partridge is always a good choice for a soft hackle.

Tom Whiting of Whiting Farms is raising a chicken that is a very good partridge substitute. He is doing some amazing things with poultry these days and is breeding a hen chicken with outstanding coloration and an amazing range of sizes. Tying size 18 soft hackles without fighting short, fragile feathers should be possible soon.

So our version of the Stripped Gear was done. We put together bead-head versions, standard versions, light and dark colored versions, and sized them from a 10 to a 16. They looked good, but would they work? Hilton was pleased, claiming it as the fly he "would not leave home without". I fished a small pond here in the Front Range and it took trout instantly—I mean as soon as it hit the water! The trout in the big freestone rivers I fish regularly have also found the Stripped Gear a welcome change to their diet.

It seems to have a very good triggering effect on trout. Is it color? All the colors seem to work. Is it the transparent effect of the body? Maybe that has something to do with it. Is it simply the animation of the soft hackle? I really don't know since I have not spent time under water observing and I have yet to find a trout that I understand.

Stripped Gear

Hook: Nymph 2X long, size 10-16 Daiichi 1710

Bead: Black for original version. Gold can be used when water clarity is suspect.

Thread: 8/0 or 6/0 UNI-Thread, light Cahill

Body: Clear Tiers Lace, by D's Flyes. Size medium.

Overbody: New Dub or Magic Dub, olive or brown

Hackle: Partridge or mottled hen saddle feather. There are several sources for hen saddles. Whiting Farms has several selections and very possibly a quite good partridge substitute.

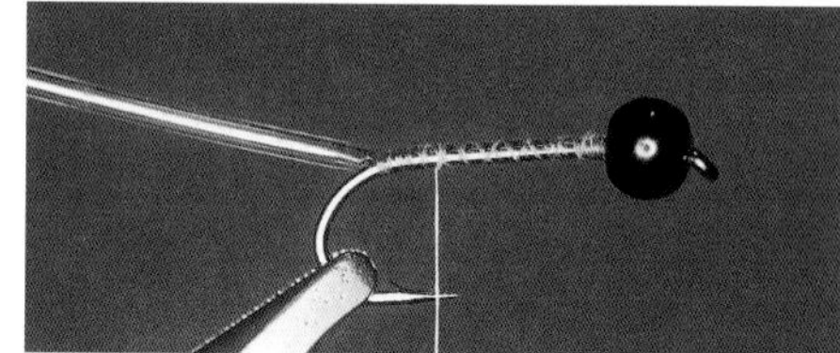

1. Slip a bead over the bend of the hook. Start the thread behind the bead.

Tie in Clear Lace right behind the bead and wrap down to the back of the hook. Make sure it stays on top of the hook.

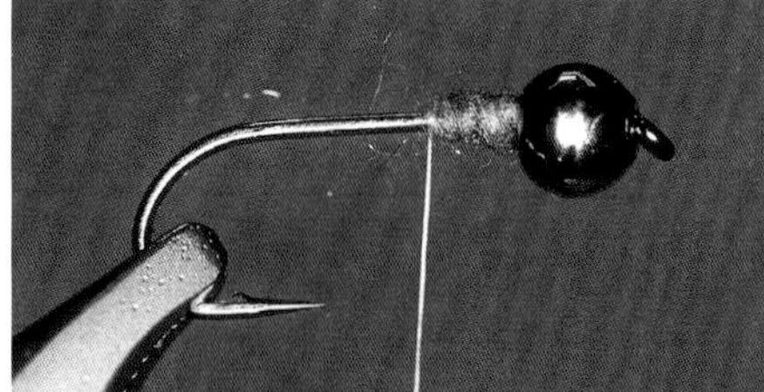

Note: Here is a little tip for those of you who have a problem with the bead sliding back into the fly. This usually happens while you're unhooking a trout and the bad part is that it sometimes destroys the fly. I normally like to apply a small amount of dubbing to the hook behind the bead and push it into the back of the bead. This helps lock it in place. This keeps the bead from sliding back into the fly when you have to get rough with it while fishing. This procedure does take a little extra time, but the added durability makes it time well spent.

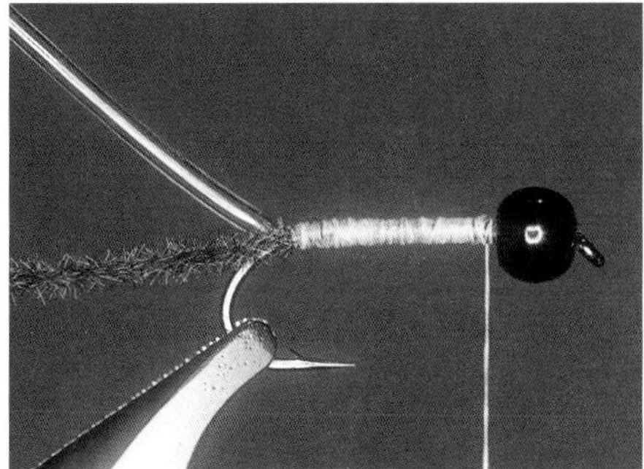

2. Take the thread forward a few wraps and tie in just the tip of the New Dub on your side of the hook. (Making sure the New Dub is on your side of the hook allows the first wrap of New Dub to lie in the gaps left by the Clear Lace in the next step.) Secure with four very tight wraps of thread as you again move to the back of the hook. Wrap thread forward, forming a smooth thread underbody.

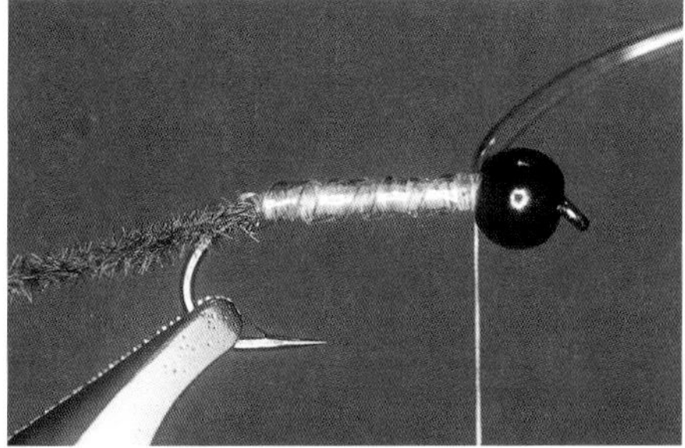

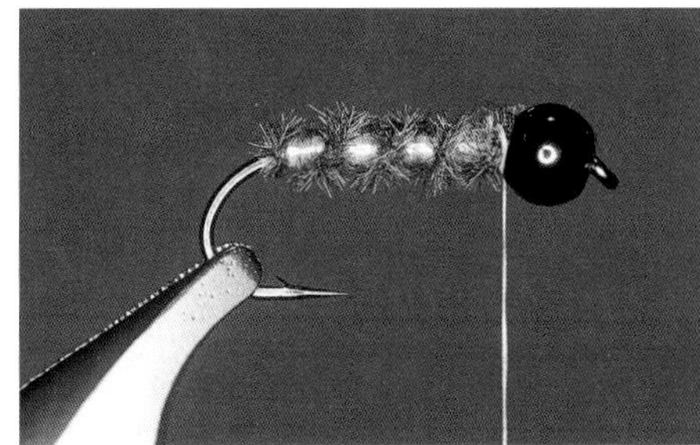

3. Wrap the Clear Lace forward with evenly spaced gaps so the thread shows through. This move is as though you were ribbing the body. Secure behind the bead. Trim excess lace. Wrap the New Dub forward in between the gaps left by the Clear Lace. Secure the New Dub behind the bead and trim excess. New Dub is pretty expensive so try to

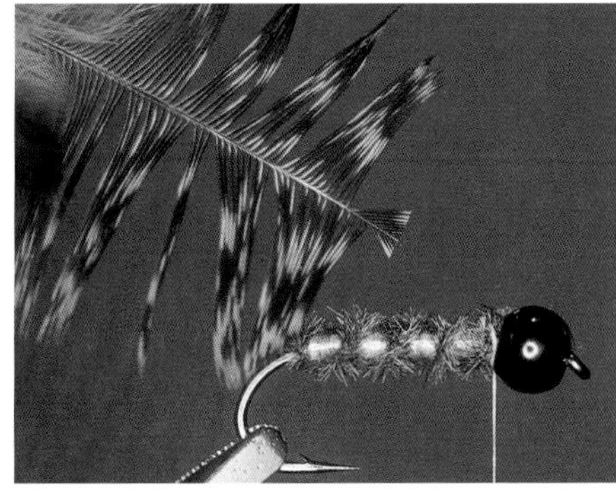

use that last little piece by using a pair of hackle pliers to wrap it in.

4. Prepare a hen saddle feather or a partridge feather by pulling the fibers back away from the tip and trimming the tip to about 1/8 of an inch. Tie in the feather by the tip with the convex side up and wrap the feather two times to form a soft-hackle collar. The number of hackle turns depends on the length of the feather and what you want your fly to look like. Usually a couple of turns will let the segmentation of the body show through and give you plenty of fibers to add the animation a soft hackle provides. Sweep it back with three fingers of your left hand and whip finish.

Teardrop Caddis

Contributed by Fred Vargas

This fly was developed by Bob Braendle, at the time an employee for the Great Lakes Fly Fishing Company. Braendle co-authored the book *Caddis Super Hatches* with Carl Richards where the fly was debuted. This book covers the super caddisfly hatches from around the country. Fred assisted them in gathering caddisfly specimens from local waters for the research needed to put the book together. Braendle set up an aquarium in the basement of the fly shop and put a number of caddisfly larvae in the tank. He would spend hours watching the movements of these caddisflies and actually got to see them emerge and hatch. The time spent watching the aquarium, along with hours of on-stream observations of the caddisfly's lifecycle, gave him the idea for this pattern.

Since it imitates an emerger or stillborn, the best way to fish this fly would be with a drag-free float or with the addition of a minute wiggle or shake that mimics the struggle of the insect trying to free itself. This pattern can be tied in any body color combination to match the angler's local hatches. The teardrop made with Darlon should be tan or gold on most versions to match the shuck as it is shed by the insect.

The poly wing on this fly can be treated with Water Shed, a permanent waterproofing agent that keeps the fly afloat very well. Hareline Inc. is the distributor of this waterproofing solution.

Cinnamon Teardrop

Hook: Wide-gaped scud, light wire, size 10-18 Tiemco 2457
Thread: Brown 8/0, Gudebrod
Body: Fine & Dry dubbing, cinnamon
Overbody: Darlon, gold
Legs: Brown hackle
Wing: Polypropylene yarn, gray-dun

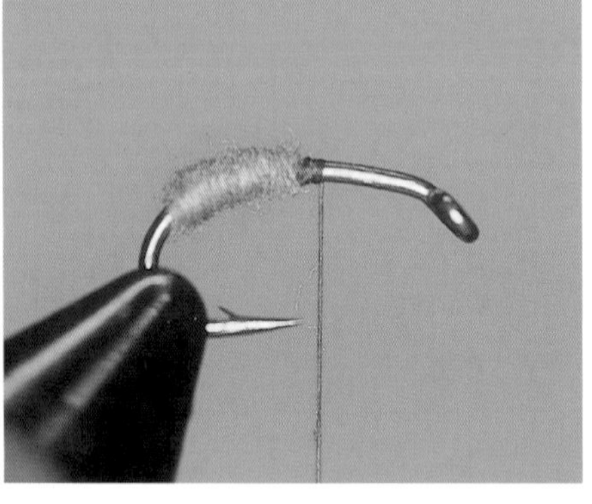

1. Start thread on the shank at the spot even with the hook point and wrap a thread base to the back of the hook just beyond the spot even with the barb. Dub a thin body from this point to where you started the thread.

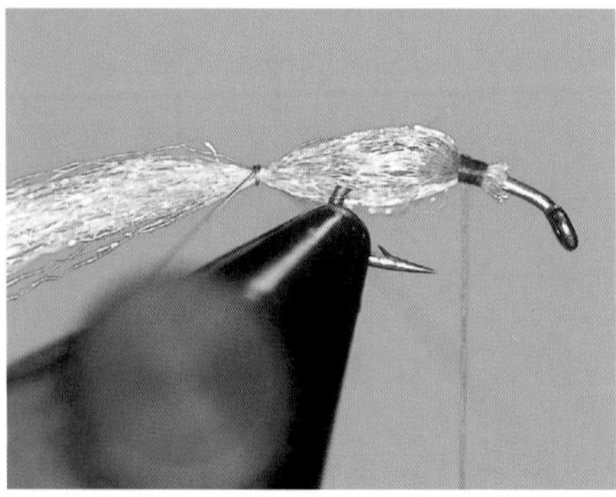

2. Secure a bundle of Darlon in front of the body with two soft wraps of thread, no thread torque at all. Take a thumbnail and press on the fibers from the top of the hook. This forces the fibers down the sides of the shank allowing the fibers to encompass the hook shank. Tighten the thread and make a couple of wraps back towards the body. Using a fine, clear thread or 8X tippet material; make a simple overhand knot around the Darlon. The knot should be about a 1/2 hook shank length beyond the bend of the hook. You are making an extended trailing shuck with the Darlon, which looks very much like a teardrop, hence the name of the fly. The shuck should be 3/4 of the body length.

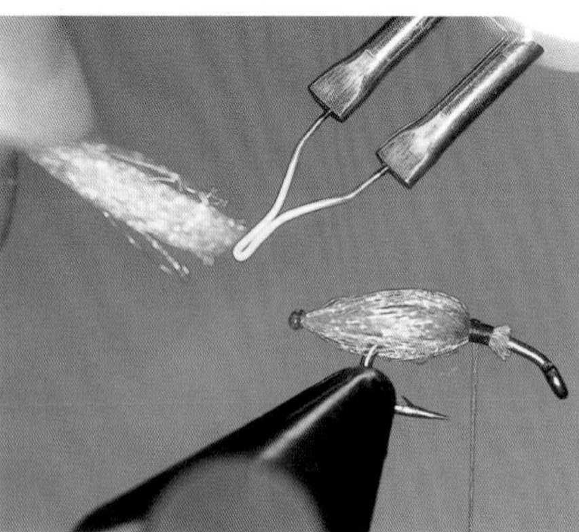

3. Fred uses a medical instrument used to cauterize blood vessels to melt the Darlon at the knot. You push a button on this thing and it is red hot instantly. A hot bodkin or needle will work, but you need to keep a candle burning to heat it up for each fly. This is also the reason for using monofilament for the knotting material. It melts right along with the Darlon to help hold the individual strands together. Nifty little trick!

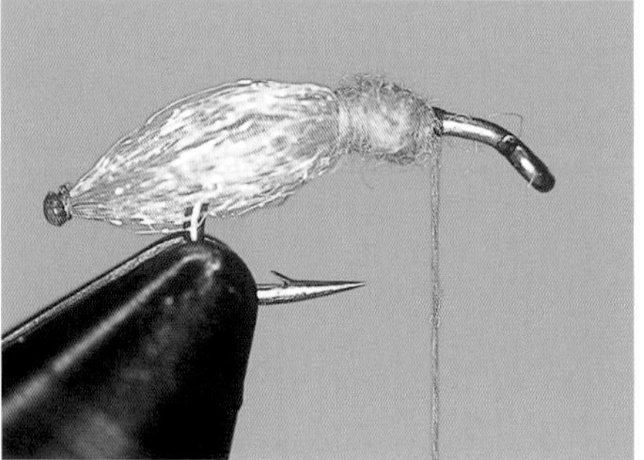

4. Add a small amount of dubbing in front of the Darlon teardrop.

5. Secure a brown hackle in front of the body and make two or three turns with the hackle for the legs on the fly. These turns of hackle do nothing for the floatability of the fly. Secure the hackle and trim excess. Trim hackle on the top and bottom of the hook, leaving the barbules on the side for the legs.

6. Take a bundle of polypropylene yarn and secure it with several tight wraps of thread on top of the hook in front of the legs. Whip finish and trim wing to length. Trim fibers hanging over the eye of the hook even with the very front of the hook. Pushing on the top with your thumbnail spreads the poly yarn. The

wing will float the fly much better if the poly yarn is spread evenly on top of the body and on both sides of the hook at the tie-in point. Dress only the wing with floatant so that the body and the shuck are below the water surface.

Chapter 4

MAYFLIES

Ausable Brown Drake (Parachute)

Contributed by Dennis Potter

This fly is a variation of an old Au Sable mayfly pattern tied many years ago by Clarence Roberts.

The original was tied as a *Hexagenia*. It used yellow thread, pheasant-tail fibers for the tail, and light to medium colored deer hair for the body. The wing was bright white calf tail and the hackle was the short spade hackle from the side of the neck. This hackle was a major problem with the original. Back when this fly was first tied, the quality of the feathers was poor. The tier would wrap in too much of the webbed part of the hackle, which was not stiff enough to hold up the big fly and it would collapse under its own weight. In addition to poor feathers, the limited choices for deer hair often made this pattern a one-fish fly. It would sink after a couple of drifts or often the hair would blow up once a sharp-toothed brown trout grabbed it. We have access to some incredible materials these days, so it is not the fault of the originator of the fly that Dennis has redesigned it.

Do not grab just any old chunk of long deer hair for the body of this fly. It should be selected carefully. Soft corky hair that flares a lot is not strong enough. The soft corky hair also acts like a sponge and that is not good for a dry fly. Elk hair will work because of the added durability, but Dennis uses the dyed belly strips from Wapsi Fly Company. The hair should have a waxy consistency to it, no broken tips, and should flare to about 45 degrees.

Top-quality hackle is a must for parachute-type flies. Stiff barbules of proper length with a stem of extraordinary length are necessary. Feather products from Whiting Farms can be special ordered to fit this need.

The pheasant-tail fibers do nothing to support the back end of this fly and may not be as durable as synthetics available out there; however, they do look more natural on the water as the fly is drifting. The *Hexagenia* and the drakes have very long tails and you should not use a stiff fiber for them.

Dennis adds, "Hi-Vis Winging Material has been touted as a replacement for calf tail. LL products in New York distributes it. Anything you can do with calf tail or calf body, from a winging standpoint, you can do better with Hi-Vis. With one bag, at the cost of $2.25, I have tied as many as 75 dozen size-14 parachute wings and you don't have to take extra time stacking the hair."

Dennis has tied this type of pattern as small as a size 16; however, it is most often tied in size 12 and 10 to imitate the brown drakes and mahogany duns. Since learning how to tie this pattern, I have put together western green drake and gray drake patterns that have worked in Colorado and Wyoming.

Para-Brown Drake

Hook: 2X Dry fly, size 10 Tiemco 100
Thread: 10/0 Benichie, dark brown
Tail: Pheasant-tail fibers
Body: Whitetail deer hair, yellow (Wapsi)
Wing: Hi-Vis Winging Material, gray
Hackle: Grizzly, dry-fly quality (Whiting Farms)

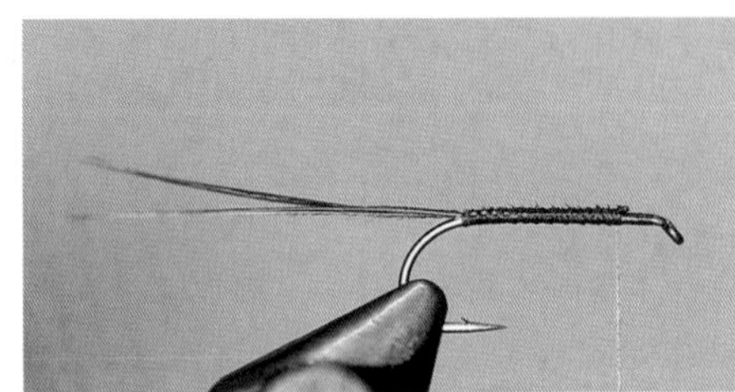

1. Start thread about 1/16 of an inch behind the eye and wrap back laying down a base of thread. Bring the thread forward again to the starting point. Measure a few high-quality pheasant-tail fibers to 1 1/2 hook shank length. Secure the tail in place using a pinch loop method and wrap back. Holding the fibers up as you wrap back avoids letting thread torque roll the fibers over to the side of the hook. The exact number of fibers is not important, just try to maintain consistency. Bring thread forward to the initial starting point.

2. Prepare and stack a clump of deer hair; a clump about twice the size of a wood matchstick is a good starting point. Dennis recommends starting with more hair than you would think is needed because of the short hair fibers and fluff at the base of the hair that end up in the trash. Make sure the thread is at

the 5/8 point of the hook. Measure the hair so that the tips extend just beyond the hook bend. Trim butt ends of the hair at the 3/4 point. Hold the butt ends of the hair just in front of the thread, and make two soft wraps of thread around the hair. Pull thread tight letting the hair roll around the hook and flare. Do not cover up the little tuft of flared hair in front of the thread wraps. You need this tuft to butt the wing against in a later step. Notice this particular hair flares to about 45 degree to the hook shank. Make two more wraps of thread to lock the hair in place. Sweep the hair back, letting it encompass the hook shank. Wrap, with evenly gapped turns of thread, to the back of the hook shank trapping the hair down. Very tight thread wraps add to the durability and floatability of the hair. Make several turns of thread at the back and then wrap forward crossing over the first thread wraps, again, equally as tight as the first wraps of thread through the hair. This procedure makes a very durable, segmented body. Move thread to just in front of the hair body.

3. Tie in a clump of gray Hi-Vis winging material over the body and trim off the excess. On a size ten, if you stretch this winging material out it should be about the thickness of a wooden matchstick. Jam the wing against the tuft of spun hair at the front of body with several turns of thread to make it stand up. To form a smooth thread base for the parachute hackle to wrap around, make a wrap of thread around the wing post while latching onto the tuft of hair at the same time. This connects the wing to the hair, making it stand upright. Wrap thread up the post about 1/4 of a hook shank. It is very important, especially while using this type of material for a wing, to have a substantial thread base to wrap the hackle onto. Bring thread down the wing post and move thread back onto the hook shank in front of the wing post.

4. Its news to most, but the hackle is a very important part of a parachute fly. If the hackle is too small, the fly will inevitably tip over. Use a hackle that looks too big rather than undersized. Measure a hackle so the diameter is 1 1/2 wing height. In other words, if the wing height is 1/2 inch, choose a hackle, when wrapped around the post, that is 3/4 of an inch in diameter. On a size-ten fly, a neck hackle may need to be used since large saddle hackle is pretty hard to find. However, if you do have saddle hackle that size, use it because the overall hackle is so much longer. Use two hackles if need be. With the convex side towards the tier, trim the fibers at the butt end of the hackle as shown in photo, about 1/4 inch off the top and about 1/8 inch off the bottom. Tie in the hackle on the fore side of the hook, in front of the wing post. With one quick turn, wrap the hackle clock-wise up to the top of the thread post. Then wrap back down the post, one wrap directly under the last. Don't skimp on the hackle, using as much as possible. Secure hackle on top of the hook shank, trim excess, and whip finish. Trim the wing height to a full hook shank length. Trim off a small corner section from the backside of the post to give it the shape of a mayfly wing.

Bead Head Twist Nymph

As described by Gary LaFontaine

The Bead Head Twist Nymph is a take from the original Twist Nymph designed by Gary LaFontaine. The original, with its crest of hackle on top of the thorax area, was designed as a mayfly imitation for stillwater situations. The original is a slow-sinking fly that an angler fishes within the top foot and a half of the surface. An easy fly to fish, the angler's only concern is to hang on and wait for the take.

Anybody that has followed his career knows that Gary LaFontaine does not develop flies at the vise. He develops them at the point of contact with the fish. He is one of very few fly developers who has donned scuba gear to see what the real insects look like and how trout feed on them. After solving one of the mysteries of hatching caddisflies with the Emergent Sparkle Pupa he turned his focus to other insect species. Mayflies in particular. (See the essay on the Emergent Sparkle Pupa (ESP).

One of the first fallacies he immediately found upon close observation was that mayfly nymphs were not opaque. He saw, up close and personal, that mayfly nymphs were a very vibrant, lively insect. In fact, you can see parts of the nymph such as blood vessels, the digestive tract, the beating of the gills as they breathe, and the tiny air bubbles that attach themselves to the gills. The air bubbles added a certain amount of brightness to the insect. The standard patterns of the day did nothing to imitate either this brightness or its vibrancy.

During my interview with Gary, I found that he had a real passion to answer questions and solve mysteries about our beloved sport. He didn't go to the vise and tie a fly, take it to the river, catch a trout and call it a success. He delved deeper into what the trout really sees and actually looks for to make its decision to eat. As with the Emergent Pupa, the mayfly nymph imitation needed a slight aura of brightness around it. Gary knew the qualities of Antron were just what he needed to develop a more effective mayfly pattern. However, the typical tying procedures used with Antron previously didn't produce the desired effect. It took some time at the vise and some serious thought, but the Double Magic technique was developed.

The Double Magic incorporates two of the most amazing materials we have available to us, peacock herl and Antron fibers. A strand of herl spun inside a loop with chopped-up Antron, also called touch dubbing, creates the amazing effect of liveliness and vibrancy of a mayfly nymph. Gary created the Twist Nymph, which imitated the naturals perfectly. Too perfect, as he found out in further tests. The new fly was such a good imitation that it blended into the "background" of the other nymphs so well it became a matter of presentation rather than the fly. One more question, one more answer. The goal now was to make the Twist Nymph a super fly.

Gary changed the look of the fly ever so slightly by changing the color of the Antron touch dubbing. The more natural color of olive or gray was changed to orange. This "odd"-colored aura around the fly was all it took to get the trouts' attention. Totally ingenious, if you ask me.

Then the bead-head revolution came along and just about every fly worthy of a name had a bead-head counterpart. Bead-head nymph patterns, if allowed to drift correctly, have a natural jigging action, which has been known for years to be a key triggering motion that just about every fish will notice. This turned the Bead Head Twist Nymph into a fly with two triggering aspects and an invaluable fly for moving-water situations.

Here is a comment from a successful New York angler. Glenn R. Wilkes exclaimed, "No bull! I tied my first Twist Nymph and caught fifteen wild browns on Oatka Creek. I had little hope of doing well because it was a hot August day at noon hour. Low, clear water and no rises in sight. My old standbys, the Hare's Ear and Pheasant Tail, hadn't produced, but a Twist Nymph was a winner this particular day."

I have fished the bead-head version of the Twist Nymph for years in all types of conditions with continued reliability. A standard dead drift in the feeding lane of a trout proves to be the most effective. So, Gary began working on a new nymphing style called the Constant Motion Technique.

If you ever got the chance to talk with Gary you will knew he was a vault of information, and as far as he knew this technique has not been published. So you are the second person (next to me) to hear these words of wisdom.

Gary explained, "It works especially well with an area with a high concentration of fish. If you like to smoke a few whitefish for the winter, the fall is a great time to find whitefish concentrated in certain areas of a stream. This is when this technique proves exceptionally effective.

"When trout are noticeably feeding heavily is another excellent time to experiment with this method." Gary added, "By the way, this is also a method the Europeans often use in the World Championships."

Now for the gist of the technique: "Step into a riffle that you think is going to be filled with fish. Make a normal cast of about 15 or 20 feet up into the riffle. Raise the rod without detouring the fall of the nymph. The Bead Head Twist Nymph would be a perfect choice since it will sink fairly quickly. When you know it is near the bottom in the prime area of the riffle, let it drift a few feet, then strike with an exaggerated roll cast. Basically, a blind strike. The more obvious action this move makes is that the fly will rise up from the bottom, like a Leisenring lift. However, this move might trigger a strike, so be ready. If there is no strike, let the fly drop again and continue drifting. Depending on the length of the drift and the speed of the current, you may have to make a new cast. Another roll cast upstream and the fly is back in motion." He adds, "This is a very efficient way to cover water completely. The fly is in the water longer than on most other nymphing techniques and the fly is in Constant Motion.

"If you want to catch a larger trout still feeding on insects using this method, remember that a big trout could very well be within the school of whitefish. The reason is that trout are not good at rooting around in the gravel, so they feed more actively as open-water feeders as the food source is drifting free," Gary continued, "But as the whitefish are rooting around kicking up insects, the trout are picking off nymphs as they are turned loose. You may take twenty whitefish but the two or three trout you hook up will be well worth your time."

Bead Head Twist Nymph

Hook: Nymph, size 12-20
Thread: 8/0 or 6/0, tan, light.olive
Bead: Metal bead, gold or black
Tail: Marabou, olive
Body: The Double Magic: Peacock herl and Antron touch dubbing. Orange, yellow, or pink
Thorax: Touch Dubbing, gray or olive

1. Slide a bead onto your nymph hook. Note: This is not etched in stone, but gold or brighter colored bead can be used for stained or off-colored water,

and black or dark-colored bead could be used for clear, low-water conditions.

2. Attach a small clump of marabou for the tail. Break the marabou to length instead of cutting it. The broken or torn marabou leaves a more natural-looking tail. The overall tail length should be about 1/4 to 1/2 the hook shank length.

3. Trim about 1 to 1 1/2 inches off the butt end of a strand or two of peacock herl. Use one strand for any fly size 16 and smaller and two strands for size 14 and 12. This fly is a mayfly imitation and should be tied as thinly as possible. Tie in the butt end of the peacock herl. Wax the thread with BT's Wax. If you apply wax to both sides of the thread the dubbing will cling to the thread better. Touch dub the thread with a counter colored Antron such as orange, yellow or pink.

4. Pull peacock herl down so it is parallel to the thread and dubbing. Make sure the peacock does not get caught up on the point of the hook. Using the True Spin loop tool, hook the thread and peacock herl in the hook of the tool and form a loop as you take the thread back to the hook shank. Attach thread to the shank right at the back of the hook

and move the thread to the front of the fly. This technique is referred to as Double Magic. Peacock herl and Antron are considered magical materials when it comes to trout flies, hence the name. Lift your bobbin out of the way and give the True Spin a spin. The weight of the tool gives the turning action momentum, so just wait a couple of seconds for it to twist the herl and touch

dubbing together. When the herl and dubbing are twisted tightly together all the way to the hook shank, you can stop it.

5. Wrap the herl and dubbing rope forward to a point just behind the bead. Leave it attached to the True Spin tool as you wrap forward. Notice how the Antron forms a fuzzy body, which when wet creates an incredible aura around the fly. Secure herl and trim excess.

6. Wax thread and touch dub with an olive dubbing and fill in the thorax area just behind the bead. This touch dubbing also adds to the overall fuzzy look of the fly and helps keep the bead in place.

7., Touch a drop of head cement onto the top of the bead. As you are whip finishing the fly, drag the thread through the glue. This gluing technique is a great way to increase the durability of the fly without disturbing the valuable Antron fibers.

Here is a gold-bead version of the Twist Nymph. Try the Double Magic technique on other patterns such as the body of a damsel nymph or the head of a pupating midge. It produces an amazing effect.

Black-Eyed Sparkling Hare's Ear

Contributed by Paul Stimpson

Here is another example of combining two flies to come up with something totally different. Gary LaFontaine combined the standard hare's mask dubbing with his old standby, Antron, and created a fly called the Sparkling Hare's Ear. John Gierach ties a pattern called the Hare's Ear Soft-Hackle.

While reading Gierach's book *Good Flies*, Paul found a technique for blackening bead chain. Dipping a regular silver bead chain in nickel blackener will blacken it.. Nickel blackener is a corrosive substance that actually rusts the metal in the chain. Paul Stimpson had the brainstorm to combine the Sparkling Hare's Ear with the Soft Hackle and then incorporate the blackened bead chain eyes. Hence the name.

Paul said, "I had tied a few of these things and didn't actually have the time to go get them wet. Then a friend of mine called and said he was headed out to hook a couple of trout. I told him to come by and get a couple of new flies I had just come up with."

He took them out and had a great day on a small stream in the Uinta Mountains, fishing them with a simple dead-drift nymphing technique.

As soon as I saw Paul tie this pattern, I knew I would have some in my fly box. I am kind of partial to the Hare's Ear since it was one of the first patterns I tied as a commercial tier and I love seeing new versions of it. I scaled it down just a little, tied it with olive dubbing, and used small black metal eyes of some kind to make a darn good western green drake nymph. It worked throughout the green drake season on every stream and river I fished. The eyes definitely get the fly down in a hurry and it actually drifts with the hook point up. It is almost snag proof and, as with the soft-hackle design, it is a very lively fly in the water.

I hope this fly will give you some creative ideas for reinventing some old pattern that could use a face-lift.

Black-Eyed Sparkling Hare's Ear

Black-Eyed Hare's Ear

Hook: Curved Nymph or 3X long, size 14- 8
Thread: 8/0 brown
Tail: Mottled hen back feather
Eyes: Bead chain, black
Ribbing: Flat gold tinsel
Body: Hare's ear dubbing mixed with brown Antron fibers
Legs: Mottled hen back feather
Thorax: Hare's ear dubbing, same as the body

1. Start your thread at the 1/4 point of the hook and wrap back to the 1/2 point. Move thread forward to the 3/4 point and attach a pair of bead-chain eyes using simple X-ing wraps with the thread. Finish with figure-eight wraps to lock the eyes in place. Move thread to the 1/4 point. Place a drop of super glue on the thread wraps around the eyes to lock them in place. Tie in a clump of hen back feather fibers for the tail and wrap to the back of the hook. The tail length should be no more than 3/4 of the hook shank, preferably 1/2 the hook shank length. Hold on to the tail clump as you wrap back to ensure it stays on top of the hook. If you let go, the tail will roll to the backside of the hook.

2. Dub the thread to form the body, leaving about 1/2 inch of bare thread

between the dubbing and the hook shank. Use this bare thread to tie in the ribbing and wrap back. Let the tinsel roll to the far side of the hook as you are wrapping back. Do not let go of the ribbing in your holding hand. When the thread ends up at the back of the hook, the dubbing should show up and can now be wrapped in place without stopping motion. Change directions and start wrapping the dubbing forward, forming the body. Rib the body with 3-4 evenly spaced turns. Secure ribbing. Adjust the amount of dubbing you apply to keep the body sparse with a slight taper going forward. The body should be kept as smooth as possible, so any guard hairs or fuzz that may be protruding from the body could be trimmed away.

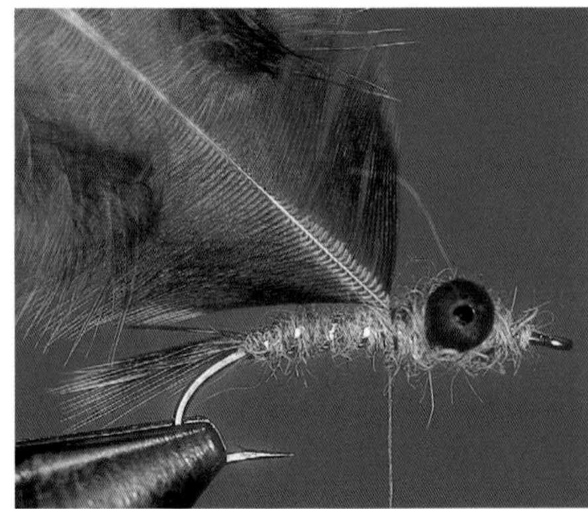

3. Prepare a hen back feather by separating the barbules at the very tip of the feather and sweep the bulk of the feather back. Tie in the tip of the feather behind the bead eyes, convex side of the feather up. Dub a small amount in the thorax area and around the eyes. Make a couple turns of hackle behind the eyes, allowing the stem of the feather to bury in the dubbing. This helps protect the feather from getting snagged on a sharp tooth.

Finish dubbing in between the eyes and the thorax area. Whip finish.

Boxwood Parachute Mayfly

Contributed by John Hagen

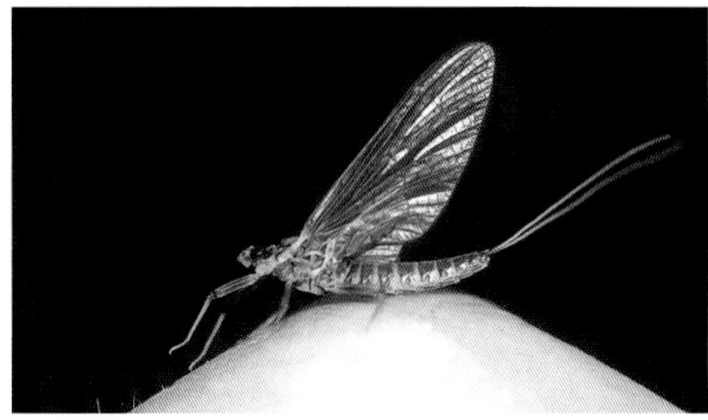

Boxwood Gulch Ranch is a private fishery where John Hagen and I both guide. It's on the North Fork of the South Platte River, 40 miles west of Denver. The ranch has a great location, huge trout, and lots of them. Well over 200 days a year are booked up there for fly-fishermen only. Check out www.boxwoodgulch.com.

Guiding up there is fun. A good angler can net more five-pound fish in one day than most fishermen do in a lifetime. An inexperienced angler who doesn't know what a good drift looks like might get lucky and get a couple. These struggling anglers are always asking (Hell, everyone asks), "What fly are they eating?" We guides have a standard answer to the question, "A good drift!"

The trout are big eaters and not particularly selective, but they are in tune enough to know the difference between a good drift and a dragging fly. However, when a mayfly hatch does happen, these trout can get as picky as any in the West.

The hatches are seldom heavy. John and I have discussed this situation many times. We check the bug life in the stream often and find there is a good number of mayfly nymphs: Green drakes, slate drakes, pale morning duns, blue-winged olives, and a few of this and that. There are lots of caddis, stoneflies, and midges as well. We have a wild theory that the fish are feeding on the emerging nymphs so heavily during the hatch that very few bugs actually make it to the surface to enjoy adulthood. When you do see a dun make it to the surface, these gluttonous trout waste little time rising to scarf it up. A special fly pattern is required for this predicament.

This is a situation every fly-angler finds himself in at one time or another. Trout are rising and feeding selectively so we must choose, or ultimately tie, the proper imitation. We catch some bugs (if we can get to them before the trout do) and lock into memory a visual picture or put the macro lens on the camera and take photos. Then we head to the vise for a brainstorming session.

When designing flies, the silhouette of the fly as viewed by the trout needs to be addressed. One other situation John noticed at Boxwood was how long it took the duns to actually get off the water and get airborne. Upon further inspection, he found a large percentage of the adults were crippled and unable to get off the water. A low-riding type of dry fly that could be seen easily was in order. The parachute style came to mind immediately.

John tied the fly specifically to imitate a couple of mayflies that hatch on this stretch of the North Fork. One is a size-12 green drake and the other is size-14 *Isonychia* that we call a slate drake. Both are relatively big flies that sit low in the water.

Since John was developing this fly to use when guiding other anglers he needed a fly they could see. John says, "It's hard to believe, but there are people out there that can't see a size 8! The white foam parachute post on this fly shows up as well as any fly I've tested. There are other materials such as calf body hair or calf tail that can be used for Parachute wings, but they produce a very heavy fly that has a tendency to tip over. This foam wing is much easier to tie and it shows up very bright on the water. It also hits the water and rides correctly every time without manipulation. Even a well-tied, standard-hackled type of fly won't land on the water correctly every time because of a poor cast. And, believe me, I've seen a few of those while guiding. So this fly also cures that problem."

John has one more reason for tying this fly: "Another problem exists on this stream for the angler who does not see a fly on the water very well. As with many other streams across the nation, smaller mayflies, midges, tiny yellow stoneflies, and caddisflies hatch during the prime dry-fly season. This complicates the sight problem, but I'm paid to catch fish no matter what the situation. I usually get more money when I net a lot of fish, so I fix problems for a living. The Boxwood Parachute Mayfly works great as an indicator fly. I will tie a length of tippet to the bend of the big parachute fly with a smaller-sized, harder-to-see dry fly attached. I can tie on whatever fly the trout may be eating at the time and the big parachute lets the client see the general area where the smaller fly is located and can set the hook when a rise occurs." John adds: "This set-up is also a great teaching aid when trying to show someone what a good drift should look like. This may seem like a put down, but there are a lot of experienced anglers who don't have any idea what a good drift looks like. Anyhow, if you show them how to mend the big parachute dry and keep it upstream of the smaller fly, the smaller fly will drift perfectly."

John is a very meticulous fly tier. Not only must his flies look perfectly proportioned (which they do), fish well (which they do), he has a great eye for color. He has a particularly good eye for blending dubbing and dying hackle to match any situation. He blends dubbing and tests it until he finds the color that works best during the hatch periods.

John likes to keep up on new materials, so he can be found in the local fly shops on his days off looking for new ones. One day he discovered a new parachute winging material called, Rainy's Foam Parachute Posts. John found them to be ideal for his large parachute mayfly patterns. They tie in with a minimum of bulk, they help the fly stay afloat, and can be seen easier on the water than any winging material he had used.

Boxwood Para Mayfly

Hook: Dry Fly 2x long, size 12-14
Thread: Olive, Danville 6/0 #60
Wing: Rainy's Foam Parachute Posts, 1/16
Hackle: One grizzly dyed olive and one brown
Tail: Moose body hair
Body: Super Fine Dubbing (Wapsi), gray olive, light Cahill and cinnamon caddis blended together.

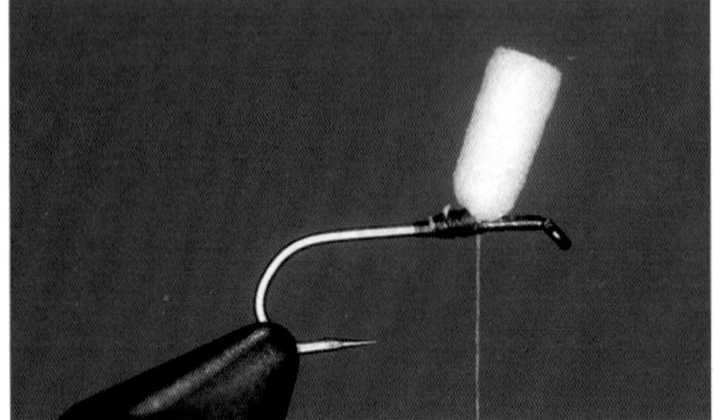

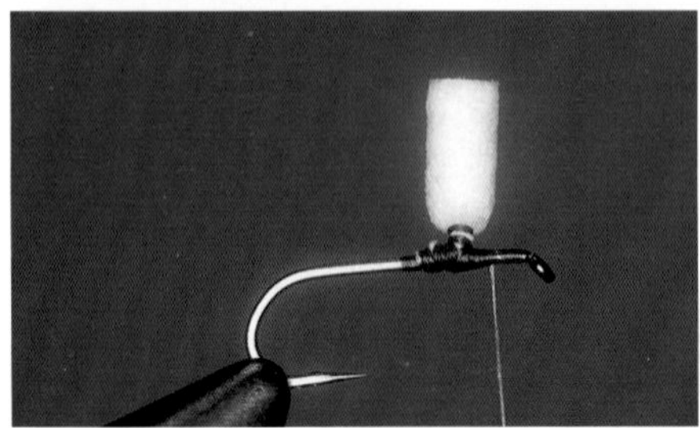

1. Start thread behind the eye and wrap back to the 1/2 point. Then move the thread forward to the 2/3 point of the shank to form a thread base for securing the wing. Leave the foam parachute post material in its full length, measure the height of the wing to no more than 1/2 to 3/4 of the hook shank and secure at the 3/4 point of the hook. (The height of the wing will be trimmed short later.) Wrap back to the 1/2 point and trim excess foam. Move thread in front of the wing. Build a dam of thread in front of the wing to stand it upright. Wrap thread up the foam wing to make a landing for the hackle to wrap around.

2. Prepare a brown and olive grizzly hackle. John suggests using hackle sized to the hook you are tying on. Use a size-12 hackle for a size-12 hook. Some tiers like to use a hackle one size larger on parachute flies. This thought works fine on the water, but I have to agree with John, the fly tied with the correctly-sized hackle looks more to proportion than with an oversized hackle. Oversized is good for golf clubs, but not for hackle. Secure the two hackles just in front of the wing and lash the hackle to the wing post as you wrap the thread up and around the post. Make sure the dull side of the feather is facing you as shown in the photo.

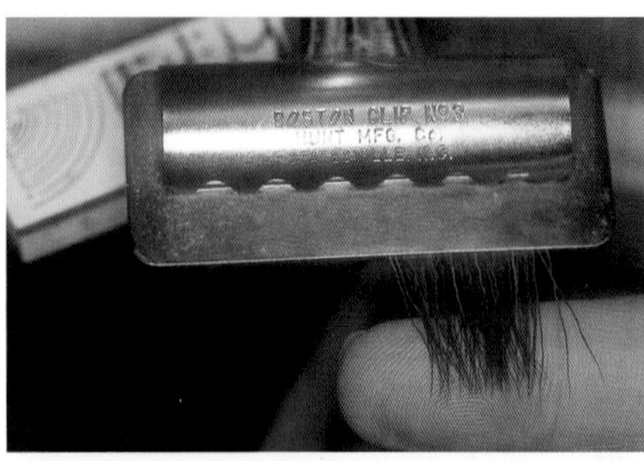

3. Wrap thread to the back of the hook then forward to just behind the wing post making a thread base for tying on the tails. Check out this time-saving tool for hair tails. It is a wide paperclip called a Boston Clip #3 made by the Hunt Manufacturing Co. Maybe you would recognize it as a bull clip. John attaches it directly to the 3/8 stem of his vise just above the C-clamp. Stack a bunch of moose hair, remove from the stacker and clamp the butt ends of the hair in the clip. If you take a little time measuring the length of hair you need for the tail, you could set the hair in the clip at a point where you just cut it off and tie it in. The butt ends of the hair should be tied in just behind the build up from the wing post. This will ensure a nice level base for dubbing the body. A note on thread torque when tying in hair tails: As you near the back of the hook, use less torque as you wrap to prevent the hair from splaying too much.

4. Dub the fly all the way to the front. Make sure it is tapered correctly and leave a small amount of bare hook at the eye to secure the hackle and finish the head.

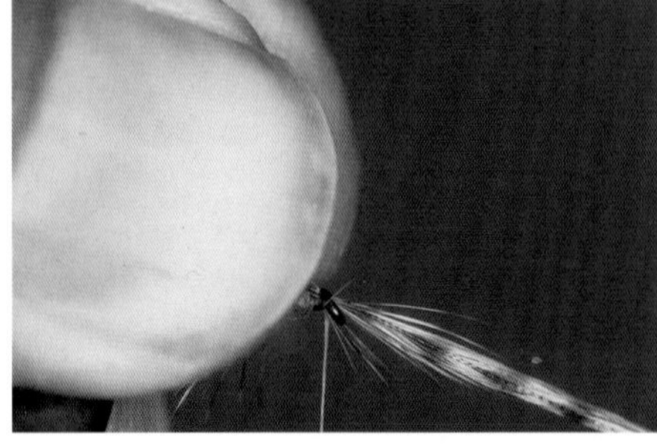

5. As soon as John started wrapping the hackle into place I asked him which direction he turns the hackle around a parachute wing. John said, "It really doesn't matter, it can be wrapped either clockwise or counter-clockwise; however, I do turn mine counter-clockwise. Another remark on turning two hackles, wrap them both at the same time. This is much easier than trying to wrap and

secure them separately. Just make sure the dull side (or concave side) of the feather is down as you wrap." With two hackles, four to five turns should be plenty. While holding the hackle tight, lift it up at the front of the fly and secure the tips of the hackle with three tight wraps of thread. Hold the hackle tips up, position your scissors points at the same angle as the eye of the hook and trim. Whip finish.

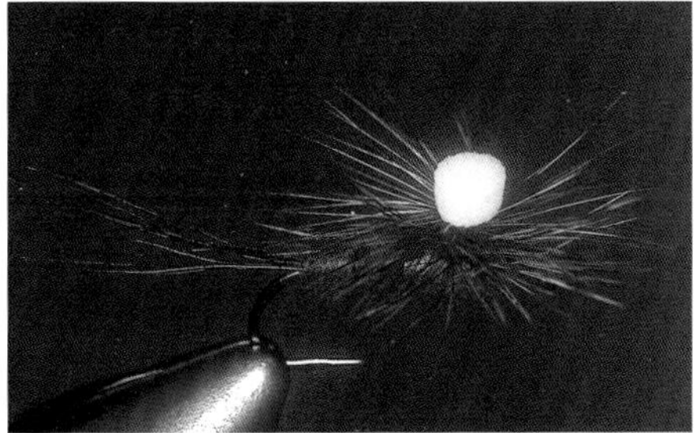

6. Trimming the wing short is optional; however, John likes to cut it short so the overall weight of the foam doesn't interfere with the balance of the fly.

Callibaetis

Contributed by John Hagen

John Hagen has tied as many dry flies as anyone I've watched behind the vise. His knowledge of winging and hackling techniques is immense, so I coaxed as much information out of him as time would allow.

John is an avid waterfowl hunter and saves just about every feather he can. So I thought I would put him to the test with duck flank wings. His eyes widened, he started pushing storage boxes to the side until he found "the box." It had bags of mallard feathers, woodduck feathers, pintail and gadwall flank feathers, and who knows what other fluff we could have found. "What would you like to see?" he asked. I guess I pestered the right guy!

We talked about a standard Cahill pattern with woodduck flank wings. They are pretty, but John thought it might be overkill to include them here since so many books cover these types of patterns. With all these feathers in front of us, we wanted to use a feather that is not used or talked about very often. The pintail feathers looked like the perfect wing for a *Callibaetis*, so that was our choice.

As all pro tiers do, he found and prepared his materials beforehand.

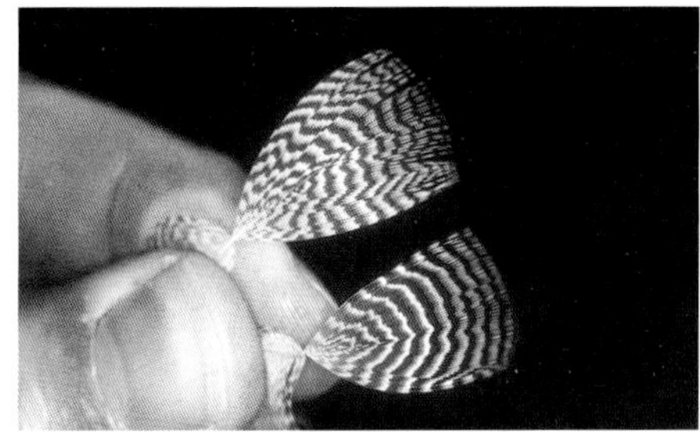

- He chose the pintail feathers meticulously, looking for just the right sizes and shape; nice full feathers with flat tops and no flaws. The pintail feather is a beautiful, heavily barred feather. The actual location on the duck where the feathers John picked was probably just forward of the flank area, so more of a body feather than a flank feather. The location is not important; the size and shape of the feather is. When you pluck the feathers from a duck it is pretty difficult to separate flank feathers from body feathers and body feathers from shoulder feathers so just bag them all together. Select the feathers you need just prior to tying.
- He grabbed a bag containing about five capes worth of size-14 dun hackle.
- He then prepared a dun spade hackle for the tails.
- Finally, he threw together a batch of dubbing.

John proceeded to put this fly together like he had tied a hundred dozen of them yesterday. (Once he got started, it seemed to irritate him that I had to get in there with the camera and take some photos. However, he dealt with it gracefully.)

I think dubbing always has been and always will be a very controversial subject for pro fly tiers. We all try to produce the perfect color, the perfect effect, or the perfect action for the fly we are tying. John's attitude about dubbing is as individualistic as any of us.

As he selected the colors to blend together to match the *Callibaetis* He has seen, he noted, "Mayfly body color is a very complicated issue. There is no mayfly out there that has a single, solid-colored body. Even though this bag says the color is *Callibaetis*, it isn't. It's close, but does not produce the right color for the mayflies on the water that I fish. It needs highlights and shade changes to make it look right on the hook. Dubbed bodies with light-colored highlights add a look of segmentation to it. A pinch of gray olive and a little tan added to this *Callibaetis* color should be just right for this fly."

The dubbing colors were not just random choices; they had a purpose. He mixed the *Callibaetis* and gray olive together by hand, folding it, pulling it apart, putting it back together, until it was blended well. "Just changing the shade a bit," he said. "Now I blend in the tan dubbing, mixing it well also. The lighter-colored dubbing adds the highlights that help show segmentation. It makes it look more alive."

John adds, "Don't take the dubbing manufacturer's labels for granted. I hardly ever take olive dubbing right out of the bag and use it. I think that most dubbing blends are too dark. The underside of a mayfly is normally much lighter than most people think, so I mix in light colors to add highlights and liveliness. In fact, don't take my word for it. You don't have to be as meticulous as I am. However, if you see the color and can make it by mixing different colors of dubbing together, why not do it? It takes just a couple of minutes. Try your best to match the color of the insects in your back yard. Only you know best."

This is why we tie our own flies! We have the option of making the best imitation of the insect we have seen through our own creativity. This eliminates the need to go to the fly shop and pick just a so-so pattern that is just almost the right color.

The technique explained here has a unique effect on the outcome of the finished fly. It gives you options, as if we don't have enough options already. It gives you the opportunity to be individualistic; you can be the developer. This is why one of the goals of this book is to open the door to your creativity.

Callibaetis

Hook: Standard dry fly, Daiichi 1180, size 14-18
Thread: Olive, Danville 6/0 #60
Wing: Pintail duck feathers
Tail: Medium dun, stiff hackle fibers
Abdomen: Super Fine Dubbing (Wapsi) *Callibaetis*, gray olive, and tan blended
Hackle: Medium dun, dry-fly quality (Whiting Farms)

1. Start thread just behind the eye of the hook and wrap back to the 1/2 point, then forward to the 2/3 point. John suggests, "Most books tell you to tie in the wings at the 3/4 point, which in turn can crowd the front of the fly as you try to finish it. Everybody thinks it is too far back. However, if you get in the habit of securing the wings at the 2/3 point, it automatically allows enough room to finish the fly so that you don't have hackle sticking out the front covering up the eye of the hook." This procedure of laying a thread base on the hook where the wings will be tied in is always a good idea, not only for duck flank wings but also for hair wings. There is less chance of the wings rolling to the side of the hook when they are tied in. Take the two pintail feathers and meld them together so the tips are even. Also, make sure the curvature of the feathers is the same when melded. In other words, lay the concave side to the convex, don't try to put the feathers with the convex sides together forming a V-wing. This will make splitting the wings later more difficult. Measure wing fibers to a height equal to or just shorter than the hook shank. John adds, "Along with the heavier hair-wing flies, I always make this type of wing slightly shorter to allow for the extra weight. If these types of wings are too tall, the fly will ride nose down every time. With the tips of the feathers extending over the eye of the hook, hold the feathers so that the concave side is facing you and tie in at the 2/3 point. You may also hold the feathers at a slight angle to the hook before tying them in and allow the thread torque to roll the fibers on top of the hook shank. Make sure the wing fibers are on top of the hook shank when finished. Secure the wing in place by wrapping thread back to the 1/2 point and trim butt ends. Leave the wing alone for the time being. We will stand it up and split it in a future step. Also leave the thread at the 1/2 point.

2. Dub thread, leaving 3/4 inch of bare thread between the hook shank and the start of the dubbing. This bare thread is used to tie in the tail. The overall length of the dubbing noodle depends on the size of the fly. This size 14 needed a length of about an inch and a quarter to complete the abdomen. As always, this varies from size to size as does the thickness of the dubbing noodle, but it is important to figure out, with the first couple of flies, the amount needed for the size you are tying in order to gain speed and rhythm. Select a clump of tail fibers. The tail should have enough fibers to balance the fly with the heavier wing. Too many fibers in the tail is better than too few. The tail is measured equal to or slightly longer than the hook shank. Trim the tail fibers so the trimmed end butts up to the back of the wing, that is, the 1/2 point; this will help make a level area for dubbing the body. Wrap back to the back of the hook. Then tie in the tail. There should be one turn of thread before the dubbing shows up, eliminating bulk at the back of the fly.

Wrapping the dubbing forward, finish a nicely tapered body to a point just behind the wing. This single step is one of those situations where you basically combine two steps into one, which increases your tying speed.

3. Pull wing back with your thumb and forefinger and make several wraps of thread in front of the wing to make it stand upright or slightly back. The wraps of thread in front of the wing should taper forward towards the eye and then back into the wing, making sure the wraps are very tight at the base of the wing. Build up the thread until the wing is in position.

4. John now uses his thumbnail to separate the wings into two equal parts. With pressure directly on top of the hook and in the middle of the wing fibers, the

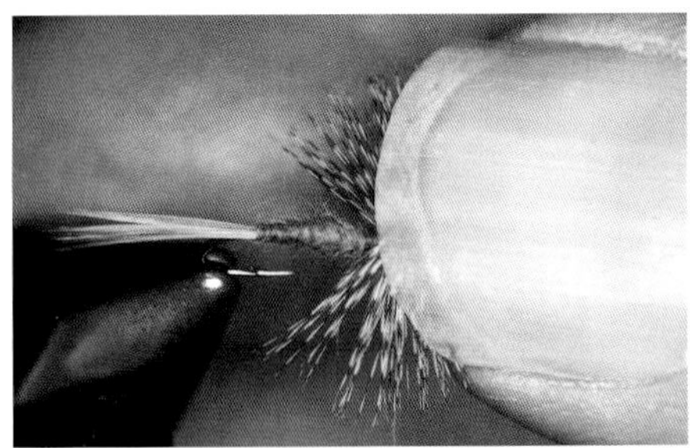

wing divides evenly and stays separated. This gives you a chance to visually inspect the wings, making sure they are divided correctly. Amazingly, this procedure works every time.

5. A simple X-ing pattern is all that is needed to permanently separate and set the wings. Hold the fore wing in the position where you want the wing to end up, ideally at a 45-degree angle. Wrap thread across to the back of the far wing. Make three wraps total, making sure the pressure or thread torque is applied to the front of the fore wing. Make one wrap around the hook in back of the wing, locking the thread wraps in place. Grab and hold the far wing up in the position where you want the wing to end up, ideally at a 45 degree angle, making a total of 90 degree between the wings. Make three wraps of thread from the back of the fore wing across to the front of the far wing. Make sure the pressure or thread torque is applied to the front of the far wing as you are making the crossing wraps. Again, make a wrap of thread behind the wing, locking the wing in position. The wings are done! John said, "Careful attention should be paid to the thread pressure applied to the wings. The tendency of the wings is to wander or lean forward, so keep the thread torque on the front of the wings." When I looked at the wings at this point, I was totally amazed that that was all it took to finish these wings.

6. Choose a properly sized hackle, (the hackle should be prepared ahead of time), trim the fibers at the butt end of the feather and secure the hackle in front of the wing. Since the hackle is secured in front of the wing, it is inevitable that you make a half turn of hackle in front of the wing. However, the second half of the first turn of hackle should be angling to the back of the wing. As you complete the first full turn, it will lie immediately behind the wing. Make a couple of turns back towards the body and then start forward carefully, laying these wraps in between the last wraps. This causes the hackle fibers to splay towards the back of the fly, giving the impression of rear legs on the mayfly. Depending on the length of the hackle, make 3-5 wraps behind the wing and cross the hackle forward to in front of the wing. Make sure this turn of hackle lies immediately in front of the wing in the notch where the hackle was originally tied in. Make 5-7 wraps in front. Along with the impression of legs, this crossing hackle action provides a denser thorax area. Secure hackle, trim excess and whip finish (See Steps 6 and 7 of PMD Quill, page 96.)

Eastern Green Drake

Contributed by Ken Mead

Here are a couple of patterns that can be very important to fly anglers in the Northeastern part of the United States. When this colossal mayfly hatches, trout and trout fishermen take notice.

"The Eastern Green Drake Nymph is more or less an original pattern of mine. It has a bit of Ernie Schwiebert influence and a little Caucci and Nastasi thrown together with a few of my own tying ideas," Says Ken Mead.

"I came up with the idea for this pattern while fishing the Beaverkill River in New York and some local small streams. I wanted a pattern that would double as a standard nymph and as an emerger. I also wanted a pattern that would swim well in still waters, as I have some small reservoirs locally that harbor great hatches of some of the larger mayflies. This pattern did it for me, particularly on the West Branch of the Lackawaxon River in Northeastern Pennsylvania. The stream, which harbors some very good-sized brown trout, can be pretty narrow in places, but supports a very good hatch of *Ephemera guttulata*." Ken adds, "The hatch can be tough to hit, but if you plan your trip within a few days of Memorial Day you should be in the ballpark."

A great opportunity to fish the nymphal pattern is when the nymphs start actively moving a few days prior to the hatch. Dropping the nymph in at the head of a pool with a simple dead-drift bouncing along the bottom is very effective. However, as the mayflies start to pop to the surface, it can be used as an emerger with a hand-twist retrieve while the fly is swinging slightly downstream. You can get a pretty good thump when a trout takes this big nymph, so maintain a tight grip on your rod.

"You can take advantage of this nymph after the hatch is over, as the trout have become accustomed to feeding on this particular food source. And don't forget the West Branch of the Delaware. When the trout are on these mayflies you can have a ball!"

Ken has used this nymph as a searching pattern on several lakes and ponds in his area, many of which have hatches of the various big eastern mayflies, including the green, brown, and yellow drakes. One particular impoundment near his home holds a very good population of native brook trout. While working the fly parallel to the brush-lined bank, a 15-incher came out and whacked this nymph for all it was worth. This tactic has worked again and again.

It looks like a good all-around nymph that could be tied in several color variations and sizes to imitate many aquatic fares.

Ken really enjoys the hatch: "Green Drake duns are a sight to behold. On the Delaware River they are huge. Minimum hook would be a size 10 2X and you would feel more comfortable tossing a size 8 2X or 3X long. They literally look like butterflies."

Unfortunately the hatch is short lived, typically about seven days of consistent hatches in any one particular area. Another problem to be aware of is weather, the old adage, April showers bring May flowers, doesn't always apply. Some of the more significant rainfall of the season, which is hurricane season, occurs around the green drake hatch. Water levels can be screwy. Conversely, water levels can be low depending on releases from dams, especially on the Delaware. However, there are several small streams with very good green drake hatches that are unaffected by water control factors.

Traveling to follow the hatch is also an option. Starting in Pennsylvania just before Memorial Day, one could follow the hatch all the way to Maine. The cycle would end the middle to late part of June.

Typically, *Ephemera guttulata* hatch during the evening hours but they may start hatching in the early afternoon if there is cloud cover. You might also see green drakes hatching sporadically all day long on smaller streams with a heavy canopy of trees overhanging them.

Ken finds this true most of the time on the West Branch of the Lackawaxon and on the Pohopoco River. These little streams have wonderful canopies over them, making them somewhat in the clouds all the time. It makes for a full day of great dry-fly fishing. The hatch can be sporadic, but there always seem to be a few bugs on the water. The trout are keying in on these duns almost exclusively, as I seldom see a natural actually get off the water before getting eaten. Watch for the spinners to start dancing above the water very late evening to dusk.

"This particular hatch on the main stem of the Delaware River can be pretty terrific also. By the second or third week of May, we start to see the March browns, which is another very large mayfly. When Memorial Day rolls around and the green drakes start to hatch, the trout are really focused on looking up to large mayflies. They carry over to the green drakes very well."

"A lot of anglers concentrate on the football field-sized pools on the Delaware when these mayflies come off. The trout in these pools can be very snotty, so I like to fish the riffles where good pods of strong rainbows hold. If you can get into the riffles at the right time with a big fly like this, you can have a tremendous fishing experience."

Ken reminded me that a stout leader is a must to turn these big flies over and to play the robust trout of the Delaware. He uses a ten- to twelve-foot leader with 4X tippet minimum, 3X tippet being the norm. "With the advantage of fluorocarbon tippet material, larger-diameter tippet is a definite possibility. This also reduces the leader-twisting effect of large air-resistant flies." Ken adds, "Make sure to slow your cast down a bit."

Ken saw this particular dry-fly pattern for the first time in the early 1980s at Barry and Cathy Beck's fly shop. He started using it with remarkable success and fell in love with the pattern immediately. He is not sure who originated it's unique wing style but feels that Marinaro's thorax type of flies may have had some influence. The wings on this fly are a pair of hen back feathers set with the concave sides together, in effect making just one wing much like a thorax style. Then, in the late 1980s Ernest Schwiebert tied a whole series of flies imitating early-season mayflies from size 10 to size 24, all with this same wing style.

Ken was honored when Barry and Cathy asked him to tie this series of flies for their shop shortly after their inception. He tied several hundred dozen of these flies. Gathering feathers for the production was a challenge. Ken found hen backs from Al's Grizzly, which were wonderful feathers. The grizzly hen backs were dyed in several colors, including the olive for this Green Drake pattern. White hen backs dyed dun were also a favorite of Ken's. "Today the most consistent feathers are from Whiting Farms and are in great supply. Dr. Tom Whiting has set a standard in the industry that is unbelievable. It is a joy for an old-time tier like myself, who basically took what he could get at the time, to have available such a wide variety of quality feathers," says Ken.

The wing style does work very well for a number of mayfly patterns. Just pick hen back feathers according to the size and color needed. For the very smallest of patterns, burning or actually trimming the wings to size is not out of the question. They work equally as well.

The dubbing mix on these flies is primarily Australian opossum, which is Ken's favorite. However, a touch of Angora goat can be mixed with the nymph dubbing to strike up some highlight colors. A few fibers of tan, yellow, and gray can add a nice appearance to this fly, but don't over-do it though. The technique of blending Angora goat into just about any type of dubbing is an old Randall Kaufmann standard. This makes the dubbing more shiny and spikier. The nymph looks more alive in the water with the added sheen and movement. Seal's fur used to be the standard, but is now prohibited.

The fly does look pretty light in color compared to the natural, but remember that when the fly gets wet it will darken up and take on some of the highlight shades.

Ken uses woodduck flank feathers for the tail and legs on the nymph. Some might say that these feathers are too expensive to use on a nymph, but he has plenty and likes the looks of true wood duck. If you have a supply, you can use the imperfect, asymmetrical feathers, as well as the ones with uneven or broken tips. Even the tips by grasping the longer fibers with your thumb and forefinger and breaking or tearing the tips away. Unlike cutting them with scissors, this method leaves a very natural looking group of fibers. Make sure that the feathers you use are well marked. For those in short supply of wood duck, mallard flank feathers dyed wood duck will work fine.

Have some turkey tail feathers prepared before hand. Glue the sides of the feathers with Dave's Flexament or spray the feathers with clear Krylon. (See Material Preparation under Turkey Tails, page 39.) The sections or slips of turkeytail fibers used for the wingcase should be about the width of the hook gape for the size you are tying. Ken has a unique way of using these feathers for the wingcase on this nymph. Actually it is an old method which has been somewhat forgotten. I like it and it looks very good on this fly.

Preparation of materials for the dry fly is also important to save tying time. Size and trim all the hackle needed for the fly. Ken suggests tying at least a dozen of any one pattern, so count out 12 ginger, 12 grizzly dyed olive, and 12 grizzly hackles. To acquire hackle large enough for this dry fly, neck hackle would be the best choice. It is getting hard to find long saddle hackle in size 8 or 10 these days.

Match up pairs of hen back feathers for the wing on the dry fly. They should be the same width and the tips should be the same shape. Try to pick a feather from the left side of the patch and one from the right side, so whatever curvature the feathers may have can meld together more uniformly. If the patch has feathers with very straight stems, this step is not as important.

Eastern Green Drake Nymph

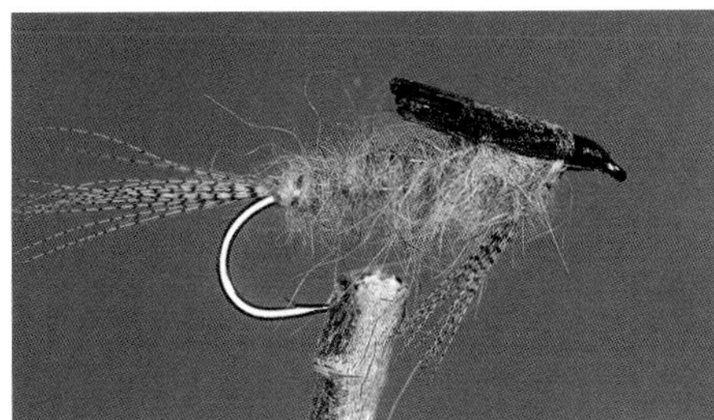

Hook: 3X long nymph, size 8-10, Daiichi 1720, Tiemco 5263
Thread: Danville 6/0, tobacco
Tail: Woodduck fibers
Body: Australian opossum dubbing, light gray, with a touch olive and yellow mixed together
Ribbing: Yellow floss
Thorax: Australian opossum dubbing, same as body
Legs: Woodduck fibers tied in beard style
Wingcase: Mottled turkey tail, folded

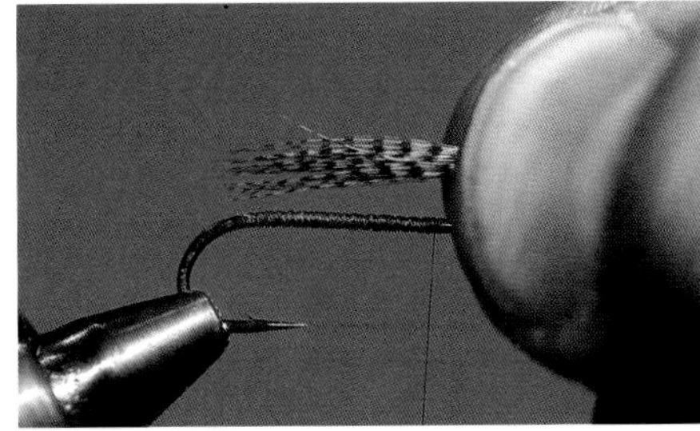

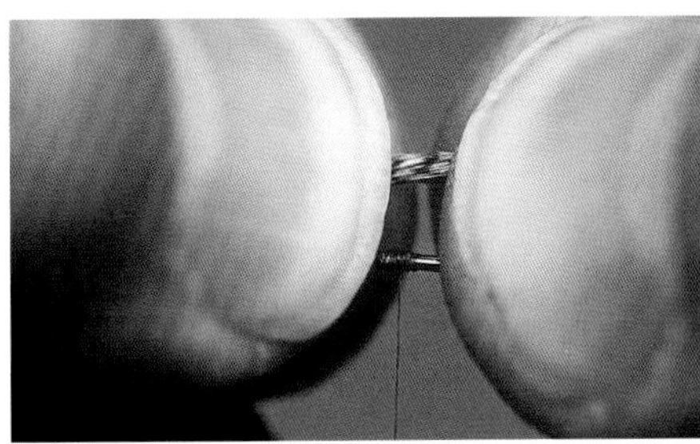

1. Start thread at the 2/3 point and wrap to the back of the shank making a good thread base. Using this starting point as a proportion, measure the woodduck fibers for the tail to 2/3 the hook shank length. Transfer the fibers into your other hand, using your thumbnails as the point of exchange. Trim the butt ends of the tail fibers prior to tie in. Tie the tails down at the back of the hook with a few tight wraps of thread.

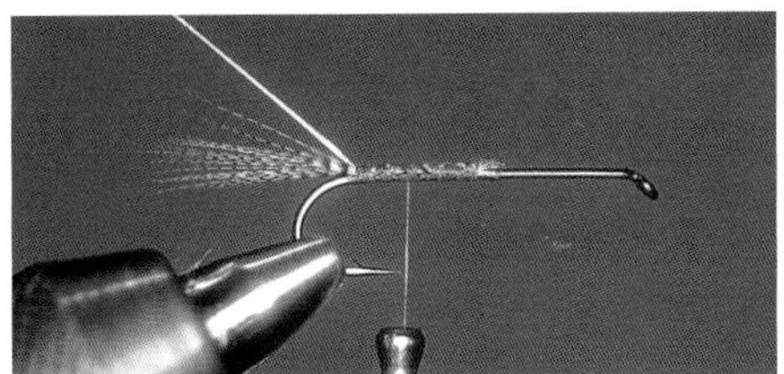

2. Secure a length of yellow floss at the back of the hook and wrap forward to about the 1/4 point. This procedure, along with the tail tie in, is one of the things Ken refers to as "economy of movement".

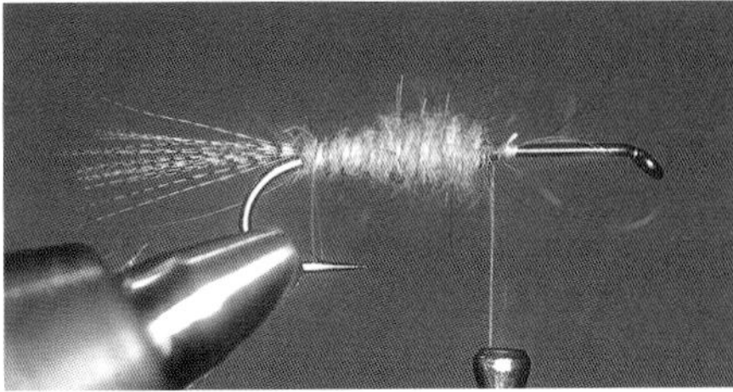

3. Dub the body of the fly to the 2/3 point. Don't skimp on the dubbing. This is a big nymph and the body should be thicker in proportion than smaller flies. Many tiers may use a dubbing loop on this size of fly; however, Ken can dub conventionally faster than doing a loop. I concur, since I dub pretty fast also. The key is to dub a short section of thread, apply it to the hook, and then repeat until the body is done. Leave the dubbing source in your hand while you are wrapping the dubbing so you don't have to pick it up for each application. (Refer to the Material Preparation section under Dubbing, page 26.) Ken calls it "power dubbing". Rib the floss with six or seven evenly spaced turns through the body and secure. Trim excess floss.

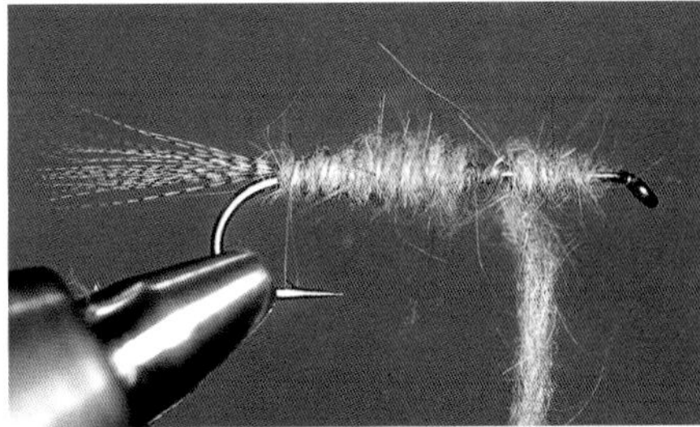

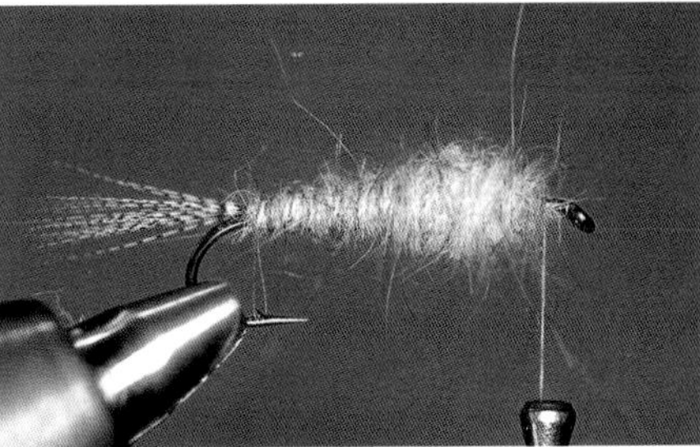

4. Dub a thorax about twice the thickness of the body. By starting the dubbing at the front of the fly and wrapping back to the body and then wrapping forward, another layer of dubbing should result in a thorax of the thickness required.

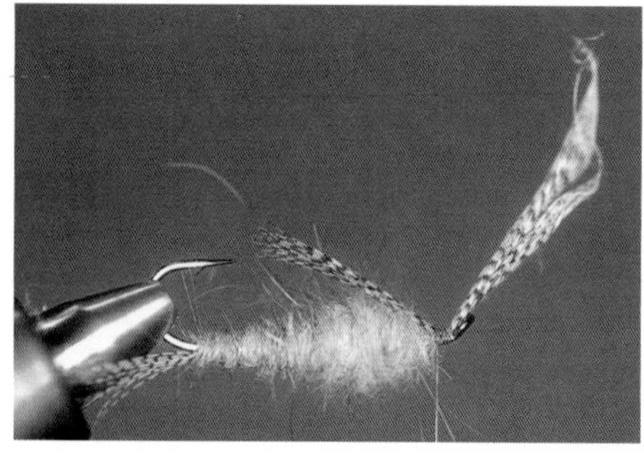

5. If you have a rotating vise, turn the fly upside down to tie in the legs. If you don't, you might want to take the fly out of the vise and turn it over to make this procedure easier. Tie in several wood-duck fibers for the legs of the fly. The tips of the fibers should extend to the hook point. This is essentially a beard hackle.

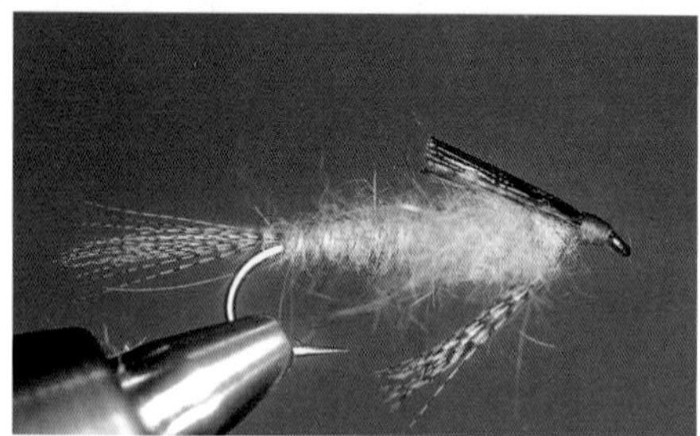

6. Turn the fly to the up-right position. Just in front of the thorax, tie in a slip of turkey tail with glued side up and the more colorful side of the feather down. Use with three or four very tight wraps. The tip of the slip should extend to the back of the thorax and the butt section hanging over the eye. It should be about the hook gap in width, which is equal to 1/4 to 5/16 of an inch. Pull the turkeytail fiber back over itself and secure. Whip finish the fly. Pick out the dubbing on the sides of the abdomen for gills and on the thorax for added life-like action. Add a coat of cement or nail polish to the wingcase for durability. Recently, Ken has been coating the wingcase with epoxy, which makes it virtually indestructible and actually adds a bit of weight. The weight adds a jigging type of motion when doing the hand-twist retrieve. Adding a few twists of lead wire to the hook shank prior to tying the fly will also aid in creating this motion.

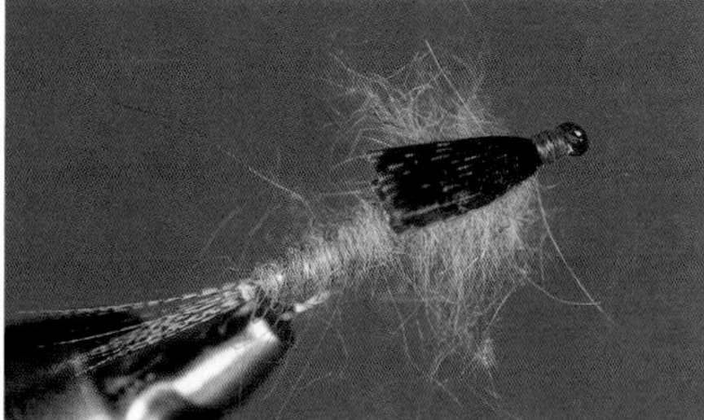

A Green Drake nypmh as viewed from above.

Eastern Green Drake

Hook: 2X dry fly, size 10 Tiemco 2312
Thread: Black 6/0, Danville
Tail: Micro Fibetts, dun
Body: Aussie Possum dubbing, cream
Wing: Grizzly hen back, dyed olive
Hackle: 1 Ginger, 1 grizzly, and 1 grizzly dyed olive. Whiting dry-fly quality hackle is preferred.

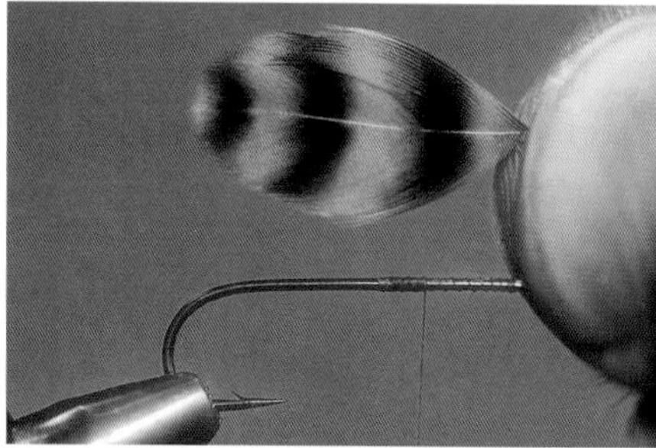

1. Start thread at the front of the hook and wrap back to the 1/2 point making a smooth thread base. Move thread forward to the 5/8 point. Take care with proportions on this fly, as it is a 2X long hook. Prepare two grizzly hen back

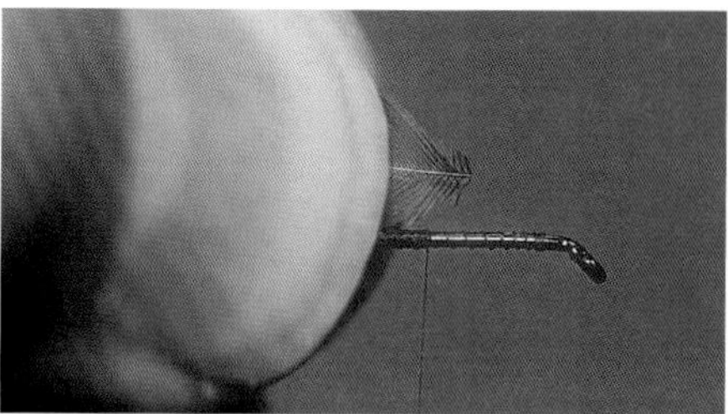

feathers, dyed olive, by putting the concave sides of the feathers together. Make sure the tips are even. Measure the wing to a full hook shank length. Switch hands and trim butt ends of the feathers.

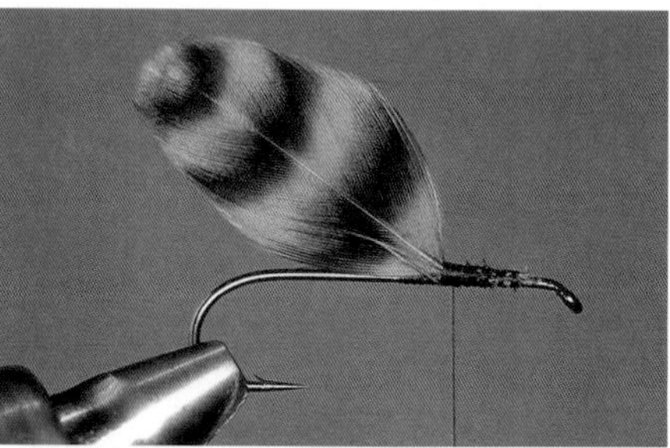

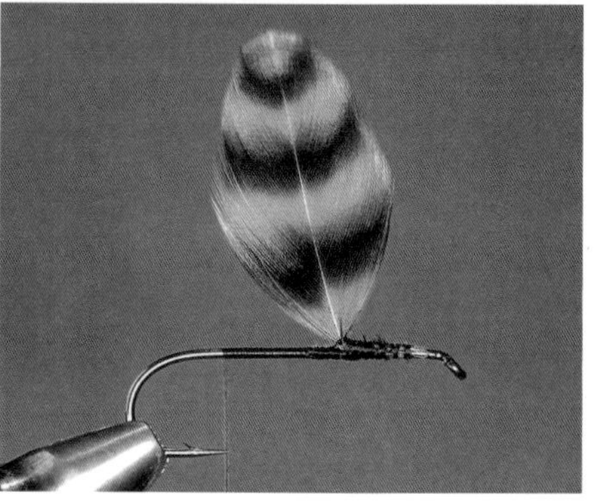

2. Tie in wing at the 5/8 point of the hook with the tips towards the back of the hook being tied in this way keeps the wing from slanting forward; you always want mayfly wings to cant back in their more natural position. Pull the wing forward and make a few wraps of thread behind the wing to stand it up.

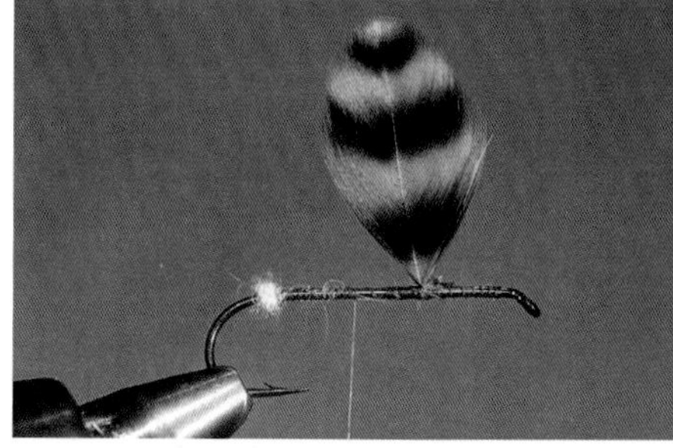

3. Form a dubbing ball at the back of the hook so the tails can be split.

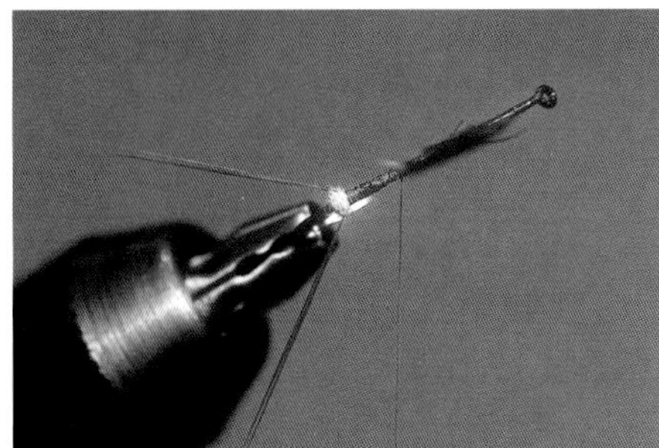

4. Measure ten micro fibbets to a full hook shank length. Trim the butt ends, tie in at the 1/4 point on top of the hook and make a few tight wraps back. Use a fingernail to stand the fibbets up so they can be counted and split evenly. Position 5 fibbets on each side of the hook and wrap them up against the dubbing ball to produce a 90 degree split of the tails.

5. Dub the body to the 1/2 point.

6. Size and prepare one ginger, one grizzly dyed olive, and one grizzly dry-fly quality hackle. Tie in hackles behind the wing with the concave sides away from you. Wrap the two grizzly hackles first and at the same time. Making a half or even a full wrap of the hackle before you attach the hackle pliers will aid in getting the hackles to wrap together. A good pair of hackle pliers helps considerably. Dorin Teardrop hackle pliers are Ken's favorite. Secure hackles. Now wrap the ginger hackle. Weave it through the other hackles as you wrap it forward. Use this third hackle to tweak the wing into position if need be. Secure hackle.

7. Dub a small cream head and whip finish. Mark the back of the abdomen with a black permanent marker. You and I both know the fish are not going to see these marks, but let's face it, if there was a fly with markings on it and another without, which one would you buy?

8. Depending on the type of water you plan on fishing, a V can be trimmed on the bottom side of the hackle to let the fly ride more flush in the water. Flat, smooth water types would be ideal for this method. The fly should be left with its full hackle when fishing in riffles and faster water types.

This pattern can be modified slightly to make a very passable Coffin Fly, which is a green drake spinner. Omit the hen back wing, use over-sized dark grizzly and dark ginger hackle, use white dubbing instead of the cream dubbing used on the dun, and simply trim the bottom and top of the hackle so it lies flat on the water.

Extended Body Mayfly (Green Drake)

Contributed by Dale Darling

This is a unique extended-body mayfly pattern because it's put together with dubbing and does not require any kind of glue. Most extended-body flies made with dubbing require some kind of glue for a binding agent.

Dale Darling is always looking for easier, more efficient ways to tie patterns that he likes to fish. He then passes along those ideas to his friends and students in fly-tying classes. However, this pattern wasn't so much a need for simplicity as it was out of necessity. Dale has an aversion to glues and epoxies. It is not that he dislikes them so much, he is actually allergic to them. He liked the looks of an extended-body fly and enjoys the way they fish so he had to figure out a way to tie them without the aid of an adhesive. He knew that most extended bodies originated on a sewing needle so he clamped one in the vise and went to work.

Lo and behold, another fly pattern was born. This fly design incorporates the stiffness of moose body hair for the under body and a strands of Antron or floss to hold the body together. The versatility of this tying technique can make a body of any color. It can easily be tied as a parachute, and works for flies down to a size 20. To speed up the process of tying several of these flies, do a dozen bodies and set them aside, then get the hooks out and tie the finished flies. You will feel like a real pro when you get these done.

Extended Body Mayfly (Green Drake)

Hook: Special Curve, Dai-Riki 305, Tiemco 2487, size 12-20
Thread: 6/0 Danville, olive. 14/0 Sheer for smaller flies
Ribbing: Antron yarn, brown. Floss or thread can be used for smaller flies
Tail: Moose body hair. Micro Fibetts or natural spade hackle can be used for smaller flies.
Body: Fine & Dry dubbing, olive
Wing: Hen tips, dark dun
Thorax: Fine & Dry dubbing, olive
Hackle: Grizzly, dyed olive and brown

1. Clamp a sewing needle into the vise with the point of the needle away from the jaws. Start thread back from the point about 1/2 inch. Tie in a length of brown Antron yarn on top of the needle with the excess length hanging over the point of the needle. About 10-15 strands

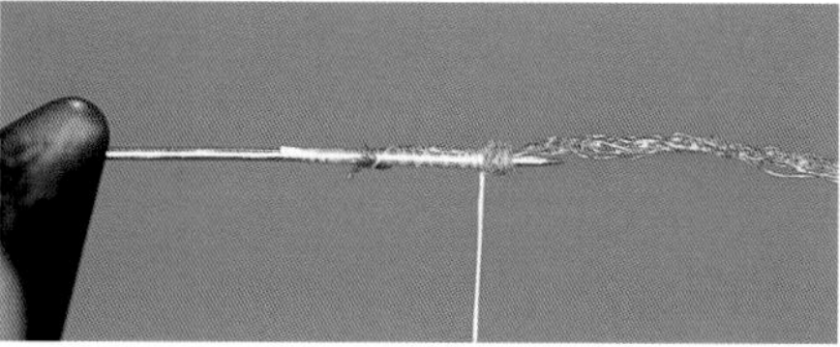

should be sufficient. Waxing the Antron fibers or floss will aid in keeping the fibers together. Wrap thread forward to just behind the point.

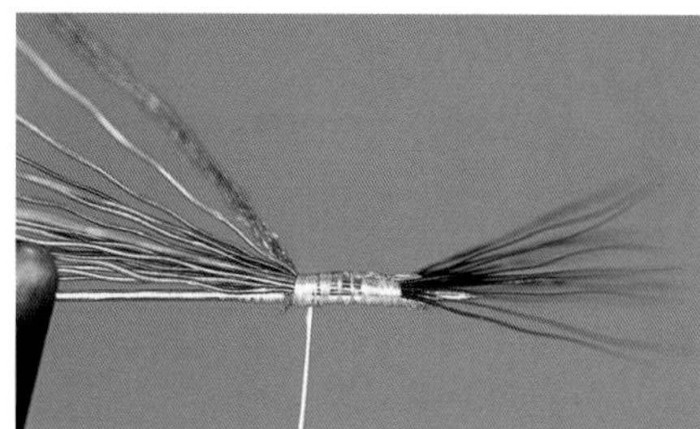

2. Stack a clump of moose body hair for the tail. The length of the tail will be judged more by eye than measuring against a hook shank. You be the judge of how long a tail should be for a certain sized hook. Remember, the tails on a green drake are pretty short. After tying a couple, you should be able to keep the tail length pretty consistent. Secure the moose fibers, tips over the point of the needle, wrap back to the starting spot on the needle. DO NOT cut the butt ends of the moose hair. Split the tail fibers evenly and pull the Antron back through the tail fibers and secure Antron at the starting spot.

3. Hold the strands of Antron over the point of the needle again and move thread forward to the tail. Dub a tapered body. Twist the Antron fibers tightly and rib through the dubbing, making even segmentations through the body. Whip finish and remove thread. DO NOT trim ribbing material or the moose body fibers.

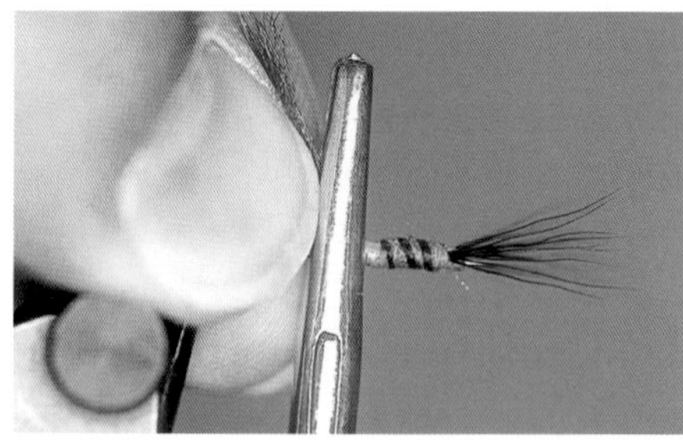

4. Slide the extended body off the needle; a pair of smooth-jawed hemostats may help in this process.

5. Clamp a hook in the vise and start the thread at the 1/2 point of the hook shank. This hook has a shorter shank than a normal dry-fly hook, so make certain of the proportions for the hook. Make a smooth thread base to the back of the hook. Move thread to the 1/4 point. Secure the moose fibers adjacent to the dubbed part of the extended body on top of the hook and wrap forward to the 1/2 point again. Grab the length of the Antron used for the ribbing and lay it down to the back of the hook with the thread. Trim off the butt ends of the moose body hair. Finish the body by dubbing a thin layer to the 1/2 point of the hook. Twist the Antron yarn and make a few final ribs through the dubbing for the segmentation. You should actually reverse rib so it is going the same direction as the original ribbing. Move thread to the front of the hook.

6. Prepare a matching pair of hen tips for the wings. With convex sides together

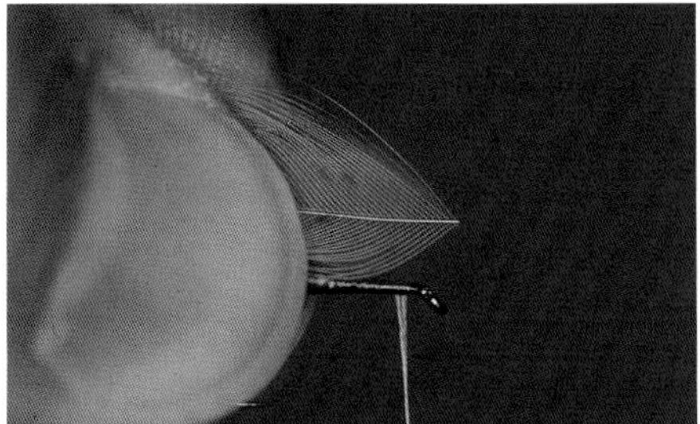

and the tips of the wings pointing back over the body, measure the wings to a full body length. Switch hands and trim hen tips even with the eye of the hook. Secure the tips of the hen feathers on top of the hook at the front of the hook. Hold the feathers up slightly while keeping the stems of the winging feather in plane with the shank of the hook and wrap them down with thread back to the 5/8 point of the hook.

7. Pull the wings up and forward and make a few wraps of thread behind the wings. Use a fingernail to push the wings forward and splay the wings. The wings should spring back to the upright position as shown in photo.

8. Make sure the thread is just behind the wings. Size and prepare the hackle.

Here is a little trick Dale uses to make sure the hackles wrap into place correctly and look uniform: After sizing the hackles for the hook, instead of simply cutting them to the same length, match up the web lines in the hackle. In other words, find the point where the web is about 1/4 of the total barbule length on both feathers and trim butt ends of the feather off at that point. Trim barbules off the stem for tie in. Apply a thin layer of dubbing to the thread, leaving about a 1/2 inch of bare thread between the dubbing and the hook shank. Secure the hackles on the fore side of the hook, behind the wing, with the brown hackle on top, using the bare portion of thread. As the dubbing shows up, apply a thin layer behind the wing then a layer in front of the wing. Dale likes the hackle to be buried in dubbing to improve its durability.

9. Wrap the brown hackle forward first and secure behind the eye. Wrap the grizzly next, weaving it into the first hackle, trying not to mash down many of the brown fibers. This is accomplished by moving the hackle side to side as you wrap forward. Make sure each hackle has a wrap adjacent to the back and front of the wing base. The last wrap of hackle in front of all others should be a turn or two of grizzly. It just looks a little nicer for some reason, I'm not sure the fish much care. Secure the hackle by making a couple of wraps forward to just behind the eye then back to the last wrap of hackle. This locks the hackle very securely. Trim both the brown and grizzly hackle tips at the same time by setting the scissor points at the same angle as the hook eye to avoid cutting thread. Whip finish from the eye to the hackle to complete the fly.

A parachute extended body mayfly can be tied by standing up a post of Antron yarn, dubbing forward and wrapping a parachute hackle.

Flashback Pheasant Tail Nymph

Contributed by Randy Smith

If you have tied any flies at all, I'm sure a Pheasant Tail Nymph has come out of your vise at least once or twice. It's taught in most fly-tying classes. It is one of the most popular flies in history, next to the Hare's Ear Nymph, the Adams dry fly and the Woolly Bugger. It is fished as an imitation for the early season *baetis* nymph, it can imitate the midsummer pale morning dun nymph, and tied in very small sizes without legs can easily imitate a midge just as the snow starts to fly.

Randy suggests fishing the Flashback on sunny days where the flash can be accentuated. Stained water, dark stream bottoms, or stream bottoms with an overabundance of moss are also conditions to try the Flashback P.T. Needless to say, it is a very important pattern to have in your fly box and equally important to learn how to tie.

I have seen P.T.'s tied in several different ways; the options are seemingly endless. The old standard pattern in natural, black, olive, and gold, the bead-head version, the Flashback, and the Bead-Head Flashback just to name a few. If you can't find a pattern somewhere in there to imitate a nymph in your local water, you aren't searching hard enough. The creative mind can go way overboard on this pattern.

I would bet the trout farm that every pro tier who has sold a dozen flies has had orders for Pheasant Tails. Randy ties them for several shops. I used to tie them in five different sizes in three different colors for a couple of shops. Five dozen a size, if my math is correct, comes to about 150 dozen P.T.'s a year, give or take fifty dozen. Just about every tier that is mentioned in this book has a similar story about tying P.T. nymphs. As pro tiers we have had to dedicate a portion of our business to the Pheasant Tail and have had to come up with the most efficient way to tie it.

Following are a couple of the best ways to tie a P.T. Nymph. Randy will show you the Flashback P.T. Nymph and I will show a standard Black P.T. Nymph (see page 92). Both are very similar in structure, yet slightly different in philosophy.

Before we start tying this fly, I should mention a few ideas for material preparation. Randy has a very ingenious layout for a small section of the top of his tying desk. He has rows of dots about a

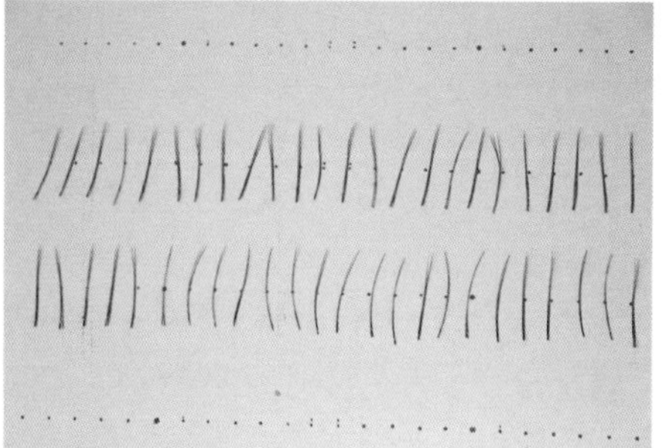

1/2 inch apart made with a permanent marker. It starts with five small dots then a larger dot for the sixth dot, then five more small dots and a double dot for the twelfth location. One dozen. He has enough dots on his tying desk for twelve dozen rows of just about anything you need to prepare before you start tying. This layout lets him prepare up to twelve dozen clumps of pheasant-tail fibers ahead of time. If he is going to tie five dozen, he starts by laying out five dozen clumps, without counting to sixty. Basically, the start of an assembly line.

Here is a formula for the number of pheasant-tail fibers in relation to hook size:

Hook Size	Number of Fibers
20	3
18	4
16	6
14	8
12	10

As you increase the fly size, add more fibers to suit the look you want. For example, I tie a big fat olive P.T. size 10 to imitate the western green drake nymph on which I may use as many as twelve to fourteen fibers.

Take several strands of peacock herl and trim off the tips and lay them out in front of you. Separate some Krystal Flash into groups of five strands. Open up a box of hooks and lay them out. Another great thing about Randy's layout method is you no longer have to count hooks. When you run out of piles of pheasant-tail fibers, you know you're done.

The last thing you need to get ready is the fine copper wire. Randy has a slick wire tender also. Start with a 3/4-inch dowel about an inch long. Drill a 1/4-inch hole centered in the top of the dowel 3/8 to 1/2 inch deep. Drill another

1/4-inch hole in the side of the dowel about the same depth. (A small block of wood could replace the large dowel, but dowel is nice because it is round, with no sharp edges.) Take a quarter inch dowel about two inches long and glue it into the top of the larger dowel. Take another section of 1/4-inch dowel about an inch long and glue it into the side of the larger dowel. Drill a 1/4-inch hole in the side of your desktop to accommodate the 1/4-inch dowel. Put a spool of wire on the top dowel and you're ready to go to work. Make sure you keep the wire under control with a rubber band.

Flashback Pheasant-Tail

Hook: Dry, size 18-24, Dai-Riki 310 (ring eye) or 305
Thread: 8/0 camel
Ribbing: Fine copper wire
Tail: Pheasant-tail fibers (all one clump)

Body: Pheasant-tail fibers (all one clump)
Legs: Pheasant-tail fibers (all one clump)
Wingcase: Krystal Flash
Thorax: Peacock herl, or dubbing

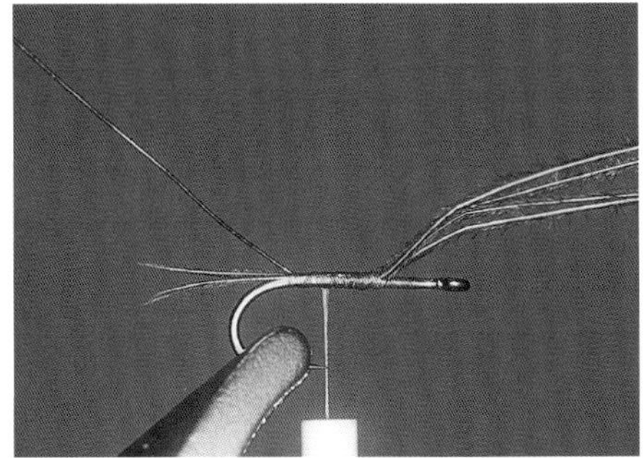

1. Start thread mid shank and secure the copper wire on top of the hook. Wrap to the back of the hook making sure the wire maintains its position on top. Measure tails so they extend beyond the back of the hook about half the hook shank length. Tie the tails in at the back of the hook and wrap forward to the 1/2 point, lashing the fibers down as you go.

2. Pull pheasant fibers back and lash them down as you move to the back of the hook again. Move thread forward to the 1/2 point.

3. Wrap the pheasant fibers forward to the 1/2 point and secure. DO NOT trim pheasant fibers yet. Randy suggests, "Anchor a hand on the vise so a finger can be used to hold the fibers down as you reposition your other hand to make the next wrap. Also, give the fibers a

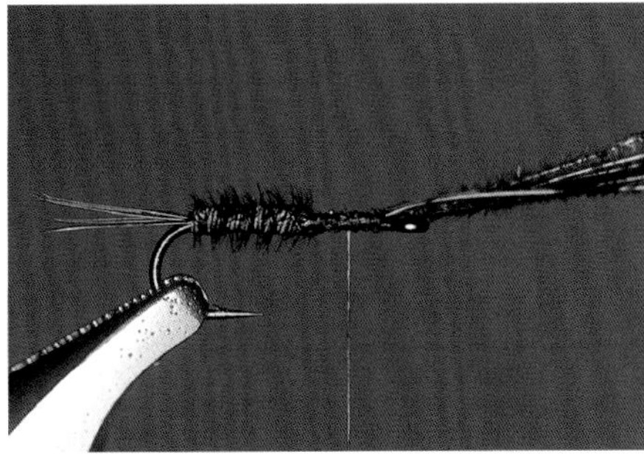

little roll so they stay bunched together as you wrap. If they roll into a tight rope, the fibers will not flatten out and makes an uneven looking body. The flatter you keep the fibers, the more control of the shape and proportion of the fly you will have."

Continue wrapping forward with your thread lashing the pheasant fibers down as you go. Take it all the way to the front of the hook. Now move thread back to the 1/2 point. Counter-wrap the wire forward with evenly spaced wraps, also to the 1/2 point. Secure wire. Instead of going to the vise with your scissors to cut the wire, simply work the wire back and forth a time or two at the tie-in point and it will break very easily.

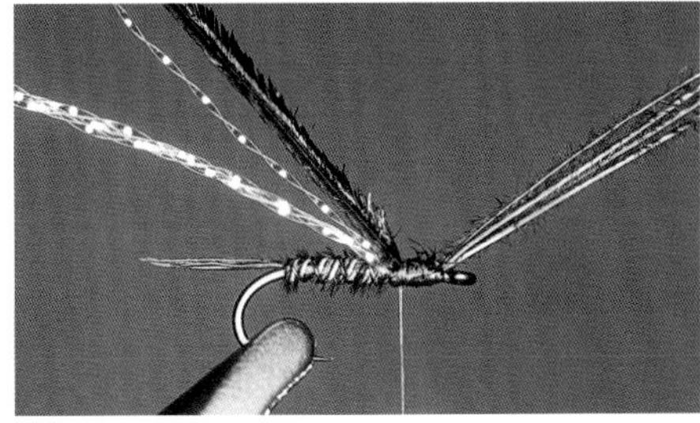

4. Tie in strands of Krystal Flash for the wingcase. Randy likes using Krystal Flash because you can easily adjust the size of the wingcase by the number of strands used for different sized flies. Five strands work well for a size 18 Flashback. Krystal Flash also does not build up bulk at the head as does Mylar and Flashabou. It adds more facets to the fly by conforming to the thorax area and forming a nice dome. Finish this step by tying in a couple of strands of peacock herl in front of the wingcase. Move the thread to the front of the fly.

Another tip from Randy is to trim your material square before tying it in.

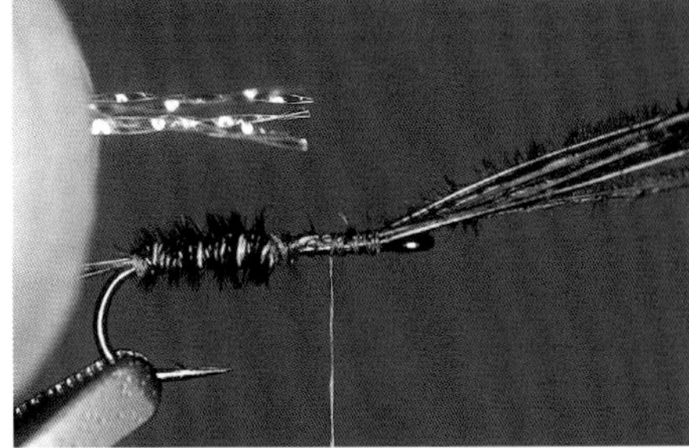

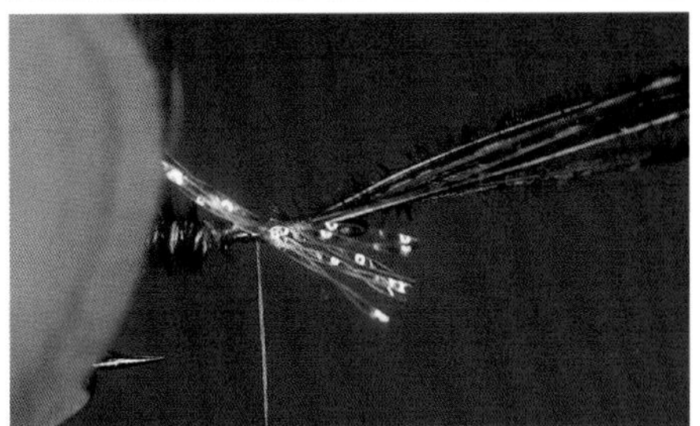

Then lash the strands down with a single wrap and pull the material back until just the tips of the material are being tied down. Secure with a few more tight wraps. Peacock can be tied in the same fashion. This is such a great speed tip, I can't exaggerate its importance enough. I see all the great pro tiers use this technique. Nothing expends more time than grabbing excess materials with one hand and bringing the scissors up and trying to cut it flush with the hook. The thread often gets severed or the point of a blade draws blood.

5. Wrap peacock herl forward making a smooth thorax. Secure with a couple of wraps of thread and pull herl back towards the bend of the hook quickly to break the excess off. Pull the Krystal Flash over the peacock herl, stroking it a couple times, which stretches it slightly

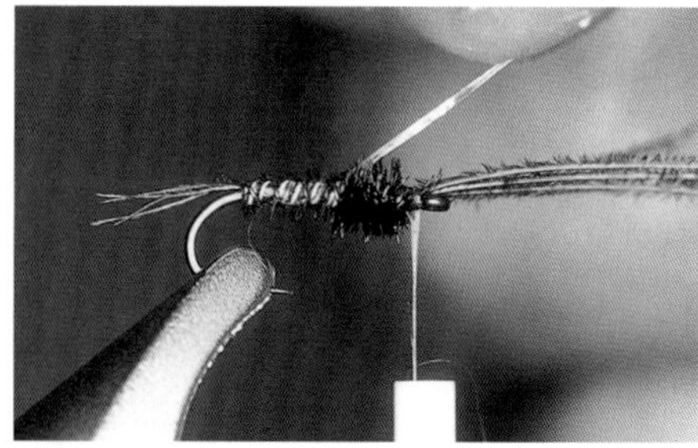

and smoothes out the kinks. Tie the flash down right on top of the hook at the front of the fly with a few tight wraps of thread. Cut excess strands of flash off and keep it in a bundle for the next fly. A little saliva helps keep them clustered together.

6. Split the pheasant fibers left hanging over the eye into two equal sections. These are now going to be used for the legs. Size 18 and smaller only need one fiber per side to give the impression of legs. Sizes 16 and 14 should have two or three per side. Secure legs down the sides of the hook. Whip finish. Hold legs under the hook and trim to length.

Hexagenia

Contributed by Dennis Potter and Fred Vargas

The Midwest, particularly Michigan, is well known for the Hex hatch. It still has a huge following, even though the numbers aren't as good as in the old days. There is folklore linked to the hatch where townships along the Au Sable River needed to get out the street sweepers, sometimes bulldozers, to rid the streets of the spent mayflies.

The "fish fly", as the Hexagenia was once known, got its name because the stench the decaying bugs rose during the warm June days after a couple of nights of spinner falls. They smelled liked rotten fish.

Without running on about too much history we are going to introduce a couple of patterns to imitate the Hex hatch that will work anywhere Hexagenia are found. The Parachute, Extended Body Hexagenia is a pattern that imitates the hatching adult and the Chernobyl Sparrow is a spinner pattern used while the Hex is on the water laying eggs.

Before you go out and find the special hairs it will take to tie these flies, read the following story about Hex fishing. It may give you second thoughts about sporting a headlamp in the dark and casting size-six, 6X-long streamer hooks with dry flies tied on them.

I had the opportunity to fish the Hex hatch with a couple of old pros, an experience I will not soon forget:

The Three Knights of Zen

As I stood in total darkness with the Holy Water of the Au Sable River flowing at my feet, I was attempting to replay what had just transpired in the last three days. I was in the Wolverine State for the first time and had just had one of the most memorable experiences of my life. I ventured to Michigan to interview a couple of professional fly tiers for this book, with every intention of doing some fly-fishing. I hoped to catch some of the *Hexagenia* action. This was the first time I had chased *Hexagenia* and really didn't know what to expect. My homework was not complete and one major piece of information escaped me—*Hexagenia* primarily hatch at night! I was not expecting to fly-fish with a light clamped to the bill of my hat.

They call it Zen fishing.

The Knights warned me that it was pretty early in the year for the *Hexagenia* hatch (It's only Father's Day), but they expected to see some late-evening spinner falls. Maybe we would see some Sulphurs, the tail end of the brown drake spinners, or the start of the gray drakes. We would most likely fish after dark.

My host was Dennis Potter, a retired businessman and commercial fly tier from Grand Rapids who owns a second home on the Au Sable River, which he calls the Riverhouse. Fred Vargas, a guide and commercial fly tier who works out of the Great Lakes Fly Fishing Company, also located in Grand Rapids area, was taking a couple of days off to help with this book. Both are contributing some of their fly-tying skills for the project. Needless to say, they both have years of experience fishing the Au Sable and were well prepared in the Art of Zen.

The Knights of Zen are serious about their *Hex* fishing. "Zenoids" from around the world flock to this area for the opportunity to blind cast, under the cloak of darkness, huge dry flies to the mystifying sound of a rising trout.

Hexagenia limbata is a large mayfly about two inches long with a wing that is at least an inch high. This particular mayfly hatches primarily at night, which adds to the intrigue. The trout really get going when these bugs are on the water, making the experience all the more exciting. The very largest brown trout finning the Au Sable are notorious night feeders. Accordingly, this is one of the best times of the year to take these brawny trout on a dry fly.

This is not a long-leader, delicate-casting game. Light rods can be used (maybe a 4-weight), but leaders need to be cut in half and knotted to at least 3X tippet to get this big fly to turn over.

There are a couple of ways to approach the art of Zen fishing. Unless you are local or experienced in the art of Zenning, hiring a guide is highly recommended. The guide will recommend you change your sleep schedule to compensate for the late hours. I guess you could call it the midnight shift of fly-fishing. One approach is to find a certain stretch of water and wait for the bugs to show. By and large, the most popular approach is to float the river. The Au Sable riverboat, a beautiful piece of workmanship, is the craft of choice. It looks much like a wooden canoe with a flat bottom and can be 24 feet in length. A short pole instead of oars is used to maneuver the boat down this winding river. Anglers float along until a hatch or spinner fall occurs. Then they drop chain and start listening for rising trout. The "chain" is not quite an anchor but slows the boat considerably.

Since we had an agenda during the day and could not spend it sleeping, we chose a stretch of water and waited. The wait was very short lived.

Night 1

We were on our beat about 8 p.m., but I was ill-prepared for Zenning. (Out West, we spend the hours after sunset driving to the water we plan to fish the next day.) To get into a superior state of Zen consciousness one must sit on the bank and wait.

We have very unpredictable hatches out west, so we just fish. Whether it is nymphing, streamer fishing or those wonderful moments when we do get to toss dry flies, we just fish. And we normally fish all day. Watching the clock instead of my fly drifting on the water was very unnerving. I saw a couple of small trout rising to small olive stoneflies, so I was forced to break Zen. Since I fish small streams as much as I can in Colorado, small fish are not at all indecorous for my ego. So I caught a few small browns to scratch my itch and then was able to sit again.

It seemed an eternity waiting for it to get dark. We did see a couple of big fish rise at last light, so I got to hear the sound of the big fish. They sound like a toilet flushing; you can almost hear their jaws click together as they inhale their first morsels of the night. The distinct sound of big trout rising became more consistent with the fading light. Soon I could no longer see the tip of my rod. The Zen started with a beautiful drum roll from a nearby ruffed grouse. It was somewhat late in the season for a grouse to beat his wings trying to attract a mate, but was one of the rewards Zen had set before us.

Just before total darkness set in, I picked a spot to stand and got my casting range down. I tried to spot any likely looking trouble and soon found out that it didn't help.

Fred had situated himself at the tail end of a riffle just before it turned into the deeper run where I was positioned. The sun had been down for some time when the bugs started to show. Fred called out after noticing a batch of gray drake spinners hovering in the air above the riffle. I had a few risers in my line of sound and when I turned on my light I could see a number of the spinners already on the water. I made a couple of casts in the general direction of the rise and was instantly hung up on a snag. I have no idea where it came from and had to break the fly off.

My eyesight is still very good, but it took a while getting used to the blue light we were using. They use a blue filter over a flashlight that clamps to the bill of a baseball cap to reduce the problem of night blindness. Perhaps it helps, I just didn't notice.

I tied on a new size-12 spinner and heard what sounded like a good fish rise near the opposite bank. Two casts later I was hung on a branch on the other bank. To make matters worse, Dennis started yelling from downstream, "*Hex* spinners!" and barks out the time, "It's 10:15."

Sure enough, the spinners are everywhere. I could hear them flapping around my head and can feel them crawling on my hands. But alas, the hook point on my snagged fly was buried and I had to break my fly off again. I turned on my light to see my first *Hexagenia*. They are GIGANTIC mayflies.

Dennis was hooked up in no time. At the last minute before heading to the river, he loaded a small fly box with *Hex* flies and placed it in the back of his vest. Like I said, it was early in the season and we were not really expecting the *Hexes* to be out, but he wanted to be on the safe side. I'm not sure if he was a Boy Scout in his younger days, but there is nothing like being prepared. He netted a sixteen-inch brown.

Fred didn't bring his *Hex* flies and, of course, I never had any to bring. I was tying on the biggest fly in my box, a size 10 Royal Wulff on which I quickly pressed the calf tail down into the spent wing position. Fred hooks up a nice trout on a streamer. I finally got the tag trimmed on my knot and began to cast to a fish rising about a rod's length in front of me.

Dennis is hooked up again and all I can hear is, "It's a good fish!" as the laughter is vibrating upstream from his position. The thrashing of the fish in the middle of the current definitely got my blood cooking. I wish I could have seen it! "An 18-inch female!" He confirms.

The riser finally takes my Wulff on about the fifteenth cast. I released a foot-long brown, not extraordinary, but rewarding.

Some Zenoids have hunted the *Hex* hatch for years without even seeing a bug. I feel very fortunate to have had such a wonderful experience my first night. I entered into the Knighthood with my fellow "Zen Heads" by taking that first fish in the shroud of darkness during a spinner fall. I landed my fish just minutes before the trout stopped rising. It was over as quickly as it began.

We could have waited for hatchers, but we decided this was a grand introduction to Zenning and headed back to the Riverhouse. As we were stumbling along the bank trying to locate our point to cross the river, Dennis noticed, under the beam of his blue light a 4- or 5-inch brook trout that had met an untimely death.

"It must have choked on one of those mayflies," I smirked.

Night 2

Before hitting the river, we grabbed a hearty dinner at the local fishing lodge. Other fly-fishermen were there preparing for another night of their own. Guides popped in and out meeting with their clients, while everyone was trying to get information on the previous night's fishing. Most of the *Hex* fishing the night before was done on the lower river near Mio. We did not divulge our previous night's success. I don't think anyone was expecting the hatches to be as high up in the river as we had been and we were not going to let the cat out of the bag just yet.

A light fog was hanging over the water when we walked up to our sitting bank. Fog may present a problem for the *Hex* spinners, but we remained hopeful. The smaller trout were active again and I just couldn't resist casting to at least a few. After all I came to fish, not sit. The little stone pattern took a couple again.

As Zen time neared, to my horror, I realized that I had left the half dozen

Chernobyl Sparrows I had tied that afternoon back at the Riverhouse. I had to beg Dennis and Fred for a couple of *Hex* patterns to get me through the night. The price of flies is outrageous at times such as these!

I went back to the same position I was in the night before and made the usual casts to get my range and see how the fly would drift. Darkness came sooner tonight.

Fireflies were flickering in the trees close to the bank. The regular bugs were out again, but no *Hexes* yet. I heard a good rise below me and turned sideways to make a downstream drift. Attempting to expand fly coverage on the water, I redirected my backcast only to get hung in a tree. It was bad, I had wrapped my leader around a jack pine branch, right at the leader/fly-line connection. My Sparrow was dangling just out of reach. It wasn't just my fly that would find a new home that night, my leader would join it as I had to break the entire length. I waded up to the bank and dug in my vest for a leader. There I was, in the dark, with a blue light hanging on my hat twisting up a nail knot feeling a little dismal.

I looked at my watch and it was 10:12 p.m. I hurried the fly knot and took up my position in the water again. At 10:17, Fred yelled out that the *Hex* spinners were on the water. I heard what sounded like a good rise upstream at about a 45-degree angle, maybe twenty feet out. My third cast was close, I heard the water displace in the vicinity and raised my rod, connecting to my second Zen trout. Although it was not a big trout, once again it was very gratifying.

Then, as I was kneeling to release my trout, across from me and about fifty yards up the hill I heard a ruckus. It was a scream like nothing I have heard in the outdoors. It sounded like a monkey getting its tail pulled. (I knew it couldn't be a monkey, but that is what it sounded like.) The crackle of low-hanging branches told me the sound was getting closer. The screams were more intense. The rustling was right along the water's edge now, right in front of me. I don't know if these guys up here know the San Juan Shuffle, but I have to tell you I had nervous feet. All of a sudden, an animal fell in the water. Maybe it was pushed or maybe it was making a last ditch effort to save its life, but nonetheless, this is one of those times I would have felt safer with a .45 strapped to my wading belt. It sounded like the animal was 25 to 30 pounds. I composed myself long enough to turn on my light and saw something in the water, but the fog was just thick enough that I could not make out the animal. Dennis had his light on by this time and saw a pair of eyes bobbing in the water but couldn't tell what it was either. My Zenster friends were pretty freaked by all the commotion. I will wonder until the day I die what took place on the bank of the Au Sable, not 40 feet from where I stood.

Maybe being a Zen Head is not what it's cracked up to be?

We could still see *Hex* spinners on the water, but the trout had stopped rising. They must have been freaked too. We waited a while, but nothing began to feed. Again, we left deciding not to wait for hatching *Hex*.

Night 3

The Au Sable watershed is a unique and beautiful system that looks quite different under a bright afternoon sun. As we toured the countryside, inspecting the North and the South Branch of the Au Sable, it was hard to believe that just a hundred years ago these streams were used to move timber to saw mills. The area around Grayling was deforested to supply the demand for building materials to fuel the growth all around the Great Lakes region. However, the leftover logjams constructed fantastic shelter for the local trout. The current has cut deep runs and undercuts around the jams. The new growth of timber supplies the cover and forage needed for the populations of whitetail deer, wild turkey, raccoons, squirrels, possum, and even the old buzzard we saw on our drive.

The streams all have fine-gravel bottoms rich in biomass. They support prolific hatches of mayflies, caddisflies, and stoneflies throughout the system. The mature trout set up along these fallen timbers to feed when the insects are plentiful. The finicky browns will not move far from their feeding lane, so your presentation needs to be within an inch of the log for them to even take a look, let alone eat your fly. I can see why the Au Sable has such a wonderful legacy as a trout stream.

On the way back to the Riverhouse I suggested we invest in a bottle of wine with dinner. The Rivergod, as Dennis is known by his friends, declared he had a few bottles down in the cellar and suggested we take one to the river that night. I agreed! I figured my Zen consciousness needed an added buzz tonight.

After a wonderful bowl of pasta with red sauce, I made sure that I had my *Hex* flies and we were off to stake out a new section of water. It was only a short distance from where we had fished the previous nights, but the Rivergod assured me that there were bigger trout there. You see, I had been giving him grief about the size of his little trout compared to the brutes we have out West. So, gracious host that he is, the Rivergod was more than happy to accommodate. We slathered up with insect repellant; the mosquitoes and no see'ums can be brutal on this river when it gets dark. We checked our leaders and headed to the river to find a comfortable bank to sit.

The Rivergod uncorked a 1989 Kenwood Cabernet Sauvignon and let it breathe a refreshing Au Sable River zephyr. It was wonderful and just got better as the evening progressed. I was feeling very Zen-like. Even the small trout rising tonight did not faze me. I tied on my Chernobyl Sparrow, sat and watched, nary shifting an inch from my perch. I was learning that, when in the presence of locals, you do as the locals do.

A couple of good fish started working early. It was as if they were anticipating the *Hexagenias* as much as we were. It was as if they were practicing their rise, gauging the water depth, focusing their vision in the low light and working on their timing. Whoa, I sure hope this is the Zen talking and not the buzz!

Well before dark, a couple of *Hex* spinners fluttered right in front of us. They dropped to the water almost instantly. The Rivergod had told me two nights before about the movement a *Hex* spinner makes on the water and this turned out to be a great demonstration. The wings went down into the spent position and the water shook as it deposited its eggs. The commotion on the water made a circle that was nearly ten inches across. The movement would stop, and about twenty feet downstream it would start shaking again. Pretty neat! The Rivergod said he imitated this motion with his fly the first night to entice the trout he caught. He calls it the *Hex* Rumba.

I got up and made a short cast to try it out. I tugged on the fly the first couple tries, which produced a very unnatural movement on the water. The Rivergod instructed me to "rumba from the elbow" while pushing the rod forward to prevent aberrant movement of the fly. After a couple more tries, I had it, so I sat back down to wait.

It was not quite dark when a large trout started rising very consistently. I felt the Zen tell me it was OK to make a couple casts. (After all it was a big fish.) I took four or five casts, all were good drifts, but the fish did not take, so I backed off. I found it very easy to sit down again.

At 10:10, I took up the same casting position to go for the same trout, and sure enough at about 10:15 we noticed the big mayflies hovering around a porch light on a house downstream from our position. A quick check with the blue hat light verified our assumption that the spinners were on the water. Although not as many as the first night, there were enough. My range was good and I knew the fly was in the proper area. Suddenly, it sounded like somebody had stepped into the water and scooped a pail of water, so I lifted my rod to set the hook. The fly zipped over my left shoulder. There was no fish attached.

I had been casting over my right shoulder so when I felt the slight resistance as I brought the fly forward I knew I had done it again! My fly had whipped off in a tree, loud enough that the Rivergod said he heard it pop off. I stepped back and retied another Sparrow under my headlamp. This one seemed to take forever. I would like to say that I was taking my time ensuring I tied a good knot, however, that was not the case. I couldn't get focused on my tippet and with Mr. Bucket Mouth still rising, my nerves were a bit rattled.

Once retied, I stepped forward into position. The Rivergod instructed me to get as close as I could without stepping off into the deepest part of the run. About five Rumba drifts later, the big fish rose in the general area of my fly and I set. A deep bend formed in my rod as I horsed him out of his lie. I kept him in the middle of the stream away from the downed timber along the far bank. My fellow Knight moved to my side to cheer me on as the trout thrashed near the surface. "Is it sixteen inches?"

"Yes," I said, "It's a good fish!"

The fight was short as the 3X tippet held firm. My light was fixed on a beautiful 22-inch male brown as it slipped into my hands.

I felt total elation. This wonderful fish had spent the prime of his life feeding by the light of the stars, the instinct passed on by many great brown trout before him. This instinct had provided him safety and kept him out of sight of so many anglers before me. I felt honored to feel his strength and gaze upon his greatness. If I were a Knight, then he must be the King!

There I was, an outsider looking in to the art of Zen. I stood there in total amazement and awe. I apologized to my friend for my comments about the Au Sable's small trout and shook his hand in reverence.

I had had a bonafide Zen experience and felt like a Zen Knight of distinction. Now that, my friends, is *Hex* fishing!

Parachute Extended-Body Hexagenia

Contributed by Fred Vargas

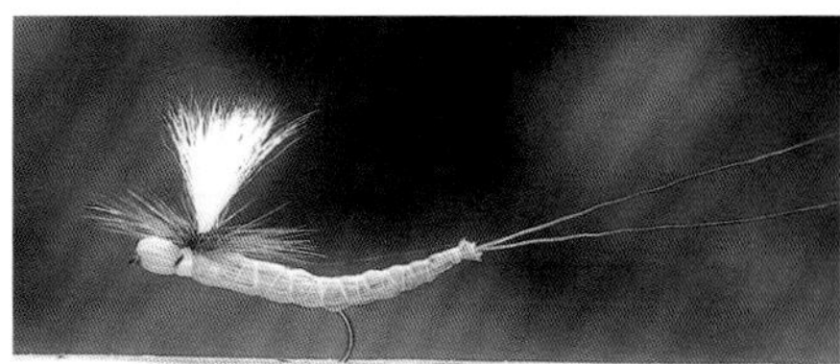

Hook: 3X dry fly, size10 Tiemco 5212, Daiichi 1280
Thread: Yellow G thread, Gudebrod
Tail: Moose body hair, long and straight fibers (two hairs)
Wing: Calf body hair
Body: Yellow whitetail deer hair, the longest body hair you can find
Thread: Yellow 6/0 Gudebrod thread for tying in hackle
Hackle: Brown dry fly, a size-6 hackle from a saddle, if you can find it

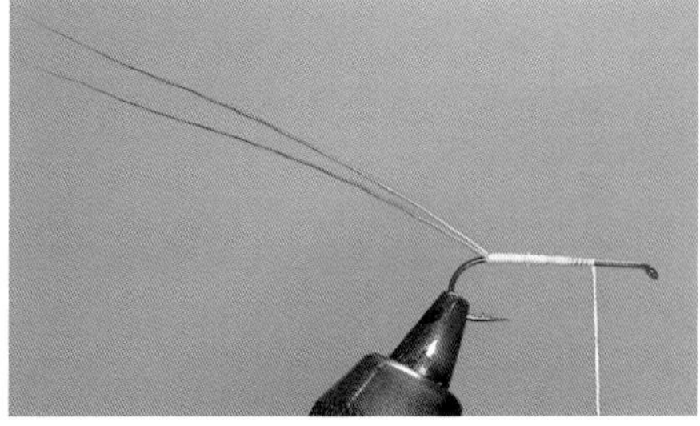

1. If your vise will allow it, set the jaws at a more vertical position than where it would be for normal tying. The Dyna-King vise that Fred uses can be set from 90 degree straight out to the side, to a point nearly straight up. Clamp the hook in the vise so the hook shank is parallel to the desktop. Start thread at the 2/3 point of the hook and wrap back to the bend and then move thread forward to the 1/4 point. Secure two moose body hair fibers at the 1/4 point with the hair tips extending beyond the bend of the hook at least two full hook shanks. Wrap to the back of the hook making sure the fibers stay on top of the hook.

2. Move thread forward to the 2/3 point. Stack a bunch of calf body hair for the wing. This hair should also be as long as you can find. Measure the calf hair for a wing height of a full hook shank. With the tips of the hair over the eye of the hook, secure the hair at the 2/3 point with several very tight turns of thread. Wrap back to about the 1/2 point and trim off the butt ends of the hair. Cover the butt ends of the hair with several wraps of thread. Pick up the wing post and make several wraps of thread forming a dam in front of the wing to make it stand up. Make a few wraps of thread around the wing post just to clump it up nicely.

3. Trim off a clump of deer hair a little larger than the size of a regular pencil. Comb out the under fur and short hairs then stack the hair. After the hair is stacked, it should be just smaller than a pencil. Move thread to just behind the eye of the hook. Measuring the hair for the body length is no more than just using as much of the hair length as humanly possible. Using the same patch of hair, you will find that the body lengths on a couple of dozen flies will all be very close. For a quick reference, the actual length of the hex is 1 1/4 inches to 1 1/2 inches. A primo patch of hair will tie you several dozen. Fred ties about 100 dozen Hex a year; just imagine the amount of hair he goes through. Hold the hair by the butt ends on top of the hook. The tips of the hair are over the eye of the hook at a slight angle going away from the tier. Using your thumbnail as a thread guide, make two soft wraps of thread around the hair. Secure the hair by gradually applying thread torque letting the hair encompass the hook. Make another wrap and tighten even more. Do not let go of the butt ends of the hair. Wrap back to the wing. Try to trim the butt ends of the hair with one snip. Clean up the area in front of the wing with wraps of thread and leave the thread just in front of the wing post.

4. Sweep the hair back initially with your fingers, and then slip a half-hitch tool over the hair to the base of the wing. Using the half-hitch tool will render your heads consistently the same size and thickness. Make a few tight turns of thread in front of the wing to secure the hair in place. Remove the half-hitch tool. Sweep the hair back and with just enough thread torque to collapse the outside hair, wrap the thread over the hair with evenly spaced wraps. You don't need to squeeze the pulp out of the hair. Continue back past the hook shank to form the extended body. Make sure to encapsulate the moose tail fibers with the deer hair. With the vise set at this vertical position, you can swing the thread and bobbin under the body without banging into the back end of the vise. When the thread reaches a point just in front of the tips of the deer hair, make six or seven tight wraps. Now wrap the thread forward with evenly spaced wraps, crossing over the previous wraps. Continue to the point in front of the wing. Whip finish and remove the G thread.

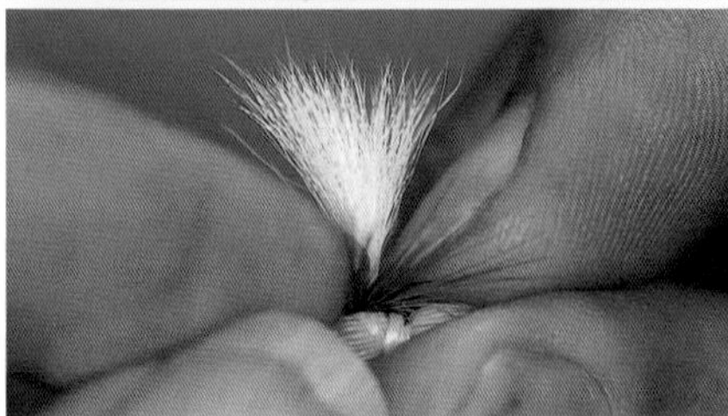

5. Start the 6/0 thread in front of the wing. Wrap around the wing post now to make a base for wrapping the hackle. Prepare a brown hackle and secure the butt end of the feather, concave side down, in front of the wing. Notice in the photo that the feather is on the far side of the hook. Wrap the feather counter clock-wise up the post and then back down with each wrap under the last until as much of the feather is used as possible. Secure the hackle in front of the wing. Using your fingernails, push the hackle wraps down to compress them closer to the deer-hair body. Either use a half hitch or lift up the hackle and whip finish.

Here is the finished Parachute Extended-Body *Hexagenia*. Notice the even crossing pattern of the thread as it was taken back over the first wraps. Beautifully done.

Fred adds, "The Hex and the Brown Drake were the first patterns I had tied commercially eight years ago. They still look the same."

Chernobyl Sparrow

Contributed by Dennis Potter

Hook: 6X streamer, size 6 Tiemco 300
Thread: Brown 6/0, Danville
Tail: Pheasant-tail fibers
Body: Whitetail deer hair, yellow or natural
Hackle: Cream saddle hackle, long dry-fly quality
Wing: Calf tail, white
Indicator: Hi-Vis, yellow

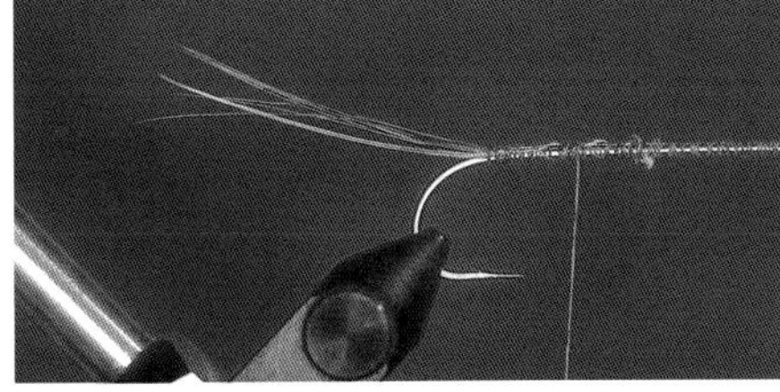

1. Start thread at the mid point on the hook and wrap back to the 1/4 point. Tie in three to five pheasant-tail fibers for the tail. They should extend beyond the bend a full hook shank in length. Move thread forward to the 7/8 point.
2. Trim off a clump of long deer hair as close to the skin as possible, about the size of a pencil. Comb out the under fur

and short hairs, then stack the hair. After the hair is stacked, it should be just smaller than a pencil. Measure the hair so that the tips extend just beyond the bend of the hook and trim the butt ends right at the eye of the hook. Secure the hair at the 7/8 point of the hook letting the butt ends flare immediately behind the hook eye. Hang onto the hair as you move the thread back with evenly spaced wraps. Once at the back of the hook, make several tight wraps. Secure a cream hackle at this point. Move thread forward crossing over the first wraps with equally even wraps.

3. Jump the thread to the 3/4 point of the hook and make a smooth thread base for the wing.

4. Acquire a calf tail with the longest hair you can find. Comb the hair with a fine-toothed comb or pet brush. Trim out a clump of calf-hair half the size of a pencil, shake out the fluff and short hairs, and stack the calf tail hair for the wings. The wing should be a full hook shank in length and secured on top of the hook with the tips over the eye. Trim off the butt ends of the hair and wrap thread over the exposed ends. Evenly separate the hair into two parts and split the wings using simple X-ing wraps. Maneuver the wings so they lie in a spent position and lock them in place with figure-eight wraps.

5. Take a three-inch length of fluorescent yellow Hi-Vis and secure it on top of the wings with an X-ing pattern so that an inch and a half is on each side of the hook. Pull both portions of the Hi-Vis up and wrap around the base of the material to make a parachute post. Here is a view from underneath the fly with the thread moved to just behind the eye.

6. Palmer the hackle forward, much like you would on a Woolly Bugger. Tie off the hackle behind the eye, trim excess hackle and whip finish.

Last Night's Emerger (Male Hendrickson)

Contributed by Ken Mead

What better place to develop a new pattern than on your trip to someplace special, trying to imitate the insect of the day. This excursion just happened to be his annual trip to the upper Delaware

River with fishing partner Phil Campbell where they were trying to imitate the well-known Hendrickson hatch. The experience was what they expected: Lots of hatching *Emphemerella subvaria* that made the fishing, to say the least, challenging.

As with many trips away from the confines of home, the nectar was going down easily and the fly-tying vise was clamped to the hotel table. (Have you ever noticed that the tables in motel rooms are not made for C-clamps? I would suggest taking a pedestal vice on your next trip if you have one.) They were tying an assortment of flymphs for the next day's fishing.

A flymph is an imitation that is no longer a nymph but not quite a full-blown adult insect. You could say it is imitating a bug going through serious labor pains. Pete Hidy designed the wingless fly that, when wet, looks a lot like the snarled mess of legs, tails, and emerging shuck of a hatching insect. In this case it is tied as a hatching mayfly, but with a slight adjustment in design could easily be converted to a struggling caddisfly.

Phil was making his own creations with Z-lon for the trailing shuck and hen hackle for the snarled mess at the front of the fly.

Ken was looking for more of an emergent type of pattern when he came up with his new creation. He wanted a fly that would still ride low in the surface, but had a more developed wing that would be easier to see. While fooling around with some CDC they had with them, their creative minds leapt into action. Or was it the single malt finally kicking in? Either way, Ken found this amazingly easy technique of palmering a few CDC feathers through the thorax of the fly, which in the end would be the wing and legs. At first it looks like quite a mess, (not to be confused with Gary LaFontaine's pattern) but with a pull here and a wrap of thread there and a couple of quick nips of the scissors he had a pretty decent, buggy-looking fly. As we all know, however, the real test of a new pattern is the moment it touches the water.

As Ken took fish after fish on his new pattern during the Hendrickson hatch the next day, Phil was forced to ask the inevitable question, "What are you using?"

Ken's reply was simple and to the point, "Last Night's Emerger!" Somewhat anecdotal, but the name stuck.

I just love those stories of how a fly was developed. Hope you do too.

Ken adds a bit of information about the materials he uses on this pattern. "Craig Mathews's Z-lon from Blue Ribbon Flies is my favorite. It seems more economical and is slightly softer than most on the market. Craig's dyed colors are outstanding and the selection is very adequate."

Whenever possible, Ken uses goose CDC on this fly if he can find it. He says, "It is cosmic! It has thicker barbules and is denser than CDC from a duck. A few friends of mine hunt geese so I get the opportunity to gather a couple of handfuls each year."

Try to find a goose hunter, you will not be disappointed in the quality of the CDC. Look under the tail (don't be shy) for a soft, often oily, patch of feathers about two inches in diameter. Start plucking! However, easily attainable brown-gray duck CDC from Spirit River is also very good.

Mayfly emergence is the stage on which trout feed most heavily during a hatch. Not only on the Delaware River, but all around the world. This is the time when the insect is most vulnerable to trout, so a good emerger imitation is a must. This fly floats well and is very easy to see, even in smaller sizes. Try this easy-to-tie pattern during your next mayfly hatch, you will not be disappointed.

Last Night's Emerger

Hook: Tiemco 2487, size 12-16
Thread: Danville 6/0, tobacco brown
Trailing Shuck: Z-lon, medium brown
Body: Aussie Possum dubbing, reddish-brown
Wing: CDC, natural dun
Thorax: Aussie Possum dubbing, reddish-brown

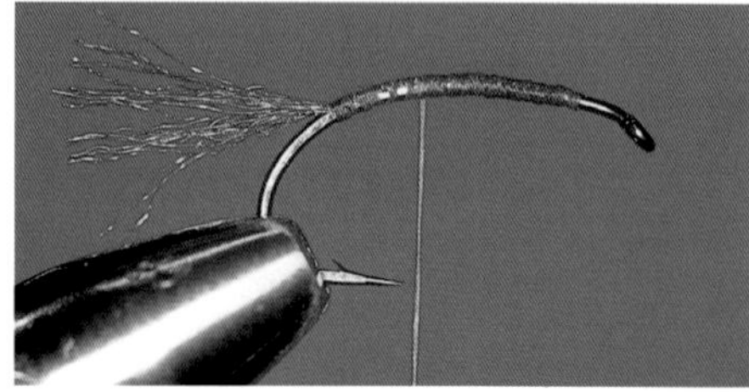

1. Start the thread at the 3/4 point of the hook and wrap back to the 1/2 point. Prepare the Z-lon for use. Z-lon comes packaged with several clumps of material tied together. The clumps need to be divided further into smaller groups of individual fibers. Ken only uses about 3/4 of a whole clump or an estimated 15–20 strands. He adds, "Use less than you think you need." Tie in the strands of Z-lon for the trailing shuck and wrap to the back of the hook. Trim the Z-lon to length, about 1/3 the hook shank length.

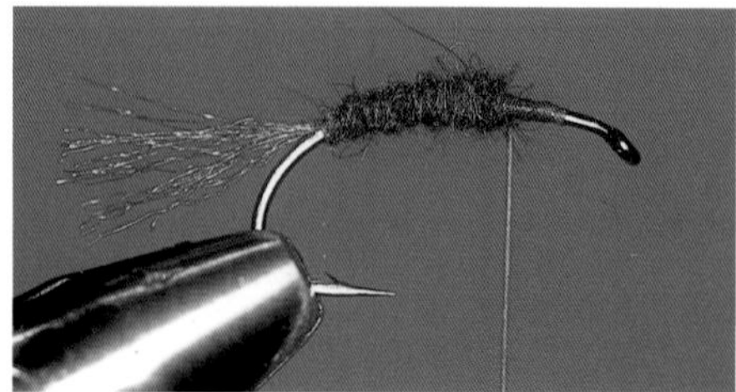

2. Dub a nicely tapered body to the 2/3 point of the hook.
3. Prepare three heavily barbed CDC feathers by laying them all together with the tips even. Pull the fibers back, away

from the tip and hold them back with your thumb and forefinger as shown in the first photo. Make sure the convex sides of the feathers are towards you. Trim the tips to ready them for tie-in as shown in the second photo.

4. Apply a small amount of dubbing to the thread leaving 1/2 inch of bare thread between the dubbing and the hook shank. Tie in the CDC feathers by the tips and allow the dubbing to form a base in which the CDC will be wrapped.

5. Make a couple of wraps with the CDC feathers, palmering them forward slightly through the dubbing. Secure the CDC and trim the butt ends of the feathers. Sweep the fibers back and up to maneuver most of the fibers to the top of the hook. Dub another small amount of dubbing for the head of the fly and whip finish.

6. Trim the CDC to shape. Trim the fibers under the fly to the gape of the hook to represent legs and then trim the wing to length. This should be a very slight trim, as you want to cut just the longest straggling fibers. Leave the overall wing longer than you would think. Eastern tiers like this look, and believe it or not, it is correct. The wings on most mayflies are longer than the normal tie-in procedure of a single hook shank length.

Here are a couple of different color combinations for the Last Night's Emerger, a pinkish-tan dubbed body for the female Hendrickson and a soft yellow to imitate E. *dorthea* or E. *invaria*, also known as the Sulphur.

Loop-Winged Baetis

Contributed by Brad Befus

Developing flies is so much fun. Getting the creative juices flowing, trying new materials, recreating old patterns, and improving on new ones. The Loop-Winged *Baetis* is a combination of old ideas on tying with the addition of relatively new techniques. The Loop-Winged *Baetis* is a sleek, old-fashioned, thread-bodied fly with thread ribbing for segmentation. With the addition of a fairly new wing and a very seldom-used thorax-style hackling technique, the Loop-Winged is a great accessory to a boring fly box. This is one great-looking mayfly pattern and it has a couple of outstanding ideas on fly construction that everyone should know about.

One of the first flies ever tied was one man's impression of an insect he saw on a stream called the Astraeus. AElian noticed fish feeding on a fly that looked much like a wasp. A wrapping of red wool fastened to a hook with two feathers from a cock's wattles fixed to the wool was as close as he could get with what he had at that time, about 200 A.D. Brad Befus is no different than old AElian. Although the blue-winged olive is very common to all parts of the world, Brad sees it a little differently than anyone else. He has shelves full of materials at his disposal, just about any and every material that can be used to tie a fly. His view of the actual insect and his experience of the many tying techniques available to him, brought about this lovely version of the "Olive".

Brad noticed that the abdomen color of a *Baetis* is much lighter than most people think. He assumed this was because most dubbing blends are mixed too dark. When looking at the top of the abdomen on a *Baetis* dun, it is a much darker olive than the underside. However, the underside is the business side as far as trout are concerned because that is what they see as the insect drifts by. Brad experimented with many materials to come up with this body color. He tried biots, which are very popular as a mayfly body. Stripped quills, which A.K. Best popularized, also looked great. These materials make a very natural, segmented mayfly body, but the tedious work of dyeing them to just the right color is time-consuming.

Some older fly patterns use thread for the body on mayflies. Why not? Threads come in several colors so the options seemed endless. After testing several colors of thread, Brad discovered the perfect color: Danville Beige #41, all it needed was ribbing to imitate the segmentation. Danville olive #60 fit the bill.

As far as the rest of the fly goes, I was totally amazed when I saw Brad split the tails on this fly. It is a slick technique for splitting tails without the use of a dubbing ball or build-up of thread, which in turn increases the speed at which you can tie the fly.

The Antron yarn for the loop-wing is a fairly new technique that adds a very realistic silhouette and shimmer to the fly. Prepare the yarn before tying. Antron usually needs to be separated into smaller, individual strands. The strands of Antron yarn used for the wing don't need to be thick and bulky.

The loop-wing is a very good blend of old and new as it depicts this popular mayfly. As we go through the steps for this fly, notice Brad's attention to details on the fly proportions as they are directly related to what he has seen by observing the real insect.

Loop-Winged *Baetis*

Hook: Standard dry fly, size 16-22
Thread: Olive, Danville 6/0 #60
Tail: Coq de Leon or Micro Fibetts, medium gray
Abdomen: Beige, Danville 6/0 #41
Ribbing: Olive, Danville 6/0 #60
Wing: Antron Yarn, light gray
Thorax: Tan Beaver dubbing
Hackle: Medium Dun (Whiting Farms)

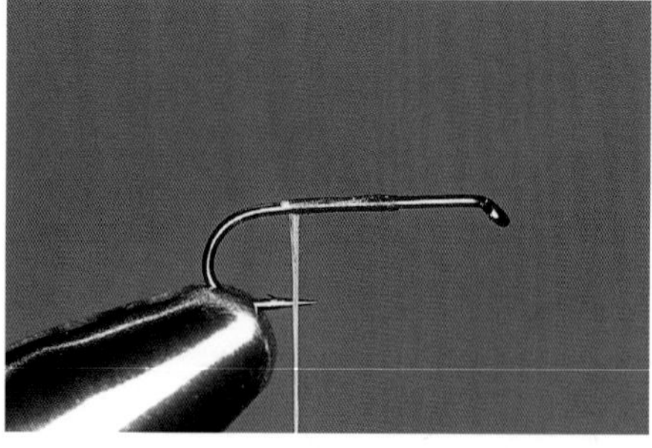

1. When looking at mayflies, notice that the abdomen and the thorax are not perfectly divided 50-50. The body (or abdomen) is longer than thorax. In an attempt to get just the right proportions on this pattern, Brad suggests dividing this fly so that the body represents 60% of the fly with the thorax taking up the other 40%. Another trick Brad uses, especially when instructing others in the fine art of fly tying, is to start the thread at the breaking point from one part of the fly to the other to set up the initial proportions. For example, the point where the body ends and the thorax starts. This is a great idea for setting proportions and it can be right there every time you start a fly. With practice, this procedure will become a subconscious move that develops consistency on all the flies you tie. With that said, start the olive Danville #60 thread at the 5/8 point of the hook and wrap back to the 1/4 point.

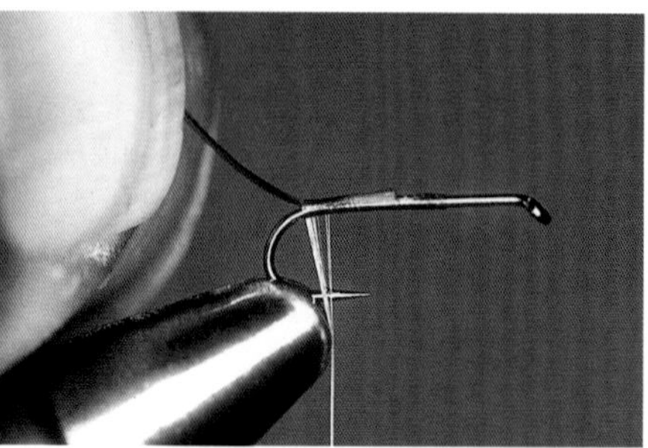

2. The Loop-Winged *Baetis* is usually tied smaller than a size 16, so the number of fibers you use for the tail should not be many. One or two fibers of Micro Fibetts on each side for the split tail are usually plenty. More fibers from a natural feather will be required; as many as four or five on each side is not uncommon. With tailing material in your right hand, measure tails to a length that is equal to the distance from the eye of the hook to the bend of the hook. This is slightly longer than the normal length used by most tiers because the tails on the mayfly are actually longer. Transfer into your left hand and tie tails in at the 1/4 point of the hook. When using Micro Fibetts for the tail, make sure the Fibbets stay on top of the hook as you wrap to the back of the shank. Simply making a couple of wraps back from the tie-in point and then lifting the tips of the tail as you wrap back can do this. Due to the stiffness of the Fibbets, it will be easier to control splitting the tails if they are positioned on top. When using natural fibers, such as those from a Coq de Leon feather, the tie-in position of the fibers is not as critical because they are not as stiff as the Micro Fibetts and can be manipulated more easily when it comes time to split the tails.

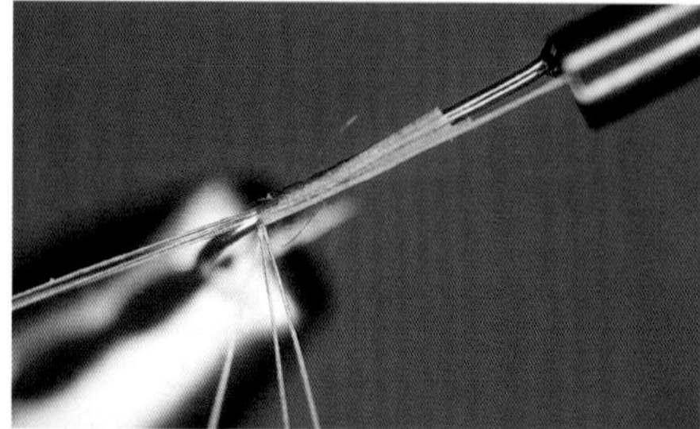

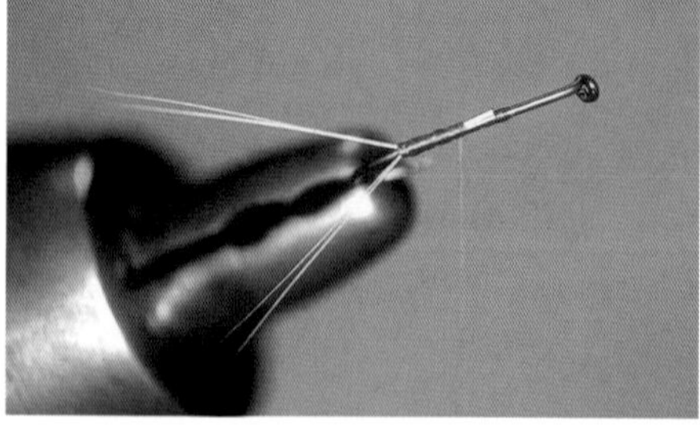

3. And it is time to split the tails! Move thread forward a few wraps. With a fingernail, push the tails up to separate them so they can be counted. Separate the fibers evenly by hand and coax them to each side of the hook shank. (Note: Photos 1 and 2 of this step were done with a lighter-colored tailing mate-

rial so the tails would show up better. Pay close attention to the direction the bobbin is pulled away from the tails.) Take the thread, from under the tail, up in between the tail and the hook shank on the fore side of the hook. Pull the bobbin forward, parallel with the hook shank until the tail is split sufficiently. Hold the tails with your hand and make a wrap or two around the hook to lock the tail into position. Now take the thread, from the top, and drop it in between the tail and the hook shank on the far side of the hook. Pull the bobbin forward, parallel with the hook shank, until the tail is split sufficiently. Hold the tails with your hand and make a wrap or two around the hook to lock the tail into position. If the tails have a downward cant to them, a single wrap of thread under both tails and pulling the bobbin forward parallel to the hook should fix the problem. Three wraps of thread have just split thc tails on this fly. Brad has found that most tiers try to use too many wraps of thread to "fix" the tails using this method and urges you not to make more wraps than is absolutely needed. This is a very simple and effective way to split tails without a dubbing ball. Move thread to the back of the hook and position bobbin out of the way, maybe lay it over the vise with the thread in your material clip. DO NOT cut the thread off.

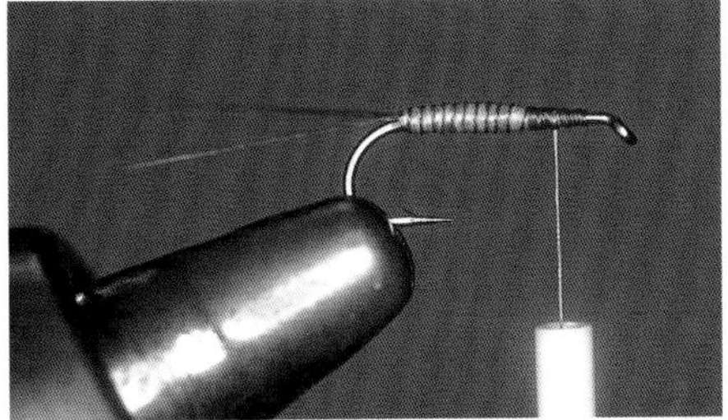

4. Start the beige Danville #41 thread and build a nicely tapered abdomen from the back of the hook to the 5/8 point. Spinning the thread counterclockwise occasionally will let the thread lie flat and ensure a smooth body. When the abdomen is done, whip finish or half hitch the beige thread. Cut and remove the beige thread. Take the olive thread and spin it clockwise to make a tight, thin rope. Rib the abdomen with this olive thread, making sure space between the ribs is very close.

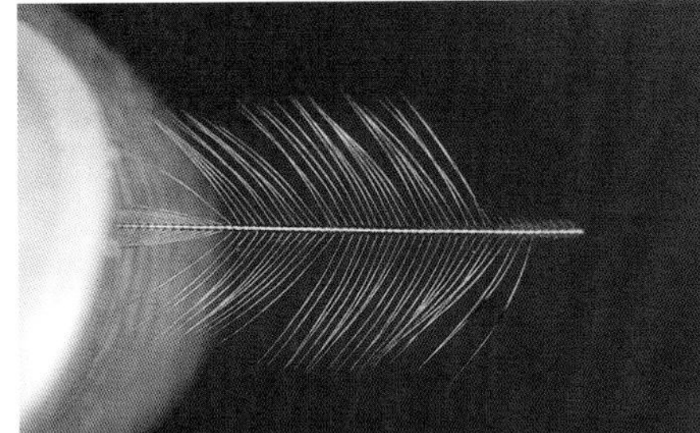

5. Tie in the Antron for the loop wing right in front of the body as you would a wingcase. Dub about an inch noodle of the tan beaver dubbing on the thread, leaving a half inch of bare thread between the thread and the dubbing. Since the hackle on this fly is wrapped through dubbing, an undersized hackle can be used. (It is not mandatory but it is an option.) In other words, a size-18 hackle could be used on a size-16 fly. Brad explains, "Trim hackle before tying in; do not pull barbs from the stem as this weakens the stem. A noticeable amount of barbs should be trimmed from the top of the stem and a short nip trimmed from the bottom. (See photo) This allows the hackle to be wrapped on a bare stem the first 1/4 turn to ensure it is set in motion accurately." Use the section of bare thread to tie in the hackle on the fore side of the hook with the shiny side towards you. This allows a 1/4 turn on top of the hook to make sure the hackle is set in place and will wrap correctly. As the dubbing shows up, form a level thorax to the front of the fly. Brad adds, "Getting just the right amount of dubbing to finish the thorax with one dubbing noodle may take a couple of flies. Just pay attention to the length of the noodle and adjust for the next fly. However, if you end up with too much dubbing it should be removed. An easy way to do this is to unwrap the dubbing a few turns, then tear the dubbing off and redo the end of the noodle and wrap back into place."

6. Palmer hackle the thorax to the front of the fly. Depending on the size of the fly, 3 or 4 wraps should be enough to get through the dubbing. Secure hackle in place and trim excess.

7. Pull the Antron over the thorax so that it encompasses the hackle. This can be a little difficult to get correct. However, if the Antron is secured at the front of the fly with two loose wraps, a bodkin can be used to adjust the height of the wing. When the height of the wing is correct, secure in place with a few tight wraps. Hold the excess Antron up and make a few wraps in front of the wing and whip finish in front of the Antron. Trim the Antron so there is a little tuft above the eye forming a head. This maneuver also locks the loop in place and keeps the wing from pulling out of place after unhooking several trout.

8. Turn the vise so you can see the fly from the front. Carefully trim the hackle

under the hook so the fly will ride more flush in the surface of the water. Notice the V-shaped cut under the hook. With the direction the feather is turned, the hackle needs to be trimmed off center to the right making sure the "outriggers" are level so the fly will ride perfectly in the water.

Pheasant Tail Nymph

Hook: Nymph 1x long, size 18-12, Daiichi 1560
Thread: 8/0 camel
Ribbing: Fine copper wire
Tail: Pheasant-tail fibers
Body: Pheasant-tail fibers (same as tail)
Legs: Pheasant-tail fibers
Wingcase: Pheasant-tail fibers (same as legs)
Thorax: Peacock herl, or dubbing
Note: This is a follow-up nymph pattern mentioned in Flashback Pheasant Tail Nymph on page 82.)

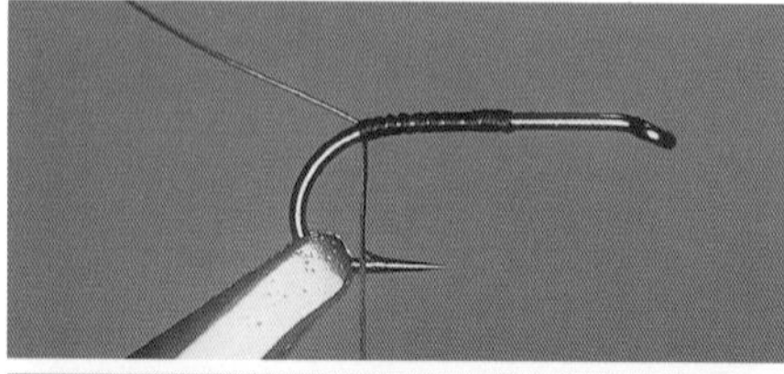

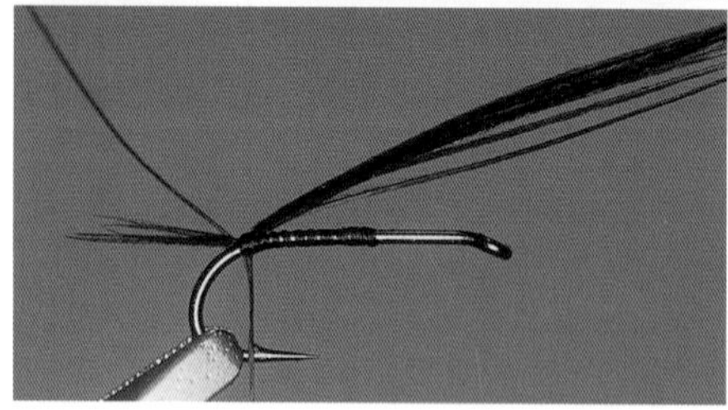

1. Start thread mid shank and secure the copper wire on the far side of the hook. Wrap to the back of the hook making sure the wire maintains its position on the far side. Measure tails so they extend beyond the back of the hook about half the hook shank length. Tie the tails in at the back of the hook and make four tight wraps on top of each other, right there at the back of the hook.

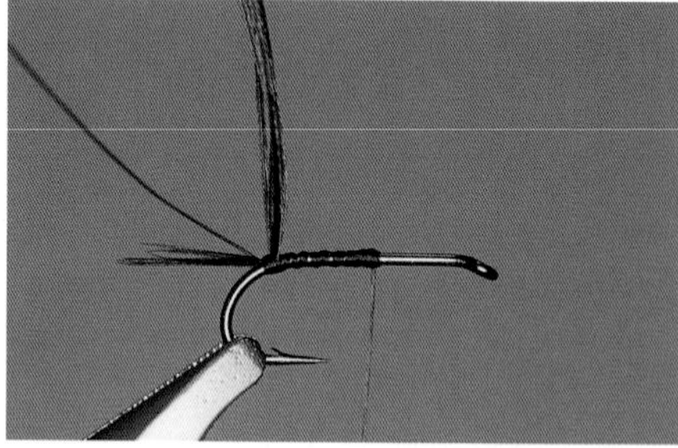

2. This next technique is quite different from the way Randy showed you how to tie the Flashback P.T. Just lift the pheas-

ant fibers up and move the thread to halfway point of the hook.
3. Wrap the pheasant fibers forward to the 1/2 point and secure. DO NOT trim the fibers yet. Wrap the wire forward over the body with evenly spaced wraps. I do not counter-wrap the wire, I wrap it the same direction as I wrap the thread and body fibers. Also, with the wire on the backside of the hook, your first turn of ribbing will go under the hook then on top so as not to interfere with the tail position. The theory of counter-wrapping the wire is to make sure all the body fibers get lashed down with the wire so they will not fall apart after a couple of good fights with strong rainbows. I make six or seven wraps with the pheasant fibers for the body and four wraps of wire with the ribbing. All the fibers are getting lashed with the wire: I have caught several fish on the same fly without it falling apart. OK, where were we? Secure wire. Hold the wire and the pheasant fibers up together and trim both as close to the hook as possible.
4. Select a new clump of pheasant fibers for the legs and wingcase. I use at least

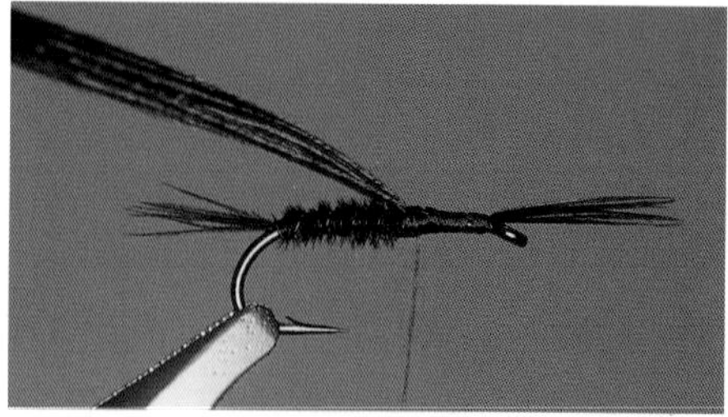

six fibers so I have three legs on each side of the hook. However, I will use as many as ten or twelve for bigger flies. The additional fibers not only make the legs more predominant, but also make a fuller wingcase. Tie the tips of the fibers in so they hang over the front of the hook the same length as the tail. Lash the fibers down as you wrap back to the 1/2 point of the hook. Make sure they

stay on top of the hook; the butt ends of these fibers are used for the wingcase.
5. Tie in a few strands of peacock herl. Wrap peacock herl forward making a smooth thorax. Secure with a couple of wraps of thread and pull herl back towards the bend of the hook quickly to break off the excess. Dubbing can also be used for the thorax. It all depends on what you want your fly to look like. Since material selection is not etched in stone, anything is legal.

6. Split the pheasant fibers hanging over the eye into two equal sections. These are now going to be used for the legs. Pull half the fibers back on the far side of the hook and secure with one wrap of thread. Lay the other half of the legs down the front side of the hook with your thumb. Secure with one wrap of thread.
7. Pull wingcase over the top of the thorax and secure just behind the eye. Trim excess fibers and whip finish. This fly

will take a little longer to tie than some methods (about 2 minutes and 30 seconds). However, for those of you who like the look of finely tapered legs, which can be achieved by using the tips of a pheasant-tail fiber, then this is the fly for you.

PMD Quill (Pale Morning Dun)

Contributed by John Hagen

The quills used for this particular fly come from the large feathers from a Whiting Farms brown or a medium ginger neck. Pick the lightest brown neck or the darkest medium ginger you can find that does not have the black furnace webbing. Hold on Marty, a PMD quill from a brown neck? Yes, a brown neck! You may be able to find natural quills from just about any brown neck, but John prefers the quills from a Whiting rooster. "They are very round, they're supple, and resistant to cracking." As John would say, "They are perfect."

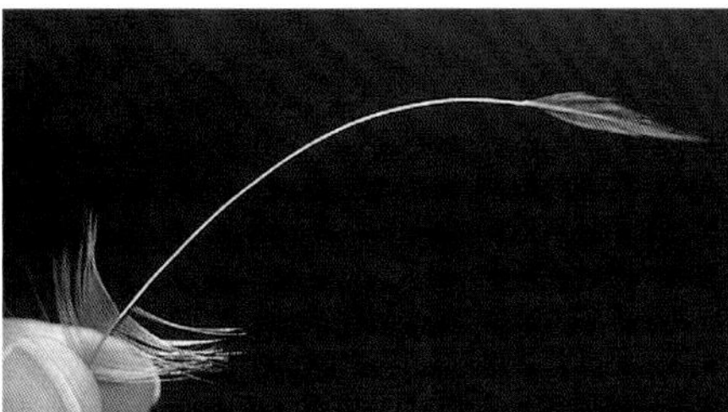

John simply strips the barbs off by hand so he can use the natural color of the quill. Do not burn the barbs off with the bleaching process explained later, as this will bleach the natural color that led you to the quill in the first place. After the barbs are stripped off they have a light peachy color which is perfect for some of our local pale morning dun hatches. An added benefit of stripping the barbs by hands is the bi-colored effect you get. The area on the quill where the barbs were stripped ends up being a cream color. So as the quill is turned into place, the peachy color and the cream color mingle to break up the solid appearance, giving the illusion of segmentation.

Before you start tying, prepare the quills by pulling off several feathers from the neck and pre-strip them. A trash can, a stereo or television, and a little patience are all you need to prepare enough quills to tie several dozen flies. Before tying with these quills soak them in water or lay them in a wet towel to soften them. This prevents them from splitting as you turn them around the hook.

Mayflies in your area may not be exactly the same color as the ones in Colorado—in fact ours vary in color from river to river—but there may be a natural neck hackle quill out there that will produce the correct color for you using this same idea. Again, when you find natural quills with the color you need, do not bleach them because they will end up cream colored and you will have to dye them.

If you cannot find the correct color in a natural feather, dyeing quills to match the shade of your mayflies is the next step to take. John has a unique way of preparing neck hackle quills for mayfly bodies.

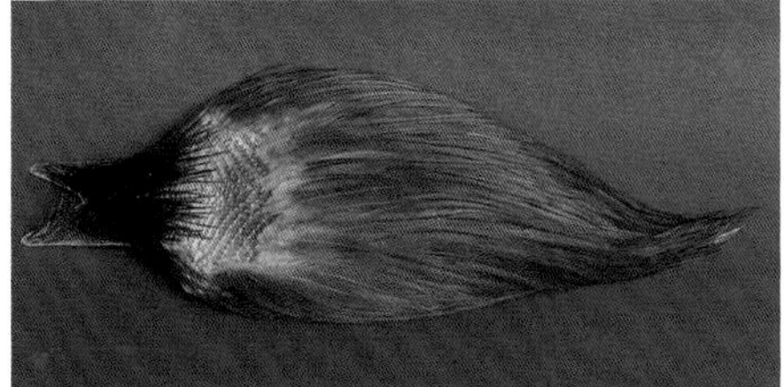

John's main source for hackle quills comes from the rooster necks from which he has pulled all the usable feathers. In other words, after all the size 12, 14, 16, 18, and 20s are pulled from the neck, he cuts off the top section where the big feathers are (see photo) He leaves the smallest feathers, size 22 and smaller, intact along with the valuable feathers on the sides. These we refer to as spade hackle and can be used for dry-fly tailing.

These big neck hackle feathers always seem to be left over, unused, when all the good dry-fly quality feathers are gone. In fact, these feathers are not even good for streamer wings. So in an effort to reduce waste, and ultimately cost, John takes this patch of feathers and 'burns' the barbs off with a bleaching process and ends up with quills ready to dye. Here is a patch of feathers that would have been eaten by bugs and now they are used to tie quill-bodied flies. By the way, trout like them!

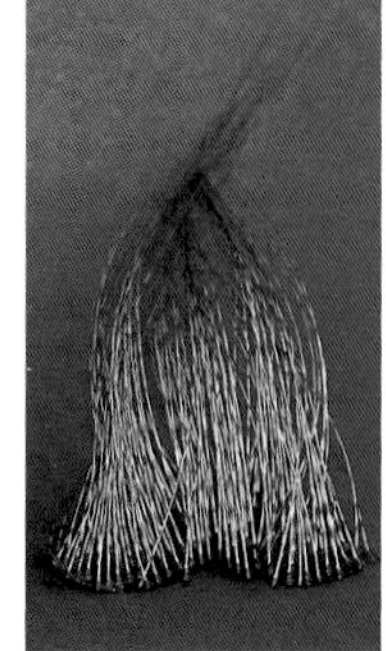

Here is the patch of grizzly feathers stripped and dyed. John refers to this patch as a "quill dispenser". Just leave the quills on the skin and dispense them as needed. It easily helps you pick the correct sized quill for the size fly you are tying.

Things you will need to burn neck:

- hackle quills:
- Clorox bleach
- Warm water
- 2 glass bowls that hold at least a quart of liquid
- Rubber gloves
- Tongs
- Baking soda

Using a glass bowl, mix Clorox bleach and warm water together 50-50. (Use a well-ventilated room or the back porch to do this project. Also unplug the phone, you do not want any interruptions.) Rubber gloves and a pair of tongs are also needed to protect your skin from any exposure to the bleach. Place the patch of feathers in the bowl, swishing and rotating during the whole process. Soon after the patch is dunked in this solution, it will start to foam. The 'burning' has started.

Check the feathers frequently as the barbs start to disappear. The fluffy marabou at the butt ends will disappear first. The barbs in the middle and the tips of the feathers take much longer. You may need to rinse the patch with clear water to see this disappearing act. If the bleach and water mixture loses its strength before the barbs are cleared off, mix a new batch. You will be able to tell if the bleach mixture has lost its zip by the lack of foaming and the fact that the barbs have stopped coming off the quills.

As soon as the barbs have been removed from the quills, extract the patch from the bleach and rinse thoroughly with water. This 'burning' process normally takes 10-20 minutes. **DO NOT** leave the feathers in the bleach too long or the enamel on the quills will be damaged. Worse yet, the quills will totally disintegrate. In fact, I may leave some barbs on the very tips of the feathers because the tips are trimmed off before using. This helps keep the bleaching time to a minimum.

Transfer the patch of quills to a bowl of water with two tablespoons of baking soda added to it. Leave in this solution for at least 20 minutes. The baking soda reverses the bleaching action and protects the enamel coating on the quills.

To do another patch of feathers, start with a new mixture of water and bleach.

The quills can now be dyed to the color of your choice. Olive, brown, rusty brown, yellow, and tan are all popular colors for quills used for mayfly bodies. If you do not have an old neck to burn, strung neck hackle can be found at most fly shops. Make sure it is neck hackle not saddle hackle. The same procedure can be used on strung feathers, but you will need to use a rubber band to hold the quills together. A quick note on dying quills, don't dye them too dark. Remember the underside of a mayfly is much lighter than you think, so resist the urge to get the color too rich. This is especially true when you are planning to tie small dry flies. The tips, or thinner part of the quill which you will be using for these smaller flies, absorb dye quicker than the butt ends of the quill. Make sure the thin part of the quill is the correct color, not the butt ends.

If all this seems like too much trouble, pre-made quills in several different colors are available through "D's Flyes", also available at most fly shops.

PMD Quill (Pale Morning Dun)

Hook: Standard dry fly, Daiichi 1180, size 14-20
Thread: Pale yellow, Danville 6/0
Tail: Light to medium ginger, stiff hackle fibers
Abnoman: Stripped brown neck hackle, light peach
Wing: Medium dun hen neck feathers Whiting Farms
Hackle: Light to medium ginger, dry-fly quality, Whiting Farms

1. John is among the many pro tiers who believe in the method of starting the thread at a point on the hook that will set a proportion for the fly. As with many of the other dry mayfly patterns in this book, the abdomen is longer than the thorax or hackled section of the fly. John has picked a spot on the hook shank he refers to as the 2/3 point and this is where he starts the thread. Wrap to the back of the hook shank.

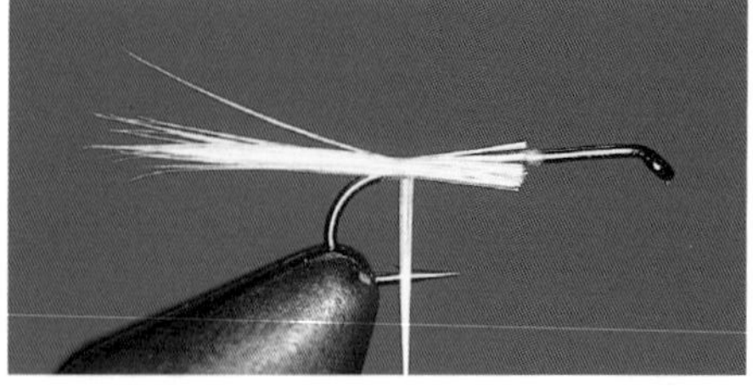

2. Pull several fibers from a spade hackle feather for the tail. Measure tails to a length just slightly longer than the hook shank and trim butt ends so that when tied-in the butts end up at the 2/3 point of the hook. (The starting point.) The number of fibers will vary with the size fly you may be tying. John says it is a visual thing, "Pull some off and tie it in. If it looks good to you, use it. If it doesn't, add or reduce the number of fibers." After you feel comfortable with the amount, remember how much you take from the stem and use that same amount on the next fly. John adds, "A tail that looks a little heavy is better than one that looks too sparse. The balance of the fly will be better with a slightly heavier tail. Eventually it comes down to the way the fly floats on the water. Tie a couple and go fishing. If they float accurately you have done well, if they take a few fish, more the better. There is much more to be said about the functionality of the fly compared to the accuracy of fiber numbers in the tail. "Tie in tail at the back of the hook with **ONE** wrap of thread. **ONE** wrap of thread?" John explains, "I know this isn't the easiest thing in the world to do, but it is imperative to make as few turns of thread at the back of the hook as possible. This reduces the bulk at the back of the fly, especially in hook sizes smaller than an 18. Use a couple of wraps until you get the hang of it. Practice, practice, practice."

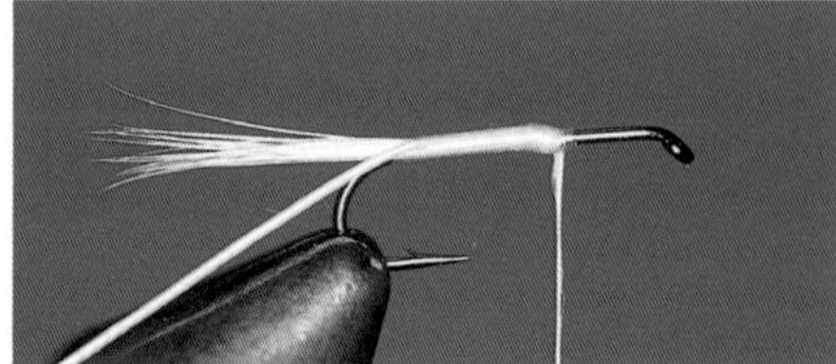

3. Pick a quill and trim about an inch and a half from the tip of the quill(s) or

to a point that removes the thinnest, least durable part of the quill. Quill size or thickness depends on the size fly you are tying. Pick thinner, shorter quills for smaller flies and the longer, thicker quills for larger flies up to a size 14. This can be done easily if you are using the quill dispenser. Tying quill flies up to a size 12 is nearly impossible because quills are just not long enough. If you try to wrap a quill too far into the butt end it will split. Hold the trimmed tip of the quill(s) at a 45 degree angle to the hook shank and tie in the tip of the quill at the back of the hook and wrap forward. A quick twist or thread torque may be needed to set the tails in place. After a couple of tries you will be able to get the quill on the hook and not disturb the tail at all. This step is a great time saver; you really should learn how to do

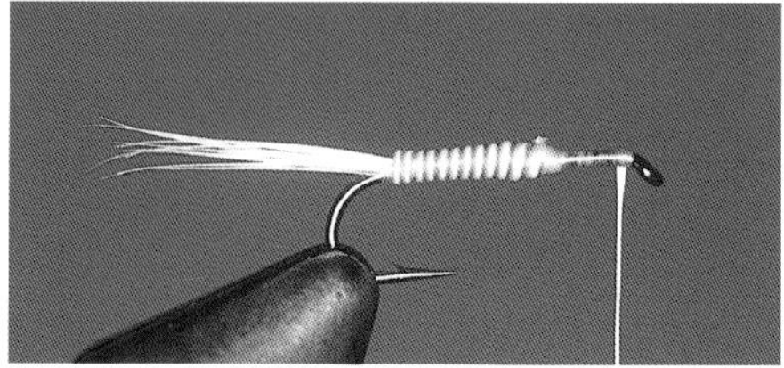

it. Wrap the quill(s) forward to the 2/3 point, where you started the thread at the beginning of the fly. (The abdomen proportion.) Secure in place, trim excess quills, and smooth the tie-down point with enough wraps of thread to cover the trimmed quill ends. Wrap forward to the eye of the hook forming a thread base on which to tie the wings. Then wrap back two wraps back from the eye of the hook. The wings are much easier to tie in if the thread is moving back into the wing than if the thread has been moving forward. This is a very particular thought, but it is one of those techniques that only a person who has tied thousands of flies would notice.

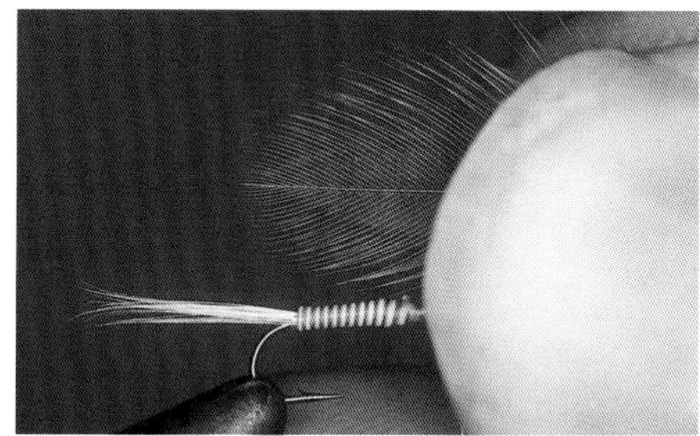

4. The hen tip feathers used for the wings should be much wider than you would think. One and a half times wider than the gape of the hook is a good starting point. When trimmed and tied in place their width is reduced markedly. The reason for this is the way the birds are raised these days. Birds raised for fly-tying feathers are genetically streamlined towards dry-fly hackle. This process eliminates the web from a feather. Hen feathers used to be very soft and webby. The hens these days could pass for dry-fly hackle in some cases. A product available years ago was a hen pullet neck, basically a young farm bird, which was perfect for hen tip wings. They were wide soft, webby feathers. They did have one downside though, they were greasy and dirty. The skins needed to be scraped, degreased, and soaked in whatever soap you could find that would clean them enough to dye to the correct color. Literally, a major pain in the butt. Whether this is good or bad for the fly tier, depending on how you look at it, these feathers are almost impossible to get these days. Sexing these birds has become so good that the growers are killing them within a couple days so they don't waste the grain it takes to feed the extra birds they can't sell. (I hope the PETA people aren't reading this.) With all that said, the webbier the feather, the less wide it needs to be. The spikier, less webby the feather, the wider it must be for it to look like a mayfly wing. The height of the wing is measured from the eye of the hook to the back of the bend, which is a bit higher than most tiers are used to. However, if you look at a mayfly closely, you will see that the wings are wider than you would think and much taller than you had initially realized. Pair the wings with the convex sides of the feathers together. This will form a V shape when separated. With the feathers in your right hand, hold them above the hook with the tips of the feathers even with the bend of the hook and your thumbnail above the eye of the hook. Make adjustments until this measurement is correct. Switch wings to the left hand, not moving their position, and trim the butt ends of the feathers at the eye of the hook. Hold the feathers directly above the hook, tie down the

trimmed ends and wrap back to the point where the quills were secured. To ensure that the stems of the hen tips remain on top of the hook shank, hold them firmly in place with a slight rearward pressure. Do not let go of them until you have wrapped back to the 2/3 point.

5. Pull the wings forward and make a few wraps behind the wings to secure them in the upright position. To separate the wings, simply push down and forward with your thumbnail. They open up and look just like a pair of mayfly wings. "There are several ideas written on setting the hen tip wings but when you look at these wings, they are perfect. How do you improve on perfect?" John says, "No wasted turns of thread, no bulk, just perfect. Stop, stop with perfect, perfect is good!" The point where the wings are located on the hook may now seem to be back farther than most traditionally tied wings, but if you look at mayflies at rest, their wings are back over their body. This location also gives the fly the balance required to ride on the water correctly. And as John says, "Everyone tries to tie everything on the hook too far forward."

6. Choose a properly sized hackle, (the hackle should be prepared ahead of time), trim the fibers at the butt end of the feather, and secure the hackle in front of the wing.

7. Since the hackle is secured in front of the wing, it is inevitable that you make a half turn of hackle in front of the wing. However, the second half of the first turn of hackle should be angling to the back of the wing. As you complete the first full turn, it will lie immediately behind the wing. Make a couple of turns back towards the body, and then start forward, carefully laying these wraps in between the last wraps. This causes the hackle fibers to splay towards the back of the fly, giving the impression of rear legs on the mayfly. Depending on the length of the hackle, make 3-5 wraps behind the wing and cross the hackle forward to in front of the wing. Make sure this turn of hackle lies immediately in front of the wing in the notch where the hackle was originally tied in. Make 5-7 wraps in front. Along with the impression of legs, this crossing hackle action provides a denser thorax area. Secure hackle, trim excess and whip finish.

This makes a beautiful, full-hackle collar that fly tiers dream of. Your dream just became reality.

PMD RS-2

Contributed by Pat Dorsey

I have read or at least looked at just about every fly-tying instruction or pattern book on the market and the RS-2 is not well represented. In fact, I haven't seen it at all and it is one of the most popular and most effective patterns for Colorado tailwaters. Trout living in the South Platte, Blue, Frying Pan, Taylor, and Dolores rivers have all fallen for this simple pattern. It's also been very productive on any freestone river with spring and fall *Baetis* hatches, which means it should work just about anywhere. Ed Engle has mentioned the RS-2 in articles written for major fly-fishing magazines, primarily as a productive fly for western waters where hatches of minute insects take place.

I have fished this pattern for trout all over the country with consistent success. There have been a few patterns similar to the RS-2 that have shown up here and there, but nothing quite as simple and effective as the original.

Pat Dorsey demonstrates in this section that the RS-2 can be tied to imitate just about any emerging mayfly by changing the size of the hook and the color of the materials. This particular pattern, the PMD RS-2, represents the emerging pale morning dun, which is popular throughout the country. His pattern uses slightly different materials than the original tied by Rim Chung. (See RS-2 Emerger by Marty Bartholomew, page 104 for more information on the RS-2 and Rim Chung.) It shows you, once again that patterns can be manipulated to suit your own taste, or better yet, the taste of the trout.

Pat guides clients on a number of the tailwaters and streams local to the Denver area. His knowledge of these streams is immense, including trout location, timing of the annual hatches, and the patterns these trout tend to fall for.

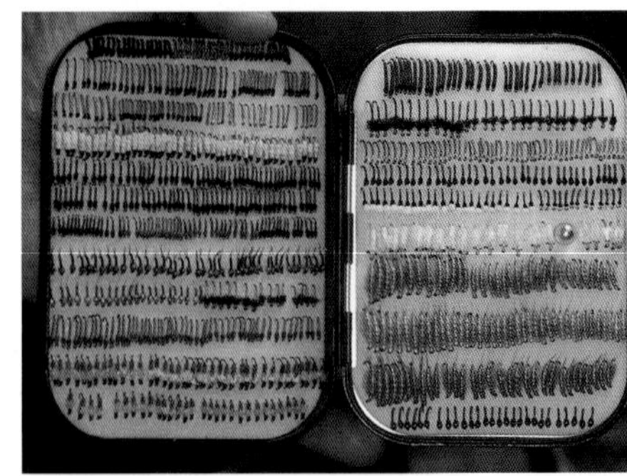

His fly boxes are loaded with tiny patterns he uses on these streams and just about every other row is some type of RS-2. "My clients bring a lot of trout to net using this fly, so I maintain an ample supply of them."

The RS-2 is a very simple fly to put together and I recommend that you tie a few for yourself. Take them to your local water and see for yourself how productive this pattern can be.

PMD RS-2

Hook: Dry fly ring-eye size 16-20, Daiichi 1110 Tiemco 101
Thread: Light Cahill 8/0 UNI-Thread
Tail: Brown hackle fibers
Body: Fine & Dry dubbing, Pale Morning Dun (Spirit River)
Wing: Brown Z-lon
Thorax: Fine & Dry dubbing, pale morning dun (same as body)

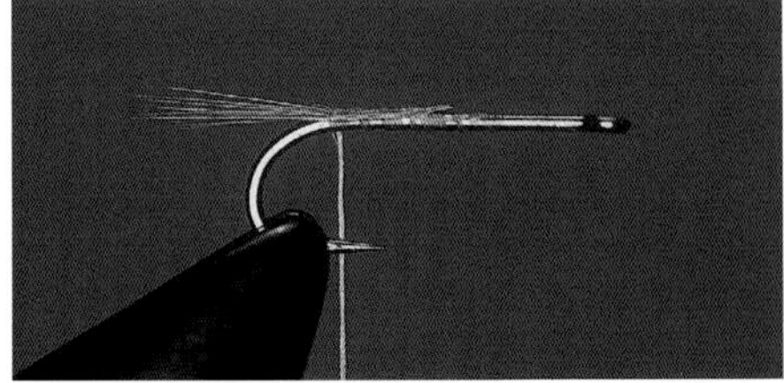

1. Start thread at the 1/2 point and wrap back to the bend laying down a thread base. Select a brown spade hackle with stiff barbules. Pull about 8-10 fibers

from the stem, measure tail to 1/2 hook shank length, and tie in the clump of hackle fibers for the tail.

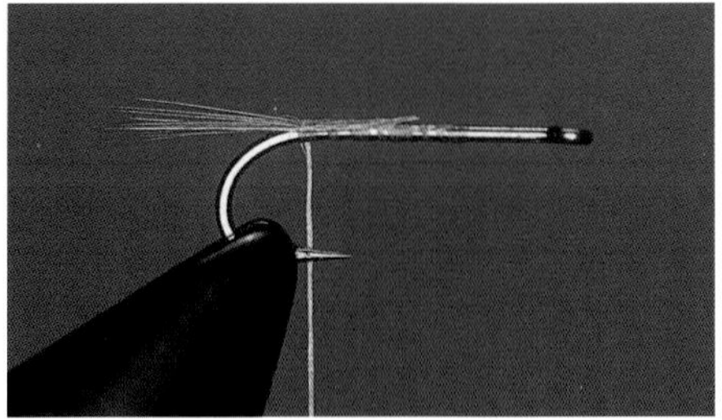

2. Dub a very thin noodle of Fine & Dry for the body. This is a very fine denier dubbing and can be applied so as to just change the size of the thread. Pat suggests, "Start the dubbing noodle very thin and gradually make it thicker. This produces a tapered noodle that, when wrapped into place, will create the natural taper of a real insect." Wrap the dubbing forward to the 3/4 point of the hook. Wrap thread forward to just behind the eye.

3. Trim the end of a clump of Z-lon square and tie it in right behind the eye and wrap back to the front of the body. Dub a very thin noodle of Fine & Dry and cover the butt ends of the wing forming the thorax. Whip finish and clip the Z-lon emerging wing to a length just above the point of the hook.

Here are a couple of variations of Pat's most productive RS-2s. First, a *Baetis* RS-2 is usually tied in a size 18 and smaller. Another good one is a

standard gray RS-2 with a glass-bead head. Pat was the first tier to put the bead-head version of the RS-2 together. How do we know this? He was working with Spirit River Inc. on a few projects and was given samples of the first glass beads that were introduced. His creativity and expertise put them to good use right away.

Quigley Cripple (*Callibaetis*)

Contributed by Richard Pilatzke

In this age of genetic engineering, it is possible, perhaps even probable, that some fly-fishing scientist will create the perfect mayfly. The perfect mayfly would be big enough to easily thread tippet through the eye of its imitation but not so big as to be difficult to cast. It would be a prolific insect that hatches not once but many times in a season, and the emergence would be in the pleasant middle hours of the day. Most important, the perfect mayfly would be graceful and pleasing to the eye of both the angler and trout. He would invent the Callibaetis.

—*Ralph Cutter*

Throughout the Western United States, Colorado in particular, the annual hatch of *Callibaetis* is eagerly anticipated. The emergence generally starts anywhere from late May to early June and continues until August as a fishable hatch. The hatch provides an early feast for lake-dwelling trout as they gorge themselves on all stages of this mayfly's life cycle. This prolific lake mayfly has been observed on the water as late as October, but these moments are usually very rare and you will only see a few bugs.

The *Callibaetis* nymph is a very good swimmer, but it spends most of its immature life clinging to the succulent cover of weed beds. Nymph fishing can be productive in the early part of hatching activity.

The process of hatching is quite disturbing for the *Callibaetis* nymph. As the nymph gets ready to emerge, the nymphal shuck fills with carbon dioxide. This starts both the separation of the shuck from the mayfly trapped inside and aids the nymph's ascension to the surface. As the carbon dioxide is produced, the nymph becomes buoyant and is lifted away from the cover of the weeds or its lakebed structure. The nymph struggles to swim back into the cover. Soon the buoyancy of the gas is too much and the nymph is lifted away from the cover. The continuing struggle of the nymphs in and out of the weed beds can really get the trout going. On some mornings, trout will see thousands of *Callibaetis* nymphs bobbing up and down, teasing them into a feeding frenzy. I have found a size 14 ginger-colored Hare's Ear Nymph to be especially effective under these conditions. A good set-up is a floating line with a long leader and a split shot close to the fly to aid in the jigging action.

Eventually the buoyancy becomes too much and the nymphs are lifted for a final ride toward the surface. When they reach the underside of the surface film, the nymphs rest briefly before the exoskeleton splits between the wingpads. The winged but sexually immature dun pokes its head through the split, and the gas pressure squirts it forward until the legs and wings are free. At this point it rests again, half in and half out of the nymphal shuck until its limbs harden to the point where it can pull itself free and fly away.

At this point the mayfly is literally helpless and the trout have figured this out. The trout can lose all control and feed voraciously on this plentiful meal. This is by far the best time to be fishing a *Callibaetis* hatch. And Bob Quigley's *Callibaetis* Cripple is one of the best fly patterns to use during the emergence.

Spectacular hatches of this mayfly occur on rich alkaline lakes with thick weed beds. Lakes in Colorado include those in South Park, such as Antero Reservoir. Delaney Butte Lakes in North Park are very good and have some enormous trout that feed on *Callibaetis*. Trappers Lake is a beautiful piece of water on the edge of the Flat Tops Wilderness Area that is loaded with Colorado River cutthroats. Henry's Lake in Idaho, Hebgen Lake in Montana, Crane Prairie and Hosmer Lakes in Oregon and Chopaka Lake in Washington are just a few of the many productive lakes across the western United States where fly anglers enjoy *Callibaetis* hatches.

Richard Pilatzke spends 95% of his angling time on still waters and has been chasing *Callibaetis* hatches for a number of years now. Richard exclaims, "As a new member at Arrowhead Ranch, one of my initial goals for the year was to learn all I could about the *Callibaetis* hatches. I knew from talking to other anglers there that all four of the lakes on the ranch had excellent *Callibaetis* hatches.

"I was almost beside myself as I looked for a target to toss my fly toward. I was sitting in my kickboat on East Lake at Arrowhead Ranch and I was completely surrounded by trout rising to *Callibaetis* duns and emergers," Rich conveys. "The water was literally boiling. At any one time I probably had 25 or more rises I could cover from my boat. This activity continued, from 10:00AM to 1:00PM, which was absolutely the most beautiful part of the day. With variations in intensity, the trout worked the mayfly hatch for the best part of these three hours. I had heard about hatches like this, but this was the first time I had actually experienced one firsthand.

"I was fishing with Matt Miles, a guide for Blue Quill Angler and an old friend of mine. We were field-testing the Quigley Cripple pattern, meant to imitate a crippled *Callibaetis* dun," Richard adds. "We were able to hook and land somewhere over 40 trout during those memorable hours. Needless to say, I would have to classify the test as a resounding success!"

Richard knew from some basic research that the mayfly duns were about a size 14 at the beginning of the hatch and decreased in size as the season progressed. "The standard pattern for the hatch was a Parachute Adams, but from my observations of the mayflies in the field, I felt that the body color of the Adams was too dark. The duns are a very light gray on the underside and that was the color the trout would see from underneath. There are many other fly patterns to imitate *Callibaetis* duns and emergers; however, year in, year out, the Quigley Cripple is by far the most productive."

A fly angler really has a choice of strategies during the emergence: You can dangle nymphs around the weed beds or fish adult imitations such as a Parachute or standard Adams and Comparaduns. Patterns such as the Quigley Cripple, a crippled mayfly pattern, can be especially effective during the peak of an emergence. Bob Quigley developed the Quigley Cripple for the Hat Creek area in California to imitate PMD (pale morning dun) mayflies. The Quigley can be tied to imitate any mayfly. Standard patterns for the green drake, PMD, and *Callibaetis* are in the fly archive on the www.flyshop.com posted by Bob Quigley.

During the hatch a fly angler may also fish emergers such as a gray RS-2 in a size 14. I have carried this pattern in my fly box for several years and have caught fish on it as a subsurface pattern or dressed with floatant and fished in the film. You can also fish a nymphal imitation just above the weed beds during the hatch. This is not as much fun as dry flies, but can put a serious bend in your rod. Rich says, "I favor a pattern that is essentially a Gold Ribbed Hare's Ear tied mayfly-style (thin body like a mayfly nymph) with light hare's ear dubbing for the abdomen and a green wingcase over the thorax. I use a parrot feather. Any lake that has a good population of *Callibaetis* will have nymph activity all year long, so the nymph pattern in a size 16-14 is a good subsurface pattern any time on these waters."

Richard had carried Quigley Cripples in his fly box for over three years and never used them. They were just filed away for use at a later date. In the three years, he had used them only briefly and with limited success. "My original Quigleys were tied from the pattern in Jack Dennis's book *Tying With Friends*. There are a number of different versions of the Quigley around and I don't think I have seen the same pattern twice. They generally have a tail made with moose body hair or a shuck made with Antron, macramé yarn or ostrich herl. A light gray body may be ribbed with wire. Some use spun gray deer in the center of the fly or gray foam and they all have a deer-hair wing tied at a 45-degree angle over the hook eye and a few wraps of grizzly hackle."

After looking at and testing several of the patterns out there, Richard started customizing the fly to his own specifications: "I fished those early Quigley versions at Arrowhead and had some nice reactions from the fish, but I wasn't quite satisfied. I continued experimenting with the pattern until I came up with the version that Matt and I fished at Arrowhead."

The Quigley Cripple pattern Richard is using now, described in the following recipe, has a sparse tail of gray macramé yarn, the body is made with gray ostrich herl, the wing is deer hair dyed light blue dun, and two wraps of grizzly hackle for legs. Rich touts, "I have personally caught over 100 trout at Arrowhead in the month of June alone with the Quigley, so it appears to be working quite well. Other fly-fishers that I have shared the pattern with have done equally as well. Adding a slight twitch to the fly after it lands on the water seems to trigger strikes. This seems to get the fish's attention when they are cruising just under the surface of the lake. It has worked reasonably well in perfectly still water, so I am satisfied that it is an accurate representation to the fish."

Fly-fishers need to be willing to experiment with new patterns and tinker with existing patterns to optimize their fly-fishing experience.

Quigley Cripple (*Callibaetis*)

Hook: Dry fly, Tiemco 100, size 14
Thread: 6/0 UNI-Thread, gray

Mayflies

Tail: Macrame yarn, gray
Body: Ostrich herl, gray
Wing: Deer hair, dyed blue dun
Hackle: Grizzly, dry-fly quality (Whiting Farms saddle)

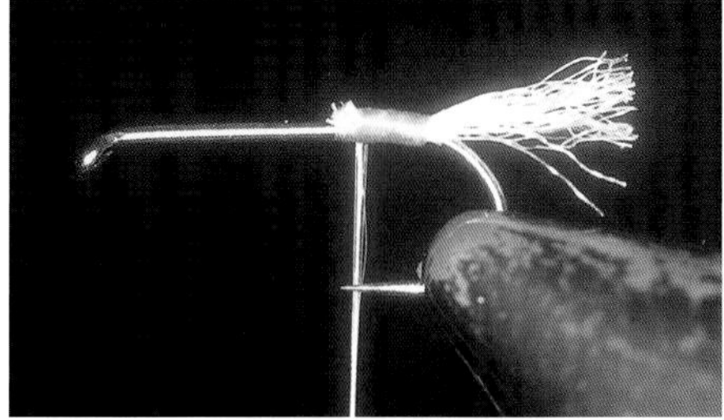

1. Start thread at the 1/4 point. Tie in a length of gray macramé yarn, about 20 fibers or so, and wrap thread to the back. Move thread forward to the 1/4 point again.

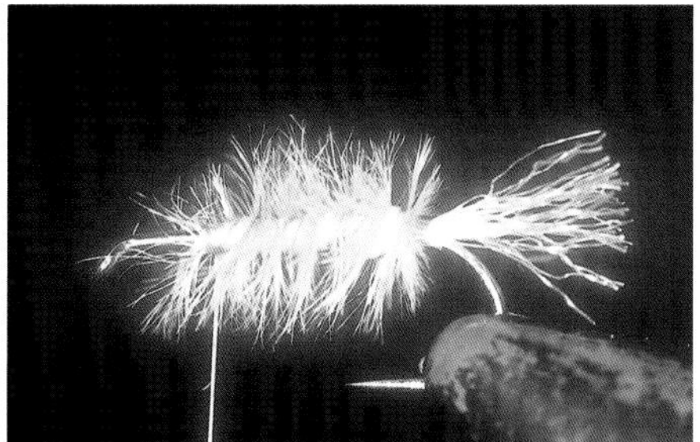

2. Tie in three ostrich herl fibers for the body and move thread forward to the 3/4 point. Wrap herl forward to the 3/4 point and secure.

3. Stack a clump of deer hair about the size of a wooden match. Measure the hair to a full hook shank length, and with the tips over the eye of the hook secure the hair on top of the hook shank. Trim the butt ends of the hair short, but do not attempt to cover the butt ends with thread. Just leave them.

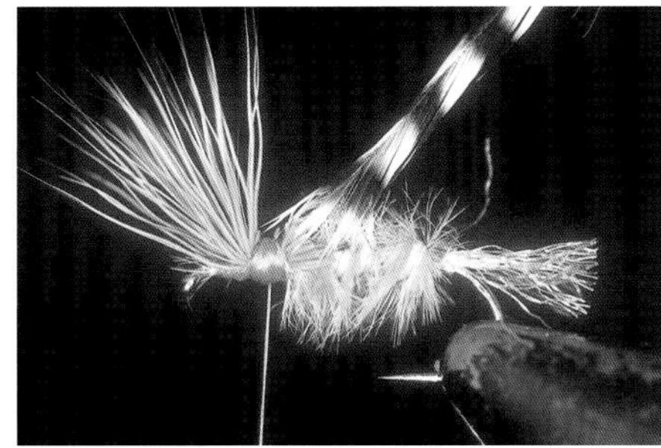

4. Tie in a grizzly hackle by the tip, shiny side up, at the wing tie-in point. Make two turns of hackle behind the wing and secure.

5. Lift up the wing and make several turns of thread in front of the wing to stand it up slightly. It should angle upwards no more than 45 degrees over the eye. Hold wing up and whip finish. Here is the finished fly.

9. The Quigley can be tied to imitate several struggling mayflies like the PMD and western green drake shown here.

Randy's *Baetis* Nymph

Contributed by Randy Smith

Over the years, I have had the opportunity to name a couple flies, but I wouldn't consider myself a real creative tier. I tweak a pattern here or there to make it look or fish the way I want it to, but what I find most interesting about new fly patterns is how they were developed. What is the thought process a tier uses to create a new pattern? What is their trial-and-error process all about? How do they pick materials?

Randy Smith, on the other hand, is the creative type and is very meticulous about detail. When I talked with Randy about his *Baetis* Nymph he was able to share a short story about the creation of this fly. It might just give you some ideas to create that special pattern of your own.

"The insects intrigued me when I first started fly-fishing and one of the first bugs I ran into was the blue-winged olives in Cheesman Canyon on the South Platte River just outside of Denver," Randy explains. "Everyone told me that if you fly-fish Colorado, you need to know how to fish the blue-wings. The other thing I found out was our hatches are not like clockwork. They are much less predictable than in the eastern part of the United States so we have to spend some time nymph fishing as we wait for the bugs to come off."

While in the canyon he concentrated on gathering some of the nymphs for closer inspection. What he found was an outstanding feature of the nymph that he hadn't noticed before, a very dark, almost black wingcase. Randy adds, "After a bit of research I found that this is the stage in a nymph's lifecycle where it develops pubic hair. In other words it is a point in time just before they hatch so this is when the nymphs must be most active and available to the trout."

Randy had an idea of what his fly would look like. His first flies looked just like the pattern here but the wingcase was made out of sections of a dark wing quill of a Canada goose. The problem was durability. The wingcase would just fall apart. "It did catch fish but as a commercial tier it would be hard to sell. As you know, we have to sell it to the fisherman before a trout ever gets a look at it!" Randy said, "Then a friend of mine, Dave Lawson of Evergreen, Colorado, turned me onto Tyvek paper. It was just what I needed. It was durable, easy to prepare and easy to get. It is the paper a Fed-Ex envelope is made of. Tyvek paper is a very good material for a wingcase because it conforms around the thorax area and it looks very realistic."

It did catch fish again and it did sell. Then the old, "got to sell it to the fisherman before you sell it to a trout" kicked in. Shop owners wanted such and such a color, so Randy tweaked the color. What we go through to make a buck!

To this day it is one of the best-selling and most effective *Baetis* nymphs available in the Denver area. I think it will work on your stream also. Randy adds, "The type of water where you fish this nymph is very important. I suggest trying the area right below a riffle, just as it gains a little depth as the top of the water smoothes. Drift it along the bottom with split shot, fish it under the surface as an emerger, or even try imitating the rise from the bottom. The *Baetis* actually live in the well-oxygenated riffle and as they start to get active and hatch, the water directly below the riffle becomes a very good feeding area."

Before starting to tie the fly, prepare the Tyvek paper by thoroughly saturating both sides of it with a black permanent marker. Then cut the Tyvek into strips for the size of fly you may be tying. For example, a size 18 nymph would use a 3/32-inch-wide strip. A little wider for bigger flies and thinner for smaller flies. Put the strips into bags and mark them according to fly size. Store them for the next time you tie. Remember, Tyvek paper has many uses and can be colored any color with a permanent marker.

Prepare several mallard flank feathers by stripping off the fluff and unusable fibers from the lower or butt end of the feather. What is unusable? Fibers

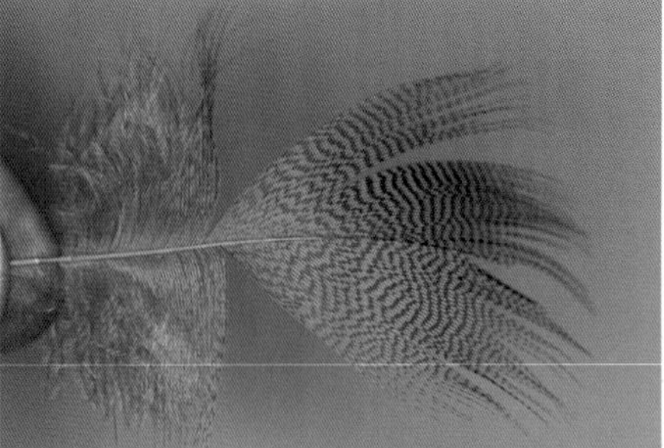

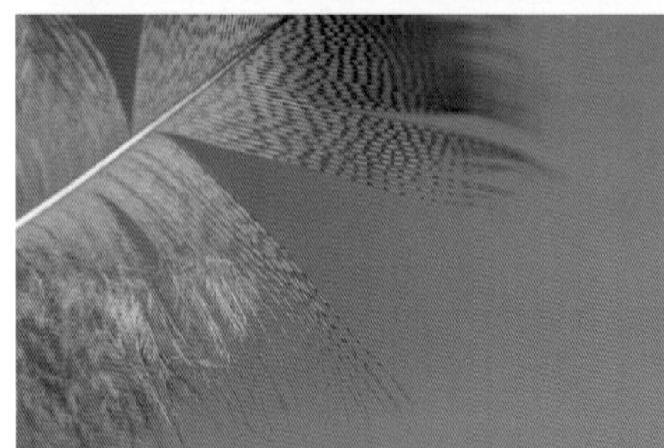

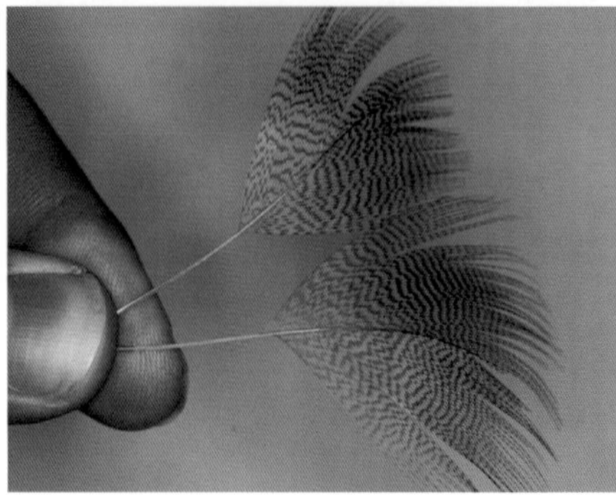

that are thin and do not have a good texture or fibers that do not have a defined barred look are not desirable. Notice the separation in the second photo. The thinness and lack of good markings on the lower part of the feather are not desirable so just pull those fibers off. The length of the fibers should also be a consideration since the mallard fibers are being used for the tails and legs with the same section. When in doubt, always go for the longer, better-looking fibers. Nothing makes tying flies more frustrating than using inferior materials.

Randy suggests having a wet sponge or small towel on your tying desk when you plan on dubbing a batch of flies. This helps remove oils you might pick up from touching your face or hair. When your fingers get slick, dubbing the nice tight, thin noodle that is required for this fly becomes more difficult, and dubbing wax will not adhere to your fingers as well.

Randy's *Baetis* Nymph

Hook: Dry, size16-24, Dai Riki 310 (ring eye)
Thread: 8/0 camel
Tail: Mallard flank (dyed as close to the same olive as the body dubbing color)
Body: Rabbit fur, 60% medium olive and 40% rusty brown
Thorax: Rabbit fur (same as body)
Legs: Mallard flank (same as tail)
Wingcase: Tyvek paper colored black with permanent marker

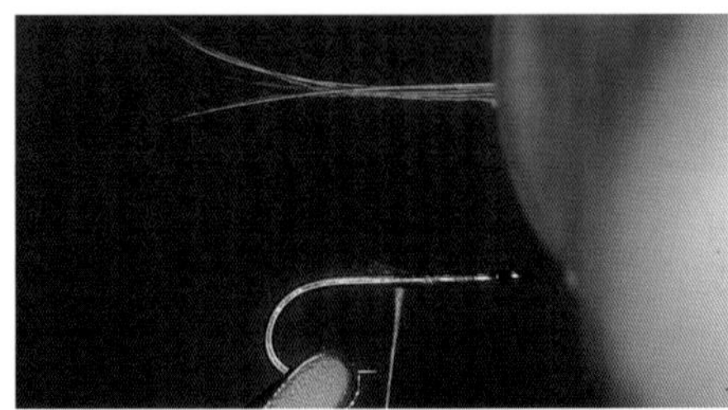

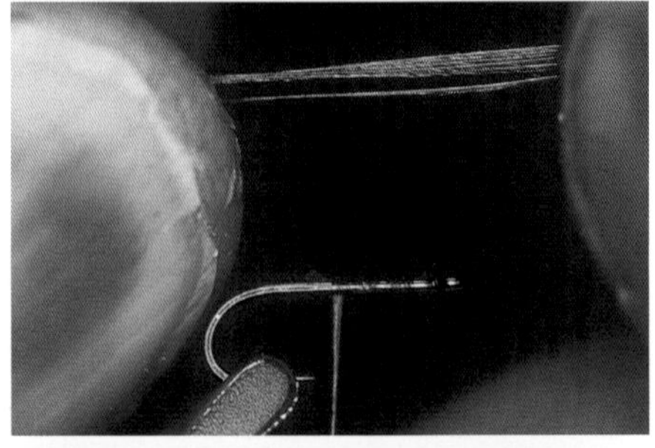

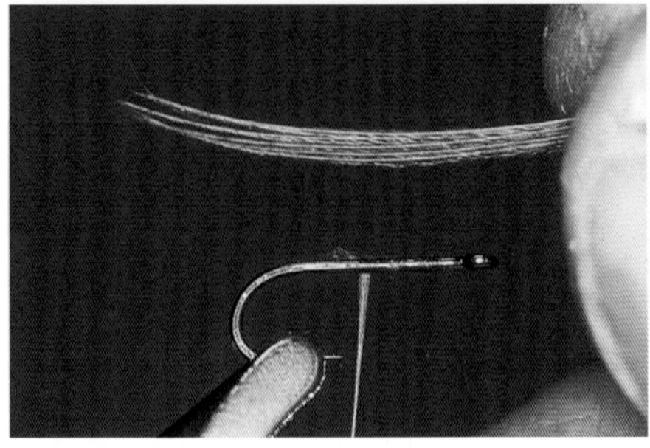

1. Start thread behind the eye leaving a small amount of bare hook behind the eye and wrap to the back of the hook. Pull six fibers from the mallard flank feather. If the tips of the fibers seem

Mayflies

too thin but the rest of the feather has good texture and coloration, the tips can be broken off. Do this by severing a small section of the tips off between your thumbnail and your index finger. This leaves a more natural-looking tip than cutting them with scissors.

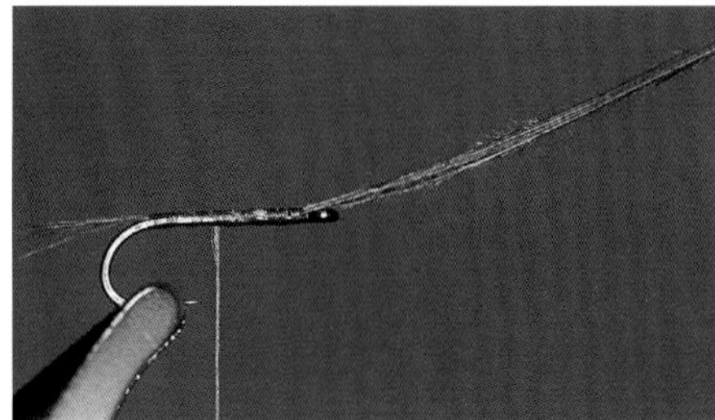

2. With the tips of the mallard flank fibers used for the tail, gauge the tail length to about half the hook shank length and tie the tail in at that point. Move the thread forward, lashing down the fibers as you wrap to just behind the eye of the hook. **DO NOT** trim the butt ends of the mallard fibers. They will be used as the legs in a future step.

3. Apply dubbing to the thread in two sections. Dub a noodle about an inch or so long (depending on the size of fly you are tying) with a slight taper to it. This noodle will be used for the body. Leave about 1/2 inch of bare thread and dub another thin noodle about 1/4 inch long. This noodle will be used for the thorax. The longer, tapered noodle helps set-up and define the overall tapered appearance of the natural insect. Applying the body dubbing and thorax dubbing at the same time eliminates the need to pick up the dubbing twice, basically doing two steps in one, which in turn will speed up your tying. One of those "pro tips" you have been waiting for all your life!

4. Wrap dubbing forward to about the 3/4 point of the hook. Notice the nicely tapered body. NOTE: If you run out of dubbing before achieving this look, add

more dubbing. If you end up with too much, it's not as easy to pull the dubbing off, so play it to the short side and add. Randy says too much dubbing, either too thick or too long, is one of the most common mistakes fly tiers make, so pay close attention to how much you are applying. After a couple of flies you will know exactly how much dubbing to put on in the first place without having to add or subtract material. This will speed up the process! As you wrap the body dubbing forward with your right hand (for right-handed tiers), pick up a strip of Tyvek in your left hand.

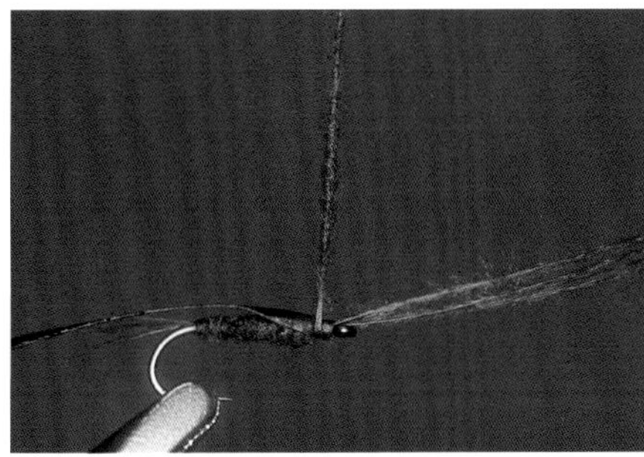

5. Just as you complete dubbing the body, use the short section of bare thread to immediately tie in the tip of the Tyvek strip with just two wraps of thread. With a little practice this can be done without stopping the motion of the bobbin. The wingcase should be just in front of the body and directly on top of the hook.

6. Separate the legs evenly, pull half the fibers down the backside of the hook. Make a half wrap of thread to secure them. Pull the other half of the fibers down the fore side of the hook. With the same wrap of thread used to tie down the legs on the backside, secure the legs on the fore side. Laying them down with the left thumb is a good way to accomplish this. Now the next noodle of

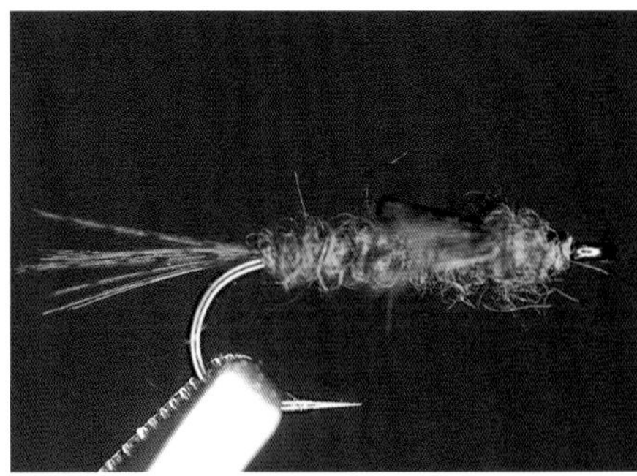

dubbing shows up and will cover all the thread wraps and form the thorax region. At this point Randy suggests untwisting the thread. Simply rotating the bobbin counterclockwise as it hangs below the hook can do this. This helps prevent thread breakage, especially with 8/0, and makes for a nice, smooth clean head. Whip finish the fly. Now pull the legs under the fly and trap both sets against the sides of the vise. Bring the scissors points even with the point of the hook and trim both sets of legs to length at the same time. Trim wingcase to length and Randy's *Baetis* Nymph is done.

Randy's ZDZ Blue-Winged Olive

Contributed by Randy Smith

When Randy originally set out designing this pattern, he wanted a *Baetis* dry fly pattern that was durable and floated well. (Don't we all!!) The fly needed a slender profile and one that sat flush on the water, very much like the natural when it is hatching.

The configuration of this pattern was a brainchild of the many dry flies out there using Z-lon. Most of these patterns were totally dependant on floatant, but did work well. CDC is also a very popular material for dry fly wings so why not mix them. CDC is not dependant on floatant, but loses its shape easily. The original prototypes worked but Randy did notice one more interesting factor. "Another thing I found in general was the wing color ended up much lighter than that of the naturals and takes were inconsistent. I went back and used a darker CDC with the Z-lon and it matched much better." Randy adds, "The shade of natural, unbleached and undyed, CDC was perfect."

When the *Baetis* were thick on the water, the wing color on the newly developed flies matched the naturals so well that the fly was much harder to see, but the takes increased dramatically.

The two winging materials benefited each other very well. The Z-lon helped the CDC hold it shape and last longer, while the CDC made for better floatation and enhanced the wing color for a more natural look.

Randy tied the original patterns on a ring-eye dry fly hook which allowed the fly to sit flush on the water. It worked well, but the new curved emerger style hooks he uses now give it a much wider gape and in turn more hooking power.

Finally, the foam thorax gave the fly better buoyancy and for those who are "dubbing challenged" made it easier to tie a good thorax profile.

The fly pattern is easy to tie and this configuration can be adapted to many other species of mayflies. This pattern portrays the standard Blue-Winged Olives we are so used to seeing in the spring and fall, but can be changed to a blue dun with a new thread color and Pantone marker. I can't wait to try a #18 PMD next June!

Randy's ZDZ Blue-Winged Olive

Hook: Dry size 16-24, Dai Riki 125 or Tiemco 2488
Thread: 6/0 Danville, Olive
Tail: Micro Fibetts, White
Body: 6/0 Danville, Olive
Wing: 60% natural CDC (Two feathers) 40% Kinky Z-lon
Thorax: Evasote foam, cut in strips and colored with a Pantone marker.

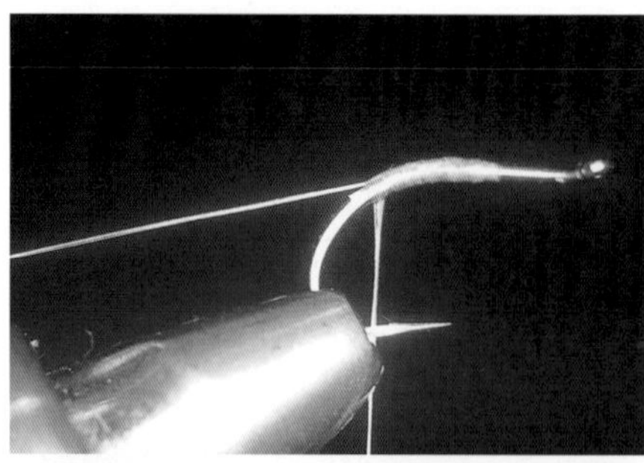

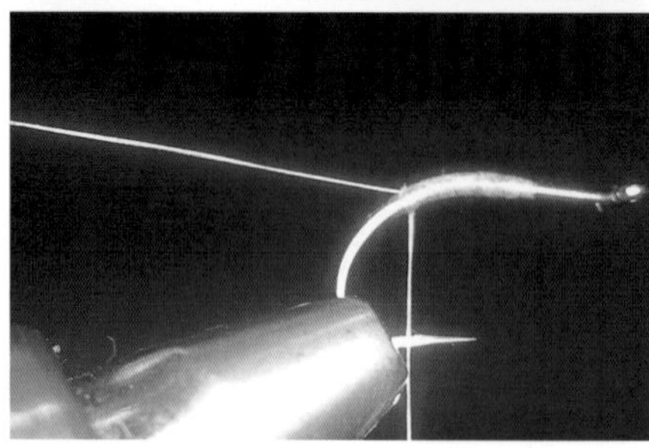

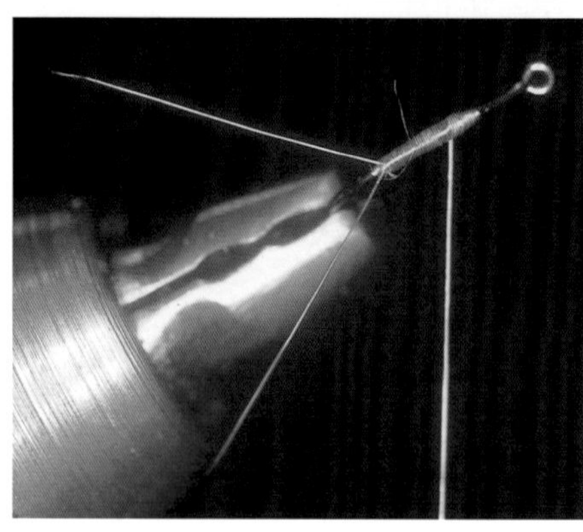

1. Start thread at the 2/3 point of the hook and tie in two Micro Fibetts. Wrap to the back of the hook keeping theFibetts on top of the shank. To set the tails, make two horizontal wraps of thread under the tail fibers to cant them upwards slightly. Then split the tails by making a wrap under the fore tail (in between the tail fiber and hook shank) and over the hook. Lock it with one wrap around the hook shank. Using light thread pressure, make a wrap over the top in between the tail fiber on the far side of the hook and the hook shank. Make one more locking wrap. As you move the thread forward, form a thread body. **DO NOT** make it too thick nor longer than the 2/3 point of the shank.

2. Lay two natural CDC feathers, tips opposite each other, on top of 15-20 strands of Kinky Z-lon.

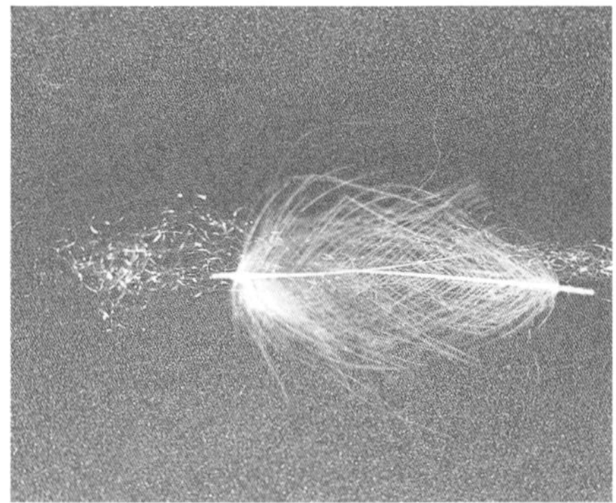

3. Clump the combination of materials together and tie in perpendicularly at the 3/4 point of the shank using one simple x-ing wrap. Gather up both sides of the winging material, holding it above the hook shank. Make one horizontal wrap around the wing base. To

finish the wing, pull up on the wing material and down on the thread at the same time. Make a locking wrap in front of the wing. Before letting go of the wing, trim it at an angle to desired height with the front of the wing being higher than the back much like a natural mayfly wing. Randy suggests that his field research indicates the fly works slightly better if the wing is shorter than a normal wing.

3. Prepare the foam for the thorax by cutting it into narrow strips and running a Pantone marker over it for the desired color. Trim it to a point at one end and attach it in front of the wing. Make a wrap with the foam in front of the wing, then behind the wing. Bringing the foam under the fly and forward to secure in front of the wing. Whip finish.

NOTE: The thickness and size of the thorax is reliant on how much you stretch the foam as you wrap it. Stretch it tighter as you wrap it for smaller flies and looser for larger flies. If stretching the foam causes the color to change too much, you can touch it up with the marker.

Rivergod Spinner

Contributed by Dennis Potter

While discussing the flies he wanted to contribute to this book with Dennis Potter, I was drawn to this pattern for several reasons. The unique method for attaching the highly visible parachute post, the trimmed parachute hackle for the actual spinner wing, and his thoughts on a thread body were a few things I thought the up-and-coming tiers of the world would want to know about.

All of Dennis's spinner patterns, from a size 14 and smaller, have thread bodies. All parachutes from size 16 down and all emergers from size 16 down have thread bodies. After several field tests, fishing the thread-body fly a few inches from the dubbed version, he found 8 out of 10 trout took a thread-bodied fly over a thinly dubbed body. Hendrickson and Sulphur hatches were the testing arenas, 7X tippet was the standard, and the browns and brook trout from the Au Sable River were the subjects. They proved to be honorable combatants and very selective to the question at hand.

"I have had anglers on the river tell me they have the right fly for the hatch, but excuse their lack of success to the tail being too long, tail is too short, hackle is too big, or wings are too long on their pattern. In reality, the body on the fly looks like it has a goiter stuck to it. It is just way out of proportion on the fat side." Dennis recalls, "I feel it is terribly, terribly important, so I do thin thread bodies whenever possible!"

The thread body is much more durable than a quill body, and the thread does accept floatants. With the vast variety of thread colors out there, the body of any fly can accommodate any "match the hatch" situation. With the addition of a contrasting-colored thread, segmentation can be added to the body easily.

The fluorescent yellow wing post is a great addition to the late-afternoon and early-evening spinner patterns, providing added visibility. Tests have also proven fluorescent yellow is much easier to see late in the day than a white wing. The same tests have shown that fluorescent hot pink is the easiest color to see during the middle of the day.

The wingpost positioning and tie-in procedure reduces bulk on the fly, which is otherwise substantial when using standard calf body hair or even turkey flats. Pay close attention to the details on this technique when tying this pattern.

I have seen several spinner wings using hackle, but never from a para-wrapped position. A hackle wrapped in the standard fashion can be separated with thread wraps; however, the ones I have seen don't look quite right to me. A standard collar hackle can be trimmed, bottom and top, to make a pretty respectable looking spinner wing. However, the fly still looks bushy on the water. I think a good spinner should be hard to see because the real ones are hard to see.

So the Rivergod Spinner gives us the best of both worlds: a fly that has a flat wing riding low in the water film and a highly visible wing post for those of us with failing eyesight. I think it is an outstanding, well-thought-out creation. My hat's off to you, Mr. Rivergod!

("Rivergod" is a Registered Trademark of Riverhouse Fly Company.)

Rivergod Spinner

Hook: Dry fly, size 14 Tiemco 100
Thread: Brown 12/0, Benichie
Wing: Hi-Vis Winging Material, fluorescent yellow
Egg Sack: Yellow dubbing
Tail: Micro Fibetts, dun
Body: Thread
Thorax: Rusty brown dubbing
Hackle: Grizzly

1. Start thread at the 7/8 point of the hook shank and wrap back to the 3/4 point. Move thread forward to the 7/8 point again. Secure a length of yellow Hi-Vis Winging Material midway to its length. Make a couple of simple X-ing wraps with the thread to make what

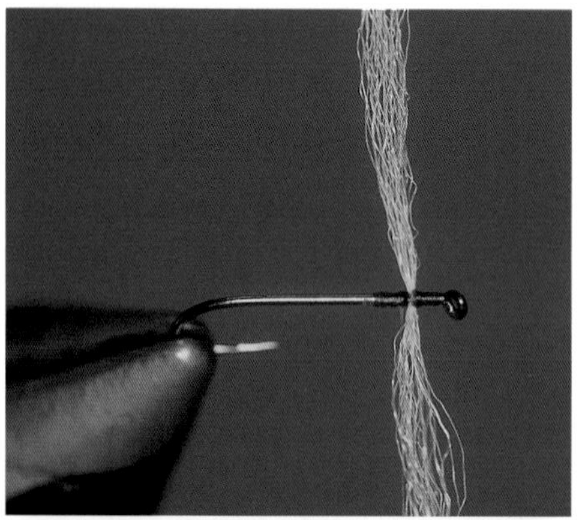

looks like a spinner wing. Fold both parts of the wing straight up and make three or four very tight wraps of thread to initially stand the wing up. Then take several turns of thread up the material, forming the parachute post and a smooth thread base for a hackle to wrap around. You need to wrap a lot of hackle on this post, so make sure the thread base on the post is a good portion.

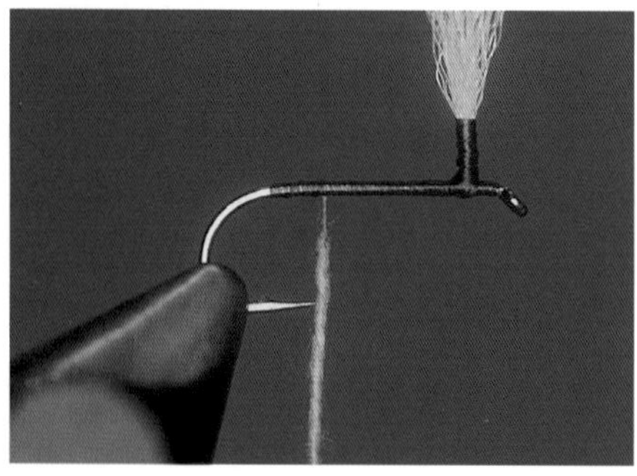

2. Apply a thin dubbing noodle to the thread. Apply a downward press with

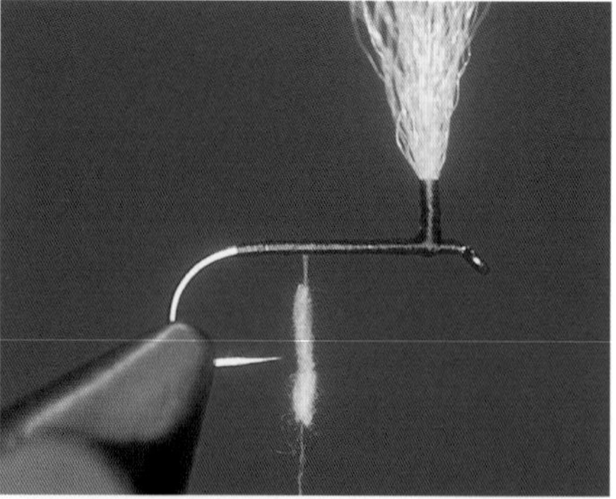

the finger and an upward press with the thumb as you twist the dubbing. This in effect will push the dubbing together into a thicker noodle, reducing the number of turns around the hook needed to get the egg sack in place. Wrap the dubbing around the hook, forming a ball at the back of the hook for an egg sack and to split the tails against. Move thread to the 1/4 point.

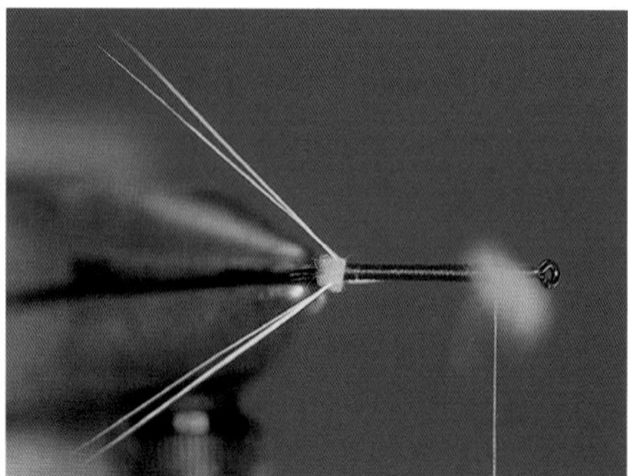

3. Measure 6 micro fibbetts to a full hook shank length. Tie them in on top of the hook, separate the Fibetts and secure an equal number of them on each side as you wrap back. Split the tails against the dubbing ball.

4. Wrap forward making a smooth thread body. Dub a small amount of brown dubbing in front of and behind the wing post to create the thorax of the fly. This is a very important proportion for a spinner. A spinner has such an emaciated appearance, the thorax stands out as

a substantial portion of the actual insect. Measure and prepare two grizzly saddle hackles. Whiting Farms saddle hackle has such a high barbule count, it is really the only hackle to use for this application. Secure the hackles in front of the wing post, convex side up, on the fore side of the hook shank.

5. With one quick clockwise turn, wrap the hackle up to the top of the threaded part of the post. Then wrap back down the post, one turn directly under the last. Secure hackle on top of the hook shank and trim excess. Whip finish. Looking at the hackle from the top, trim away small amounts of the hackle fibers in front of and behind the wing post. Do not get carried away trimming the hackle. Take little cuts of hackle at a time; it is very difficult to glue them back in place! This will give the parachute hackle the look of a spinner wing. The grizzly hackle adds nicely to the look of a spinner wing giving it the broken, venation look. The yellow post can be trimmed to any height since it is there only to hold the hackle and to serve as a visual indicator.

RS-2 Emerger

The RS-2 (Rim Semblance 2) was invented by Rim Chung to imitate the *Baetis* mayflies on the South Platte River. Rim questioned the need for so many similar patterns as he browsed through the fly bins at the local fly shops. There are a number of patterns between size 18 and size 24 that are so much alike that you would need a masters degree in "Fly Tying Manuals" to know all their names. He had a notion that he could simplify this enigma. Basically all he wanted to do was make an improvement on these basic patterns available at the time.

What he had created turned out to be one of the top producers on the Platte year after year. To this day, twenty-five years later, it is still considered the most effective fly pattern when you head to the South Platte River.

Rim says, "I feel the addition of the emerging wing is the key. Selective fish, whether it be on the South Platte or the Bighorn River in Montana, like to key in on the activity of the emerging insects." However, Rim says not to limit the time you fish the RS-2 to the emerging stage of the hatch. "Fish it all the time!" It is the ONLY fly he fishes. "The color and size combinations are unlimited so there is no reason it can't imitate small caddis, stoneflies or midges."

I agree, but it is not the only fly I fish. Early and late in the season, when *Baetis* activity is expected, I like to start out fishing it deep with a Pheasant Tail Nymph or an Olive Biot Nymph. When trout start to rise, I take the split shot off, fluff up the CDC wing, and fish it in the surface with the nymph close behind.

My version of the RS-2 is modified slightly from the original. The original is tied with Micro Fibetts for the tail, the body is beaver dubbing that has the longest fibers available, and the wing is the fluff from the bottom of a hackle. (Review the section on dubbing and find out how great minds work. It was very interesting to me as I talked with Rim that he is so adamant about long fibers in his dubbing.) I use moose body for tailing, muskrat or synthetic dubbing, and CDC for the emerging wing. I like the floating qualities and the visibility of CDC so I can fish it as a dry. The choice is yours as far as materials go. Use what you are comfortable with.

Rim also has a very interesting system he uses to fish the RS-2. He is an advocate of a very light fly line. He uses a level running line only .027 thick with a 10' to 11' leader tapered to 7X. He takes a normal 10' 6X leader and cuts the butt section off down to about .017 then adds back 6X and 7X tippet to achieve the overall length. He adds, "The thinner the system, the less drag that can be induced during the drift." You can find out more about Rim Chung and the RS-2 at http://home.att.net/~ferenc.

The RS-2 is a very easy fly to tie, something all pro tiers look for when they take on work. I was very fortunate to have it as one of my major production flies. I used to tie a few hundred dozen of them a year. If you tie a lot of any one fly, there is always the chance that you will eventually find out how to really tie it and tie it well. With the techniques I use on this fly I went from tying a dozen and a half flies an hour to close to three dozen an hour.

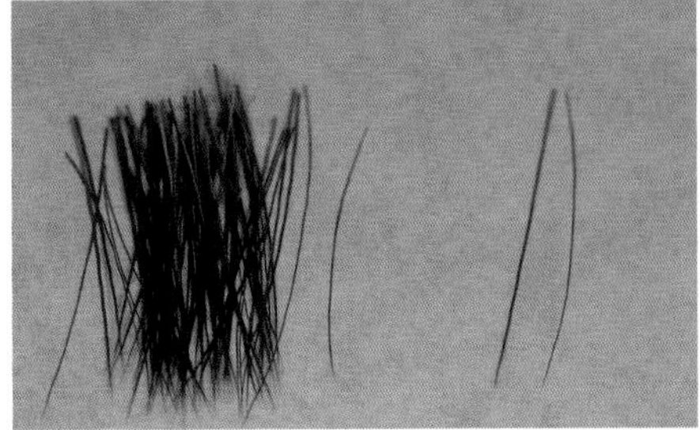

Preparation always helps in your overall production. Get your hooks out, pull out some CDC feathers, and prepare a ball of dubbing. Lay them in some order and easy to reach. Stack a clump of moose body hair for tails. I like to trim the moose hair to about an inch long and lay it near the edge of my tying table. As you can see, it is pretty easy to separate out two fibers and get the tips together so they are ready to tie in.

This is one of those flies with a couple of very good techniques that I hope will become a major part of your repertoire. If you can dub the thread first and then tie in a tail or ribbing, it will speed up your tying tremendously. Always keep this in mind. You will be surprised just how often this opportunity presents itself, especially with smaller flies.

After you dub the thread, make sure you leave an amount of bare thread between the dubbing and the hook. Usually a minimum of a half-inch is necessary for this technique.

This is also a good time to add one more of my thoughts on tying in tails, in a way that also speeds up your tying. In this case we are using moose body hair fibers. However, this approach works with any tail. Take two fibers, even the tips and put them in between your left thumb and fore finger (for a right-handed tier). Take them to the hook and make one wrap of thread over the tail. Remove your left hand and take a look at the length of the tail. After a little practice, you should be able to look at the tail and tell if it is too short or too long. Adjust the tail length by grabbing the tail again, loosening the thread tension and pushing or pulling the fibers to length. After you do this a few times you will know just how much tail you need and no adjustment will be necessary. You can do this with any tail, on a nymph or dry. (Measuring the tails by holding them in your right hand over the hook, then switching them to the left hand will save time by making only one trip to the vise.) It will be a big surprise to see how consistent your tail lengths have become!

RS-2 Emerger

Hook: Dry fly, size 16-26
Thread: 8/0 gray
Tail: Moose body fibers or Micro Fibetts
Body: Muskrat or Fine & Dry dubbing
Wing: CDC light gray

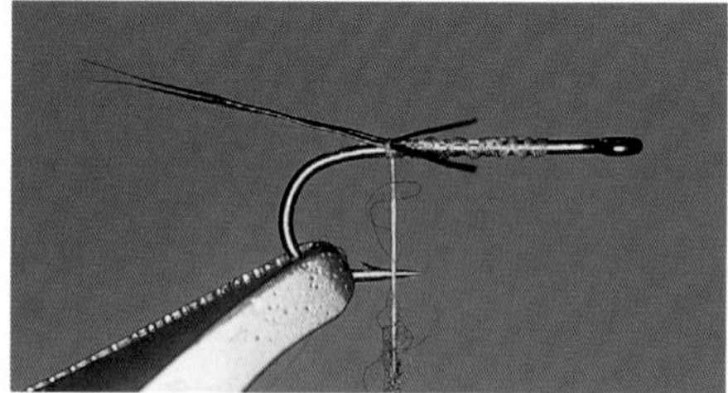

1. Start the thread at the 3/4 point of the hook and wrap back to the 1/4 point. This helps set up the proportion of the fly. Dub thread, leaving about 1/2 inch of bare thread between the dubbing and the hook. Take two moose body fibers, even the tips and make one wrap of thread over them to make the tail. Check tail length. It should extent beyond the back of the hook a full shank length. Make any adjustment by loosening the thread tension and pulling or pushing the fibers under the one wrap of thread. One small adjustment is usually all it takes to get it the right length.

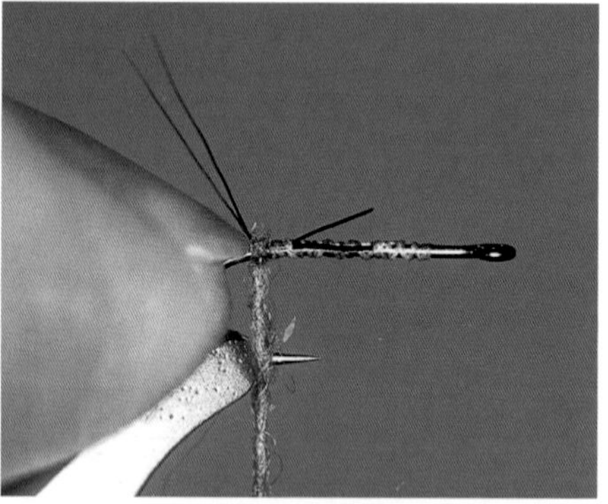

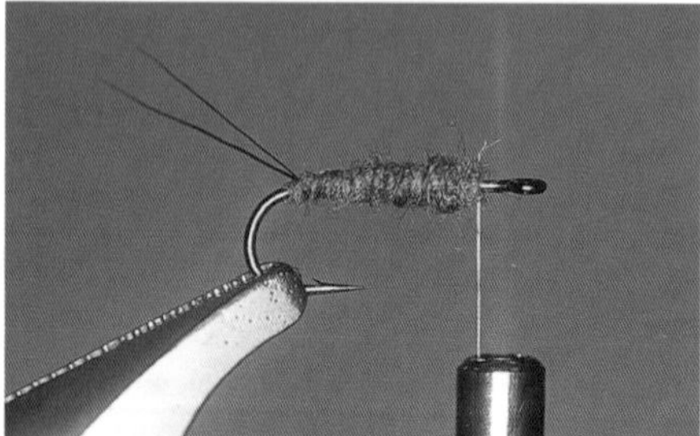

2. Wrap the thread to the back of the hook, holding the tail up so it stays on top of the hook. The dubbing should show up at this point. Make sure there is one wrap of dubbing in front of the tail. Push the tail up with a fingernail from your left hand, either the thumb or index finger. Notice how the tail fibers split naturally. Make one wrap of dubbing under the tail to prop it up at a slight angle. Continue the dubbing forward to make a thin, carrot-shaped body.

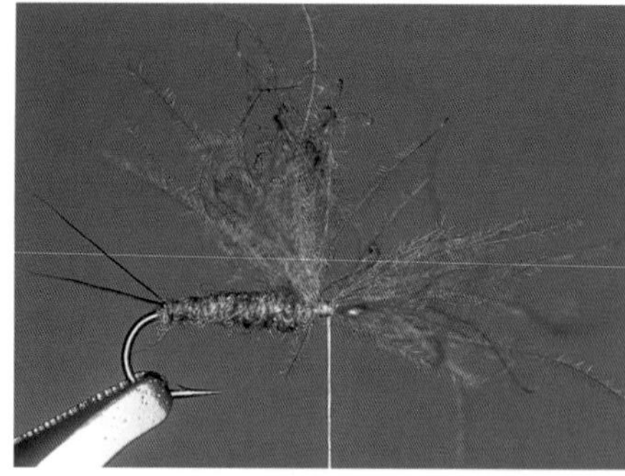

3. Take a CDC feather and pull a clump from the stem. Bunch the CDC together and secure the clump on top of the hook in front of the body. Make sure you tie in as close to the middle of the clump of CDC as you can.

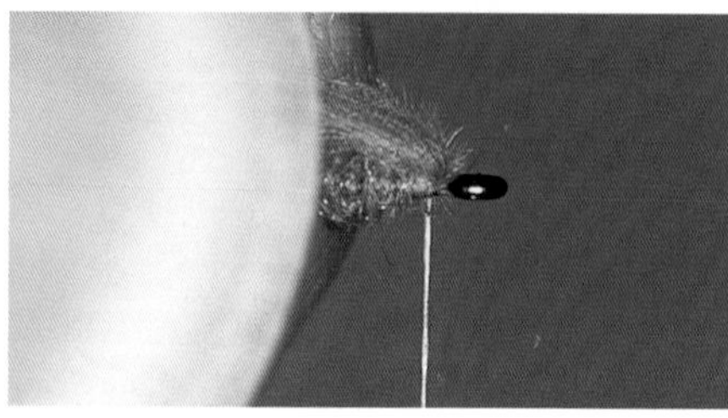

4. One night while tying a few dozen RS-2s, I realized that a lot of the CDC was ending up in the trash. Looking at the fly as pictured in Step Three, the thought came to me that if I just pulled the whole clump back and tied it down I would save some waste. It worked great. I nearly doubled the useable amount of CDC I was tying in and it saved me a trip to the vise with my scissors to trim the tips hanging over the eye of the hook.

5. Whip finish and trim wing to length. Since this is tied as an emerger, I trim the length of the wing by pulling the fibers back over the fly and cut at a spot just above the point of the hook. This is a perfect length to imitate a newly hatched mayfly.

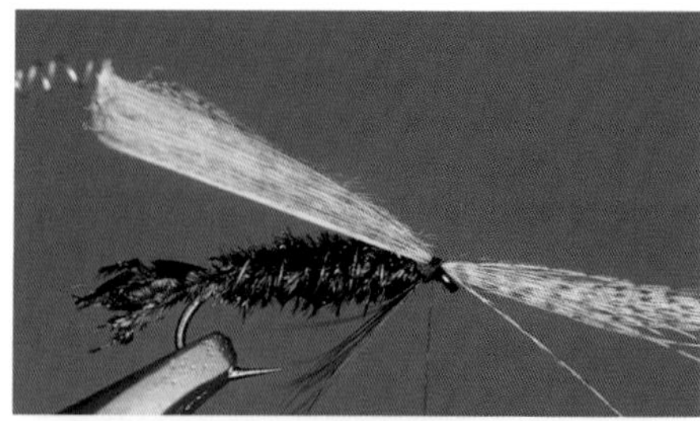

Come to find out the technique used to make the emerger wing on the RS-2 worked great for the bronze mallard wingcase on a Zug Bug. Here is a sequence of photos of a wingcase for a Zug Bug.

Sassy Dun

The Sassy Dun is not a new fly. I don't want to give you the whole history of fly development, but the overall style of this fly falls on the same page as the Comparadun and its predecessor, the Haystack. The wing material is the only change that has been made here. I use the hair from the bottom of a snowshoe hare foot for the Sassy Dun. I first heard of using snowshoe hare feet for tying from John Gierach. He wrote about saving the hare's feet to use for some of his personal flies. So I got some rabbit feet, and gave them a try.

It has turned out to be my favorite winging material for my personal collection of Comparaduns. I use it in the natural creamy color for the pale colored

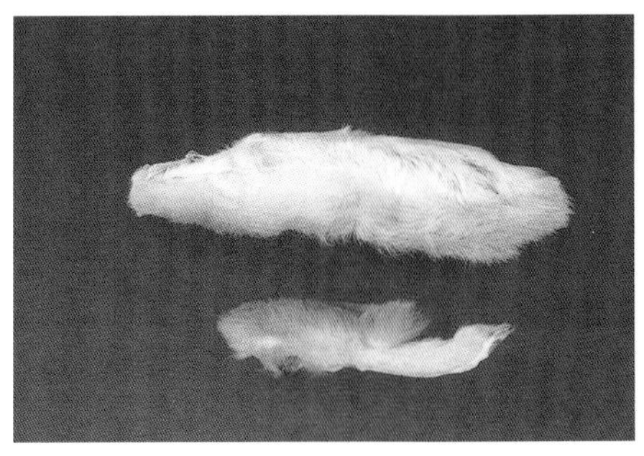

mayflies and dye it into some dun colors for the olives and drakes in the region.

Snowshoe hare has great qualities for use as the wing on a no-hackle type of fly. It has a natural resistance to water, making it very buoyant. Its visibility is superior to that of deer-hair. It also does not build up as much bulk as does the Deer-hair Comparadun, which makes it great for tying flies down into the size-20 range. What else could you ask for?

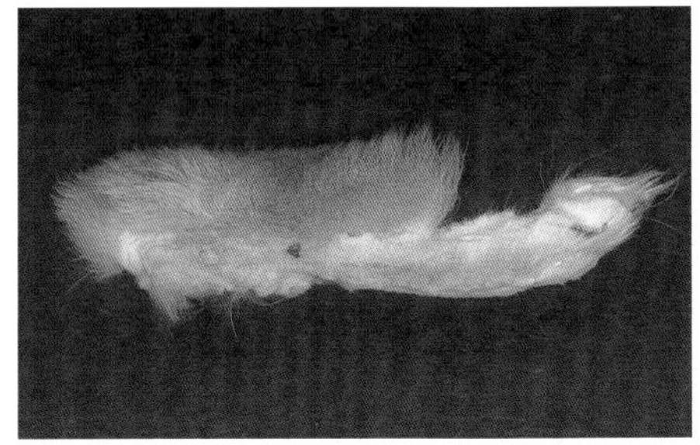

I trim the hair off the top of the foot and blend it in with my rabbit dubbing. This makes the foot much easier to use as I start clipping out clumps for use as wings. I have also found that cutting the first clumps of hair from the front of the foot near the toes makes the process of making wings much easier. I try to cut the hair out in rows so that the size, or weight, of the wings is more consistent. See the chapter on deer-hair wings in the "Material Preparation" section for more information on this process.

As with any hair-wing fly, the most important aspect of the wing is the tie-in procedure. It is very important to make sure the clump of hair stays on the top half of the hook. If the hair rolls around the shank of the hook, the height of the wing will be uneven. Advanced split-hair wings creates an additional problem. The wings will be uneven and also very difficult to split evenly. This becomes an issue of balancing the weight of the wing and consistency of proportion.

Since this wing is not split but fanned around the top half of the hook in a 180 degree semi-circle Comparadun style, you should concentrate on placement of the wing (proportion) on the hook and make sure the hair stays on top of the hook.

You can make a quick check to be sure the wing is in place by turning the fly over and making sure you can still see the thread base and the bare hook shank without hair interfering with the view. Here is a close-up of a deer-hair wing to illustrate what the tie-in should look like from the bottom.

Sassy Dun

Hook: Dry fly, size 12-20
Thread: 8/0, color to match
Tail: Micro Fibbetts, color to match pattern. Natural spade hackle fibers can also be used for tail
Body: Fine & Dry dubbing by Spirit River, colors to match your local BWOs, PMDs, Light Cahills, Hendricksons'
Wing: Snowshoe hare foot hair

1. Start thread at the 3/4 point on the hook and wrap back to the 1/2 point. Jump a couple wraps forward back to the 3/4 point. This thread base is very important to any hair-wing dry fly. It gives the hair something to grab onto as

you tie it down, helping to keep the hair from rolling.

2. With the rabbit foot hair no stacking is needed. This is what gives it the sassy look: Using your thumbnail as a guide, measure the wing height against the hook shank so that it is the same length. Slide your thumbnail forward to the 3/4 point. One of the main problems tying in a hair wing is that it wants to roll as the hair is tightened into place with the thread. You can use that fact to your advantage by tilting the hair tips down on your side of the hook at about a 15 degree to a 30 degree angle. Bring thread up in front of the wing and pinch it between the fingers holding the hair. Drop the thread over the backside of the hook. Pull the bobbin toward your left shoulder quickly (for a right-handed tier, to the right shoulder for left-handed tiers). The thread torque from this pull will roll the hair on top of the hook, right in the position you had your thread. Make a second wrap, tightening to the point the thread is about to break. Start wrapping back to the 1/2 point of the hook. Do not let go of the hair as you wrap back. Trim hair and cover the butt ends with thread and you should have a perfectly placed wing. Check the bottom of the fly to make sure the wing is directly on top of the hook shank.

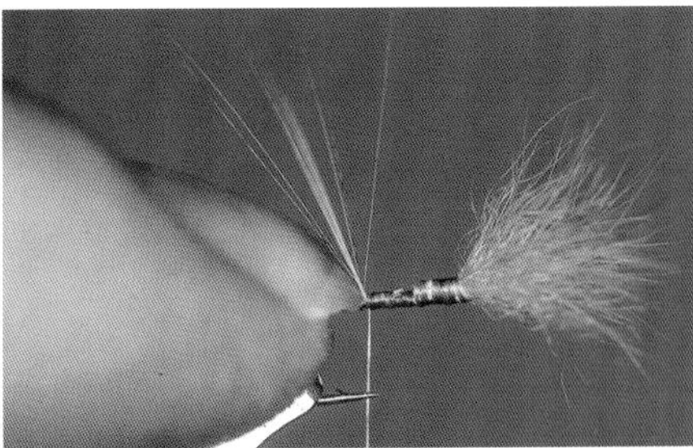

3. Make a small dubbing ball at the back of the hook to split the tails against. Tie

in Micro Fibetts so they are just a little longer than the hook shank and wrap to the 3/4 point of the hook. Holding onto the tails as you wrap will ensure they stay on top of the hook. I have found that 5 fibers on each side of a #12, 4 fibers on each side of a #14, 3 fibers on each side of a #16, and 2 fibers on all flies smaller than a #16 works out very well. I push the tail fibers up with a fingernail so I can count them more easily. Grab half of the fibers, pull them down and towards you. Starts wrapping to the back of the hook, locking the fibers you are holding to the side of the shank. Amazingly, the other tail fibers are rolling over to the other side.

As you near the dubbing ball let go of the near tail and adjust the far tail with a wrap or two to make sure it is also on the side of the shank. Here is the finished tail.

4. Dub a nicely tapered body to just behind the wing.

5. Dub the thread again, leaving about a 1/2 inch of bare thread between the hook and the dubbing. Pull the wing back and slightly down. The downward motion helps splay the wing around the shank into the 180 degree formation. Wrap thread tightly in front of the wing, building a dam of thread for the wing to stand up against. As the dubbing shows up, move forward slightly towards the eye of the hook. Now go back again with the dubbing to the base of the wing, again anchoring the wing into the upright position. This slight move forward with the dubbing then back to the wing keeps the dubbing from falling off itself as you try stacking it in front of the wing. You must make one wrap of dubbing behind the wing to fill a gap of bare hook that occurs under it. Move to the front of the fly and whip finish.

Here is a time-saving move for you: I have found the amount of dubbing it takes to finish the thorax area of the fly to be about the same as the amount it takes to do the body.

Here is a frontal view of the Sassy Dun.

Spectrumized Mayfly Nymph

Contributed By John Hagen

One of John's favorite nymph patterns is a Pheasant Tail Nymph. He has used it successfully everywhere he has fished and has tied them commercially. As I mentioned in the section on the Flashback Pheasant Tail by Randy Smith, the P.T. Nymph is a bread-and-butter-type fly for a pro tier. Everybody uses them and someone needs to tie them. John says, "I've tied a bazillion of them!"

Pheasant Tail Nymphs are normally tied on your tippet to imitate small mayfly nymphs. A P.T. Nymph has a close resemblance to an early and late-season *Baetis* nymph or if tied in a size 16 or 14 could be a PMD nymph in mid summer. The overall shape of the P.T. must have a lot to do with its productivity. It simply looks like a mayfly nymph.

Most P.T.s are tied with a peacock herl thorax. Not that there is anything wrong with tying them with herl, but mayfly nymphs generally don't have a dark thoraxial region. Yes, they do have a dark back, but John with his keen eye for detail, has noticed that their underside is lighter in color.

John's theory on the P.T. Nymph is a bit different: "I think the P.T. Nymph is a better midge imitation than a mayfly pattern. Even though the shape of the nymph could easily match any number of mayflies, the overall color, especially in the thorax area, matches a midge more closely. The dark thorax and the sprouting legs could imitate a hatching midge while the tail has the correct color of the trailing shuck. It may sound a little weird but hey, that's my opinion, and I may be wrong!"

In fact, under closer inspection, if you take a look at the nymphs in the water and turn them over you will see several different colors throughout their underbody. As with adult mayflies, the underside of a mayfly nymph is generally lighter in color than the top of the insect. You'll see reds, oranges, yellowish olives, and pinks mixed in with the natural dark olives and browns. Reds and oranges are definitely the most common colors you will see.

John said, "Tying the Spectrumized Mayfly Nymph is an attempt to depict what the mayfly nymphs actually look like as viewed from the underside, which is a view that a trout could see. The Awesome Possum dubbing I use for the thorax is very easy to work with. It blends easily, comes in many colors, and works very well for nymphs with a shaggy appearance.

"Essentially we are tying a P.T. Nymph but we are making it with a light-colored thorax, which more closely resembles a mayfly nymph. However, in designing this nymph, I wanted to use the effect of gills provided by the pheasant-tail fibers on the body. Another advantage of this fly is the ease of dubbing the thorax, creating the legs without using the pheasant-tail fibers for the legs."

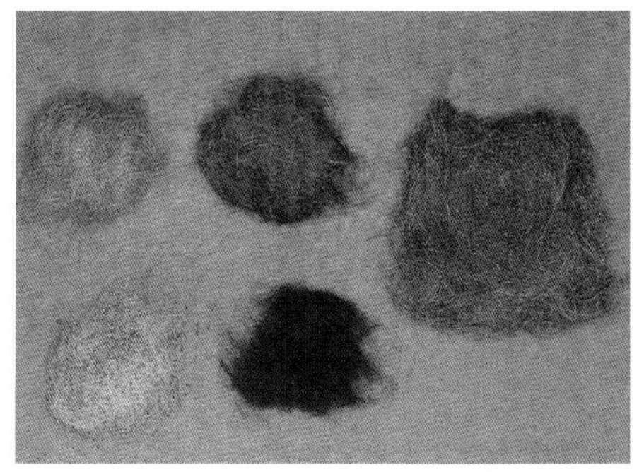

The base of the dubbing is Australian Possum, specifically, a brand by Wapsi called Awesome Possum. A natural tan and olive are used for the base color, then a red Awesome Possum (looks like magenta) and another Wapsi dubbing product called Sow Scud in a shrimp pink color is blended with the base colors. The Sow Scud has some kind of synthetic in it that adds some sparkle to the dubbing mix. John explains his simple recipe, "If you started with equal parts of each, it comes out just about perfect. Surprisingly, it looks like a lot of red and pink but trust the mix; it looks good."

If you find nymphs in your areas that are colored differently, tweak the mixture to match your bugs. The ball of dubbing on the left is a mix with orange instead of red. The one on the right is the standard mix with red in it.

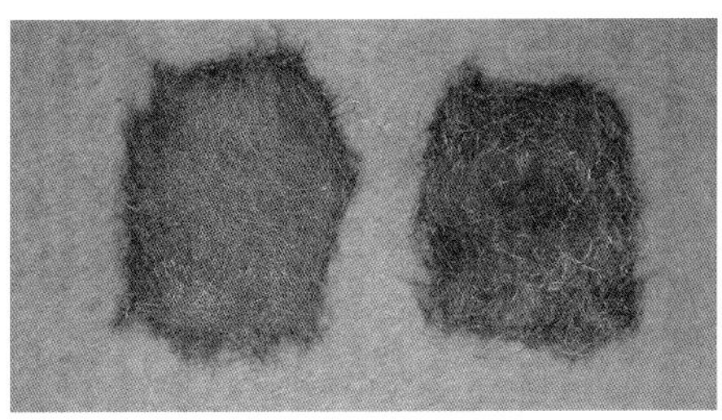

Spectrum Nymph

Hook: Nymph 1x long, size 12-20, Daiichi 1560, Tiemco 3761
Thread: 6/0 olive Danville #60
Ribbing: Fine copper wire
Tail: Pheasant-tail fibers, dyed olive
Body: Pheasant-tail fibers (same as tail)
Wingcase: Pheasant-tail fibers, dyed olive
Thorax: Awesome Possum distributed by Wapsi. Natural tan, olive, red, and a Wapsi dubbing called Sow Scud in a shrimp pink all blended together.

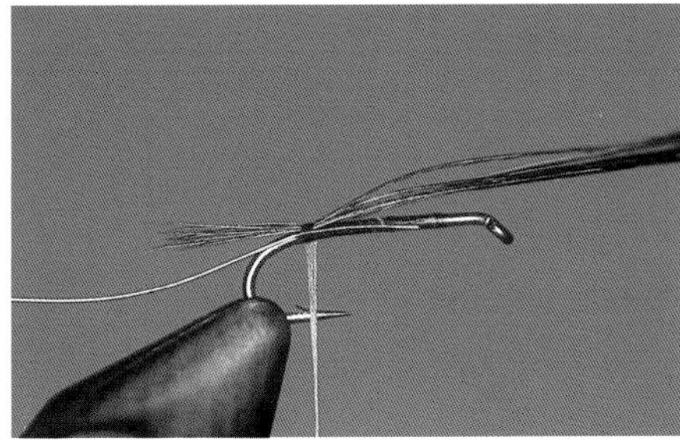

1. Start thread at the 2/3 point and secure the copper wire on the near side of the hook. Wrap to the back of the hook making sure the wire maintains its position on the near side. Don't get weird with the number of pheasant-tail fibers you use for the tail. Smaller flies only need a few, while a larger fly can have as many as seven or eight. Measure tails so they extend beyond the back of the hook 1/2 a hook shank length. Tie the tails in at the back of the hook and make a couple of tight wraps right on top of each other at the back of the hook.

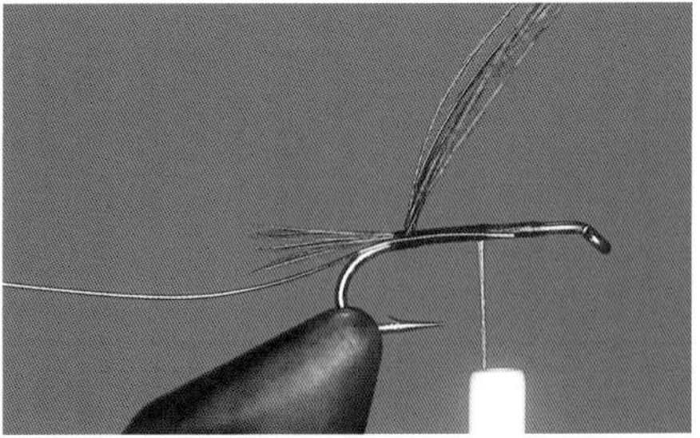

2. This is one of the best speed techniques around for Pheasant Tail Nymphs: Just lift the pheasant fibers up and move the thread to the 2/3 point of the hook. When John saw this photo he wanted me to pass this along: "The photo of this step shows the bobbin very close to the hook only to give the location of the thread after the tails are tied in. I don't tie with the bobbin this close to the hook. I like some distance between the hook and my bobbin. I know a lot of tiers like to keep the bobbin close to the hook for better control but I like the thread longer for better feel. I like to feel the thread stretch as I'm applying torque on a material. I also think it is easier to tie in materials without the nose of the bobbin in there so close. It may sound a little weird but hey, that's my style, and I can't be wrong!"

3. Wrap the pheasant fibers forward to the 2/3 point and secure. DO NOT trim pheasant fibers yet. Reverse wrap the wire forward with evenly spaced wraps over the body. With the wire on the near side of the hook, your first turn of ribbing will go under the hook then on top so as not to interfere with the tail position. The theory of counter wrapping the wire is to make sure all the body fibers get lashed down with the wire so the fly will not fall apart. Secure wire. Hold the wire and the pheasant fibers up at the same time and trim both as close to the hook as possible. Wrap thread forward

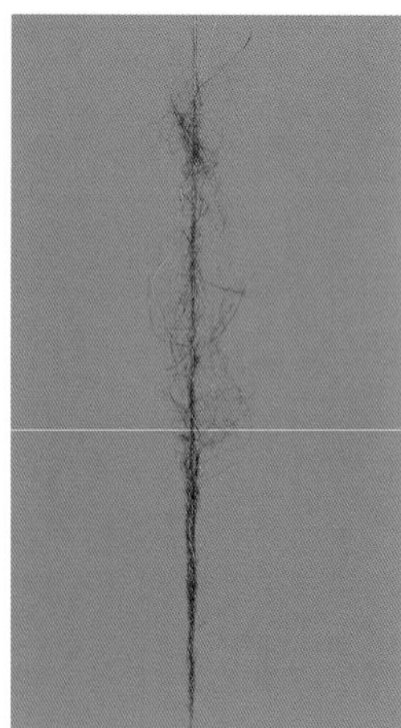

to the eye, then back to about the 3/4 point. This forms a thread base on which to wrap the wingcase and dubbing.

4. Wax thread and touch dub a length of dubbing, leaving about 1/2 inch of bare thread between the hook and the dubbing. After it is touch dubbed, tighten up about 1/2 of its length by twisting it as you would for normal dubbing. (See Step 1 of the Exploding Caddis,) Again, the overall length of the dubbing will depend on the size of fly, so tie a couple and adjust the amount of dubbing until it works out so you have just enough to finish the thorax. Select a new clump of pheasant fibers for the wingcase. John likes to use a new clump of fibers to ensure he gets the true olive color of the fibers and not the darker butt ends. This also guarantees you enough length to hang onto when pulling it over while finishing the fly. He uses several fibers so he can make a wide wingcase. More fibers should be used on larger flies. Trim about 3/8 inch off the tips to remove the thinnest part of the fibers. Secure the tips of the trimmed fibers at the 3/4 point using the short section of bare thread. Wrap back to the 1/2 point of the hook or just on top of the front of the body, making sure they stay on top of the hook as you go. Wrapping back to the 1/2 point ensures that there is a smooth transition between the wingcase and the body. In other words, when you pull the wingcase forward, there shouldn't be any bare thread showing behind the wingcase or in front of the body. Now move the thread to the front of the hook and the dubbing should show up and be ready to wrap. John does this dubbing in two layers. Wrap the section of "normal" dubbing back to just in front of the wingcase. The section of shaggy touch dubbing is now wrapped forward. The last couple of wraps of dubbing should be swept back to keep fibers out of the eye of the hook.

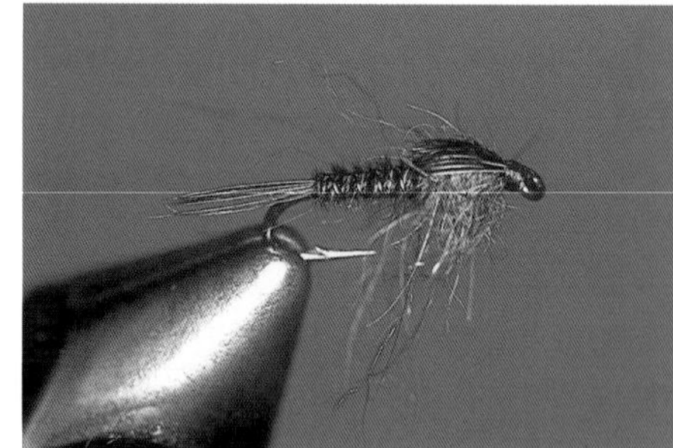

5. John says, "People look at my flies and say they look way too bushy. I like bushy; it makes the fly look alive! I like my nymphs to look they are kind of exploding alive, kind of messed up in an organized sort of way." Stroke the dubbing fibers back and pull the wingcase over and secure behind the eye. Whip finish and take a look at this fly from underneath.

Tiny Gray CDC Spinner

The Tiny Gray Spinner filled a void in what seems to be an endless number of patterns needed for highly selective trout in tailwater and spring-creek situations. With the South Platte River out my back door and the Frying Pan River a mere four-hour drive away, the ability to tie on the right fly at the right time is imperative to fly-rodding success. Both streams are very well known for their early spring and fall *Baetis* hatches, which leave many a fly-fisherman (including myself) mumbling obscenities as the rod is laid to rest at the end of a long, hard day.

"Ah, what fun!" we say.

There are nymphs tied to exacting proportions with three tails and six legs for these hatches. The emergers and crippled dun patterns are nothing short of artistic genius. Hey, I've seen size 18 dun patterns with little red eyes pasted inside the hackle. But one stage of the life cycle is left out in most fly boxes, the egg-laying stage, better known as the spinner.

I am assuming this of course, because I rarely talk with anyone who says they take fish on a spinner during this popular hatch. That may be intentional. They don't want to let the cat out of the bag and give up one of their best patterns. They do talk about the Trico spinner patterns they use on the South Platte in late summer, but fail to mention spinners during the *Baetis* hatch. A comment I do get occasionally when talking about spinners is a lack of visibility. "Those things are just too hard to see," they say. I know it's nice to be able to see your dry fly drifting on the water, but I also know it's not imperative.

With this in mind, I'm going to continue with my assumption.

My first success with a spinner pattern was on the Taylor River below Taylor Park Reservoir. Green drakes and PMD's hatched in the afternoon. Anglers were as thick as the duns, but as the sun faded over the western peaks, several SUVs followed, leaving me with a quiet evening to myself.

Trout were rising sporadically along the bank and the inward seams, but were still as finicky as they had been all day. This was my first trip to the Taylor and I had only been fly-fishing for two years, tops. Unable at that point to just react and let it happen, most of my thoughts were going back to what I had read in the recent past about riseforms and certain times of the day. (Thank God I read as much as I did in those first few years.) The trout rising were anything but aggressive, in fact I saw a trout rise near the surface and follow something back several feet before slowly slurping in the invisible morsel. That is when the light came on. The books said slow, deliberate rises were usually to spinners or adult midges. I did see some insects buzzing around and I knew they weren't midges. The books said some spinners fall late in the evening so I felt I had only one choice of flies, a size

14 Rusty Spinner. I will always have fond memories of that evening.

With that experience under my belt, I continued to use my "go-to" fly. Spinner patterns worked everywhere (and still do), not only in the evening, but also in the morning. I fish it right in the middle of the afternoon as an attractor pattern. I started tying the Tiny Gray Spinner several years ago just for the South Platte River. Those guys were correct, spinners are hard to see on the water. And the smaller they get the harder they are to see! However, they did work. When CDC came around, that problem became non-existent. CDC floats this tiny fly very well and stands out like a sore thumb on the water. After trying several patterns in small sizes and slightly different styles, this version of the Tiny Gray Spinner became my favorite. The simple tail and standard quill body are pretty basic, but the wing can be a little tricky. Once you tie a few with this wing style, I'm sure you will find it very quick and easy to put together. Picking a good CDC feather not only makes the fly easier to tie but also conserves your CDC inventory. You should be able to tie three, maybe four flies with one feather.

Fishing a spinner pattern is almost as easy as tying one. You should observe the time of day the actual hatch occurs to pick the best time to try a spinner pattern. For quick reference, a *Baetis* hatch that takes place in the morning should produce spinners that evening, while an afternoon hatch may bring on spinners through the night and into the early morning hours. My disclaimer is apparent with my reference to "should produce" and "may happen". Temperature, wind, and any number of elements can change the course of history for delicate mayflies. Try this sometime: When the hatch comes off during wet weather, be it rain or snow, and the mayflies are having a difficult time getting off the water, cut one of the wings off your spinner and fish it as a stillborn or crippled fly. You may be pleasantly surprised. (Amazing how far you can come from just reading a couple of books.)

Tiny Gray Spinner

Hook: Dry fly, size18-22
Thread: 8/0 Gray
Tail: Spade hackle fibers, dun
Body: Stripped quill, Whiting natural dun rooster neck
Wing: CDC, watery dun
Thorax: Aussie Possum dubbing, gray

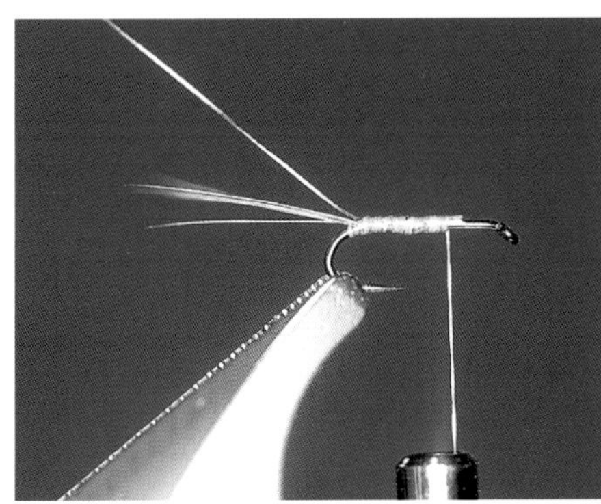

1. Start thread at the 5/8 point of the hook and wrap to the back. Add a couple of wraps right at the back of the hook. Tie in 4 or 5 spade hackle fibers for the tail with just a couple of turns of thread. Do not move thread. (Note: The short feathers with long barbules from the side of the natural dun neck work fine for this application.) When tied in place they should be just slightly longer than the hook shank and butted up against those last couple of wraps of thread. This will naturally splay the tail fibers, eliminating the need to do any additional splitting of the tails. Strip the fibers off of a Whiting Farms natural dun rooster neck hackle. Use one of those big long butt feathers that always remain on the neck long after the rest of the feathers are used up. I used to use any old dun hackle quill for this fly until I found these natural dun necks. They have the genetic remnants of grizzly coloration in the stem, which makes the segmentation of the body really stand out. These quills are also very round and turn into place with ease. One last thing: This quill usually doesn't need to be soaked in water or moistened in any way. You can if the quill wants to split as you turn it, but this doesn't usually happen. If you have burned the fibers off with bleach, then soaking them in water may be a good idea, as this process does seem to make the quill somewhat brittle. Trim the thinnest part of the quill away and tie in the tip of the quill in front of the tail. Wrap thread forward to the 5/8 point of the hook.

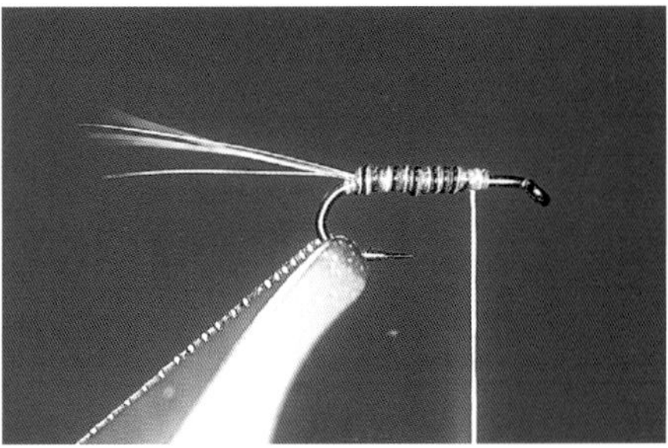

2. Wrap the quill forward making one turn right in front of the last. Secure at the 5/8 point. Trim excess quill and smooth the tie-down area with a few turns of thread.

3. Select a CDC feather that has fairly uniform consistency in barbule thickness and length. Pull about a 1/4-inch clump of fibers off one side of the stem. Hold the fibers or lay them on your tying desk. Pull the same amount of fibers off the other side of the stem. Meld the two clumps together so that the butt ends are away from each other. In other words, lay the tips of one clump with the butt ends of the other clump. Tie the CDC fibers in at the 3/4 point with a simple X-ing pattern. Notice how the denser butt ends of the fibers are

protruding outward. This gives the wing a nice wide appearance, just like that of a mayfly. Also, notice the impression of veins running through the wings.

4. Apply a very thin dubbing noodle to the thread and dub the thorax. Making a couple of wraps directly behind the wing, a couple in front, and finally crossing in between the wings seems to be the best way to lock the wings in position. Whip finish and trim wings to shape.

A size 14 is about as large a spinner you can tie effectively with CDC using this method. Anything larger usually needs a feather tip on each side to make it work correctly. Here is a size-14 Rusty Spinner, which easily falls into my top five favorite trout flies.

Trico Spinner

Contributed by Pat Dorsey

When was the last time you saw a Trico spinner fall? Not one of those late-September spinner falls when there are a few spent insects swirling in the back eddies, I mean a real Trico spinner fall. I'm talking about one of those in late August when millions of these tiny mayflies are hovering above the water in their annual mating dance. Clouds of literally millions of these mayflies are flitting up and down, some finishing their molt, some males actively fertilizing the females and every trout within sight has its eyes fixed to the surface. Then it happens. The females descend to the water, letting go of their eggs to drift to the bottom of the river ensuring next year's mob. The males flutter lifeless to the water's surface and the water shimmers with the glassy wings of these tiny mayflies. What a sight!

You could be viewing this from the bank of one of your favorite rivers or perched atop your catamaran on a high-desert lake. Tricos are found in many types of water and just about anywhere in the world. On top of that, this mayfly hatch and ensuing spinner fall can last as long as any insect hatch of the year, sometimes a couple of months.

Trout will rise relentlessly to this mayfly spinner every day, trying to get their fill. I've seen trout rise and take a spinner, move to the side and take another, drift back and sip another, taking four or five flies on one rise. This can be an amazing sight; however, being prepared for this carnage is imperative.

The most difficult and frustrating part of this type of fishing is the size of the insect. I compared a natural Trico spinner on the South Platte River below Spinney Mountain Reservoir to a size 24 I had tied to 7X tippet and my size 24 looked like a gorilla. I had nothing smaller than the gorilla, so I trimmed the bottom of a size-20 Griffith's Gnat and actually took a couple fish. They must have thought it was several spinners stuck together. (I still don't carry anything smaller than that gorilla.) If the minute size of the flies isn't enough, the hordes of spinners on the water make the trout very selective, adding to the challenge.

If I haven't convinced you to stay home at this time of year, then I would load up a box of Tricos in several tiny sizes and change the abdomen color on a few. Female spinner abdomens can be much paler in color than their male counterparts, which are mostly black. Females can be light olive to almost white in color, while others have been found with yellowish or even orange abdomens. Don't be fooled into thinking the trout can't tell the difference in the color of the abdomen of these spinners, so tie a few oddballs just in case. Two very distinctive features of any Trico spinner are that they are short and they have a black bulky thorax.

Pat Dorsey shows you here how to tie a very quick Trico Spinner pattern. The key to this fly is its simplicity and the use of very basic materials. However, don't feel tied down to these basics. Thread color can be changed for the body of the fly, natural hackle fibers can be used for the tail, and the wing material can be changed to a favorite yarn of your choice.

Again, I would like to stress the idea behind this book. The patterns in this book and the tiers who contributed to the book are using ideas to help you speed up your tying and to help with tying techniques. There are many Trico spinner patterns to choose from out there, so let these ideas fit into your own style of tying and let your creativity tell you what materials you should use.

Trico Spinner

Hook: Ring-eye dry fly, size 18-26, Daiichi 1110 Tiemco 101
Thread: Black 8/0 UNI-Thread
Tail: White Fibetts, a nylon tailing material (Spirit River)
Body: Black 8/0 UNI-Thread
Wing: White Z-lon
Thorax: Black Fine & Dry dubbing (Spirit River)

1. Start thread at the 7/8 point of the hook and wrap back a few turns. Measure three Fibetts to 1 1/2 hook shank length for the tail. Tie in the Fibetts and wrap them down to the back of the hook, making one wrap right next to the last, giving a smooth level thread base for the body. Make sure the tails

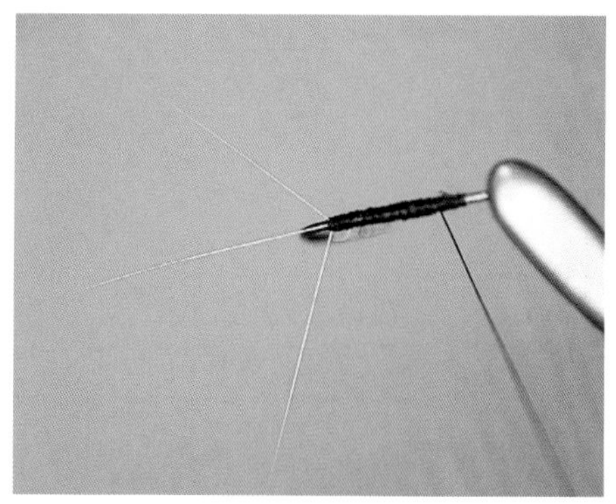

stay on top of the hook as you go back. As soon as you reach the back of the hook, make one wrap of thread under the tails to prop them up slightly. Initially separate the Fibetts by pulling one Fibett on each side of the hook to a 45 degree angle. They will not stay in this position permanently so you need to lock them in place. Make a wrap of thread, from over the top of the hook, in between the Fibett and the hook shank on the far side of the hook. Grab the Fibett and hold it at a 45 degree angle to the shank. Tighten the wrap and then make a turn around the hook shank to lock the tail in position. Let go of the fibet. Make a wrap of thread, from under the hook, in between the Fibett and the hook shank on the near side of the hook. Hold the fibet at a 45 degree angle to the shank. Tighten the wrap and then make a turn around the hook shank to lock the tail in position. Let go of the fibet. Amazingly, those four wraps of thread make the perfect split tail. Wrap thread forward to the 1/2 point of the hook making a smooth thread body.

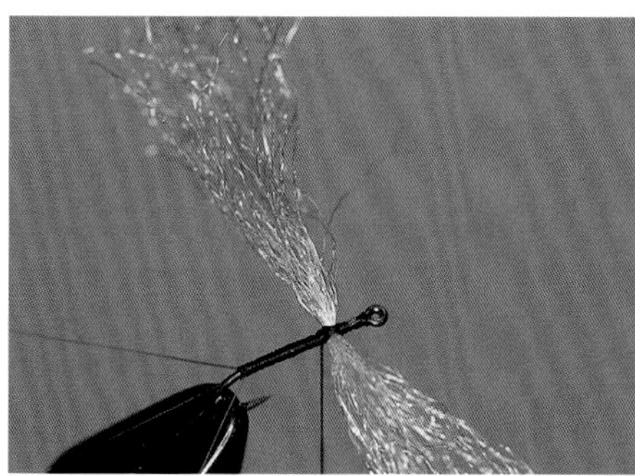

2. Cut a section of Z-lon about 1 1/2 inches long. Z-lon is packaged in clusters of strands that will be separated as needed for different sized hooks. So the number of Z-lon fibers used for the wing will vary from hook size to hook size. A safe reference point may be a half a cluster for a size 18 and then fewer fibers as the hook size gets smaller. Move thread to the 3/4 point of the hook and tie in the Z-lon with equal lengths of the Z-lon on each side of the shank for the spinner wing. Making a simple X-ing pattern in the middle of the wings will lock them at a 90 degree angle to the hook shank.

3. Dub thread with black Fine & Dry and start wrapping the dubbing behind the wing. Dub an equal amount in front of the wing, then from in front of the near wing, cross over the top to the back of the far wing. Bring dubbing to the back of the near wing and cross over the top to the front of the far wing, making an X-ing pattern. Repeat if necessary to make a uniform, well-defined thorax. Whip finish.

Chapter 5

MIDGES

Biot Midge

Here is one of those seemingly simple flies that has taught me a couple of very fine points about tying flies for speed and durability. They are so subtle that even after you hear them you will think I am absolutely nuts.

The biot midge was another of the flies that I tied several hundred dozen of every year for nearly six years. When you tie that many of any fly you will figure out its nuances and find the tricks to tie it fast and consistently, no matter how many flies you have to tie.

Wrapping the biot can be done a couple of different ways, but one thing I had to figure out in the beginning was how to get the flash we use for ribbing in between the little raised edge on the biot without interfering with its appearance. It didn't take many flies to figure this out. I had to tie the flash on my side of the hook so the first wrap would lie in between the first wrap of the biot. No big deal.

The first real problem I encountered while tying this fly was the biot wanting to unwind itself at the slightest loosening of the thread after it was tied in. Since it is a small fly, I didn't want to build up too much thread. Three or four turns were all I wanted to use, but if I bumped the bobbin and loosened the thread, it would unwind, so I was very careful not to bump the bobbin. Inevitably it would happen at a very inopportune time, just when I was in a hurry trying to get five dozen done to deliver the next morning. Most of the time I would have to tie in a new biot to make the fly look right. Very frustrating and time-consuming! Then one night it came to me. You will think I'm nuts. To secure the biot, I made two turns over the biot then raised the biot up with the hackle pliers and made one wrap of thread onto the hook. I took total pressure away from the thread by raising the bobbin up; the biot didn't move. I have no idea how many hundred dozen of those things I tied before I fixed that problem!

I have been teaching this trick to each of my beginning fly-tying classes ever since. I use it when securing anything from chenille to peacock herl, from a pheasant-tail body to wingcases. The only difference is that I tell them to make three wraps, lift up the material and make two wraps on the hook shank. One, two, three,,,,,,one, two.

If ever there were a problem a novice tier would be guilty of, (me included), it would be making too many wraps of thread in the overall fly, in turn causing too much bulk. This trick is a great teaching aid to eliminate that problem.

I was tying a solid two-dozen Biot Midges an hour with my standard tying procedures, so it wasn't as if I were looking for something to speed up the process. But again a light went off one night as I was tying them. I realized this technique after I figured out the biot dilemma, so I know I was getting close to a total of six hundred dozen tied.

I figured out that if I picked up the biot and the flash at the same time, then I could tie them in one after the other. I tied in the flash first, on my side of the hook, then immediately tied in the tip of the biot on top of the hook so I would make only one trip to the vise instead of two. This sped my tying up to at least two and a half dozen an hour. And it only took me six hundred dozen to learn it!

Material Preparation

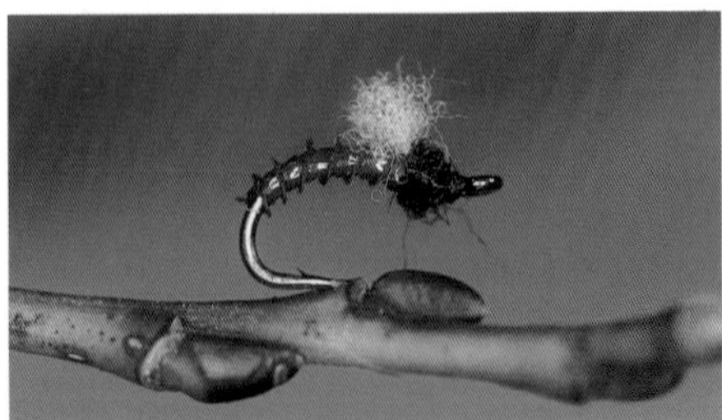

Hook: Curved nymph, size 18-24 Daiichi 1140 or 1150
Thread: 8/0, color to match
Body: Goose biot, black, olive, gray, red are common
Ribbing: Krystal Flash
Wing: Antron yarn, Aunt Lydia's rug yarn
Head: Dubbing, slightly darker than the body

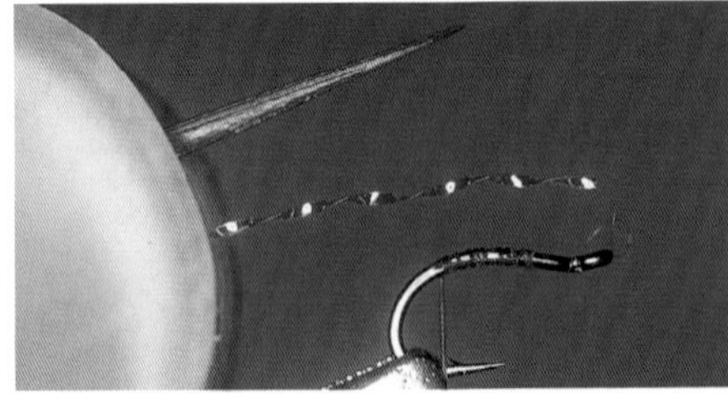

1. Start thread at 3/4 point of the hook and wrap back to the 1/2 point. Pick up a biot so that its straight edge is on top and the notched edge is on the bottom. Also pick up the flash, positioning it below the biot in the same fingers.

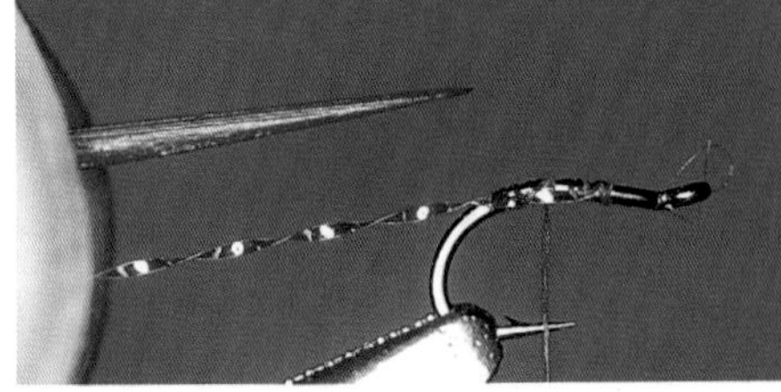

2. Tie in the flash and wrap to the back of the hook making sure the flash is

secured on the tier's side of the hook. Not on top, not on the far side of the hook.

3. Tie in the tip of the biot at the back of the hook and wrap the thread forward to the 3/4 point. Attach hackle pliers at the butt end of the biot. Again, make sure the straight edge of the biot is on top.

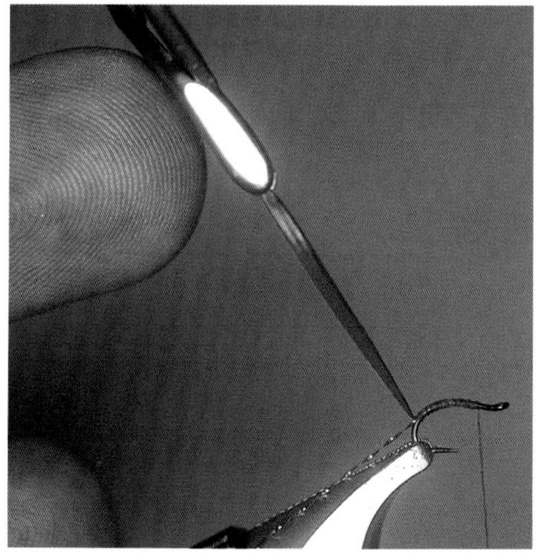

4. Here is the trick to turning a biot. As you raise the hackle pliers to begin wrapping, make a 180 degree counter-clock wise turn of the hackle pliers so the straight edge of the biot is now to the back of the fly. This will start the biot without a twist, allow the nice little raised segmentation to stand up, and let the flash wrap in between the segments of the biot.

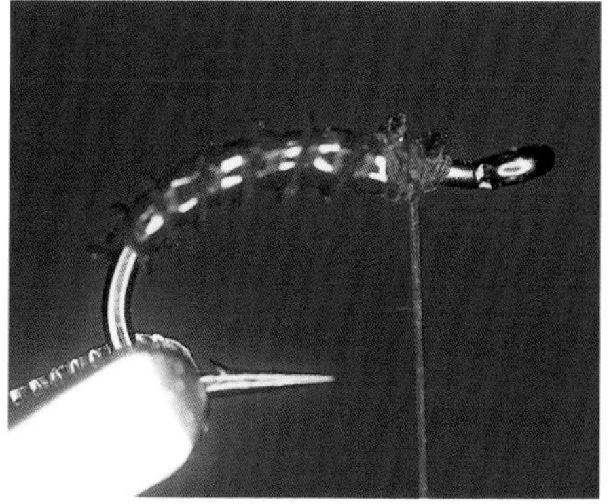

5. Wrap biot forward and secure with two wraps over the biot, then lift the biot straight up and make a wrap of thread back onto the bare hook. Trim the butt end of the biot. Wrap flash forward in between the segments of the biot, leaving the raised edge of the biot unimpaired. Secure flash and trim close to the hook.

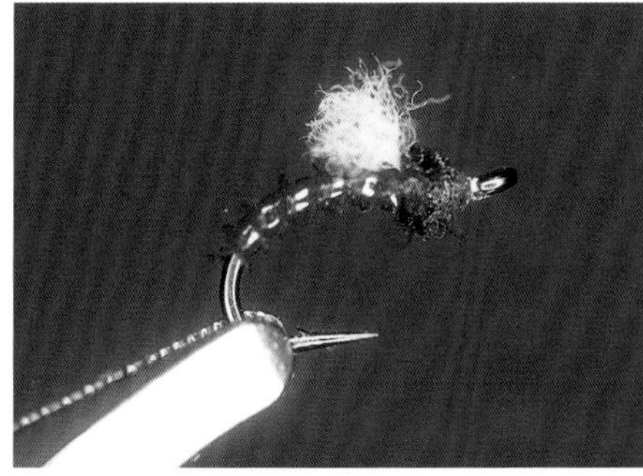

6. You can use a standard dubbing trick here. Dub about a 3/4-inch noodle of dubbing to the thread, leaving about a 1/2 inch of bare thread between the dubbing and the hook. (You must experiment with a couple of flies to determine the right amount of dubbing it will take to finish the head so that no adjustments will have to be made.) Now use the bare thread to tie in the wing. As you finish securing the wing into place the dubbing should be showing up. Use the dubbing to make a small head and whip finish. Note: Dubbing is not absolutely necessary. A thread head is adequate, especially on the size 20's and smaller.

Griffith's Gnat

Contributed by Pat Dorsey

The Griffith's Gnat is one of those obscure patterns that doesn't look like it imitates any insect. (There are a quite a few of those patterns around.) And that is true enough. It is not tied to imitate any ONE insect, it is tied to imitate a cluster of insects, namely a midge cluster.

This very simple pattern can be used in many situations. There are several streams around the nation that have unbelievable midge hatches. In fact, they can be so heavy that the adult midges have a tendency to run into each other, sticking together, forming clusters of midges as large as an 8x10 sheet of paper. More commonly, the clusters range in size from about the size of a Tic-Tac to a fifty-cent piece. The Griffith's Gnat is tied to match those small clusters. Trout on these streams have figured out that rising to a cluster is more satisfying than picking off a single insect. Why fish a size 26 adult midge pattern when you can tease a trout up to twenty adult midges with one size 18 dry fly?

I have found it to be an especially great searching pattern on high-mountain lakes and small streams. The fly imitates just about anything that could get trapped in the surface film. Yes, it can imitate midges, but the Griffith's Gnat can look like a beetle, any of several other terrestrials, or a water boatman. With the hackle trimmed a little, it may be a reasonable impression of a hatching *Callibaetis* or a Trico spinner. I hate to admit it, but I have caught carp on this fly when they were feeding on cottonwood seeds.

The peacock herl and the light-refracting grizzly hackle is a great combination of fly-tying materials. Pat says, "I like to dress this fly with a dry-fly powder called Frog's Fanny. It is absolutely the best floatant I have ever tried. This fly will ride high, making the visibility greatly improved."

Pat's one suggestion for tying the fly: "Make as many turns of hackle through the peacock herl as hackle length will allow. You want to make as tight a cluster as you possibly can. While tied without a wing, it does not have an obvious orientation on the water, so it could ride upside down and still look like a Griffith's Gnat." Charles Brooks referred to this situation as being "tied in the round", much like his black stonefly nymph and the common Woolly Bugger.

I have no idea how far-reaching the Griffith's Gnat's range really is; however, wherever you might be is not far enough. I have confidence this fly will take trout anywhere, at just about any time of the year. You owe it to yourself to tie a few, then go out when the midges are covering the water and fish a size 18 while your buddies are drifting a size 24. I think you may win a bet or two!

Griffith's Gnat

Hook: Ring-eye dry fly, sizes 16-24, Daiichi 1110 Tiemco 101
Thread: Black 8/0 UNI-thread
Body: Peacock herl
Hackle: Grizzly, dry-fly quality neck hackle or saddle hackle (Whiting Farms)

1. Start thread behind the eye and wrap back a few turns. Trim the tips of three strands of good quality, very fluffy peacock herl. Tie in the herl and lash it down to the back of the hook. Size and prepare a grizzly neck hackle. Pull 1/4 inch of the barbs off both sides of the stem. Tie in the hackle in front of the herl. Allow enough room between the stem of the hackle and the herl so as to make one wrap of herl behind the hackle. This lets the hackle bury into the herl on the first turn as you palmer it forward, making the fly more durable. Move thread to the front of the hook.

2. Make a wrap of herl behind the hackle stem and then wrap it forward to the eye. Secure and trim excess herl. Notice the wide, fluffy appearance of good peacock herl.

3. Palmer the hackle forward, making sure the dull side of the feather is forward as you turn the hackle. This will let the curvature of the hackle point forward. Make as many turns of hackle as you can. If you have hackle left over when you think you are done, unwrap

the hackle a ways and cram another turn in before you finish the fly. Secure and trim excess. Whip finish.

Mercury Midge
Contributed by Pat Dorsey

Midges are a very important food source for many species of fish, if for no other reason than the sheer abundance of this insect. Midges live in every type of water, but they thrive in stillwater and tailwater situations. If you fish these types of waters, midge patterns should take up more room in your fly boxes than any other pattern. A mixture of colors and sizes including a good selection of larval, pupa, and adult stages should be considered.

We have known for years that a white midge pattern can be very effective on many tailwaters from the San Juan River in New Mexico to the Bighorn in Montana. An old pattern called the Miracle Nymph, which is tied with white floss in the shape of a small cigar with copper wire ribbing, has been a go-to fly for many tail water fishermen. Overall though, the white pattern is probably the most underutilized in the small-fly category.

The Mercury Midge, tied by Pat Dorsey, is an attempt to improve the old Miracle Nymph by tying the fly much thinner to better imitate a midge. The Mercury Midge got its name from the silver-lined, glass bead tied in at the head of the fly, which looks like a little ball of mercury. Pat fishes this pattern as the point-fly on a dual-fly setup. Attach about 12 inches of 6x or 7x tippet to the eye of the first fly and tie on a Mercury Midge. A scud, an RS-2, a Pheasant Tail Nymph, or a small Hare's Ear could be used as the first fly in this setup. With the extra flash the bead provides, Pat uses this pattern as somewhat of an attractor pattern. However, the thread color can be changed to match the color of any midge you may run into.

This is a very quick tie that is great practice in the small details of fly tying. Thread control and rhythm can be improved by tying numbers of these small patterns. Before you know it, you will be tying a couple dozen an hour. The better you get at the small details, the better overall tier you will become.

Mercury Midge

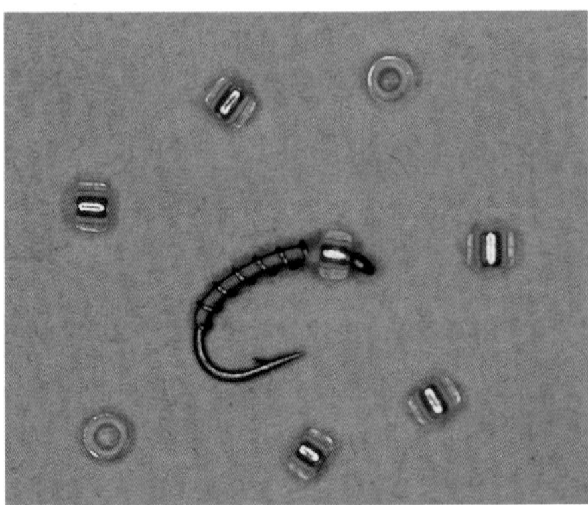

Hook: Curved scud, sizes 18-22, Daiichi 1130
Thread: White 6/0 Danville #001
Bead: Extra-small, silver-lined glass bead (Spirit River #260)
Ribbing: Small copper wire
Body: White 6/0 Danville #001

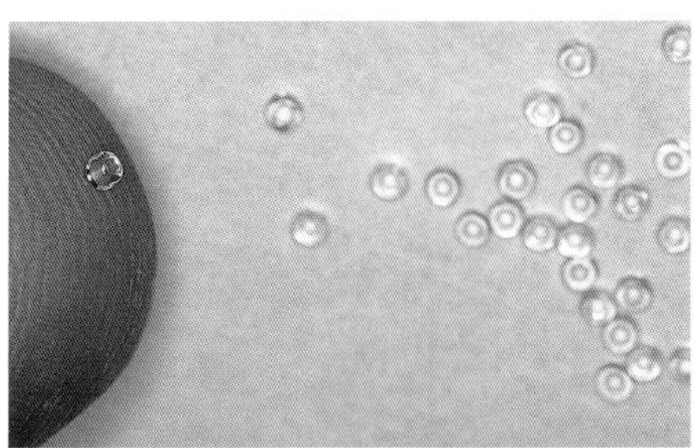

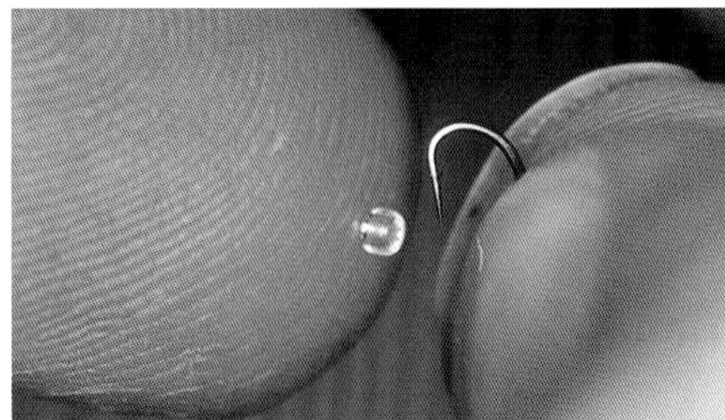

1. Slip a silver glass bead onto the hook. Pat holds the hook between his right thumb and index finger with the hook point exposed. With the beads lying loose on the desktop, he just presses his left index finger on top of a bead and picks it up. These small glass beads will temporarily adhere to your finger long enough to get them on the hook point. If your hands are dry and you have a difficult time picking up the beads, you might need a little dubbing wax on your finger.

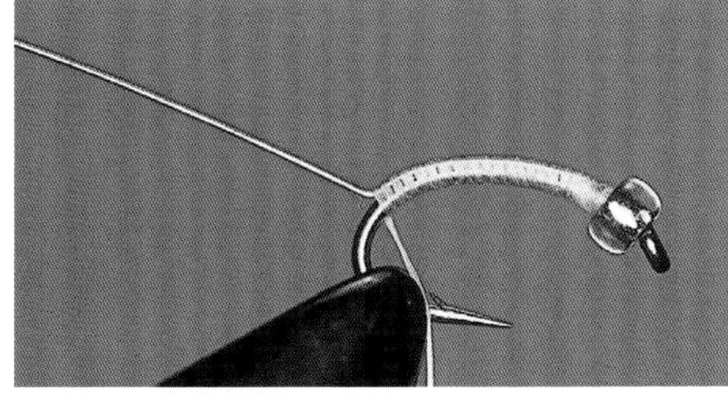

2. Make sure the bead is at the eye of the hook and start thread right behind the bead. Immediately tie in the copper wire on top of the hook and lash wire down to the back of the hook. Make sure the wire remains on top of the hook as you wrap back. You want the wire to stay in place so the body of the midge will not have any unevenness to it.

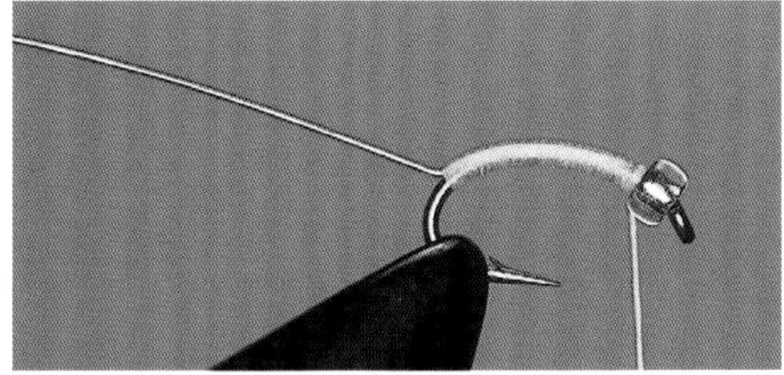

3. Move thread forward making a smooth white body without the hook or the wire showing through.

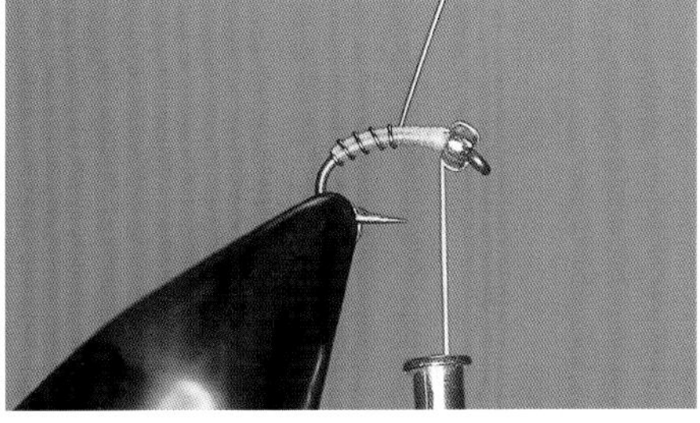

4. Reverse wrap the wire forward with evenly spaced turns. Avoid building up too much bulk by securing the wire with just two wraps of thread behind the bead. Bend the wire back and forth a

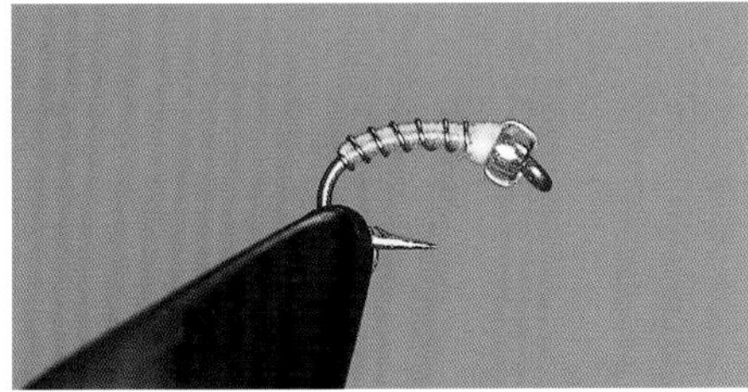

few times and break it off instead of cutting it. Make a two- or three- turn whip finish and this fly is done.

Rojo Midge

Greg Garcia fishes every Monday. (It's his day off) When we chat I always find out how the fishing was. Usually the first thing he boasts about is the absence of the normal weekend crowds! Now, understand that Greg is a good angler and is very humble, but about three years ago his stories held much more conviction and excitement. He was mumbling something about the RoJo: "This is the best fly I have ever fished on the Platte!"

At this present time, Greg is part owner of Trout's Flyfishing, a local fly shop here in Denver. The life of Riley!

Since he is the creator of the fly, he has every right to be proud of it, but calling it the "Best Fly" may be pushing it a little bit. I asked how to tie it and he gave me a couple to try. Sure enough, it was very productive, not only on the South Platte, but just about every other difficult tailwater where I fished it. It is a great early-season fly when midge activity is at its peak.

The fly is just different enough from the basic midge patterns to give it appeal, not only for the angler but also the trout. And I must say that bright red bead can't hurt.

The RoJo Midge is a simple pattern, yet an interesting fly to tie. It should bring a bit of creativity to your own tying.

Rojo Midge

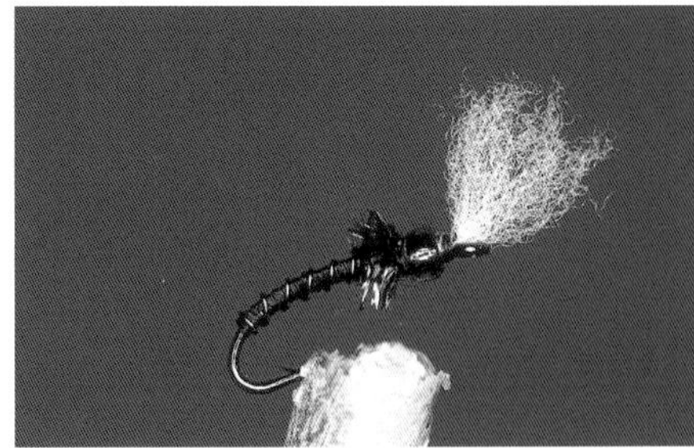

Hook: Curved nymph, Daiichi 1270, sizes 18-22
Thread: 8/0, black
Bead: Ruby (silver-lined) glass bead, X-small by Spirit River
Wing: Oral B dental floss
Body: Thread
Ribbing: Fine copper wire
Head: Peacock herl

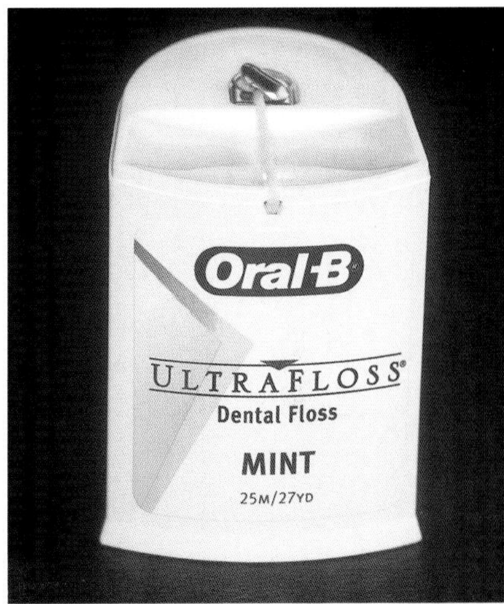

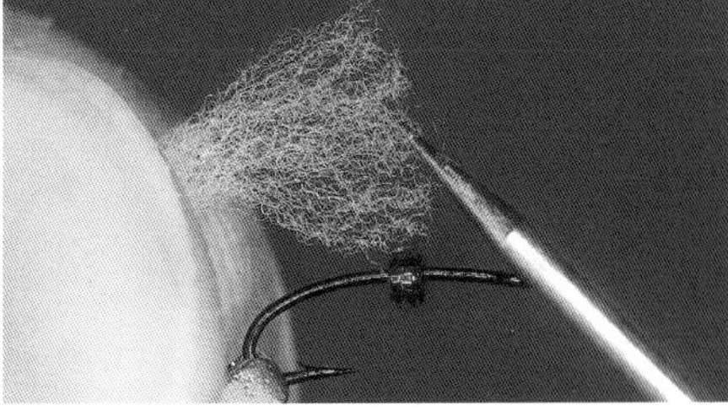

1. Slip the red (RoJo) bead onto the hook. Start thread right behind the eye of the hook. Prepare the emerging wing by shredding the tip of dental floss with

Midges

a bodkin. Don't laugh, you know fly tiers find some of the wildest things to tie with and this is some neat stuff! All you need to do is loosen up the fibers. Tie in the strand of floss so that it extends over the eye of the hook. Use as few turns of thread as possible. Trim emerger wing to length and make a three-turn whip finish.

2. Push bead up over the base of the wing. Take thread over the top of the bead and start it again behind the bead. Don't worry about the bare thread over the bead as it will be secured later when you whip finish just behind the wing.

3. Tie in the very tip of a piece of copper wire and wrap it down to the back of the hook, keeping the wire positioned on top of the hook. By tying in just the tip of the wire, you will eliminate the need to go to the vise with your scissors and trim any excess.

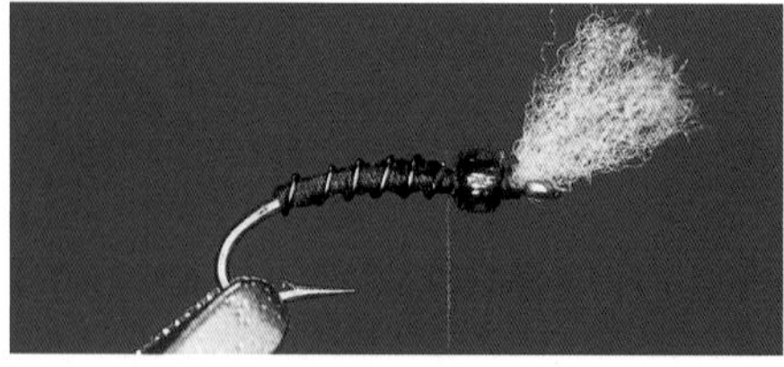

4. As you wrap forward, lay the thread as evenly as possible. This will form a thin, smooth body. Evenly space five turns of wire forward and secure wire. Bend the wire back and forth a couple times and it should break off, again eliminating the need for scissors.

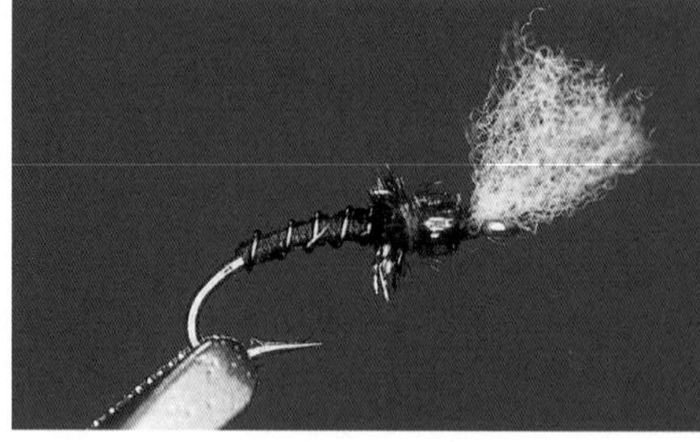

5. Tie in one strand of peacock herl and make a few turns right behind the bead. Secure the herl and make a three- or four-turn whip finish right behind the bead.

Z-lon Adult Midge

Contributed by Randy Smith

If ever there were a fly that a commercial tier would want to have on his list of things to do, it would be the Z-lon Midge. It is a speed tier's dream: three materials and small in size. This means very few steps and the ability to develop a quick, smooth rhythm.

Believe it or not, the great numbers of speed tiers I know don't look like they're tying fast. They have impeccable rhythm and make very few mistakes, such as breaking thread, dropping materials, or having to redo proportional errors. Everything just seems to flow together. When added to the trivial amount of material used on a small fly, this fly can be tied in less than two minutes. The materials are synthetic, can be found in abundance, and are very easy to use.

For the people who tie for themselves, this is a great fly to learn rhythm and proper proportions for a small fly. Not only pro tiers, but all tiers need to pay close attention to proportion to make a great-looking fly that performs on the water the way it is supposed to.

John Betts originally designed the Z-lon Midge. The way Betts constructs a lot of his flies and the materials he uses always makes them interesting to study. The simple nature of this fly does not mean there wasn't a lot of thought put into it. The legs are a very important proportion, requiring close attention. Too little Z-lon for the leg material will lead to an unstable fly on the water and too much material will lead to a bulky unnatural look.

The wing material had to be thoughtfully considered for the same reasons. Zing Wing is the perfect choice because it is such a thin material that does not build up bulk and it looks as close to the natural midge wing as any material around.

Here is a formula for the number of strands of Z-lon for legs in relation to the size of hook.

Hook Size	Strands of Z-lon
20	24
22	21
24	19
26	15

Randy adds," This is not the original formula given to me. I've refined it slightly to make the fly perform better. I guess I'm being anal about these amounts for the legs but this formula makes a correctly proportioned fly and creates enough surface tension to allow the fly to float well. Prepare the bundles of Z-lon ahead of time. Separating six or eight bundles of twenty-four strands of Z-lon is not as nerve-racking as it may sound."

John Betts popularized Zing Wing. At first glance it looks like a white plastic rope. It is actually strapping material used to ship certain foreign goods. Betts found it in a trash dumpster behind a Pier-One Imports store. After it is separated and untwisted it is actually thin sheets of clear film. Easily cut into strips of any width, it can be used for several different winging applications, including mayfly and caddis wings.

Prepare the Zing Wing by cutting it into strips about 1/16 of an inch wide for size 20 and 22 flies, a little thinner for size 24 and 26.

Again, this prep work before you start tying is done in the spirit of speed and consistency of proportion.

The Z-lon Midge is a simple yet effective pattern for just about any midging situation. Early spring and late fall is usually the best time for midge activity, but they can be the insect of choice for feeding trout anytime of the year. Just match the color and size of the fly to the midges you will be imitating. In larger sizes, it can be a great stillwater midge pattern.

Randy says, "In the tiny sizes, it ranks as one of my favorite tailwater dry-fly midge patterns. An important thing to remember about fishing this fly is that it will be hard to see, and has a tendency to sink before the drift is over. Don't be too quick to pick up and make another cast. It works very well just under the surface also."

This is a floatant-dependant fly, so make sure you carry your favorite silicone gel.

Z-lon Adult Midge

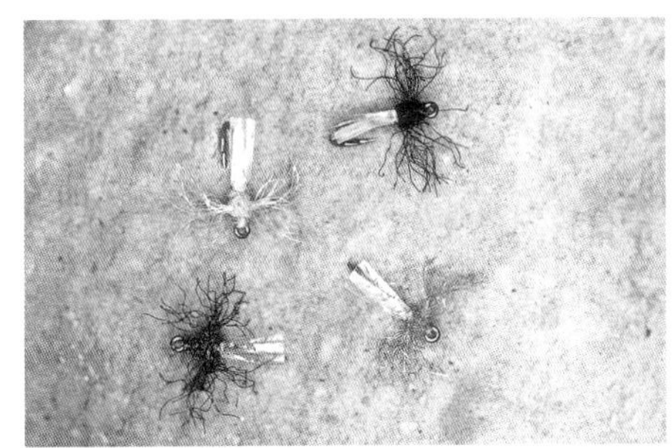

Hook: Dry fly, sizes 20-26, ring-eye preferably
Thread: 8/0 to match fly. Black, brown, tan, and gray
Body: Thread
Wing: Zing Wing
Thorax: Fine 'n Dry dubbing, same color as thread (Spirit River)
Legs: Kinky Z-lon to match body color

1. Start thread at mid shank and wrap forward to just behind the eye. Tie in a slip of Zing Wing material about an inch long as close to the middle of the slip as possible.

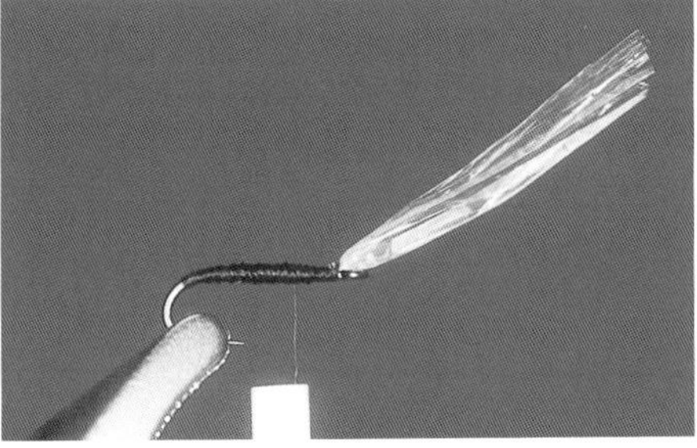

2. Fold the wing material so that both sections are over the eye of the hook and secure into place with a few tight wraps of thread. Create a slightly tapered thread body over the back three-quarters of the hook.

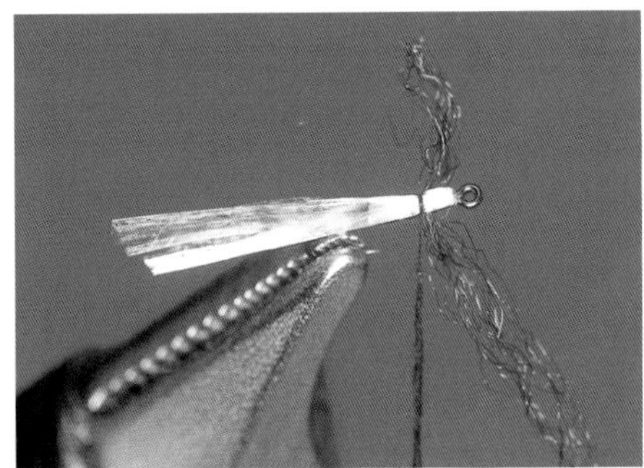

3. Tie in a bundle of Z-lon for the legs at the 7/8 point of the hook. When tying with this kinky Z-lon, wetting the bundle with saliva helps keep it manageable and easier to tie into place. This bundle should be tied in with a simple X-ing pattern so that a half-inch of the material hangs out one side and the rest hangs on the other. When the time comes to trim the legs to length, the longer bundle can be used for the legs on the next fly. Move the thread to behind the legs, about the 3/4 point. Dub a very thin noodle of Fine n' Dry to the thread. The length of the noodle depends on the size of the fly you are tying, but about three-quarters of an inch of dubbing is a good starting point. Adjust this length as needed. Make sure to leave about a half-inch of bare thread between the hook and the dubbing. Now pull the winging material back over the top of the body and use the section of bare thread to secure the wing into place.

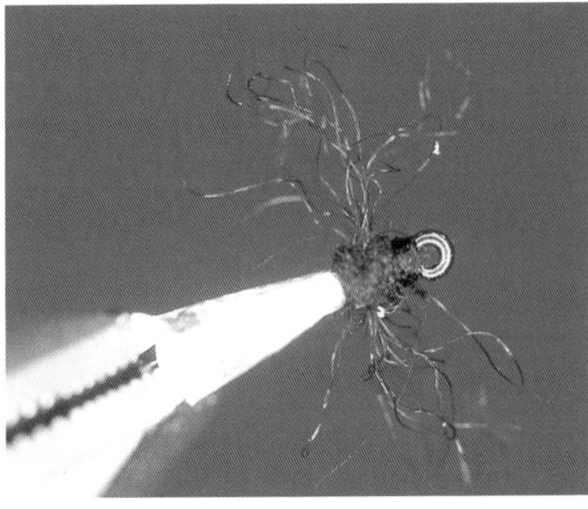

4. Continue wrapping thread until the dubbing shows up. Make a wrap of dubbing in front of the legs then behind the legs. Make a wrap from behind the fore wing to the front of the far wing, then from in front of the fore wing to behind the far wing. Again, just a simple X-ing pattern. By adjusting the thread tension as you wrap, the legs can be adjusted back and forth so they are in perfect position. Also make sure to cover up any thread wraps or part of the white winging material that may be showing. Whip finish. Trim wings and legs to length. The wings on an adult midge are not very long so trim accordingly. A simple way to do this is to butt a blade of your scissors against the bend of the hook and cut the wing. This procedure is repeatable; ensuring the length of the wings on all the flies you tie will be the same. Before you trim the legs to length, remember this kinky Z-lon has some spring to it, so don't trim them too short. Separate the legs by pulling them to the sides or just pushing a finger directly into the cluster on both sides to make them slay out. This will also provide better support for fly when it is on the water.

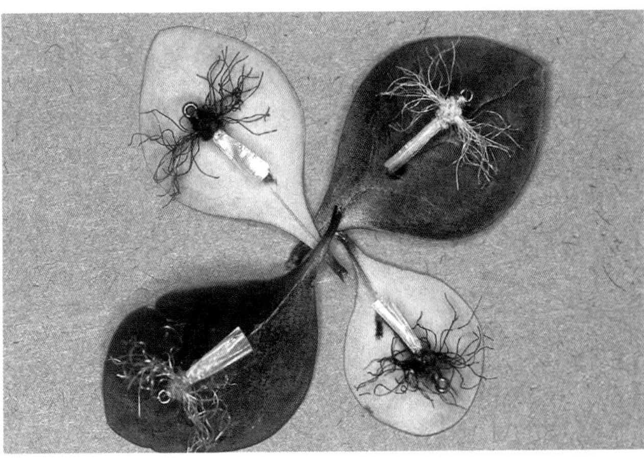

Chapter 6

STONEFLIES

Braided Golden Stone
Contributed by Pat Dorsey

The stonefly is one of the last great hopes of all fly anglers. It's a symbol that lets us know we don't have to fish tiny midge and mayfly patterns all the time. Trout actually do eat large insects, at least during certain times of the year. When the stonefly nymphs start their migration to the shore in late spring, they are constantly ripped loose from the rocky bottom they travel, becoming available to any trout downstream.

Inquire about your local waters and find out which ones hold stoneflies. Find out the best sections of the river, which species of stoneflies live there, and what time of year they become active. You won't be sorry. Whether drifting nymphs deep along the bottom of a swift riffle or plopping big dry flies under the overhanging willows, stoneflies can produce many exciting days of fishing each year.

The Braided Golden Stone is another version of the ever-so-popular stonefly nymph. I think all stonefly patterns are unique, but this one is a real work of art. The braided body on this fly creates a very realistic and unrivaled fly.

A quick note to remember about this book: It is full of techniques and ideas from some of the best tiers in the business. Even though you see several golden stone patterns in this section, it is not meant to limit your use of the techniques for them. Feel free to let your imagination get the best of you. Any one of these golden stones can be turned into brown stones, black stones, or albino stones by changing the color of the materials used. Change the size and color to match the insects in your area.

The one thing that amazed me about this fly was the fact that Pat Dorsey tied this one commercially for a while, selling many to several local shops. I told him he was a glutton for punishment. But, all pro tiers have been punished at one time or another, usually on their own accord. However, that is how the skills of pro tiers are honed so sharply. We rarely turn down a good challenge or a chance to use a new technique.

This pattern will challenge you in all phases of fly tying. But the result will be worth the effort. It is a multi-stepped fly that has a definite order to it, so pay close attention to the tying steps. It has many different materials and provides a unique opportunity to learn a half-hitch weave. The real challenge of this fly is to get it all on the hook and still have room to slip your tippet through the eye. Take the challenge!

Braided Golden Stone

Hook: Nymph 3X long, sizes 8-10, Tiemco 5263
Thread: 6/0 Danville (multi-strand) brown
Tail: Gold or Sulphur-colored goose biots
Body: Larva Lace, one brown and one yellow tied with a half-hitch weave
Underbody: Yellow floss
Wingcase: Brown Swiss straw
Thorax: Golden yellow Furry Foam
Legs: Brown hackle
Antenna: Gold or Sulphur-colored goose biots

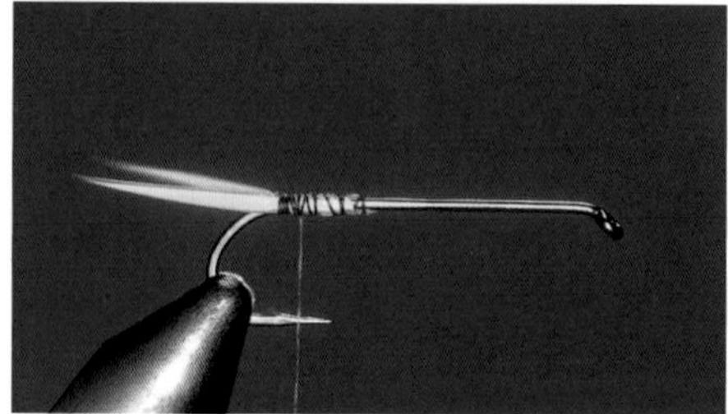

1. Start thread at the 1/4 point of the hook and wrap back a few turns. Pat ties in one tail at a time and does it with great efficiency. He feels he can control the flare of the split tail better that way. Tie in a biot on the far side of the hook so its convex side is against the hook. The tail should be 1/2 the hook shank in length. As you wrap back, adjust the thread torque as to make the biot flare. Try a couple of wraps to see how far the biot will flare. A tighter wrap flares more; a looser wrap produces less flare. Continue wrapping back to the bend of the hook. Then move forward with the thread and tie in a biot on the near side of the hook, convex side toward the hook. Make sure it is the same length as the far tail. Wrap back adjusting the thread torque so the flare is the same as the far tail. It was surprising to me how quickly Pat had the tails in place; and they were split perfectly.
2. Wrap thread forward, making a level thread base, to the 7/8-point of the hook. Tie in a length of yellow Larva Lace on the far side of the hook and wrap back to the tail. Make sure the lace remains on the far side of the hook as you wrap back. Move thread to the 7/8-

point and tie in a length of brown lace on the near side of the hook and wrap back to the tail. Again, make sure the lace remains on the side of the hook. You are trying to create a flat underbody.

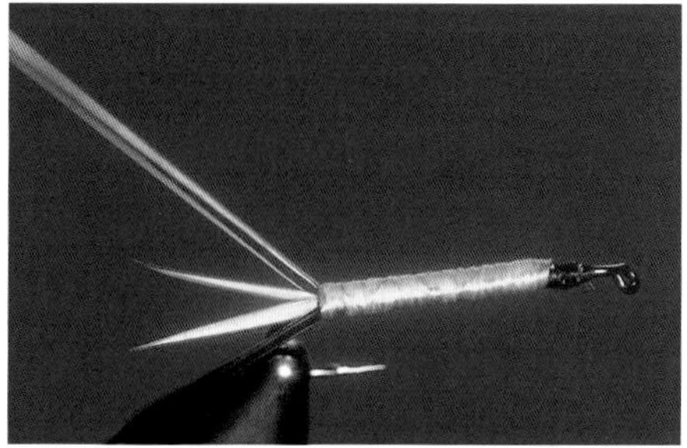

3. Move thread to the 7/8 point and tie in the yellow floss. Lash down the floss to the back of the hook. Move thread forward to the 7/8 point again. Wrap floss forward making a smooth yellow underbody. Secure at the 7/8 point and trim excess floss. Whip finish and remove thread.

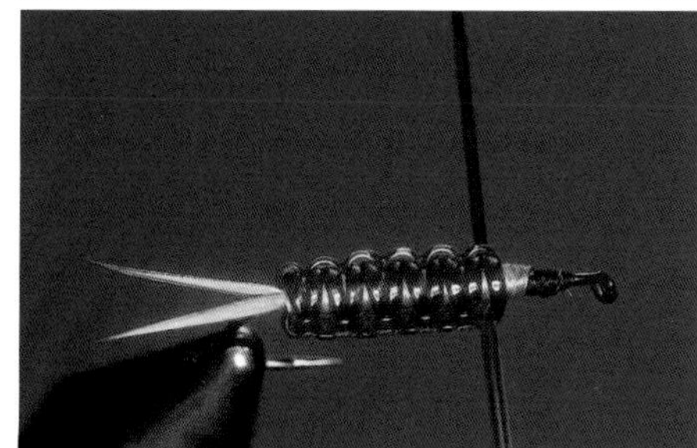

4. The half-hitch weave is easier to do if you turn the vise so the eye of the hook is facing you. Start the weave by crossing the yellow lace over the brown lace and pull the yellow through making a half-hitch knot. Slip the knot over the eye of the hook. Tighten the knot as you position the lace in front of the tails. The brown lace should have crossed over the top of the hook and the yellow will be under the hook. Tighten the knot making sure the actual knot stays on the side. Cross the yellow lace over the brown lace and pull the yellow through making another half-hitch knot. Slip the knot over the eye of the hook, making sure the brown lace is on top and the yellow is on the bottom as you tighten the knot. Position the knot in front of the last one and tighten. If at any point the yellow lace crosses over the top of the hook, the half-hitch needs to be taken apart and redone. Repeat until you are at the end of the yellow floss.

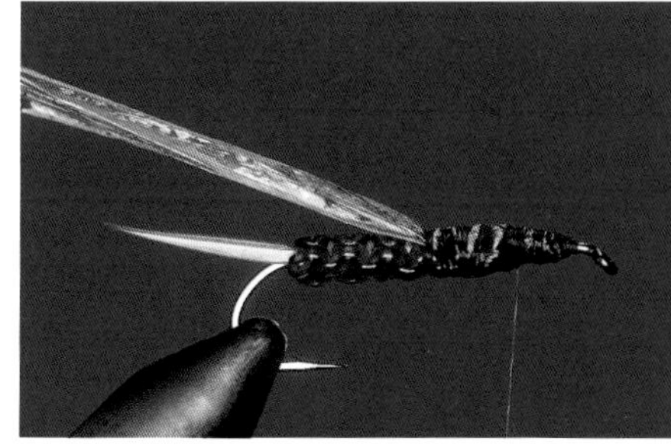

5. Restart the thread in front of the body and secure the lace. Trim excess lace. Prepare the Swiss straw for the wingcase. Swiss straw comes folded in many layers, so take a piece a few inches long and unfold it. Cut a strip about 1/2-inch wide and fold it in half, making the width of the wingcase 1/4-inch wide. Tie in the wingcase in front of the body and wrap back over the weave to the 1/2 point of the hook.

6. Tie in a length of Furry Foam for the thorax. Pick a brown hackle equal to or one size larger than the hook size. Trim the butt end of the feather and strip 1/2 inch of the barbs off both sides of the stem. Tie in the hackle as shown in the photo. Move thread to just behind the eye of the hook.

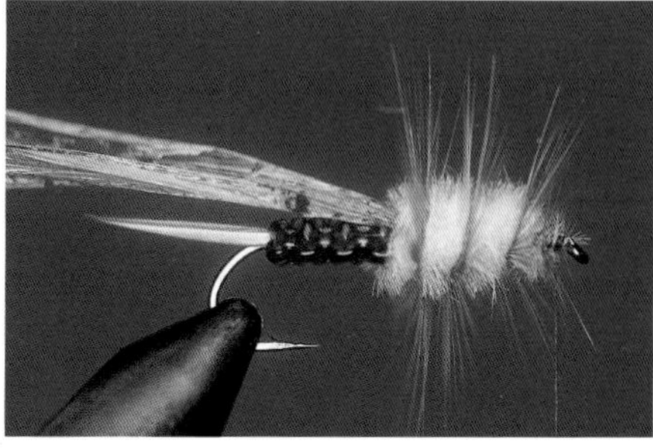

7. Wrap the Furry Foam forward, filling the thorax area. Make sure the fuzzy part of the foam is showing as you wrap. Secure and trim excess foam. Palmer the hackle forward through the thorax. Secure and trim excess hackle.

8. Pull wingcase over the thorax and secure behind the eye. You are looking for two gold biots that are slightly thinner than what you used for the tail. These thin biots can be found near the tip of the quill. Secure a biot on each side of the head for the antenna and whip finish.

Elk Hair Foam Stone

Contributed by Rich Pilatzke

The idea for this fly came years after a fishing experience on the Gallatin River in Yellowstone National Park. Rich Pilatske and his father-in-law, Pete Peterson, trekked to the park on the 4th of July in 1980. The water was roaring down the narrow channel and catching trout was tough.

With mobility limited, Rich was hitting the banks with a new hopper pattern he developed made with Art Foam tied in for a body and elk hair for the wing. A thick hackle collar finished this size-6 fly. It was pretty much a standard pattern in those days except for the foam body. "It may have been a little early in the year for hoppers, but streamers and nymphs seemed to be a waste of time also. A big dry fly was at least enjoyable to cast and watch drift. As the day went on, salmonflies started to show themselves. Eventually, while working a large bend pool, a nice trout came to my yellow-bodied hopper," Rich says. "I'm positive the trout took it for a salmonfly,"

This experience is what got the creative juices flowing, but the salmon-colored body would elude him for years because of the limited number of colors available in the foam market.

"I was fascinated with foam as a fly-tying material the first time I saw some. My mind was racing furiously thinking about flies I could tie with my new material," Rich proclaims. "Since I was already infatuated with terrestrials, I would eventually tie Madam Xs and Elk Hair Hoppers from this foam. They were highly successful fished as grasshopper imitations. These early foam flies did work; however, the foam lacked durability and did not float well for any length of time. It was actually what I would call an open-cell foam."

Rich continued to work with foam and kept his eyes open for any new foam materials that came on the market. Eventually, the closed-cell evasote type of foam made its way into the craft stores. Tying flies just took a huge turn for the better at Rich's vise. The closed-cell foam was much easier to work with, it came in a number of great colors, it floated much better, and his flies were lasting much longer.

This version of the adult stonefly, with the salmon-colored foam body, emerged from that grasshopper pattern he tied at least twenty years ago. This size 6 makes an excellent *Pteronarcys* imitation and has worked effectively on the Madison River hatch as well as the upper Rio Grande River in Colorado. Changing the color and size of this pattern will help you imitate any stonefly anywhere in the world.

Elk Hair Foam Stone

Hook: Nymph 3x long, size 6, Tiemco 5263 or Daiichi 1720
Thread: Black 6/0 UNI-Thread
Tail: Elk hair
Body: Orange Rainy Sheet Foam 1/8"
Wing: Elk hair
Hackle: Brown

1. Start thread at the 1/4 point of the hook and wrap back slightly. Stack and measure a clump of elk hair for the tail. It should be about 1/3 the hook shank length. Secure tightly and move thread to the 3/5 point of the hook.

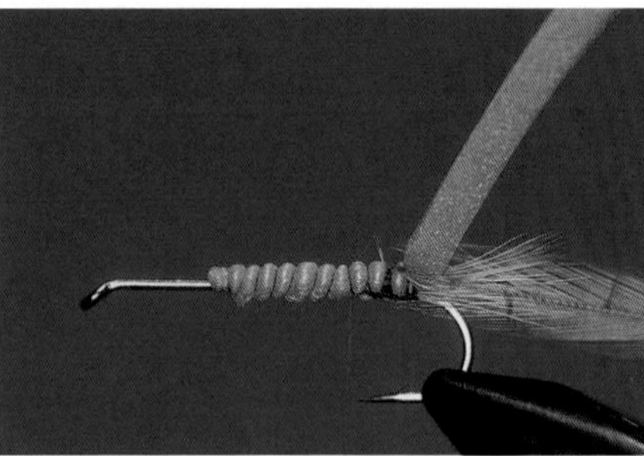

2. Tie in a strip of orange foam and wrap to the back of the hook. Tie in the tip of a brown hackle at the back of the hook. On this size 6 hook the hackle should be

measured to about a size 10. Move thread to the 1/5 point of the hook. Pull foam over and secure it in place with a couple of turns of thread. Lift the foam up and move the thread to the 2/5 point of the hook. Secure the foam down again with a couple of turns of thread. Lift foam up and move thread to the 3/5 point of the hook. Secure the foam down with a couple of turns of thread. Now wrap the hackle forward through the segmentations in the foam. Make two wraps in each segment if hackle length will allow. Secure the hackle at the 3/5 point of the hook. Trim the hackle and foam at the same time. Make a few turns of thread to clean up the trimmed foam to make a landing area for the wing.

3. Stack and measure another clump of elk hair for the wing, which should extend to the back of the body. Secure the wing in front of the body. Cover the butt ends of the hair, smoothing out the hook shank for the hackle.

4. Prepare another hackle. This one should be a size larger than the one wrapped through the body. A size 6 or 8

will work nicely. Tie in the hackle by the butt end of the feather, in front of the wing, and wrap forward. Secure behind the eye and whip finish.

Enchanted Prince Nymph

Contributed by Paul Stimpson

The Enchanted Prince Nymph, as tied by Paul Stimpson, is a fine example of tying creativity, exemplary material handling, and fine tying technique. Paul has tied for Gary LaFontaine a number of years and has taken on many of his ideas for creating new fly patterns—the willingness to try different things, experiment with different looks, and use different materials are among them.

Paul took a very effective fly pattern in the Prince Nymph and tried to create something slightly out of the ordinary. He had tied the Twist Nymph for Gary and was amazed at the value of the Double Magic technique, so he started by changing the ordinary peacock herl body of the Prince to a Double Magic body. It worked at least as well, if not a small percentage better. The sparkle the Antron adds to this fly was how it got its name, the Enchanted Prince. (I always find naming a fly very difficult.)

Most Prince Nymphs are tied with the white biot wings lying down over the body with the concave side down. Paul thought he would try the pattern with the wings canting upwards with the convex side down. It made a very noticeable difference in the number of hookups. Paul thinks the increased movement of the wings may give the fly added life or even cause a slight attractive vibration as it drifts through a run. He also uses this pattern in lakes. It may be a great imitation of a backswimmer when tied in the correct size. Again, the added movement may wake up trout as it is stripped through the water.

There should always be a reason a fly works better tied one way rather than another, but oftentimes the answer to our questions eludes us. This is what keeps us behind the vise trying new things!

Now some ideas on material handling and fly proportion: To start with, a little preparation is in order. Pre-load all the beads on the hooks first.

Biots for the tails and the wings on this fly should be selected carefully. The biot's width should equal the size of the hook. In other words, use a biot that is wide enough for a large fly and a thinner one for smaller flies. As they come off a goose wing, the biots are wider at the base of the feather and thinner at the tip. This relates to correct proportioning and proportions should always be of utmost importance when tying flies. Paul also suggests leaving the biots intact on the strip so they can be pulled off in order of width, rather than pulling them all off and then trying to match up pairs as you go.

Paul also proposes an often-overlooked idea about peacock herl. The herl should be left in the bag it comes in and then you can pull the strands out as you need them. The herl has several lengths when it's sewn together, however, if you leave it in the bag it can be pulled out according to length also. Paul finds it amazing how consistent the number of strands he pulls out at a time. He strives to use the same number of strands on each fly. With a little practice, it is easy to pick out just the right number. Five strands is a good starting point for a size-10 hook.

Let's give one a try.

Enchanted Prince Nymph

Hook: Nymph 2X long, size 14-10 Daiichi 1710
Bead: 1/8 gold
Thread: 8/0 black
Tail: Biots, brown
Body: Peacock herl and orange Antron touch dubbing, using the Double Magic technique developed by Gary LaFontaine
Hackle: Brown saddle, Whiting Farms
Wing: Biots, white

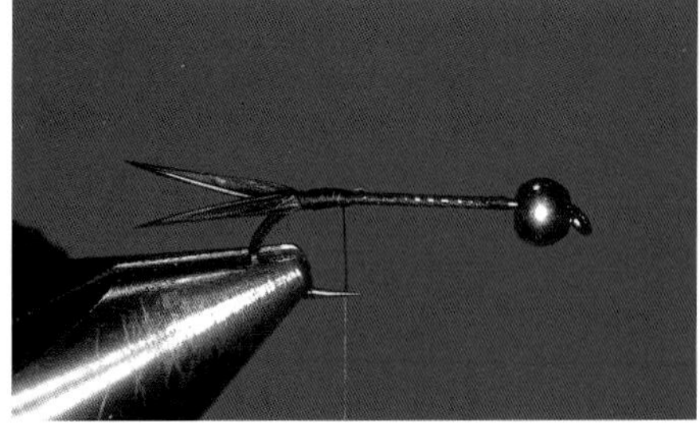

1. Slip a bead over the bend of the hook. Start the thread behind the bead and wrap back to the 1/4 point, laying down a thread base. Secure a pair of brown biots, one on each side of the hook shank, and wrap back to the bend. The thread butting up against the bend of the hook will naturally split the tails into the common stonefly position. Move thread to the point behind the bead.

2. Trim the tips of the peacock herl and tie in five strands right behind the bead and wrap them down to the back of the hook shank. This tie-in procedure will maintain a nice level body for the herl to wrap around. Paul has found in his own tying that five strands of herl is just right for a size-10 hook. Adjust the number to four strands on the next size smaller and so on. Apply a tacky dubbing wax to a couple of inches of the thread. B.T.'s Dubbing Wax is one of the best on the market for this technique. Apply the Antron touch dubbing to the waxed thread. Now loop the thread back to the hook, essentially making a dubbing loop. Wrap your thread back

slightly to lock the loop in place and then move the bobbin forward to just behind the bead. Cut the loop at the opposite end from the dubbing. (See photo.) Pull the peacock herl down and meld the thread with the herl. Using an electrical clip or hackle pliers, clamp the herl and the touch-dubbed thread together and spin. Wrap peacock and Antron (Double Magic) forward and secure at a point behind the bead, leaving room enough for the hackle and wings to be put in place. This technique makes beautiful peacock chenille with Antron fibers protruding from the herl. This Double Magic method was made famous by Gary LaFontaine and has proven to be a great combination of materials that trout find irresistible.

3. Measure and prepare a brown hackle one size smaller than the hook being used. For example, use a size-12 hackle on a size-10 hook. Tie in the hackle behind the bead, shiny side up. Make two wraps of hackle, secure and trim excess. Do not build up too much bulk with the thread, as there are still a couple things to do behind the bead.

4. Separate two white biots and put them together with the concave side up. Secure the biots on top of the hook for the wings. Snug them back against the body to help prop them up at an angle near 45 degrees. Again, use as few turns of thread as possible. The tips should extend just short of the back of the Double Magic body. Trim the butt ends of the biots.

5. Tie in two or three more strands of peacock herl behind the bead and make a couple turns to clean up the area in front of the hackle and behind the bead. This peacock collar is for esthetics only, making the transition between the wing and hackle to the bead more appealing to the tier's eye. The trout could give a rip. Whip finish to complete the fly.

Prince Nymph

Contributed by John Hagen

The dreaded Prince Nymph! I don't know anyone who really enjoys tying this fly, except maybe John Hagen. He suggested tying the fly for the book, not only because he has tied thousands of dozens of them, but especially for his thoughts on how he puts it together based on what he has learned from tying so many Prince Nymphs. After watching him tie the few flies he has contributed to the book, I can tell he has paid his dues figuring out the finer details of speed and proportion for just about all phases of fly tying. Here is a guy, without hesitation, who sits down and whips out whatever fly is needed for the fly shop or whatever empty space he has in his own fly box, no questions asked. John really enjoys the challenge.

Any tier with a fly in their hat has at least attempted to tie this thing. Out here in the West, a Prince Nymph is the go-to fly when the fishing is good (fishing is always good) and the catching is a bit slow. We have all learned to tie it out of necessity rather than enjoyment. Although a bit goofy looking, it is a particularly effective pattern on most streams. I mean really, what does this thing actually represent? I know we pass it off as a stonefly nymph, or as I call it, an attractor stonefly. Then you take it to a lake and it works in still water! What is it now, a dragonfly nymph? Who knows? It sounds like it just needs to be wet to work. A Prince Nymph drifted in tandem with a small midge larva, a Pheasant Tail Nymph, or a Buckskin can be a deadly set-up in just about any situation.

Doug Prince, the fly's originator, couldn't have known the havoc he would wreak on the commercial tiers of our time. It is a time-consuming fly, requiring several different materials, several steps, and those white biot wings. However, there are few pro tiers who haven't filled an order of Prince Nymphs primarily from a predicament called supply and demand. Fly shops just can't get enough of them. So, we all have our own ideas and strategies for putting this fly together, which is good and sometimes bad.

I have had discussions (oftentimes arguments) about the many ideas about putting this fly together. Some tiers split the tails differently, some use different ribbing materials, but in general, everyone seems to be in agreement on the construction of the back of the fly. It is those white biots that bring out the hostility. For those of you who have had trouble with those white biots, John may just have the answer for you.

I think John's real strategy for doing this fly here was to win this argument once and for all. No one can disagree, or at least he doesn't have to hear it. If you don't like his ideas, I hope you look him up and give him the business.

Prince Nymph

Hook: Nymph 1x or 2x long, size 8-18
Thread: Black, Danville 6/0
Tail: Brown biots
Ribbing: Gold woven oval tinsel
Body: Peacock herl
Hackle: Brown hen saddle, Whiting Farms
Wing: White biots

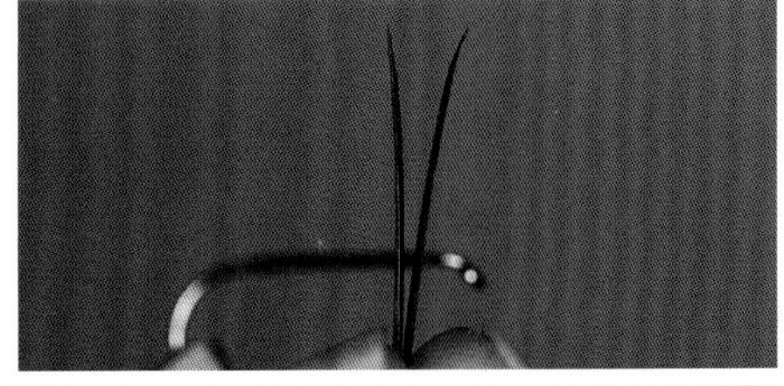

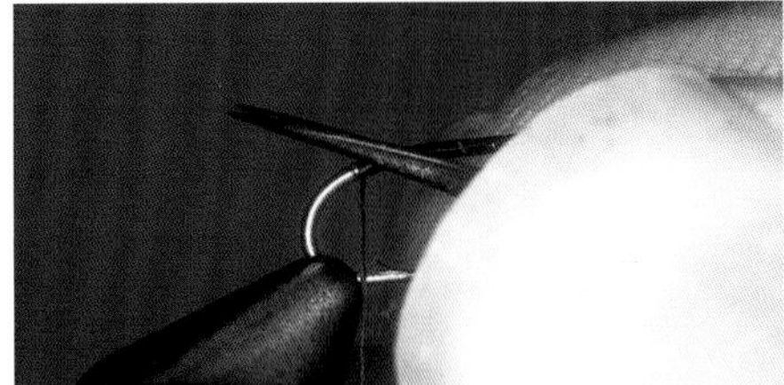

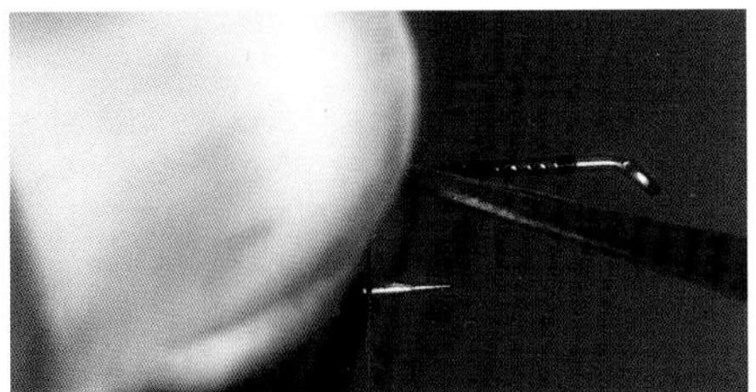

1. Start thread at the 3/4 point of the hook and wrap to the back of the shank. Separate two brown biots and put the convex sides together so as to form a V with the tips. Slide the biots from under the hook shank, one biot on either side of the hook. Tail length is 1/2 the hook shank length. Switch hands without changing the position of the biots and secure with several tight wraps of thread. The tails split nicely and are locked into place. Trim the excess.

2. Tie in ribbing so that it is on the fore side of the hook. Tie in several strands of peacock herl by the tips at the 3/4 point of the hook and wrap back to just in front of the tails. This procedure makes the underbody level before wrapping the herl into place. You can be the judge of the number of peacock herl strands. Make a chubby fly or an anorexic little Prince, it's your choice. As you will see, John's royalty eats well.

3. Wrap the herl forward to the 3/4 point. **DO NOT WRAP TOO FAR FORWARD**.

Secure with three tight wraps of thread. Reverse wrap the ribbing forward with evenly spaced wraps, also to the 3/4 point. **DO NOT WRAP TOO FAR FORWARD**. Secure and trim excess herl and ribbing at the same time as close to the hook as possible. **NOTE: It is very important that you DO NOT WRAP THE MATERIAL TOO FAR FORWARD.** The lack of bare hook shank behind the eye is one of the major problems tiers have with this step. It becomes very difficult to finish the fly without a huge thread head **IF THE MATERIALS ARE WRAPPED TOO FAR FORWARD**. If after a couple of flies, you have had trouble finishing the fly, reread this step. What you have ended up doing is trying to finish a size-14 fly on a size-16 hook. In other words, you have run out of hook before you have run out of fly. If you have a problem finishing the fly, secure everything at the 3/4 point of the hook and **Do Not Wrap To Far Forward**.

4. When choosing a soft hackle, pick a hackle so that the length of the barbs extends from the eye of the hook to the point of the hook. This is not terribly important, so if they extend beyond the hook point it is OK and likewise if they are too short. Prepare a brown hen back feather as shown in Step 2 and 3 of the Exploding Caddis. With the shiny side of the feather towards you and tip of the feather over the eye of the hook, strip the barbs off the top half of the feather. Trim the tip of the feather to tie in. With the shiny side of the feather up and the bare side of the feather away from you, tie in the tip of the feather at the front of the hook. Wrap soft hackle three of four times and secure right behind the eye of the hook and trim excess. As you wrap this feather you will notice that it lies in place by itself, swept back like a perfect soft hackle, without manipulation.

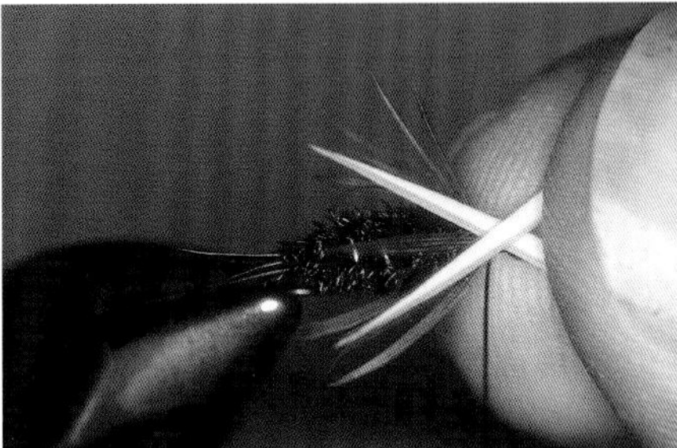

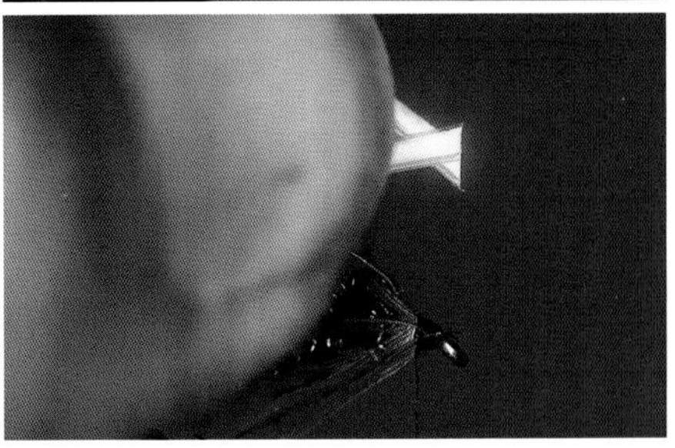

5. OK, those white biots. Take two biots and put them together in a cross with the concave sides down so the tips of the biots point down. With the biots in your right hand, gauge the length of the wings from where they cross, so they extend from the eye of the hook to the back of the body. Switch biots into your left hand, trim the butt ends of the biots off to a point just in front of the cross, but do not let go of the biots. Hold the biots slightly to the side of the hook and secure in place behind the eye. Make a couple of tight wraps letting the thread torque roll the biots on top of the hook, but do not let go of the biots yet. Make 5 to 7 more tight wraps of thread and then let go of the biots. Immediately whip finish and notice the very small thread head you've made. You have just tied yourself a great-looking Prince Nymph!

A variation of the Prince called the Golden Prince Nymph

Randy's Golden Stone

Contributed by Randy Smith

Tying stonefly nymphs can be a double-edged sword for most commercial fly tiers. On the one hand, it is usually a complicated, multi-step fly pattern that takes more time to tie than most pro tiers want to spend. We usually charge more for these type of flies, but the more time it takes tie a fly, the less money to be made, pure and simple. On the other hand, a lot of fly-fishermen don't like to tie them or have difficulty tying them for themselves. The result is a fly high in demand for fly shops. So, somebody has to tie them.

The pro tier is always figuring out a way to tie a fly faster, either reducing the number of steps or changing materials to make the fly easier to tie. Randy's Stone Nymph is a great example of the resourcefulness and creativity of a seasoned tier. With the use of a material that can be wrapped around the hook instead of dubbing and a wingcase that is doubled as the top of the abdomen, the time it takes to tie this fly is cut in half. By making it a viable production fly, a tier can make money and it also becomes a much easier fly for the novice to tie.

A big piece of Furry Foam looks just like a blanket you might see at a hotel—

because that is exactly what it is. A friend of mine dragged me over to J.C. Penney's one day to buy a blanket. I politely asked him, trying not to deprive him of his manly duties, why he did the shopping for bedding. He said, "Hey, it's fly-tying material." It can be found in fly shops now, cut to a manageable size. It does need a little prep work though. It is actually two pieces of foam stuck together which need to be separated before it can be used properly. Starting at a corner, carefully pull apart the two pieces of foam. Randy suggests doing this while watching television; it can take a while to get the two pieces apart. When separated, it is a dual-sided foam. One side is furry and the other side is smooth and kind of tacky. Starting with yellow Furry Foam, prepare the foam by coloring the furry side using a Pantone pen #470-T Rust Brown. After it is colored, cut it into 3/4 inch strips. Furry Foam is very easy to use, speeds up tying tremendously, and is very versatile. This color works well for a golden stone nymph, but with the vast number of stonefly species available to trout, making nymphs of different colors is as simple as changing the color of the foam and/or the marker color.

Split tails on a stonefly nymph present many challenges for tiers. Splitting the tails evenly and handling the biots are a couple that always seem to come up in discussion. Prepare the tails by separating the biots into individual fibers by pulling them from the main stem. Loose biots are much easier to work with than having to pull the fibers off for each fly. Randy has a unique procedure for this process, as you will see in the tying instructions.

A great thought Randy has about tying in general, tails in particular, is to make adjustments as necessary. In other words, if the tails are not in the position you want them after tying them in place, move them. If you have to untie them to make the fix, untie them. However, most of the time a little twist here or a tweak there will do the trick.

Bodi-Stretch, sold by Spirit River, is a material some of you may have seen used as the back on a scud. It can be dyed just about any color and by stretching it can be made to any width you like. The great thing about Bodi-Stretch for the wingcase on this stonefly is its durability. Randy's original stonefly nymph patterns were tied with goose-quills. His experiences fishing the goose quills fly proved to be good for about four or five fish before it would fall apart. Soon after Spirit River introduced Bodi Stretch, Randy made the switch. The fly looks better and does not come apart.

Stonefly activity usually peaks in late spring or early summer. This is the time of year when most fly anglers concentrate their efforts with stonefly patterns, working both nymphs and big dry flies to fool aggressive trout. Don't be fooled by the typical hatch charts though. In rivers where great numbers of stoneflies exist, stonefly nymph patterns can be effective year round.

Randy related to me a story about the Colorado River in October. He was assisting a group of eighth graders at a whirling disease project on the Kemp Breeze section of the Colorado River. They had a wildlife biologist talking about the problem of whirling disease and several stations set up on the river for the kids to study. They took stream-velocity readings, water temperatures, and seined the stream bottom for samples of the bug life. Randy, helping at the seining station, found an abundance of stonefly nymphs in these samples. Golden stones, black stones, and several smaller species were netted. Later in the afternoon, after the kids left, a chance to fish presented itself. He tied on a black stone nymph, not really expecting it to work (thinking it should work only in the spring) and another smaller nymph that should work in the fall. In the next couple of hours a dozen rainbows, ranging from fifteen inches to six pounds, hammered the black stonefly nymph. Simple lessons learned: Pay attention to what the river is telling you and never say never!

Reports from customers using this fly pattern and reorders from fly shops prove the fly's effectiveness.

Randy's Golden Stone

Hook: Curved Nymph 3X long, size 8-#12, Dai Riki 270 or 710
Thread: 6/0 Danville (multi-strand) brown
Weight: .020 wire
Tail: Brown goose biots
Back: Bodi-Stretch, brown (Spirit River)
Ribbing: Medium copper wire
Body: Yellow Furry Foam, with Pantone Rust Brown #470-T

Wingcase: Bodi-Stretch, brown
Thorax: Yellow Furry Foam (same as body)
Legs: Speckled brown hen back feather

1. Wrap the front 1/3 of the hook with .020 lead wire. Resist the urge to put on

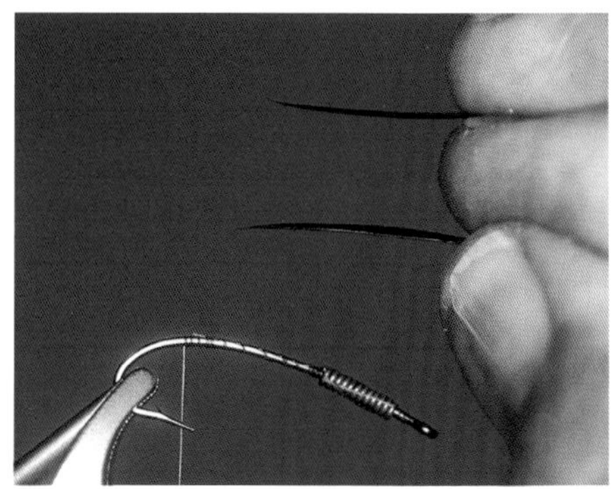

too much wire. A heavily weighted fly has a tendency to drift somewhat awkwardly in the water making a natural presentation more difficult. When a fly is tied in the round the amount of weight really does not matter. "In the round" means the fly does not have a top or bottom, it looks the same from whichever angle you look at it. (A Woolly Bugger is a prime example of a fly tied in the round). Start the thread behind the wire and lock the wire into place with a few wraps. Move thread to the back of the hook. Loosen the vise and reposition the hook so that it is canting downwards. Notice the easier access at the back of the hook for the tail tie-in procedure. Randy has a unique method of separating a pair of goose biots for a split tail. With the convex sides of the biots together, he grabs one between his thumb and index finger and the other between the index finger and his middle finger. Moving the thumb or the middle finger will line the tips up very quickly. When the tips are even and tail length is determined, switch to the left hand and tie in at the back of the hook. For speed purposes Randy does not take the time to build up a ball of thread or dubbing at the back of the hook to assist in splitting the tails. When the tails are tied directly on the sides of the hook, they naturally split a certain amount. If this is not enough for you, a wrap or two of thread between the tail and the hook will help separate them a bit more. A thread ball does work better for size-12 flies and smaller. I have tried this method of splitting tails since Randy showed it to me and it does work very nicely.

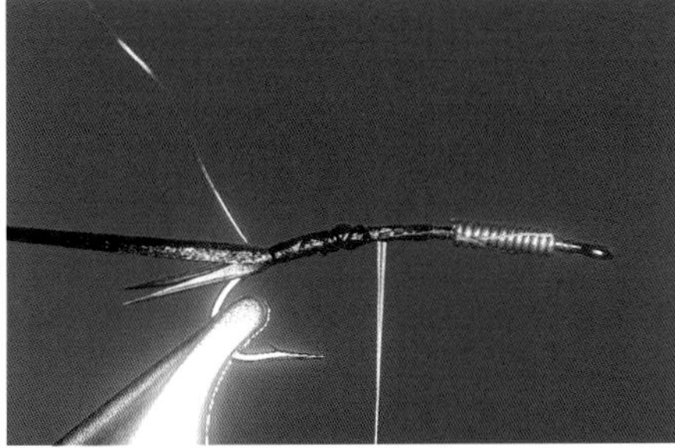

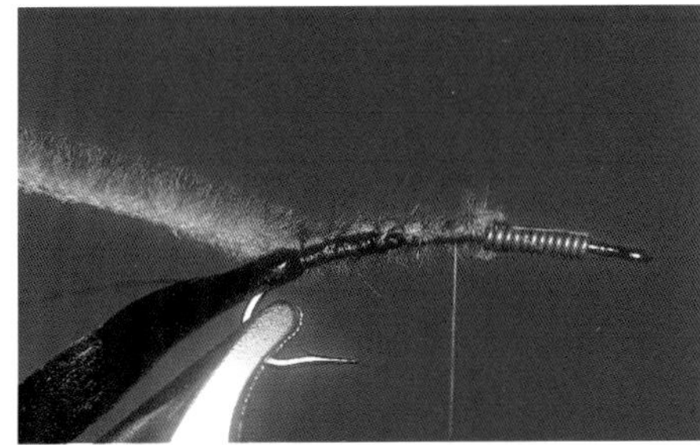

2. Once the tails are in position, the ribbing, back, and body material are tied in. Tie in copper wire on the backside of the hook and wrap it back to the tail tie-in point. Trim a piece of the Bodi-Stretch to a point, making tie-in easier and reducing the bulk of material that would end up at the back of the hook. Using as few wraps as possible, tie in the Bodi-Stretch at the 1/4 point and wrap back to the tail, pulling it tight as you go. This also reduces the amount of material that gets tied in at the back of the hook. Make sure there is a clean transition between the tail and the back. A quick note about the back: A stonefly nymph does not have a real back. Many stonefly nymphs are tied to imitate the top of the abdomen, which is darker. This is done most often with slips of turkey tail fibers. They have mottled coloration, but are not as durable. The darker top of the abdomen is a natural camouflage that makes the stonefly nymph blend in with the rock on which it lives. Tie in a strip of Furry Foam and also wrap to the back of the hook.

3. Pull the Furry Foam tight at first (without breaking it off) and start wrapping forward. Make sure the fuzzy, colored side is showing as you wrap. As you move forward, loosen the tension on the foam to create a nice taper to the abdomen. Secure at the 1/2 point of the hook but DO NOT trim the foam off.

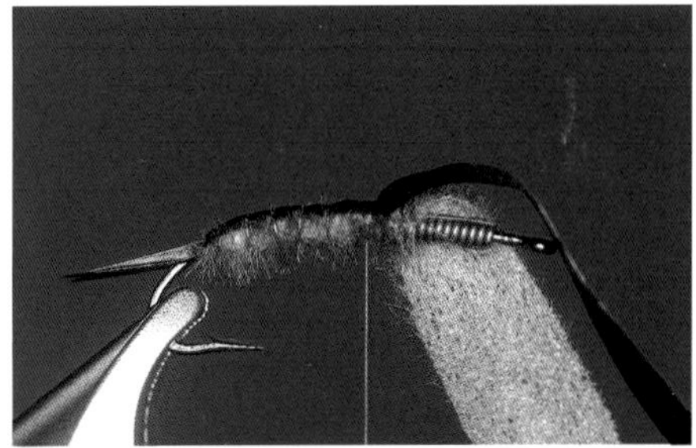

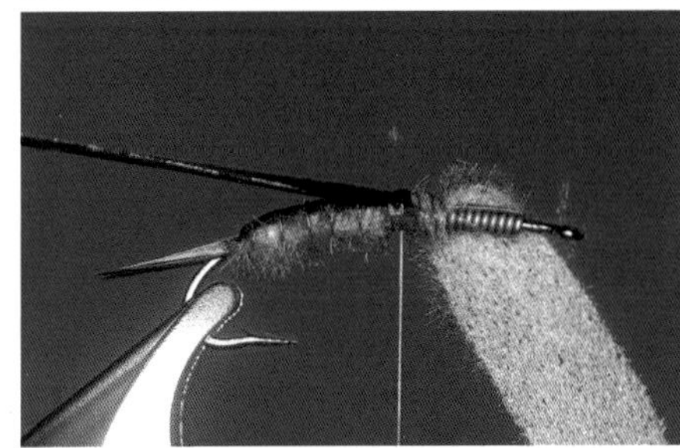

4. Pull the Bodi-Stretch over the abdomen just like you would a wingcase. Stretch the material until it is the width you like and tie it off at the 1/4 point of the hook. DO NOT trim the Bodi-Stretch. Rib the abdomen with five or six evenly spaced wraps of the copper wire. Trim the wire and lay the Bodi-Stretch back over the tail. Secure in place in front of the abdomen. The Bodi-Stretch will be used for the wingcase in a future step.

5. Prepare a hen saddle feather by pulling the fibers back away from the tip

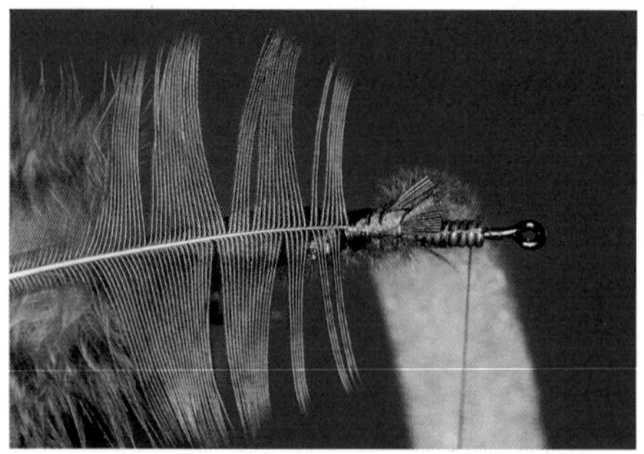

and trimming the tip to about _ of an inch. Secure the tip of the feather in front of the abdomen with the concave side of the feather up.

6. Take the Furry Foam that is left over and wrap it forward forming the thorax, again making sure the colored side of the foam is showing. Secure foam behind the eye of the hook and trim excess. Pull the hen back feather over the thorax with your right hand to make the legs. Take care not to put too much tension on this feather as you pull it over for the legs. The stem in the tip of a hen feather is very thin and can break easily. Separate the barbs at the eye of the hook. With the bobbin in the left hand secure the feather in place behind the eye of the hook. Trim excess feather.

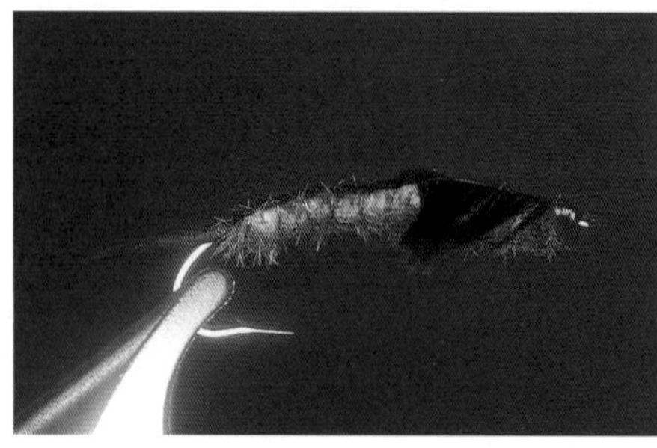

7. Pull the Bodi-Stretch over the top of the legs and thorax to make the wing-case. Stretch the material to a width wider than what is pulled over the back, secure behind the eye and trim excess. Whip finish.

Stimulator

Contributed by John Hagen

In 1980, when Randall Kaufmann invented the Yellow Stimulator, he surely had no idea the impact he would have on the world of fly-fishing, let alone fly tying. This is one of the most effective dry flies available to fly anglers. Primarily tied as a searching or attractor pattern, the "Stimmy" has the versatility to be tied in many sizes and different colors. It can be tied specifically as an adult stonefly, a hopper pattern, or any of several species of caddis. The possibilities of this high-floating dry fly are seemingly endless. Kaufmann figured that out very quickly as he added the Green, Orange, Royal, Golden, and Black Stimulators to his repertoire.

The original Yellow Stimulator, and likely the most popular, when tied in smaller sizes is an excellent pattern for the little yellow stoneflies found out here in the West. The Madison, Frying Pan, Roaring Fork, Bighole, and Clark's Fork all have important hatches that draw trout to the surface. I should also mention the Deschutes, since this river is in Kaufmann's back yard.

A very effective way to fish the Stimulator is with a dropper. On a tippet of 18 to 24 inches tied directly to the bend of the Stimulator, tie either a smaller dry fly or a nymph of your choice. The Stimulator takes its share of trout, but it can also draw the fish's attention to the surface only to notice the smaller dry or nymph drifting in its wake. Two chances are always better than one. We call it the Hopper Dropper set up.

What makes the Stimmy so effective is unknown. There are several patterns out there similar in nature, but they are not as popular or lively. Some feel the fully palmer-hackled fly rides so high in the water that the trout never gets a real good look at the fly but it looks "alive" enough to eat. Maybe all this hackle emits a realistic light source through the water to make the bug look realistic. Who knows for sure? Until we find a trout that can explain all this technical crap to us, we will just have to keep preaching our theories and inventing flies that are effective, which in turn produce new theories.

Everyone should send Randall Kaufmann a "Thank You" note for saving us the trouble.

I would like to thank John Hagen for putting this Stimmy together for your enjoyment. John's version is tied just as Kaufmann's original, except for a slight color variation; a brown hackle through the body instead of badger and an orange dubbing for the thorax instead of an amber color. However, notice the very short tail and the wing that stands tall above the body just as Kaufmann suggests. John has also thrown in a couple of speed techniques that make the fly a bit easier to tie.

Stimulator

Hook: Curved Dry Fly, Tiemco 200R, Daiichi 1270 #6-#16
Thread: Fluorescent Fire Orange, Danville 6/0 #505
Tail: Bleached elk body hair
Ribbing: Fine gold wire
Body: Yellow yarn
Rear Hackle: Brown, one size smaller than hook size
Wing: Bleached elk body hair
Thorax: Rusty orange dubbing
Hackle: Grizzly, one size smaller than hook size

1. Start thread at the 3/5 point of the hook and wrap to the back. Go forward to the 3/5 point again laying a thread

Stoneflies

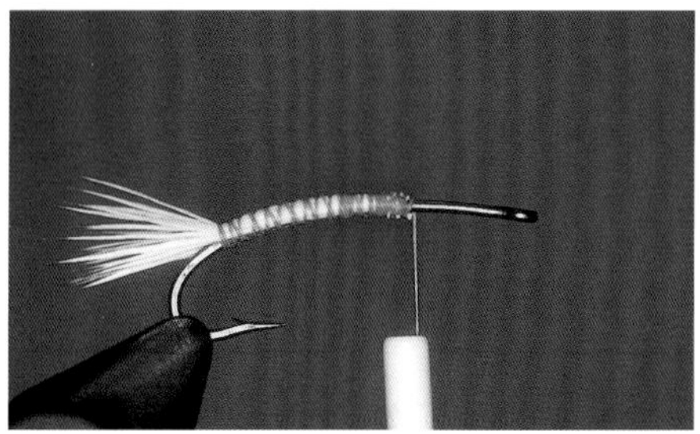

base for the tail to be tied onto. Stack a bunch of bleached elk body and transfer it to the clip. (Here is a close-up photo of how the hair should be spread out in the clip and cut for use as the tail. I show you this technique with the thought that you should be tying at least a dozen of these at a time.) Measure tail to a length of 1/3 hook shank or the gape of the hook, whichever you find easier. Trim hair so that the butt ends of the tail can be secured at the 3/5 point. Tie in and wrap to the back of the hook. As you near the back of the hook, release some of the thread torque so the tails will not splay too much. Wrap forward, reapplying thread torque, to the 3/5 point.

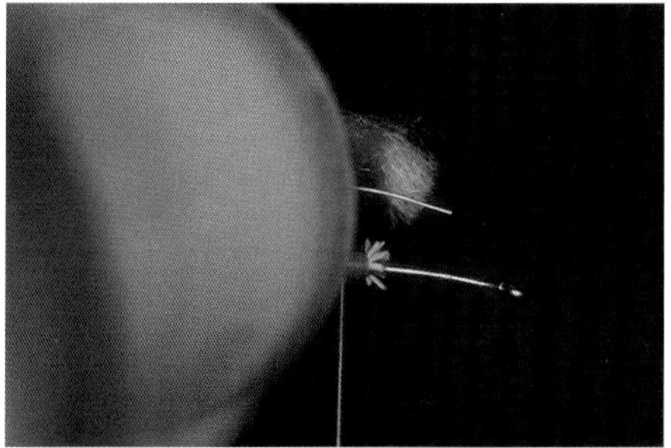

2. Tie the wire ribbing and the body yarn in at the same time. Wrap to the back. Move thread forward to the 3/5 point and wrap body yarn forward. Secure and trim excess yarn. Prepare a brown hackle, remembering to use a hackle one size smaller than the actual hook size being used. Tie in the brown hackle at the 3/5 point.

3. Palmer the hackle to the back. Holding the hackle up with the left hand, grab the wire with the right hand and make a wrap with the wire, securing the hackle at the back of the hook. Carefully rib the wire forward through the hackle and secure at the 3/5 point. Trim wire. (Note: This step is exactly like the procedure used on the Al Troth Elk Hair Caddis.) Wrap thread to the front of the hook then back to the 4/5 point, laying down a thread base for tying on the wing. In the photo I have left the tip of the hackle intact just to show where it is, but it needs to be trimmed at this time.

4. Stack a clump of bleached elk body hair for the wing. Measure wing length to the back of the body while holding the hair in your right hand. Switch the hair to the left hand, maintaining the wing position on the hook, and trim the butt ends of the elk hair at the 4/5 point of the hook. Here is a down-wing tie-in procedure that Dale Darling showed John as he was becoming one of the fine commercial tiers of our day. John explains, "With the hair directly over the hook and in the position it should be tied in, bring thread up and split the hair in half with the thread. Start wrapping the thread around the hook, lashing half the wing in place. Continue around the hook with the thread and lash down the other half of the wing. Two more tight wraps will lock the wing in place and keep it from rolling around the hook. Finish the wing by wrapping back to the 3/5 point, basically butting the wing against the body. This is what causes the wing to push upwards and stand tall as it lies over the body. Cover the wing butts with thread, making a smooth landing area for the dubbing and hackle to wrap onto." NOTE: The amount of hair needed will vary from hook size to hook size, however, a clump of hair taken from the skin that would measure one quarter inch square is a good starting point. Then decrease or increase the amount for the next fly. Cut the same amount from the patch of hair for future flies. (Refer to the section on "Preparing Hair" for help in getting the same amount of hair for every wing.)

5. Dub thread leaving about 1/2 inch of bare thread to tie in the hackle. Prepare a grizzly hackle, also measured one size smaller than the actual hook size. Secure hackle in front of the wing and as the dubbing shows up, dub a level thorax. Palmer the hackle forward through the dubbing and secure at the front. Trim excess and whip finish.

Chapter 7

STREAMERS

Articulated Flash Fly

Contributed by Todd Sabine

It always amazes me how a fly is developed. Sometimes it's out of pure creativity, some newfangled material tied an old-fashioned way, or an old material tied with a new technique. Sometimes it comes from brainstorming after seeing a fish feed on an insect or some waterborne creature that you have not encountered before. Oftentimes flies are developed to solve a problem by making a fly drift differently, look different, or act differently. When you see this Articulated Flash Fly and understand how it was created, you will see a wonderful blend of both problem solving and amazing creativity.

Check out the names of some of these color combinations for the Articulated Flash Fly:

Fort Knox: Gold/Gold
Silver Dollar: Silver/Silver
Margarita Ville:
Chartreuse/Pearl/Silver
Tequila Sunrise:
Chartreuse/Orange/Gold
Fruit Cocktail:
Orange/Pearl/Pink/Gold
Victoria's Secret: Pink/Pearl/Silver
Shirley Temple: Purple/Pink/Silver
Steelie Blue: Dark Blue/Light
Blue/Silver
Mardi Gras: Black/Purple/Red/Silver
Blue Midnight: Black/Light Blue
Ruby Slippers: Red/Orange/Gold

Only a true-blue steelhead fisherman could come up with such a fine array of colors. Todd Sabine happens to be one of those guys. A steelhead fisherman since the age of eight, and a guide off and on since his late teens, Todd has been an avid fly-fisherman for over 20 years.

At season's end Todd treats himself to an annual fly-fishing trip to British Columbia for the elusive steelhead. Todd has fly-fished British Columbia's Babine River for years under all sorts of conditions. It is these tough conditions along with unexpected circumstances that led to this brilliant revolution. He has a few silver hairs behind his ears now, so I know he has the experience to match the many chrome-bright steelhead he has taken. I will let him tell his own story as it sounded when he relayed it to me:

The motivation behind my Articulated Flash Fly is a story that spans a lifetime. As a youngster I spent many summers in Alaska pursuing salmon with conventional gear and the ever-popular "Pixie" lure. It was always amazing to me how effective that flashing steel was at hooking fish. Over time, as I evolved into a fly-fisherman I took pride in catching these great game fish with a fly rod. Now older and a little more refined in my angling methods I don't feel as if I need dozens of hook-ups in order to have a great day of fishing, but getting a few hook-ups is always nice.

In the fall of 1999, we had a group of anglers on the Babine River steelhead fishing. Some of the guests at the lodge were spoon fishermen and over the course of the week the spoon fishermen ou fished the fly-fisheren by a significant margin. Not unusual,l but a bit aggravating to me. The fly-fishermen certainly caught some nice fish and worked hard for every tug, but the number of fish hooked on spoons versus. flies was about 5 to 1 under late-season, chilly conditions. With water temperatures in the 35-38∞F rang,e the added flash and motion of those spoons was what it took to move fish consistently.

One of our guides commented on the success of the spoon fisherean and said to me, "We just can't make our flies move like those spoons. It's the flash and motion that gets'em!"

To me that statement was a challenge to create a fly tied by conventional methods with standard materials. It would be considered a fly yet move with flash and motion like a spoon.

I spent considerable time that winter pondering such a fly. What makes a fly a fly? Where is the line drawn between fly and lure? I imagine that a hundred people would give you a hundred different answers on the subject,t so I set off to create the ultimate flashing, moving fly.

The problem after many of the earlier concepts were completed was that I was not sure if what I had created would be considered a fly. I discarded many attempts because I did not feel they met the proper criteria for a fly.

In the end I came to these conclusions:

- *I had to create flash without metal (except for the eyes).*
- *I had to create motion without plastic lips or excessive amounts of epoxy.*
- *The pattern had to be tied without fins or the use of snap swivels.*
- *The fly had to be light enough to cast with a standard 8 wt. fly rod or larger.*
- *And most of all I had to create dramatic motion that would not twist your leader.*

The two flies already in existence that held the most promise were the Articulated Leech and the Alaskan Flash fly. Both are outstanding patterns for late-season steelhead, but I felt there might be something more there.

The Alaskan Flash Fly had the elements that I needed with the use of Flashabou: flash and some motion. However when tied in it's traditional form, if the wing material got really long, say 4-5-inches, the Flashabou would often foul around the hook. The great thing about the Flashabou material is that it has little resistance and moves through the water easily. On the

ther hand, the Articulated Leech had another lement of motion in that its design has articu-ation. Each fly works very well on its own, so why not combine the two?

A change in the connection material and he length of the connection, the position of the weighted eyes on the rear hook, and proper hook selection (after much trial and error) cre-ated the dramatic flash and motion I was look-

ing for. When the B.C. steelhead guides saw its movement in the water for the first time, all they could say was, "OH MY GOSH!"

In the late fall of 2000, the Babine River reared its nasty head and produced super tough, high and cold water conditions. But this year I was armed with the Articulated Flash Fly, and it delivered!

It is not the pattern I would fish under optimal conditions, as I prefer a more traditional approach to steelheading, but when conditions are steadily deteriorating and one is faced with not fishing at all or going home, then it's time to turn to this save-the-day pattern.

Todd Sabine

If you have ever ventured off to catch steelhead in British Columbia, you know it is a daunting task. To start with, you are after a sea-run rainbow trout that doesn't want to eat. Then the weather can be an issue. The months of October and November can bring anything from warm sunny days to miserable blowing snow. One rainstorm can wreck a week's vacation and a few thousand dollars by taking that wonderfully low, clear river and turning it the color of creamed coffee, blowing it way out of proportion.

Preparation is the key to a successful trip. I have heard it said, "There is no such thing as bad weather, just bad gear!" Whether it is warm socks or the correct fly pattern, gear is of the upmost importance. If a single fly pattern could give you the edge when the going gets tough, I would make sure I had that pattern.

If you come home with a few pictures of big steelhead, you have had a great trip and bragging rights that will drive your fishing buddies nuts for a whole year. Bragging rights or no fish? Not a difficult question. Put together a few of these amazing flies and see if you can come home and drive your buddies crazy with envy.

We are going to tie a simple purple and silver pattern we will call Purple Rain.

Articulated Flash Fly

Rear Section

Hook: SS Hook, Tiemco 811S, size 2/0-2
Thread: 3/0 waxed monocord, color to match
Weight: Lead barbell eyes
Underwing: Chenille, color to match
Wing: Flashabou, just about any color combination
Connect Rear Section To Front Section: 30-pound. Dacron backing

Front Section
Hookshank: Salmon hook, Tiemco 7999, #2/0-#2
Thread 3/0 waxed monocord, color to match
Underwing: Chenille, color to match
Wing: Flashabou, to match rear section

Tying the rear section of the fly.

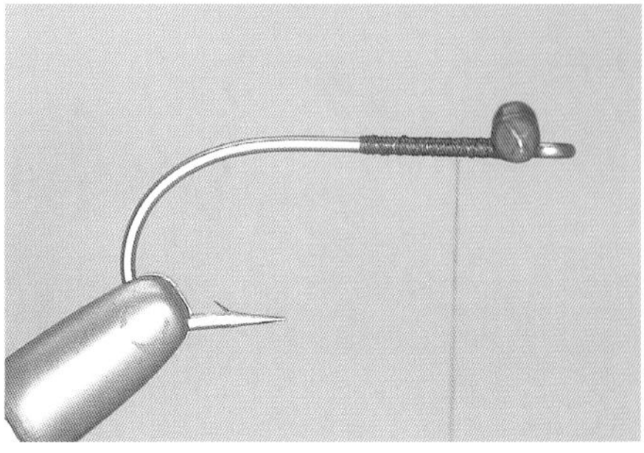

1. Start thread at the eye of the Tiemco 811S stainless-steel hook and wrap back to the 1/2 point of the hook. Move thread forward to the 7/8-point of the hook and attach the barbell eyes on top of the hook shank using a simple X-ing and figure-eight pattern.

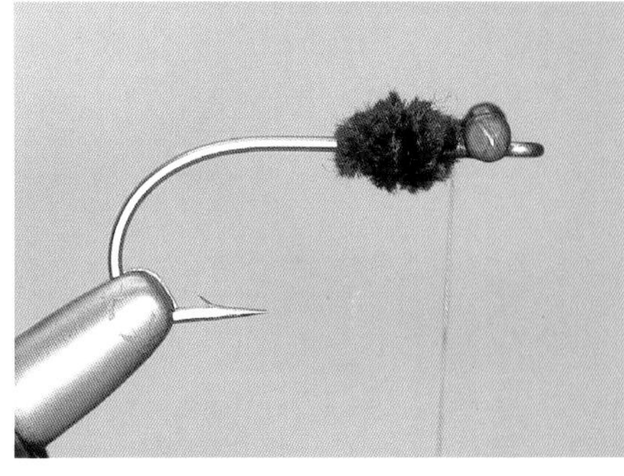

2. Tie in a length of medium purple chenille behind the barbell eyes and wrap it down with thread to the 1/2 point. Move thread to the eye. Wrap the chenille to the barbell eyes, then back and forth, forming a large ball of material behind the barbell eyes. Secure chenille. Note: Dubbing could be used to form the ball but chenille is much faster.

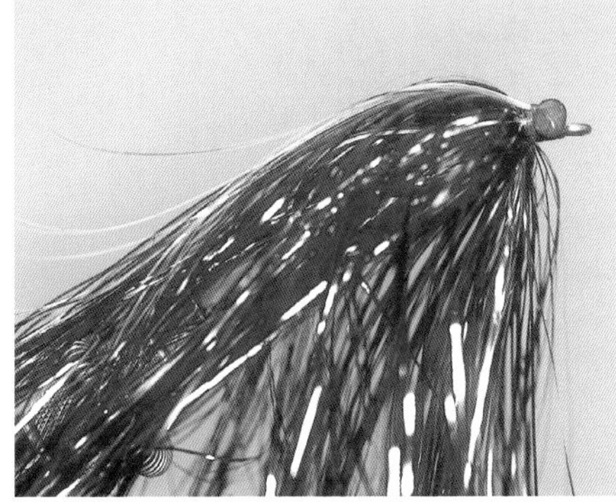

3. Cut a bunch of purple Flashabou, about half the overall length as it comes in the package. The number of fibers in the bunch is hard to judge: it's really an amount you feel you can comfortably handle, say about 50 strands. Secure

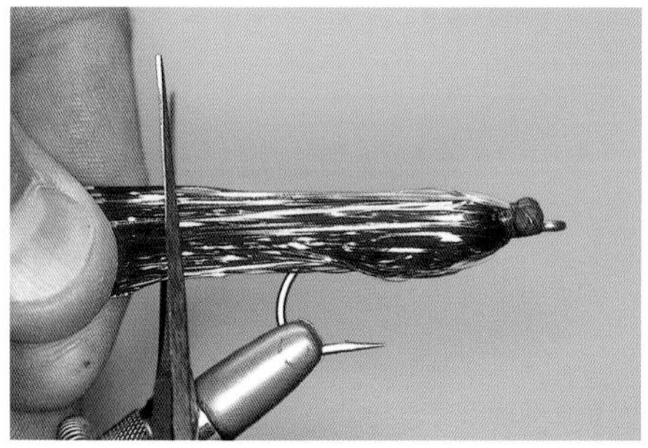

the Flashabou, in the middle of bunch, with several wraps of thread between the barbell eyes and the chenille ball. Maneuver the fibers to the underside of the hook, letting the fibers spread evenly and lock into place with a few wraps of thread. Repeat with another bunch of purple Flashabou, holding half the fibers on one side of the hook and the other half on the other side. Lock into place with a few wraps of thread. You are encompassing the hook shank with Flashabou, like a feather as it would be tied as a soft hackle, allowing the chenille ball to flare the material. Repeat with silver, then another purple, and finish with silver Flashabou. The hook shank should be totally encompassed with Flashabou. Whip finish and cement the head of the fly. Pull all the Flashabou fibers back and trim to length. About a half-inch beyond the hook bend works very well.

4. Here is the rear section of the fly up to this point.

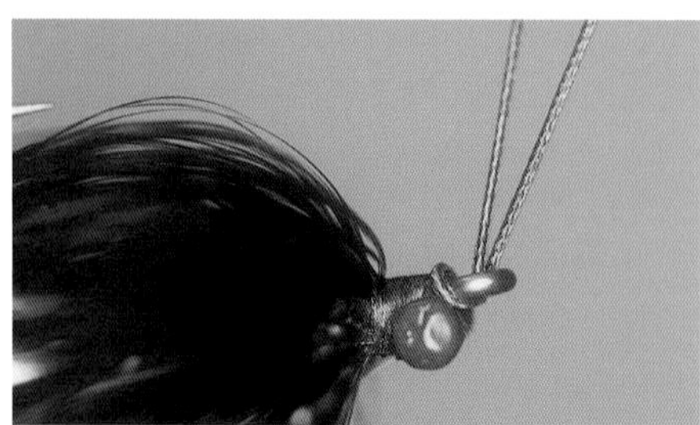

5. Loop a foot-long piece of 30-pound Dacron backing through the eye. Make sure the two ends of backing exit through the bottom of the hook eye. Most backing comes in orange, white, or green, so you will have to color it with a dark permanent marker. Remove from vise.

Attaching the rear section to the front section.

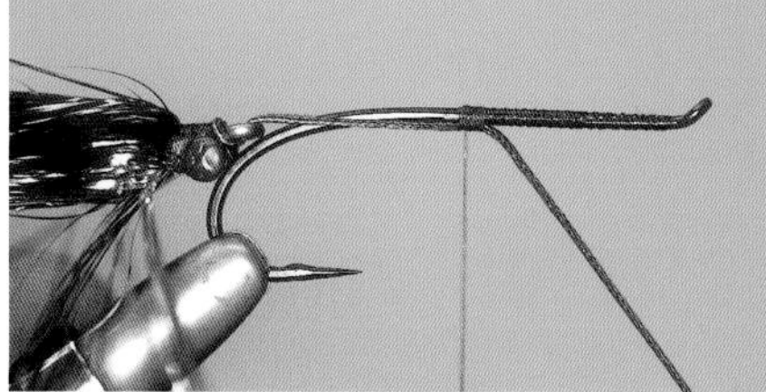

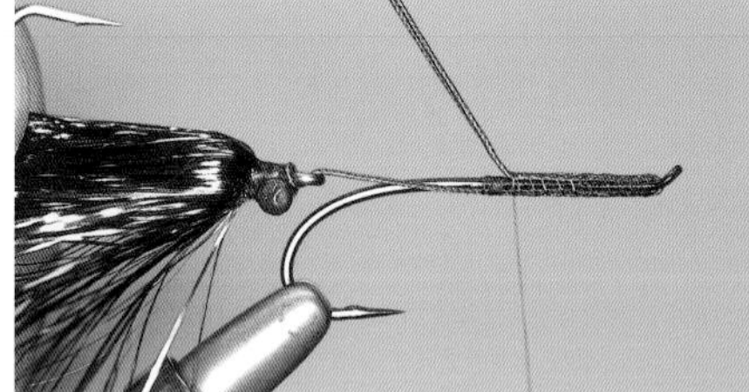

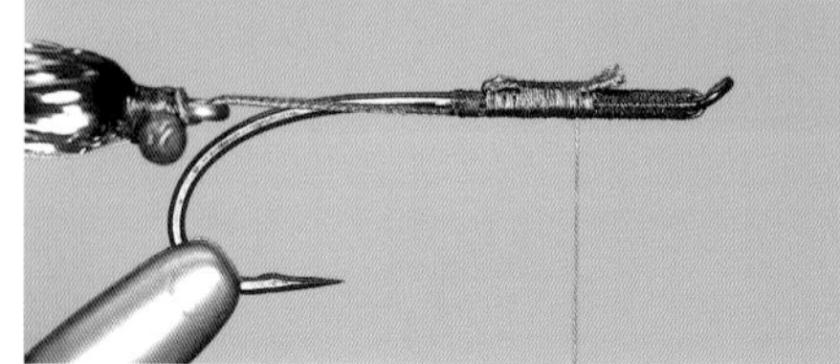

6. Place the Tiemco 7999 salmon hook in the vise. Start thread behind the eye and wrap back to the 1/2 point of the hook. With the hook point up, bring the hook eye of rear section of the fly to the bend of the salmon hook as shown in photo. Secure the two strands of backing to the underside of the hook, wrapping them down to the eye of the hook. Feed both strands of the backing up through the hook eye. Wrap the backing down to the 3/4 point, fold it over forward, and wrap it down to the 1/2 point of the hook. It may seem like overkill, but when the steelhead fishing is tough and you get hooked up with a big fish, you do not want anything to go wrong, especially your fly coming apart!

Tying the front section of the fly.

7. At this time you may want to secure the rear hook to something so it does not flop around and get in your way. A rubber band around the hook bend attached to something on your tying desk works well. A long piece of tippet

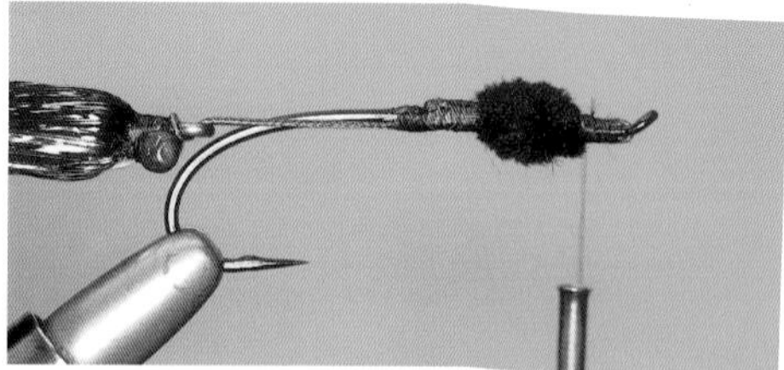

material looped around the bend of the hook tied off to some point on your desk could work also. Tie in a length of medium purple chenille behind eye and wrap it down with thread to the 3/4 point. Move thread forward to the eye. Wrap the chenille to just behind the eye, then back and forth, forming a large ball of material behind the barbell eyes. Secure chenille.

8. Cut a bunch of purple Flashabou, about half the overall length as it comes in the package. Secure the Flashabou, in the middle of bunch, with several wraps of thread between the eye and the chenille ball. Maneuver the fibers to the sides of the hook, letting the fibers spread evenly and lock into place with a few wraps of thread. You want to cover only the top half of this section of the fly. You want the under-side of the shank to be open so it doesn't interfere with the movement or "articulation" of the rear section. Repeat with another bunch of purple Flashabou, covering another section of the top of the hook shank. Lock into place with a few wraps of thread, allowing the chenille ball to flare the material. Repeat with silver Flashabou to finish off the top of the fly. Whip finish and cement the head of the fly. Pull all the Flashabou fibers back and trim to length, about a half-inch

Streamers

beyond the hook bend works very well again.

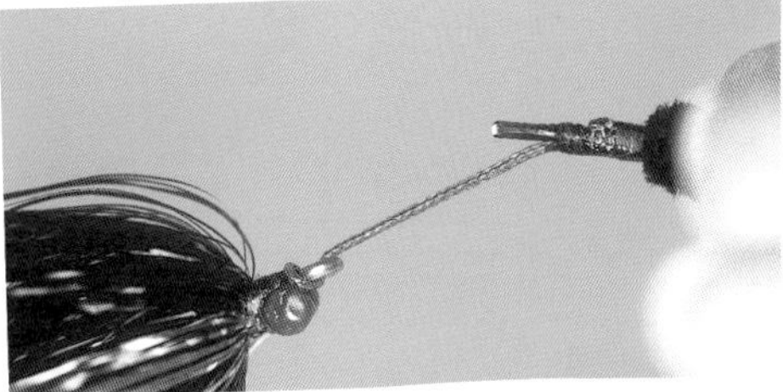

9. With a pair of heavy-duty wire cutters, cut the hook bend off the salmon hook (the front section of the fly).

Brad's Shad

Contributed by Brad Befus

Brad is what you would call an all-around angler. He is very knowledgeable in all aspects of fly-fishing. He can be found standing belly deep in the Gunnison River hooking up the local brown trout, or just over the hill tossing poppers on a farm pond for bass. A week later he could be found on a flats boat in Belize casting fake shrimp to a bonefish, then he is chasing northern pike in Alaska. I guess I would call him versatile.

His stacks of fly boxes show his versatility also. The thing I noticed initially was the carryover of patterns from one box to the next. I saw trout flies in his bass boxes, bass flies in his pike and muskie boxes, and pike flies in his saltwater boxes. However, the one pattern that showed up in all his boxes was the No Name Shad. After Brad tied the shad for this book, I told him I thought we should give the No Name a name. I figured Brad should get the credit, so Brad's Shad is the name of record.

Always experimenting, always trying new materials, Brad is continually developing and testing new patterns. He attained a splendid addition to his repertoire with this pattern. The versatility of Brad's Shad runs the gamut from large predatory coldwater fish to popular warmwater species to saltwater varieties. Brad has caught northern pike and tiger muskie on this fly, in fact it could be one of his favorite flies for tigers. Smaller sizes have been good for wipers, especially in dirtywater situations. Largemouth bass have fallen for this seductive pattern as have a couple of catfish in a Nebraska lake. In saltwater, tarpon, jacks, snook, and barracuda have grabbed onto it also.

It is a pretty simple fly to tie, and has all the aspects of a great streamer pattern. Great natural baitfish colors (with several options for just about any color combination you would like), lots of lifelike movement, and those big eyes. Brad says, "I think eyes are a very important addition to any streamer. Predators like the realism that eyes accentuate on a moving fly."

This fly would be a great addition to your fly boxes. Get a bag of new materials and try your hand at this one.

Brad's Shad

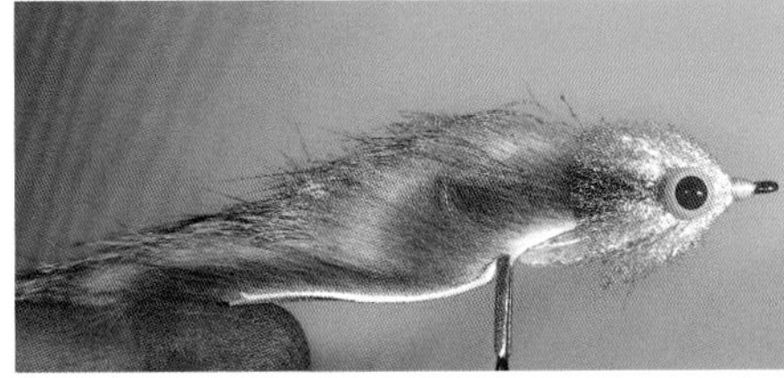

Hook: Tiemco 911S 3X Long Stainless Steel, size 4/0-2
Thread: White, single-strand, flat waxed nylon
Body: Pearl Reflash Tubing (by D's Flyes)
Rattle: Glass rattle, 3mm
Overbody: 5 minute epoxy
Wing: Grizzly-colored Rabbit Zonker Strip (Std. Width) "Fur, Feather & Fly" is one of the better brand names for rabbit strips.
Gills: Red Darlon (D's Flyes)
Head: Saap Body Fur
Eyes: Solid plastic eyes, white or yellow 7mm

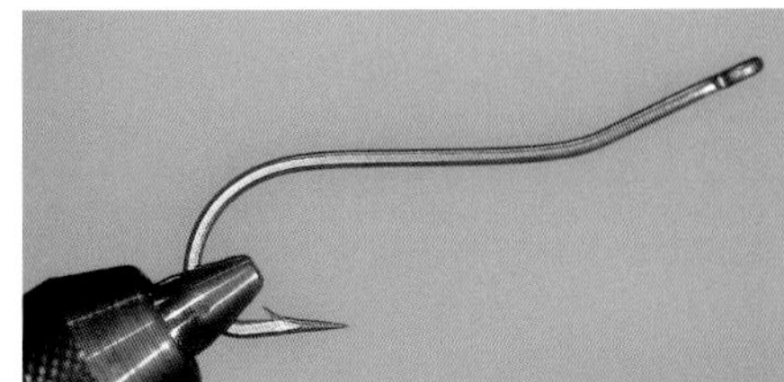

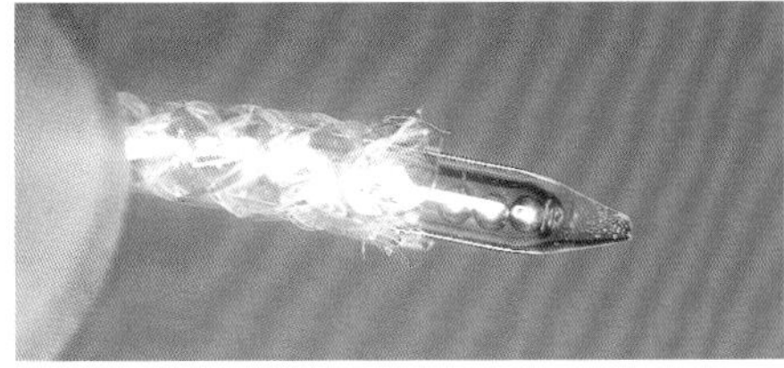

1. Brad doesn't use a traditional bent-back hook for this fly. He likes to bend the hook himself. "I like to bend the hook a little farther back than the store bought hooks, about 2 to 2 1/2 hook eyes back from the eye. Hold the eye of the hook in a pair of pliers where the bend will be and bend the hook against a table." A slight bend is good; there is no need for a radical angle on this pattern. Prepare a number of hooks ahead of time. Cut a length of the Reflash Tubing and insert the rattle into the tubing. The rattle has a pointed end, which we want at the end of the tubing we secure to the hook. A length of tubing about 2 inches is a good starting point and should vary from hook size to hook size. You should tie a couple and find out just how much you need to avoid wasting too much of the tubing. The rattle is optional, but Brad makes sure the flies he plans to fish in off-colored or stained water has a rattle. If a faster sink rate is desired, a Twist On or lead wire can be inserted into the tubing. Prepare the tubing and rattle ahead of time also.

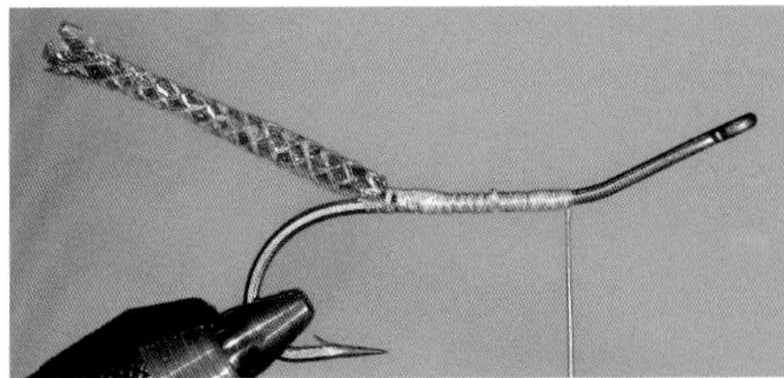

2. Insert hook in the vise in the normal, hook-down position and start thread at the man-made bend. Wrap back to a point just past where the bend starts.

Tie in the Reflash Tubing at the back and wrap thread forward to the bend. Make sure the hook has a clean thread base so the shank does not show through. Pull the tubing over as if it were a wingcase and secure at the bend. Trim excess tubing and either half hitch or whip finish. Remove thread. Repeat this procedure on the rest of the hooks. (Somewhere along the way Brad had mentioned that he does thirty at a time, but I would imagine a dozen flies would be the norm for personal use.) Mix up a batch of five-minute epoxy and coat the entire body. Be as liberal with the epoxy as you can without having the epoxy drip on the floor. This fly rides hook-up when fished, so you want as much weight at the body and rattle position as possible. A rotating wheel that holds several hooks is a great tool for the drying process of the epoxy, as it will keep the coat of epoxy even. There are several types of hook-turning machines available on the market, so check with your local fly shop.

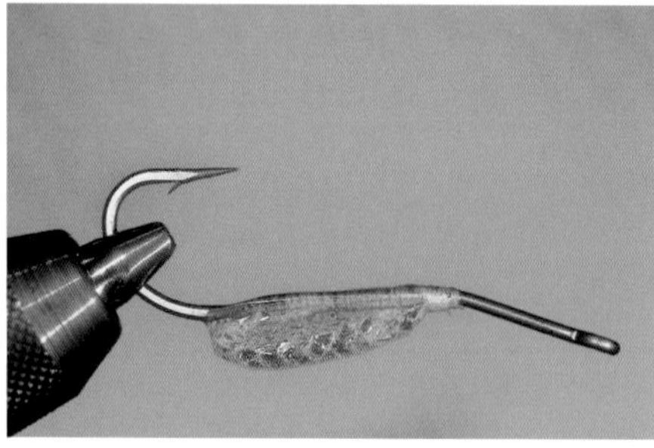

3. While the epoxy is drying, prepare the rabbit strips. Cut strips to a length where a full hook shank of skin is hanging past the hook bend and the tip is tied in at the bend. A 6-inch ruler clamped to your tying desk would speed this process up tremendously. Strips cut to a length of three inches is a rough starting point. For northern pike and tiger muskie, a long rabbit strip is desirable for the added motion. Shorter strips are better for species such as wipers. Brad says, "I normally like to make them long and trim them shorter if need be while fishing. If I get a lot of short strikes, fish grabbing the tail end of the fly and letting go, I'll cut the rabbit strip shorter. Now if they grab the tail, they get a mouthful of hook." Measure the strips to a point equal to the hook shank. (The ruler comes in handy again.) Poke a hole in the hide of the rabbit strip at this point with a dubbing needle. Brad does not recommend trying to poke the strip directly with the hook point. He reports that you will tear more strips than it's worth. He has also tried using a razor blade to make a slit in the strip before slipping it over the hook but then durability becomes a problem. After they get wet, the stress of a couple of long casts with the now-heavy fly will tear the strip and end up destroying the fly. When the epoxy is dry, slip the point of the hook through the hole in the rabbit strip and push it all the way to the body. Insert the hook in the vise upside down and start the thread at the kink again. Position the strip on the hook shank as shown in the photo. Stretch the rabbit strip forward and cut the hide just ahead of the bend. Trim a small patch of hair from the strip to give the thread something to latch down on. Secure the end of the strip with several tight wraps of thread right at the kink.

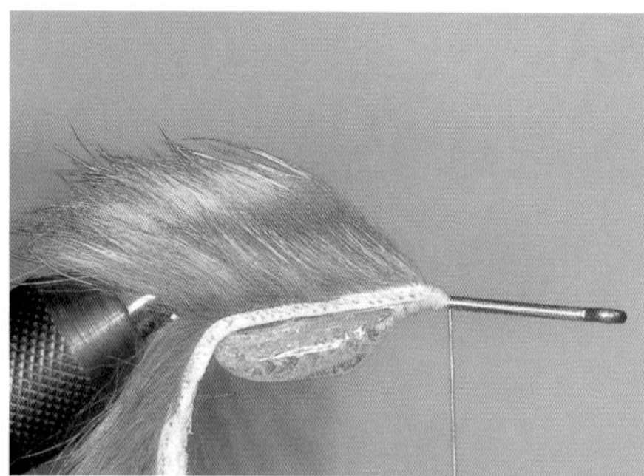

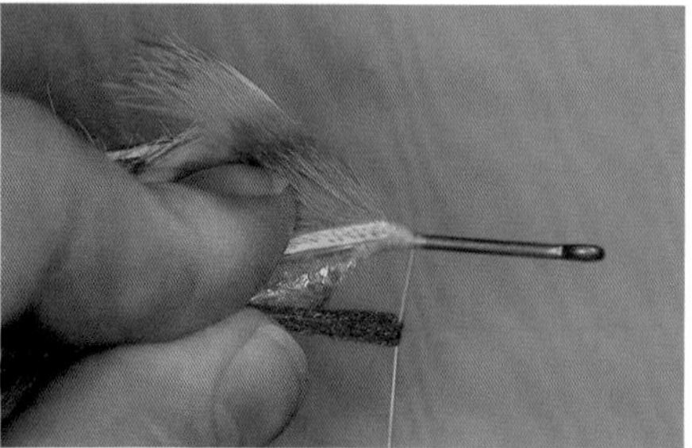

4. Cut two strands of red Darlon about 2 inches long for the gills. Fold the Darlon over the thread, slide it up to the side of the hook, level with the hook shank, and secure with two wraps of thread. Repeat on the other side of the hook. Do not worry if the ends of the Darlon are uneven because the head of the fly will be shaped in a later step.

5. Take the Body Fur material and secure the end in front of the body. Move thread forward to just behind the eye. Wrap the Body Fur forward four or five wraps as you would a soft hackle. The core of this Body Fur is very strong, so you can really crank it down very tight on the hook. Secure behind the eye, trim excess, and whip finish.

6. Trim the head to the shape of a baitfish. Brad likes to use a curved pair of scissors to shape the head on this fly. He turns the scissors so the concave side is towards him, avoiding the possibility of trimming something you don't want to trim. It may be necessary to lift and maneuver the material around to taper and thin the Body Fur. The thinning of the material helps the gills show through also. Remember not to trim too much at once; it's pretty hard to glue it back on. You can always trim more as you go. Cut the red Darlon gills even with the Body Fur. Glue the eyes in place near the points where the gills were tied in on each side of the head. Brad suggests using Goop or Shoe Goo

for the eyes because these glues stay flexible and the eyes stay on better in tight cover while dragged over rocks and downed timber. Super Glue and some other types of adhesives that dry hard become brittle and will not hold the eyes in place as well. Check your local hardware store for these sticky products.

Copperhead

Contributed by Ken Mead

"The Copperhead is just an all-around good pattern," says Ken Mead. "How could you go wrong? The fly is tied with an overall appearance of a Woolly Bugger with the color-coordinated look of designer clothing."

It has root beer colored marabou instead of just brown. (I haven't been able to find the dye yet.) It is dressed in the finest of peacock herl instead of plain old chenille. The furnace hackle deceives the eye, making it look much thinner than the old meat-and-potatoes pattern it emulates. The glitter of woven copper wire dresses the fly up and holds the whole thing together. And what would this exceptional piece of attire be without a red necklace and a fine copper globe to top it off?

Ken came up with the pattern while looking for a streamer type of fly to use on the Little Lehigh River in Pennsylvania. "I have always been intrigued by brown-colored flies after reading some of Randall Kaufmann's work. Kaufmann always said brown was one of the most under-utilized colors used in fly tying."

The trout on the Little Lehigh are pretty spooky from all the attention they receive. Since they see a lot of flies, Ken tried to combine several effective and different materials together.

"Peacock herl works well anywhere and on just about any fly. The addition of the copper wire and the copper bead gave the fly the subtle flash I was looking for."

Ken doesn't want to take credit for the color combination because there are a number of brown flies out there, but when this fly was published in the *Flies of the East*, he had no one complain that the Copperhead was their pattern.

Success with the fly came quickly. The first outing with the Copperhead produced a 20-inch brook trout on the Little Lehigh. It has become a popular pattern locally and has done a bit of traveling. Barry and Cathy Beck have used it with very good results in the Arctic Circle for char. Jeff Curry used it in South America, and many trout in the Rocky Mountain region have fallen for this seductive-looking Bugger.

If you show something to enough people, human nature has a tendency to want to "burst your bubble". Ken showed this fly to a fellow fisherman and he said, "No wonder the fly works so well, it looks like a damn earthworm."

Opinions vary, but success is the name of the game and this fly does work. Trout do eat worms, don't they?

"It doesn't matter if I'm tying three flies or thirty dozen, I like to get my materials laid out in order and in correct quantities for each fly," Ken adds. "First, I will slide all the beads on the hooks. I like to use a pair of tweezers to grab the bead for this step. I count out the marabou plumes, prepare my hackle, and lay out individual clumps of peacock herl."

Here are a couple of notes on the materials used in this fly. The old standard for palmered hackle was the use of saddle hackle. Ken doesn't use saddle hackle anymore. Most saddle hackle these days is not wide enough for this application. He now chooses the big feathers from a good-quality dry fly cape, which have a nice tapered look when wrapped into place. And for a guy with numbers of capes lying around, plentiful too.

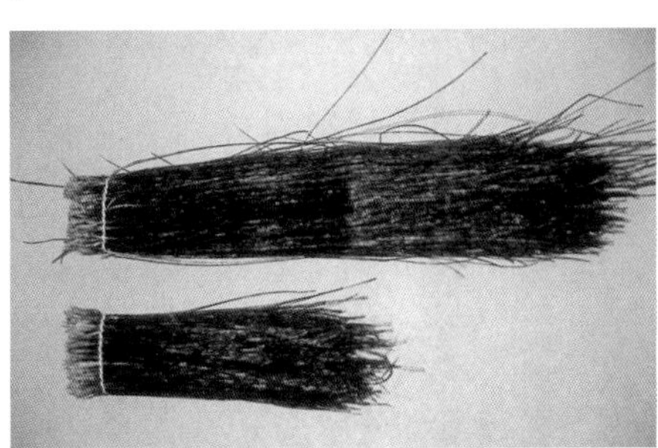

Ken also chooses to use the long 8"-12" peacock herl instead of the shorter 6"-7" herl for this fly. The added length helps ensure that the body of the fly has good full herl with fewer stems. In other words, the better part of the shorter herl will usually get used up before the body is fully wrapped. What you end up with is the front end of the body with more stem, or "woody," than nice fluffy herl. With the longer herl you may get two flies out of the same clump.

Copperhead

Hook: Streamer 3X or 4X long, size 6-10 Daiichi 1720
Bead: 5/32 copper bead
Thread: Danville 6/0, red
Ribbing: Medium copper wire
Tail: Marabou, root beer. A popular version of the fly has yellow marabou tail topped with the root beer colored marabou. This is the version we will tie in this sequence
Body: Peacock herl
Hackle: Furnace brown

1. Slide a 5/32 copper bead onto the hook. Place hook in vise and start the thread at the front of the hook and lay a thread base to the back. Tie in a smaller yellow marabou plume and wrap it down with thread to just behind the bead. Tail length should be close to a full hook-shank long. Move thread to the back of the hook once again.

2. Tie in a plume of brown marabou over the top of the yellow by making 5 or 6 tight wraps of thread right at the back of the hook. The length of the brown marabou tail should be the same as the yellow. Do not move thread forward yet. Prepare a brown furnace hackle and tie it in by the tip with the concave side of the feather away from you. Now secure the marabou in place by wrapping it down to just behind the bead. Trim the butt end of the marabou.

3. Tie in the tip of the copper wire right behind the bead and wrap it down to the back of the hook. Tie in the clump of peacock herl and move your thread to the front of the fly. To speed up the tying process you can wrap the herl and hackle together at the same time (that is why we like to use the 8"-12" peacock herl) or wrap the herl to the front then wrap the hackle and wire at the same time. Either way is pretty slick. In this sequence we will wrap the herl and the hackle at the same time. A little hint that will help this procedure go better: Make a full wrap with the herl, then latch onto the hackle and wrap them both forward. Secure both the hackle and herl behind the bead. Trim the herl and make another wrap or two with the hackle to form a nice full collar. Secure hackle and trim.

4. Sweep the palmered hackle forward, making the hackle fibers stand more upright instead of swept back. This tip aids in the wrapping of the wire through the body by reducing the number of fibers that get trapped against the body. Weave the wire forward through the hackle trying not to trap many hackle fibers. Secure wire and make several wraps with the red thread to form a throat on the fly. Ken incorporates this red throat technique on many of his streamer flies. Does the fly with the red throat work better when it comes to catching trout or catching fishermen? The answer is up to you in the way you tie your own flies. Pro tiers tend to make flies that sell, while remaining very effective for the purpose intended. Whip finish and toss it in your favorite stream or pond and see for yourself whether it works or not.

Epoxy Woolly Bugger

I'm sure you have heard some wild stories about how a certain fly pattern got its beginning, but this one has to take the cake. In fact, if I didn't have the witnesses to back me up, I wouldn't blame you if you discarded this as a line of crap.

I wish I had a date for you but I don't. I know it had to be the fall of 1991, or maybe '92. A good friend of mine, Barry Conyers (a.k.a. Conman) and I (a.k.a. Buggermaster) decided to cook up some T-bone steaks for Jack Sayers (a.k.a. Gray Ugly). Gray had done us a favor or two somewhere down the line so we thought we should render a good deed in his benefit. Anyone who knows Gray knows food is a great benefit to him.

Plans were made. Greg Berdick (a.k.a. Greg), a friend of Conman, was invited because he makes an unbelievable acorn squash baked with butter and nutmeg, or maybe it was cinnamon. Gray showed up on time and we all had a Crown Royal on the rocks and pulled off a couple of good stories. Conman is turning the steaks and I was pouring four more Crowns.

After dinner, drinks were iced down and we settled into some easy chairs. Before long, Gray said he just got some samples of a new material at the Fly Tackle Dealer Show here in Denver (this is how I know it was the fall). Out to the car we went and Gray carried his fly-tying tackle box in. He carried it because I don't think the rest of us could walk without leaning on something. Gray is a much bigger man and can handle booze better than the rest of us.

Out came this sparkly flat ribbon in just about every color a trout fly could dream of. This material is made by Kreinik and comes in purples, greens, olives, browns, and what I would call a dead ringer for peacock. Gray proclaimed, "I want to see what you pros can tie up with this stuff!" (Note: I use Poly Flash Tubing by Spirit River for my Epoxy Woolly Buggers now.)

Conman said, "It's all yours, Bugger."

I got behind the vise and whipped up a Prince Nymph using the peacock-colored stuff, then some caddis larvae out of the green stuff, a stonefly nymph, and then a Woolly Bugger. The flies were looking pretty good until someone brought up the idea of using epoxy. It got ugly, and in a hurry. Epoxy was everywhere and on everything. (I had to trim a glob of it out of my left eyebrow the next morning) However, before all was said and done, we did figure out how to get the hackle wrapped through the epoxy without turning it into a glorified piece of trash.

The Epoxy Woolly Bugger was born! Epoxy had been used for many saltwater flies at the time, but this was the first time anyone had turned hackle through epoxy for a trout fly. Epoxy did catch on very quickly and the real creative tiers out there have come up with some fabulous flies and many new techniques for it.

Epoxy Woolly Bugger

Hook: Streamer 4X-6X long size 6-10
Thread: 6/0 black
Tail: Black marabou
Flash: Holographic Flash mixed in with the tail
Body: Poly Flash Tubing (Spirit River)
Hackle: Black (Whiting Farms Bugger pack)

I have a little trick for you users of marabou. It is faster to take just a single plume, bunch it together and tie it in for the tail on a Woolly Bugger, but I like a very thick tail on my Buggers. I realized that most of the feather was ending up in the trash with the standard tie-in procedure. So instead of using two feathers I found that if I just pulled some of the lower feather off and bunched it together with the tip I could achieve the look I prefer and it doesn't take that much more time.

1. Notice that the tail is tied in just at the back of the hook. You don't want to build up a thick body on this fly. Add a few strands of flash down each side of the tail and trim to the length of the tail.

2. Move thread to the front of the fly. Tie in the Poly Flash body material and wrap back to the point in front of the tail. With your first wrap, go under the hook shank and back so that the tail tie-in point gets covered with the first wrap of Poly Flash. As you wrap the body material forward make sure you keep it as level as possible.

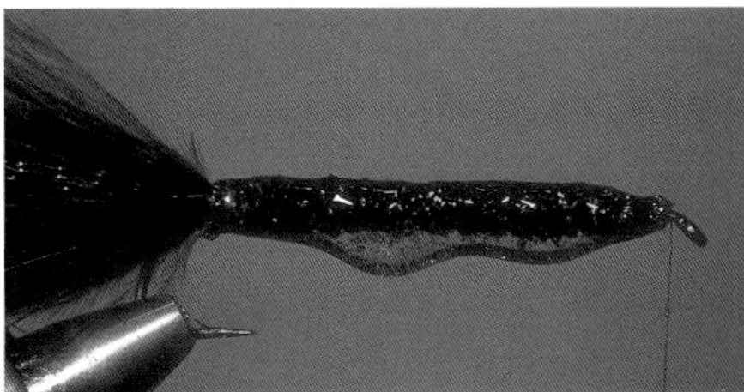

3. Mix up a small amount of 5-minute epoxy. Cover the body with epoxy. You may notice the epoxy starts to sag after a few seconds. If your vise rotates, just turn the Bugger over and let the epoxy run the other direction. If your vise doesn't rotate, take a bodkin or tooth-

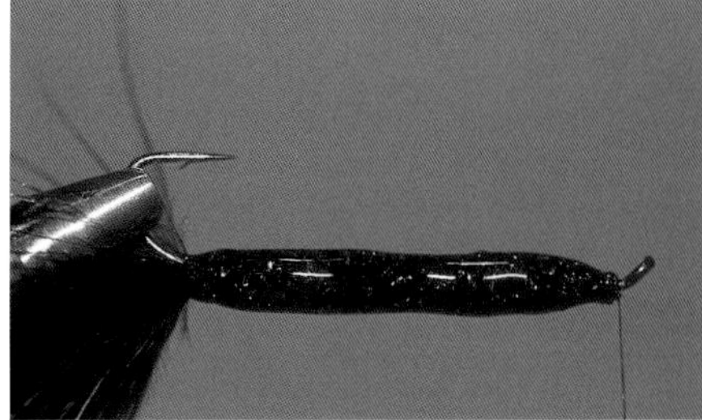

pick and move the epoxy back up on top of the hook or just remove it if there is too much.

4. Now the fun begins. Prepare a hackle by trimming about 1/8" of the fibers off both sides of the butt end of the feather. I prefer the feathers from a Whiting Farms Bugger Pack. The feathers are long enough for flies up to a size 6, 6x-long hook, the barbules have a nice taper to them, and they look great on the finished fly. Tie in hackle at the front of the fly. The epoxy should be past the point of sagging by now. Attach hackle pliers to the feather and palmer-wrap the hackle through the epoxy to the back of the fly.

5. Let hackle pliers hang as the epoxy sets up. Whip finish. After the epoxy

sets up (about 5 minutes) remove excess hackle and hackle pliers.

6. Here is the finished fly after whip-finishing.

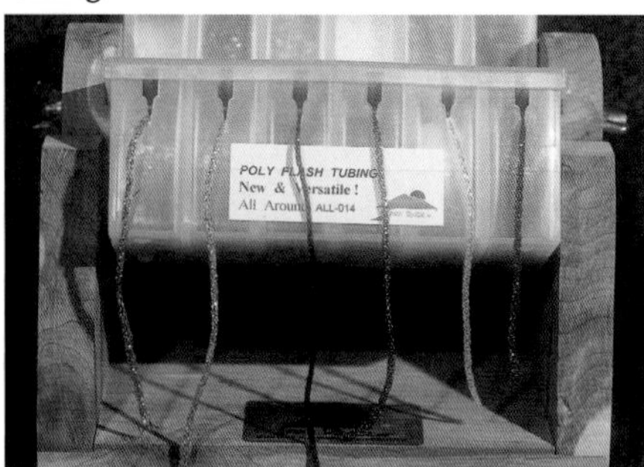

Let your creativity take over when tying this fly. You should be able to come up with some great patterns using this technique. Oh, by the way, I haven't found a trout that can break the hackle on this Woolly Bugger.

Magic Minnow

Contributed by Brad Befus

The Magic Minnow is probably the quickest and easiest streamer you will ever tie. The original pattern was tied on a regular trout streamer hook with a white, olive, and black color combination to imitate a fat-head minnow. Brad started tying the fly for carp in 1993 or 1994. He wanted a fly design that could be fished in shallow water, that would sink rather slowly, and take on the profile of a small baitfish and be semi-weedless.

Brad continued with the evolution of the fly, "Then I put it on a stainless -teel hook and started catching redfish, bonefish, and baby tarpon because of the same needs. Again, a shallow-water situation. It has also been a good fly for smallmouth bass and crappie. It has recently become a popular pattern for surf perch in California and stripers on the East Coast. The striper guys back east have told me that chartreuse-and-white Magic Minnows produce very good results for the big fish that ride in the shallow water. They think the smaller profile type of streamer works because these fish never see anything this small. The big stripers have these big 6-10-inch lures tossed in front of them all the time and have become wary of them."

This is a pretty small streamer tied on a size 8 Tiemco 411S bent-back hook. It is unique in that it is smaller than all the other bucktail streamers out there. It's kind of a micro streamer, something that has not been addressed as a pattern design.

As with many of Brad's flies, the Magic Minnow is a very versatile pattern. It can be stripped in front of many species of fish. Streamer fishing is a hoot and probably the most underutilized method of fly-fishing. It wouldn't hurt to stash a few of these away to cap off a day of fishing with a couple of late-evening strikes.

Magic Minnow

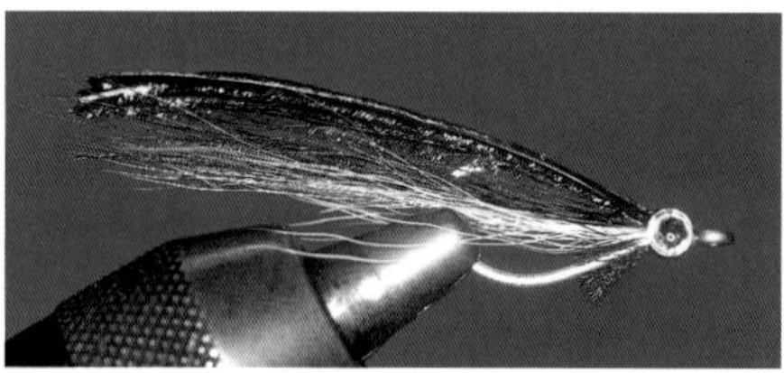

Hook: Tiemco 411S, size 4-8
Thread: Monofilament thread
Wing: Bucktail, white, olive, black layered
Flash: Holographic flash
Gills: Red Darlon (D's Flyes)
Eyes: Prismatic Tape Eyes, 1/8 for size 6 & size 4, 3/32 for size 8

1. Preparing the bucktail wing is the most important part of this fly. In fact, it is the only preparation you need to be concerned with. Even thought the wing is very short, Brad says, "I prefer bucktail to synthetics for this wing. I like to use bucktail that is fine in nature. The hair from the very tip or the pointed end of the bucktail is ideal for this purpose. The coarser hair from the lower part of the bucktail tends to flare too much and loses its liveliness when wet." Cut a small amount of white bucktail from the hide. A sparse wing is desirable on this fly so don't overdo it. (The photos for this step are using more hair than truly needed. However, more hair is needed for visual instruction.) Remove any unruly hair that is bent or with broken tips. Finger stack the bucktail instead of using a hair stacker. The photos depict an example of finger

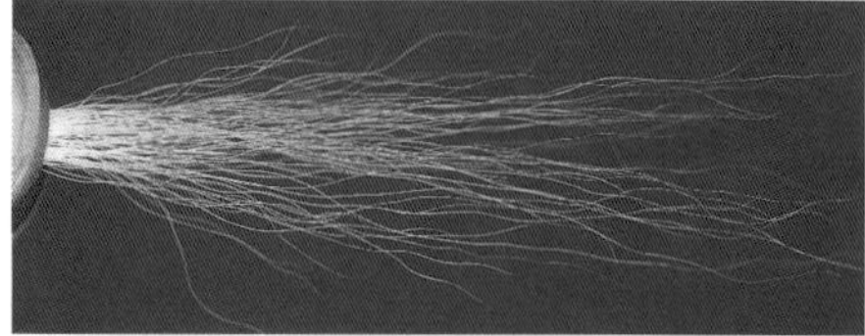

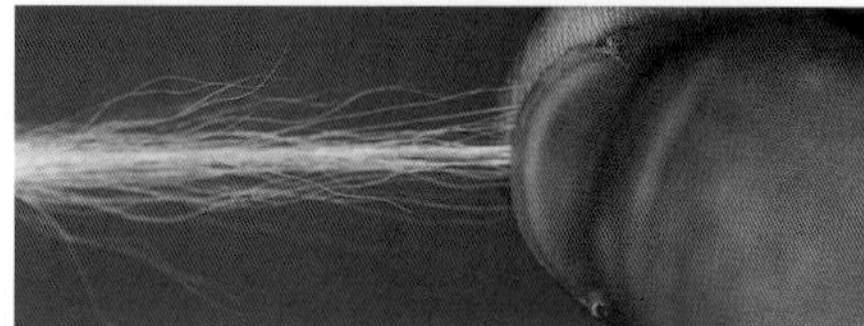

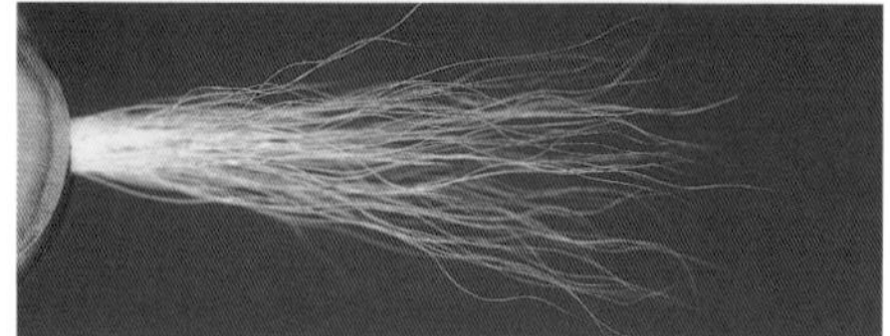

stacking. Notice in the first photo that the hair has roughly three different lengths: A few real long fibers, then fibers of medium length, and then fibers just longer than the thumbnail. The second photo shows the longer hairs being pulled from the clump. Now, simply lay the tips of the longer fibers into the original clump so that they are even with the shorter tips. Repeat a few times until the tips are more uniform, but not totally stacked. The slightly uneven tips of the wing look much more natural when wet than a wing that has perfectly even, square tips. Note: Most bucktail is very long and curly in nature, making it hard to stack. You could beat the top of your tying desk with a hair stacker for several minutes and never get the hair stacked.

2. Insert the hook upside down in the vise. There is no body on this fly, so

start thread just behind the eye of the hook and wrap back to the bend in the shank. Wing length should be equal to about two hook shanks. Measure the white bucktail to length and trim butt ends. Tie in the bucktail at the bend and wrap forward to the eye, making sure the hair stays on top of the shank.

3. Cut a small amount of olive bucktail and finger stack the hair. Measure to a length equal to the first part of the wing and trim butt ends. Tie in the butts just a bit behind the butts of the white hair. We are tying to form a slight taper to the head so the position of this tie-in is important. Secure the olive section of the wing to the hook by wrapping back to the bend. Take one strand of Holographic Flash, fold it over the thread, take it to the top of the hook right over the wing and lash down with a couple of wraps of thread. Trim to length.

4. Repeat the same procedure with the black bucktail for the third layer of the wing. Fold about half a strand of red Darlon over the thread and take it to the bottom of the fly for gills. Lock in the little red beard with a couple of wraps of thread. The mono thread will let the red show through on the bottom of the head. Prepare a few strands of peacock herl for the topping on the streamer. Even the tips, measure to the same length as the bucktail, trim butt ends, and tie in on top of the hook. Finish the head and whip finish. Since the head will be finished with epoxy, you could just slap a couple of half hitches on to finish the fly. If you want the herl to follow the wing contour a little bit, place a dubbing needle under the wing, pinch the herl and the needle and stroke it back, curling it under slightly as you pull. Don't apply too much pressure on the herl or it will break. Note: Here is a little secret for you. If the herl happened to be a bit long, you can trim them with scissors then singe them with an open flame, either a lighter or match, and regain the natural-looking tips. Be careful using this method, you could end up with a bare hook again if you get carried away with the flame. If you were tying several flies, this would be a good place to stop and go to the next fly. After you have tied the number of flies you want, go to the next step.

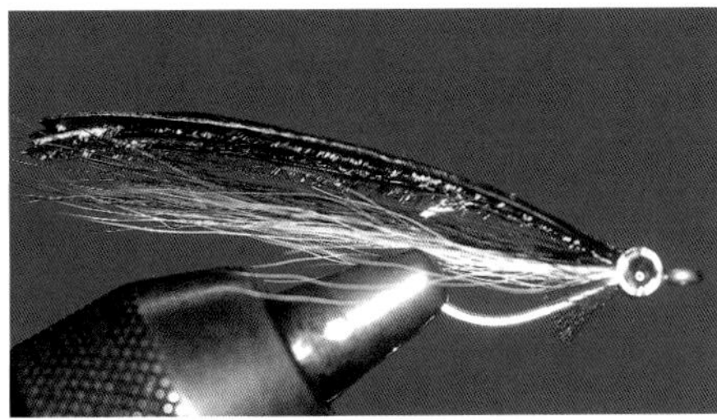

5. Stick a prismatic eye on each side of the head. Mix up a small amount of 5-minute epoxy and cover the head and eyes on the fly. The great thing about the mono thread is the epoxy used to finish the fly will soak through the thread and bind the bucktail directly to the hook very well.

Soft Shell Crawfish

Contributed by Brad Befus

This crawfish pattern evolved from the need to imitate the young soft-shelled crawfish in a local pond near Boulder, Colorado. In the spring, large numbers of these immature crawfish were available to the carp that cruised the shallows of this well-structured gravel pit.

One of the best patterns fishermen were using at the time for carp was a Clouser Swimming Nymph. Bob Clouser tied the swimming nymph to imitate a large *Hexagenia* nymph found in his local waters back East. Since Colorado doesn't have *Hexagenia* mayflies, Brad wanted to be more specific in his patterns. He got the idea for the Soft Shell Crawfish from the Clouser, but built it to imitate the little crawfish. A case of matching the hatch for carp!.

The shellback and the tail are made of peacock herl. It's not the typical translucent material used on most crawfish. Brad had noticed a dark gut line on these little crawfish, so in an attempt to reveal this part of the fly, figured peacock herl was as good as anything. "After all, peacock herl on a fly never hurts."

Even though smallmouth bass and largemouth bass have been known to chow on a few of these, the pattern was actually tied for carp. Trout in Elevenmile and Spinney Mountain reservoirs here in Colorado, bodies of water well known for their populations of crawfish, have succumbed to this meaty-looking pattern. By the way, Elevenmile Reservoir has a very good carp population that can be caught on this pattern in June.

If you need to fish the fly in deeper water, let's say for smallmouth bass, a cone weight slipped on the leader gets the fly down. However, a better idea might be a Teeny 5-foot mini-tip line with a type-three sink rate and a short leader.

Brad's patterns always seem to have great crossover capabilities. They usually represent a food source that is foraged upon by numerous species of fish. If you love the challenge of adapting to different water and different fish as much as Brad does, then I'm sure patterns such as the Soft Shell Crawfish will fit the bill for you.

Soft Shell Crawfish

Hook: Tiemco, 947BL size 8-10
Thread: Olive, Danville 6/0, #60
Claws: Olive, rabbit fur from small Zonker strip works well
Antennae: Silicone Leggs, pumpkin/blue black

Shellback: Peacock herl
Rib: Monofilament thread
Legs: Grizzly dyed golden olive Chickabou Soft-Hackle, (Whiting Farms)
Thorax: Olive rabbit dubbing (same color as claws)
Abdomen: Olive rabbit dubbing

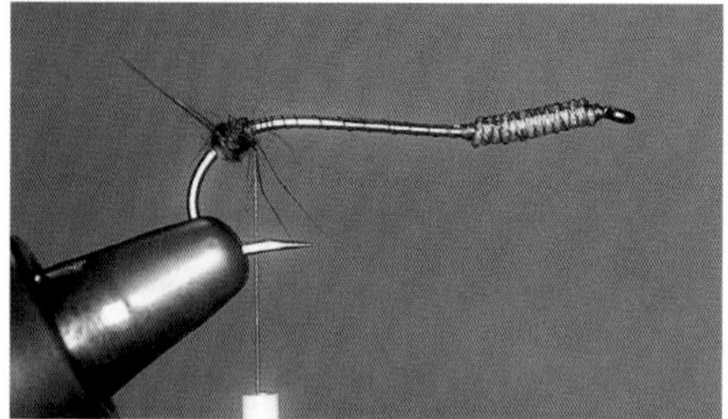

1. .020 lead wire from the kink in the hook to about a hook eye length behind the eye. In other words, leave just enough bare hook behind the eye to finish the fly. Start the thread behind the lead, lock the lead in place and move thread to the back of the hook. Make a dubbing ball slightly down the bend, just past the straight part of the hook shank.

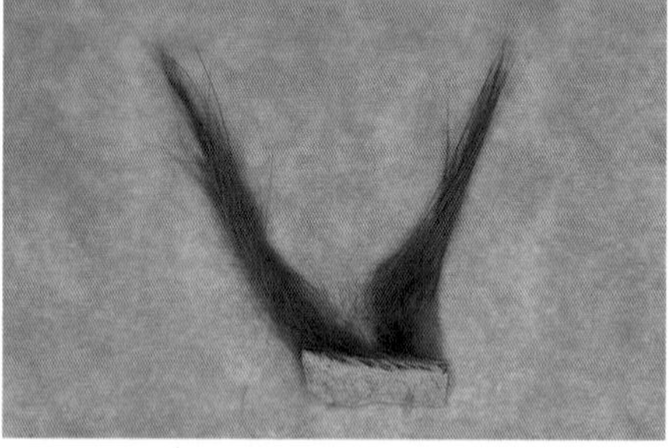

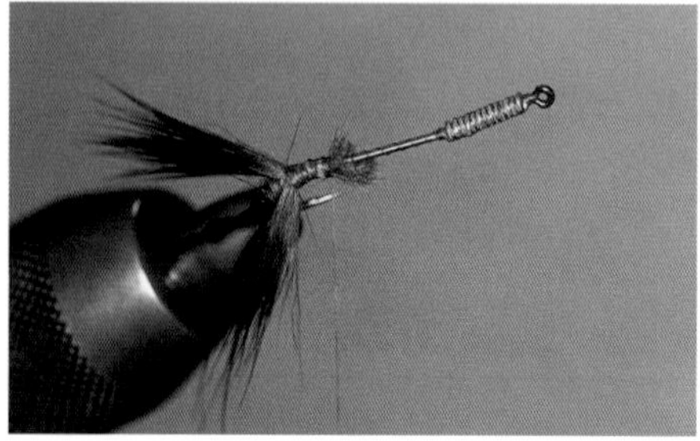

2. Take an olive rabbit strip about an 1/8 inch wide and cut a piece of hide off about 1/8 to 1/4 inch long. You now have a very small piece of rabbit strip with guard hairs and under fur still attached to use for the claws. Here is a nifty trick for making the claws on this crawfish. Without cutting the fur off the skin, separate the fur evenly (a little saliva will help keep the fur separated), measure it to 3/4 of the hook shank length, and tie in half of the clump on the far side of the hook. Wrap back against the dubbing ball, making sure the claws angle out away from the hook and slightly downward. This fly rides hook up, so when turned over, the claws are angling up in their natural defense mode. Take the other half of the clump and secure it on the fore side of the hook. Wrap back against the dubbing ball, making sure the angle is the same as the claw on the far side. Trim close to the hook, removing the little chunk of skin. Take one strand of Silicone Leggs a couple of inches long, fold it over the thread, slide it up to the hook and lash down the antennae back to the bend. Move thread to just behind the lead weight.

3. Turn the hook over in the vise. Trim the tips of 10-12 strands of peacock herl for the soft shell back. To help build a little bulk so less dubbing is needed, tie in the tips of the herl right behind the weight and wrap to the back of the hook. Hold the herl up as you wrap back, to ensure the herl stays on the underside of the hook. This will also keep you from stabbing your thumb with the point of the hook. The herl should butt up against the claws. Tie in the mono thread for ribbing at the back of the hook. Tie in the olive grizzly soft hackle by the tip, also at the back of the hook. There is a lot going on here at the back of the hook, but don't worry, there is a method for all this madness. Dub thread with olive rabbit dubbing and wrap forward to about the 1/2 point of the hook, filling in the thorax area of the fly.

4. Make a few turns with the soft hackle forward through the thorax. Secure and trim excess. Rib mono thread through the thorax and hackle with three or four evenly spaced wraps. Secure and pull mono back out of the way so you can rib the rest of the fly later. Dub thread again and wrap dubbing to the front of the fly, tapering the body thinner towards the front of the fly.

5. Pull the peacock herl over for the soft shell and secure behind the eye. Rib the mono thread forward with evenly spaced wraps to the front of the fly. Secure and trim excess. Lift the peacock herl and make a few wraps of thread directly on the hook under the herl. The thread wraps under the herl cant the tail up slightly. Whip finish. Trim herl to a 3/4 hook shank length beyond the eye of the hook for the tail. Splay the tail and the fly is done.

Spider

Contributed by Fred Vargas

The Spider is primarily used as a streamer pattern to hook up with the mighty Great Lakes steelhead. It was actually one of the first patterns that

Fred Vargas tied when he started fly tying. He was looking for fairly simple patterns to tie and this was one of them. This particular tie is a Vargas version of the Wet Spider originally tied by Al Knudson in 1930. He found it in Trey Combs' *Steelhead Fly Fishing and Flies*.

The main difference in the fly pattern is the use of a stinger hook and the way the tail is tied in with matching mallard flank feathers that move in the water like a natural tail. The original pattern uses a small clump of mallard for the tail. Maxima 40-pound Chameleon is stiff enough that the stinger hook holds its position very well and does not flop around at the back of the hook. The original used yellow chenille for the body, but Fred has found that Lite-Brite dubbing from Spirit River Inc. is a great substitute that adds a subtle flash and extra life to the fly.

The most important feature of this fly is the way the front hackle is wrapped. Fred had an eye for fly tying even before he knew what was really going on. He noticed that all the well-tied flies he saw had small thread heads. Looking at his, he knew he had to improve that aspect of his tying. The fact that he was new to fly tying and that he was self-taught made this all the more remarkable. Not knowing any better, he looked at the flank feather he was getting ready to tie in. He saw the butt end of the feather was thicker than the tip. So he tied in the butt first and after a little maneuvering was able to wrap the feather forward, developing a beautifully small tapered head. He has perfected this technique, so pay close attention to the tying instructions when the front hackle is donned.

This technique is a great example of how pro tiers troubleshoot and solve problems in the act of tying flies.

Vargas took his first steelhead on a fly with this pattern and it continues to get hook-ups to this day. The seductive motion of the hackle has enticed smallmouth bass, walleye, and several saltwater species to eat this fly.

The most effective way to fish this pattern would be with a full-sinking line or a Teeny sink-tip line with a leader no longer than four feet. Fish it quartering downstream and let the fly swing across, or use an active retrieve from a boat.

Fred's version of the Spider is great example of letting your creativity take over and viewing a pattern from a new angle.

Spider

Hook: Streamer 7X long, size 4 Daiichi 2370
Stinger: Special curved scud, size 10 Daiichi 1150
Thread: Yellow 6/0, Gudebrod
Tail: Matching mallard flank feathers
Body: Lite-Brite, yellow (Spirit River Inc.)
Hackle: Large mallard flank feather

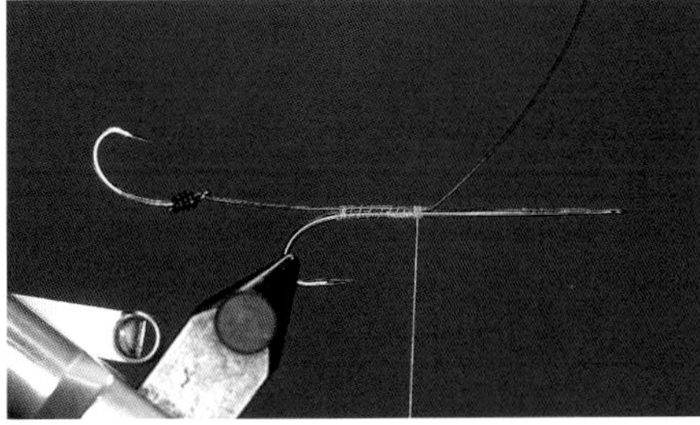

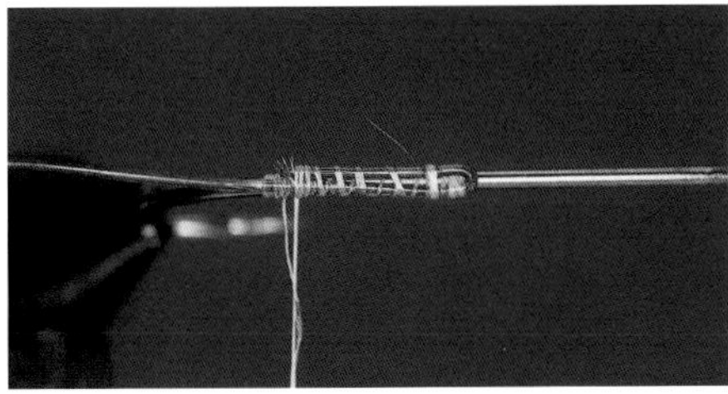

1. Prepare the stinger hook before tying this fly. Any stiff bite tippet of 40-pound test will work to attach the stinger hook to the main hook. We are using brown Maxima (chameleon) on this example. Snell the stinger hook using a nail knot tool. This works real slick with a three-turn nail knot. Start the thread on the main hook at the 1/3 point and wrap to the back creating a smooth thread base. Move the thread back to the 1/3 point. With the hook point up, secure the stinger hook on the top of the hook, favoring the fore side and wrap to the back of the hook. Move thread forward again. Pull the tag end of the bite tippet back and lay it on the top, favoring the far side of the hook, and wrap back with very tight wraps. Trim excess tippet and drop a spot of super glue on the thread wraps to lock the stinger hook in place.

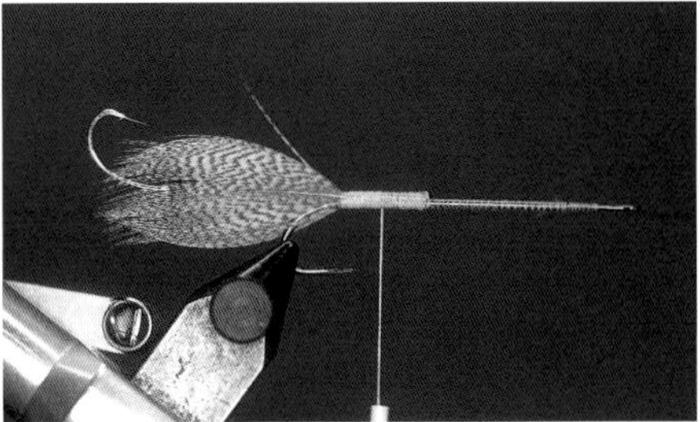

2. Match up a pair of medium-sized, barred mallard flank feathers for the tail. With the concave sides together, attach one feather on the far side of the hook and the other on the fore side of the hook. Length of the tail is up to you. It is there to disguise the stinger hook and add a square-looking tail to this baitfish imitation.

3. Dub the body to the front of the fly leaving plenty of room to turn the hackle and finish the fly. Lite-Brite is a very coarse dubbing and should leave a raggedy, loose-looking body. A quick tip to help a tier put the dubbing on this long hook shank: Apply about 3 or 4 inches of dubbing to the thread and wrap it in place. Keep the dubbing ball in your hand and apply another 3 or 4 inches and wrap it in place. Repeat until the entire body is done. This is much more efficient than trying to dub 6 or 8 inches and hitting yourself in the chin with the bobbin. With a little practice this procedure will soon become second nature. Stop the dubbing at about the 3/4 point on the hook shank.

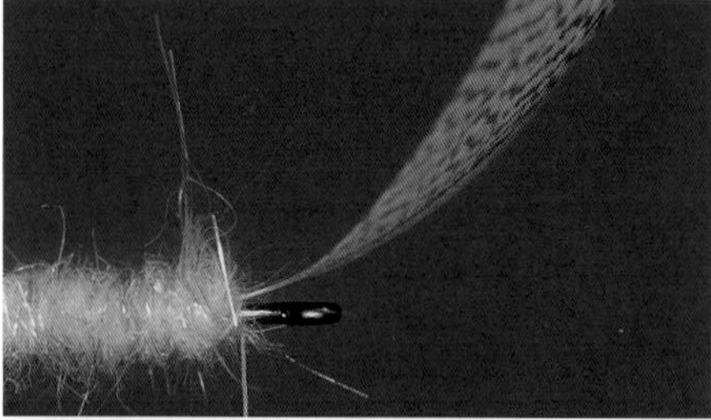

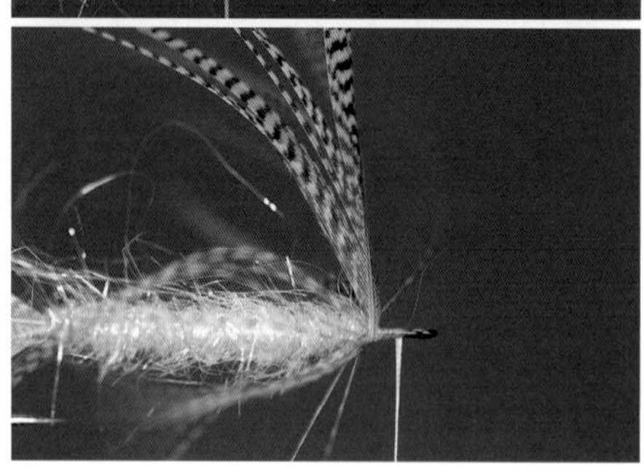

4. Pull the fluff off a large mallard flank feather, cut the stem of the feather off at the point where the nice part of the feather starts. Tie the flank feather in by the butt, concave side up, and out over the eye of the hook at the 7/8 point of the hook. Wrap the stem down to the 3/4 point. Apply more dubbing to cover the hackle stem up to the hackle tie-in point. Move thread to the hook eye. Make a half wrap under the hook shank and hold the feather straight up, making sure the flat part of the stem will wrap on the hook shank. Sweep the barbules of the feather back into a soft-hackle position and make the first full turn around the hook shank.

5. Wrap the flank feather forward, one wrap right next to the last. Fold the bar-

bules back after each wrap to ensure that all the fibers are swept back in a typical soft-hackle position. Use as much of the feather as possible, with the help of a pair of hackle pliers if need be. By wrapping the butt end of the feather first, the head of the fly will have the natural taper already built in and give you a fuller look. Notice the tiny little head that is formed by wrapping the feather in this fashion. You can also save the step of trimming off the excess flank feather by simply pulling it back and tying it down with thread. The stem is so small at this point in the feather that it will blend in very nicely with the rest of the soft hackle. Whip finish.

The Universal

Contributed by Randy Smith

I really don't know what it is about this fly, but as soon as Randy described it to me I knew I had to include it in this book. After I had seen him tie it, there was no doubt at all. The wild thing is that it's nothing special. It doesn't have a super-secret tying technique. It's not real pretty, so it wouldn't be a big seller at the fly shop. (The main reason is because fly anglers don't fish streamers enough.) Not many people know of its existence, so it's never been the so-called "hot fly". However, what it is is different.

As the story goes, a truck driver dropped by a fly shop here in Denver looking for someone to tie a batch of streamers for him. He showed them a sample to go by and no one in the shop had ever seen anything like it. He called it the Universal. Randy was in the shop at the time and ended up tying a few for him. He thought it was a cool fly and brought it to my attention, so I will do the same for you.

Randy said, "When I first started tying I tried to tie as many different patterns as I could. I think it had a lot to do with my relatively quick progression in fly tying. With that in mind, I wanted an abundant variety of fly patterns to help improve your tying skills, so I thought the Universal fit right in."

I hope it is a reminder that a full fly box should have more in it than nine different stages of a mayfly and thirty-one different flavors of a caddis. Randy didn't have any experience fishing the fly so I took it upon myself to put the Universal to the test. I have fished it several times now and have taken fish on three different pieces of water. On one stretch, I hooked five trout in 45 minutes; with one of them breaking 3X tippet. I hope it is a reminder that big flies catch big fish. I hope you will tie a couple and get them wet.

We have no idea who developed it or if it is in some other book somewhere. So, if you are out there, thanks for the great addition to the world of fly patterns and if it is published elsewhere, please don't sue me for copyright infringement.

The Universal

Hook: Streamer 3X long, size 8, Dai Riki 730
Thread: 6/0 Danville, black
Weight: 020 wire

Streamers

Ribbing: Copper wire
Body: Pearl Poly Flash (Spirit River)
Underwing: Two black and one yellow streamer-quality neck hackle
Overwing: Mallard flank feather, tied horizontally
Collar: Light dun neck hackle, very wide and webby

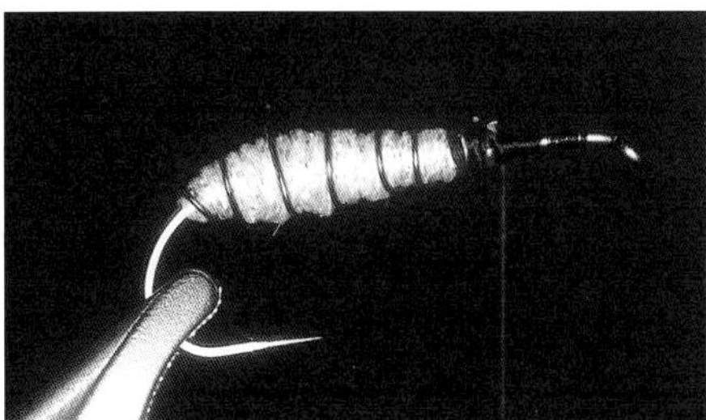

1. Wrap about half the hook with .020 lead wire. I counted fifteen wraps as Randy was preparing the size 8 hook. Position the weight towards the back of the hook. Start thread behind the wire and lock the wire down with thread. Tie in a piece of copper wire on the backside of the hook and wrap to the back of the hook. Move thread to the front of the weight and tie in the Poly Flash. Lash the Poly Flash down as you wrap to the back of the hook. I prefer leaving it on the spool, I'll wrap what I need then trim, eliminating any waste. Move thread to a point in front of the weight and wrap the body material forward, forming a reverse tapered body while covering the lead weight completely. This taper of the body ensures that the underwing feather will lie over the body correctly. Secure and trim excess.

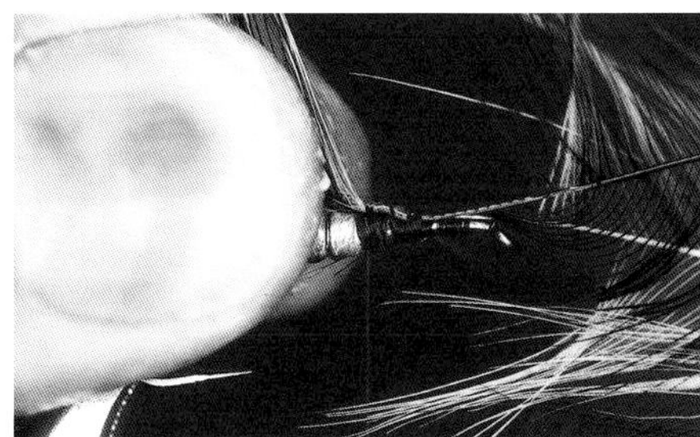

2. Prepare two black neck hackle feathers and one yellow. If you are using feathers that are still on the skin, pull a feather from the left side of the neck and one from the right side. This ensures that the curvature of the feathers match. The yellow feather just needs to be the same size as the black feathers. Meld the yellow hackle inside the two black

hackles. Be sure that the black hackles have the concave sides together and the tips of the three feathers are together. Measure the length of the hackle for the underwing so that it is two times the shank length. Now strip the barbs off a small section of the feathers where they will be tied down. Tie the wing in right in front of the body, making sure the stems of the feathers stay on top of the hook. If the stems do not stay on top of the hook they will twist and separate. Trim the butt ends of the feathers.

3. Find a large mallard flank feather for the overwing. It should look symmetrical, having very even length barbs on each side of the stem. If you have a bag of loose feathers, find the best possible one. A small bag may only have a couple of good feathers. A bag of an ounce or more should have several dozen good feathers. On skin the best feathers will come from the rear part of the flank. The length of the overwing should be the same as the underwing, maybe just a bit longer. After getting the right length, strip the excess fibers and fluff off the stem. Place the feather horizontally over the top of the underwing and secure in place. Trim the excess stem.

4. Pull two large hackles from the top of a quality light dun dry-fly neck. These are those big nasty hackles on a neck that can be used for the wings on a Gray Ghost streamer or end up getting dyed black for Woolly Buggers. Wide, webby

feathers are just right for the collar on this fly. With the tips of the feathers together, make a separation in the feathers about an inch from the tip. This is where the real width of the feather starts. Trim the tips, leaving about 1/4 to 3/8 of an inch and tie in on top of the hook in front of the wings. Move your thread to the front of the hook. Wrap the feathers forward, sweeping the barbs back as you go. Secure at the front of the hook and trim butt ends off. Make a nice clean thread head and whip finish.

5. Carefully trim the hackle collar to shape being careful not to cut the wing. A slight angle from front to back is desirable.

Wet Burrito

Contributed by Fred Vargas

Fred Vargas watched Dave Whitlock tie this type of fly and liked the simplicity of the pattern. It also intrigued him because he knew it would work on his home waters of the Muskegon River. Fred liked the overall design and the materials used on the fly, but he thought he needed to eliminate a few of the bells and whistles. He guides fly anglers on the Muskegon River and needs flies that are simple to tie, yet effective, simply because of the nature of the river. The Muskegon was a logging river, so there are snags lurking at the bottom that devour flies when an angler is trying to get them down to the fish. The depth and current requires the use of a 300-grain sinking line to get the fly down to the popular steelhead on the Muskegon River. With this type of rig an angler can lose a lot of flies.

Fred explains, "Patterns used for guiding have to be effective, yet easy and quick to tie. When I find something that I think will work with a few minor changes I will tie them. In this case, the Wet Burrito was an instant success."

Whitlock's original is called the Sheep Minnow. Tied as a bass streamer, the pattern is varied to imitate bluegill, crappie, and shad. Some were tied sparely to run deep in the water, while others were laden with wool to make them swim with more action. You can find this pattern in *Fly Patterns of Umpqua Feather Merchants*.

"I added a flash tail and the dubbed body to this pattern while leaving out the outer wing and eyes. When you look at Whitlock's original recipe in the book, I think you'll understand about the bells and whistles," Fred says.

He enjoys the simplicity of the fly, but that does not take away from its effectiveness. The flash and overall white color of the fly work very well on steelhead rivers, especially when the water is somewhat off color or murky. The red throat adds the strike-triggering color and represents gills. And trout like it.

Wet Burrito

Hook: 7X Streamer, size 4 Daiichi 2370
Stinger: Scud Hook, size 10 Tiemco 2457
Thread: White 6/0, Gudebrod
Tail: Krystal Flash, pearl
Body: Lite-Brite Dubbing, white (Spirit River Inc.) Lite-Brite Dubbing red
Belly: White wool
Underwing: Krystal Flash, pearl
Wing: White wool, topped with gray wool
Overwing: Krystal Flash, peacock colored

1. Prepare the stinger hook before tying this fly. Any stiff bite tippet of 40-pound test will work to attach the stinger hook to the main hook. We are using brown Maxima on this example. Snell the stinger hook using a nail knot tool. This works really well with a three-turn nail knot. Start the thread on the main hook at the 1/3 point and wrap to the back creating a smooth thread base. Move the thread back to the 1/3 point. With the hook point up, secure the stinger hook on the fore side of the hook and wrap to the back of the hook. Move thread forward again. Pull the tag end of the bite tippet back, lay it on the far side of the hook, and wrap back with very tight wraps. Trim excess tippet and drop a spot of super glue on the thread wraps to lock the stinger hook in place. Add several turns of .030 lead wire in front of the stinger-hook tie-in point to about the 3/4 point of the hook shank and lock it in place with thread.

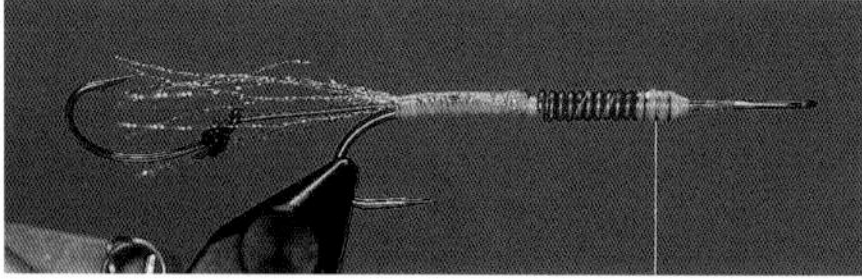

2. Secure 13 strands of Krystal Flash at the back of the hook for the tail. Half jokingly, I asked Fred to be more precise about the number of strands. He jumped right in and said he does count them because he wants all of his flies to be consistent. Consistency is an inherent, spiritual trait of a pro tier. Length is up to the tier, however, cutting the strands right at the point of the stinger hook looks pretty good. Save this bundle of flash for later use. Wet them with a little spit to keep them together.

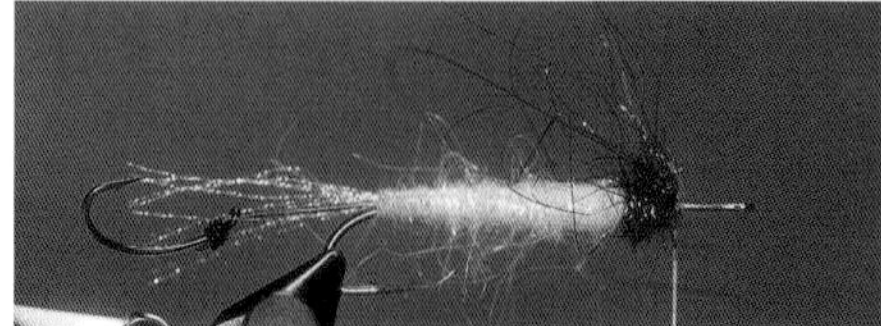

3. Dub the body to the 3/4 point of the hook. Taper the dubbing slightly as you go forward. Dub a red throat area to the 7/8 point of the hook. The dubbing should be pretty rough looking with loose fibers of the Lite-Brite sticking out around the hook shank.

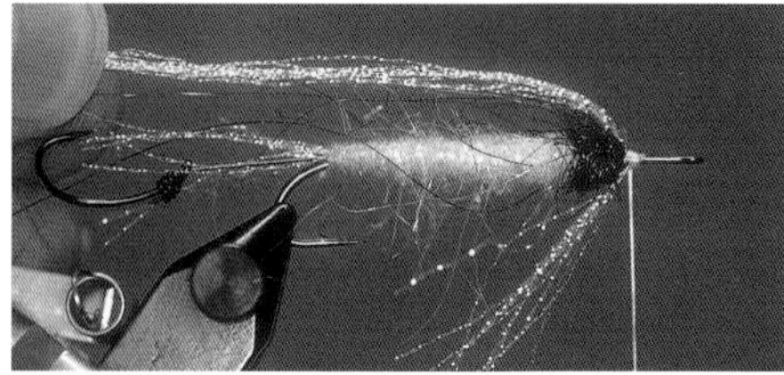

4. Take the 13 strands of Krystal Flash you used for the tail and secure them on top of the hook. Make sure the strands extend beyond the stinger hook on the back. Separate the strands hanging out over the eye and pull them back and under the hook shank. Make a wrap or two to lock them in place. Trim the strands under the hook at the hook point. Trim the strands on top of the hook to the point of the stinger hook, even with the tail.

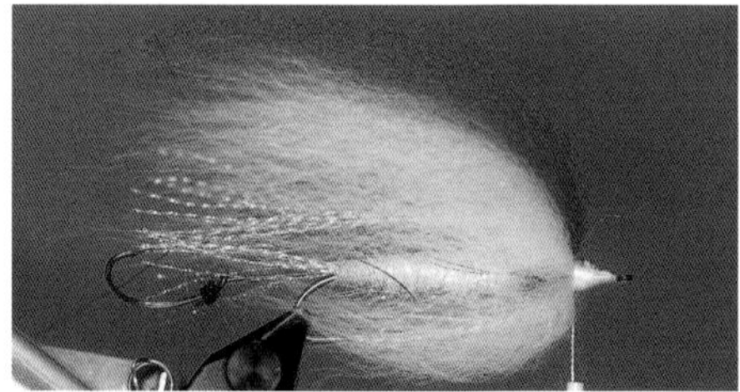

5. Take a patch of white wool and comb out the fibers with a fine-toothed comb. A pet brush works very well to fluff the fibers up. Snip out a clump about the size of a wooden match stick. Secure it under the hook so that the tips extend back to the inside of the bend. Trim excess. Cut out another

clump of white wool about twice as thick as the first. Secure it on top of the hook with the tips extending back to the point of the stinger hook. Comb out a patch of gray wool and snip out a clump about the size of a wooden match stick. Secure it on top of the

white wool so the tips of both clumps are even. Make sure to put a drop or two of head cement at the wool tie-in point to help lock it in place.

6. Add 8 or 10 strands of peacock-colored Krystal Flash for a topping and whip finish.

Chapter 8

TERRESTRIALS & ATTRACTORS

Ausable Skunk

Contributed by Dennis Potter

Here is an ancient Au Sable fly that was originally called Madson's Skunk. Developed by Earl Madson years ago, it is still one of the go-to attractor patterns for the Au Sable River and many still waters in the area. Dennis adds, "Some of the old-timers still call it Madson's Skunk. There is also a wet fly with the Skunk name; so many of us locals just call the dry fly a Dry Skunk to differentiate it from the wet."

For trout and smallmouth bass alike, it is best fished when both the water and air temperatures are warm. It works especially well around cover, such as fallen logs, brushy banks where limbs dangle above the water, and behind rocks. Be prepared for the fish to absolutely crash this bug. They abandon all elegance when eating this thing.

It is a great pattern to toss while covering lots of water from a boat. Tactics include those used for hopper fishing. It's a good pattern for windy days. Work the structure, the edges of slow water such as eddies, and water hidden by shadows. One of the favorite techniques of the dedicated skunk head is to slap it on the water, let it travel dead drift for a foot or two and then give it the slightest twitch. That minute kick of the legs often draws an explosive hit. However, much like any attractor pattern, if the fish show no interest in the bug after a half hour, forty-five minutes, take it off and try something else. There is no miracle fly out there, including this one. It has its time and place and it is up to a challenged angler to find that time and that particular place where the fly will produce.

"I have had great success with this fly on the Missouri River below Holter Dam and it has been wonderful for the big cutts on the Yellowstone River. However, one of my favorite places to use this pattern is on Wakely Lake, a local still water near the Riverhouse," Dennis adds, "It is flies-and-lures-only, catch-and-release water where no motors of any kind can be used. It is only open from June 15 to August 31 and is full of bluegills, sunfish, big bass, and pike. Its 137 acres are totally undeveloped, owned and managed by the Forest Service.

"Most of my time on Wakely Lake is spent chasing the gills and sunnies. One of my favorite Wakely flies is a size 6 2X long Skunk, never smaller! I have had countless fish in the 10 to 21- inch class totally inhale the big fly." Dennis exclaims, "The bluegills and smallmouth bass are canoe pullers. My daughter, then 16 years of age, had a bluegill on in Wakely Lake that turned the canoe and pulled it a few feet before breaking off, not in the weeds, just by pulling. I got a good look at it when it rolled close to the surface and my best guess was 13-14 inches. It was a Moby Gill!"

When you first look at this fly and its flared head it givse the impression of being some kind of popping bug. It could easily be used as such, however Dennis thinks the most effective part of the fly is the rubber legs. The lifelike action of the legs is what he thinks attracts the trout to this particular pattern. "I creamed 'em while on Sixteen Mile Creek in Montana one year. Pretty much out of disgust because of my lack of success on the lower part of the creek, I tied this pattern on and slammed it on the water in the upper reaches of the canyon and had three browns come out of hiding to take a look. I hooked up and landed nearly 20 trout that day until there was only one leg and about half the wing left on the fly. They quit taking the pattern until I put a fresh bug on with new legs. They got right on it again."

A trick Dennis has found with this bug involves the subtle movement of the legs. This works especially well on stillwater situations. If a trout comes up and hangs under the fly but is hesitant to eat, just a slight wave of the rod tip will make the legs wiggle without effectively moving the fly, producing explosive takes.

Most of the flies tied in the Midwest using hair are tied with whitetail deer. Whitetail is easy to acquire there and the hair does work relatively well. However, Dennis chooses Craig Mathews' Select Elk from Blue Ribbon Fly Shop in West Yellowstone for the wing on this fly. He has found it to be the finest elk hair on the market. Clean tips, very good hair length, and hair durability makes this an outstanding choice for all elk body-hair needs.

Materials needed for attractor patterns can range from the truly exotic, like New Wave Chenille, to something as simple as rubber legs. The types of rubber legs vary from square, speckled silicone, and the basic round rubber in as many colors as you might find in a big box of Crayolas. Dennis relays, "I think they all may have their special purpose in the fly-tying world, but for a simple attractor dry fly like the AuSable Skunk, medium round rubber works best. The natural flowing action and unrestricted motion of round rubber is much more appealing than the stiff, bi-directional square rubber."

Pre-cut the rubber legs to about 2 inches in length. Prepare enough for two lengths on each of the hooks laid out. A dozen hooks would be a good start.

Ausable Skunk

Hook: 2X dry fly, size 10 Tiemco 2312
Thread: Black 6/0
Tail: Calf tail, white
Body: New Age Chenille, black
Wing: Elk body hair, Craig Mathews Select Elk
Legs: Medium round rubber legs

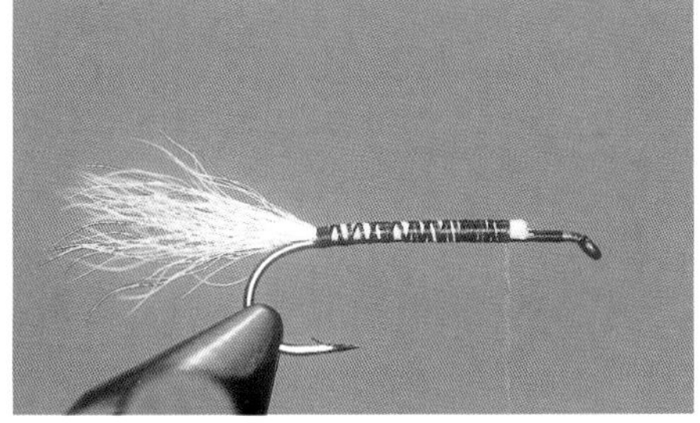

1. Start thread at the front of the hook shank and wrap to the back of the hook. Stack and measure a clump of calf-tail hair to a full hook shank in length. The first photo shows the thread position at the barb, what we refer to as the back of the hook, just for illustration purposes. Move thread to the 3/4 point of the hook. Move hair to opposite hand and trim the butt ends of the hair at the 3/4 point. Secure the butt ends of the hair at this point and wrap to the back of the hook. Hold the calf hair up slightly as the thread is wrapped over the hair so the hair will remain on top of the hook shank. Move thread forward to the 3/4 point.

2. Strip off about 1/8 inch of the chenille down to the thread core. Tie in this length of chenille at the front of the fly. Leave thread at the front of the hook. Wrap chenille back to just in front of the tail. Now wrap the chenille forward over the top of the first layer. Secure chenille at the 7/8 point of the hook and trim excess. Make sure not to crowd the last turn of chenille too close to the eye of the hook.

3. Clean the under fur and short hair fiber, stack and measure a clump of elk body hair for the wing. The tip of the wing should extend back to the tip of the tail. Trim the butt ends of the hair. Let the butt ends of the hair remain over the eye and make two soft wraps of thread over the hair. Tighten the thread

to secure the clump at the front of the hook allowing the butt ends of the hair to flare. Add a few tight wraps of thread to lock the wing in place. Sweep the elk hair back, making sure the hair is over the top of the body. Jump the thread back to the 3/4 point of the hook shank and make several wraps around the hair so that it lies flat over the body. Apply enough thread torque to flare the hair slightly without making it explode into some modern hairdo.

4. Cut two pieces of medium round rubber legs to about two inches in length. With the thread remaining at the 3/4 point, secure one on the far side of the hook with two soft turns of thread and then the other on the fore side of the hook with two soft turns. Slide the legs so there are even amounts to the front and back making a clear X pattern with

the legs. Make sure the rubber legs are even or horizontal to the hook shank so they ride on the water correctly. Secure with several tight wraps of thread that dig into the hair and rubber legs. This will pop the legs out into the X-ing position. Pull the front legs back out of the way and make one wrap of thread though the middle of the flared head and pull tight to lock everything into place. Whip finish directly behind the eye.

Bead Head Marabou Worm

As described by Gary LaFontaine

The Marabou Worm is a simple concept. This fly represents a technique that creates a certain action that trout recognize as a live, edible food source.

There are two types of worms that trout feed on. One is an aquatic worm called an annelid. The other would be of the terrestrial type, basically an earthworm that gets washed into the stream. One can be a constant food source while the other is a sporadic food source.

The key trigger of these worms is the way they tumble in the water, so the development of the Marabou Worm had to incorporate this natural tumbling action. To make this happen the fly has to be weighted in a certain way. The head of the fly has to sink and the tail needs to float. The head sinks to the bottom where the current is very slow, while the tail rises up into the faster currents. This design causes the fly to sumersault as it drifts. It is very important to maintain a very good dead drift to produce this action. Any tension on the leader will reduce this triggering action.

The original pattern incorporated lead wire on the front half of the hook with marabou wrapped over the top. This gave the fly the weight at the head. The tail floatation is just a piece of high-density foam glued to the marabou tail. This works, but then a friend, Ben Bracken from Green River, Wyoming, came up with a bead-head version of the fly that works even better.

Here is what Bracken has to say, "The Bead Head Marabou Worm is my secret weapon. The first time I tried it on the Green River in Wyoming, above the famous tailwater in Utah, was on a nothing piece of water on a very slow day. On six casts I caught four big trout from a place that had never produced a big fish for me before. The secret is in the way the fly tumbles."

The entire concept of feeding trout lies in the trigger. Gary LaFontaine explains: "When a trout is feeding on a freestone stream, he is looking at all sorts of food items. Believe it or not, the trout is using all of its brain power deciphering what it is looking at. What is that? Is it food? What is this floating by? Is it food? The trout is feeding opportunistically. He has to really think about what the shapes, sizes and colors are telling him about the items. Are they food?"

"Now let's say the trout is in the Henry's Fork feeding on a pale morning dun hatch. The trout has a chance to lock into one visual pattern. He thinks less and less as he locks into that pattern. He becomes more and more brain dead with each passing moment." Gary adds, "In effect, the trout becomes dumber by the moment. Selectivity is not a function of intelligence, it is a function of less thinking. So, the dumber a trout is, the harder he is to catch."

Think about it. It is just the opposite of what most fly-fishermen think.

All trout feeding is based on triggers. These concepts all came from Gary's work in behavioral psychology. The phrases that we see, such as "triggering characteristics" and "exaggerating the trigger", come from professional papers that were published for his masters thesis on "The Selective Feeding of Trout".

A fly must have a triggering characteristic that is just like the insect it is trying to represent.

This is triggering in a nutshell. Gary explains, "Let's say you are walking down a stream and you see your buddy Joe. You didn't recognize his face, or his big hands, or his old wading boots. What you did see was his goofy fishing hat, his blue vest, or that he towers in at 6' 5." One recognizable feature was the trigger. It was the unique characteristic about Joe that you could see before any other characteristic. When a trout is feeding in a stream and there is a hatch on, there is one characteristic about the insect that stands out."

The importance of a fly pattern is number one, the size; number two, the shape; number three, the color. This will vary according to the insect. With a salmonfly, size may be the most important feature. However, as a bright green caddisfly is drifting towards a trout, color may be the most important feature of that insect. An emerging caddisfly displays the undeniable characteristic of brightness.

The triggering characteristic of the insect is going to be the most prominent aspect of that insect. That is what the trout sees first. This is what Gary found with his scuba-diving work.

A worm has a triggering action, not color, not size, not shape. The important thing is movement. The Bead Head Marabou Worm imitates the action of that worm. And this action is what the trout recognizes from the furthest distance. This action mimics life, which tells the trout that this object is edible.

As I said before, a perfect dead drift is imperative to produce the correct action, but timing is also very important as far as availability of this important food source goes. High-water periods are very good times to fish the Bead Head Marabou Worm. This period will dislodge worms by the thousands. Rainstorms also make earthworms available. A quick: Try fishing below a golf course after a hard rain shower.

Bead Head Marabou Worm

Hook: Nymph 2X long, size 12-16
Thread: 8/0 or 6/0, color to match marabou
Bead: Metal bead, gold or black
Tail: Marabou, orange, tan, gray, brown, red

Tail Float: EdgeWater foam, 1/8-inch diameter disk
Body: Marabou, same piece used for the tail

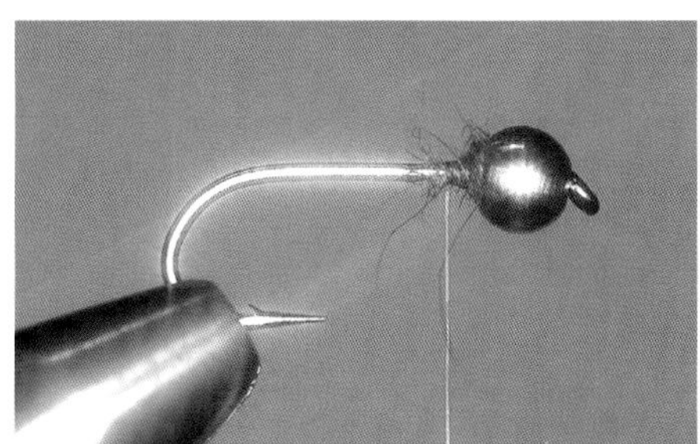

1. Start the thread behind the bead and dub a small amount of dubbing on the hook. With your fingernails push the dubbing ball into the void at the back of the bead. This helps keep the bead in place as you tie the fly and, more importantly, as you are fishing the fly.

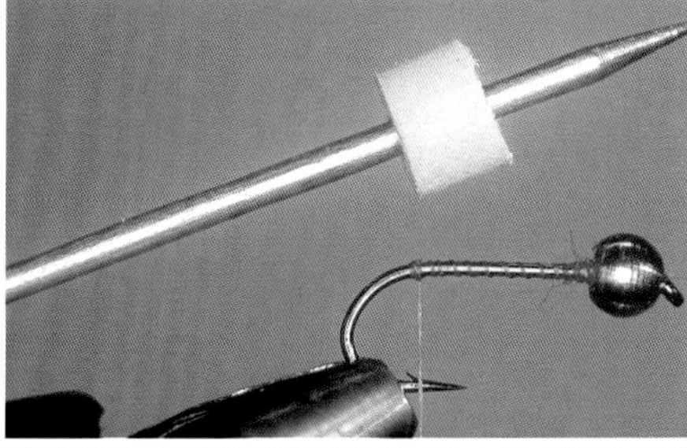

2. Move thread to the back of the hook. Let's say a minimum of a dozen flies are going to be tied in this tying session. Select twelve high-grade blood marabou feathers and strip both sides of the stem about half way up. Make sure to leave the excess stem attached. With a bodkin, poke a hole all the way through an EdgeWater foam disk. These foam disks are pre cut into a cylinder shape about 1/8 of an inch thick. Remove the foam from the bodkin and immediately feed it onto the marabou stem. Slide the foam ("tail float") up to a point where two hook-shanks' length of the tip of the feather is beyond the foam disk. Finish all twelve up to this point.

3. Measure the marabou so that two hook shanks length of marabou is beyond the bend of the hook, which should be just in front of the tail float. Attach the marabou to the hook with several tight wraps of thread.

4. Grab the end of the marabou stem and make a half wrap. Make a counter-clockwise turn of thread around the marabou and wrap both forward to just behind the bead. Separate the marabou from the thread. Hold the marabou up with your right hand and with the bobbin in the left hand secure the marabou behind the bead. Place a drop of head cement on the bead and whip finish. As you whip finish, drag the thread over the bead, picking up the cement as you finish the fly.

5. After completing all the flies to this point, secure the tail floats with a drop of super glue directly on the marabou a hook-shank's length beyond the bend of the hook. Carefully slide the tail float back to the super glue. It will lock in place immediately. Repeat and you have a dozen flies ready for the water.

Here are some popular colors for the Marabou Worm: Gray, brown, red, orange, and tan.

Chernobyl Ant

Contributed by Rich Pilatzke

This is a pattern that originated on the Green River in the 1980's to imitate Mormon Crickets. It was tied in the one-color black version such as this particular pattern, also known as the "BBB" (Big Black Bug), but I see no reason a two-tone version with yellow, tan, or orange mixed in wouldn't work. This fly won the Jackson Hole One Fly contest twice, (in 1995 and 1996) and is being discovered all over the country.

It is a go-to fly in late summer, but can be especially effective in high-water situations by drifting it near the bank. I have had clients worried about my abilities as a guide when they saw me tie this gaudy-looking thing on their tippet, that is until the first slashing rise nearly jerked the rod out of their hands. This fly draws attention, not only to an unsuspecting angler, but also to just about every trout in the river.

It is one of those flies that get the big fishes' attention. Rich Pilatzke notices, "I think the amount of foam on this fly makes it soft to the immediate touch of a fish, making them hang on longer and giving the angler plenty of time to set the hook."

I have had reports of its productivity on Slough Creek and the Lamar River in Yellowstone National Park. When the trout wouldn't take a regular hopper and ignored the Elk Hair Caddis, they hammered a dual-colored Chernobyl with a tan underbody. It has also worked with great success on high-mountain lakes, up to a size size 4, when the wind is kicking up its heels.

The Chernobyl Ant is a very easy pattern to put together. Grab some foam and rubber legs and get to it.

Chernobyl Ant

Hook: Nymph 2x long, size 6-12, Tiemco 2302
Thread: Orange 6/0 UNI-Thread
Body: Black 1/8" evasote closed-cell foam
Legs: Medium or large round rubber
Indicator: Yellow 1/8-inch evasote closed-cell foam

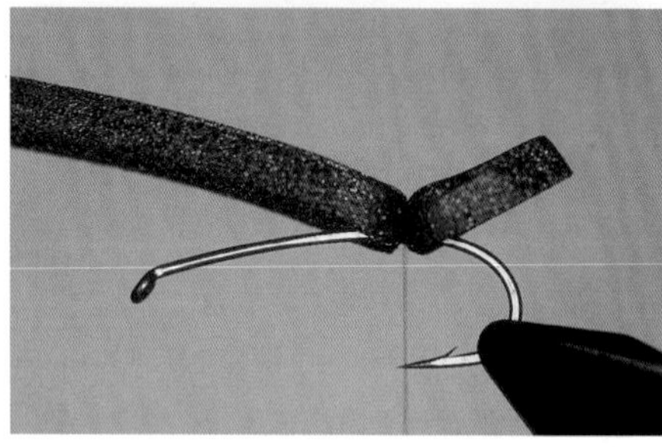

1. Start the thread at the back of the hook. Cut a strip of 1/8 inch black evasote foam about 1/4 inch wide. Trim corners of the foam as shown. Tie the strip on top of the hook shank, right at the back of the hook. This portion of the body should extend just past the bend of the hook.

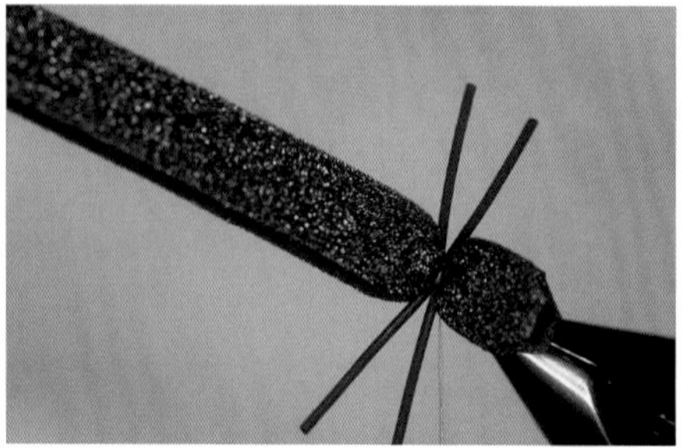

2. Fold a section of round rubber around the thread, slide the rubber to the far side of the hook and lock into place with a couple of loose wraps. Even the length of the legs with a careful pull here or there, repositioning the round rubber to make the legs the correct length, then snug up the thread. This procedure makes a nice pair of V shaped legs. Repeat on the near side of the hook. Preparing several sets of legs all the same length beforehand will speed up your tying and make all the legs uniform in length when tied in place. Sections an inch and a half long are about right. This also eliminates the need for trimming the legs on the hook. Large round rubber is the correct for size 6 and larger hooks, while medium round rubber is best for sizes smaller than 6.

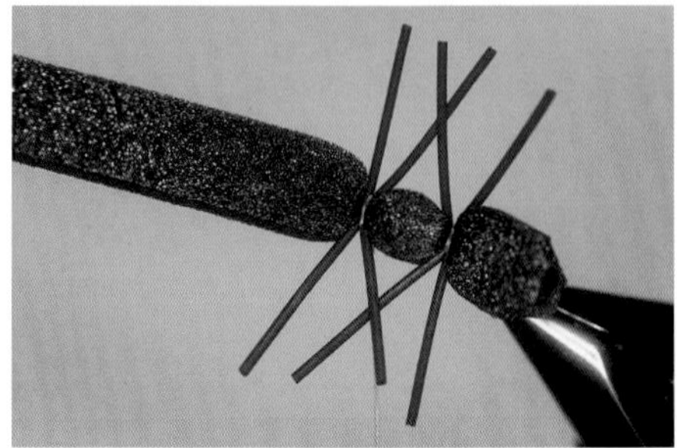

3. Lift up the foam and move thread to the 1/2 point on the hook. Secure the next section of the body foam with a few turns of thread. Repeat the steps for tying in another set of legs on both sides of the hook.

4. Tie in a strip of yellow foam for the indicator on top of the hook. Make sure the yellow indicator foam is cut as wide as the black foam. Lift up the foam and move the thread to the front. Secure the black foam, trim excess, and whip finish. Trim excess yellow foam, super glue the indicator in place with Zap-a-Gap, and you have a finished Chernobyl Ant.

Crystal Beetle

Contributed by Rich Pilatzke

The first foam patterns I tied were black foam beetles. They were a design by Craig Mathews, a master tier and one of the owners of Blue Ribbon Flies. He called it the Blue Ribbon Beetle. It is a very simple pattern of foam with black deer-hair fibers for legs. The Crystal Beetle, however, is the creation of Nick Niklas. He is a very talented Blue Ribbon Flies guide from West

Yellowstone, Montana. Nick, a very wise gentleman, heads south during the winter and guides salt water, where he specializes in catching redfish. The main difference in the Crystal Beetle is the flashy chenille for the body.

Rich explains, "One of my first sources of good-quality evasote sheet foam ended up being Blue Ribbon Flies in West Yellowstone. They carried Traun River Polycelon foam in several different colors. I immediately liked this as a tying material and bought a good supply of it. I am still using it today, fifteen years later; that's how much I bought. It is my go-to material for patterns such as the Foam Ant, Chernobyl Ant, Madison River Stopper, and of course beetles. "

The fly typically is tied on a size-12 dry-fly hook, however, Rich started using the Tiemco 102Y terrestrial hook, which added a new look to the fly and is sized differently. A size 13 is very close to a size 12. It would be a number of years before he figured out that black foam ants and beetles, while highly effective patterns, worked much better with a strike indicator of yarn or foam on their backs. (They worked better for me because I could see them on the water, making it easier to detect a fish taking the fly.) So with the addition of the yellow foam strike indicator on top of the fly it became a revised version of an already very good fly.

Rich says, "My fascination with foam only grew stronger as different types and colors of foam started to become available. I began to experiment with other fly patterns tied with foam. I was always on the lookout for unusual sources of foam and flies that could be modified with foam in its construction."

Before you get any preconceived ideas about foam flies or using a beetle pattern, note that Mike Lawson has the black beetle listed as one of the top ten producing flies on the Henry's Fork. That's impressive enough for me to carry a couple!"

Crystal Beetle

Hook: Dry fly, size 9-15 Tiemco 102Y
Thread: Black 6/0 UNI-Thread
Body: Bailey's Medium Flash Chenille, either pearl/black or lime/black

Overbody: 2mm thick closed-cell foam or a strip of Larva Lace pre-sliced foam
Legs: Black deer hair
Indicator: Yellow 1/8" evasote closed-cell foam

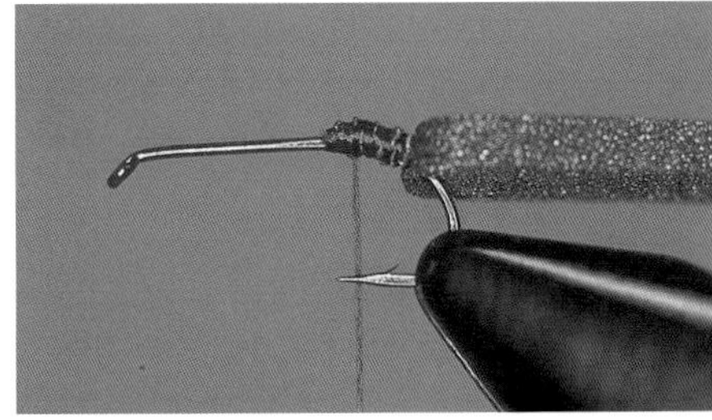

1. Start thread at the 1/4 point of the hook and wrap back slightly. Tie in a strip of the black foam at the back of the hook and wrap thread down the bend slightly. Move thread to the 3/4point of the hook and secure a length of Crystal Chenille. Wrap it down to the back of the hook. Move thread forward to the 3/4 point.

2. Wrap chenille forward to the 3/4 point and secure. Trim excess. Pull foam over and secure it in place with a couple

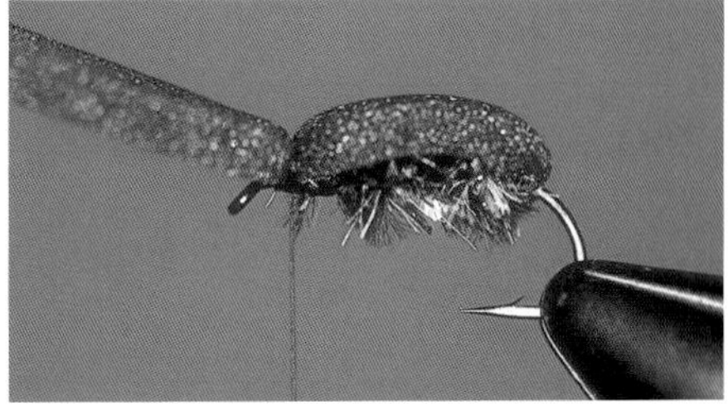

turns of thread. Leave the foam extending over the eye until a later step.

3. Tie in three black deer-hair fibers for the legs using a couple simple X-ing wraps.

4. Tie in a strip of yellow foam at the 3/4 point as shown in photo. The yellow foam is strictly for better visibility. Lift up the foam and whip finish behind the eye.

5. Trim the foam and deer-hair legs. By pushing in on the legs lightly you can put little knee joints in if you like. Here is the finished Crystal Beetle.

Deer Hair Wooly

Contributed by Char Stimpson

Gary LaFontaine introduced me to Paul Stimpson at the Denver Sportsman's Show in January 2001. He suggested that Paul, an outstanding professional tier, would be a great contributor for this book. As with most people in the fishing industry, when Gary talked, I listened. Paul and I chatted about this project and he agreed to help out.

Paul had been tying hundreds of dozens of flies for Gary's newsletter, the "Book Mailer" and I could see through the work he was doing that he was very adept at tying patterns that Gary markets in the newsletter. In March, we met again at the Western Colorado Fly Fishing Expo in Grand Junction, CO. It was there that I met his wife, Char. She was right in there tying beside Paul, demonstrating her talents. And talents she has. She was spinning deer hair with ease; in fact it looked so easy and the Mohawks she was tying were so consistent, that I could not help but be impressed. I asked her if she would like to disclose her techniques in this book along with Paul. She agreed and we set a date to meet the following June at their home in Ogden, UT.

While Paul had been tying all the easy patterns, like the Double Wing and the Duck Butt Dun for Gary ha ha, Char got stuck with the hair spinning duties. I say, "Got stuck with hair spinning" because it would be gruesome, sweaty work for me, but it seemed that Char actually enjoyed the task.

Char suggests using a fine, thin-shafted hair like whitetail deer for the spinning, especially on smaller flies. This hair flares and spins easily and compacts very tightly. Pay close attention to Char's technique on spinning this hair in the following instructions. It is by far the most efficient and durable way to spin hair. This method is what caught my eye when I was watching her tie.

The Deer Hair Wooly is a great pattern to practice the spinning technique. A grizzly hackle, whitetail deer hair, and a thread that will flare hair is all it takes. On top of that, when the fly is done it is a most effective generic terrestrial fly. It can be fished whenever a hopper or beetle would be used. When nothing specific is happening on the water, try it. Toss it in there tight to the bank, under the over-hanging limbs of a willow, or those dark, shadowy spots where you just know the biggest fish in the river is holed up. This fly just might take the biggest fish of the day, but you won't know unless you try it.

This is a pattern that can be tied in stages or what might be referred to as assembly-line tying. When a tier is planning to put several of these together, tie in hackle, spin the hair, and set it aside until all of them are done. Then trim them all to shape and finish off the head. It does increase the speed of tying dozens of this pattern.

Deer Hair Wooly

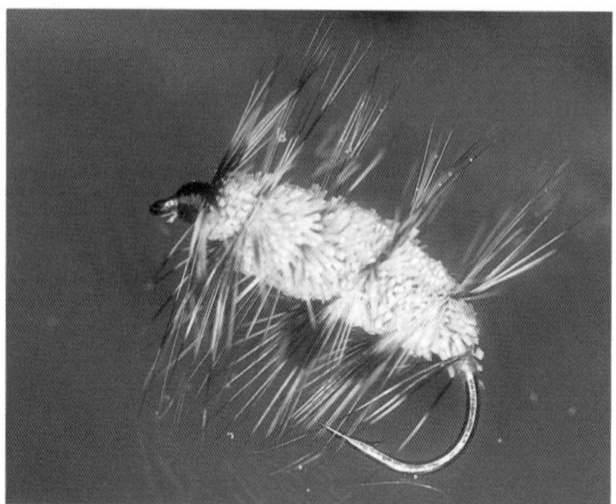

Hook: Dry fly, size 16-10, Daiichi 1180
Thread: Gudebrod G, tan
Hackle: Grizzly saddle, (Whiting Farms)
Body: Spun deer hair
Head: 8/0 black thread

1. Start thread at the very back of the hook and tie in a grizzly saddle hackle. The hackle should be measured to one size smaller than the hook being used. The hackle is wrapped through the deer hair, effectively causing a standard hackle to be oversized.

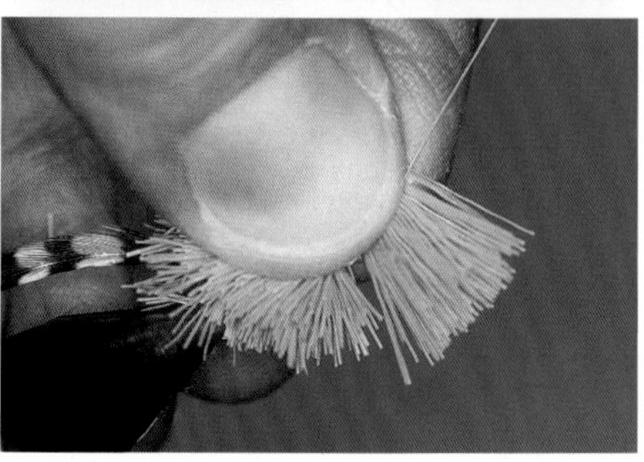

2. Trim out a clump of deer hair to start spinning the body. Start with a clump about the size of 2 wooden kitchen matches. Cut the hair to an overall length of 1/2 inch using the corky portion near the base of the hair. With the thread still at the back of the hook, hold the hair above the hook. Using the pinch method, make two loose wraps of thread around the mid-section of the hair. Gradually pull the thread tight. For the first clump only, hold the hair so it won't spin. Simply hold the hair with a finger on the backside of the hook as the thread is being tightened letting it flare in place. Char now wraps the thread back through the hair 2 or 3 times towards the bend to assure the back of the hook is covered. Then cross wrap the thread forward to the front of the hair to tie in the next clump. This procedure keeps the hackle from rolling out of place and reduces the amount of hair hanging up in the hook point. It is also what makes spun hair look tightly packed and easy to shape. So the next time you spin hair for any fly, instead of making wraps on top of the initial wraps, (which is what most tiers are taught to do) crisscross from the middle of the hair clump to the back of the clump. Then cross the thread over to the front portion of the clump. A tier can easily make 4 to 7 wraps of thread through one stacking of hair. This effectively locks the hair to the hook with several angling

wraps of thread making the hair body much more durable. It also flares the hair very tight to the hook shank. This eliminates the gaps in the hair fibers close to the shank that show up after shaping the body. Sweep the hair back and make two wraps of thread directly on the hook shank in front of the hair. Continue by spinning another clump. This time hold the hair up to the hook shank at a 45 degree angle, make the two soft wraps, and tighten the thread. Let go of the hair and let this clump encompass the hook shank as it flares. Char makes this point, "This technique is more like displacing the hair around the hook than it is spinning the hair. After it is displaced, flare it with several crossing wraps of thread." Stroke the hair back, and make two turns of thread on the hook shank in front of the hair. Compact the hair by squeezing it together with your fingernails or with a hair-packing tool such as a Brassie. This procedure stands the hair up perpendicular to the hook, so the next clump can be tied in without trapping hair fibers from the last clump. Repeat the process until the hook shank is totally covered with spun hair. Make a couple of half hitches and remove thread.

3. Using a straight pair of scissors or a double-edged razor blade cut the hair on the bottom of the fly first to open up the hook gape. With a curved pair of scissors, shape the body of the fly into a cigar shape. Get the rough shape of the fly, then finish with more precise cuts. Do not cut too much at a time, as it is very difficult to glue hair back on! Hold the hackle down and out of the way as you trim near the back of the hook to avoid severing the hackle from the fly. Notice how the hair at the back and the front of the body is tightly compacted.

4. Restart the thread and make 4 or 5 palmering wraps of hackle through the hair. Secure the hackle, trim excess, and whip finish.

Double Wing

Contributed by Paul Stimpson

Much of the design of this fly was done with light, color, and reflection in mind. It was a study of attractor-fly design and why trout take them. All parts of the fly were tested. With hackle, without hackle, thick bodies, thin bodies, bright versus dull. All bases were covered. After the Double Wing had been thoroughly assessed over extra difficult trout and examined in as many lighting conditions possible, it was found to have a special place in the fly boxes of Gary La Fontaine and his research assistants. It was named the Agitator. I have a feeling it wasn't because the fly agitated the trout as much as it agitated and aggravated its developers. The story behind the development can be found in Gary's book *The Dry Fly*.

As the fly is actually tied, the wing layers the body in such a way that Gary described the fly as prismatic. In fact, the Prism was the second name given for the fly. However, when mentioned among the group the pattern always went by its nickname, "Hey, let me try one of those Double Wings." So, the nickname was changed on its birth certificate and it has stuck.

Instead of laboring over all the details about Gary's research, let's just say the Double Wing is a fine tribute to all of his findings and contributions. He never held back any "trade secrets" that many so-called experts wanted to keep to themselves. He gave freely and was a wonderful writer and storyteller. I will let you have the joy of researching it yourself.

Here are all the color combinations for the Double Wing pattern.

DOUBLE WING

White Double Wing

Tail: White sparkle yarn
Tag: White floss
Rear Wing: White elk hair
Body Hackle: Silver badger
Body: White sparkle yarn (touch dubbed)
Front Wing: White calf tail
Hackle: Grizzly

The White Double Wing is a fantastic, all-around attractor dry fly, especially on a stream where brown trout are the predominant species. Gary LaFontaine suggest shady overhangs and late in the afternoon around dusk.

Cream Double Wing

Tail: Cream sparkle yarn
Tag: White floss
Rear Wing: Pale yellow elk hair
Body Hackle: Ginger
Body: Cream sparkle yarn (touch dubbed)
Front Wing: White calf tail
Hackle: Grizzly

The Cream Double Wing is more subdued than the White Double Wing and is designed more for streams with terrestrial moths. The Laramie River in Wyoming comes to mind.

Gray Double Wing

Tail: Dark gray sparkle yarn
Tag: White floss
Rear Wing: Rust-colored elk hair
Body Hackle: Cree
Body: Dark gray sparkle yarn (touch dubbed)
Front Wing: White calf tail
Hackle: Grizzly

This is a great pattern for those dark, dreary days with complete cloud cover. The Gray Wulff used to be my favorite for these conditions.

Orange Double Wing

Tail: Burnt orange sparkle yarn
Tag: White floss

Rear Wing: Brown elk hair
Body Hackle: Brown
Body: Burnt orange sparkle yarn (touch dubbed)
Front Wing: White calf tail
Hackle: Grizzly

Orange is the best color to use when the ambient light reflects the colors of autumn. These same ambient light conditions exist at sunrise and sunset. This is my favorite along the front range of the Rockies.

Lime Double Wing

Tail: Lime green sparkle yarn
Tag: White floss
Rear Wing: Lime green elk hair
Body Hackle: Olive grizzly
Body: Lime green sparkle yarn (touch dubbed)
Front Wing: White calf tail
Hackle: Grizzly

The Lime Double Wing is a very good fly pattern for those streams with lots of foliage that reflectsshades of green ambient light. Try it during the bright midday hours also. This is a hot pattern.

Royal Double Wing

Tail: Green sparkle yarn
Tag: Red floss
Rear Wing: Brown elk hair
Body Hackle: Coachman brown
Body: Peacock herl
Hackle: Coachman brown
Front Wing: White calf tail

What else can be said about the Royal family of flies? Show it to a trout during dry-fly season and you should have a better than 50% chance of getting hooked up. That's my opinion and I may be wrong, but I may be right.

Midnight Double Wing

Tail: Black sparkle yarn
Tag: White floss
Rear Wing: Black elk hair
Body Hackle: Black
Body: Black sparkle yarn (touch dubbed)
Front Wing: White calf tail
Hackle: Grizzly

Do you like fishing at night? If so, this is the pattern for you. Believe it or not, black shows up best in the dark as it silhouettes against the sky. Don't limit the possibilities of this fly though. How many black crickets and beetles have you seen on the water?

Charm Double Wing

Tail: Silver sparkle yarn
Tag: Yellow floss
Rear Wing: Pale gray elk hair
Body Hackle: Bright Medium Blue
Body: Silver sparkle yarn (touch dubbed)
Front Wing: White calf tail
Hackle: Grizzly

This is a wild-looking fly to be considered trout fare; however, when nothing else in the fly box is working it may be good for a last ditch effort. If tied big enough it might take a steelhead.

Brown Double Wing

Tail: Brown sparkle yarn
Tag: White floss
Rear Wing: Tan elk hair
Body Hackle: Furnace
Body: Hare's Ear Dubbing Mixed With Brown Sparkle Yarn
Front Wing: White calf tail
Hackle: Grizzly

The sparkle yarn makes this a bright attractor fly. The shape of all the Double Wing variations is build to attract trout. The Brown Double Wing is another good late-afternoon fly and can be used when bright colors are getting refusals.

Yellow Double Wing

Tail: Yellow sparkle yarn
Tag: White floss
Rear Wing: Pale yellow elk hair
Body Hackle: Golden badger
Body: Yellow sparkle yarn (touch dubbed)
Front Wing: White calf tail
Hackle: Grizzly

Bright days call for a bright fly and the Yellow Double Wing is a bright fly. Tie it down to size 16 for the small yellow stoneflies. There are a number of yellow-bodied terrestrials also.

Consider the ambient light presented to you during the day (or night) before choosing a Double Wing.

I will pass along some of Paul's thoughts on materials used on this fly. The Antron yarn (sparkle yarn) is a given. It can be found in most fly shops, however, the best touch dubbing is called Quick Fingers. Paul was very selective about the hair he used to tie this pattern. The elk body hair used for the back wing does not flare as much as most deer hairs so it's the kind to use. It was precisely dyed to the right color and had nice clean, unbroken tips.

My jaw hit the floor when I saw the box of white calf tails Paul pulled out. They were the finest tails I had ever seen. I couldn't help but ask where he acquired them and he said, "Everywhere!" He adds, "I check out every calf tail in every store I go into. Good ones can be found. I look at the hair at the very base of the tail to make sure it's full, the hair has to be especially straight and fine in diameter. I take them home and rinse them in Woolite, dry them, comb them out, and put baby powder on them."

It sounds like a lot of work, but when you see them in the "ready state", you will know it was time well spent. They are a brighter white than usual and the hair stacks extremely well, which makes using calf tail much less of a headache. This prep work beforehand will always save you time when the real tying starts.

Pink Double Wing

Hook: Dry fly 2X long, size 16-8
Thread: 10/0 pink, Benichi
Tail: Antron yarn, pink
Tag: White floss
Rear Wing: Elk body hair, dyed gray
Hackle: Ginger
Body: Antron Touch Dubbing, pink
Front Wing: Calf tail hair.(Choose the best hair you can find.)
Hackle: Dry fly, ginger (Whiting Farms)

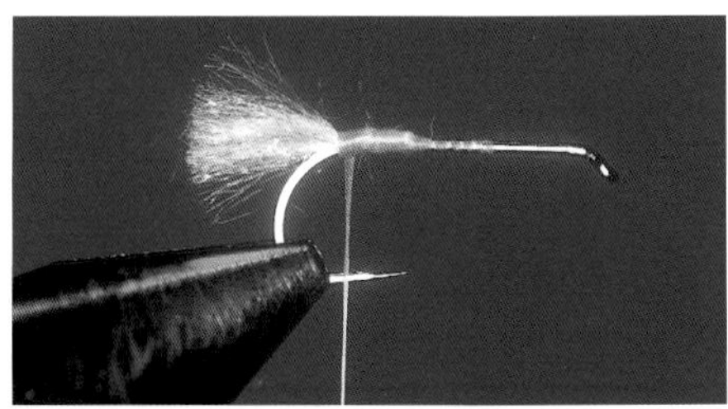

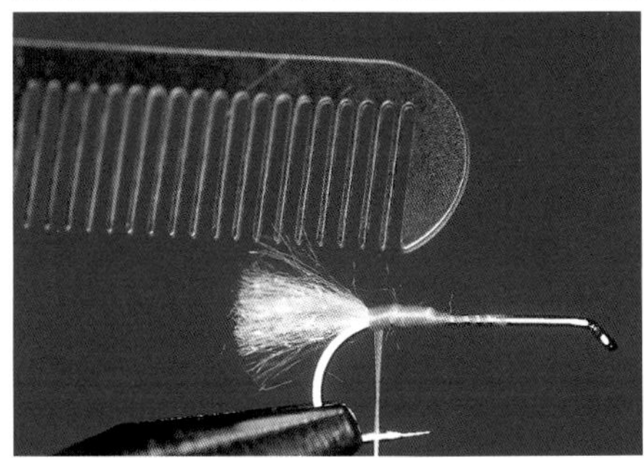

1. Start the thread at the 3/5 point and wrap to the back of the hook shank. Antron yarn normally comes in 3 or 4 plies; you will want two plies for the tail. Tie in a short length of Antron yarn for the tail. Trim the yarn to the length of the gape of the hook. Take the time to comb out the Antron with a fine-toothed metal comb. Gary LaFontaine designed a comb especially for this procedure. It is distributed by Upmqua Feather Merchants.

2. Tie in a piece of white floss (always wet the floss before you use it because it behaves itself better than when it is dry) and form a tag in front of the tail. The tag should stop at the point of the hook. This creates a hot spot at the back of the fly which may be a reason why this fly design is so effective.

3. Prepare and stack a clump of elk hair about the size of a wooden match. With the tips of the hair even with the tail length, secure the hair on top of the hook right in front of the floss tag. Cover the butt ends of the hair and make a smooth base with the thread.

4. Prepare and measure a dry-fly hackle. Tie in hackle, shiny side up, right on top of the hook shank. Apply dubbing wax to the thread and touch dub an Antron body to the 3/5 point of the hook.

5. Wrap the hackle forward to the 3/5 point, secure hackle and trim excess. Trim the hackle on the top and bottom of the body, leaving the barbules sticking out the sides of the fly.

6. Prepare and stack a clump of calf-tail hair. Secure hair on top of the hook shank with the tips of the hair extending back to the same length as the underwing. Notice how straight this hair is. This is primo calf-tail hair. Tie in a dry-fly hackle in front of the wing and make a smooth thread base to wrap the hackle.

7. Make sure the thread is directly in front of the wing before starting to wrap the hackle. This is an amazing little trick to keep the hackle from sliding forward on the slope of thread that inevitably is formed on this type of dry fly with a down wing. Now wrap the hackle forward making sure to stay behind the thread. The thread will move forward with the hackle, keeping the hackle from sliding down the ramp. Secure the hackle when it reaches the front of the hook. This course of action also helps keep hackle fibers out of the eye, making it easier to whip finish a clean head.

Here is a look at the Double Wing from a trout's point of view. Notice the "hot spot" created by the floss tag. The body is more of a warm color, unlike the hotter yellows and oranges of some of the other variations. The Pink Double Wing is another good early morning and late-afternoon attractor pattern.

Foam Madam X

Contributed by Rich Pilatzke

It seems like the past several years I haven't set out to fly-fish either streams or lakes without a fly box of terrestrial patterns. My box of terrestrials contains a good supply of beetles, ants, hoppers, and crickets. It even has some wasps that I tied specifically for Quincy Reservoir, an impoundment for the City of Aurora's water supply. These flies have become a major part of my fly-fishing arsenal.

I have tied the Foam Madam X in one form or another for over fifteen years. It is an excellent grasshopper imitation and with an orange or yellow body is a good imitation of caddis and stoneflies. A number of fish species find terrestrials a real treat which they can rarely resist. First, most terrestrials are tied in quite large sizes, especially when compared to the usual fare on which a trout feeds. A hopper or beetle represents quite a large food source to a fish that has been feeding on size-24 midges. I feel this is the reason that I have been able to take many midging trout (and an occasional yellow perch) on size-10 Madam X patterns on several of my favorite waters. Second, many terrestrials land on the water awkwardly with a loud splat and then struggle enticingly on the surface for several minutes, driving most predators crazy. This audible splat and the motion of the insect in the water seem to trigger aggressive strikes in trout and other fish. I think that rubber legs tied on a terrestrial pattern, such as those on a Madame X, can help to trigger strikes when they are twitched. Third, I believe that fish can really develop a taste for specific terrestrials, such as ants, and may feed preferentially on them.

This version of the Foam Madame X is definitely one of my favorite terrestrial patterns, mainly because it is relatively easy to tie, a great imitation of a hopper, and is extremely durable. I once caught 22 green sunfish in about 20 minutes on a size-10 Foam Madam X. It got pretty chewed up, but was still good enough to fool number 23, who finally broke through the worn tippet. I like to tie a cricket pattern that is simply a black Madame X, which I call a Black Widow. It has worked very well, especially for bass and panfish. I have taken a number of Madame Xs that have been chewed to shreds and cut off the old fly, examined and sharpened the hook, and tied a new fly on it.

Remember that any live terrestrial will drown and eventually sink, especially the bigger hoppers and crickets. So don't be afraid to experiment with an intermediate sinking line or split shot when it comes to hopper patterns. The Madison, the San Juan, and the Gunnison are just a few outstanding rivers to nymph-fish hoppers in late summer. I have had many fish take a waterlogged Madame X that was several inches under water.

So the next time you load up your fishing gear during the summer or fall for a trip to your favorite stream or lake, don't forget to throw in a few extra terrestrial patterns. You may find that they prove to be a smashing success.

Foam Madam X

Hook: Nymph 1x long, size 6-14, Tiemco 3761 Daiichi 1560
Thread: Yellow 6/0 UNI-Thread
Tail: Deer hair, red or orange
Body: 2mm closed-cell foam, in yellow, green, or orange
Wing: Whitetail deer hair
Legs: Medium or large round rubber

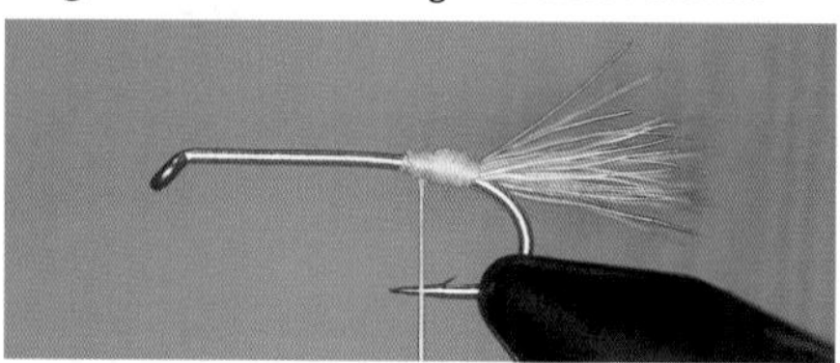

1. Start thread at the 1/4 point and wrap to the back. Stack and measure a clump of deer hair for the tail. The tail should be about 1/2 hook shank long. Tie into place and wrap down the butt ends of the hair. Move thread forward to the 1/4 point.

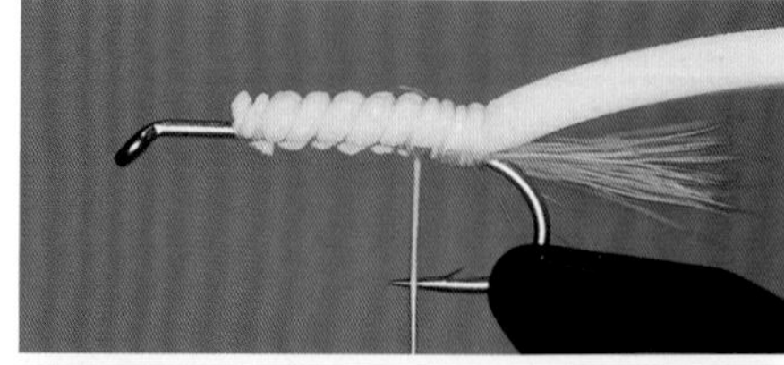

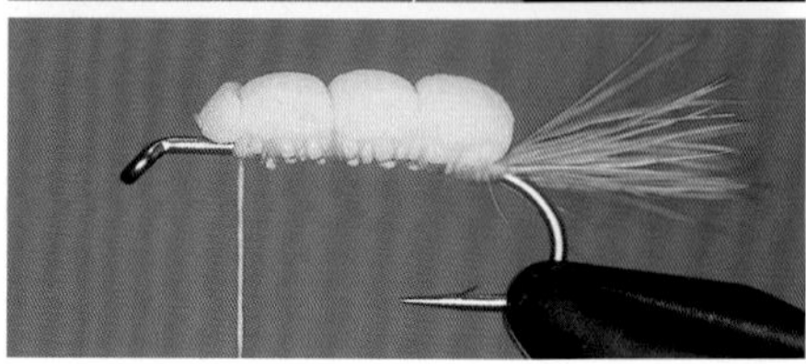

2. Tie in a strip of foam and wrap to the back of the hook. Move thread forward to the 1/4 point and pull the foam over and secure in place with a few wraps of thread. Lift up the foam and move thread to the 1/2 point. Lay the foam down on top of the hook and secure in place with a few wraps of thread. Lift up foam and move thread to the 3/4 point. Again, lay the foam down and secure in place. Trim excess.

3. Stack and measure a clump of deer hair. The wing is tied in over the eye (points to the front) just behind the hook eye. The tips of the hair should extend over the eye about 1 and a 1/4 hook shank length. Wrap the hair down to the 3/4 point and trim out the butts.

4. Sweep the hair up and over the top of the hook. It is pulled over the shank to form a semi-bullet head, with all the hair on top of the hook shank. Secure in place with several tight turns of thread.

5. Fold a section of round rubber around the thread, slide the rubber to the far side of the hook and tighten into place. This procedure makes a nice pair of V-shaped legs. Repeat on the near side of the hook. The two V-shaped legs on either side of the hook create an X, hence the name Madam X. If the legs are tied in unevenly, a careful pull here or there can easily reposition the legs to make the correct length. Whip finish.

The Foam Madam X can be tied in just about any color combination you wish. Don't worry about it; just whip some together. This fly pattern has been a top-producing attractor pattern for years.

ICU Carpenter Ant

Contributed by Richard Pilatzke

There are several foam ants out there these days, but this one is unique in the way it is tied. A strip of foam is attached at the back of the hook and tied down in three sections to form the three gasters that make up an ant's anatomy. With the addition of the yellow foam sight indicator this fly is a dream to fish. The ICU ("I see you") Carpenter Ant was named by Rich Pilatzke's wife, Cheryl, because she could see it so well on the water.

"I first tied this ant to fish Clear Creek, just outside of Denver, in the mid-1980's," says Richard.

Anybody who fly-fishes for trout knows that the fish have a tremendous liking for ants. And if you didn't know this, you should put a couple of these together and try them out next summer. Ants can be available to trout from mid spring all the way into November. They are effective in moving water and possibly more so in stillwater situations.

Here is a fishing experience from Rich Pilatzke that might give you some ideas on fishing ant patterns.

Terrestrial Time

The sun was well up and the temperature was already in the low 70's when I wheeled into Cordell Smith's driveway in Morrison at about 7:00 AM. It was the second week of August and Cordell had invited me to enjoy a day's fishing at the exclusive Arrowhead Ranch in South Park.

I had a cup of coffee with Cordell and got a quick tour of his tying room. This is where he ties his very effective saltwater patterns, which are his fly-tying specialty. We transferred my fly-fishing gear to Cordell's vehicle and quickly headed west on Highway 285 toward Fairplay. We went about ten miles past Fairplay and turned into the main entrance to the ranch. The ranch is a 4400-acre private ranch that is being developed as a membership fly-fishing resort. It has six miles of the South Fork of the South Platte and four lakes ranging from 3 to 10 acres in size. We checked in at the Registration Building and picked up our badges and keys for the South Lake. The South Lake is a three-acre spring-fed lake that is typical of many South Park lakes—it is alkaline, weedy, and is a veritable fish factory— fish in these lakes typically grow an inch a month during the summers, about six inches per season.

I knew from Cordell that this lake contained primarily Kamloops rainbows and brown trout and I was anticipating a good day's fishing. Because of the elevation of the lakes, about 9200 feet, I felt fairly confident that many of the fly patterns I had developed and used for the past five seasons at the Highland Lakes area near Divide would be effective here.

We started fished from the shore of South Lake at about 9:30 AM. The fish were rising intermittently, taking what looked to be midge pupae just under the surface of the water. Their dorsal fins sliced through the surface of the water as they slowly gathered in the emerging midges. I also noticed several flying ants on the water, in both black and dark brown colors in about a size 10.

We found a nice pod of trout working, so Cordell and I waded into waist-deep water and took up casting positions. I decided to start off with a size 10 black Foam Carpenter Ant, a pattern that had been producing well for several months already this season. I gave Cordell several freshly tied ants to try also. He was awarded with an almost immediate hookup and quickly landed a feisty three-pound Kamloops rainbow. I quickly followed his lead with several hookups from my casting location. The fish were wary, but they could be enticed into taking this large ant imitation attached to a 5X tippet.

We were thoroughly enjoying ourselves! And if that wersn't enough, near the head of the lake where the springs came in, we could see several large fish working the shallows. I worked my way up to the area and began casting to the risers that I had seen there. I quickly hooked up with several fish, finally landing one. I found that netting these large fish while fishing from the shore was difficult. The large trout headed straight for the weed beds and were able to "weed me". (I was dreaming of sitting atop my pontoon boat, which was in the garage at home, confident that I could have landed most of them.)

I signaled for Cordell to come down to the inlet where I was fishing and we both worked on the rising fish for a while. I switched over to a size 13 Crystal Beetle after having a large rainbow break the ant off in its jaw. I continued to get hookups. I was able to get several fish to take my fly in less than a foot of water; they were rising in extremely shallow water, but if you approached carefully and gave them a well-presented fly, they would take it. I was still able to land only about half of my solid hookups, as several fish either took me into the weeds or popped my tippet. I did manage to land several fish over 20 inches, including one that went about 22 inches.

We finished up the day at about 4:30, both pleasantly tired after casting all afternoon to rising fish. We were able to enjoy this beautiful Colorado summer day casting dry flies to rising trout, and as an added bonus, able to catch a bunch of them. As we drove back I chatted with Cordell and marveled at how he could fish just as hard as I did. Cordell is getting ready to turn 74 in less than a month. (Sounds like fly-fishing is the cure for aging.) I sure hope that I'm able to fish like that at that age. (If I keep fly-fishing it may be possible.)

We enjoyed a beautiful sunset going back and decided that we would have to do this again, maybe next year, but definitely again.
Notes From The Far Side
By Richard Pilatzke

Icu Carpenter Ant

Hook: Dry fly, size 10-16 Fenwick Barbless
Thread: Black 6/0 UNI-Thread
Body: Black 1/8" evasote closed-cell foam
Legs: Black deer hair
Indicator: Yellow 1/8" evasote closed-cell foam

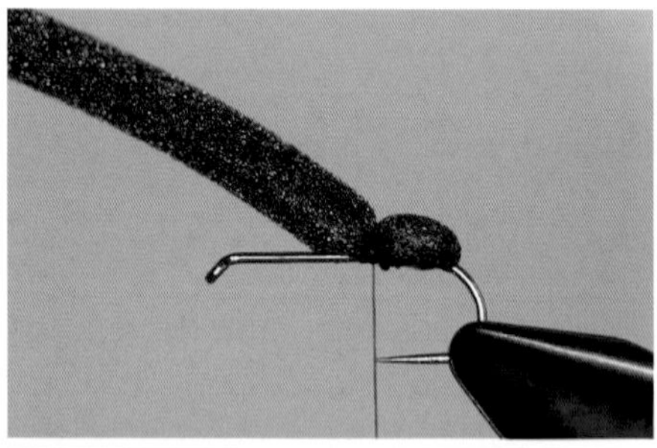

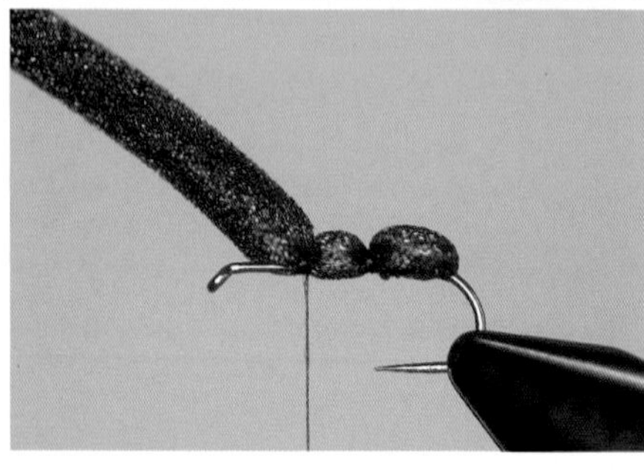

1. Start thread at the 1/3 point and wrap back. Tie in a length of black foam and move thread to the 1/3 point. Pull the foam over and secure it on top of the hook shank with a couple of wraps of thread. Lift up the foam and move thread to the 2/3 point of the hook. Secure the foam in place with a few wraps of thread.

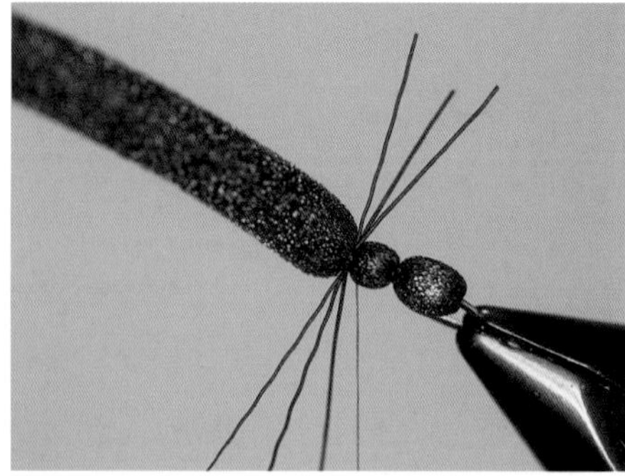

2. Tie in three black deer-hair fibers for the legs using a couple of simple X-ing wraps.

3. Tie in a strip of yellow foam on top of the hair at the 2/3 point of the hook as shown in the photo.

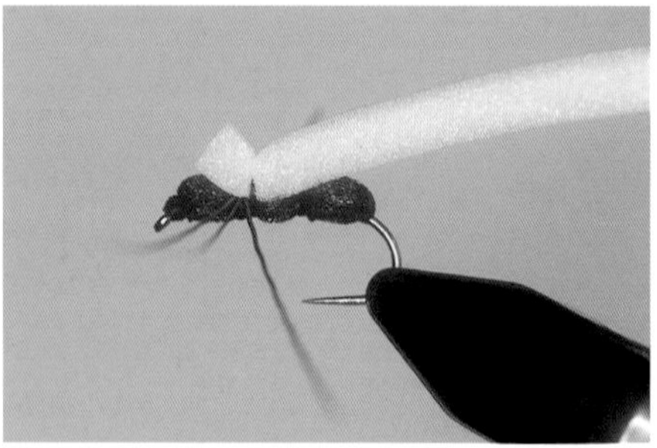

4. Lift up the foam and move thread to the front. Secure the black foam at the eye, trim excess, and whip finish.

5. Finish the ICU Carpenter Ant by trimming the foam indicator and the legs. Super glue the indicator with Zap-a-Gap. Pushing in on the deer-hair legs lightly, you can put little knee joints in if you like.

Klod Hopper

Contributed by Paul Stimpson

The name was catchy, but after Paul Stimpson described the pattern to me, I knew the tying technique used to construct the fly was unique and needed to be in this book. The original prototype of this hopper pattern was named the Red-Legged Hopper. After a modification or two, Paul renamed the pattern after his good friend Claude Ashby. So the Klod Hopper came to be.

Paul admits, "I hate tying hoppers, but I love to fish them. I took this problem to the vise to develop a quick, easy way to tie a pattern that would imitate a mature grasshopper, float well, and fool some of the "intelligent" fish I've had to deal with lately. I started with Denny Breer's Cicada Trude, a foam-body cicada pattern. This fly floats well, but needed some modification for a hopper. I changed the color, switched to a dubbed body, and started fishing."

"My fishing days were interrupted with periods of hopper chasing. I had forgotten just how hard those guys are to catch," Paul adds. "The ones I did catch were unceremoniously tossed into the water for observation purposes. I watched how they floated and moved. They floated in the surface film, not on it and kicked to escape. I never did see a hopper attempt to fly from the water, the wings were in the "at rest" position the whole time. A few of the persistent ones were actually able to kick to shore and escape."

Paul said, "I've seen thousands of live hoppers before, but I really hadn't inspected one up close. I did find the hoppers in my area that weren't the standard yellow-bodied version you find at the local fly shop. The naturals I was able to capture were of a tan and brown variegation. The most surprising feature I observed were the kicker legs. They were large and red."

Back to the vise Paul went in pursuit of a better imitation. He changed the foam and dubbing to a tan and tied the fly with dark brown thread. He used red rubber legs tied in the "X" fashion to allow them to rest on the water. The typical knotted pheasant-tail fibers or trimmed hackle legs did not provide the movement that he had noticed on the water. Sizing the body hackle down allowed the fly to set more flush in the surface film.

"I couldn't wait to test my new hopper," says Paul. "My wife Char and I fish a private pond near my home in Utah. The fish in this pond have seen every hopper known to man and are very selective. The first iterations of the new idea for the hopper were disappointing, but the latest modification with the tan body and red legs was the answer. I'm convinced the trout in this pond were keying on the red legs."

As Gary LaFontaine warns, "You never want to trust the creator about his own fly." So try this one yourself on selective fish, I'm sure you'll be pleasantly surprised.

Klod Hopper

Hook: Dry fly, 2X long, size 12-6
Thread: Flat waxed nylon, brown
Body: Closed-cell foam, tan
Overbody: Brown dubbing
Hackle: Dry-fly saddle, brown (Whiting Farms)
Wing: Elk hair or fine whitetail deer hair
Thorax: Closed-cell foam, tan
Legs: Grizzly Legs, red (Spirit River)

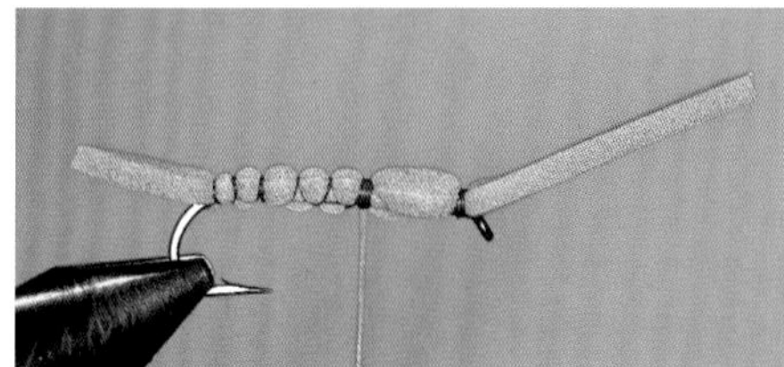

1. Cut a piece of 1/8" tan closed-cell foam into a strip about 2 inches long and as wide as the gape of the hook. Trim one end to a point. Start thread at the back of the hook and lay down a

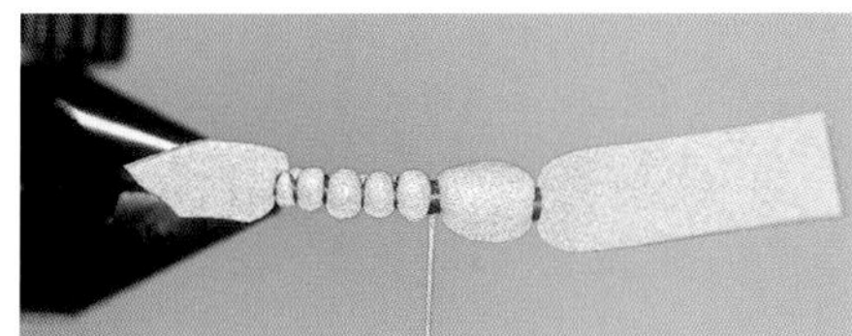

base of thread to the front. Tie in the strip of foam just behind the eye on top of the hook. Leave 1/2-inch extending over the eye. Jump the thread to the 2/3 point and secure the foam again. With evenly spaced wraps, move the thread through the foam to the back of the hook. Go forward with evenly spaced wraps to the 2/3 point again. Even though we are going to cover this part of the fly with dubbing in a following step, do not wrap the foam down with any more turns of thread. We want the foam to retain much of its shape to help the fly float. Trim the end of the foam that is hanging over the back of the hook into a point. This is a simple extended body. Jump thread to the back of the hook.

2. Prepare and measure a rooster hackle with the barb's length the same as the width of the gape of the hook. Secure the hackle at the back of the hook. Dub the body forward to the 3/4 point.

3. Palmer hackle forward to the 2/3 point and secure hackle.

4. Stack a clump of elk hair and tie it on top of the hook in front of body. Trim the butt ends of the hair and make a landing area for the legs to wrap on.

5. Secure a silicone leg on each side of the hook at the 2/3 point, in plane with the hook shank. The rear part of the legs should be slightly longer than the front legs. The legs can be tied in longer than needed and then trimmed. Pull the foam back over the front part of the fly to form a bulky, hopper head and secure at the 2/3 point. Whip finish.

Orange Humpy
Contributed by Dale Darling

When I first realized that this book would become a reality, I knew I would contact Dale Darling and have him reveal the secrets of this fly. Dale tied this fly several years ago at a local tying clinic that I attended and I was convinced then that I would never tie a Humpy the standard way again. Not only was I intrigued by the way the pattern was tied, it became one of my go-to patterns for small-stream fly-fishing. The orange-bodied fly has also fooled several well-educated trout on the South Platte River.

The wing tie-in procedure is unique for this Humpy. It makes measuring the wing much easier and the consistency in wing height it presents is ingenious.

Dale recognizes Jack Dennis as the master of tying the Humpy in the traditional fashion. I have watched several great tiers that do a very consistent job tying this pattern, but for the most part it is consistency that becomes the challenge. Proportions on the fly, starting with tail length, are of utmost importance while tying the Humpy in the traditional way. The other proportion that needs to be considered is the length and fullness of the hair used for the hump and wing height. If the tail is too long or short, so goes the wing height. If the hair is secured a fraction too far back or forward, the wing height is off. If the body thickness is not consistent from one fly to the next, the wing height will vary on the flies tied.

Dale just thought there were too many variables for the average tier while tying this fly. For the average tier to be consistently successful tying this pattern a new tying technique needed to be created. Dale and good friend, Tom Finn, were tossing ideas around and came to the conclusion that if they could take the number of variables down to one, the wing height, the fly would be much easier for the tier just trying to fill his fly boxes. After a few tries the Humpy wing tie-in procedure was perfected. They found the only variable to be considered was the size and thickness of the hump. And that is not a big deal when proportioning the fly.

I think this was one of the truly greatest, creative ideas in all of fly tying. I know I would have never thought of it! I'm just glad someone came up with it.

I do fish the Humpy often. Dropped into a blanket of caddisflies on the Arkansas River, the Orange Humpy has moved brown trout out of their rhythmical feeding. The hatching caddisflies are so thick there is no way to see a caddis pattern on the water, let alone get a trout to take notice of your size 16 amongst the millions of bugs on the water. After several hook-ups, I determined the Orange Humpy must have looked like dessert to the gorged brown trout.

This new method of tying the Humpy is not limited to just the orange-colored fly. Yellow or red thread bodies, dubbing color of choice, and peacock herl make excellent bodies for the Humpy. Tie a Humpy with orange thread, a peacock herl body, and brown hackle; it should be outlawed.

Orange Humpy

Hook: Dry Fly, Dai-Riki 300, Tiemco 100 or 2312, size 10-20. An optional hook could include a 2X long nymph like a Dai -Riki 730 or Daiichi 1710 for the added strength of the heavier wire
Thread: 6/0 Danville, fluoresant orange, red, yellow
Tail: Moose body hair
Wing: Elk mane or elk body with very long fibers
Body: Thread, fluoresant orange, dubbing or peacock herl
Hackle: Dry-fly quality, brown and grizzly mixed
Thorax: Orange dubbing

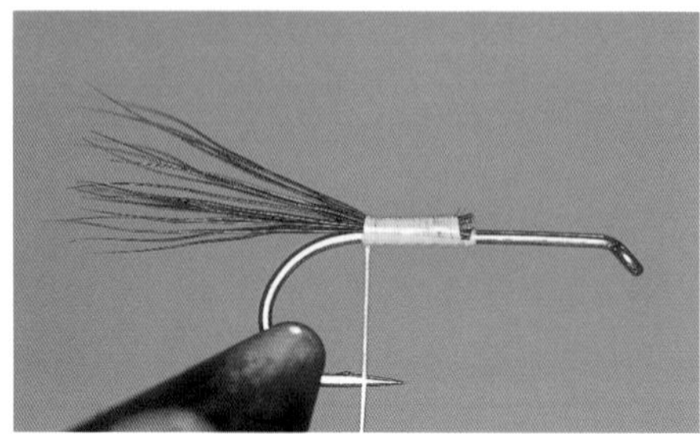

1. Start thread at the 1/2 point of the hook and wrap to the back of the hook. Move thread forward to the 1/2 point laying down a thread base. A quick note about the 1/2 point of the hook used for this fly: Dale emphasizes that with this fly the 1/2 point on the hook shank is measured *after* the area for the head of the fly is taken out of the equation. So make sure to set the 1/2 point back slightly to accommodate the head of the fly. Do not crowd the head of this fly. Stack and measure a clump of moose body hair for the tail, maybe 20 fibers for a size-12 hook. Measure tail material from the front of the eye to the back of the bend. Clip hair in front of the eye and secure butts at 1/2 point with several tight wraps of thread. Make sure to hold the tail up slightly as the thread is wrapped to the back of the hook shank. This ensures that the hair stays on top of the hook shank. As the thread wraps get closer to the back of the hook, loosen the torque on the thread so the tail does not flare too much.

2. Move thread forward to the back of the head, then move thread back to the 3/4 point. The thread hangs in the right spot on most hooks when it will bisect the point of the hook and the front of the eye of the hook. Stack a clump of elk hair for the wing. Always try to start with more hair than you need. You will lose some of the bulk from the short hairs and under fur at the base of the hair. Remember it is always easier to take hair away than it is to add more. Dale prefers elk mane hair for its length. Measure the hair from the tail tie-in point (or barb of the hook) to the back of the hook eye. Dale prefers the wing on this fly to be just a fraction short of a full hook shank high. Secure it on top of the hook at the 3/4 point. Wrap back with few tight wraps to the 1/2 point. Make sure the thread does not go in front of the first wrap, as it will change the wing position or proportion. Trim

out several fibers and move thread back a few more turns. Trim out more fibers and wrap back some more. Repeat again before wrapping to the back of the hook. Trimming out some of the bulk of the elk hair helps form a tapered body without excess wraps of thread. It also reduces the bulk of hair that is pulled over for the hump. Form a thread body covering up all the elk/moose material with thread. Dale encourages folks to use their dubbing of choice for the body, which also works fine on this fly.

3. With the thread at the 1/2 point on the hook shank, pull the butt ends of the elk hair over the top of the body to form the hump, and secure. After securing the hump trim the excess material behind the wing and cover the butt ends before standing the wing. Again, do not wrap forward of the original wraps used to secure the wing. Very important! Notice that the wing has remained in the down position over the eye up to this point. It has been out of the way while building the body and making the hump.

4. Lift the wing up and pull it back. Make several wraps of thread, forming a dam in front of the wing. Now crimp the hair between your thumbs to spread the hair out evenly on top of the hook. The wing should be in an upright position and perpendicular to the hook shank when the dam is complete.

5. Separate the wing into two even clumps. This can be accomplished by making the separation by hand, with a scissor point, or bodkin slid into the hair directly above the middle of the hook shank. Turning the vise to position the fly for a head on view helps determine the centerline. When the separation is complete, make a wrap of thread from in front of the fore wing to the back of the far wing. The next wrap should be from behind the forewing to the front of the far wing, making an X-ing pattern. Repeat the X-ing pattern three or four times. The wings will end up in a flat posture, much like a spinner wing.

6. Make a few wraps around the base of the far wing. Lock the thread by making a wrap around the hook behind the wing. Repeat the same procedure for the forewing. Figure-eight the wings. Push up on the wing clumps from under the hook with your fingers. Move the wings to the 45-degree position, or 90 degrees to each other by bending the hair into the position. They will stay in this position very nicely.

7. Size and prepare a brown and a grizzly hackle. Here is a little trick Dale uses to make sure the hackles wrap into place and look uniform: After sizing the hackles for the hook, instead of simply cutting them to the same length, match up the web lines in the hackle; that is, find the point where the web is about 1/4 of the total barbule length on both feathers and trim butt end of the feather off. Trim barbules off the stem for tie-in. Apply a thin layer of dubbing to the thread, leaving about a 1/4 inch of bare thread between the dubbing and the hook shank. Secure the hackles on the fore-side of the hook with the portion of bare thread, behind the wing, with the brown hackle on top. As the dubbing shows up, apply a thin layer behind the wing, then a thicker layer in front of the wing to help compensate for the thickness of the wing tie-down area. Dale likes the hackle on this fly to be buried in dubbing to improve its durability.

8. Wrap the brown hackle forward first and secure behind the eye. Wrap the grizzly next, weaving it into the first hackle trying not to mash down many of the brown fibers. This is accomplished by moving the hackle side to side as you wrap forward. Make sure each hackle has a wrap adjacent to the back and front of the wing base. The last wrap of hackle in front of all others should be a turn or two of grizzly. It just looks a little nicer for some reason, if that matters to anyone. I'm not sure the fish much care. Secure the hackle by making a couple of wraps forward to just behind the eye then back to the last wrap of hackle. This locks the hackle very securely. Trim both the brown and grizzly hackle tips at the same time by setting the scissor points at the same angle as the hook eye to avoid cutting thread. Whip finish from the eye to the hackle to complete Dale's Orange Humpy.

Here are a couple of options for the Humpy, a yellow dubbed body and one with tied with orange thread, a peacock herl body and brown hackle.

Rivergod Trude

Contributed by Dennis Potter

Dennis Potter originally called this fly the Pearl Trude. This particular bug was first used in 1989 during the One Fly Contest on the Snake River. Somewhere along the way Dennis got the nickname of the Rivergod. With that distinction, most of the flies that he has developed or plagiarized, have received the Rivergod moniker, including the Rivergod Trude. Dennis often says, "Fly tying is such a great sport because you can take some fly pattern and change it, tweak it, make it better and stick your moniker on it. I know that tiers have done it with some of my bugs but that is OK, because they are so damn good they can't be improved upon. Please excuse me while I puke."

The overall look and sparkle of the fly was developed to entice the cutthroats on the Snake. Dennis knew these trout liked bright attractor flies and wanted a dry fly for the contest. Even though nymphs or streamers would probably be the best bet for numbers of trout, one snag and a lost fly would take you out of the running. The original adaptation bore close resemblance to the Trude flies first fished in the 1940s on the Harriman Ranch of the Snake River.

"There have been a few modifications over the years, however, this fly has by far and away been my favorite searching attractor fly," says Dennis. "Most Trudes of old have a simple fore hackle and many incorporated a tail. This unique-looking fly does not have a tail and has a palmer-hackled body. It does not look like a traditional Trude, but I stuck the Trude name on it years ago and haven't bothered to get rid of it."

Rivergod Trude

Hook: 2X dry fly, size10-16 Tiemco 2312
Thread: Brown 12/0, Benichie
Ribbing: Fine gold wire
Body: Pearl tinsel, medium
Hackle: Grizzly dyed wood duck or dark barred ginger, dry-fly quality, preferably Whiting Farms saddle hackle
Wing: Hi-Vis, gray or white
Thorax: Peacock herl
Hackle: Grizzly-dyed wood duck or dark barred ginger, dry-fly quality preferably Whiting Farms saddle hackle

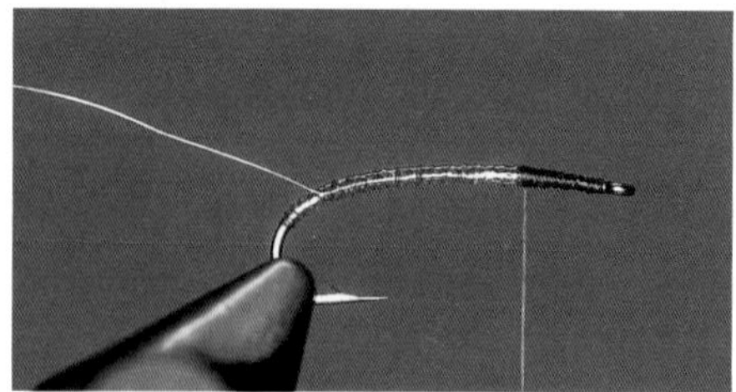

1. Start thread at the eye of the hook and wrap to the back laying down a level thread base. This hook has somewhat of a sweeping back to it and Dennis likes to take the thread beyond the barb 6 or 8 wraps so he can wrap a tag of tinsel out the back of the fly. Move thread forward again to the 2/3 point and tie in a length of small gold or silver wire. Wrap it down with thread to the back of the hook shank. Move thread forward to the 2/3 point and tie in the tip of a length of pearl tinsel. Leave thread at the 2/3 point. Wrap the tinsel back to the wire, skip behind the wire and make 2 or 3 turns of tinsel for the tag. Change directions and wrap the pearl tinsel forward over the top of the first wraps. Overlap each wrap slightly so there is total coverage. Secure the tinsel at the 2/3 point and trim excess.

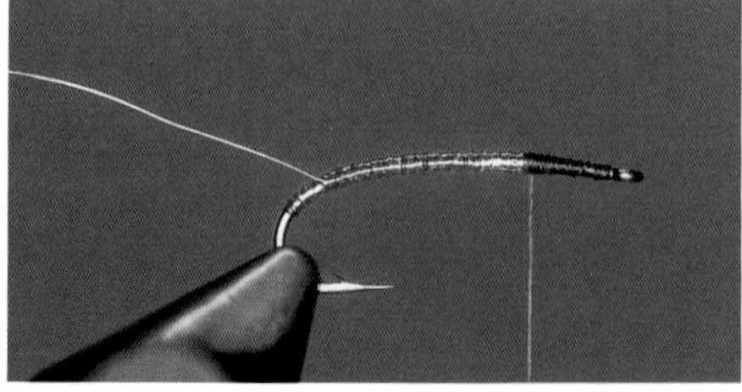

2. Measure and prepare a saddle hackle. The hackle should be one size smaller than the hook size you are using. In other words, use a size-16 hackle for a size-14 hook. Tie in the hackle at the 3/4 point, in front of the body with the hackle over the back of the body.

3. Palmer the hackle to the back of the hook. Hold the hackle up and secure it with three turns of the wire. Let go of the hackle and rib the wire forward through the hackle. Move the wire back and forth as it is wrapped forward to prevent the hackle from being mashed down. About 7 turns of wire through the hackle should be sufficient. Secure wire and then work it back and forth using friction to break the wire instead of cutting it with scissors.

4. Do not cut any of the hackle from the top of the fly. Make a separation in the hackle with scissors and then use a couple of fingers to sweep the hackle down to the sides of the fly. This leaves as much hackle on the fly as possible and

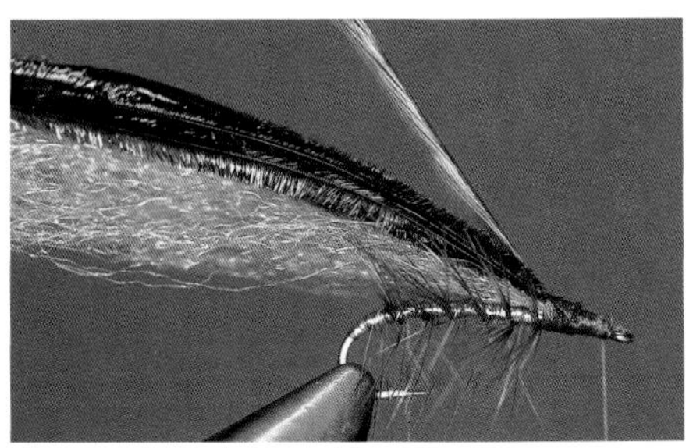

still opens up a gap for the wing to lie in. Tie in a clump of Hi-Vis for the wing. Do not trim wing yet. Tie in 6 or 8 strands of peacock herl in front of the wing. Measure a saddle hackle to match the size of the hook and secure it in front of the wing. Move thread to just behind the eye. Half hitch so the thread will not induce slack.

5. Make a couple of turns forward with the peacock herl and secure behind the eye and on the side of the hook. Securing the herl on the side of the hook eliminates the chance of one of the stems from the herl ending up interfering with the opening in the eye. A good thought process now prevents the frustration of unable to get a tippet through a fly later on the stream. Trim excess herl. Throw another half hitch in so the peacock herl will not come loose. Wrap the hackle through the peacock herl and secure behind the eye. Trim excess hackle. Whip finish the fly and cut wing to length. The wing should extend just beyond the bend of the hook, however, since it is a down wing the length is up to the individual tying the fly. This is a dandy bug!

Royal Coachman Trude

Contributed by John Hagen

John proclaims this fly as one of the two flies that made him famous. As a fly-fisherman, he has learned that trout do have a mind of their own, but can be fooled with out-of-the-ordinary techniques. As a guide, he has been a hero during tough hatch situations with the Royal Coachman Trude, putting more trout in the net than any one person should. At the vise, he has been able to show his expertise in proportion control, winging techniques and beautiful hackle collars, while often going against the grain of tradition.

John's other fly of fame is the Renegade. "The Renegade and Royal Coachman Trude are "soul mates". The versatility of these two flies is amazing. With all the new materials giving us the ability to tie very intricate, perfect imitations, these two nearly ancient flies by and large catch more trout on the surface in a year than any other combination of dry flies. Hell, the Renegade pulled under with a split shot or two, takes its fair share of fish!"

John likes to use the Royal Trude during periods of mixed hatches when there are many different types of insects on the water. "When you can't decide if they are eating size-22 Trico spinners, some dinky little size-24 western *Baetis*, a size-16 tan caddis, or an odd PMD drifting by, the Royal Coachman Trude is a great fly to try. A situation may occur when several trout in the same hole are feeding on different bugs. I've caught a trout on a size 18 Rusty Spinner and then shown it to other risers in the pod and not even get a lazy refusal. Hey, he ate it, why isn't anybody else eating it? They must be eating something else. Now what?"

Why aren't the other fish eating it? What am I missing? How do you go about choosing the correct pattern? These are questions all of us have asked ourselves at one time or another. John's answer has come from experience and experimentation, "I'll fish bugs like this one, the Royal Coachman Trude which I love, not so much that it looks like any one particular bug but because it could look like a number of different things to the fish. I like to fish it one or two sizes larger than the bugs on the water. Local fly-fishermen fish a lot of tailwaters, so let's say we have size 18, 20 and 22 bugs coming off, I'll go to a size-16 Royal Trude."

"I'll mention the Renegade in the same breath here because it's the same

kind of a deal. It doesn't look like anything in particular; it's a fore and aft type of fly that has a list of great ingredients. It's got brown and white hackle. It's got peacock herl. All of this can make the fly look like a number of different things. Either of these flies could look like a small terrestrial, maybe a beetle, cricket, or flying ant. They could imitate several bugs stuck together, possibly crippled or dead insects. I feel the Trude looks like a bug struggling to get off the water. That's why I like to use it!"

John adds, "Since the Trude has that lovely white wing, I fish it as an indicator fly with an emerging nymph or difficult-to-see tiny dry-fly attached."

When the trout seem especially stubborn and obnoxious, get off the beaten path and try a pattern that's a little old and a technique a little odd to see if the rod will get bent.

Royal Coachman Trude

Hook: Dry fly, Daiichi 1180, Daiichi 1280 2X long, size 6-16
Thread: Black, Danville 6/0
Tail: Brown spade hackle fibers

Body: The Royal body, a band of peacock herl, a band of red floss, and another band of peacock herl
Wing: White calf body hair
Hackle: Brown, one size smaller than hook size

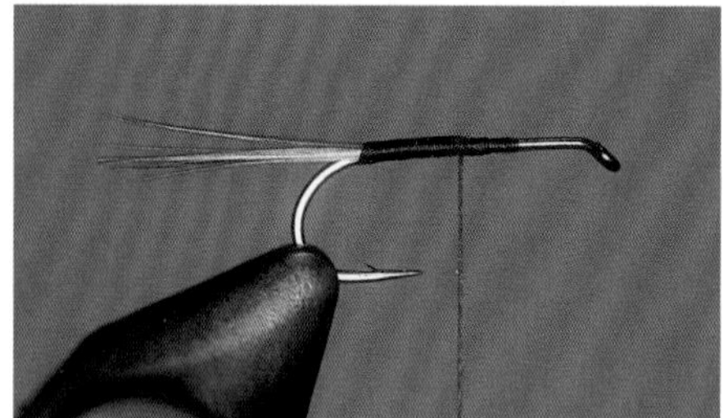

1. Start thread at the 3/5 point of the hook and wrap to the back laying a thread base for tying on the tail. Measure tail to a length equal to the hook shank, trim hackle so that the butt ends of the tail are at the 2/5 point. Secure tail at the back of the hook and wrap forward to the 2/5 point. John explains the brown hackle tail: "Traditionally this fly has a tail made from the orange and black golden pheasant tippets. I still use a few tied that way but I thought the orange was a little too bright for what I was using it for. I'm using this fly on a lot of tailwater situations, and I didn't want a lot of bright stuff hanging off the back of the hook. The brown hackle tail better imitates the color of a trailing shuck of a bug struggling to get off the water. The fly is traditionally thought of as an attractor pattern, but I'm tying it as a tailwater emerger, crippled looking, whatever."

2. Trim the tips of a few strands of peacock herl and tie it in. Wrap to the back of the hook. Move thread forward to the 1/5 point and make a few turns of herl forward. Secure herl and lash it down at the 2/5 point. Do not trim the peacock herl.

3. Tie in a strand of red floss and lash floss down back to the 1/5 point. Move thread forward to the 2/5 point and make a few turns of floss forward and secure at the 2/5 point. Trim red floss as close to the hook as possible.

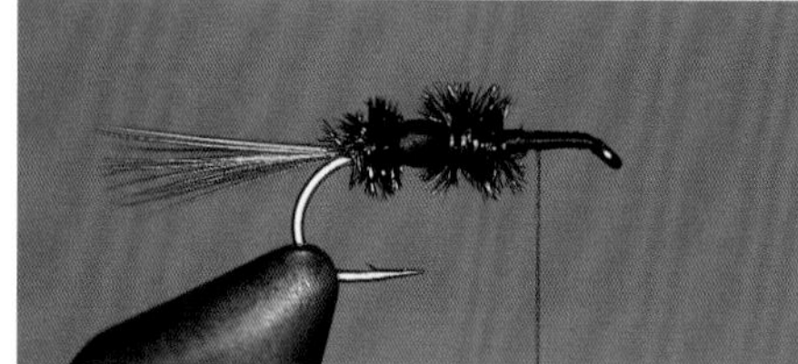

4. Move thread forward to the 3/5 point and make a few turns of herl forward and secure at the 3/5 point. Trim excess peacock herl. Wrap thread forward to the eye of the hook and wrap back to the 4/5 point, laying a thread base for tying on the wing.

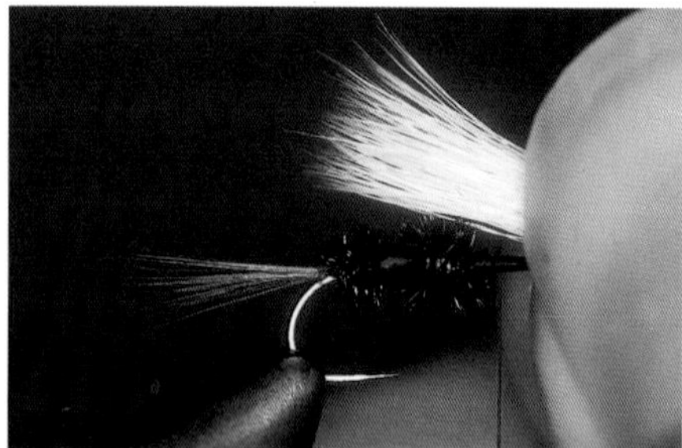

5. Stack a clump of calf body hair for the wing. Calf hair has a lot of fuzz and crappy short hair at the base of the hair so make sure to take more hair than you think you would need. On flies, say size 12 and larger, calf tail may be used for the wing. It is pretty kinky, hard to stack and arduous to work with, but makes a sassy-looking wing. The amount of hair needed for the wing definitely varies from hook size to hook size. A clump of hair taken from the skin that would measure 1/4-inch square is a good starting point. Then decrease or increase the amount for the next fly. Cut the same amount from the patch of hair for future flies. (Refer to the section on "Preparing Hair," in the Material Preparation Chapter, page 34, to help getting the same amount of hair for every wing.) Measure the wing so the tips of the hair are at the back of the body.

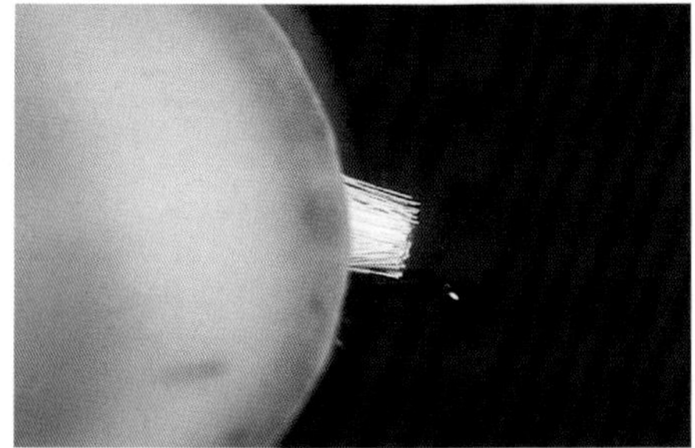

6. Switch hair to the left hand without changing its position; trim the butt ends of the hair as shown in photo. With the hair directly over the hook and in the position it should be tied in, bring thread up and split the hair in half with the thread. Start wrapping the thread around the hook lashing half the wing in place. Continue around the hook with the thread and lash down the other half of the wing. Two more tight wraps will lock the wing in place and keep it from rolling around the hook. Finish the wing by wrapping back to the 3/5 point, butting the wing against the body, then cover the wing butts with thread, making a smooth landing area for the hackle.

7. John likes to use a hackle one size smaller than the hook size being used, e.g., a size-16 hackle for a size-14 hook.

This procedure helps balance the fly and gets it closer to the water. A larger hackle has a tendency to tip the fly over on its nose with these down-wing type of patterns. Secure hackle in front of the wing and wrap forward a nice thick, full hackle collar. Secure hackle at the front. Trim excess and whip finish.

Soft Hackle Peacock

Contributed by Randy Smith

One question I always ask these exceptional tiers before we get started is, "What are ***your*** favorite patterns you carry to fish with?" I am always hoping the answer will fall into the simple criteria that I set for the topic of this book, showing either speed techniques, durability, or consistency of proportion. With that in mind, Randy had several excellent ideas.

Randy's great passion is backpacking into and fly-fishing high-mountain lakes, so this is where we started. We discussed several patterns and decided on the Soft-Hackle Peacock because of the unique wrapping technique for the peacock herl.

There are several ways to wrap peacock herl to increase durability. Ribbing the herl with a fine wire of some kind is normally the first choice for many tiers. You can spin it in a loop, which makes a nearly indestructible body. However, it takes several steps to complete and thus more time than most of us speed tiers like to spend. Then Randy brought it to my attention that a lot of tiers like to reinforce peacock herl with thread. By making several wraps of tying thread around the herl before wrapping it into place adds durability. Less durable than previous suggestions, but much quicker.

Randy's method is the quickest of them all. Similar to the technique of using the tying thread, Randy makes a single, clock-wise turn of thread around the peacock herl and simply starts wrapping. Just like magic, the thread continues to twist into the herl as you wrap forward. This accomplishes the same result as before without the extra time to wrap the thread and peacock herl together.

Again, this is less durable than wire ribbing or a loop but it is very quick to accomplish. What we have is a simple point of give and take with this technique. On the one hand we could ***give*** up several minutes to tie a very durable, simple fly that may catch several trout. On the other, we could tie a simple fly with a simple technique that takes less than two minutes to tie and have a peacock fly that is somewhat more durable than what we would have if we had just wrapped in the herl. Now the real kicker. Whichever fly you decide to tie could be lost in a watery grave hung on a deadfall or dangling from a 25- foot blue spruce. If we *take* three or four hungry cutthroats on a single fly before it is shredded, has time been well spent? Of course!

I have gone through pounds of peacock herl in my fifteen years as a pro tier and had never seen this technique so we thought it needed to be brought to your attention.

The Soft-Hackle Peacock is not a new fly pattern nor is it hugely popular in these days of fancy-dancy materials and precision patterns. It is one of those generic patterns in a group of many variations of the soft-hackle fly. And it is one of those fly patterns that has caught its fair share of trout and pan fish. In larger sizes you will see patterns with very long soft-hackle that take salmon and saltwater fish on a regular basis. The undeniable success of this type of fly is reason enough to have it in your fly box.

Randy uses the Soft-Hackle Peacock for cutthroat and brook trout in the high lakes of the Rocky Mountains. It is also a go-to fly in beaver ponds and the drainage above and below said beaver ponds. It sounds like it is the only pattern he carries, "No, I do carry a couple of dry flies. A Parachute Adams and a caddis or two.

"This fly does excel as a subsurface pattern for our native cutthroats and the elusive golden trout. Maybe it is the red tail, or the peacock herl, but more than likely it's just the animation and life-like action the soft-hackle provides." Randy adds, "Work the fly with a slow, rhythmic action, stripping it at different depths until the trout find it."

Soft Hackle Peacock

Hook: Nymph 1X or 2X long, size 8-16 Dai-Riki 075
Thread: 6/0 Danville (multi-strand) black
Tail: Red hackle fibers, large rooster neck hackle used for saltwater flies works well, or a Streamer Pack by Whiting Farms would be the most economical way to go. A dyed red hen saddle feather could work also.
Body: Peacock herl
Hackle: Mottled hen saddle feather. There are several sources of hen saddles. Whiting Farms has several selections, including the Hebert Miner line of birds which has exceptional selection and quality.

1. Start thread at the 3/4 point of the hook and tie in tail. Wrap tail down to the back of the hook. Tail length should be 1/2 to 3/4 of the hook shank length. Move thread forward to the 3/4 point again, tie in 6 to 8 strands of peacock herl, and wrap to the back of the hook. Leave thread at the back of the hook. Remember to trim the tips of the peacock herl before you tie them in so trimming at the vise is unnecessary. Make a half wrap with the peacock herl so the clump of herl is now under the fly. Make a single wrap of thread around the herl in a clock-wise direction. I think an explanation is in order: The peacock herl is wrapped under the hook and the butt-ends are facing the tier. The thread

is in front of the herl and pulled out straight, basically at the 3:00 position. Then the thread should go under the herl towards the 6:00 position, around to the 12:00 position and back to the 3:00 position. This is the single wrap of thread around the herl.

2. Now pull the bobbin down a short distance, grab the herl and thread at the same time, and wrap forward to the 7/8 point of the hook. Separate the herl from the thread, hold the herl above the hook and secure it in place with the thread. Trim excess herl. As you will experience here, a single wrap of thread around the herl will turn into several as we continue to wrap forward. Another one of those pro techniques that save us time.

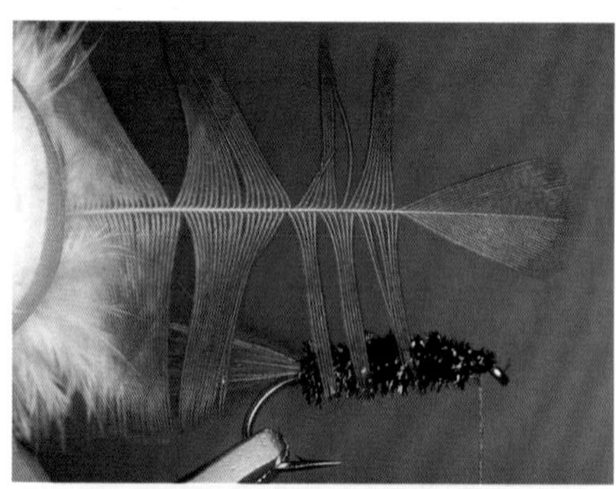

3. Prepare a hen saddle feather by pulling the fibers back away from the tip and trimming the tip to about 1/8 of an inch.

4. Tie in the feather by the tip with the convex side up and wrap the feather two or three times, forming a soft-hackle collar. For speed purposes, Randy doesn't take the time to fold the hackle. He just wraps it in, secures it, sweeps it back with three fingers of his left hand and whip finishes. It looks amazingly good. I think I will quit folding mine. The number of hackle turns depends on what you want your fly to look like. Usually a couple will suffice. Whip finish and you are done.

SALTWATER FLIES

Carolyn's Shrimpi
Contributed by Mark Hatter

An essay from Mark Hatter on developing a pattern and the successes that followed.

Many winters ago, my long-time fishing partner Charlie Madden and I ventured out to Mosquito Lagoon, a vast shallow saltwater estuary on the east coast of central Florida. Redfish were our target. Upon arriving, we were surprised to find a howling north wind that churned the deeper flats into a turbid soup. Only the really skinny water was clear enough to fish. Since sight-fishing was out of the question with the stiff wind, the only prayer we had was to blind cast down and across wind as the boat skated along.

Die-hards, we elected to set the skiff up on long north-to-south drifts and blind-cast while the boat kited downwind. Heavy grass matted the foam-streaked surface making stripping difficult without fouling the fly after only a few feet. Neither of us had an intermediate sinking fly line to cut through the surface clutter.

I was doubtful we would even register a strike when Charlie surprised me by hooking a very nice redfish. I staked-out the skiff to stop our drift while Charlie battled the red. After a short tussle, he released the fish and we continued the drift. Maybe, I thought, there was a chance to make the proverbial silk purse out a sow's ear after all.

Minutes later he bagged another red, which measured just over the maximum slot length. Again, he released it in short order. I had just pulled the push pole from the muddy bottom to again set our drift when, incredibly, Charlie hung a third decent redfish on his next cast.

I could not believe his luck! We were fishing nearly identical tackle. Only our flies were different. I was using a trusted Lefty's Deceiver, but I didn't know what he was throwing. Finally, after a fourth fish, I caved in to my envy and curiosity. "What ***are*** *you throwing Charlie?" I demanded with some annoyance. "Gotta new fly I tied up!" He stated glibly. "Last Friday I came over to wade the west shore of the lagoon before dark. There were 'tailers' everywhere and I tried several patterns and colors but I only caught one redfish on a pink Clouser. I took the fish home to eat and when I cleaned it I found its stomach loaded with small brownish-colored grass shrimp. I thought about what I wanted in a fly designed to imitate these shrimp while taking into consideration weedless capability. A couple of experiments later at my tying bench and I came up with this little gem." He tossed me one of his shrimp imitators.*

"I wanted a little weight to get it down to tailing fis,h but I also wanted the fly to ride hook up like a Clouser, so I added bead-chain eyes to the back of the hook and used bucktail as a weed-guard wing under the hook eye. Tied this way, the bead-chain eyes and hook point never snag in the grass," Charlie added.

Analyzing the fly, I concluded that Charlie seemed to have a potential winner. Still, I was skeptical. I rummaged through my fly box and found a weedless pattern I had weighted with lead wire. Although a minnow imitator, it was similar in color to Charlie's invention. I tied it on my tippet.

An hour later I was down seven fish to nothing. "Alright, gimme one of those flies!" I snarled.

Charlie handed me one of his creations. I tied the shrimp imitator to my tippet while worrying that this acid test might tell me something I didn't want to know. Fortunately, two casts later my line tightened as the hook point of Charlie's new pattern found the lips of a fat slot red. Relieved it was the fly and not the angler, I have to confess, Charlie indeed had a real winner. While the bucktail wing coupled with the heavy palmered hackle made his fly virtually weedless, more importantly, his invention outfished the venerable Clousers, Sea-Ducers and Deceivers I had grown accustomed to using. Clearly the redfish were selectively choosing to eat his invention!

"I'm gonna call this little jewel Carolyn's Shrimpi!" Charlie proclaimed, "In honor of my wife who tolerantly puts up with my addiction to fly-fishing!"

And so, on that winter day, it was anointed.

Years have passed since that fateful trip and the Carolyn's Shrimpi has accounted for many a redfish, trout, snook, jack, tripletail and Spanish mackerel. This successful fly pattern has even taken skittish Florida Keys bonefish.

The pattern is easy to tie and can be crafted in a variety of colors. Over the years I have settled on two primary color patterns though: a brown/orange color scheme and grizzly yellow.

Mark Hatter
"Fly Fishing in Saltwater"
Nov/Dec 2000

Carolyn's Shrimpi

Hook: Stainless-steel saltwater Daiichi 2546, size 1/0-2
Thread: Brown, flat waxed nylon
Tail: Brownish-tan elk or deer hair
Antenna: Red Krystal Flash
Eyes: Silver bead chain
Legs: Grizzly hackle, dyed orange
Body: Medium brown chenille
Wing: Brown bucktail

1.Start thread at the front of the hook and wrap to the back of the hook shank laying down an even thread base. Stack,

then measure a couple dozen strands of brownish-tan elk or deer hair to about half a hook shank length. Tie in the hair at the back of the hook allowing it to flare at a 45 degree angle above and below the hook shank by adjusting the torque on the thread. Next, tie in four to eight long strands of red Krystal Flash by folding the strands around the thread, hold the thread up, slide the flash down to the hook shank, and secure on top of the hook shank. Wrap forward over the butt ends of the hair ensuring that the hair and flash are secured in place. The red Krystal Flash imitates the shrimp's antennae and should be trimmed to a length of about four inches once tied in.

2. Attach a pair of medium bead-chain eyes immediately in front of the hair using an X-ing pattern and figure-eight thread wraps to lock the eyes in place. A drop of nail polish or head cement will help make the connection more secure. 3, Tie in a six-inch length of medium brown chenille in front of the eyes. (Any

brown rug yarn would work also.) Do not move thread. Wrap the chenille forward to the eye. Now, double back and wrap to the bead-chain eyes. Make a single figure-eight wrap with the chenille around the bead-chain eyes and secure.

4. Immediately behind the bead-chain eyes tie in a long, webby brown or orange dyed grizzle hackle. Move thread forward through the chenille to the eye of the hook. Palmer the hackle to the hook eye and secure. A long hackle is imperative in order to build some bulk to the body of this fly. If you have short grizzly hackle, a second or even third hackle may be required to build up the needed bulk on this fly.

5. Rotate your vise or turn the fly over in the vise for this next step. The wing on this fly is primarily used as a weed guard, so a stiff hair with minimal flare is desired. The hair from the tip of the bucktail where fewer hollow hairs are found will provide the maximum weedless effect. Stack, then measure, a clump of bucktail slightly longer than a full hook shank length. (Remember, hand stacking is usually the best way to even the tips of bucktail.) Secure the clump of brown or tan bucktail just behind the eye on the underside of the hook. Make a smooth clean head and whip finish. Use a clear nail polish or head cement to add durability.

The Carolyn Shrimpi can be tied in a wide variety of colors from black to yellow or even pink. The bead-chain eyes will provide enough weight to sink the fly but still allow for a soft presentation to fish in skinny water. Lead eyes can be used on flies for deeper-water presentations. We have tied them in a wide variety of colors and weights with consistent results.

Dale's Bonefish Fly

Contributed by Dale Darling

"Bonefish are adrenaline-laced caffeine addicts!" says Dale Darling. "They must think they are constantly in danger and spook as quickly as any fish that swims."

A good bonefish guide will give you lessons in walking on the flats hoping to prevent unnecessarily spooking bones. Toe first, and then lay the heel down. Move slowly. Cup your hands around your polarized glasses to reduce glare. Slather on the sunscreen. They are just full of helpful information. For a beginner in the sphere of bonefishing, they are essential.

Dale's Bonefish Fly is not much different from most bonefish patterns on the market. It has a few subtle, personal changes. The body on the fly is made with Ice Dub, a UV-enhanced attractor dubbing, and the wing has both calf tail and grizzly tips, which Dale feels adds more realism to the pattern. However, Dale admits that many patterns will fool a bonefish if presented correctly.

Presentation is the key to successful bonefishing. One major point to remember is to cast to one fish. Don't go on a flock shoot. Picking one target will calm the nerves and focus the mind for a precise cast.

The next thing to consider while pursuing bonefish is to pick a good angle for the cast. In other words, cast to a bonefish so the odds are in your favor that the fly will be presented in a natural fashion. From the bow of a boat, pointing at 12 o'clock, the best angle to present a fly is when the fish is coming at you from about 11 o'clock to 1 o'clock. The fly can be cast well ahead of the interception point to avoid spooking the bonefish prematurely and stripped in the direction the fish is traveling. The farther away you are from this straight-on cast the harder the presentation becomes. Lead-time, casting distance, and spooking the fish become more critical. A good guide can position the boat for an effective presentation only when the wind and tide movement are in their favor.

While wading for bonefish it is easy to turn your nose, with your nose being 12 o'clock, to these high percentage angles. Remember, bonefish are the ones moving; you need to take your time and watch the water. Bonefish are much harder to see from this lower angle and may be closer to you when you do spot them, so have your fly in hand and be ready to cast in an instant.

Mudding or tailing bonefish have to be approached with tremendous stealth. A wave slapping the side of a flats skiff is a no-no. The fly line casting flashes of light and shadow over a shrimping bonefish is the same as throwing rocks at it. Bye-bye! Bonefish won't "tail" for it; Dale says, "They have Beam Me Up Scotty technology. They are there one second and gone the next. Bonefish spook themselves; they do not need any help."

The fly design is itself useful in many cases. "In some areas, I really think a lot of flash is bad; it has a tendency to scare fish these days. Along that line, while I like the Ice Dub, I often use rabbit or some other natural material that is purposely tied without flash." Dale adds, "If I get into particularly spooky fish, I'll switch to the more subdued pattern."

Do a little homework on the area you plan to fish, Find out what type of water you will be in; sandy bottomed or covered with turtle grass? Matching the color of the fly with the color of the bottom is a good idea. Some expert bonefishermen feel this theory should not be overlooked. Is the angling pressure high or is it a very remote area? Finding out just a few small items about an area and determining the type of fly patterns it will take to be successful is well worth the time spent. Did you know the color of the bottom of the flats at Christmas Island is a pale yellow? (Hint, hint) Good luck!

Dale's Bonefish Fly

Hook: SS Salt Water, Dai-Riki 930, Daiichi 2546, or Tiemco 811S, size 8-2
Thread: Single-strand floss and orange Danville 6/0 or UTC 70 to match the body color
Eyes: Medium bead-chain eyes, black
Tail: Marabou, to match the body
Flash: Krystal Flash, Root beer/pearl

Body: Ice Dub, tan, orange, pink, chartreuse, yellow, olive, white, pearl
Wing: Calf tail, or craft fur, tan or white
Hackle: Grizzly hackle tips, natural, or dyed to match body
Weed Guard: 25-60-pound monofilament, depending on size of hook

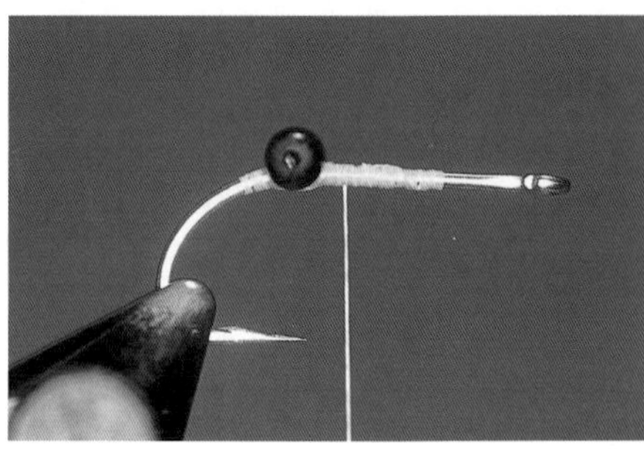

1. Start the single-strand floss thread at the 1/2 point and wrap to the back of the hook. Move thread to the 1/4 point and secure the chain eyes on top of the hook. Using X-ing wraps, the single-strand floss makes quick work of attaching eyes. It is much stronger than regular 6/0 thread, so it does not cut on an exposed sharp edge of the chain eyes and will not break under a heavy thread torque. Start the orange 6/0 thread on top of the floss. Trim tag ends of the thread and remove the floss. Move thread to the back of the eyes.

2. Tie in a small clump of orange marabou for a tail. Tearing off the fibers rather than cutting them is the best way to adjust the length of the tail. This

Saltwater Flies

leaves a natural look to the tail. Tie in a strand of Krystal Flash so that it lies on the side of the tail, then pull it around the hook to the other side of the tail and secure it in place. It is pretty sparse this way, but adds just a bit of flash. Trim to the length of the tail.

3. Turn the hook over in the vise and dub the body. "I do like using a dubbing loop for the body; however, around the eyes, I like to dub by hand to keep the stuff tight without building up too much bulk," Dale says. "Either way works fine, it is totally up to the tier." If one is compelled, a strand of Krystal Flash can be used for a rib through the body. Make sure to dub in front of the eyes and taper the dubbing thinner towards the eye of the hook.

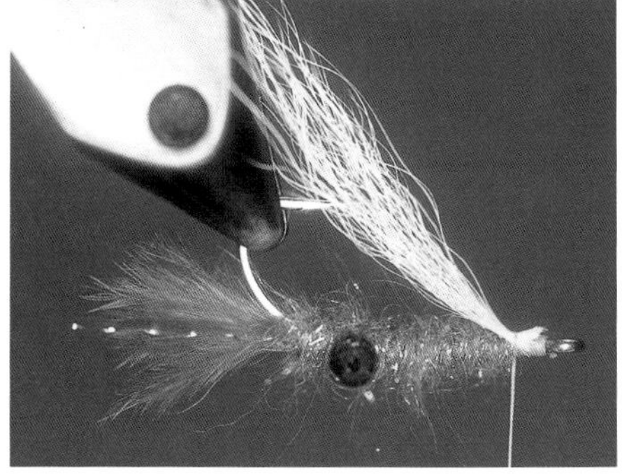

4. Choose bucktail, calf tail, or synthetic craft fur for the underwing. The hair should be evened by hand, what we call finger stacking. Pull out the very longest fibers and lay them back into the clump with the tips even to the bulk of the tips. Repeat three or four times until the hair is reasonably even. Totally stacked, square-looking hair is not required. In fact, a slightly feathered look is desirable. Measure the hair to extend to a point even with the tip of the tail. Secure at the 7/8 point of the hook, making sure to leave room at the head of the fly so it is not crowded in later steps.

5. Prepare and measure a pair of grizzly hackle tips for the over wing. The feathers should be the same length as the under wing. With the concave sides together, secure the feathers on top of the wing letting the feathers encompass the hair on both sides. In other words, you should have the shiny sides of the feathers facing out. Add a couple strands of Krystal Flash into the wing.

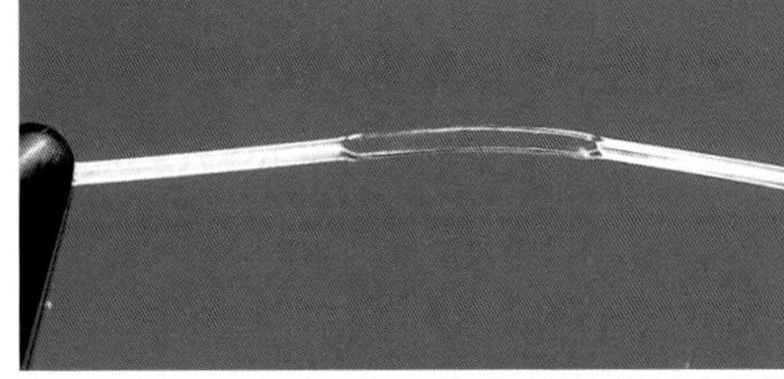

6. The weed guard is a length of monofilament attached just behind the eye of the hook. With smooth-jawed pliers, smash about 1/4 of an inch in the middle of the monofilament. Bring the flattened part of the monofilament under the eye and fold it upwards. Secure in place with tight wraps of thread. Adjust the monofilament with thread wraps so it forms a V shape and lies on both sides of the hook point. Whip finish and trim monofilament to a length just above the plane of the hook point. For sandy bottoms, the weed guard is not necessary. Often though, over turtle grass or coral, having a weed guard is the difference between you catching or not catching bones.

Dale's Crab

Contributed by Dale Darling

There are a number of crab patterns out there these days, and nearly every one is time-consuming and awkward to tie. After tying a variety of crab patterns for a number of years, Dale Darling has been in pursuit of an easy-to-tie, yet effective crab pattern.

The spun-hair crabs with all the bells and whistles are gorgeous but time-consuming. Epoxy crabs are very realistic but Dale is allergic to glues and epoxies. The crabs made from yarns weaved around the hook to form a flat crab-like body are effective, but all of the above take time and special materials to construct. Dale said, "I tied many of these types of patterns because I knew I would need crab patterns for the permit and redfish I may have a chance to cast to. I knew there was an easier fly to tie out there; I would just have to create it!"

"A new material came out a few years ago called E-Z Shape Sparkle Body. E-Z Shape Sparkle Body is a thick, non-toxic liquid right out of a squeeze bottle with great sparkle to it. It is an easy substance to shape that dries hard and its ease of use lends itself to several creative applications." Dale adds, "As soon as I saw it in use, I instantly knew what I could do with it for a crab pattern."

Everything was actually right there on his tying desk: dubbing, bead-chain eyes, hen back feathers, and calf tail. He had to dig through a drawer or two to find the silicone legs, but that isn't bad compared to the labor involved putting the traditional patterns put together. Dale said, "The first one went together just as I had imagined it would."

His first chance to use the new crab fly was in Belize. He and his wife were on their annual getaway to take in the sights, relax, and yes, get in some saltwater fly-fishing. While wading the flats near their bungalow, they suddenly had two permit come into sight. He bombed an 80-foot cast in front of the cruising permit. The lead fish turned to take a look and swam right on by. The second ate the crab immediately. The battle was on! The permit that refused the fly was following the other around like a lost puppy (there is video of the fight) until the struggle got too close to the four bare legs sticking in the water. Through all the thrashing, the tippet and knots held long enough for a photo.

"The photo is nice to have for the album and for use during slide presentations, but the memory of that day will be etched in my brain forever. The experience of tying a new pattern, spotting the permit, making one cast and having the fish eat it is totally amazing! Don't you love it when a plan comes together!"

The pattern can be tied in an assortment of colors, but tan and olive seem to be the best. Instead of the suggested Ice Dub used for the framework of this fly, regular rabbit dubbing can be used. Cut enough Silicone Leggs to length before you start tying so there are two pieces for each fly. Depending on the size of the fly, two-inch pieces should be sufficient. They can be cut much longer and trimmed when you reach your fishing destination.

Dale's Crab

Hook: SS Salt Water, Dai-Riki 930, Daiichi 2546, or Tiemco 811S, sizes 2-6
Thread: Single-strand floss and Danville 6/0, tan, cream, olive
Eyes: Medium bead-chain eyes
Tail: Calf tail, tan
Claws: Hen saddle tips, light mottled tan
Body: Ice Dub, UV tan, olive, cream
Shell: E-Z Shape Sparkle Body, sandy crab, olive, pearl
Legs: Silicone Leggs, pumpkin (Spirit River)l.

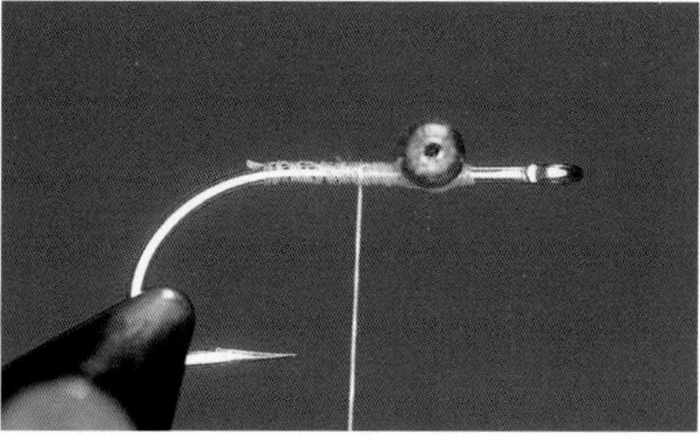

1. Start the single-strand floss at the 3/4 point of the hook and secure the bead-chain eyes in place with a simple X-ing pattern. Finish with several figure-eight wraps to lock the eyes in place. Start the 6/0 thread right over the top of the floss and trim tag ends of the thread and remove the floss. Move thread to the back of the eyes.

2. Even the tips of a small clump of tan calf tail by hand for the tail. Calf tail is very hard to stack, but this hair does not need to be totally stacked. Measure the tail to half a hook shank in length, trim the butt ends so they are just behind the eyes, and secure tail on top of the hook. Hold the calf-tail fibers up as the thread is wrapped back to ensure that the hair stays on top of the shank. Wrap the thread down the bend of the hook slightly so the tail has a downward angle. Let the thread hang at the back of the fly.

3. Match up a pair of mottled tan hen back feathers for the claws. With the convex sides together, measure the feathers to about 3/4 of a hook shank in length. Hold the feathers in place, making sure a feather is on each side of the hook, and secure the feathers just in front of the tail. These feathers can be tied in separately if both feathers together are too hard to manage. The claws should flare out slightly and have a nice V appearance. Trim the butt ends of the feathers. Dub a body with the Ice Dubbing. A dubbing loop should be used if preferred by the tier. The dubbing should be thinner at the tail, much thicker in the middle of the body and thinner again at the front. Make sure to dub around the eyes. Whip finish and remove thread. Note: Dubbing can be rabbit or another natural material for a more natural look. Olive, tan, and cream colors are good.

4. With a bodkin or dubbing brush, pick the dubbing out of the sides of the body. This is preparing the flat, rounded body of a natural crab. Trim the dubbing fibers to a round or almond shape. Make sure to trim the top and bottom of the fly so it is, in fact, flat. On smaller hooks trim to the size of a dime, while on larger hook sizes go to the size of a quarter. Your destination will determine what size to tie. This would be a great time to start another fly and leave this one to rest. After a dozen flies are tied to this step, start squeezing out the E-Z Shape Sparkle Body in the following step.

5. Turn the hook upside down in the vise and squeeze a generous amount of E-Z Shape Sparkle Body over the dubbing. Spread it over the body with a

toothpick or bodkin. Add more as needed to cover the body area with a thick, even coat. Lay two sections of the Silicone Leggs across the body in an X-ing shape so you have two legs on each side of the body. Bury the legs in the Sparkle Body so they are totally covered with the substance. Make them a bit on the long side so they can be trimmed to the desired length when you see the fly in proportion. Tweak the shape of the body by hand if need be and set aside to dry. It will take a couple of hours to set up totally and should cure overnight before use. Using purple Silicone Leggs is not a bad idea with a cream-colored crab; believe it or not, the critters are purple.

Kumiski's Fuzzy Crab

Contributed by Mark Hatter

There is much to say about the function of a fly. When designing a fly, its function should be at the top of the design feature list. The way it looks (from below) as it rests on the water, how it looks in the water, what color it appears to be in the water, how it acts in the water, or any combination of these constitutes its functionality. The main reason a fly is eaten by a fish is because of one or more of these features.

I hate to say it, but there are thousands of fly patterns out there that are tied strictly for looks. (Hey, I'm as guilty as anyone.) Yes, they are beautiful! The creator used the best of his or her imagination to make a fly that is very impressive. To their fellow tier and angling friends, the fly is the greatest thing they have ever seen; it's the cat's meow, the belve in their dere, a pattern that just has to be in their collection of other beautiful, impressive flies. You wouldn't dare put it in a working fly box and take it to the water and actually use it! It is quite possibly a good thing, because more than likely it wouldn't "function" very well if it did get wet. However beautiful the fly is, it has to have functionality to be effective.

The reason I picked Kumiski's Fuzzy Crab was to better illustrate the importance of the function feature in a fly. This fly is not particularly pretty; in fact, I could see most anglers pushing it to the back of the fly box. As you read this experience, Mark Hatter had while standing in front of hundreds of redfish, think about the guy before him, John Kumiski, who must have had a similar experience and gone home to the vise to create this magnificent fly with great functionality.

Recently, my good friend Mel Schubert and I took a long needed 3-day vacation from the rigors of work to the beautiful expanses of Charlotte Harbor off Florida's southwest coast to hunt for redfish and snook. As luck would have it, the snook were difficult to find but the redfish were plentiful.

Late on the first day, while searching for snook along a quiet mangrove shoreline, we encountered a shallow flat adjacent to an island literally covered with tailing redfish. Neither Mel nor I had ever seen so many redfish tailing at the same time. Several schools of 50 to 100 fish, plus scores of pairs and singles, were rooting around in thick ***thelassia*** *turtle grass in less than 12 inches of water. It was much too shallow for Mel's 18-foot skiff to work effectively. Fortunately, the bottom was surprisingly firm and we could quietly wade into casting range without spooking fish. We staked-up Mel's skiff and bailed out to attack the fish.*

I was armed with a chartreuse/white Clouser Minnow, a venerable and time-proven weapon. Within minutes, I had three clean shots at different fish from a single position. It was purely Nirvana! I cast to the first fish once, twice, then a third time before beaning it on the head with the fourth cast. It blew out in a puff of sand and turtle grass. No problem, two more within range.

Amazingly, the same scenario repeated itself on the next two fish. The thick-bladed turtle grass was problematic; my Clousers were not weedless and fouled on the first or second strip. Thick grass had never really been a hindrance to me, at least not so where I fish on Florida's east coast where another thinner-bladed grass thrives, but here, the situation was clearly different.

I poked around my fly box for another selection and settled on a weedless Carolyn's Shrimpi. The Carolyn's Shrimpi is a weedless shrimp imitator developed by another friend of mine, Charlie Madden, specifically for Mosquito Lagoon redfish.

I heard Mel whoop for the third time as I tied on the shrimp pattern. Looking over my shoulder, Mel's Thomas & Thomas eight-weight was doubled over...again...for the third time in 15 minutes!

An hour and five pattern changes later (three shrimp, two crabs) I was still without an eater. Meanwhile, Mel was racking up some impressive numbers. It was getting dark, the tide was flooding the flat and the fish were not showing as well in the deeper water. Defeated, I slogged back to the boat. Mel followed shortly and I soon discovered his secret.

"At this time of year the fish are feeding heavily on small crabs," Mel reasoned. "I figured that a weedless crab pattern would be the key to getting their attention. I was right!"

"But I tried a couple of my weedless crab pattern," I complained. "They kept hanging up in the grass, what were you doing differently?"

Mel handed me a dark brown fly with a disk-shaped "shell" made out of a two-sided fuzzy material that sandwiched a thin layer of foam. A pair of ginger hackles splayed outward at the bend of the hook with a clump of tan calf tail between the hackles. A heavily palmered grizzly hackle around the shank under the foam shell completed the pattern. Lead dumbbell eyes tied under the "shell" just behind the hook eye added the weight required to get the fly to the bottom.

"This," Mel stated with a bit of drama as he held the fly up between two fingers, "Is a Kumiski's Fuzzy Crab! Bar none, it is the best crab pattern I've used under these conditions. It has weight, provided by the lead eyes, so it gets to the bottom. The relative bulk of the fly causes it to push water, making it more noticeable to a fish whose head is buried in the bottom. The palmered hackle and the splayed hackle provide life-like legs and claws. Finally, and most important, the "shell" material is tied to the shank in a manner that elevates it to the point of the hook. Look! See how the "shell" makes the hook weedless?"

Mel was right, the fly did exactly what he described and proof was in the numbers of fish he had posted earlier.

Kumiski's Fuzzy Crab is the ingenious creation of author and shallow-water guide John Kumiski. Many anglers have found this fly effective for redfish, black drum, bonefish and even permit. I had heard a lot about the effectiveness of the fly, but never tied nor fished one until my trip to Charlotte harbor.

That evening after an excellent meal of fresh blackened redfish, compliments of Chef Schubert, Mel tied me a batch of Kumiski's Fuzzy Crabs while I finished the dishes.

For the next two days, an abundance of redfish held on the same flat and I joined Mel in racking up some impressive numbers...all on Kumiski's Fuzzy Crab!

By Mark Hatter

Kumiski's Fuzzy Crab

Hook: Stainless Steel Salt Water, Daiichi 2546, sizes 1-4
Thread: Brown, flat waxed nylon
Tail: Calf tail, brown or tan
Flash: Pearl Krystal Flash
Claws: Hackle tips, ginger, furnace, or grizzly
Shell: Brown Furry Foam
Body: Grizzly hackle
Eyes: Lead barbell eyes

1. Start thread at the front of the hook and wrap back laying down an even thread base. Tie a clump of tan or brown calf tail so that the tips extend beyond the bend of the hook about 1/2 inch. Add a few strands of Krystal Flash.

2. Prepare four hackle tips. You can use ginger, furnace or grizzly, preferably two from each side of a neck cape. Match the tips of two feathers from one side and two from the other. When tied on either side of the hook, you get opposite curvature of the feathers. Tie in a pair of hackle tips on the far side of the hook and a pair on the near side of the hook so they extend beyond the calf tail. Allow the tips to splay outward.

3. Trim a piece of Furry Foam material into an almond or disc shape leaving a tab of material on both ends of the piece. For size 4 hooks the Furry Foam material should be approximately the size of a dime. For larger crabs tied on size 1 hooks, a quarter-sized piece is about right. Rotate vise or turn the hook over. Take the trimmed Furry Foam shell and tie one tab down on the inside bend of the hook as far back on the straight portion of the shank as you can manage.

4. Carefully move the foam shell out of the way without tearing it out of place. The stuff is pretty durable. Tie in two or more natural grizzly hackles at the back of the hook and palmer them forward toward the eye of the hook. Use the longest hackles you can find for this part; you also want the barbs to extend out beyond the shell. Thick palmered hackle also adds a small degree of lift to the underside of the shell when the fly is completed, adding to its weedless capability. The palmered hackles should finish immediately behind the hook eye.

5. Tie in a pair of lead dumbbell eyes.

6. Take the other tab end of the Furry Foam shell and tie it to the hook shank

behind the eye and in front of the dumbbell, whip finish and fix the head with nail polish or head cement. Trim the shell as required to balance the width on either side of the hook shank.

When the fly is completed, the Furry Foam material should spring or bulge upward from the inside hook shank toward the hook point. This feature makes the fly completely weedless when properly tied. The Furry Foam is very soft and compresses easily when inhaled by a fish, making the hook-set easy.

Mad-Hat Sprat

Contributed by Mark Hatter

As a beginner in the arena of fly-fishing for tarpon, I'm always on the look-out for any information pertaining to the subject. Yes, I have caught a couple and have a travel bag full of tarpon flies, but as many other unknowing angling souls know, the first time you have one of these metallic-scaled 'poons' leap in front of you, you become obsessed.

I had a recent experience (I almost missed) that will help lead you up to the information on the Mad-Hat Sprat. It is funny how life hands you opportunities when you least expect it.

A local fly shop contacted me to help them with a guide trip. A couple of guys from out of town wanted to photograph a five-pound rainbow for a magazine article. All the guides at the shop were busy or out of town, so I said I needed a day out of the house and could use a little pocket change. Arrangements were made and I was waiting for a phone call to confirm the plans. No phone call. Eleven P.M. and still no phone call (I was supposed to pick these guys up at 6:30 A.M.). I thought the deal fell through, that the out-of-towners had stiffed me. I called the private ranch I had booked for the day and cancelled, turned on the answering machine, and off to bed I went.

I rolled out of bed at 6:20 A.M. to let the dog out and the phone rang (Now I noticed five new messages flashing that I had received through the night). It is the shop owner confirming the trip and telling me where to meet the guys! A little after 7 A.M., I pulled into the parking lot on Interstate 70 and met Dennis Porter and Mark Hatter. They gave me a load of crap for being late and I told them to stick it, (it's a guide thing we do here in Colorado) and we got along just great for the rest of the day and late into the night.

Mark, the photographer and outdoor writer, is from the Orlando area in Florida and is quite the saltwater fly-fisherman (fly-fishing for tarpon is his passion). Dennis, a business owner, is from Phoenix, Arizona. Go figure. They could both fish a bunch so I had a pretty easy day. We got the photos and they actually let me fish some.

Mark had only fly-fished for trout one time before this trip and I was wondering why he was hooked up so often. He is a beautiful caster, tossing a great loop with the unfamiliar five-weight. But it takes more than just a good cast to catch trout. You have to know where the trout lie, how to get the fly in the current so it floats over the trout naturally, and know how to set the hook on a trout, instead of a tarpon. I discovered he was carrying more than a camera in his bag. It turned out he knew where the trout were because they were right below him. Dangling in the water at his feet was a chum bag full of ground shrimp he had brought from Florida! He couldn't help but hook up because the trout were eating everything that floated by. I will have to say it was working much better than the stinky cheese I was using.

All joking aside, Mark sat up front with me on the two-hour ride back to Denver and we talked about tarpon fishing. (I will be in Florida sitting up front in Mark's boat next year.) He talked about some of the flies he had developed and I coaxed him into sending me information on a few of these flies for this book.

Mark was very benevolent in his efforts and information, passing along this piece of information about the fly. Mark, thank you for your contributions.

Before a recent trip to Trinidad and Tobago for a tarpon feature article I'd been asked to write for a fly-fishing magazine, I hooked up with Dan Jacobs a good friend who lived for a time on the islands. Jacobs is an expert on "TT" tarpon, having taken many with conventional tackle.

I asked him if there was a particular forage species that these Florida cousins keyed on when feeding.

Jacob's reply was to the point: "Sprats are the live bait of choice. They are exceedingly abundant and are the only bait the 'Trini' captains use."

The Sprat is the vernacular term used for a type of pilchard baitfish that is ubiquitous in both Trinidad and Tobago and, apparently, a tarpon staple in the region. Jacobs provided me a photo of a sprat before my trip so I could tie a bunch. With the photo he also threw me several packages of 6/0 Eagle Claw circle hooks. "You ever tie flies with these?" He questioned. "That's all the "Trini" captains use down there; they never lose fish on this circle hook."

I had never used c-hooks for tying flies but was intrigued to give it a try and was astonished with the results: not a fish was lost when it ate on a c-hook fly. Hook-set is easy when using c-hooks, simply hold tight to the line as the fish comes tight. The hook will lodge either in the fatty part of the upper lip or the corner of the mouth at the jaw hinge every time.

While I was impressed with the hook-up results of the c-hook, Captain Gerard "Frothy" de Silva of Tobago was impressed with the sprat-imitator fly pattern. In two days we burned through the dozen I had tied before the trip switching over to conventional patterns when the sprats were gone. Interestingly, the conventional patterns yielded lackluster results com-

pared to the sprat fly. When I told de Silva the fly had no name, he was quick to respond, "Fine, I will name it the Mad-Hat Sprat! Now, where can I purchase three dozen?"

By Mark Hatter

Fly Fishing in Saltwater, *Nov/Dec* 2000

Mad-Hat Sprat

Hook: Eagle Claw Black Pearl Circle Hook, size 6/0
Thread: White, flat waxed nylon
Wing: White Icelandic sheep or Streamer Hair with pearl Krystal Flash or hot yellow Flashabou
Head: White or pale yellow lambs' wool
Eyes: Solid plastic doll eyes
Markers: Permanent ink: Bronze or olive and black

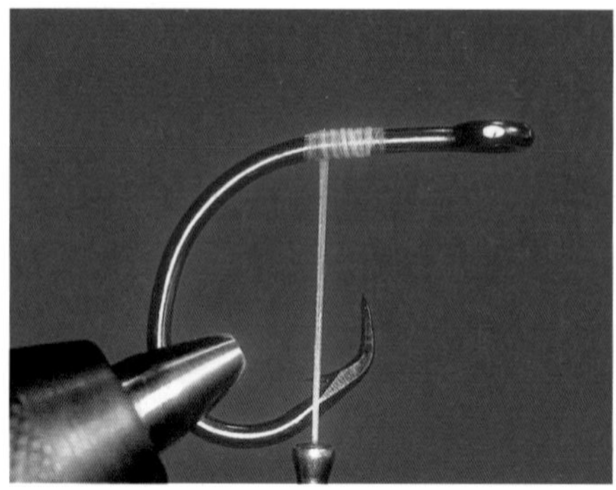

1. Here is one wicked-looking hook. Since the actual proportions on the hook may be hard to derive, we are going to tie all the materials for this fly on the front, most straight portion of the hook. Start the thread near the middle of the straight part of the shank and wrap back to where the bend starts. Looking at it, the thread should hang right through the barb, as with most other hooks, however, this one just looks weird.

2. Tie in a clump of white Icelandic sheep hair or Streamer Hair first above and then below the hook shank. Tie in about twice as much winging material above the shank as below the shank. Don't worry about the length of the wing at this point since it will be trimmed later. Add a few strands of Krystal Flash with each clump on top of the hook

3. Repeat the previous step, adding hair above and below the hook while throwing in a few strands of flash. Stop adding wing material about 1/4 inch from the hook eye.

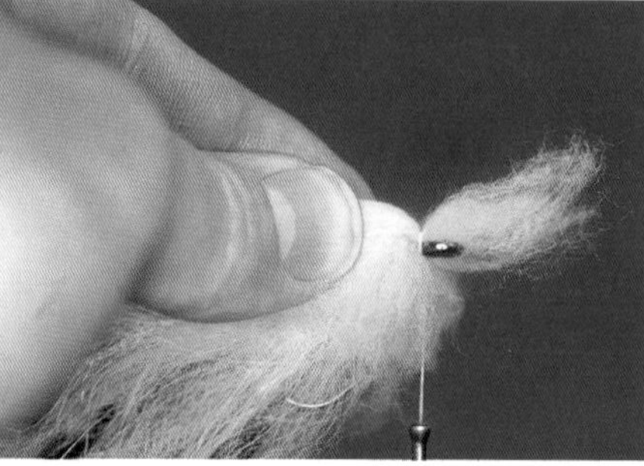

4. Using either white or pale yellow lambs' wool, spin the wool in the 1/4-inch area between the hook eye and the

front end of the wing. Wool does not actually spin, so you need to take a clump of wool and make two loose wraps around the clump, maneuver the wool so it encompasses the hook shank, then tighten the thread. Sweep the clump of wool back and position the thread in front of the clump. Repeat the process until the hook shank is covered. Between each clump, make sure to compress the wool much like you would while spinning deer hair. Whip finish the thread at the hook eye and cut thread. Fix the whip finish with either thread cement or clear nail polish.

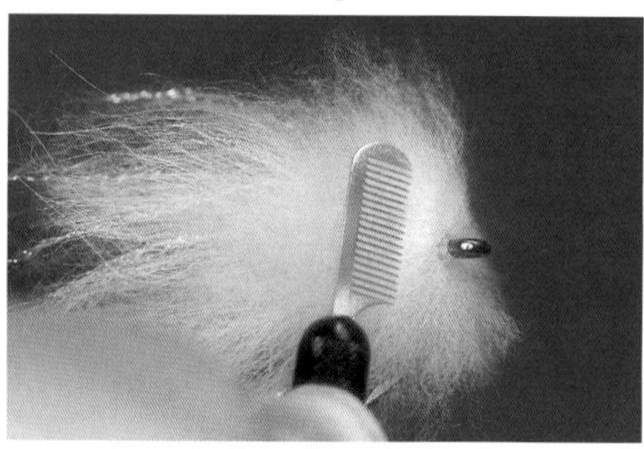

5. Tease out the wool head with a fine-toothed comb and comb it back toward the hook bend. Blend it with the wing as you comb it back.

6. It looks like this Sprat needs a haircut! Carefully trim the wool head and wing in roughly a laterally compressed teardrop shape taking more material from the sides of the fly than from the top or bottom. The finishing touches should be to smooth the shape of the head and carefully taper the wing back.

7. Color the top of the head and wing with the bronze or olive permanent-ink marker. Add a black gill spot with the black permanent ink marker. Glue solid doll eyes on both sides of the head with either Aqua Seal or Shoe Goo.

The finished Mad-Hat Sprat.

Nail Spoon Fly

Once upon a time there was this Floridian who got transplanted to Strasburg, Colorado. His father was in the military, so new surroundings were not uncommon to him. He was funny, had a thunderous laugh, played the guitar, and sang a little. He fit in; I guess he was used to it. I was a freshman in high school when I first met him. We called him Yo-Yo.

By and by, Dave Baskin (that is what we call him now) made his way back to his hometown of Homestead, Florida. He married, had kids, and lived through Hurricane Andrew. (Actually he stayed in his home as the storm ripped through the area. He has a picture of a huge palm tree in his front yard and to this day has no idea where it came from.) He raises orchids and, with the Everglades literally just out his back door and Biscayne Bay out his front, spends a lot of time fishing. He found out through an old schoolmate from Strasburg that I had written a book on fly-fishing in Colorado. Dave had just had an article written about one of his fishing excursions in the *Miami Herald*, so he felt we had something in common and gave me a call.

A half hour of male bonding, you know, his fish are bigger than mine, but I can catch more than he does type of stuff, sets the tone for a fishing trip. Mind you, he does not fly-fish at this time, but is willing to take me out and show me around the Everglades.

The trip comes off well and he got to see a "buggy whipper" in action. I caught some of his Florida bass, a couple of baby tarpon, some snapper looking thing, and missed a couple good shots at snook. When we got back to his place he was coming down with a fever. His temperature was fine, but all he could talk about was fly-fishing. (We all know how that sickness sets in!) "What did you catch 'em on?" "What is that fly called?" "Does that rod really weigh 8 pounds?" He was actually more interested in the flies than he was in the fly-fishing, but still amazed by the whole act.

At the airport, I promised to send him some fly-tying stuff, an old vise, and a Lefty Kreh saltwater tying video. Life as he knew it was over.

Dave started tying as soon as he got the stuff in the mail. Thank the tying Gods for e-mail or his phone bill would be huge. Question after question, I was beginning to think I had created a fur-and-feather monster.

He did start fly-fishing some, but only when he was by himself. His fishing buddies were relentless at the thought of him becoming a "buggy whipper". He started catching some fish, searching the web for anything he could find on the subject, and tied more flies. He found this "Spoon Fly" on the web (www.stripersurf.com). According to an article in the summer 1998 issue of *Fly Tier Magazine*, Marty Edgar originated this fly. He called it the Nail Spoon Fly. Dave finds it pretty interesting and put a couple together. And you know, he caught a bunch of fish on the fly. The bass loved it, the jacks hated it, redfish and snook ate it, and Dave took his first tarpon on a fly with it.

We met up again the next year for more of the same, only this time he has a fly rod and a box of his creations from tying over the past year. He had come a long way in such a short period of time; his flies were pretty clean and he actually had a pretty good, self-taught cast. He was tossing at least 75 feet with ease. We fished with his Spoon Flies and he showed me some modifications he had made to make them work better for his situation.

Dave fishes mostly the backcountry of the Everglades with mangrove roots and down timber being the major obstacles. He found himself hanging up and losing his fly quite often. "I hate losing these things; they take 24 hours to finish," he said. (He had not discovered 5-minute epoxy yet. That revelation changed his attitude about tying the fly, not the resolve to fix a problem.) "Anyhow, I started adding a couple of metal beads to the underside of the fingernail so the fly would ride hook up, making it virtually weedless, or should I say rootless. The action of the fly, its bobbing and weaving and fluttering didn't change; however, and I seldom get hung any more," Dave added.

Tying flies is just a series of solving problems.

I thought the intrigue of the birth of a fly-fisherman and fly tier would be of interest to you. It always fascinates me how people get started in this crazy sport and then to find a guy with troubleshooting skills and some real fish smarts only adds to the story.

As long as you use 5-minute epoxy to put this fly together it is very simple and tying numbers of them at once really speeds things up. The pattern tied here has a yellow scheme, but any color of your choice can be incorporated.

Nail Spoon Fly

Hook: Stainless Steel Salt Water, Daiichi 2546, size 2/0-2
Thread: Yellow flat waxed nylon
Tail: Yellow bucktail
Flash: Krystal Flash
Body: Yellow yarn or dubbing to take up the epoxy
Overbody: Fake fingernail set with 5-minute epoxy
Weight: Metal beads or small split shot
Legs: Grizzly hackle points
Eyes: Prismatic eyes

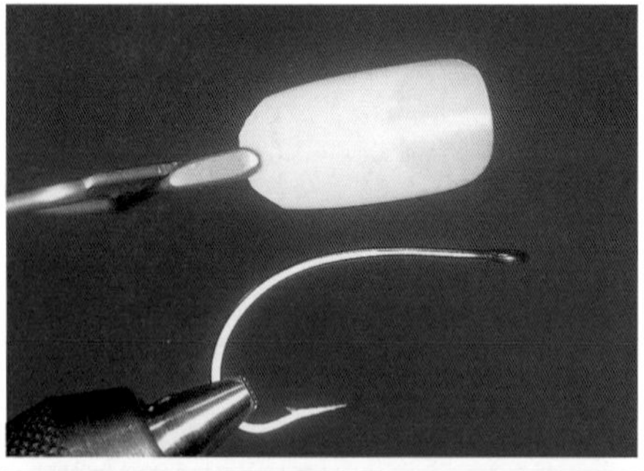

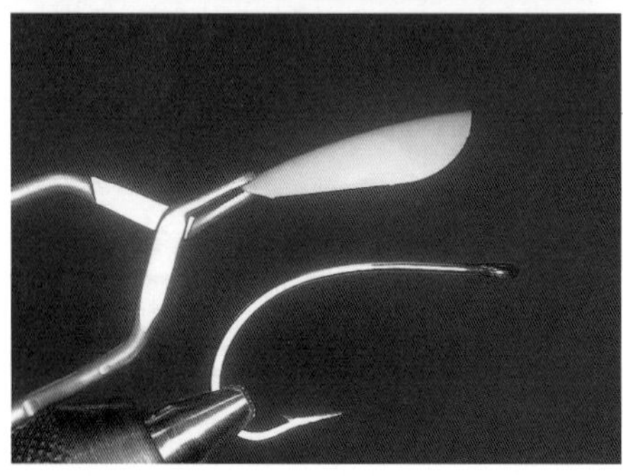

1. Bend the hook shank so it fits neatly inside the curve of the fake fingernail. The shank should be long enough to fit inside the curve of the fingernail, but leave the bend and eye of the hook exposed. Trimming the fingernail slightly to make it fit the hook is OK.

2. Start thread at the 7/8 point of the hook and wrap to the back of the hook. Move thread forward laying down a thread base. Hand-stack and measure a clump of yellow bucktail for the tail on the fly. NOTE: Just about any material could work for the tail on this fly. Craft fur, Streamer Hair, Flash-A-Boo, and hackle feathers are options. The tail should be at least a hook shank, if not longer, in length. Trim and tie in the butt ends of the bucktail at the 7/8 point, securing the bucktail on top of the shank. With very tight turns of thread, wrap to the back of the hook making sure the hair stays on top of the shank. Add several strands of Krystal Flash. Move thread forward to the 7/8 point again.

3. Tie in a length of yarn (do not move thread) and wrap the yarn to the back of the hook. Now, reverse direction and wrap the yarn forward to the 7/8 point and secure with thread. Whip finish. The yarn is for filler only so you don't use much epoxy. If you are planning on tying a dozen flies, prepare as many hooks up to this point, then continue on to the next step.

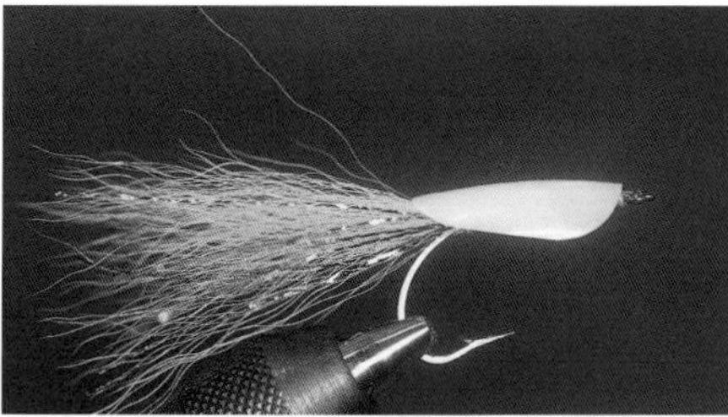

4. Dab the top of the yarn with Shoe Goo or super glue and set the fingernail in place. Make sure the fingernail is centered on the hook.

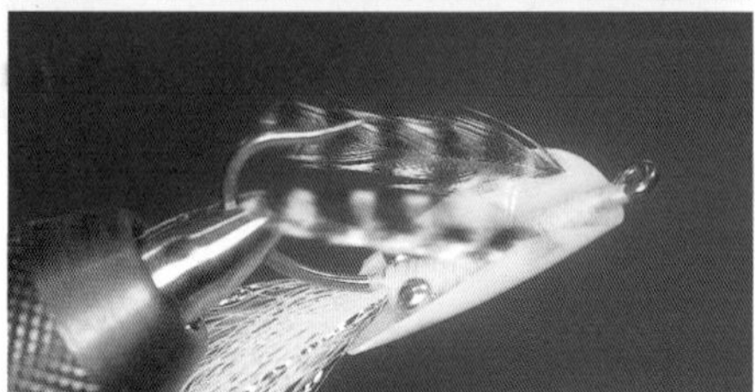

5. After the glue has dried, turn the fly over so the nail is on the bottom. Set a bead on each side of the hook with Shoe Goo, positioned at about the 1/4 point of the shank. Remember that the beads are used to make the fly ride hook up, making it virtually weedless. The original version does not use the extra weight and will ride hook down and fish closer to the surface. This step is optional, depending on the type of water you are fishing. Glue a grizzly hackle tip on each side of the fingernail near the front of the fly, pointing back slightly.

6. I have discovered a pretty neat trick with epoxy that may or may not eliminate the next step. I have to give credit to Mark Hatter (See Pale Lagoon Crab

also in the Saltwater section). If you are after a certain color for the body (fingernail), a drop of acrylic paint mixed in the epoxy will do the trick. A basic acrylic craft paint you can get at a hobby store is the best that I have found. It comes in many very good colors; it comes in small quantities, and is inexpensive. One caution though: DO NOT USE TOO MUCH PAINT! If too much paint is added to the epoxy it will turn into bubblegum and becomes very hard to work with. Fill the fingernail with epoxy and allow it to set up.

7. Once the epoxy has hardened and you have not added color to the epoxy, the fly can be painted instead. Paint the top and bottom of the fly as desired. Amazingly, fingernail polish works pretty well. Enamel paint used on toy models works well also. However, if you do add paint to the epoxy for the inside of the fingernail, you could mix up another small batch of epoxy with the same color (or a different color as far as that goes) and paint the top of the fingernail. This makes a very durable, high-gloss finish. Glue on a pair of prismatic eyes.

Here are a few options for you to consider when using the Nail Spoon Fly.

A fly with grizzly-dyed orange feather tips instead of bucktail for the tail could imitate the Myan Perch, a very well-known food source in the Everglades. Then a frog pattern and another favorite warmwater pattern, a crawfish, just to open up the door to other possibilities.

Pale Lagoon Crab

Contributed by Mark Hatter

As I watch tiers, whether they have tied thousands of dozens or are just starting the thread on the hook for the first time, I find everyone really trying their best to put the fly together as precisely as possible. A seasoned angler that ties for him or herself attempts to imitate the fish species' food source as closely as possible, while the beginner simply attempts to follow instructions. I believe it is human nature to try your best.

As Mark Hatter was telling me his story about developing the Pale Lagoon Crab, all my thoughts and perceptions about fly anglers were correct. Here is a guy doing his homework trying to imitate a food source as closely as possible with the goal of fooling a favorite saltwater species into thinking it is real. The story of life for most of us seasoned anglers.

I will let Mark weave this marvelous tale as I heard it for your enjoyment.

One of the aspects I find so intriguing about fly-fishing is the unpredictable nature of fish species on any given day. Thank goodness fish behave the way they do, otherwise our fly boxes would contain only a single pattern in a single color and we would always catch fish. A very boring proposition, wouldn't you say! The good fortune of enigmatic fish behavior has driven fly-fishers to create ever-changing fly patterns in search of the "holy grail" pattern. Along the way, the pleasure of inventing new patterns or mutating existing designs often leads to art forms more fit for shadowbox displays than saltwater emersion.

I too am driven by both art and the science of "building" a better imitation. The Pale Lagoon Crab pattern described here is artful; however, it was the result of necessity. That is, all other patterns failed to entice any redfish into eating during a particularly difficult January a few years ago in the Mosquito Lagoon on Florida's east central coast.

Cold weather had killed most of the grass (a normal occurrence) on the shallowest of flats. The denuded seascape exposed a profusion of quarter-sized, pale-colored crabs, which the redfish consumed with abandon. Quite literally, characteristic patterns including Clouser Deep Minnows, Sea-Ducers and various shrimp imitations failed to produce. The Anderson McCrab would likely have worked, however, I wanted to create a pattern closer to the real McCoy. The Mosquito lagoon crabs had an almond shape and I wanted to see if I could get rid of the lead eyes used on the McCrab.

Armed with a few live models in a small jar I set out to create my own design. Trial and error and numerous "lake tests" in my swimming pool finally led to a crab pattern with the correct shape and, more importantly, the correct balance which insured the crab would land on the bottom, legs down every time. In fact, if the fly lands topside down on the cast, it will right itself within the first three inches of water column.

Satisfied with my production version, I trekked to the lagoon to conduct a "live test". As I had previously found, tailing redfish shunned my standard offerings. My "control group test" in place, it was time to unveil my secret weapon. Shortly, I spied a pair of redfish laid-up on a table-sized sand spot. I made the cast and the crab landed on the water about two feet from the closest fish. Like in the pool, the fly righted itself on the way to the bottom. Almost imperceptibly, the redfish moved to the fly and stopped. I was just about ready to twitch my offering to impart some action when the redfish began to move off, my fly line trailing closely behind. The redfish had eaten the fly as it had laid there, legs down, claws up in its defensive posture. I didn't even move the fly!

Since that day, the pattern has proven to be quite effective for laid-up redfish, tailers and those on the move. I have even taken bonefish on this fly in small dime-sized versions. Although I have yet to have a permit eat this fly (I can't seem to get them to eat any fly!), I'm sure it would be at least as effective as the Anderson McCrab.

The Pale Lagoon Fly can be tied weedless; however, I prefer to tie it without weed guards. Crabs generally do not move much when pursued by predators; rather they head for the bottom and take up a claws-splayed defensive posture. Accordingly, only very small strips are required to work this pattern, obviating a need for a weed guard.

When you complete your Pale Lagoon Crab, you may be tempted to frame it rather than fish it, so make at least two; one for display and one for the flats!

By Mark Hatter

Pale Lagoon Crab

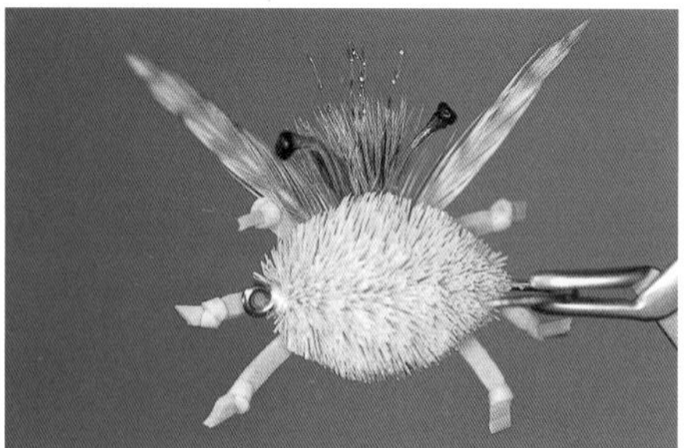

Hook: Stainless Steel Salt Water Daiichi 2546, sizes 1/0-4
Thread: White, flat waxed nylon
Body: Natural deer hair, or a coarse hair good for spinning such as antelope or caribou.
Legs: Rubber bands
Claws: Bleached grizzly hackle tips
Eyes: 25-40-pound-test monofilament
Eyebrows: Tan marabou. Whiting Farms has a feather called Chickabou which works very well for this application.
Flash: Pearl Krystal Flash
Weight: 020-.030 lead wire

1. Start the white, flat-waxed nylon thread at the 1/4 point of the hook and wrap to the back of the hook. Selection of the correct hair for spinning is important. The more hollow or coarse the hair shaft, the better the hair will spin on the hook. A spongy feeling hair such as the lighter-colored hair from the belly or rump of a whitetail deer, just about any hair from a pronghorn antelope, caribou body hair, and the body hair from a mule deer are all good choices for this procedure. After selecting the best hair, take a clump of the hair about as thick as a pencil and comb out the fluff at its base. It is not important to stack the hair before spinning, as you will trim most of it off to obtain the final shape. Hold the clump on top of the hook and make two soft wraps around the hair. Let the hair encompass the hook shank and slowly pull the thread tight letting the hair go as it starts to flare. Continue tightening until the hair has stopped spinning. Make one more wrap through the hair and sweep the hair back. Position the thread in front of the spun hair and make a couple of wraps around the shank. Prepare another clump of hair and repeat the spinning process in front of the last clump. After spinning two clumps of hair, pack the hair. Hold the hair in place at the back of the hook with your left thumb and first two fingers and push the hair back with the thumb and first two fingers of your right hand. Use a Brassie" in place of your fingers on the right hand, reducing the chance of spearing a finger with the hook point. Continue until the hook shank is completely covered with spun hair. You will be surprised at the amount of hair you can apply to the hook in this fashion. When you reach the eye, whip finish the thread, sealing it with either nail polish or whip-finishing cement. If you are planning to tie more than one of these flies, which I would highly recommend, set this fly aside and do another up to this point. Six is a good number, but a dozen would be better. I always recommend doing at least a dozen of any fly; you just start to get the hang of it after about ten flies.

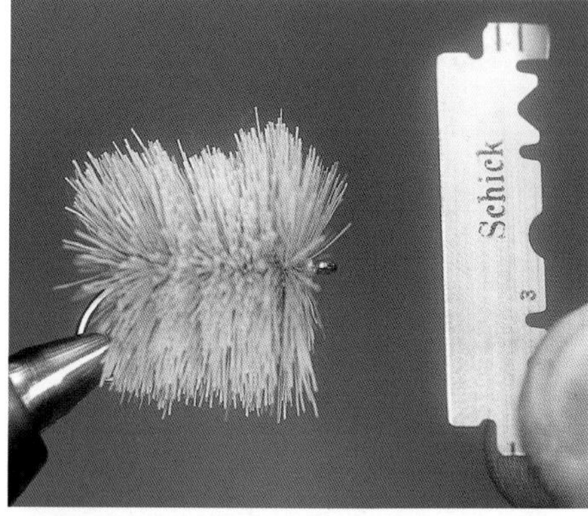

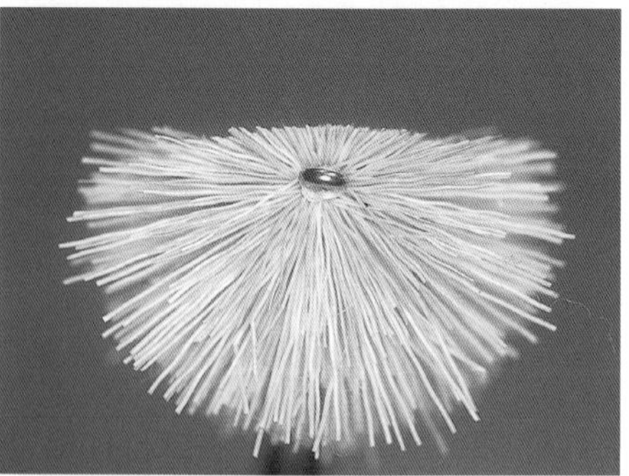

2. With a pair of sharp scissors or a double-edged razor blade, trim the hair into an almond shape. The bottom of the crab fly, which is actually the top of the hook shank, should be trimmed flat. While the top of the crab, between the hook point and shank, should be trimmed into a dome shape.

3. Curve-tipped scissors or half of a double-edged razor blade can be used for the final trimming to achieve a perfectly uniform almond shape.

4. Make the crab's legs by tying knots in rubber-band strips and trimming them to proportional lengths. Super glue the

legs one at a time to the bottom of the crab. Again, preparing twelve sets of legs beforehand will speed this fly up.

5. Next, super glue grizzly hackle tips that curve or splay outward to make the crab's claws. Melt the tips of two lengths of 25-40-pound-test monofilament to form eyes. Super glue them to the bottom of the crab.

6. Take a small tuft of tan or cream marabou or a Chickabou feather and super glue that on the bottom of the crab between the eyes. Also super glue a few strands of pearl Krystal Flash in place. The marabou and Krystal Flash will impart a subtle, lifelike action to the fly even if it is just sitting on the bottom.

7. Coil a small length of .020 or .030 lead wire and super glue it to the underside of the crab. The coil should be oriented toward the rear end of the shell so the crab will sink tail end first. At this point the crab can be water tested for balance. The super glue will hold the legs, claws, eyes, mouth parts and lead-wire coil in place during the water test, but will also allow the lead-wire coil to be easily removed and replaced as required. Readjust the lead-wire coil as required to get a consistent balance.

8. Once the crab has been balanced (and dried if water-tested, mix a small amount of tan acrylic paint into 5-minute epoxy. Do not add too much paint to the epoxy or it will become stringy and very hard to work with. When the epoxy is consistently colored, use a toothpick to spread the epoxy over the base of the legs, marabou, eyes, lead-wire coil, and hackle claws. Once the epoxy sets up, the crab is ready for use.

Pop-Eyed Snookery

The *Snookery* was the name of a houseboat belonging to Herman Lucerne. Herman was one of South Dade County's most famous snook fishermen. He was well known for his backcountry fishing, his work with children, and his love for the outdoors. Unfortunately, he was one of the many fatalities of Hurricane Andrew.

A fellow angler, South Florida guide, and good friend of mine, Captain Dave Baskin, from Homestead, Florida knew Herman and was fortunate enough to fish with him in the Everglades. He became very fond of this type of fishing. The favorite species of a Glades fisherman is the snook. This elusive predator tests the skill and wits of any angler who drifts into its mangrove-lined channels. Dave, who has been tossing flies for only a year, has found a new challenge in trying to "hook a snook" on a fly rod. Fascinated with the art of fly tying, Dave has come up with some very interesting and effective saltwater patterns. One of these is the Pop-Eyed Snookery, named after his good friend's houseboat.

Dave says, "I got the idea for the big pearl eyes from Captain Dave Sutton. He ties a crab fly with those goofy looking things and it works pretty darn well. I decided to try them on a snook pattern, one that imitates their main food source, a Myan perch. The mixture of red bucktail and grizzly hackle in the tail with the black and orange body makes for a very close resemblance. But those eyes, they are wild!" Dave adds, "I feel any predatory fish needs to look into the eyes of is prey just before it eats it!"

And eat it they did! The first time he fished this pattern Dave landed an eleven-pounder. "It was the way the snook would not give up on the fly that told me that it was a winner. Most of the time a snook will drop off a fly, or a lure as far as that goes, when it misses an attempt. This big boy would not give up on it and kept crashing the water behind it until the fourth time when he hit it hard. I just know it was those eyes."

Pop-Eyed Snookery

Hook: Stainless Steel Salt Water, Daiichi 2546, sizes 2/0-2
Thread: White flat waxed nylon
Tail: Red bucktail and grizzly hackle
Body: Medium black chenille
Overbody: Hot orange Cactus Chenille
Hackle: Large grizzly soft hackle dyed orange (American Hen Hackle from Whiting Farms.)
Eyes: Pearl eyes

1. Start thread at the 3/4 point of the hook and wrap to the back of the hook. Move thread forward laying down a thread base. Hand-stack and measure a clump of red bucktail for the tail on the fly. The tail should be about two hook shanks in length. Trim and tie in the butt ends of the bucktail at the 3/4 point securing the bucktail on top of the shank. With very tight turns of thread wrap to the back of the hook, making sure the hair stays on top of the shank. Attach a grizzly hackle tip to each side of the hook so the tips are mid way into the tail. Move thread forward to the 3/4 point again.

2. Tie in a length of medium black chenille on the fore side of the hook and wrap to the back of the hook. Move thread to the 3/4 point again. Tie in a length of hot orange Cactus Chenille on the far side of the hook and wrap to the back. Move thread to the 3/4 point. Tying in the chenille at the 3/4 point and wrapping back helps maintain a nice level body.

3. Wrap the black chenille forward to the 3/4 point leaving slight gaps between the turns. Secure with a couple of wraps of thread. Now wrap the Cactus Chenille forward, filling the gaps between the black chenille. Secure at the 3/4 point also.

4. Prepare a large grizzly-dyed orange hen neck feather by pulling the fibers back away from the tip and trimming the tip to about 1/8 inch. Tie in the feather by the tip with the convex side up in front of the body. Wrap the feather as many times as the feather allows, forming a soft-hackle collar. Secure.

5. These pearl eyes can be found at most hobby shops and some fabric stores. They come in many sizes and you want to get the biggest you can find. Cut a pair of pearl eyes from the rope and secure in place right behind the eye with X-ing and figure eight-thread wraps. You want the eyes to be slightly forward from the body, standing out by themselves, so don't let the body get too far forward. Whip finish. Paint eyes on the pearl eyes and cement them in place with clear fingernail polish.

More Fly Tying Info

The Benchside Introduction to Fly Tying
Ted Leeson & Jim Schollmeyer

Renowned writing team Ted Leeson and Jim Schollmeyer have set another milestone in the world of fly tying with this unique new addition to their Benchside Reference series. Following the incredible success of *The Fly Tier's Benchside Reference,* Jim & Ted now offer the first beginner's book of fly tying to allow readers simultaneous access to fly recipes, tying steps, and techniques. No more flipping back and forth from fly pattern to technique, hoping the wings don't fall off your mayfly. The first 50 pages of this oversized, spiral-bound book are filled with impeccably photographed fly-tying techniques. The next 150 pages are cut horizontally across the page. The top pages show tying steps for dozens of fly patterns, including references to tying techniques that are explained step by step in the bottom pages. This groundbreaking book is sure to thrill all fly tiers. Over 1500 beautiful color photographs, 9 X 12 inches, 189 pages, all-color.

SPIRAL HB: $45.00 ISBN: 1-57188-369-X UPC: 0-81127-00203-0

San Juan River Journal
Richard Twarog

New Mexico's San Juan River and Navajo Lake are gloriously featured in this well-written and beautifully-photographed book from professional photographer Richard Twarog. Rich with history and spectacular scenery, Twarog explores the history, landscape, structures, and early residents of the area. The famous San Juan Worm and other productive patterns are discussed, as well as effective fly-fishing techniques, equipment, and various fish species you'll encounter. Personal essays and interviews with local characters provide depth and personality, beyond just a guidebook this book puts you on the banks of the San Juan, heart and soul. 8 1/2 X 11 inches, 88 pages, all-color

SB: $25.00 ISBN: 1-57188-373-8 UPC: 0-81127-00207-8
HB: $35.00 ISBN: 1-57188-374-6 UPC: 0-81127-00208-5

Small-Stream Fly-Fishing
Jeff Morgan

There are many myths surrounding small streams—they only hold small fish, they're for beginners and kids, they aren't a challenge, don't allow for versatility in techniques, and so on—in this book, Morgan addresses these myths and shares the realities of small-stream fishing. Topics covered include: the myths; best small-stream equipment; ecology; entomology and fly patterns; small-stream types; fly-fishing techniques; casting; reading the water; and more. If you're up for the challenge, maybe it's time to explore this fun and unique facet of fly-fishing. 8 1/2 x 11 inches, 144 pages.

SB: $24.95 ISBN: 1-57188-346-0 UPC: 0-81127-00180-4

Ask for these books at your local fishing or book store or order from:

1-800-541-9498 (8 to 5 P.S.T.) • www.amatobooks.com

Frank Amato Publications, Inc • P.O. Box 82112 • Portland, Oregon 97282

Hatch Guide for WESTERN Streams
Jim Schollmeyer

Successful fishing on Western streams requires preparation—you need to know what insects are emerging, when and where, and which patterns best match them. Now, thanks to Jim Schollmeyer, the guessing is over.

Hatch Guide for Western Streams is the third in Jim's successful "Hatch Guide" series. Jim covers all you need for a productive trip on Western streams: water types you'll encounter; successful fishing techniques; identifying the major hatches, providing basic background information about these insects. Information is presented in a simple, clear manner. A full-color photograph of the natural is shown on the left-hand page, complete with its characteristics, habits and habitat; the right-hand page shows three flies to match the natural, including effective fishing techniques. 4 x 5 inches, full-color; 196 pages; fantastic photographs of naturals and flies.

SB: $19.95 **ISBN: 1-57188-109-3**
UPC: 0-66066-00303-4

The Fly Tier's Benchside Reference To Techniques and Dressing Styles
Ted Leeson and Jim Schollmeyer

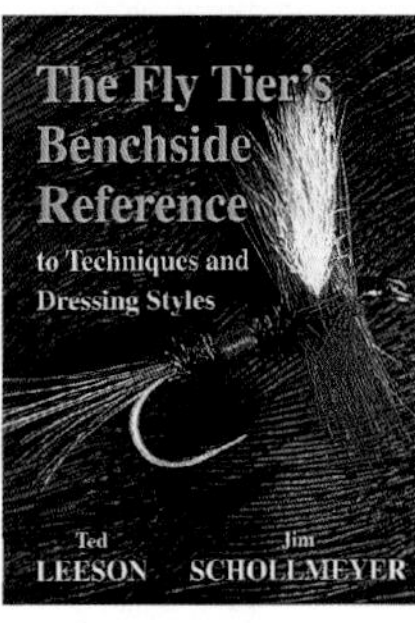

Printed in full color on top-quality paper, this book features over 3,000 color photographs and over 400,000 words describing and showing, step-by-step, hundreds of fly-tying techniques! Leeson and Schollmeyer have collaborated to produce this masterful volume which will be the standard fly-tying reference book for the entire trout-fishing world. Through enormous effort on their part they bring to all who love flies and fly fishing a wonderful compendium of fly-tying knowledge. Every fly tier should have this book in their library! All color, 8 1/2 by 11 inches, 464 pages, over 3,000 color photographs, index, hardbound with dust jacket.

HB: $100.00 **ISBN: 1-57188-126-3**
UPC: 0-81127-00107-1
CD: $59.95 For PC or Mac **ISBN: 1-57188-259-6**
UPC: 0-66066-00448-2

Federation of Fly Fishers Fly Pattern Encyclopedia Over 1600 of the Best Fly Patterns
Edited by Al & Gretchen Beatty

Simply stated, this book is a Federation of Fly Fishers' conclave taken to the next level, a level that allows the reader to enjoy the learning and sharing in the comfort of their own home. The flies, ideas, and techniques shared herein are from the "best of the best" demonstration fly tiers North America has to offer. The tiers are the famous as well as the unknown with one simple characteristic in common; they freely share their knowledge.

As you leaf through these pages, you will get from them just what you would if you spent time in the fly tying area at any FFF function. At such a show, if you dedicate time to observing the individual tiers, you can learn the information, tips, or tricks they are demonstrating. Full color, 8 1/2 x 11 inches, 232 pages.

SB: $39.95 **ISBN: 1-57188-208-1**
UPC: 0-66066-00422-2

Western Mayfly Hatches
Rick Hafele and Dave Hughes

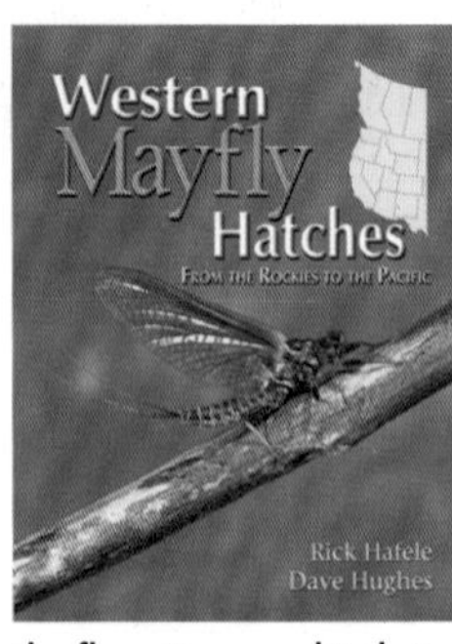

With their usual meticulous attention to detail, Hughes and Hafele turn their attention to the widespread mayfly, one of the most important insects to fly-fishermen. This book shares all that you need to know about the insect, and the fly patterns and techniques to match them, including: matching hatches, collecting and observing mayflies, recognizing species and stages, fly-tying techniques, presentations, and so much more. With 300 color photographs, 75 illustrations, and hundreds of fly patterns, this book leaves no stone unturned. 8 1/2 x 11 inches, 268 pages, all-color.

SB: $39.95 **ISBN: 1-57188-304-5**
UPC: 0-81127-00138-5
HB: $60.00 **ISBN: 1-57188-305-3**
UPC: 0-81127-00139-2
LTD. HB: $125.00 **ISBN: 1-57188-337-1**
signed by authors **UPC: 0-81127-00171-2**

Woolly Wisdom: How to Tie and Fish Woolly Worms, Woolly Buggers, and Their Fish-Catching Kin
Gary Soucie

The Woolly Bugger and Woolly Worm are among the most versatile and widely used flies; they're easy to tie, require no expensive, exotic materials, and, most importantly, they catch fish. *Woolly Wisdom* is an in-depth look at these effective fly patterns, including tying and fishing with them. With an emphasis on experimentation with tying in different styles and for various fish species—both fresh and salt water—this book is fun, informative, and extremely useful; a must for every fly-fisher who has any Woollys in their fly boxes. 8 1/2 x 11 inches, 170 pages, all-color.

SB: $35.00 **ISBN: 1-57188-351-7**
UPC: 0-81127-00185-9
HB: $45.00 **ISBN: 1-57188-352-5**
UPC: 0-81127-00186-6
Limited HB: $125.00 **ISBN: 1-57188-355-X**
UPC: 0-81127-00189-7

Innovative Flies and Techniques
Al & Gretchen Beatty

While working on *The Federation of Fly Fishers Fly Pattern Encyclopedia* it quickly became clear to the Beattys that another book was necessary. Many of the flies in the *Encyclopedia* were worthy of more than just a fly plate and dressing, so they are included in this book with step-by-step photos and descriptions. They've also included many new flies, but each is included for the same reasons: the pattern is an innovative design, a simple but effective idea, or makes improvements on an existing fly. 8 1/2 x 11 inches, 196 pages.

SB: $35.00 **ISBN: 1-57188-347-9**
UPC: 0-81127-00181-1
Spiral HB: $49.95 **ISBN: 1-57188-348-7**
UPC: 0-81127-00182-8
Limited HB: $125.00 **ISBN: 1-57188-349-5**
signed by authors **UPC: 0-81127-00183-5**

Ask for these books at your local fishing or book store or order from:

1-800-541-9498 (8 to 5 P.S.T.) • www.amatobooks.com

Frank Amato Publications, Inc • P.O. Box 82112 • Portland, Oregon 97282

Cara with her father Duncan.

Six Percent - Down's Syndrome: My photographs Their Stories

First published in the United Kingdom in March 21st 2013 by:

Photohonesty
Perth,
Scotland, UK

ISBN: 978-0-9575639-0-2

In partnership with Down's Syndrome Scotland

Please note that this book contains some words which are regarded by most as offensive. They are included here because they were spoken by those who used them as a way of communicating their real life experiences. No further offence is intended.

Front Cover: Sisters Penny and Rose

Design by: Umair Akhtar, UA Graphics

Final design, printing and binding by 52 Print Solutions

www.photohonesty.org

‘The data on outcome show that after the prenatal diagnosis of Down's Syndrome 91% of affected pregnancies are terminated and 9% are continued. Some of the continued pregnancies miscarry naturally, some end as still births, and approximately 6% of prenatal diagnosis are live births'.

Source: The National Down Cytogenetic Register for England and Wales: 2010 Annual Report

SIX PE

DOWN'S S

MY PHOTOGRAPH

HONESTY™

RCENT
YNDROME
S THEIR STORIES

Foreword

I first met Graham in 2010 when he was taking photos of families at one of our local branches. Subsequently, we met to discuss an idea he was formulating about a larger scale project – a body of work that would attempt to document the essence of the relationship between parent and child with Down's syndrome that he had witnessed in his sessions with the group.

We put him in touch with families and over the months the project inevitably grew as Graham met parents and siblings who willingly shared their stories. The scope of the project then encompassed the families' stories and Graham began to record interviews. Parts of those interviews are contained within this book and some make difficult reading, as the truth of the circumstances is set out.

It has never been Graham's or our intention that this documentary, should paint only a rosy picture of living with a child with Down's Syndrome. Having a child with Down's syndrome brings challenges for each family and the degree and timing of those challenges varies from one family to the next, but isn't this the case for every family, whoever and wherever they are? Bringing up the next generation is tough and no one can predict where their children - with or without Down's syndrome will end up.

What we've set out to do, is to make people stop and think about the lives of the Six Percent; about how they can and do live good lives, and achieve remarkable things - despite the challenges.

As the project neared completion and a draft of the book was compiled, opinion became divided as to whether the book was 'too' honest in its recounting of the experience of families and whether it would be off-putting for new or potential new families. Consequently I had to go back to first principals and think about the message both Graham and the charity were trying to communicate. I concluded that the project was indeed about trying to make people think – about the images they saw and the words they read and that we shouldn't be apologetic that some of these images and words were shocking.

It is only in the last few years that images of people with Down's syndrome as 'ordinary people', have begun to become more common. Graham and I continue to debate whether documentary photography is 'art', but what I'm sure of is that his work here raises people with Down's Syndrome out of specialised medical text books and places them firmly in the mainstream of society and I thank him with all my heart for that.

Pandora Summerfield

Pandora Summerfield
Chief Executive Officer
Down's Syndrome Scotland

November 16th, 2012

KATIE

‘And the consultant, who up until then had been a great guy, began the sentence by saying I’d just like to discuss the options available to you. And I remember getting really angry! I said, there aren’t any f**king options. She’s my child and your job is to get her out of here’.

The day I arrived to take more photographs Katie had put a line of salt across all windows and doors Stuart tells the story.

'The incident with the salt was pure mischief, you know. She went into an imaginary world, she thought she was going to keep out the gremlins and keep us all safe! So the motive was absolutely spot on. I saw the salt along the door and I thought, I swept that floor yesterday, what the hell is that salt doing there? And I thought, maybe Carol's put some ant powder down or something! What the hell has she put ant powder there for?'

On another occasion.

'The head teacher said, right you'll do this or I'm going to have to write a note in your dialogue book, and inform your parents of how naughty you've been. Give me your book. And Katie said, if you're going to write bad things in my book you're not f**king having it!'

GBR.

Mark 19, Rachael 15, Katie 13, Matthew 11

RILEY

Katie

'She was just so tiny, because she was only four and a half pounds, she was a tiny wee thing'.

'Stuart's actually not very good at talking about how he's feeling about things, he tends not to tell you what he's thinking. He's talking now, but he doesn't tend to tell me what he's thinking very much, so I didn't actually know how he felt about having a child with Down's Syndrome. You hear about marriages breaking up and things going wrong when somebody with a disability comes into the family, it's not uncommon for these things to happen, and I couldn't work out whether he was okay about it or upset and just not speaking about it. I had no idea how he was'.

goddess
goddess
goddess
goddess

Katie

JAMIE

Fiona and Ross have three children Ellie, Jamie and now baby Sam. The tenderness of this moment, where they hug Jamie as a baby became the point at which I realised I had to share what I'd seen, with the World.

Fiona and Ross received the news in the 19th week of the pregnancy that the amniocentesis had shown that Jamie would have Down's Syndrome and they had two weeks to decide what to do.

'We agreed that the hospital would text me to let me know when the results were in. I just rang, without thinking, from the car. I'm the kind of person that just needs to know how things are. I prefer to know. By Sunday we had made a decision and in reality, we had reached the same conclusion by mutual understanding'

Ross

A baby Jamie pulls his big sister Ellie's hair.

'They said just to let you know you've made your decision now but the option of termination remains open. We won't mention it again'.

'The doctor also explained that there was a higher risk of miscarriage. I hadn't thought much of it, at the time, but suddenly it came back into my head and I was stressed for the remaining four months because we wanted the baby so much and he could have been snatched away from us. Even though our second son Sam didn't have Down's Syndrome I was still very anxious to see him born'.

Fiona

'Actually when I was pregnant with Ellie, the test came back with a 1 in 152 risk, which we thought was high and then with Jamie it was 1 in 8. We agonised over the decision to have an amniocentesis'.

'As I'd felt him kicking, I had formed a relationship with him. We'd had three miscarriages after the birth of Ellie, which could have been due to chromosomal abnormalities. None of those babies had survived and he was alive, and he wanted to be born – I thought he's the way he is for a reason – he's meant to be here'.

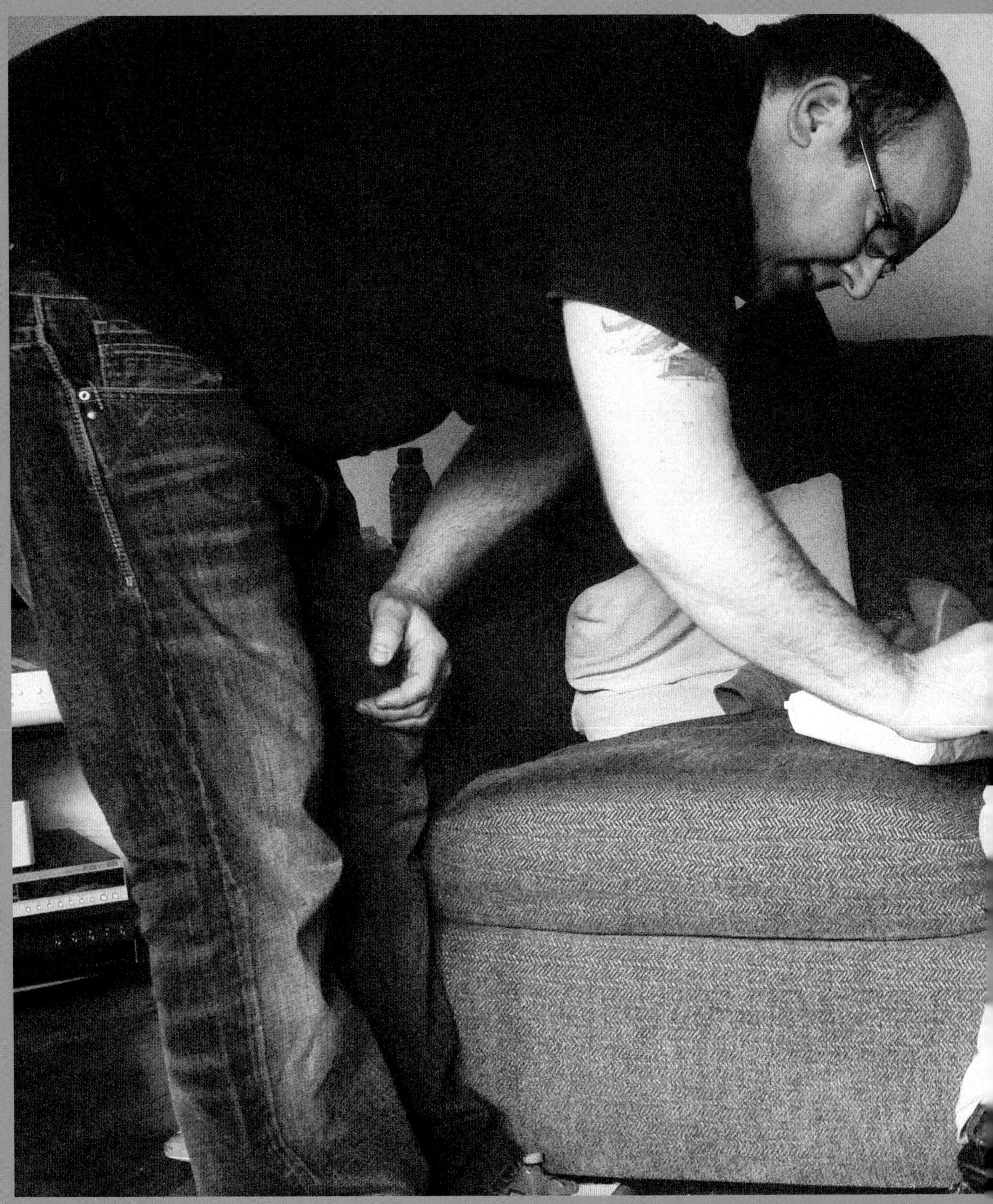

Jamie with his baby brother Sam.

‘Looking back now we think about how lucky we are. If we had made a different decision life would be very different. We just couldn’t imagine not having Jamie’.

Ross

MATTHEW

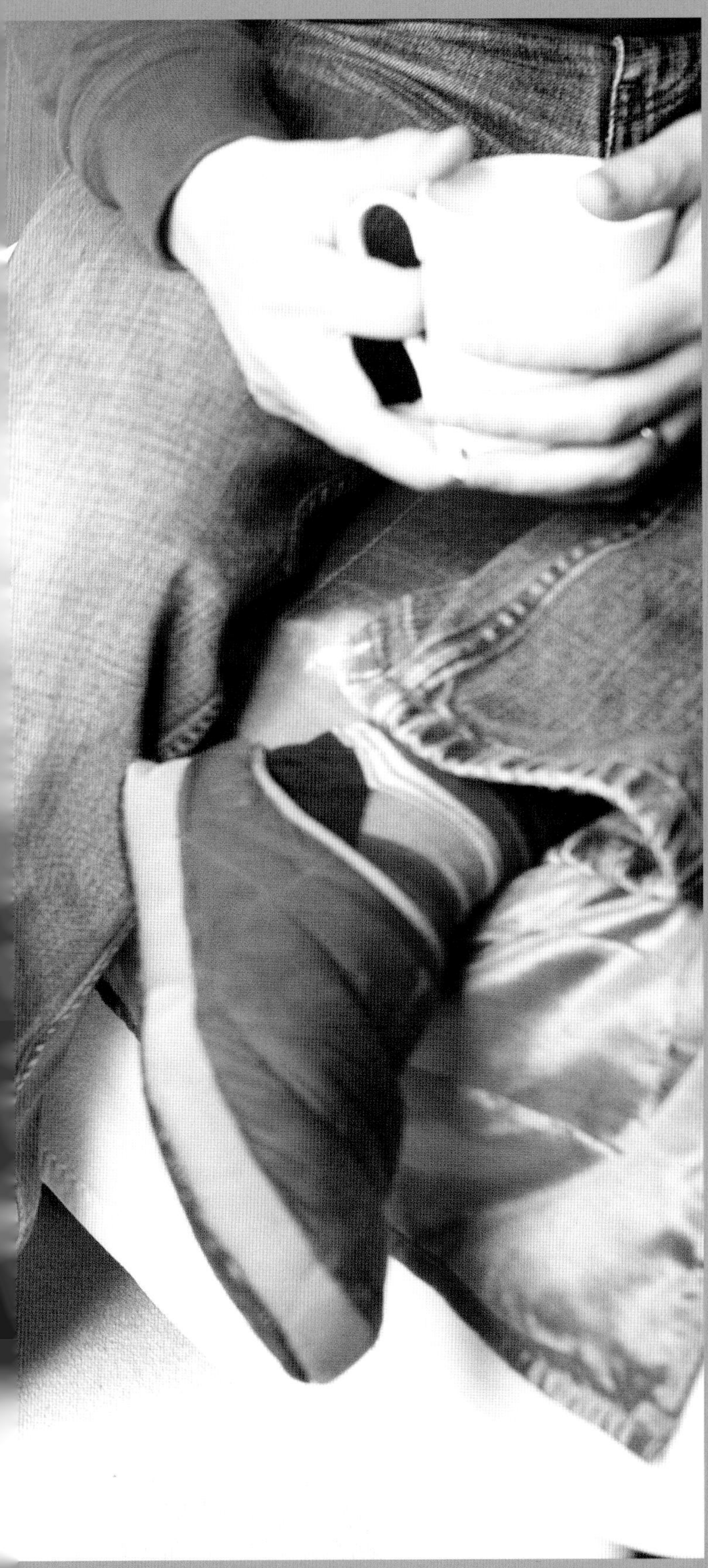

Previous page: Matthew locked my gaze as I looked down from the pews at their local church during Sunday service.

When Matthew was born, a second son to Katrina and Colin, and a brother to Adam they didn't know he would have Down's Syndrome. As they openly shared their experiences, it was clear how those early days, and the sadness they experienced was driven by the stigma attached to the condition. Like all the families I met there was a short period of adaption and then adjustment.

'As soon as Matthew was born, and the nurses had done their bits and pieces, they brought him to Katrina. As she lay in the bed, looking at Matthew, the first thing she said to me was, has he got Down's Syndrome? And I said, don't be ridiculous'.

Colin

'Show everyone your hand. You don't actually do that very often, do you?'

'I knew that it was a sign of having Down's Syndrome but I hadn't checked his hands. And then we found out further down the line that so many per cent of the population have actually got it anyway'

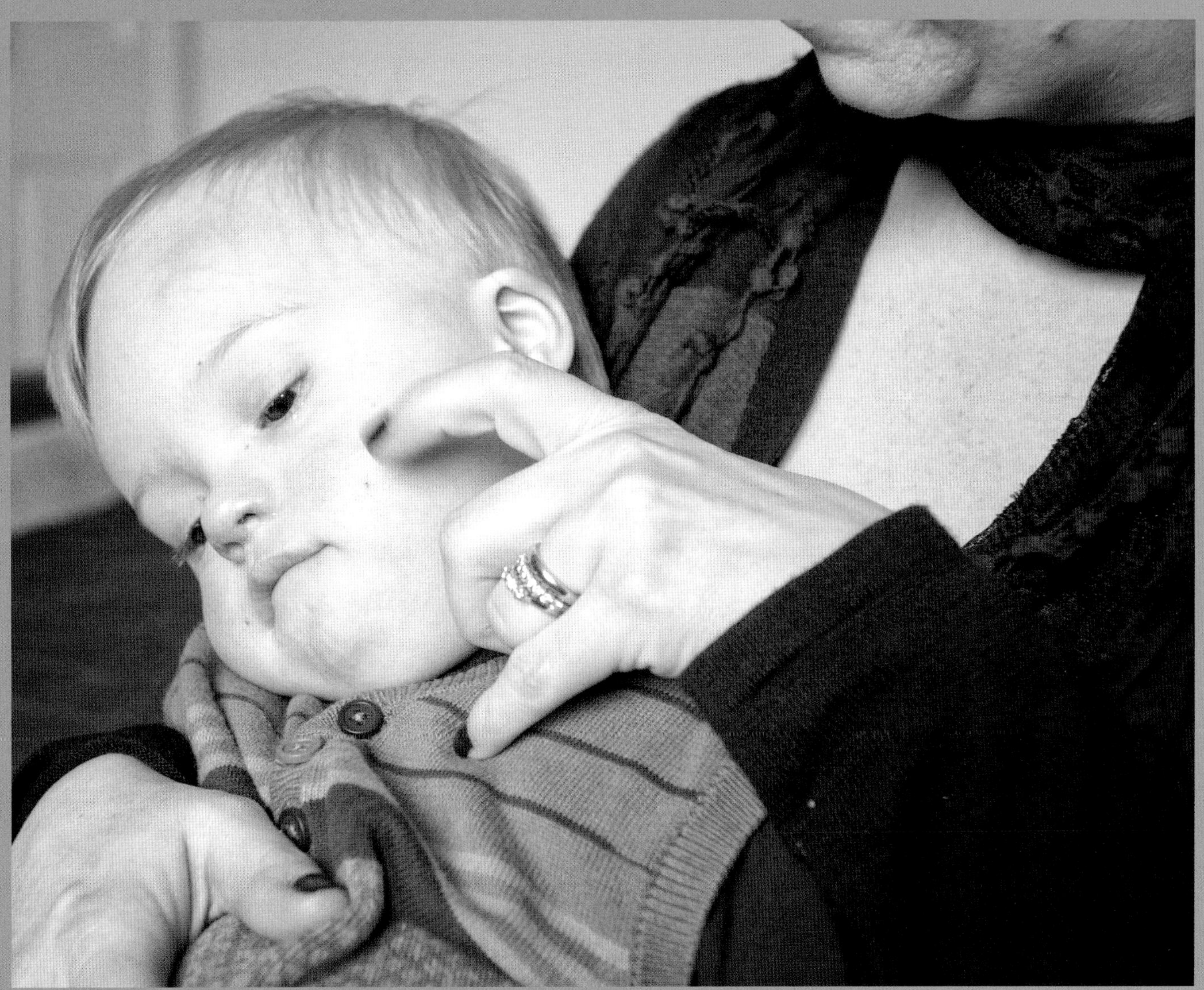

In sharing her innermost feelings, Katrina was not the only person to draw comparisons with the feeling of bereavement. It seemed a very important part of the process of acceptance to me, like moving on. It was legitimate to feel that way and an important validation for others.

'It was a horrible time. Neither of us have ever lost a parent or a very close relative. It was like a death, I would say, in terms of the feeling of sadness. I've never felt sadness like it'.

Katrina

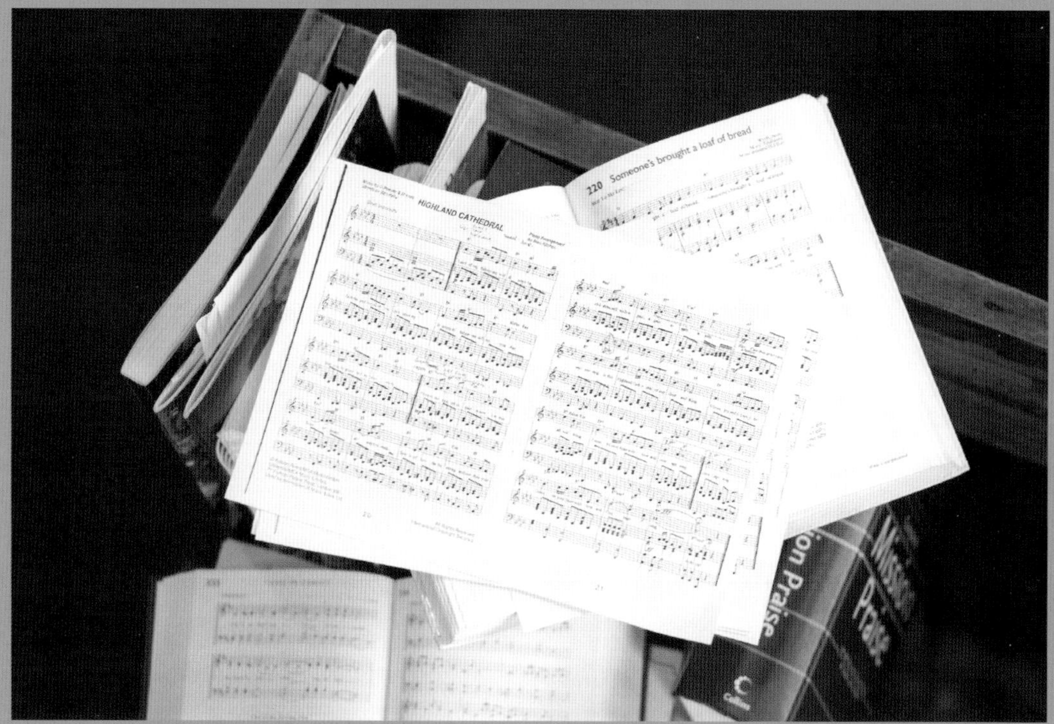

Katrina and Colin are members of the local church where she plays the organ.

'Much of what made things difficult in the beginning for us had a lot to do with the stigma attached to the condition. There is a lot of ignorance towards Down's Syndrome'.

'But now, having had Matthew, and realising how much he has to give us and how much fun we've had, it hasn't been the worst thing in the world. We just want other people to know that'.

GAP

‘I pick him out of his cot some nights. If he’s sound asleep I pick him up and put him over my shoulder. I sometimes bring him through here, don’t I ? We just look at him’.

Katrina

'Once we got Matthew home and realised he's just a baby, he's just like every other baby in the world. He was the easiest baby!'

Colin

CAMERON

The best way to
Invest your money and
make your mom proud
The place to advertise anything and everything.
www.euroawk.cz
euroawk
THE GREAT OUTDOORS.

PRO-MATIC ČR
SPOLEČNOST S RUČENÍM OMEZENÝM

PORTRÉT 10 × 15 cm

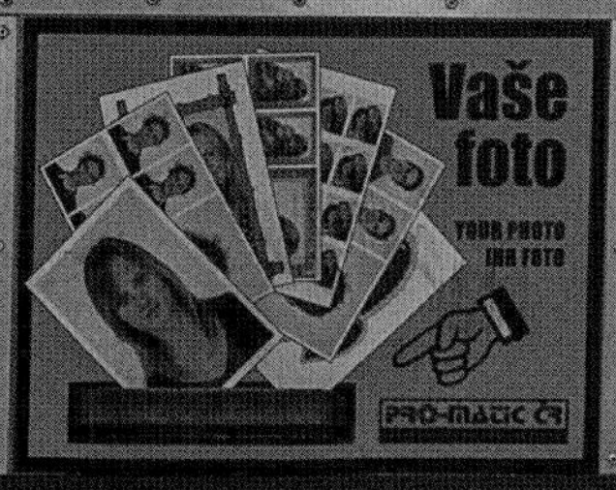
Vaše
foto
PRO-MATIC ČR

RYCHLÉ FOTO
QUICK PHOTO / SCHNELLES FOTO
DIGITAL
za 1 minutu
in ONE minute / in EINER Minute
PRO-MATIC ČR
RYCHLÉ
FOTO
QUICK PHOTO
SCHNELLES FOTO
nejlepší ceny
best prices / zu Bestpreisen
PORTRÉT 10 × 15 cm 50 Kč
PRŮKAZOVÉ FOTO 100 Kč
KALENDÁŘE, VESELÉ FOTO
100 Kč
za 1 minutu
in ONE minute / in EINER Minute

Sarah was working in Prague with her husband Bryan when she gave birth to Cameron.

They didn't know he would have Down's Syndrome and that the Czech authorities would want to take him into care.

‘They took us to the basement of the hospital where all would be explained,
we just went down and down’.

‘The Professor showed us the computer screen and it was like little kidney shapes all joined up together and then you got to chromosome 21 and there were three. He said your child has translocational 21’.

‘He wanted to take blood to find out if we were carriers. We refused as we didn't want to know or to apportion blame’.

‘They came in and said, this is a form you can sign if you like, we’ll take Cameron away. You’re in the Czech Republic, the Czech law is quite clear that Cameron is not your problem, Cameron is a state problem. Sign the form, lead your life, go off and enjoy it, you’re a young couple. We said he’s British and that’s not the way we do it, and that’s not going to happen’.

‘They weren’t being disrespectful It was just what they do but all the emotions surfaced again worse than before’.

Right: The birthing suite in Prague is prepared for the next birth.

'And then you get this feeling of being ashamed. It's really strange because when you have a Down's Syndrome kid you're actually mourning for the child that you never got, that you maybe expected to get. So you almost treat it a bit like a death which is a horrible thing to say, because we wouldn't change Cameron for the world'.

'You've lost the child you want and got the child that you've got'.

Bryan

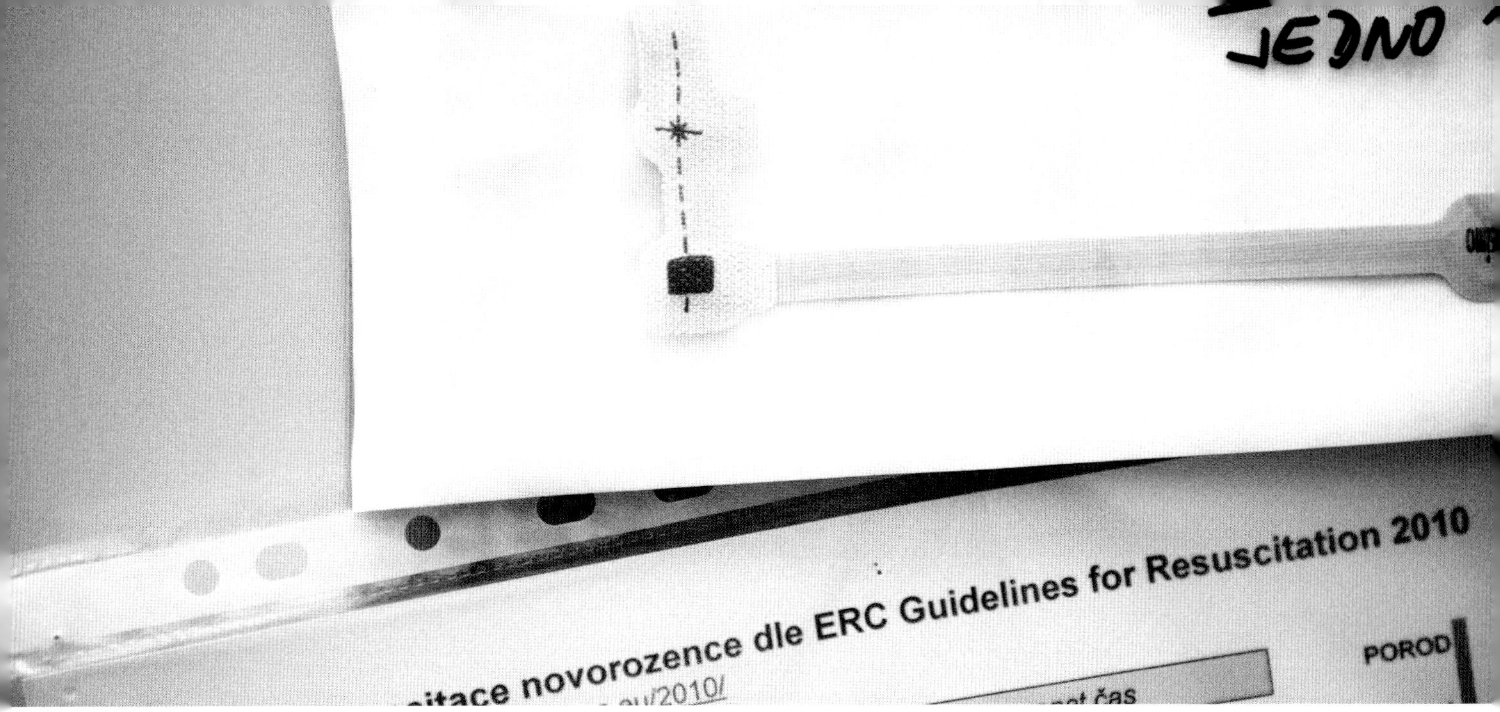

JEDNO
itace novorozence dle ERC Guidelines for Resuscitation 2010
POROD

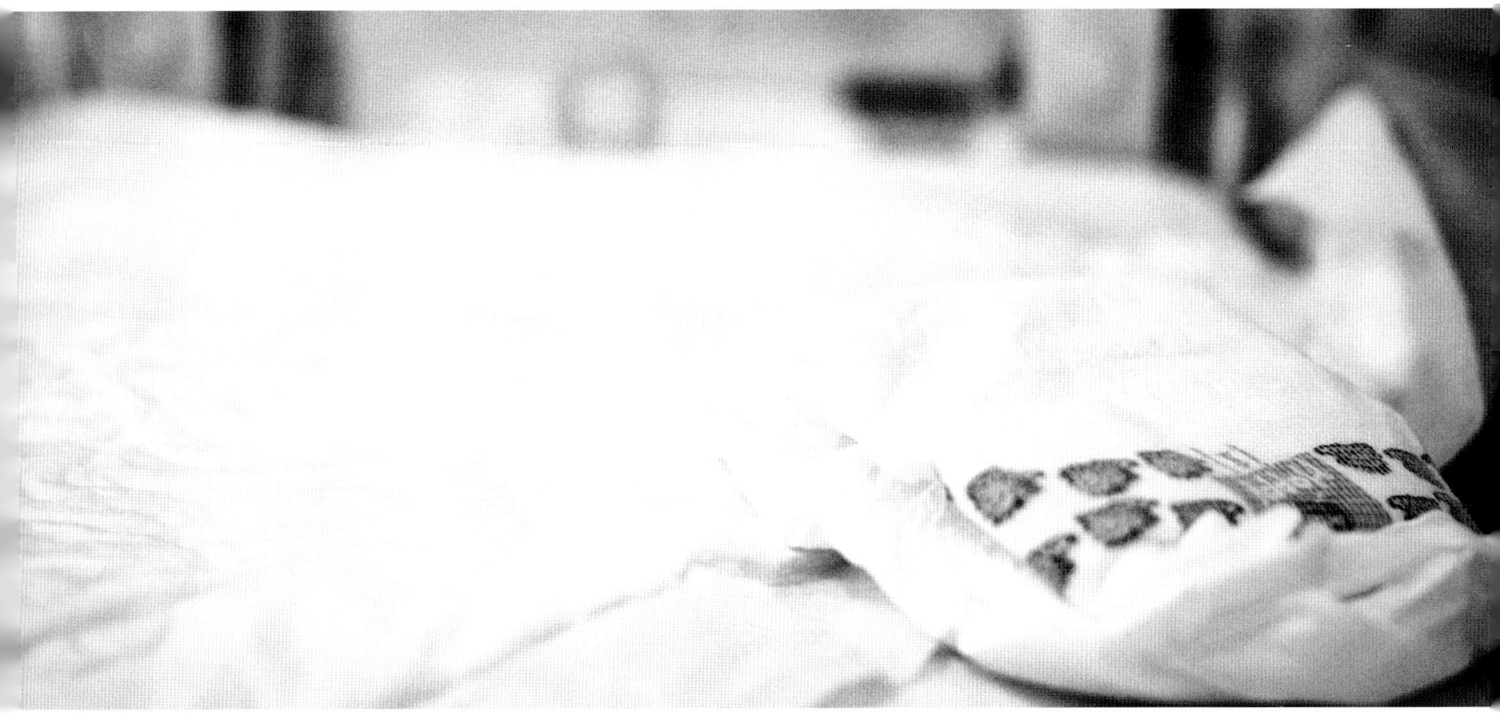

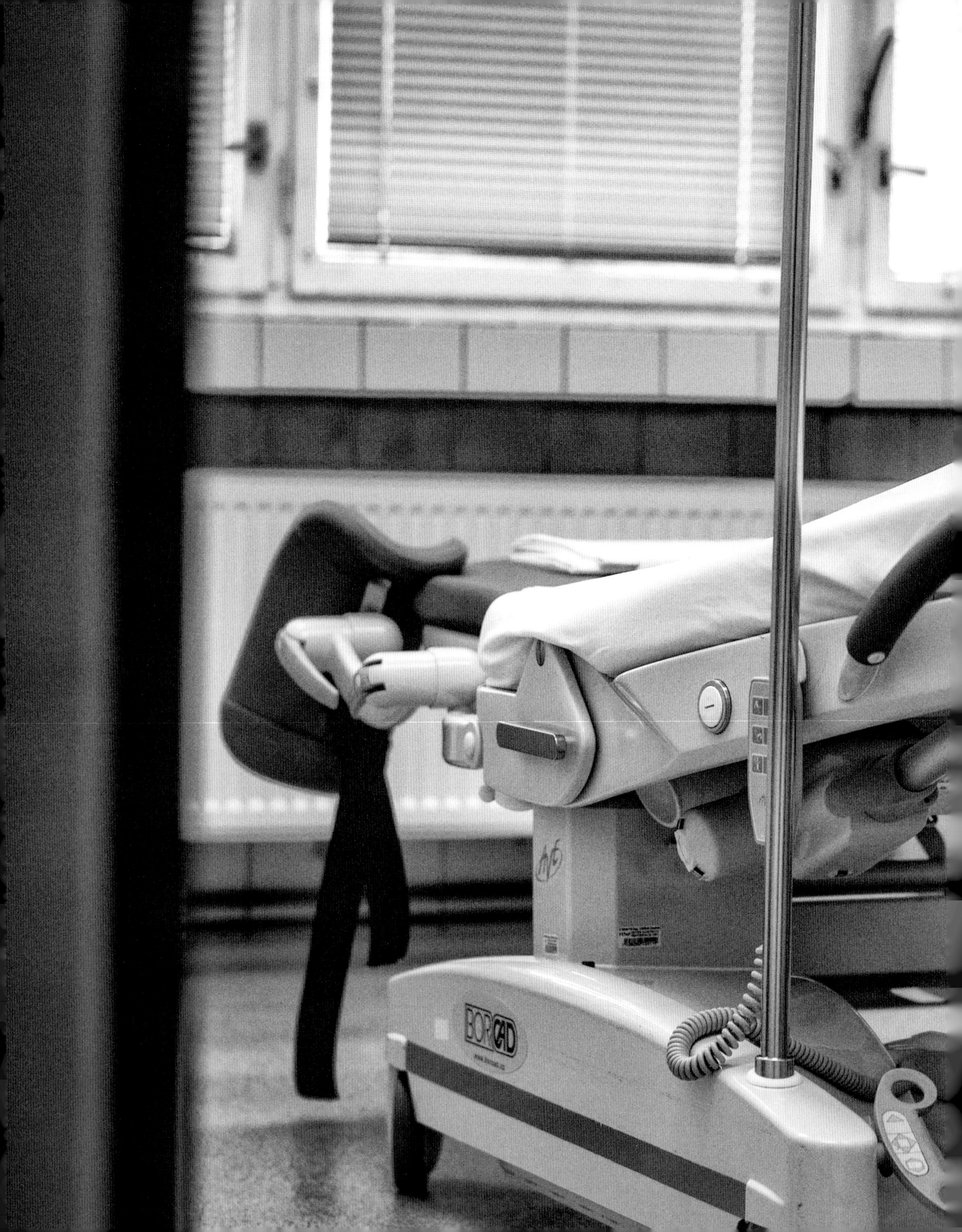
BORCAD

A white doctors coat is reflected in the stainless steel door of a birthing suite.

Jana delivered Cameron and she continued to support the family in the weeks and months following his birth.

Here she is seen meeting Cameron, now eight years old, at a clinic in Prague.

ORDINACE

Bryan: There was a lovely, lovely nurse who didn't speak much English at all and she crept in...
she was a lovely woman...she crept in and she kept on touching Cameron and looking at him and checking him and we didn't really know...we just thought it was an affectionate bond, we didn't realise it was anything other than that.

Sarah described the same kind nurse, when I interviewed her separately, and how she helped her bond with Cameron.

Sarah: The night after we had been told, that nurse came in and she seemed to know I was struggling a bit. She couldn't speak English but we got by. She just put Cameron in my arms and said 'he's a bit cold'.
I just cuddled him and that was what I really needed.

(To Cameron) We had a lovely little cuddle didn't we when you were a little baby
didn't we?

Cameron: Mummy?

Sarah: Is it my turn? (to play football)

'When my dad first picked Cameron up he said you're a lucky lad, you're one of us, nothing's going to happen to you now'.

SYLVIA

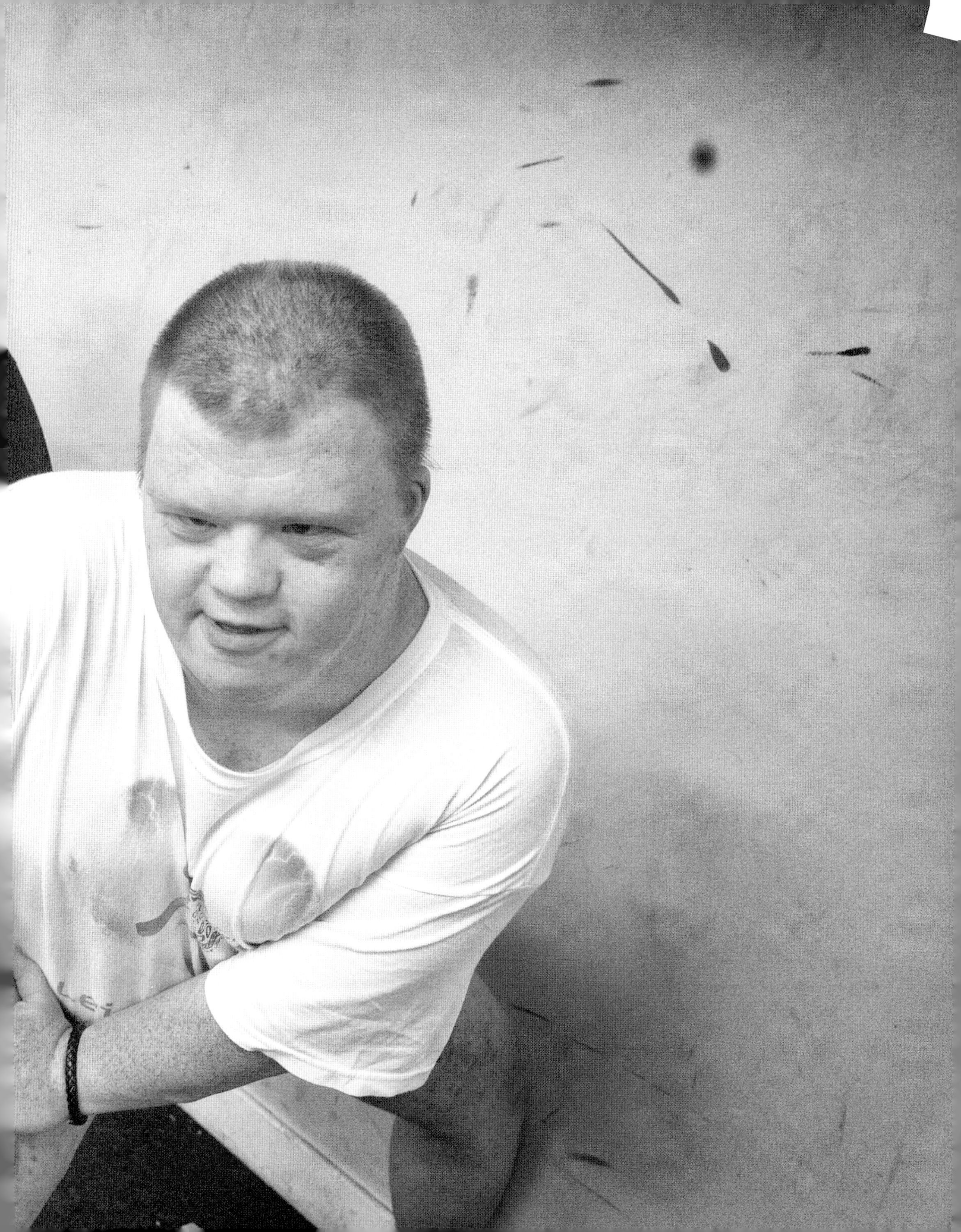

Previous page: Sylvia and her friend John at the gym.

Sylvia is in her fifties and lives with her Mum, Liz and Dad, James. She has an older and a younger sister. Sylvia is warm, funny and absolutely committed to sport having won medals for powerlifting and skiing. As I talk to her Mum and Dad it's clear that, despite encountering stares and comments throughout her life Sylvia and her family have adopted a 'lets just get on with it' approach.

They understand that much of the reaction is a fear of the unknown brought about by a lack of exposure to those with Down's Syndrome and that now that more of those who have the condition are in the community, attitudes are slowly improving. They are critical of families who won't go out with their child. James thinks those families feel ashamed when they shouldn't.

Liz says 'Sylvia is my pal we go everywhere together' and that includes travelling the globe while she competes at the highest level.

SCOTTISH
POWERLIFTING
ASSOCIATION
MASTERS
2000
IRELAND 2003
the feeling
LIFT
2004

2004 SISTER SYLVIA MOFFAT L.O.L 54
GRAND ORANGE LODGE OF SCOTLAND

SCOTTISH
MASTERS
2006

2004 SISTER
GRAND ORANGE LODGE

S.MOFFAT

SCOTTISH
MASTERS
2006

S.MOFFAT

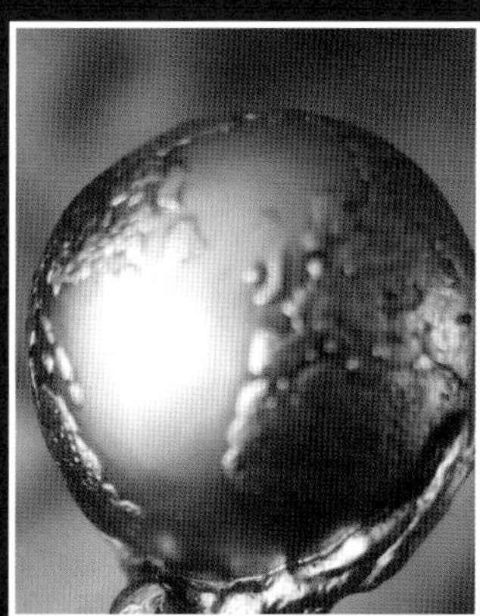

SCOTTISH
WER LIFTING
MPETITION 2011

Previous page: Just some of Sylvia's medals.

Liz: Fifty years ago it was always planned to be a home birth and after Sylvia was born, and they had cleaned her up, the nurse said 'Do you know your daughter has Down's Syndrome?'

James: They didn't call it Down's then.

Liz: It wasn't Down's they called it then – it was mongol – I hate that word but the midwife said she's a mongol. I was nineteen years old and I didn't have a clue.

She said 'Your not being very fair, you'll never be a fit mother, you'll never manage her and your other daughter (Davina was one year old). Best plan is to put Sylvia away. You'll never manage and I've never seen it so prominent. She'll never walk, never talk, won't ever be able to feed herself and you can't educate her'.

He, (pointing at James) lost the head and threw her out and we never allowed her back in the house.

'We had to force feed Sylvia for six months'.

'Sylvia was no different from any other child having to learn to live in the world. We see it as our job to help her to live in the world as it is. Right now, all she and her friend John want to talk about, is Down's Syndrome. When they are on the bus they point at people and say has he got Down's Syndrome or has she got Down's Syndrome'.

Liz

LG
Remote Man
103
MY LITTLE WHITE DOVES
C'MON ANDY

'Sylvia has always just been part of the family, just one of three, but at the same time she was special. When she was born we thought we've just had another baby so now just get on with it. Look how well she has turned out'.

A PICTURE
IS
WORTH A
THOUSAND
WORDS
1974

'Last year Sylvia and I took the train back from Blackpool and it was really busy, people were standing all over the place and there were two seats beside us which were empty. A small woman pushed her way through and said'.

'Look I'm having a seat and nobody is going to tell me I can't sit. I know you don't want to sit because of that girl. She is better than all of you'.

EVE

Eve, or 'wee Evie' as everybody calls her, lives with her mum Lesley. The relationship between her mum and dad ended six months after she was born. She spends every Thursday with Kenny, her dad, his wife Theresa and their son Kenneth. Lesley has an older son Ross from a previous relationship, as has Kenny. His son has autism. Wilson, Eve's grandad, continues to be an important part in all their lives.

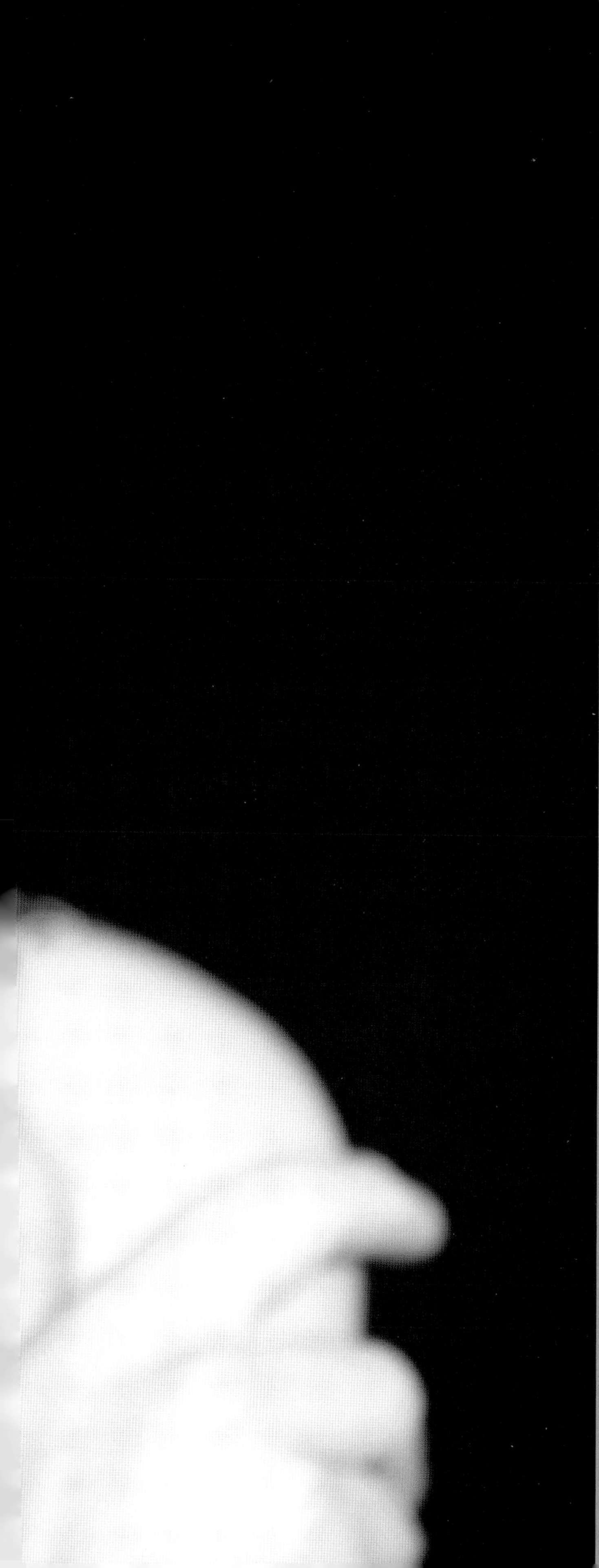

As I sat one on one, and physically close to Lesley, I asked her to think back to those few days in hospital when it became clear that something was wrong but nobody knew what.

'Kenny and I never connected somehow. I guess it might have been because I was too involved in the day to day care of Eve. I think it became a tragedy for him for a little while'.

‘It forced me to search my soul and think about what it is to be human and what we think is human. Down’s Syndrome is not as important as I first thought, but it is tough...’

'I was more concerned about how Lesley and Kenny were going to cope'.

'I wasn't sure how Lesley would manage since Eve's Dad left. I thought she might struggle but she's coped, she's marvellous. I'm fair proud of her'.

‘Eve has a memory like a computer, she loves music and dance and has a tremendous imagination now. I wouldn’t change her for the world. Down’s Syndrome or not it makes no difference’.

'Lesley noticed straight away that Eve had Down's Syndrome and then once the tests were done and they came through there was no surprise. Down's Syndrome though was immediately forgotten about and has been since. Our priority was to make sure Eve survived as she wasn't feeding and was in a special care unit.'

'I'm not going to sit here and say people are judgemental about Eve and then be judgemental about them'.

AMARENA
MENTA
CIOCCOLATO
FRAGOLA
FIOR

There was an intensity about Kenny that I detected the minute we met. As I sat just a few feet away he talked of his fierce determination to protect Eve and his frustration at the attitude of others of whom he say's.

'I have to deal with this every f**kin day'.

And of the fact that he felt that he has received little support

'Support wasn't there for me as an individual'.

The day after Kenny remarried they arrived home to find that a Sympathy card had been posted through the door containing a condom and the message.

'No more retards'.

CORINNE

Previous page: Corinne watches intently as her Mother walks up the garden path at the beginning of a weekend visit. The atmosphere of anticipation has been electric as she waits for her family to arrive.

Michelle and Mark have three children. Corinne is the oldest at 21 years old. She has a sister Ellis who is 19 and a brother Shea who is 16.

As we spent the evening together, the family shared lots of funny stories about things that have happened when they have been out and about with Corinne including an incident, when she pulled down the swimming trunks of a fellow swimmer at a local pool. They all laughed as the stories were retold and it became clear that this family were not just coping but that they were as one.

As Mark said 'We didn't know that Corinne would be born with Down's Syndrome and apart from the initial shock we were proud parents again after an hour'.

Photography
perfect planting

‘Corinne has severe and profound learning difficulties in having both Down’s Syndrome and Autism. Up until around two years old she was progressing well and then her head stopped growing for nine months before then starting to grow at a slower rate. We were told that wasn’t a good sign’.

Corinne's sixteen year old brother Shea,
holds a photograph of her first smile in his hands.

'There is stigma but as I've got older I refuse to care about it.
After all Corinne doesn't care about it – she isn't embarrassed herself
so why should I be'?

Shea

'The hardest thing for me was to realise, that to be a good mum to Corinne, I had to give her up and that's the hardest thing ever. I had not to be selfish about that and do what was best for her. It still hurts a lot but I can cope with it because I know she is happy'.

Corinne now lives in a Camphill Community and they spend every second weekend and holidays with her.

'When everyone looks at you it's really hard. I love my sister and I feel very protective towards her, but everyone seems to already know your whole life. I was the girl with the sister who has Down's Syndrome. Like any sister I get annoyed with her sometimes but I miss her not being here'.

Ellis

There were times I felt emotional and this was one of the most poignant. While the combination of Down's Syndrome and autism makes Corinne a live wire, and she seems a little out of control sometimes, there was this moment when I felt that she was comfortable in her own skin. Somehow it seemed important that she had her own sense of identity. Peaceful, quiet, serene and Corinne was at that moment Corinne.

Corinne

RUBY

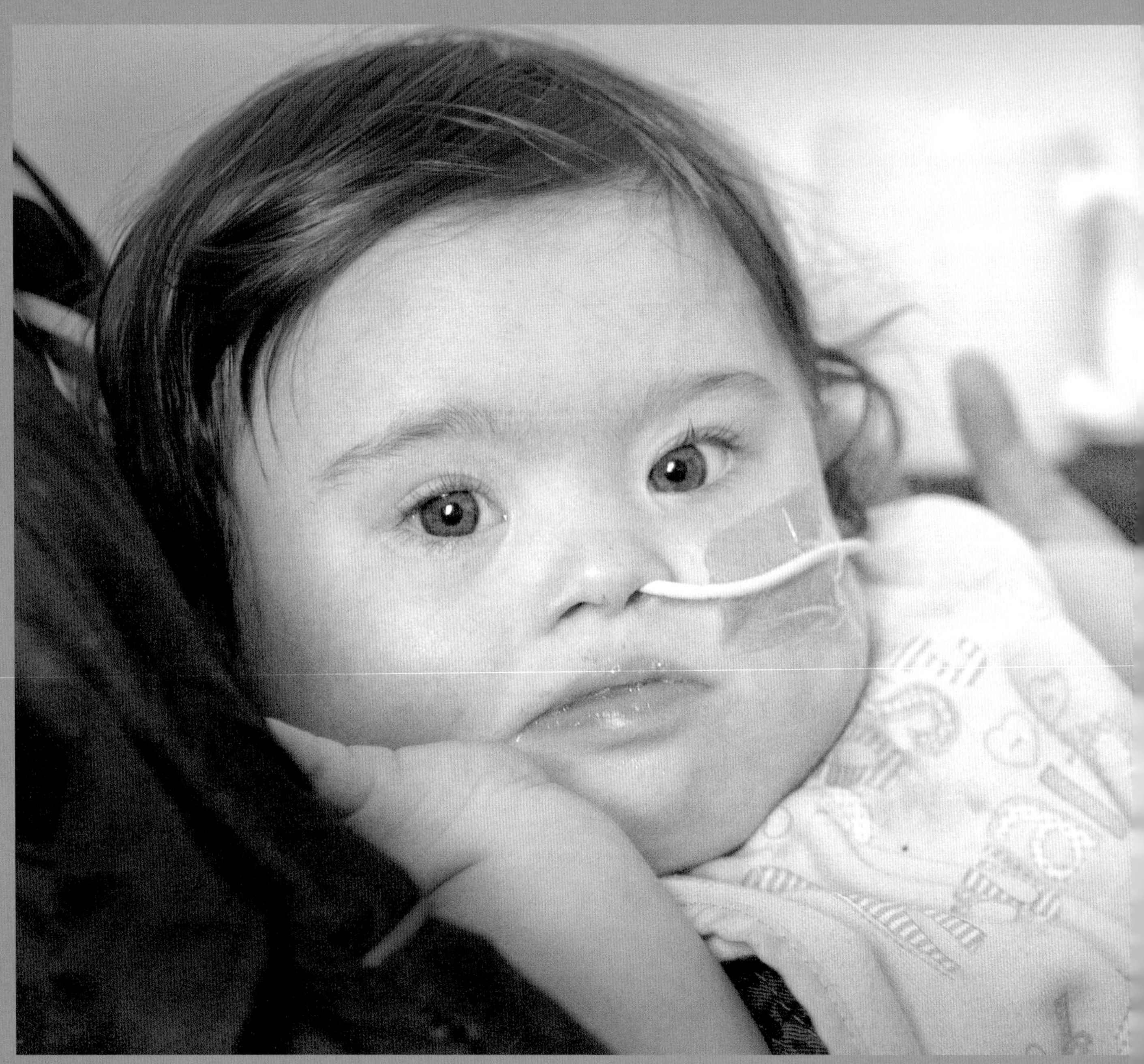

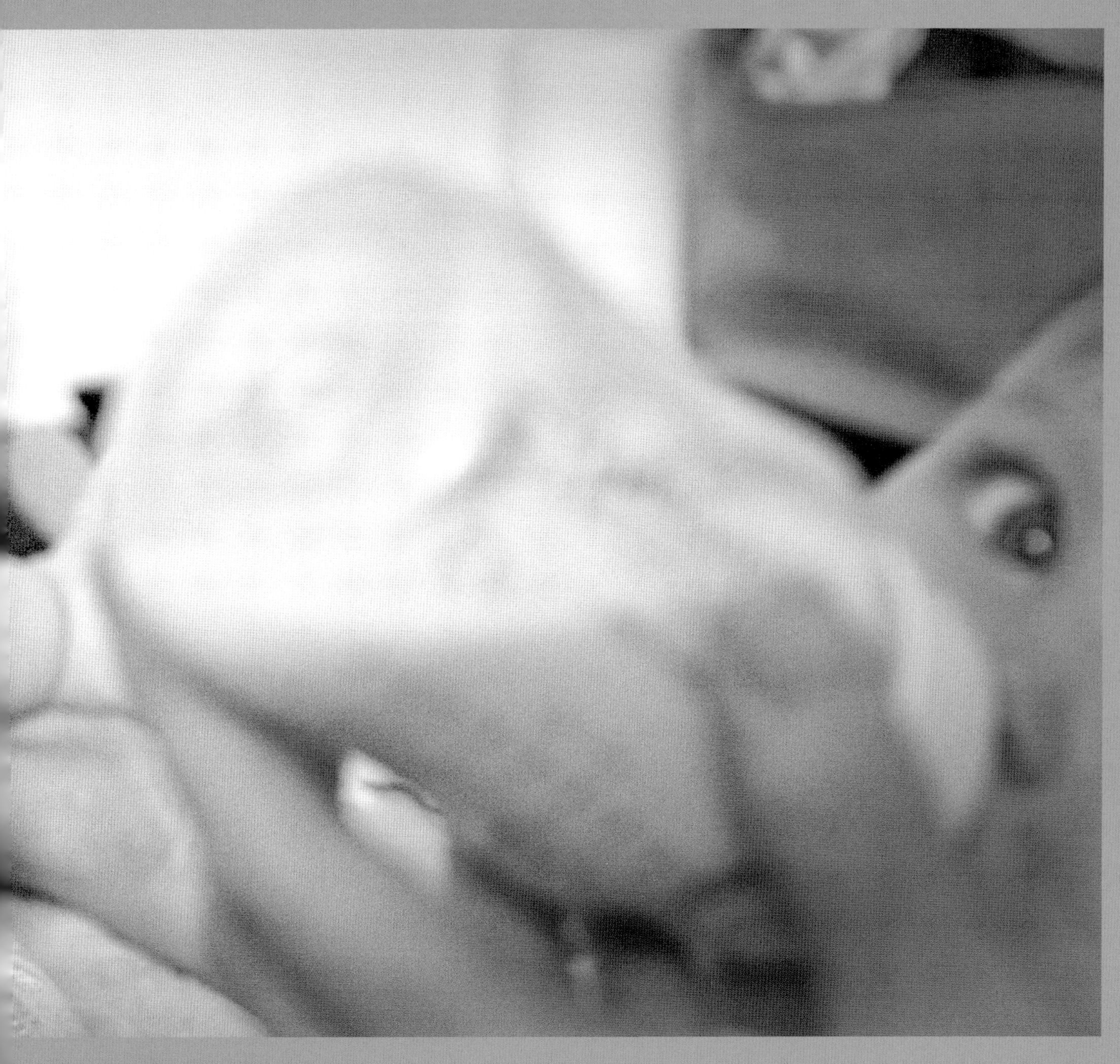

'It just seemed to be that the test didn't really tell us anything that we could act on, so we just decided to go with it and wait for the next scan. I think it was about then that they started saying, well she's definitely got a heart condition. It was sort of 50/50 whether she would be born with Down's Syndrome'.

'We were fine with that, by then and thought, well alright, the important thing is she's going to make it'.

‘So the specialist said with that amount of fluid, best case, she’s not going to get any bigger but then she probably won’t survive. So the way we looked at it was that a lot of people can walk away without a baby and we were still having one baby’.

Tracii

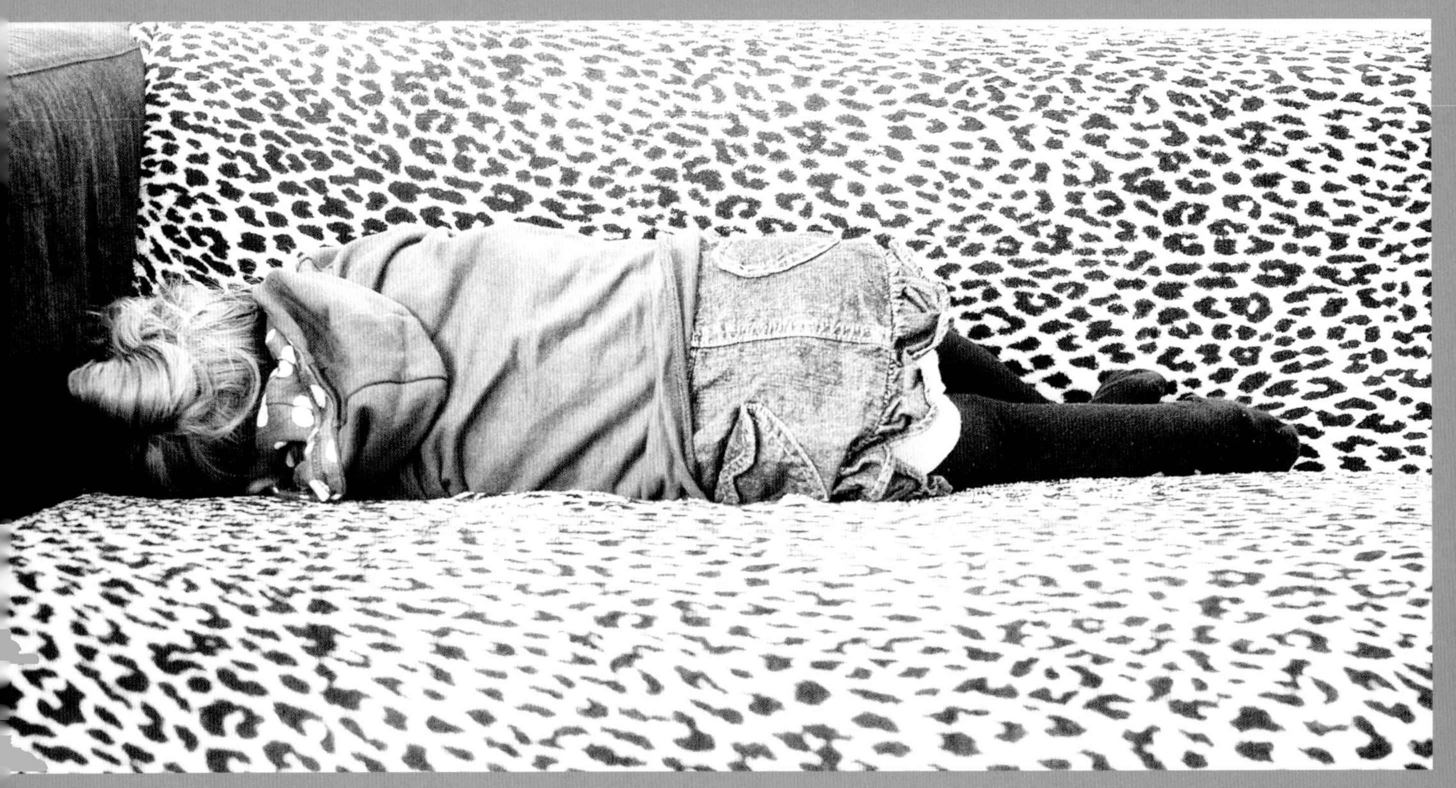

'Darby was Twin A and Ruby was Twin B because they didn't think she would survive, but she came out first so she potentially was Twin A, but on the record she was Twin B'.

Tracii

'They used the term incompatible with life throughout the pregnancy and Ruby could have died. When we found out it was Down's Syndrome we thought that is a relief'.

WAY
Make Your Sub
a Footlong
£2.79
ANTHONY
OGOGO'S
PERSONAL BEST
Chicken
Teriyaki
WHAT'S YOURS?
GREENWAY
No stopping
at any time

221
Leith Walk
2 2 3

‘And when people say things like, sorry, you can understand where they’re coming from. At the same time I just say, don’t be sorry, there’s nothing to be sorry about really’.

Tracii: It was just before Christmas when the time came to tell people and we planned to do just that. Everyone was going out celebrating, and it was that day we found out that Ruby might not make it past Christmas. That's pretty much how things were left until the New Year.

Although we didn't have a terrible Christmas, did we?

Neil: No, no.

Tracii: We figured that we were still having a baby and if you get all upset about things like that it can end up doing more damage than good.

'I had read somewhere somebody had said they wouldn't change their baby having Down's Syndrome for the world, and it's true because Ruby wouldn't be Ruby'.

Afterword

The most common question, asked of me, over the last two years has been 'Do you have a personal connection with Down's Syndrome?' While I realised that people were genuinely interested, as to why I'd chosen this subject, it was also implied that this was something you wouldn't choose to get involved in unless there was a family, or some other close connection.

I think the answer to the question is rooted in my early years. I'd been given an autograph book filled with the signatures of the entire Manchester United football team of the time, George Best, Bobby Charlton included. I showed my father the book and he took it from me and signed it 'Danny the barber'.
I was horrified thinking that he wasn't entitled to sign my autograph book. Seeing my face, and realising what I was thinking, he said 'why shouldn't I sign it, I should be there too I'm famous?' And to an extent he was right.

Part of his legacy was to leave me with hatred, and that's not too strong a word, of prejudice, stigma or any attempt to contain or classify an individual. I was lucky to have a good teacher, but the world at large has been less fortunate. They don't have such an insight and so often adopt the prejudices of others resulting in stigma. In working on this, and similar projects, I've been saddened to find individuals, affected by disability, who also believe the very same prejudices.

The way I have chosen to challenge stigma is through my photography and I will continue to seek ways to get my work into public view through projects like 'Six Percent'. The book is intended to be real and balanced, and so what you see is what I saw, and what you've read is what I've heard. It would have been entirely inappropriate to create a sugar coated image of life with Down's Syndrome in some attempt to neutralise some of the views held by others.

There is no doubt in my mind that Down's Syndrome has a profound effect on those with the condition and their families, I've seen it first hand, but what I saw was a million miles from what the world had conditioned me to expect.

Having started 'Six Percent' without a personal connection I now feel I have one.

Graham Miller

February, 2013

My fathers signature in my autograph book.

Thank to

Mike Walsh who introduced me to his beautiful daughter Charlie-May giving rise to 'Six Percent'.

Pandora Summerfield CEO of Down's Syndrome Scotland for her belief, support and courage in letting me show reality.

The board of Directors and trustees of Down's Syndrome Scotland for backing publication of the book and exhibition.

My best mate Neil Burns, of George James Ltd, who paid for Umair's design work.

Umair Akhtar, of UA Graphics, who won't mind me telling you that he is affected by Asperger's Syndrome. If you ever thought that someone with Asperger's couldn't be a designer then you now know that to be untrue.

Leon and Andy of 52Printsolutions, Edinburgh, printers and bookbinders who worked very hard to translate my ideas into something that we can all be proud of.

Paul Robertson, Curator at Summerhall Gallery, Edinburgh who sat up when he saw the draft and told me my work 'was important and it had to be seen'. I needed to hear that.

Hayley Goleniowska ,who writes an award winning blog about her experiences as a mother with a child with Down's Syndrome. She's done such a lot to push me up that final hill.

Rose my amazing wife and two beautiful daughters, Holly and Mandy, who have been incredible. At times I couldn't even live with myself and so it must have been very hard for them, but they never waivered. I owe them a break now. (A short one).

To all of the families featured in the book, who allowed me, and now you, into their very private lives. It is through their determination to let others learn from their experiences that you are holding the book now. I now count them all as the most wonderful friends. I hope 'Six Percent' is what you hoped it would be.

Martin who I had the great pleasure to work with, but whose photographs do not appear here, for reasons outside of his control. Hopefully one day they will be seen.

'Six Percent' is dedicated to;

Andrew, Cameron, Cara, Corinne, Eve, Jamie, Katie, Matthew, Penny, Ruby and Sylvia'.

They taught me more about humanity than I ever thought possible.

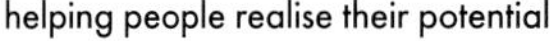

www.georgejamesltd.co.uk